# THE MACMILLAN
# STUDENT ENCYCLOPEDIA OF SOCIOLOGY

MACMILLAN STUDENT ENCYCLOPEDIA OF SOCIOLOGY

EDITED BY
MICHAEL MANN

M
MACMILLAN PRESS
LONDON

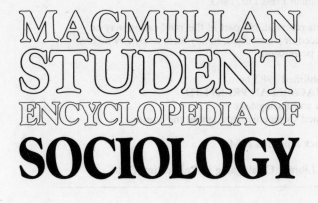

# MACMILLAN STUDENT ENCYCLOPEDIA OF SOCIOLOGY

EDITED BY

## MICHAEL MANN

**MACMILLAN PRESS**
LONDON

© Macmillan Press Ltd, 1983

First published 1983 by
THE MACMILLAN PRESS LTD
London and Basingstoke
Associated Companies throughout the world

Paperback reprinted 1984

**British Library Cataloguing in Publication Data**

The Macmillan student encyclopedia of sociology.
    1. Sociology — Dictionaries
    I. Mann, Michael
301'.3'21        HM17

    ISBN 0-333-28193-4
    ISBN 0-333-28194-2 Pbk

Typeset by Leaper & Gard Ltd, Bristol, England
Printed in Hong Kong

# Introduction

Sociology presents especial difficulties for constructing the orthodoxy of style, format and content necessary for an encylopedia or dictionary. Society does not lend itself to clean dissection and neat sub-division: not quite a seamless web, more a slightly ragged, amateurishly stitched patchwork quilt, from which some bits keep falling off, and to which new bits are added. Sociology should, and does, reflect this messiness. It offers relatively little unchanging orthodoxy, either in content or in the way the discipline divides up its internal specialisms. Sociology can only be a society's understanding of itself and this is constantly in flux and contested.

In dictionary terms the word 'sociology' itself is a hybrid, a mixture of Latin (*socius*, originally ally, then society) and Greek (*logos*, knowledge, perhaps science), hence 'knowledge (or 'the science') of society'. Sociologists argue that such knowledge is distinct from that of other disciplines. It refers to what they call the 'emergent' properties of society. Indeed, the best short definition of sociology contained in this encyclopedia is to be found under the entry *emergence*. But there divergencies will become apparent between sociologists as to whether they regard emergence as 'structure' or a 'process'. This is one of the many sociological controversies which are to be found here, but they are not decisively resolved in these pages because no orthodoxy exists. It is for the reader to decide whether to favour 'structure' or 'process', or whether to combine the two. This is the challenge, the excitement, and the subversiveness of sociology: it calls always for an independence of mind, a critical spirit, as much from the student beginner as from the established scholar.

A second aspect of the unorthodoxy of sociology is that its parts move at different speeds. The social problems of each decade differ. Some settle down and we establish quasi-orthodoxies about them. But, just as we are doing so, other problems, hitherto unsuspected, rear up and hit us in the face — usually accompanied by the polemics of contending interest groups. For the editor of an encyclopedia this creates a dilemma: to mirror this situation, so that entries in one field will reflect an established orthodoxy while those in another will reveal bafflement or polemic; or to impose a common orthodoxy of 'on the one hand, and on the other hand' type? As general editor I resolved this by inaction, allowing the specialist in each field to choose. The entries are, in varying combinations, balanced, authoritative, indecisive and polemic. On occasion I have entered the foray to add a dissenting note to an entry. I hope that these varying stylistic qualities convey the varied flavours of sociology.

Most of the contributors have covered their subject area by writing a number of short entries, which is the general style of this Encyclopedia. But a few took the opposite approach, writing only a handful of long entries. Where the information forms a coherent continuous whole, this is perfectly appropriate — as, for example, in JB's excellent account of *Psychoanalysis*, where various concepts and theories ultimately cohere into a single world-view. I confess to having let contributors have their head in another respect too. They sometimes wrote at greater length than I had originally indicated, but the value of their contribution justified extended treatment. For example, MPB's and LS's entry on *Slavery* is far longer than the institution's importance within sociology would appear to warrant — but it is extraordinarily interesting!

Finally, the entries on individual writers are obviously uneven. The length of these entries bears no direct relationship to that person's importance within sociology, and for a good reason. Anyone who has been truly seminal within sociology has developed theories and concepts which will be the subject of separate entries in the Encyclopedia. Marx, Weber and Durkheim all have entries of their own, but their pre-eminence is only truly encompassed by counting also the dozens of other entries, from *Action Theory* to *World System* which bear their imprint. Of the two Meads, Margaret rather than George Herbert has the longer entry. Yet George Herbert has been of far greater significance for sociology, and this is revealed in the content of about ten other entries from *The Act* onwards.

Despite all this liberality on my part, the Encyclopedia should still have a disciplined, uniform core. I hope that you will find interesting, informative sociology wherever you look, and that your questions are answered in our entries.

I believe my contributing editors have done a magnificent job. I would like to thank them all most warmly. Shaie Selzer and Māra Vilčinskas for Macmillan, and Margot Levy, have been invaluable; and my secretary, Yvonne Brown has coped marvellously with the peculiar typing requirements of an encyclopedia.

London School of Economics
April 1983

# Contributors

| | | | |
|---|---|---|---|
| BJB | B.J. Bullert | MM | Michael Mann |
| CGAB | Christopher Bryant | PWM | Peter Musgrave |
| DB | David Beetham | SJM | Stephen Mennell |
| DBn | Douglas Benson | HN | Howard Newby |
| JB | Joan Busfield | WO | William Outhwaite |
| MB | Martin Bulmer | JP | Julian Petrie |
| MPB | Michael Banton | KM | Ken Menzies |
| RED | Robert Dowse | MP | Martin Partington |
| JE | Judith Ennew | MR | Michael Rose |
| EG | Eva Gamarnikow | MDR | Michael Rush |
| MMG | M.M. Goldsmith | PR | Paul Rock |
| AH | Ankie Hoogvelt | RR | Ray Robinson |
| AJH | Alan Hunt | KP | Ken Plummer |
| NH | Nicky Hart | DS | David Smart |
| MJ | Michael Jackson | DRS | David R. Steel |
| JL | Jon Linzell | HIS | Hillel Steiner |
| ML | Michael Lane | JS | Jeff Stanyer |
| AM | Adrian Mellor | LS | Leslie Sklair |
| AMcC | Alistair McCulloch | BT | Bill Tupman |
| EM | Elizabeth Meehan | JW | Jennifer Wood |
| EMM | E.M. McLeery | RW | Roy Wallis |
| JWM | J.W. Moon | | |

# List of entries

# How to use this Encyclopedia

No Encyclopedia or Dictionary can wholly live up to the pretensions of its apparent format. There is no principle of verbal organization which can ensure that every word you wish to look up will appear as a separate entry. Obviously I hope that this is often, even usually, the case. But in the cases where it isn't, please do not turn away in annoyance. If you are recommended under *doctor-patient relationship* to see *sick role*, please try it. If you do not find a term at all, think for a moment of cognate terms, or of other terms with which it is usually associated, and consult the list of entries which appears on pages vii-xi. Thus an explanation of 'Despotism' will be found under *Absolutism* and *Oriental Despotism*; 'American Legal Realism' will be found under *Law, Trends in Legal Theory*. And if, having read the entry, you want more, follow up the cross-references which are given either at the end of the entry or are picked out within the entry — always in SMALL CAPITALS. Both practices are used sparingly, so that you will find directly relevant information there. Bibliographic references to relevant books and articles have also been kept to a minimum. There are no long reading-lists but references given are considered by the writer to be important.

My contributing editors and I have worked to a similar general style and format whose details will become readily apparent. One consistency might appear at first sight to the reader as inconsistency. We have used what is generally called 'non-sexist language' (e.g. 'he/she' instead of just 'he' where the gender of the person referred to is not relevant) except where paraphrasing a writer who does not do this. It is relevant information that most writers in the classic tradition, from Comte to Parsons, did not use non-sexist language.

MM

**A**

**absolutism.** Usually applied to the regimes of some formally despotic European monarchs of the 17th and 18th centuries in Europe, claiming the Divine Right of Kings and backed by centralized STATES. In most cases, these states represented a balance between the powers of the landowning ARISTOCRACY and the rising BOURGEOISIE, and their monarchs for a short but crucial period were able to take advantage of this. They were also aided by the 'military revolution' of the 16th and 17th centuries in which artillery and more complex and expensive systems of supply and drilling encouraged the growth of centralized command structures backed by the fiscal resources of large states. Absolute monarchs introduced codified law, standing armies, permanent bureaucracies, and national systems of taxation to pay for them. It is sometimes argued that absolutism paved the way for CAPITALISM, but the pioneers of commercial capitalism, Holland and England, were constitutional rather than absolute monarchies.

Loosely, absolutism can refer to any regime in which the rulers are not bound by the rule of law and in which the state has some ability to enforce its near-arbitrary powers. LS, MM

**accommodation.** See PARK, R.E.

**acephalous.** Literally 'without a head', referring to social groups that exist without centralized authority, leaders or chiefs and yet exhibit political organization. Occasionally these are referred to by the more general term 'stateless societies', which can also include groups that have chiefs or acknowledged rulers, or by the more correct and descriptive term 'segmentary societies'. Study of such groups has been particularly associated with EVANS-PRITCHARD and with societies like the Nuer in areas surrounding the southern and central Nile Valley. Such groups usually live in spatially well-defined areas and exhibit consciousness of their identity and exclusivity. Political organization means that part of the social organization which is concerned with the control and regulation of the use of force. A central component of acephalous organization is KINSHIP or LINEAGE affiliation, although AGE SETS can provide additional points of political focus. Political organization is achieved through a balance of power, both sacred and secular, between separate but associated descent groups, which are visualized as being in structural opposition (or fission) in a short-range perspective, yet associated in a complex network of relationships (or fusion) within the larger perspective that binds segments together. Adherence to a particular group, be it large or small, is claimed or achieved according to situational circumstances. Political balance can be achieved through ritual mediators, but authority is not attributed to individuals. Such systems are in perpetual flux, and are called segmentary because of the emphasis placed, at particular moments of political tension, on adherence to one or more segments of the relevant lineage.

See also STATE. JE

1

**achievement.** Performance in social positions may be measured by various criteria which differ across cultures, such as achievement in education through formal examinations, marks of physical prowess like exceeding a given height or weight or winning a fight, or improvement of social status through upward SOCIAL MOBILITY. Such social success is referred to as achievement. This concept is used particularly in the context of attitudes towards achievement, such as achievement motivation (see MIGRATION). Some social positions, however, cannot be achieved; actors are ascribed to them and movement in or out of them is almost impossible. Positions to which actors are ascribed in most societies are sex, colour and social class at birth. The last example demonstrates one of the problems arising from an over-rigid use of the concepts of achievement and ascription: though social class is ascribed at birth, movement to another class is possible through upward or downward mobility. PARSONS saw these two related concepts as so central to sociological theory that he included achievement/ascription as one of the five pairs of PATTERN VARIABLES around which he believed all societies are structured.                                    PWM

**act, the.** A basic unit of SYMBOLIC INTERACTIONISM developed especially by G.H. MEAD and BLUMER, stressing that people act, rather than simply react. Human life is composed of an ongoing stream of interpretive 'doings' both covert (e.g. 'thinking') and overt (e.g. arguing), the former often being a deliberate rehearsal of the latter. For Mead, an act is built up through four stages: (1) impulse — the generalized disposition to act; (2) perception — the organizing, selecting and defining of a situation; (3) consummation — the completion of the act with an achieved goal. Such 'acts' may be of various classes: automatic, blocked, incomplete and retrospective.

See M. Natanson *The Social Dynamics of George H. Mead* (1956; 2/1973).

KP

**action approach.** In Industrial Studies, denotes an explanation of patterns of behaviour at work by reference to variably distributed 'orientations to work', these orientations being socially generated. It contrasts with approaches that seek sources of industrial behaviour in supposedly universal, individualistic economic motivations (SCIENTIFIC MANAGEMENT), or in universal psychological wants or needs (SELF-ACTUALIZATION THEORY), or in the technological environment of work (SOCIO-TECHNICAL SYSTEM).

'Actionalists' maintain that individual economic rationality is mediated — on occasion neutralized — by a socially transmitted and sustained set of goals and perspectives. It was long ago established, for example, that in the USA country-born Protestants were more likely to respond to incentive payments than city-born Catholics. Actionalists thus insist that economically 'irrational' behaviour usually reflects the operation of some social rationality. This insistence should be distinguished from the preoccupation of HUMAN RELATIONS theory with 'social' explanations of work behaviour, since actionalists challenge that work behaviour is mainly determined by some 'non-logical' inborn drive towards face-to-face sociability. But exactly what distinguishes any given 'orientation to work'? How, exactly, is it socially created, transmitted and sustained? To what extent is it modified by experience in work itself? And is there not a danger, in attempting to grasp the subjective rationality of typical social actors, of slipping into a concern with socially disembodied 'definitions' of their (work) situation held by separate individuals, thus neglecting the manner in which 'definition' must be constrained by structured features — social and economic — of the total work situation? These aspects have generated lively debate.

See ACTOR; DEFINITION OF THE SITUATION.

MR

**action research.** Research in which the knowledge and techniques of social science are combined with practical policy initiatives to plan and achieve social change. Whereas the traditional role of the researcher is diagnosis and interpretation of past events, the action researcher is actively involved in new planned policy initiatives, monitoring the base-line situation, observing the changes initiated by the plan, and attempting to monitor the plan's effects.

Examples of action research are Operation Headstart in the USA and the Educational Priority Area in the UK. Both sought to stimulate educational innovation in selected areas to reduce social and educational disadvantage among disadvantaged families (in the USA, ethnic disadvantage especially). In both countries, community development programmes also intervene in selected local areas to identify problems, participate in suitable development programmes, and evaluate their success or failure. Research activities have been a major component of all these programmes.

See also EVALUATION RESEARCH.

See C.H. Weiss (ed.), *Evaluating Action Programs* (1972). MB

**action theory.** Approaches to sociology which emphasize how actors perceive a social situation, the ends they choose to pursue in it, and the means they adopt in pursuing them. In its emphasis on conscious orientation and purposive action, action theory stands in opposition to BEHAVIOUR-ISM.

WEBER's discussion of social action in the first chapter of *Economy and Society* (1924) is usually taken as the starting point of action theory. Weber argued that to explain an action we must interpret it in terms of its subjectively intended meaning. A person's action is to be explained in terms of the consequences he or she intended — purpose — rather than in terms of its actual effects; the two are often at variance. A 'subjectively intended meaning' is also a causal explanation of the action, in that the end in view is a cause of present actions.

Weber outlines a four-fold typology of rational and non-rational patterns of action. *Zweckrationalität* ('goal-rationality') is the highest form of rational action. The actor weighs against each other the means available for attaining a given end, the costs and benefits of using those means for one end or another, and finally various ends themselves. Weber has in mind the models of rational economic action developed in classical economics, involving concepts such as marginal utility, marginal revenue and opportunity cost. The other patterns of action are in effect treated as deviations from this pattern. *Wertrationalität* ('value-rationality') involves weighing the means towards an end rationally against each other, but the end itself is not questioned: it is accepted as a binding and absolute goal. Such action is often governed by religious belief — salvation is an example of an unquestioned and absolute end. Finally, Weber speaks of affectual action, governed by strong emotion, and traditional action, which he sees as governed by habit; the definitions of these last two categories in particular are open to many criticisms.

Another landmark in 'action theory' was PARSONS's *Structure of Social Action* (1937), a study of Weber, DURKHEIM, PARETO and the economist Alfred Marshall. Parsons claimed these authors had been converging towards a 'voluntaristic theory of action', which he proceeded to advocate and develop in numerous later works. Parsons grafted on to Weber's means/ends schema Durkheim's preoccupation with common values or CONSENSUS; shared values influenced the choice of means and ends, and helped ensure that individuals' pursuit of their own ends did not lead to a war of all against all.

Points of similarity with Weber's and Parsons's discussions are in the work of American pragmatist thinkers like William James, G.H. MEAD, and especially in W.I. THOMAS's notion of the DEFINITION OF THE SITUATION. There is also an affinity with POPPER's idea of 'the logic of the situation', which he sees as a key element in historical explanation.

Despite its merits, action theory is not a comprehensive and self-sufficient theoretical orientation for sociologists. It is irredemiably individualistic, and though individuals may perceive, orientate themselves and pursue purposes, social institutions cannot — no one now believes in the reality of a 'group-mind' (see TELEOLOGY). Social processes can rarely be explained entirely in terms of the intentions, goals or purposes of individual people. Actions of individuals usually need to be explained as much in terms of the compelling social processes in which they are caught up as those processes need to be explained in terms of intentions (see ETHNOMETHODOLOGY; PHENOMENOLOGY; SOCIAL STRUCTURE; SYMBOLIC INTERACTIONISM; UNANTICIPATED CONSEQUENCES).

This lack of theoretical self-sufficiency is evident even in the 'action theory' of Weber and Parsons. The discussion of action in the abstract is only a small aspect of Weber's work. His broader concern is with how typical patterns of action became embodied in the West in institutions such as markets, rational-legal BUREAUCRACY and rational law, or why they failed to become so in China, India and elsewhere. Similarly, much of Parsons's career was taken up with trying to effect a marriage between action theory and FUNCTIONALISM, using the inadequate apparatus of the latter to deal with the structural processes which the former was unable to explain.                                          SJM

**activism.** As with any other voluntary activity, political activity engages only a minority of people, the activists. Most people's maximum involvement in politics is voting at elections, whereas activists engage in the day-to-day work of persuasion, attending meetings, soliciting funds, canvassing etc. Although the term is conventionally used of people in political parties, there is little to distinguish them from active members of other voluntary associations such as TRADE UNIONS and PRESSURE GROUPS.

Compared to populations, activists tend to be younger, better educated, better paid, more liberal (with conspicuous exceptions), feel more politically effective, and are better informed.

Theories of why people become activists are legion. Psychological and psychoanalytic theories generally emphasize some aspect of childhood, such as early loss of parents, parental arbitrariness, feelings of weakness, hate etc engendered in the family and displaced into politics, and political activity as a learned behaviour. Others stress political activism as an outcome of social background, such as education, income and occupation. The higher a person on these scales, the higher the probability of activism. Political activity is positively associated with higher than average levels of general communal involvement.

Tracing the origins of political activism encounters methodological difficulties. Except in situations like mass revolt, most people are politically passive (see ELECTIONS). Thus only a relatively small sample of likely activists can be obtained, even in a longitudinal study starting from pre-puberty.
RED

**adequacy.** WEBER distinguished CAUSAL and 'meaningful' adequacy. The correct solution of an arithmetical problem or a 'rational' course of action is meaningfully adequate: that is, it is correct in terms of the system of meaning within which it is embedded, without reference to its likelihood in the real world. The causal adequacy of an EXPLANATION depends on the probability that what is meaningfully adequate will actually occur in reality. According to Weber both are required by sociology, since this is concerned both with meaningful action and with a scientific investigation of causes.

SCHUTZ emphasizes meaningful adequacy. His 'postulate of adequacy', variously defined in his writings, demands that a social scientific explanation 'be understandable for the actor himself as well as for his fellow-men in terms of commonsense interpretations of everyday life'. This is still widely accepted within PHENOMENOLOGICAL sociology but many sociologists disagree, regarding the 'commonsense' explanations of social actors as often confused, incoherent and causally inadequate.

See M. Weber, *Economy and Society* (1921), chapter 1; A. Zijderveld, 'The Problem of Adequacy', *Archives Européennes de Sociologie*, 1972.
WO

**adolescence.** The LIFE CYCLE is divided into a number of sequential stages. These vary across cultures and through time. Since around the mid-18th century in European cultures growing importance has been attached to the stage between childhood and adult status, which is known as adolescence. During this stage a young person has to pass from dependence to independence of the family of origin. Much social experiment occurs during adolescence through which the maturing actor becomes an adult with a more or less structured identity; more particularly, orientations towards the opposite sex are formed. Because of growing claims during adolescence by the young for independence in such socially central fields of action as sex, work and leisure activities, clashes, often defined by parents and other adults as rebellion, are likely between GENERATIONS and these can result in changes in social NORMS with respect to the family and in other areas. See DELINQUENCY.

PWM

**Adorno, Theodor Wiesengrund** (1903-69). German Marxist writer who contributed to a number of academic disciplines. Born in Frankfurt, the son of a Jewish wine-merchant and a singer (whose name he eventually adopted), Adorno studied in Frankfurt and Vienna, and was close to the Institute for Social Research, which he joined in 1931. He left Germany in 1934 for Oxford and, in 1938, New York, where the Frankfurt Institute had established itself in exile. He moved to California with other Institute members in 1941. He returned to Frankfurt in 1949 and was Director of the Institute from 1958 until his death.

Adorno was probably the most important thinker in what came to be called the Frankfurt School of CRITICAL THEORY. Main works: *Negative Dialectics* (1966); (with HORKHEIMER) *Dialectic of Enlightenment* (1947); and a vast range of work in philosophy, social psychology — especially *The Authoritarian Personality* (1950) — and the sociology of culture, especially music. He was a leading protagonist in the debate about positivism in the early 1960s.

See AUTHORITARIAN PERSONALITY; POSITIVISM.

WO

**aetiology.** The study or assignment of the causes of a phenomenon. In medicine the term is used to refer to the investigation and exposition of the causes of a disease, and often simply to refer to the causes, presumed or established, of the disease. In sociology the classic example is DURKHEIM's *Suicide* (1897).

JB

**affect.** A term sometimes used generally to refer to feelings, dispositions or emotions, but more often and specifically to refer to the complex pattern of physiological, environmental and cognitive elements of which emotion is the meaningful aspect. These elements may include a high or low level of physiological arousal, use of language, pleasure or displeasure, rage, anxiety, happiness, excitement and fear. A range of emotions may be manifested at the level of meaning, although sometimes affect is used in a more restricted way to refer to certain feelings only. K. Pribram (*Brain and Behaviour*, 1969) uses affect in another specialized sense to mean the state produced when a motivated action is prevented from occurring.

JL

**affinal.** The type of relationship, such as brother-in-law, which is claimed through marriage rather than the direct blood ties of DESCENT. Affinal relations are sometimes contrasted with KINSHIP relations.

JE

**age set.** See RITES OF PASSAGE.

**aggression.** Attacking behaviour directed towards other people, objects or oneself so as to hurt, overthrow or bring into disrepute, whether by direct physical means, by words, or by more indirect psychological means. The term is commonly used as an attribute of individuals; other terms, such as CONFLICT, violence or WAR, are generally used to refer to aggression between groups. Hence aggression in humans has largely been studied by psychologists, while group conflict is studied by sociologists and political scientists. FREUD initially viewed aggression as a natural response to frustration and this idea was further developed by other psychologists and became known as the frustration-aggression hypothesis. Freud later believed aggression to be a manifestation of Thanatos, the death drive (see PSYCHOANALYSIS). A portion of the innate self-destructiveness of individuals was diverted towards the external world and directed on to other people. It could, however, be sublimated, transformed into more productive creative energy. The idea of an instinct of aggression that must find outlet in some form, whether socially acceptable or not, has been developed by the ethologist Konrad Lorenz, who based much of his theory of human aggression on empirical studies of animals. Others, particularly the BEHAVIOURISTS, have emphasized the importance of learning in the development of aggression, and have carried out studies that indicate that aggressive behaviour can be acquired by processes such as 'modelling' (the selective imitation of behaviour).

See also GENDER.                          JB

**agrarianism.** A set of values which holds that agriculture is the most natural and desirable vocation and the farm the ideal place to live and raise children. It derives from Western European romanticism and stresses the Arcadian virtues of family as a way of life. Particularly influential in American political culture, having been codified by Thomas Jefferson and referred to as the 'Jeffersonian Bread', 'Agricultural Fundamentalism', 'the Agrarian Myth' or 'Pastoralism'.

See ENVIRONMENTALISM.              NH

**agribusiness.** A term coined by the Harvard economist John H. Davis (*Harvard Business Review*, 1956). Its meaning has expanded considerably to encompass: (1) Those economic activities which are ancillary to, and dependent upon, agriculture. These include the supply of agro-inputs (e.g. machinery, foodstuffs, chemicals) and the processing, marketing and distribution of agro-outputs. This was Davis's original meaning of the term. (2) Subsequently agribusiness has come to mean profit-maximizing, rationally organized agri-culture. This emphasizes farms which have become rationally organized in the face of prevailing market conditions, enabling contrasts to be drawn between agriculture as an expressive activity ('farming as a way of life') and agriculture as an instrumental activity ('farming as a business'). (3) Agri-business is also used as a collective noun to describe all the stages involved in modern food production ('from seedling to super-market') that are corporately controlled and rationally organized to obtain maximum profitability. This usage acknowledges that the rise of agribusiness as originally defined

has promoted changes in the overall AGRI-CULTURAL STRUCTURE.

HN

**agricultural structure.** How the component parts of agricultural production are organized and relate to each other. Changes in the structure of agriculture are recognized by those constructing a sociology of agriculture to have a profound effect upon rural society in general. Particular attention is paid to two important structural trends in modern agriculture: (1) agriculture is becoming increasingly concentrated in fewer, larger and more capital-intensive forms; (2) agriculture is becoming increasingly structurally differentiated according to a special-ized DIVISION OF LABOUR and profit-maximizing AGRIBUSINESS principles. This involves the reorganization of food-production into a number of segmented processes of which farming is only one part. Farming has become the transformation of one set of industrially manufactured products (seeds, fertilizers, pesticides, feedstuffs, machinery etc) into another (the raw materials of the food-processing sector). Both trends involve changes in the relation of agricultural production and in the structure of rural society.

See also AGRICULTURE, SOCIOLOGY OF.

**agriculture, sociology of.** A sociological approach to the study of social relations in agriculture which begins from an analysis of production systems, labour process and the impact of technological innovation on agriculture. The purpose is to elucidate the social organization of agriculture through a comparative analysis of crop industries in agricultural production.

The term has also a broader meaning, having come to summarize a more radical and critical approach to the conventional subject matter of rural sociology. The 'sociology of agriculture' has thus become a rallying cry for a 'new rural sociology' particularly in the USA since the late 1970s. Its principal research areas include the structure of agriculture (see AGRICULTURAL STRUCTURE) in advanced capitalism, state agricultural policy, agricultural labour, regional inequality and agricultural ecology.

Marxist analysis regards rural sociology as reducible to a sociology of agriculture; others view the sociology of agriculture as an important and useful starting-point in reconstructing rural sociology but not as coterminous with it. These points of view reflect deeper divisions among sociologists about the precise nature of the relationship between economy and society.

See F. Buttel and H. Newby, *The Rural Sociology of the Advanced Societies: Critical Perspectives* (1980).

HN

**algorithm.** A central concept in computing, denoting a repeated, cyclical set of steps by which the solution to a problem may be generated. It is a process defined by a programme and not, as in mathematics, an explicit solution defined by a formula. Computing techniques used in sociology (e.g. CLUSTER ANALYSIS, MULTI-DIMENSIONAL SCALING) frequently rely centrally on the algorithms they employ.

JL

**alienation.** Loss or estrangement, either from one's self or from society, or (as in MARX) from control over social and economic processes. It first appears in modern Western thought in the philosophy of HEGEL, although its origins can be traced through Hegel's Lutheranism to the ideas of St Augustine, and from there back to classical antiquity. At the hands of Hegel's critical followers Bauer, Feuerbach and Hess the notion was progressively secularized until with the young Marx it appears as a descriptive and critical account of the condition of labour in capitalist society. From the 1930s, with the rediscovery of Marx's early writings, the notion played an increasingly important role in the 'humanist' interpretation of Marx's thought, and after the World War II a more reformist and psychology-oriented version appeared in American sociology.

With Hegel, alienation is a part of the human condition. Consciousness is estranged from the world of nature and physical objects, and can only overcome this alienation through a process of growing self-knowledge, generated in history, which allows consciousness to recognize that this apparent external reality is only a projection of itself.

In taking over Hegel's concept, Marx radically altered it. He refused to accept that the production of objects is necessarily alienating, arguing that this is only the case under the specific economic and social relationships of capitalism. In the *Paris Manuscripts*, written in 1844, Marx argued that under capitalism labour is alienated in four distinct ways: (1) alienation from the product of labour, which is appropriated by others; (2) alienation from work itself: instead of being an area of fulfilment, labour in bourgeois society becomes forced labour; (3) alienation from other people, for the essence of social relationships under capitalism is that they are competitive; (4) alienation from the 'species-being', that is, essential human nature. What distinguishes the human species from animals is that whereas animals merely adapt to their environment, human beings consciously master theirs. Under capitalism, this element of conscious mastery is lost, and the worker is reduced to the status of an animal. Unlike Hegel, Marx saw alienation as a condition specific to one form of society, and one which could be overcome by changing conditions in the real world, not in consciousness. And unlike DURKHEIM, Marx viewed happiness as resulting from the liberation of individual human nature, not from its regulation (see ANOMIE).

Since the publication of the *Paris Manuscripts* in 1932, alienation has become important in rival interpretations of Marx. 'Humanist' readings, founded on the notion of alienation, have argued either that Marx's early works are to be preferred to his later ones, or that alienation continues to be the central theme of such later works as *Capital* (where it appears as 'the fetishism of commodities'). This school has been bolstered by the relatively recent publication of the *Grundrisse*, Marx's notebooks for *Capital*, in which his continuing concern with alienation is evident. The first modern Marxist to draw attention to the importance of alienation in Marx's work was Georg Lukács in *History and Class Consciousness* (1923), in which he extended Marx's 'fetishism' into the much broader concept of

8 Allport, Gordon W.

'reification'. Lukács was, however, working without the benefit of Marx's 1844 critique of Hegel and, as a consequence, substantially reverted to the Hegelian equation of alienation and objectification. But 'scientific' readings of Marx's work have stressed the importance of his later works at the expense of the *Paris Manuscripts*, arguing either that alienation is abandoned by the mature Marx or that where the concept is to be found in his later works, its meaning has radically altered (see MARX, MARCUSE, ALTHUSSER).

In the 1950s and 1960s, alienation was incorporated into mainstream sociology by purging it of its evaluative connotations and recasting it in a more operational and empirical form. Seeman (*American Sociological Review*, 1959) argued that 'alienation' could be decomposed into five separate elements: powerlessness, meaninglessness, normlessness, isolation and self-estrangement, each of which may be measured by attitude scales. Four of these (excluding normlessness) were further developed by Robert Blauner in *Alienation and Freedom* (1964). He maintained that different forms of production technology gave rise to differing degrees of alienation. Where there was a high proportion of craft labour, as in unit production schemes (Blauner himself took the case of traditional printing) levels of alienation on all dimensions were much lower than in mass-production industries such as automobile manufacture. Experience of alienated states was also less acute in process production (e.g. chemicals) where production was highly automated. This allows for historical optimism, as there is a tendency to automate mass-production, rendering it more akin to process production, which will itself expand. Thus the quantity of alienating work should fall. This hypothesis is summarised in Blauner's 'inverted U-curve for alienation': alienating tasks rapidly increase in number with the onset of industrialism, reach a peak where they becme typical of manual work as a whole, but then, with the onset of automation, begin to decline. A corollary of this was likely to be greater social cohesion and harmony in general, as workers would be integrated into plant social structure, feel a sense of responsibility and security and considerable work satisfaction.

These ideas have been criticized. (1) Blauner's data were inadequate to sustain his hypotheses: other evidence shows automation does not necessarily alter dramatically the average worker's tasks and satisfaction in the predicted directions. (2) Process production does not necessarily nourish a sense of wider social integration — just as it does not necessarily stimulate 'revolutionary' aspirations of the kind predicted by Mallet in his theory of the new WORKING CLASS. (3) In operationalizing the concept of alienation Blauner edited out much of its traditional meaning and critical force. In Marxian analysis, alienation is linked to exploitation and the exclusion of workers from control over the enterprises in which they work: it is a feature of socio-economic structures as a whole. Thus it is misleading to suggest that alienation will disappear from society simply because technical trends may reduce workers' subjective sense of it. (4) Blauner adopts a technologically determinist standpoint in predicting even the level of this sensed deprivation in work in the future. However, these hypotheses have proved stimulating both for empirical research and theoretical analysis.                AM, MR

**Allport, Gordon W.** (1897-1967). American psychologist, pioneer in the theory of personality in the USA in the interwar years. Born in Montezum, Indiana, where his father was a physician and his mother a strongly Protestant schoolteacher. Both Allport and his brother Floyd, who became the founder of modern operationalist social psychology in the USA, experienced religious conflicts which may have led to their interest in social service.

Allport was educated at Harvard. A travelling fellowship (1922-4) took him to Germany and England, where he was exposed to European ideas, including gestalt theory. Returning to Harvard, he developed the TRAIT approach to personality theory initiated in his thesis. He collected an exhaustive battery of trait names for describing personality and produced a theory of ATTITUDES and attitude-formation, published in *Personality: A Psychological Interpretation* (1937). Allport held that a SELF, or ego, was a necessary component of a psychology of the individual; following

Swedenborg, he termed it the 'proprium' or private area. The essential property of personality was its nature as an open system, free to exchange matter and energy creatively with the environment, possessing some homeostatic states and a tendency to increasingly internal organization.

In 1938 Allport became Chairman of the Harvard Department of Psychology and used this position to help bring displaced European intellectuals, including Kurt LEWIN, to the USA. He assisted war-resisters and pressed for a just peace, as well as carrying out studies on the damaging effects of rumours and PREJUDICE. These studies led to *The Nature of Prejudice* (1954) and concluded that psychological explanations of prejudice were inadequate in themselves; historical and social aspects could not be reduced to the psychological.

Allport's advanced course on the history and methods of psychology formed the basis for the well-known *Handbook of Social Psychology* (1954; 2/1969) edited by a former colleague and student, Gardner Lindzey. Allport's approach to personality allows great eclecticism, and though he created no particular school of psychology his ideas influenced a whole generation of social scientists.

See ATTITUDE; PERSONALITY; PREJUDICE.

JL

**Althusser, Louis** (1918- ). French Communist intellectual and Marxist philosopher. Born in Algeria, Althusser went to school in Algiers and Marseilles, and was captured by the Germans 1940. After the war he studied at the Ecole Normale Supérieure in Paris, graduating in 1948, and has taught there since. His thought is often interpreted as stemming from particular ideological conflicts within the Communist Party. A depressive, he spent several periods in mental hospital, including the whole of the May-June 1968 'events' in Paris. In November 1980 his wife Hélène, a research sociologist to whom he was extremely attached, was found strangled. Althusser immediately confessed guilt but was too delirious to be charged. He was incarcerated in a mental hospital, where he remains. No charges have yet been brought, but it is doubtful if philosophy and sociology will benefit more from this brilliant yet tragic man.

His works include *For Marx* (1965), *Reading Capital* (1965), *Lenin and Philosophy* (1969) and *Essays in Self-Criticism* (1976). Althusser was associated, particularly in the early part of his career, with the French-based movement of STRUCTURAL-ISM. His books have influenced the post-1968 generation of Western Marxist intellectuals, inspiring work in fields as diverse as sociology, anthropology, historical studies and literary criticism. His writings on ideology have been particularly fertile.

Althusser's career was a critical response to modern Western Marxists who, since the 1920s, reacted against both the economic determinism of vulgar Marxism and the totalitarianism of Soviet orthodoxy, with a 'Hegelian' and 'humanist' interpretation of Marx, stressing Marx's earlier work at the expense of later writings. But Althusser argues that Marx's work passed through an epistemological break in 1845, when he abandoned his early, HEGELIAN problematic, founded on the ideological notion of ALIENATION, for a mature scientific framework, founded on such structural concepts as forces and RELATIONS OF PRODUCTION. The 'problematic', borrowed from the French philosopher of science Bachelard, is important in Althusser's anti-EMPIRICIST theory of knowledge. Knowledge cannot be validated by correspondence to the facts of independent, external reality. Rather, different frameworks of thought (problematics) contain particular sets of questions which, when addressed to reality, construct different sets of facts about the world. 'Facts' cannot arbitrate between differing problematics. One must proceed by examining the theories themselves, testing their coherence by a process which Althusser has borrowed from Freudian psychoanalysis and terms 'symptomatic reading'. This examines not only questions present in the words of the text but also absent ones. Problematics are always silent on some questions and this may reveal most about them.

Althusser's style is always polemical and often abusive. He rarely discusses mainstream sociology, dismissing it in asides as 'bourgeois'. He concentrates his attack on 'vulgar Marxism' and the equally simplistic Hegelian-Marxist variant, denying that the economic 'base' is the sole determinant of particular historical situations. He maintains that the social formation consists of distinct areas — the economic, political, ideological, and theoretical — each of which enjoys 'relative autonomy' from the others. The economic area is determinant only 'in the last instance', and never without the effects of the others. Each historical 'conjuncture' is thus the result of a number of determining factors, or, in another phrase borrowed from Freud and psychoanalysis, 'over-determined' (see PSYCHOANALYSIS). This model of social structure, influential in the 1970s, did not lead to the theoretical breakthroughs it seemed at first to promise. Nobody has as yet defined closely what is meant by only 'relative' autonomy or advanced a criterion by which 'the last instance' could be recognized (but see MODES OF PRODUCTION). Althusser's work has been criticized by other Marxists. His epistemology has been attacked as idealist because it ultimately fails to produce criteria which could distinguish between science and ideology. His argument that theoretical work itself constitutes a 'practice' has been criticized for divorcing the work of intellectuals from the daily struggles of the working class. Althusser conceded something to these arguments, while defending the main tenets of his theory.

AM, MM

**analytic.** An analytic truth is true by virtue of the meanings of the words in which it is stated, whereas a synthetic truth is true by virtue of some independent state of affairs. Thus 'all bachelors are unmarried' is an analytic truth, whereas 'all bachelors have beards' would, if true, be a synthetic truth. In social sciences what are presented as empirical LAWS often turn out to be analytic truths, or tautologies.

Analytical philosophy is the name usually given to a broad tradition of English-language philosophy begun with the analysis of concepts practised by G.E. Moore and the logical analysis of Bertrand Russell and WITTGENSTEIN. It culminated in the school of 'linguistic analysis' (also called linguistic or Oxford philosophy) which flourished in Oxford and elsewhere around the middle of this century. At its most optimistic, this school believed that traditional philosophical problems could be resolved by paying careful attention to the everyday use of words, since the use of language is itself part of something more complex — what Wittgenstein called a 'form of life'. This has been applied to the social sciences by Peter Winch.

See also COMTE; KANT; VIENNA CIRCLE.
See W.V.O. Quine, 'Two Dogmas of Empiricism' in *From a Logical Point of View* (1953).

WO

**anarchism.** A doctrine holding that the absence of government would not be a condition of chaos, but of harmonious order. The STATE, with its extensive apparatus of administration and coercion, is seen as the major source of oppression and inequality in society; once it were abolished, people's suppressed social capacities would be released, and they would arrange their affairs spontaneously for the good of all. Individualist anarchists conceive of a society of small self-sufficient producers; collectivist anarchists conceive of co-operation between worker-owners in the running of industrial enterprises. In either case, society is to be organized from the bottom upwards, with wider arrangements being agreed by negotiation between autonomous units. No individual person or social unit can be compelled to accept arrangements with which they disagree.

Anarchist opposition to institutionalized authority extends to the revolutionary movement. Anarchists hold that the means used to change society should embody the principles of the future society itself. The only authority recognized should be that of ability in a specific task, not that of permanent position; non-violent action is preferred to violent. Violence is to be directed only at symbolic targets, as a spark to ignite spontaneous mass disobedience to the state. In practice, anarchists have had to compromise these principles in order to defend popular revolutions by arms, as in Russia, Spain and elsewhere. Yet their critique of Marxism on the grounds that its revolutionary organization contains the seeds of a new dominant class has been reinforced by the treatment they have themselves received at the hands of Communist parties. There are today many quasi-anarchist religious communities (see NEW RELIGIONS).

DB

**ancestor.** Defined not merely as a dead member of the same social group. As FORTES points out, an ancestor has a name and also living relatives, who ensure his or her continued social relevance after death. An ancestor can be of either sex, according to the society involved. It is not unknown to find matrilineal ancestors venerated in patrilineal societies, and *vice versa*.

JE

**ancestor worship.** A practice distinguished by the congregation involved. In the restricted sense, this is composed of members of the same lineage and, in a wider sense, of people who share the same family context. Ancestor worship, as FORTES argues, is a CULT in which only exclusive ancestors are worshipped, and is a more complex than a simple means of providing a genealogical charter for a specific SOCIAL STRUCTURE. Nevertheless, genealogical knowledge is necessary for correct ritual observance within the cults, for it is also more than a cult of the dead. Funerary and mortuary rites are not, in themselves, the means of conferring ancestorhood. Becoming an ancestor is a particular RITE OF PASSAGE, in which the dead person is returned to the social group and symbolically incorporated. Among the West African Edo, the ancestor is 'planted' in the homestead by burial of the hair and nail parings in the home compound. This resting-place of the symbolic, rather than real, whole corpse, then becomes the sacred focus of future rites.

Theories of ancestor worship in social anthropology have fallen into three types. Initially it was suggested by 19th-century writers such as Tylor and FRAZER that ancestor worship was a psychological construction which sought to ward off a supposedly universal fear of death. Later, it was held that such cults provided a means of validating the social and moral structure of society. More recently, various anthropologists have stressed the tensions inherent in particular KINSHIP relations, principally the father-son relationship. Ancestor worship is seen as an expression of an ideal relationship between the living and the dead, involving obligations and RECIPROCITY, reflecting the basic unit of authority in intergenerational relations. Thus a crucial component of ancestor worship is kinship, represented by ideas of parenthood and inheritance. Rivalry between generations, for instance between a father and his firstborn son aspiring to his property and status in a patrilineal society, is vital in ancestor worship. Fortes claimed that the Oedipus complex (see PSYCHOANALYSIS) is institutionalized in West African Talle society through the rigid avoidance systems which operate between a living father and his firstborn son, ritualizing the tensions inherent in what FREUD called an ambivalent relationship. Ancestor worship is the worship of parenthood, as well as the validation of authority. But the relationship between parent and child does not alone explain ancestor worship. It is the principle of organization inherent in the authority relationship that is the crux; through this, it represents the principles of the kinship system to successive generations.

JE

**Annales School.** The French journal *Annales d'histoire économique et sociale* was founded in 1929 by M. BLOCH and L. Febvre as a vehicle for a new theory of history which aimed to integrate the fast-growing social sciences into a reconstructed scientific history. The contributors to the *Annales* included historians, economists, geographers and sociologists (the most prominent of whom was Durkheim's student, M. Halbwachs). The *Annales* school developed a view of history as a science of human societies in contrast to the dominant view that history is primarily a collection of facts about the past. The work done by members of this school, which was never more than a loose association of scholars, proved congenial to historically minded sociologists and sociologically inclined Marxists. Those tendencies are combined and the traditions of the *Annales* continued and developed at the Braudel Centre under the direction of I. Wallerstein at the State University of New York at Binghamton.

LS

**anomie.** Literally 'without NORMS', but more usually a state of society in which substantial disagreement exists over appropriate norms. If a set of people are in complete disagreement about the appropriate norms to follow, one cannot speak of them as a society. DURK-HEIM and MERTON are responsible for the two main approaches to anomie.

Durkheim sees anomie in modern society resulting from the incompleteness of the shift from mechanical to organic solidarity. The division of labour in society has progressed faster than the moral basis for this division; thus some aspects of society are inadequately regulated, hence anomie. Durkheim relates anomie to many ills or pathologies of modern society. For instance, in *Suicide* (1897) one of the four types is anomic suicide: cast adrift from norms that define what is worth doing and worth striving for, people become more likely to commit suicide. As a society becomes more anomic, the suicide rate increases. Suicide increases in societies both in times of depression and of economic boom, since both place people in new situations where their old standards are of little use. Life becomes aimless and suicide more likely. Below this theory lies Durkheim's 'conservative' belief that human happiness and social order depend on a high level of social regulation by society and on value CONSENSUS. Without this, human nature is subject to 'malady of infinite aspiration'. This is opposite to Marx's 'radical' theory of ALIENATION in which (capitalist) social structure frustrates human NEEDS, but both rest on theories of essential human nature which cannot be validated.

Durkheim's psychological assumptions were modified by Merton. In *Social Theory and Social Structure* (1949, rev. 1957) he implicitly changed the meaning of anomie from normlessness to norm conflict. In his analysis of the contemporary USA, unhappiness results because of a disjunction between different parts of the value structure of society, between culturally prescribed goals (essentially high material achievements) and institutionalized, legitimate means of attaining them. Anomie occurs when people cannot achieve the goals by the normal means. But they may adapt to this in five different ways: by conformity or four types of DEVIANCE (innovation, ritualism,

retreatism and rebellion) in which either or both the goals and means are rejected. In Merton's discussion, unlike Durkheim's, CLASS differences are important.

While the American ideology stresses that the good life is open to all, the opportunity to succeed is different for different social classes. Rejecting the legitimate opportunity structure and replacing it with crime to achieve success is concentrated in the WORKING CLASS. The view of deviance as a response to socially structured failure and the cure it suggests — increasing opportunity — has been extremely influential. It has been part of the justification of many social welfare programmes designed to alleviate social disadvantages, particularly through education, such as Operation Headstart (see COMPENSATORY EDUCATION).

See also INFLATION.                KM, MM

**anorexia nervosa.** See MENTAL ILLNESS.

**antinomianism.** The belief that law or moral conventions do not apply to those who have attained a state of, or realized their condition of, sinlessness or membership of God's elect, or to those who possess God's dispensation from conventional morality (i.e. 'anti-NORMS'). In various forms this belief has appeared among Christian SECTS from the time of the Early Church to the present day. It is sometimes based on the assumption that the true disciple, once released from sin by the acceptance of salvation, is thenceforth freed from sin for ever and need exercise no moral control. John Humphrey Noyes in the 19th century argued that Christ came not simply to forgive sin but to give freedom from sin. Hence true followers lived in a state of perfection. As they should also love God in their fellows the way was opened for the practice of 'complex marriage' in the Oneida Community which Noyes founded. All male followers were 'married' to all female followers and might, in principle, engage in sexual intercourse with any of them. Other sects believed that disciples are not freed from sin by salvation but that, following such biblical passages as Acts 13:39 ('By him all that believe are justified from all things from which ye could not be justified by the law of Moses'), the true disciple has received a dispensation from the observances of the moral law. The contemporary Children of God interpret this to mean that the sexual attractions of members may be employed in bringing others to salvation. In the 17th century antinomianism appears among the radical Protestant sects of the English Revolution, often as an extension of the Calvinist doctrine of election. Since membership of God's elect and of the damned were foreordained those who possessed an inner conviction of their election were free to indulge themselves as they chose.

RW

**anxiety neurosis.** See MENTAL ILLNESS.

**appreciation.** Advocated by Matza (*Becoming Deviant*, 1969) as a procedure appropriate to his 'naturalistic' investigation of DEVIANCE. Naturalism was designed to supersede the alleged 'correctionalism' of CRIMINOLOGY, correctionalism being defined as a distorting stance which sought knowledge for manipulative ends. Whereas the older criminology was thought to approach people from without and describe them as if they were 'things' or 'objects', appreciation is a sympathetic version of VERSTEHEN (understanding) which attempts to understand the inner logic of others' actions. Human will and meaning are restored to a central place in sociological reasoning. Employed by Matza, appreciation is akin to the method of PHENOMENOLOGY; it consists of an introspection into one's own consciousness to establish the significance of the activity of another person.

PR

**apprenticeship.** A system of training for craft labour traditionally favoured in Britain, borrowing from a pre-industrial model in which the apprentice spent a lengthy period (unpaid or even 'unfree') learning a craft or trade, typically in his master's household, before becoming qualified as a paid workman ('journeyman'). The journeyman's aim was to become a master himself, but shortage of capital as well as mediaeval life-expectancy often frustrated this ambition. Restriction of entry and lengthy 'training' safeguarded the market power of the craft, whilst socializing the recruit into a novel

identity and integrating him into a tightly-knit, exclusive group possessing guild organization and its own technical 'mysteries'.

Skilled trade apprenticeship after industrialism often retained something from these institutions, including excessively lengthy training and special rites (such as being immersed in printer's ink) to mark graduation, but above all a stress upon learning, fierce pride in craft membership, a readiness to stand up for the quality of workmanship against the demands of rapid output, and a strong determination to resist 'interference' from outsiders such as employers, other workers, or consumers. In the British labour movement, craft unions have as a result at times been regarded as excessively preoccupied with their sectional aims, thus undermining workers' solidarity and CLASS CONSCIOUSNESS.

See also PROFESSION; SKILL; TRADE UNION.

MR

**appropriate technology.** In the course of their capitalist development advanced countries have invented technologies which are largely capital intensive and labour-saving. The transfer of these technologies to developing countries is often argued to be inappropriate to the factor endowments prevailing there. Developing countries are typically scarce in capital, abundant in labour and lack the skills necessary for the efficient utilization of the transferred technologies. The answer lies in the invention and development of 'appropriate' technologies which can make use of local resources and local skills and which make minimal demands on scarce capital resources.

AH

**aristocracy.** A ruling class whose considerable privileges derive from ownership of land and to which entry is normally restricted by (noble) birth. In classical Greek usage the term meant 'rule by the best' as opposed to oligarchy, 'rule by the rich', but this was seen even then to be an ideological distinction. Aristocracy in one society may denote a ruling oligarchy, in another a collective leadership which rules alongside a monarch, or the monarchy and the aristocracy may be locked in combat or co-exist uneasily.

See also NOBILITY.                                    LS

**aristocracy of labour.** See LABOUR ARISTO-CRACY.

**Arrow's theorem.** A fundamental result of mathematical social science, to the effect that the individual preferences of members of a community as to the distribution of its resources are together not sufficient to define preferences for the community as a whole. It was originally proved by K.J. Arrow in 1950 in the context of WELFARE ECONOMICS.

The assumptions of the theorem are that each individual has a complete and consistent order of preferences over all possible distributions of goods and services, an order that is not affected if one particular option is removed, and that the community social welfare function is positively related to each individual's ordering. Arrow proves that there is no general way of constructing a social welfare function satisfying these conditions. The theorem is important for sociology because it establishes a basic limit upon CONSENSUS in the choice of collective action insofar as this affects the distribution of goods and services. However, being a non-existence theorem it has not promoted an associated body of theory and research, and despite wide initial interest critics have seen it as not being a fruitful result within welfare economics.                                    JL

**ascription.** See ACHIEVEMENT.

**Asiatic mode of production.** The most contentious of MARX'S MODES OF PRODUCTION. It assumes the absence of private property in land in Asia, a matter of controversy. Primarily with reference to India, Marx vacillated between the views that land was held by the community or by the state. He explained this in terms of geographic and climatic conditions requiring large state-managed hydraulic works (a suggestion developed by K. WITTFOGEL). As P. Anderson suggests in a useful review of the subject (*Lineages of the Absolutionist State*, 1974), Marx and Engels's relative lack of knowledge about Asia led them into a

position in which the Asiatic mode of production became a residual category for non-European societies which seemed to be stagnating.

Recent historical research has probably established the likelihood that land formally owned by the state was often in practice at the disposal of powerful slaveowners and/or nobles (as in China). State and private ownership could also easily co-exist (as in 10th-century Byzantium). Communal ownership of land at the local level also co-existed with private ownership (as in medieval Russia), and so on. Such facts transfer attention from the legal question of ownership to the sociological question of practical possession, or in Marxist terms from the juridical expression of relations of production to the real appropriation of the surplus (of agricultural or other production). Therefore in India, while there was no private property in land in the Western sense, the organization of the CASTE system and the Hindu state ensured the privileges of the ruling class and its agents as thoroughly as any feudal aristocracy might have done.

Thus the Asiatic mode of production does not add anything distinctive to the ancient-slave or the feudal modes of production. Its geographical limitation would also make it inconsistent with a general theory of modes of production. Either there are regularities of human history encapsulated by the contradictions between means of production and relations of production, or each region of the globe possesses its own regularities.                                    LS

**assimilation.** See PARK, R.E.

**association, coefficients of.** Association is a general term in statistics referring to an orderly relationship between two VARI-ABLES, so that over a population knowledge of the value of one attribute gives some additional knowledge of the value of the other. Association gives information about relations between variables, and is to be distinguished from implication, a logical relation between theoretical propositions, and CAUSALITY, an asymmetric, temporally ordered relation between events.

Coefficients of association provide

measures of the degree of extra information by assessing the proportional reduction in error (PRE) in predicting one attribute when the value of the other attribute is known. Coefficients differ in the prediction rules they employ and in the way they define error. Both are related to the level of MEASUREMENT involved.

For nominal level variables (see MEASUREMENT), error can only consist of mismatching categories. The 'natural prediction rule' is to predict the modal category of the dependent variable when knowing nothing about the category of the independent variable and, when knowing it, to predict the modal category of the dependent variable within that category of the independent variable. The proportional reduction in error then yields Goodman and Kruskals asymmetric lambda, a widely used coefficient. Lambda, however, may take on a value of zero (no association) even when the observations of the dependent variable are unevenly distributed over the categories of the independent variable, if the modal category of the dependent variable is the same for all categories of the independent variable.

For ordinal level variables (see MEASUREMENT), error can be defined as predicting the wrong order on the dependent variable for two observations. Goodman and Kruskal's gamma uses this principle. For a $2 \times 2$ table, gamma condenses down to the easily used and interpreted Yule's Q.

Gamma has the disadvantage for some purposes that it can achieve its extreme values of 1 in situations other than when all the observations are on the diagonal of the contingency table (absolute association). Kendall's Tau-B is designed for use on these occasions, although it has no simple probabilistic interpretation. Ties on variables are ignored.

For ordinal variables where the observations can be more or less completely ranked individually, Spearman's coefficient of rank determination, Rho, measures the PRE in predicting rank on one variable from rank on the other. For intervally measurable variables Pearson's r, the product-moment correlation coefficient, or simply correlation coefficient, is almost universally used in sociology, partly out of habit, but largely because of its relation to the theory of REGRESSION and CAUSAL MODELLING. Error is defined by squaring deviations from the predicted values of the dependent variable, and the square of the correlation coefficient has a natural interpretation as the proportional reduction in the variability of the dependent variable when the value of the independent variable is known (i.e. no proportion of variance explained). Thus a correlation coefficient of 0.5 only represents a 25 per cent reduction in variability. The correlation coefficient, in addition to assuming an interval level of measurement, assumes that the variables are jointly normally distributed.

Pairs of variables are rarely isolated in sociology, usually occurring in intimate relation with one or more other variables. Partial association refers to the association between two variables when the categories of the remaining variables do not alter or, to put it another way, when the remaining variables are controlled for. All or most of the association between two variables may disappear when the effect of other variables is controlled for, or less commonly, the association between two variables may be suppressed by other variables and increase dramatically when these are controlled for.

JL

**atheism, methodological.** In general usage, atheism refers to belief in the non-existence of God. P. BERGER (*The Social Reality of Religion*, 1969) coined 'methodological atheism' to describe a sociological approach to religion which seeks to understand religion as a human construction, leaving open the issue of whether it also possesses a status independent of man. Some writers, such as R. Towler (*Homo Religiosus*, 1974), interpret Berger to mean that the appropriate methodological stance of the sociologist of religion is to assume that the beliefs being studied are false. But Berger is not making a claim about the content of the beliefs in question so much as a statement about the nature of a sociological concern with religion. He is arguing that sociology's role is to examine religion insofar as it is humanly created and to leave the issue of whether it is anything more than that to theology.

RW

**attitude.** In modern social science, the concept of attitude is a distinctive product of 20th-century American social psychology. It is a general concept connoting the cognitive, affective and behavioural orientation of an individual towards a specific object or class of objects in the natural or social environment. Conceptually, an attitude is a persistent relation between individual psychological process and the environment, unlike a motive (which is seen as existing only during the situations to which it is relevant) or a personality TRAIT, also a persistent feature but without a specific object. An attitude may involve a belief, but in general it does not imply the degree of logical organization required of a belief.

Etymologically the term attitude has two semantic components, both deriving from the Latin *aptus*: one as in 'aptitude', a fitness or ability; the other, as used in art, expressing the pose or set of a figure or statue. 'Mental' and 'motor' attitudes were initially distinguished by psychologists, and in the last quarter of the 19th century many experiments were carried out by German psychologists such as Münsterberg and Large on the degree to which responses were affected by both the muscular preparedness of the subject and the direction of his attention. The two threads were drawn together through PSYCHOANALYTIC theory, the concept of subconscious psychological processes showing a way to reconcile aspects of unconscious and conscious psychological orientation. After World War I ALLPORT combined experimental and psychodynamic approaches in his pioneering work on personality theory, producing in 1935 a definition which has been of enduring influence: an attitude is 'a mental and neural state of readiness, organized through experience, exerting a directing or dynamic influence upon the individual's response to all objects and situations with which it is related'. His brother Floyd Allport had been influenced by Münsterberg while a student at Harvard, and with the technical help of L.L. Thurstone he initiated empirical methods for measuring and scaling attitudes, an area which has generated much fundamental research on the nature of measurement (e.g. by S.S. Stevens, C. Coombs) and has contributed largely to a view of social science as

consisting of relating together variables characterizing individuals.

The concept of attitude is neutral as to the causal role of heredity and environment. Relating individual psychology with the social world, it has been a focus of research for both social psychology and sociology. As early as 1918 Thomas and Znaniecki viewed attitudes as the individual counterparts of social values, and a large body of social research has aimed to measure these social attitudes to predict or explain social behaviour. Sociologists have studied the processes of attitude change largely with a view to the implementation of social policy through the changing of attitudes, a level of intervention that to conservative political and social interests has seemed preferable to social structural change. By contrast, relatively little research has been done on the origin of attitudes.

At least since the 1950s, research has also concerned the relationship between attitudes and behaviour. Conceptually, attitudes and behaviour have an intimate relationship. Attitudes are to be inferred chiefly from overt behaviour, but they are not to be seen as behaviour. They are to be seen as underlying it and as determining it jointly with current situational factors. In practice, the measurement of attitudes has involved the use of verbal responses in isolation — QUESTIONNAIRES, interviews etc — and the correlation of these measurements with the occurrence of the relevant behaviour has proved very weak. Attitudes seem to be in part evoked by the situation of their measurement, and where this situation is widely different from the operational situation, attitude measurements have been poor predictors.

See COGNITIVE CONSISTENCY THEORY; PERSONALITY; TRAIT.

JL

**authoritarian personality.** A concept made popular by ADORNO, Frenkel-Brunswick, Levinson and Sanford's classic study of PREJUDICE, *The Authoritarian Personality*, first published in 1950. The stimulus for this immediate post-war study was FASCIST anti-semitism; it was initiated by the American Jewish Committee and some of the researchers were refugees from Hitler's persecution. The specific aim was to examine why certain individuals are willing to accept anti-semitic ideas and opinions; the concern was with the individual's relation to anti-semitic IDEOLOGY rather than with the origin and development of that ideology, or with the rise to political power of its proponents. Although the study has interested socio-logists and typifies one approach to the study of the relation of individual to society, its concerns are essentially psychological.

The study divides into two parts. The first deals with the hypothesis 'that anti-semitism probably is not a specific or isolated pheno-menon but part of a broader ideological framework'. Anti-semitism is part of a broader range of ATTITUDES, and the person who is anti-semitic is more likely to be generally ETHNOCENTRIC, and CONSERVA-TIVE in his political and economic philos-ophy. These attitudes relate to PERSONALITY. Theoretically, personality structure is conceptualized along FREUDIAN lines, and attitudes are seen as relating to basic psychological needs. According to these authors, personality is itself moulded by the social environment and is seen to determine ideological preferences. Anti-semitic and ethnocentric attitudes, they suggest, relate to underlying emotional — often primitive and irrational — needs.

To test these ideas four Likert-type ques-tionnaire scales (see SCALING) were devised; the first three conceptualized as attitude scales and designed to measure anti-semitism (The A-S scale), ethnocentrism (the E scale) and political and economic conservatism (the PEC scale). The final scale is referred variously as a measure of 'implicit anti-democratic trends', and of the 'poten-tiality for fascism' (the F scale). It is a measure of personality, and by implication as the means of identifying the authoritarian personality — a concept not formally defined, but given meaning through the components of this scale. The sub-scales include conventionalism (rigid adhering to conventional MIDDLE CLASS values); authoritarian submission (submissive, uncritical attitude toward idealized moral authorities of the in-group); authoritarian AGGRESSION (a tendency to be on the lookout for, and to condemn, reject, and punish people who violate conventional values) and anti-intraception (opposition to the sub-jective, the imaginative, the tender-minded).

The questionnaire scales were admin-istered to a sample of some 2,000 indi-viduals, mostly white, non-Jewish, middle class native Americans, contacted through formal organizations, as well as to a number of small specialized sub-samples. The CORRELATIONS between the scales were all positive as hypothesized, some relatively high (in the main sample they were as follows: A-S with E 0.80; E with PEC 0.57; PEC with A-S 0.43; F with A-S 0.53; F with E 0.73 and F with PEC 0.52). The relation-ship between ethnocentrism and education and INTELLIGENCE was also examined and a low but statistically significant negative association was obtained. The authors argue that this indicates that neither factor can really account for the phenomenon of prejudice.

The second half of the study deals with the origins and development of the authori-tarian personality. Data were obtained from in-depth interviews with 80 individuals from the main sample (half from the highest quartile on the E scale, half from the lowest quartile; half men, half women). PROJECTIVE TESTS (the TAT and some projective questions) were also used. Theoretically this was obviously influenced by PSYCHO-ANALYTIC ideas: prejudice is viewed as orig-inating in the dynamics of family interaction; more specifically parental anxieties about status produce parental behaviour that is itself basically authoritarian. Brought up with high expectations, the child represses his or her own failings and shortcomings (see DEFENCE MECHANISMS) and projects them onto others. Prejudice in relation to others results, the projection of one's own faults on to other people serving to rationalize and legitimate aggression towards them.

The study has been criticized methodo-logically for (1) sample selection (the failure to obtain a random sample); (2) scale design (uni-directional questions raising problems of 'response set', i.e. where respondents get into the habit of answering in a particular way regardless of the meaning of each new question); (3) interview bias (interviewers were shown the first questionnaires before the second interview); (4) the restricted size of the interview sample. Theoretically, criticism has focused on: (1) the psycho-analytic approach to personality structure and dynamics, and standard criticisms of this approach have been advanced (see PSYCHO-ANALYSIS); (2) the validity of the scales of attitude and personality — it has been argued that the study essentially measures an authoritarianism of the political right. Alternative approaches have been advocated by EYSENCK and ROKEACH, amongst others. Eysenck (*Psychology of Politics*, 1954) identified two basic person-ality dimensions, labelled tough- and tender-mindedness and radicalism-conservatism, arguing that it is necessary to assess both if we are properly to encompass the diversity of prejudice and authoritarianism. Rokeach (*The Open and Closed Mind*, 1960) uses the concept of dogmatism to develop a more general measure of authoritarianism, independent of political content; (3) the importance of personality in explaining racial prejudice, persecution and discrim-ination, has been questioned. Adorno and his colleagues formulated psychological rather than sociological questions about prejudice, explicitly and reasonably restrict-ing their attention to the susceptibility of individuals to anti-semitic and other ethno-centric beliefs; however, in so doing, they assume that personality structure is of considerable importance in accounting for phenomena such as anti-semitism. It may be that the contribution of personality (moulded by earlier social environment) is often of relatively little importance compared to situational factors such as the changing political and economic culture of the society, operating almost irrespective of personality.                    JB

**authority.** A particular type of power. Most sociologists, following PARSONS, define it as power which is legitimate, recognized as morally justified by both the powerful and the powerless (see LEGITIMACY). But others, influenced by CONFLICT THEORY, have argued that power is almost never endorsed morally by the powerless. Instead, they define authority as power which is thor-oughly institutionalized. Its use is un-questioned because it is routine — authority is neither right nor wrong, it just is. Both conceptions are heavily influenced by different readings of WEBER, the major theorist of authority.

See also POWER.                    MM

# B

**Becker, Howard S.** (1928- ). American sociologist. Born in 1928 in Chicago, Illinois, his father was in advertising. He took all his Northwestern University, Chicago, in 1965. 1946, AM 1949, PhD 1951), and became Professor of Sociology and Urban Affairs at Northwestern University, Chicago, in 1965. Influenced heavily by the ideas of BLUMER and Everett C. Hughes, he became noted for his contributions to LABELLING THEORY through his publication *Outsiders* (1963), to methodology (especially PARTICIPANT OBSERVATION), to field work studies of student cultures, and to SYMBOLIC INTER-ACTIONISM generally. He was a professional pianist at 15 and later studied jazz musicians, and is a keen photographer: this led to his study of 'Art Worlds' and the contribution of photography to sociology.

KP

**behaviour.** Action which may be observed, inferred or reported, as distinct from the dispositions (values, beliefs, ATTITUDES) of social actors. What people do is not necessarily the same as what they say they will do. Therein lies a major problem since much social research data is derived from statements about the dispositions of actors, rather than evidence of actual behaviour. For example, studies of race relations depend on attitude measurement to a greater extent than on evidence of actual inter-racial contact. Many studies since La Piere in 1934 have shown that expressed attitudes and actual behaviour are not necessarily consistent with one another. Yet it is only in relatively few fields (e.g. studies of VOTING,

FERTILITY, INDUSTRIAL CONFLICT) that the opportunity to compare attitudes and behaviour occurs.

See I. Deutscher, *What We Say/What We Do* (1973). MB

**behaviourism.** An influential school of psychology that, following POSITIVIST principles, makes observable behaviour, as opposed to mental events and subjective experience, the prime object of study. The term behaviourism, however, encompasses a diverse range of theoretical and methodological positions, and behaviourists differ considerably in the precise status attached to both observable behaviour and mental life. The approach in its various forms has dominated academic psychology (in part by virtue of its increasingly broad and diverse character) and has had an important influence on the social sciences. It has not only served as a model of the scientific analysis of human behaviour, but has also provided a range of theoretical and substantive ideas that have been utilized in diverse ways within the social sciences. G.H. MEAD, for instance, called his own approach SOCIAL BEHAVIOUR-ISM, while G.C. Homans used behaviourist ideas in his analysis of social interaction (*Social Behaviour: Its Elementary Forms*, 1961), and they also had an influence on EXCHANGE THEORY.

The beginning of behaviourism in the United States, according to most commentators, occurred in 1913 with the publication of a paper by J.B. Watson entitled 'Psychology as the Behaviourist views it'. For Watson, psychology was an objective, experimental branch of natural science whose goal was the prediction and control of behaviour. To this end he contended that it should 'discard all reference to consciousness' and abandon introspection as a method of study. Instead, psychology, in order to make itself properly scientific, should focus on what could be objectively measured. Mental experiences, he suggested, were essentially epiphenomenal and human behaviour could be explained without reference to them.

The dominant substantive interest of many early behaviourists, as of later ones, lay in the mechanisms of learning. Building on the ideas of physiologists and animal psychologists, including the Russian physiologist, Pavlov, and their work on the reflex, the simplest forms of learning were analysed. Learning was conceptualized as a process in which human behaviour was controlled and moulded by environmental forces, the latter viewed as a set of discrete stimuli, the former as a set of discrete responses. The task of research was to identify the processes involved in the establishment of connections between stimuli and responses (hence, the use of the term S-R psychology to refer to this type of approach to learning). The concept of conditioning was used to refer to the learning process itself, for behaviour was held to be dependent (conditional) on the presentation of a neutral stimulus, with the new stimulus-response connection held to be established through a process of reinforcement (the use of some stimulus to strengthen the new response). Much of the behaviourist study of the learning process attempted to delineate the principles of learning on strictly empirical lines, an approach epitomized by the work of B.F. Skinner (*The Behaviour of Organisms: An Experimental Approach*, 1938) and extended by him to language (*Verbal Behaviour*, 1957). There has, however, been a strong theoretical tradition within behaviourism, exemplified in the work of C.L. Hull (*Principles of Behaviour*, 1943).

The attempt to analyse human behaviour in terms of direct S-R connections has provoked considerable criticism, not least from philosophers who have pointed to the problems involved in a behaviourism that eschews all reference to mental events (an approach often referred to as radical behaviourism) on the grounds that the identification of particular human actions requires some attention to the individual's intentions (and hence necessitates some mentalistic reference). Other critics, both within and outside psychology, have objected to the atomistic, mechanistic, and asocial assumptions about human behaviour that assign a largely passive role to individual in relation to environmental forces. Such arguments were given substantive support by the fact that attempts to analyse learning in terms of direct S-R connections were by no means successful in empirical terms, even with the simple (and according to critics extremely narrow) animal learning situations used in many experiments. Experimental studies often yielded evidence of patterns of behaviour that did not fit the predictions of radical behaviourists and indicated insight, meaning, and purposive behaviour. Consequently the findings of empirical research of the 1930s and 1940s led some behaviourists to reject the more radical forms of behaviourism and to develop alternatives. Edward Tolman, for instance, in the 1930s put forward a purposive behaviourism (*Purposive Behaviour in Animals and Man*, 1932), while in the 1950s Osgood and others introduced mediational theories of learning (*Method and Theory in Experimental Psychology*, 1953). Mediational theorists argued that overt stimuli and responses were not directly connected, but were linked (mediated) by internal processes involving meaning that could themselves be conceptualised in terms of internal stimuli and responses. Other theorists contended that what is learnt is not discrete behavioural responses but information about the environment that may, for instance, consist of facts and strategies for action. What is accepted by all these behaviourists is that some reference must be made to cognitive processes (they are often referred to as cognitive or neo-behaviourists). Their behaviourism is distinctive more in terms of its methodological commitment to relate mental events to observable behaviour and its substantive interests (the focus on the learning process continues to be dominant) than in the theoretical status given to mental events. Whilst, therefore, the specific theoretical claims of the different versions of cognitive behaviourism raise many problems, many of the strongest criticisms of behaviourism cannot be laid at their door.

See also BEHAVIOUR THERAPY.

JB

**behaviour therapy.** This term refers to techniques of therapy whose theoretical rationale are to be found in BEHAVIOURIST principles of learning. Behaviour therapy or behaviour modification, as it sometimes known, was largely developed in the second half of the 1950s (the first published use of the term came in 1953) with the work of Joseph Wolpe and B.F. Skinner in the USA and H.J. EYSENCK in the UK. A little earlier J. Dollard and N.E. Miller had tried to translate PSYCHOANALYTIC concepts into the terminology of Hullian learning theory, and well before this some early behaviourists had attempted on occasions to use techniques of conditioning for therapeutic purposes.

Techniques of behaviour therapy are used by psychologists and PSYCHIATRISTS to try and modify any aspect of behaviour that is considered undesirable, including the symptoms of MENTAL ILLNESS such as anxiety. From the behaviourist point of view the symptoms of mental illness are conditioned responses or habits that are maladaptive, and the terms abnormal behaviour or DEVIANCE are to be preferred to that of mental illness. The range of techniques that has been developed is based on the different possibilities contained within learning theory for getting rid of a learned response. A widely utilized technique of therapy, used especially to treat symptoms of anxiety and phobias, is known as systematic desensitization. This involves the attempt to facilitate the acquisition of a new response (relaxation) that is incompatible with the existing response (anxiety) in order to eliminate the latter. More controversial is so-called aversion therapy where the aim is to acquire an aversion to something that has high value for the individual (for instance, alcohol or drugs) by pairing it with something unpleasant (a small electric shock or a nauseous pharmacological agent). Another technique uses rewards to reinforce (strengthen) desired behaviour. This has been applied in an institutional context in the form of what is called a token economy.

Though the varied techniques of behaviour therapy clearly derive from the principles of behaviourist learning theory and are often criticized on the same grounds, the extent to which in practice the content and therapeutic operation of behaviour therapy is consistent with the principles of behaviourism and the details of learning theory is more doubtful. Therapy sessions often include much that falls outside a strictly defined conditioning process, for instance, discussion of the patient's symptoms, and it may well be that the therapist's involvement with the patient and any warmth that is shown are of more therapeutic value than the conditioning process itself. There is much debate, too, about the value and effectiveness of behaviour therapy, with critics asserting its limited application (to readily isolated items of behaviour) and its ineffectiveness (they claim the symptom, or some other, often recurs). Eysenck contends, however, that behaviour therapy is far more effective than psychoanalysis or psychoanalytically oriented forms of therapy. The issue is not easy to settle, not only because there is little agreement on criteria of improvement or cure, but also because the clinical context in which behaviour therapy and psychoanalysis are normally given militates against systematic evaluation of effectiveness, and properly controlled comparative studies are almost non existent.

JB

**Bell, Daniel** (1919- ). American sociologist particularly associated with the 'end of ideology' debate and the concept of 'post-industrial society'. A graduate of City College, New York, and Columbia University, Bell taught at Chicago and Columbia Universities before becoming Professor of Sociology at Harvard in 1969. His publications include *History of Marxism in the United States* (1952), *The New American Right* (1955), *The End of Ideology* (1960), *The Radical Right* (1963), *The Reforming of General Education* (1966), *Towards the Year 2000* (1968), *Confrontation* (1969), *Capitalism Today* (1971), *The Coming of Post-Industrial Society* (1973) and *The*

*Cultural Contradictions of Capitalism* (1976).

Bell was a leading exponent of convergence theory, which emerged in the late 1950s. This assumed that technical and economic imperatives of social organization are more influential than political ideology in shaping social structure; capitalist and state socialist societies are therefore becoming increasingly alike. Bell contributed towards the futurology which became fashionable in the late 1960s, acting as Chairman of the Commission on the Year 2000 set up by the American Academy of Arts and Sciences. Many of the sociologists who had participated in the 'end of ideology' debate advocated, in the following decade, the thesis of the 'post-industrial society', a term Bell coined. Industrial societies are entering a new phase of evolution, most advanced in the USA; whereas industrial society is dominated by a business elite and the pursuit of profit, post-industrial society is characterized by a closer relationship between science and technology, by the primacy of theory (abstract, highly codified knowledge) over empiricism, and by the dominance of a new elite of scientists and technocrats whose power is based upon their specialized knowledge. The university becomes the key institution responsible for the production and evaluation of knowledge and in promoting technical growth. The application of theoretical knowledge can be seen in the rise of science-based industries, the use of computer-based simulation procedures in decision-making, and the application of macro-economic theory in the management of the national economy. A service economy replaces a primarily goods-producing economy, and the white-collar sector becomes the largest unit within the labour force, rendering the Marxist preoccupation with the industrial worker increasingly obsolete. The concern of the (rapidly expanding) professional, scientific and technical groups for general welfare becomes the main ethos in post-industrial society, promising greater social harmony. Economic class conflict is superseded by communal conflict over issues such as health, education and the environment. Since the political realm is treated as autonomous, structural change is examined without an analysis of political factors which may affect such change.

Bell's term 'post-industrial society' was also used in France by Touraine. It is also similar to Etzioni's 'post-modern society', Lichtheim's 'post-bourgeois society', Kahn's 'post-economic society' and Halmos's 'personal service society'. The concept of a society based on knowledge is shared with the British and American New Left of the 1960s and with writers such as Galbraith, Clark Kerr and the Marxist HABERMAS. Bell's sociology has affinities with the Saint-Simonian and Weberian traditions (see SAINT-SIMON, WEBER) and the work of other technocratic theorists.

Most sociologists accept the reality of the trends identified by Bell, but many of his critics doubt that these trends amount to a radically different form of society. They argue that he neglects the survival of the main traditional power-structures of the USA, especially capitalism and militarism. Bell himself — always an empirically honest writer — provides figures in *The Coming of Post-Industrial Society* which show that the bulk of American Research and Development is sponsored by big business and the military.                                    JW

**Bendix, Reinhard** (1916- ). German/American Weberian sociologist. Born in Berlin, Bendix emigrated to the USA in 1938 and received his PhD from the University of Chicago in 1947. Since 1956 he has been a dominant influence at the University of California, Berkeley. President of the American Sociological Association 1969-70. Best-known as a leading WEBER scholar: his book *Max Weber: An Intellectual Portrait* (1960) introduced many English-speaking sociologists to the more historical and comparative side of Weber's work and provided an important counterbalance to PARSONS's more abstract interpretation, *The Structure of Social Action*. In many other books on a variety of subjects — *Work and Authority in Industry* (1956), *Nation Building and Citizenship* (1964), *Embattled Reason* (1970) and *Kings or People?* (1980) — Bendix has pursued and developed a variety of Weberian themes in a manner only slightly less encyclopaedic than Weber himself.

*Work and Authority in Industry* is concerned with BUREAUCRACY. It traces the historical transformation of the 19th-century entrepreneurial ideology, which legitimated the private ownership of property, into a new managerial ideology legitimating the managerial exercise of control in large-scale bureaucracies. Bendix claims that in the UK the growth of the managerial ideology was associated largely with the capital-intensive industries and that it emerged within the USA in response to the bureaucratization of industry and the growing power of the trade union movement. *Kings or People* uses Weber's distinction between FEUDAL and PATRIMONIAL authority in a wide range of historical case-studies.

Bendix collaborated with S.M. Lipset on two influential works. *Class, Status and Power* (1953) attempted to reconcile European and American conceptions of stratification through a Weberian model of 'class, status and party' (see CLASS: NEO-WEBERIAN THEORIES). *Social Mobility in Industrial Society* (1959) promoted the (much-disputed) thesis that rates of inter-generational mobility from manual to non-manual labour reveal a similar pattern in advanced industrial societies (see SOCIAL MOBILITY).

LS, JW

**Benedict, Ruth Fulton** (1887-1948). American anthropologist and poet (published as Anne Singleton) who originally studied and taught English literature. She studied anthropology at the New School for Social Research (1919-21). At Columbia in 1922 she encountered the major influences of BOAS and KROEBER, under whom she began a field study of the Serrano Indians of California, writing a Doctorate on the guardian spirit in North America in 1923. Her work was always comparative; she studied the Zuñi, Cochite and Pima Indians of America and in later years turned to Asia and Europe, as well as drawing upon data from other researchers in order to analyse the characteristic 'culture patterns' of various peoples, with particular reference to value systems and what she saw as corresponding personality types. This was most clearly expressed in her best-known work, *Patterns of Culture* (1934) in which she compared the 'Apollonian' culture of Pueblo Indians with the 'Dionysion' culture of other North American Indians and the 'megalomaniac' Kwakiutl Indians with the 'paranoid' Dobuan islanders of the South Pacific. These cultural labels caused some confusion, and although her work is still read and enjoyed by many students, her framework of analysis has not persisted in mainstream social anthropology. After World War II she turned to large-scale modern societies, founding and directing the Columbia University Research in Contemporary Cultures project in 1947. Her study of Japanese value systems in *The Chrysanthemum and the Sword* (1946) is regarded as being influential in affecting public policy in America towards Japan. She taught social anthropology at Columbia, and her influence as a stimulating and sympathetic teacher upon several generations of students of cultural anthropology was considerable.

JE

**benefit.** See UTILITY.

**Berger, P.L. and Luckman, T.** Peter Berger, now Professor of Sociology at Rutgers University, and Thomas Luckman, now Professor of Sociology at Konstanz University, collaborated in the early 1960s while at the New School of Social Research, New York. Both were interested in the sociology of religion and by extension in the way in which knowledge and ideas were influenced by social structure. In their influential *Social Construction of Reality* (1966) they used the PHENOMENOLOGICAL writings of SCHUTZ, who also taught at the New School, to argue that the influence of social structure upon reality should be investigated not only at the social level, as in the traditional sociology of knowledge, but also at the interpersonal level of the common-sense knowledge of everyday life. In both this book and a number of contemporaneous papers (together, singly or with other authors) they examined the processes whereby persons create a personal view of social reality as they are socialized into any society (the subjective view of reality) and the ways in which such views are objectified as INSTITUTIONS that come to be seen as obdurate factors by the actors in any social system (the objective view of reality). Finally, they attempted to bring these two processes together under one perspective, a theoretical problem as yet only partially solved by social theorists.

See KNOWLEDGE, SOCIOLOGY OF.

PWM

**Bernstein, Basil** (1924- ). British sociologist of education, known principally for his work on language and social class. Since 1967 Professor of the Sociology of Education at the Institute of Education, University of London, and an influential figure in his field in Britain since the early 1960s and more recently in Europe and throughout the English-speaking world. His work, and some of that carried out at the Institute's Sociological Research Unit, of which he was Director, has been collected and published, particularly in *Class, Codes and Control* (3 vols., 1971-5).

His earliest work suggested that two linguistic codes, eventually named elaborated and restricted, were typically learned differentially by the MIDDLE CLASS and WORKING CLASS. Much research, both in Britain and elsewhere, has been undertaken in connection with this theory; some workers have substantiated it, but others have either suggested modifications or produced results that seemed to refute it. The failure to validate Bernstein's theory in regard to its linguistic element is probably largely attributable to its underestimation of the social context in which language is used.

This theory has clear implications for the differential socialization of the social classes, and Bernstein and others have done research to isolate various dimensions of these differences. Bernstein has emphasized ways in which aspects of language, such as questions, and other practices, such as the use of toys, are used by the social classes in bringing up children. More specifically, research seems to have identified person-oriented and position-oriented families, located respectively in the middle and working classes.

Since 1970 Bernstein has extended the concept of code to the analysis of the CURRICULUM of formal educational institutions and has used the terms classification (the degree of permeability of the boundaries of school subjects) and framing (the power of teachers and pupils over PEDAGOGY) to analyse the content of and changes in the curriculum.

Although these concepts are much used because of their research fertility, Bernstein's original analysis has been modified by some subsequent criticism.

The force and direction of Bernstein's work has led to its constant application to practical problems, particularly in the field of COMPENSATORY EDUCATION, though Bernstein himself has disavowed any belief that linguistic codes are necessarily tied to social classes or that one code or one set of socialization practices is to be valued more highly than another.

See LANGUAGE.

PWM

**best way** [the 'one']. A propagandist notion originated by TAYLOR and accepted in the early dogma of SCIENTIFIC MANAGEMENT, that there always exists one method, and one only, established by production engineering 'science', for organizing any given technical process (e.g. cutting metals) or work-task. But 'best' for what and for whom? Taylor betrayed his own standpoint by talking frequently of the 'quickest and best' way to perform work-tasks. Many simple, routine manual operations, (e.g. shovelling) can be redesigned by work engineers to render them more productive in the sense that a fixed unit of output can be secured for a smaller physical effort. But Taylor saw this as an opportunity not to ease physical exertion but to augment production. By distributing daily physical exertion more opportunely, the worker's total daily effort might actually be far higher. For more complex tasks that require substantial mental involvement (e.g. machining) the 'best way' collides with human psychological complexity, notably individual differences. The HUMAN FACTOR psychologists inaugurated the scientific battle against the 'best way', following the protests of humanitarians and the labour movement on other cogent grounds. Much later, the idea that one 'best way' must also exist for designing overall technical systems began to be doubted (see SOCIO-TECHNICAL SYSTEM): this critique remains topical and vociferous. Reaction, overall, has had positive results, and is now institutionalized in the practice of Ergonomics (which aims to offset the naïvety of production engineers about human biology and psychology) and in a growing social awareness that technology and productive systems can, and should, be designed to suit the human needs of those who operate them.

MR

**Beveridge, William Henry** (1879-1963). British social reformer and one of the architects of the WELFARE STATE. Originally trained as a lawyer, Beveridge held a range of different posts, from sub-warden at Toynbee Hall, to civil servant, to Director of the London School of Economics (1919-37). Although for many years he was not aligned to any political party, he became Liberal MP for Berwick-on-Tweed in 1944; after losing that seat a year later he entered the House of Lords as a Liberal peer.

Early in his life, influenced by the WEBBS, Beveridge campaigned for old age pensions, free school meals, and government action to help the unemployed. He had an enduring interest in the problems of UNEMPLOYMENT. In 1909 he published *Unemployment: A Problem of Industry*, a pioneering study of the extent and causes of unemployment. Throughout his academic career he published regularly on related topics. *Full Employment in a Free Society* (1944) was an influential examination of policies for dealing with unemployment.

However, Beveridge is best-remembered for his work on the reform of the social services. In 1940 he was appointed Under-Secretary in the Ministry of Labour, and in 1941 was asked to chair an inter-departmental inquiry into the co-ordination of the social services. Although it was not intended that the inquiry should be seen as a major initiative, its report *Social Insurance and Allied Services* (1942) proved one of the most important documents on social services in the UK and formed the blueprint for the WELFARE STATE legislation introduced between 1944 and 1948. The Beveridge Report, as it came to be known, detailed the deficiences of existing services and outlined a plan to attack the 'five giants' of idleness, ignorance, disease, squalor and want. The attack was to be based on a free national health service, FAMILY ALLOWANCES, SOCIAL INSURANCE, social assistance and government policies to maintain full employment.

The aim was to cover all contingencies from the cradle to the grave.

Beveridge's report was received unenthusiastically by the Government but aroused widespread public interest and support. In 1943 the Government was forced to commit itself to the Report's proposals, and though legislation was not introduced immediately, this heralded a major new departure in British social policy.

MPJ

**bias.** See ERROR.

**birth-and-death process.** A type of STOCHASTIC PROCESS in which new members are added to a population, and old members leave, according to probabilistic laws. The problem is to work out the expected growth, or decline, of the population, the effects of changes in birth and death rates, the range of variation to be expected, the probability of the population being extinguished and the expected waiting time, possibly infinite, before this happens. The general theory of birth-and-death process was developed in the late 1930s, chiefly by William Feller; while its main application in social science is in DEMOGRAPHY in modelling human population growth, it can be used to analyse many other populations.

JL

**bisexuality.** See PSYCHOANALYSIS.

**black.** In many parts of the USA the population is divided into two categories, white and black; anyone with an ascertainable degree of African ancestry is accounted black, even though his complexion may be no darker than that of someone from the Mediterranean. From the time the first Africans landed in North America in 1619, they and their descendants have been variously called Negroes, blacks and coloured. When the major American agency for combatting racial discrimination was formed (on an inter-racial basis) in 1910, it chose the title National Association for the Advancement of Coloured People. At this time 'black' was an adjective of disparagement, evaded by the used of a euphemism. With the rise of the civil rights movement of the 1960s activists preferred 'black'; insisting that 'black is beautiful' and exhorting 'black pride' they denied that being black was to be regretted. In 1966 Stokely Carmichael referred, rather loosely, to 'black power' and the expression caught on despite little agreement about its implications. The slogan appeared to challenge the whites but probably the main function of these expressions was to promote black unity and sustain an ethnic revitalization movement.

The terminology crossed the Atlantic to the UK where most of the older Caribbean-born generation identify themselves primarily by their country of origin but secondarily as blacks. Most of their British-born children and a small minority of the younger Asians identify themselves primarily as blacks, but classification is not as simple as in the USA. Asians are inclined to identify themselves by religious or ethnic attributes, for instance, as Sikhs or Gujeratis. This is generally ignored in official categorizations. In the CENSUS, the population born in the Caribbean, black Africa and Asia formerly under British rule is identified as New Commonwealth with Pakistan. In other sources it may be designated 'Blacks and Asians' or 'blacks'. As yet there is no agreed majority designation nor any overall minority self-designation.

See also ETHNICITY; RACE RELATIONS.

MPB

**black economy.** See POLITICAL CORRUPTION.

**Bloch, Marc** (1886-1944). French historian, born in Lyons and educated at the Ecole Normale Supérieure. He taught at the University of Strasbourg from 1919 until 1936, and then at the Sorbonne until forced out by the Nazis. Despite opportunities to leave France he chose to remain, joined the Resistance in 1942, and was captured and executed in 1944.

Marc Bloch was the foremost medieval historian of his generation and through his activities as a comparative historian and his key role in the ANNALES SCHOOL he has had a lasting influence on historical sociology. The work for which he is best known to sociologists is his masterly *Feudal Society*, first published in 1939-40 and translated into English in 1961. However, medieval scho-

lars tend to consider his greatest achievement to be his study of the French countryside, *Les caractères originaux de l'histoire rurale Française* (translated as *French Rural History*, 1966). His reflections on the practice of history, of considerable interest to comparative and historical sociologists, were published posthumously in 1949 (English translation *The Historian's Craft*, 1964).

LS

**Blumer, Herbert** (1900- ). American sociologist. Born in St. Louis, Missouri, his father was a cabinet-maker and his mother a housewife. He studied at the Universities of Missouri (1918-22) and Chicago (1925-8) where he came under the intellectual influences of G.H. MEAD, PARK, W.I. THOMAS and Ellsworth Faris. He taught first at Missouri (1922-25), then at Chicago (1925-52), and latterly at the University of California, Berkeley (1952-72). Throughout this time he has been noted for his inspired teaching of the SYMBOLIC INTERACTIONIST tradition (he coined the term in 1937) and for his interpretation of the philosophy of Mead, whose classes he took over upon Mead's death. Blumer was active in professional football for seven years, had extensive experience in labour arbitration, and had many close contacts in the Chicago 'underworld'. He has served in numerous positions and committees for the advancement of American sociology including the presidency of the American Sociological Association (in 1956) and the Society for the Study of Social Problems (in 1955), and has edited the American Journal of Sociology (1941-52) and the Prentice-Hall Sociology Series (since 1934).

More famed for his direct teaching than his writings, his key ideas are to be found in *Symbolic Interactionism : Perspective and Method* (1969).

KP

**Boas, Franz** (1858-1942). German-American cultural anthropologist, pioneer of the collection of detailed ethnographic data. Born in Minden, Germany, of agnostic and revolutionary parents who had discarded their Jewish faith, Boas attended the universities of Heidelberg, Bonn and Kiel, taking a doctorate in physics in 1881. From at least 1882 he showed an interest in ethnology, which was stimulated by his work as a geographer on expeditions to the Arctic and British Columbia. He changed to anthropological studies shortly before he moved to the USA in 1887. He taught anthropology at Clark University (1888-92) and held museum posts in Chicago (1894-6) and the American Museum of Natural History in New York (1896-1905). Boas was Professor of Anthropology at Columbia University from 1899 until 1936, and trained several generations of American anthropologists, including BENEDICT, KROEBER and Margaret MEAD. His organizational ability and force of personality shaped the study of culture, psychology and value systems, contrasting with the narrower sociological focus of British social anthropology.

Boas's primary interest was the collection of ethnographic data, in which he included physical, social and linguistic material as well as artefacts, to arrive at a general view of a particular culture as well as deriving general themes of cultural comparison. His interests and intellectual abilities were wide-ranging. He worked principally with North American Indians, particularly on the Northwest Coast, collecting a vast quantity of data on all aspects of their society. He was aided not only by the young anthropologists he trained, but also by the systematic collections of material from travellers and settlers in the area. One of his main purposes was a rescue ethnography, which sought to preserve information regarding changing or disappearing societies. He tried to spread his students in the field as widely as possible throughout the world, sometimes, as in the case of Mead, persuading them to change their original choice of field location.

Major works: *The Mind of Primitive Man* (1911); *Anthropology in Modern Life* (1928). Collections of his essays, such as *Race, Language and Culture* (1940), give an idea of the range of his interests and the scope of CULTURAL ANTHROPOLOGY.

JE

**Booth, Charles** (1840-1916). A shipowner who achieved prominence through his pioneering work on the extent of POVERTY, *Life and Labour of the People of London* (17 vols., 1891-1903). Booth started his work to disprove a claim made in the *Pall Mall Gazette* that a quarter of Londoners were living in poverty. His detailed investigations were based on a subsistence definition of poverty. After a survey of spending patterns in 30 families he suggested that if income fell below a certain level a family could be classified as 'poor', and if significantly below this level, as 'very poor'. The poor found it 'a struggle to obtain the necessaries of life' while the 'very poor' lived 'in a state of chronic want'. Booth found that in East London 35 per cent of people were poor and of these 12.5 per cent were very poor. When he extended his coverage to all of London nearly 31 per cent were poor, a higher figure than that in the *Pall Mall* articles.

Booth's work was the most important early study of poverty that attempted to examine the problem on a formalized, impersonal level rather than on an anecdotal basis. It was thus of major methodological importance and a pioneering piece of empirical research. The detailed way in which Booth documented the extent of poverty inspired both social reformers and other studies of the problem (*see* ROWNTREE).

MPJ

**Bourdieu, Pierre** (1930- ). Director of Studies at the Ecole des Hautes Etudes and Director of the Centre for European Sociology, Paris. After working as an anthropologist in Algeria in the 1950s, Bourdieu moved into sociology and has written widely on the sociology of education and of CULTURE, and more particularly on formal education, art and museums. In *Reproduction in Education, Society and Culture* (1970) he sees culture as differentially distributed in any society: those in power try to reproduce contemporary culture more or less in its present form, that is, favouring their interests. Education is seen as a central agency of reproduction since compulsion is possible both to force attendance and in the PEDAGOGY used. Bourdieu makes much use of the concept of symbolic violence in attempts by the powerful to ensure the reproduction of their arbitrarily chosen version of the culture to pupils at all levels of the educational system. A hidden structure, manipulated by the powerful, is working to reproduce the overall society. The differential distribution of culture ensures that some, mainly children of the powerful, have a better chance of succeeding through education and inheriting the elite culture, thereby themselves almost inevitably gaining power in later life. Central to his analysis are the concepts of reproduction, culture, violence, arbitrariness and pedogogy.

PWM

**bourgeoisie** [from the French *bourg* (town)]. (1) In origin, the merchants and leading townsmen in feudal and post-feudal Europe, distinguished from the other major CLASSES or ESTATES of FEUDALISM (peasants, nobility, clergy). Successively extended by many writers to take in (2) the owners of capital in general, sometimes distinguishing owners of the means of production from owners of other forms of capital; (3) those who discharge the functions of capital, though not legally owners, such as managers, and more contentiously, higher civil servants; and (4) all non-manual employees. These extensions have made the term imprecise and have required sub-divisions indicating vertical differentiation within it; the *grande bourgeoisie* refers to major bourgeois groups, the PETITE, or petty, BOURGEOISIE to minor ones (especially shopkeepers and other small business proprietors). Some insist on the horizontal differentiation of finance, industrial and other capitalists, sometimes termed 'class fractions'. The term 'bourgeoisie' is used more frequently by Marxists and continental Europeans, writers in the Anglo-American sociological tradition preferring the term 'middle class' (for further discussion see MIDDLE CLASS).

CGAB

**Braverman, H.** See SKILL.

**bureaucracy.** An ORGANIZATION whose structure and operations are governed to a high degree by written rules. Its core is a hierarchy of 'offices', that is to say, of carefully defined functional roles, staffed by fulltime salaried persons. Rules state the relationship of any one office to others, govern the administration of the business of any given office, and regulate the recruitment of staff to the bureaucracy and any later promotions. The organizations created in this fashion are

quite distinct from the individuals who happen to staff them, and should operate in a completely foreseeable way. The logic behind bureaucratic structure is to produce entirely determinable, impartial, and impersonal operation. To adopt one formulation, the administration of things replaces the government of persons: as far as the 'perfect' bureaucracy is concerned, there are no people; at best, there are 'cases'.

WEBER originated modern sociological interest in bureaucracy, which he never adequately defined. His work was a byproduct of his fascination with the growth of what he termed rational-legal AUTHORITY in industrialized societies. This was inseparable from the existence of bureaucratically regulated organizations, above all those concerned with state adminstrations. Weber believed that some bureaucratic features would increasingly mark the giant private business corporations emerging in his day, though he was preoccupied with public service bureaucracy. His assertions that bureaucratic organization was a summit of rationality attracted attention among industrial sociologists. It was believed that Weber argued that bureaucracy would invade the economic sphere because it was more efficient than the *ad hoc* organizational solutions adopted by entrepreneurs in practice. A whole literature demonstrating the 'dysfunctions of bureaucracy' (especially in economic organizations) thus flowered around 1950 in the USA. Yet Weber had insisted upon distinctions between the *formal* rationality of operation (which bureaucratic-type structures would guarantee) on the one hand, and, on the other, *substantive* rationality in outcomes (which 'bureaucracy' should tend to augment): neither could be equated with 'efficiency' as conceived by an entrepreneur. Despite this misunderstanding, such critics produced useful material on how a 'vicious circle' can become established in the operation of an organization, through the mutual influence of structural elements. In turn this led to the creation of new specialisms (see ORGANIZATIONS), losing Weber's interest in the impact of organizations on society. The search was for the structural conditions of 'effective' operation — though curiously, the term 'bureaucracy' was thus given even wider currency.

In certain respects, this was regrettable, for it helped to feed an entirely different type of enquiry in which the term bureaucracy is used loosely as an all-purpose critical weapon. This tradition goes back to 18th-century France, where the term was coined. Bureaucracy can equate with 'misgovernment', 'incompetent administration', 'self-perpetuating administrative elite', 'obstructive officialdom', 'unnecessary paperwork', 'social parasitism', or with similar pejorative meanings. The term is used in such senses by the press, and in political life — where Trotskyites vie with Conservatives in condemning 'bureaucracy' (by which each mean sharply different things). More than a trace of such evaluations remains in many purportedly analytical uses of the term. Likewise, the focus varies between 'bureaucracy' viewed as an abstract system (of government, or management), as a societal variable (e.g. for assessing historical change), as a specific administrative complex and its traditions (e.g. 'French bureaucracy'), as the actual professional staff of an administration ('the bureaucracy') and so on.

See also AUTHORITY; ORGANIZATION; WEBER.

See M. Albrow, *Bureaucracy* (1970).

MR

# C

**capitalism.** An economic system in which the means of production are privately owned, capital is concentrated and used to make and accumulate profits, and the mass of the employed engage in free wage labour. MARX elaborated these characteristics and tried to demonstrate the exploitive nature of this system as it developed in the early modern world through his theory of the capitalist MODE OF PRODUCTION. Sociologists have been primarily interested in the origins of capitalism, its connections with IMPERIALISM, the condition of the various CLASSES within capitalist societies, and the potential for the transformation of capitalism into something better.

*Origins.* The controversy about the origins of capitalism covers a wide area, from the debate over the PROTESTANT ETHIC THESIS and the general problem of material versus ideational factors in SOCIAL CHANGE, to the arguments about the breakdown of FEUDAL-ISM and its transition to capitalism. Much of this controversy consists in protagonists talking past each other about terms they are defining differently or imprecisely. The contemporary significance of this debate is the problem of why the non-capitalist part of the world has not, as yet, managed success-fully to develop capitalism, discussed in Weberian terms in S. EISENSTADT (ed.) *The Protestant Ethic and Modernization* (1968). The non-Weberian answer to this question focuses not on the personality structure of the prospective capitalist, but on the development of capitalism as a WORLD SYSTEM.

*Capitalism and imperialism.* I. Waller-stein (*The Modern World System,* 1974) argues that from the 16th century capitalism through colonial or imperial expansion began to divide the world up into zones on the basis of an international division of labour in which the colonies (the periphery) supplied the raw materials to the European powers (the centre) for manufacture and export which would destroy the handicrafts of the colonies and inhibit economic growth there (see CENTRE-PERIPHERY). Illustrations of this process are provided by A. Gunder Frank, *Capitalism and Underdevelopment in Latin America* (1967) and F. Moulder, *Japan, China and the Modern World Economy* (1977). An important part of this system was SLAVERY, which provided a captive labour force for the plantations of the New World. The role of government in the development of capitalism has always been complex. In some cases governments follow a policy of non-intervention (often termed *laissez faire* capitalism) in which private enterprise is permitted to operate free from restraining legislation, as was the case during the INDUSTRIAL REVOLUTION in England; in other cases governments deliberately set out to create factories, markets, credit and other capitalist institutions, as in 19th-century Germany; in yet other cases governments 'nationalize' enterprises and run them as state concerns, as in most of Europe today to the extent of about one quarter of total assets. Irrespective of the nature of state involvement, for the most successful capitalist economies imperialist expansion of an economic and/or political and/or military

30

kind is and has been a necessary operating condition for these economies to grow (see STATE).

*Capitalism as a social system.* With the advent of the WELFARE STATE in the rich countries of the world the social system of capitalism has been transformed. The significance of the so-called 'rediscovery of poverty' in the rich capitalist countries of the West in the 1960s and 1970s (see D. Bull (ed.) *Family Poverty*, 1971, for the UK; R. Will and H. Vatter (eds.) *Poverty in Affluence*, 1970, for the USA) was not that there were still poor people in Europe and North America, but that for the first time in history the abolition of famine, malnutrition, homelessness, avoidable sickness, illiteracy and ignorance was within sight for the majority of the population in many countries. The corollary to this remarkable fact is that within this sea of affluence there are innumerable, and apparently not decreasing, islands of deprivation once occupied by the whole of the unskilled WORKING CLASS and now occupied by a variety of structurally disadvantaged groups. These groups are made up for the most part of low-paid workers, coloured immigrants and their descendants, the old, the chronically sick and disabled, the long-term unemployed and unsupported single-parent families; these categories often overlap. Capitalism seems unable to provide sufficient funds and institutional help to mitigate the material suffering of such people (see UNDERCLASS). On the other hand, the mass of the working population and its dependants enjoy an unprecedentedly high standard of living and security. Yet happiness and satisfaction, as might reasonably be expected to have resulted, do not seem outstandingly to characterize the working populations of rich countries. To explain this apparent anomaly sociologists have devised a battery of concepts and theories such as RELATIVE DEPRIVATION, the FUNCTIONALIST THEORY OF STRATIFICATION, CONFLICT THEORY, and the EMBOURGEOISE-MENT THESIS. Despite their important differences, all of these address themselves to the issue of how individuals, groups or classes reconcile themselves to a society in which occupational achievement and economic and other rewards are distributed in an extremely inegalitarian fashion. There is a vast literature which documents and attempts to explain the differential economic, social, educational, political, cultural, medical etc experiences of manual and non-manual workers and their families, invariably to the disadvantage of the manual worker. Sociologists in the main have resisted the Marxist conclusion that wage labourers are exploited in capitalist societies and that such misery that persists is a direct consequence of the capitalist MODE OF PRODUCTION, and a variety of Marx-inspired theories have been developed to account for the survival of capitalism.

*The transformation of capitalism.* Marx's prediction that the continuing economic crises of capitalism would provide the opportunity for the working class to make a REVOLUTION that would bring COMMUNISM has not, as yet, been fulfilled (with the possible and marginal exception of Russia in 1917). Nevertheless, all the important theories of the transformation of capitalism can be best understood as a reaction against or an attempt to improve upon Marx. They can be divided into economic, political and cultural theories. Economic theories range from those which postulate that the next crisis of capitalism will be the last, to those who argue that capitalism has already transformed itself either through a MANAGERIAL REVOLUTION, a technological leap, or some other means to a post-capitalist or POST-INDUSTRIAL SOCIETY. An influential variant on this is the CONVERGENCE THESIS which holds that technical-industrial imperatives are turning *all* industrialized societies into a similar mould. The main political theories are based on the ideas of WELFARE CAPI-TALISM (which argues that by providing a minimum standard of living the capitalist state will effectively buy off the revolutionary potential of the masses) and CORPORATISM (in which the state averts crisis by taking over the mainsprings of economic life). The main cultural theory revolves around the concept of HEGEMONY, developed by GRAMSCI (see *Prison Notebooks*), which emphasizes the importance of destroying bourgeois ideas and the supremacy of bourgeois culture, particularly education, political theory, religion and laws that directly serve to exploit the working class. Therefore, a proletarian culture must be built up by working-class intellectuals at all levels to oppose that of the ruling class. Only then will the working class be in a position to take over the politics and economics of a revolutionary society.

Marx's fundamental criticism of the ideology of bourgeois political economy was that it saw capitalism as something necessary, natural, and hopefully eternal. All of the theories and concepts discussed here have been and continue to be fiercely contested, with the result that the necessary, natural and eternal character of capitalism appears to many and perhaps most sociologists as ever more doubtful.

See CLASS; EXPLOITATION; LABOUR PROCESS; TRANSNATIONAL.                                    LS

**career.** A term with two uses in sociology.

(1) In the sociology of work it retains its popular meaning of progressive advance through a series of functionally related occupations. It is the most ordered type of upward SOCIAL MOBILITY. Originally associated with the PROFESSIONS, in the 20th century it has become increasingly characteristic of male MIDDLE CLASS occupations in general, and has therefore become a key part of both CLASS and GENDER differences. Whereas the adult work-life experience of many, perhaps most, middle class men is one of unfolding achievement and progress, that of most adult women and most working class men is at best one of stability, at worst one of instability and disruption (see WOMEN AND THE LABOUR MARKET).

MM

(2) In the sociology of DEVIANCE it describes the stages through which a person passes on route from one status (e.g. non-marijuana smoker) to a new status (e.g. marijuana smoker) — the classic illustration of this use being H.S. BECKER's 'Becoming a Marijuana Smoker' in his *Outsiders* (1963). A distinction is often drawn between the 'objective' career which depicts the stages common to all people passing through such status change, and 'subjective' career which depicts a particular person's view of such changes. GOFFMAN uses the term 'career' in both ways in his study of the moral career of the mental patient — objectively, to describe the broad changes in 'going mad' (pre-patient, patient,

post-patient) and the contingencies involved in defining the madness status; subjectively to capture the mental patient's own changing sense of self. It is an important conceptual tool for SYMBOLIC INTERACTIONISM and is closely allied to status passage (see RITES OF PASSAGE) and LIFE HISTORY.

See DEVIANT CAREER; LIFE CYCLE.

KP

**cargo cult.** A distinctive form of MILLENARIAN MOVEMENT which occurs in the Melanesian Islands of the South Pacific. It combines elements drawn from the Western culture of the planters, traders, administrators and missionaries and from the indigenous culture. These are synthesized into ritual activity or social practices believed likely to encourage gods or ancestors to send the natives 'cargo', that is, supplies of Western goods such as cotton clothes, tobacco, alcohol, canned food, machinery or sometimes even guns. Cargo is expected to arrive by boat or plane, as do the supplies sent to the white colonialists.

The rituals or practices followed are often revealed to the movement's prophet in a dream. They sometimes involve the breaking of old taboos, and the creation of new ones. They may involve the destruction of crops and livestock, which may leave the natives destitute unless assisted by the colonial administration.

Cargo cults represent the adaptation to contemporary circumstances of the natives' traditional conceptions of culture and economic resources as being provided by gods or spirits in return for ritual observances. Thus the non-arrival of the cargo does not convince the natives that the cargo myth is false, only that they have not yet secured the appropriate ritual observance. New cults may therefore re-emerge in the same area or nearby within a short time of the collapse of a cult; see CULT.

See Peter Lawrence, *Road Belong Cargo* (1964).

RW

**casework.** A widely used social work method based on intensive interviewing, aimed at enabling the social worker to understand the problems faced as fully as possible so that potential solutions can be explored with the client. This method can only be successful if the client co-operates because the aim is to help the client work out his or her own problems rather than to impose solutions.

Interviews frequently suggest that the presenting problem is not the real or the only one. Considerable care and skill are necessary to ensure that additional problems are not missed or that the importance of the presenting problem is not obscured. A persistent criticism of casework is that social workers too often ignore the presenting problem and look towards changes in client behaviour for the solution of problems rather than to the resources and opportunities available.

Casework is strongly linked to psychodynamic theory and is one of three main social work methods, the others being groupwork and community work (*see* COMMUNITY CARE).

MPJ

**caste.** Derived from the Portugese *casta*, meaning race, lineage or pure stock, which is in turn derived from the Latin *castus*, meaning clean, pure or pious. Coined to refer to the traditional Hindu-based system of social organization in and around India. This originated in the 2nd or 1st millenium BC and was largely in place by about 500 AD. It includes ENDOGAMOUS marriage, strict rules regarding social and personal contacts, occupational homogeneity, and structured economic and ritual practices within each caste. Distinctively, each caste is 'purer' than the one below it and must be protected from physical contact with it. The original classification of castes was into Brahmin (priests), Kshatriya (warriors and landlords), Vaishya (farmers and traders), and Sudra (servile peasants). At a later stage Haryans (untouchables) were added to the scheme at the bottom. These castes still exist, mostly only as convenient fiction, sometimes as a loose framework around a further sub-division of 3,000 or so *jatis*, local associations of lineage groups, sharing many of the same restrictions and themselves further divided into sub-castes. A *jati* may exercise collective control over culture, ritual and law through a village council (*panchayat*).

The major difficulty in studying caste is the anti-historical bias of Hinduism, which presents itself as a timeless system. WEBER (*The Religion of India*, 1958) and many others noted the importance of belief in *dharma* and *kharma* for the maintenance of the system. *Dharma* refers to the order of things, natural and social, and the proper way for members of each caste to behave. If one lives by the code for one's caste, one acquires merit and, on death, is reborn in a higher caste. This, and the converse, rebirth in a lower caste for those who violate the *dharma*, is the doctrine of *kharma*. Those who observe the *dharma* in successive reincarnations finally obtain release from the wheel of deaths and rebirths. Nevertheless, both Weber and Hutton (*Castes in India*, 1946) explain its history as a unique integration of two main dynamic processes, an increasing DIVISION OF LABOUR and successive waves of tribal and religious conquest movements. But later, and in theory, persons could neither enter the caste system nor move through it in this life (though modern scholars emphasize the amount of collective mobility that *jatis* can achieve). Most writers have followed Weber in marvelling at the most perfect system of EXPLOITATION ever designed, where lower orders accept their submission as morally correct and eternal. Some materialists have seen it as an elaborate disguise for a particularly ruthless form of CLASS exploitation (e.g. Meillaissoux, *Economy and Society*, 1973). Others (e.g. Dumont, *Homo Hierarchicus*, 1970) reply that concern with class and exploitation are Eurocentric, not found in India. The relationship of caste to SOCIAL STRATIFICATION and class theory thus remains controversial.

Some writers have used the term caste to analyse societies outside Hinduism. Examples include Dollard on class and caste in relations between whites and blacks in the southern states of America in the 1930s (J. Dollard, *Caste and Class in a Southern Town*, 1937), and references to the Junkers as a caste in Prussia. Certainly some social groups have jealously guarded their privileges against equality and social mobility, preserving their purity, sometimes invoking religious justifications in the process, with the help of laws, norms and conventions about intermarriage, commensality and job reservation. Nevertheless, nowhere else is there a structure truly comparable in its ritual and economic complexity to that of the Indian caste system. Moreover, other terms from the vocabulary of class, STATUS, ESTATE and ETHNICITY will usually suffice.

See Béteille, *Social Inequality* part 7, (1969).

CGAB, MM, LS.

**castration complex.** See PSYCHOANALYSIS.

**category.** A class whose nature and composition is decided by the person who defines the category; for example, persons earning wages in a certain range may be counted as a category for income tax purposes. A category is therefore to be contrasted with a group, defined by the nature of the relations between the members. The distinction is important to the study of RACE RELATIONS since people ascribed by others to a category and treated differently because of this (e.g. Africans from different states) respond by developing a consciousness of their shared position and make themselves into a group. The distinction is also important in the analysis of attitudes towards ethnic groups, since the category that is perceived by the majority member may not be the same as the group that exists; each interacts with the other and their boundaries change (see BLACK; ETHNICITY). A parallel distinction is found between the two major uses of the term CLASS.

MPB

**cathexis; anti-cathexis.** See PSYCHOANALYSIS.

**causal modelling.** A family of statistical techniques for making causal inferences from correlational data. These techniques originated largely in econometrics and were introduced into sociology in the late 1950s and 1960s by Herbert Simon and H.M. Blalock; they are now widely used, particularly in American sociology.

That causation is not necessarily implied by a (non-zero) CORRELATION between two VARIABLES is a truism of statistics. A correlation between X and Y may be spurious in the sense that it is the result of common causation by a third variable, Z; in this case, the correlation would disappear if Z could be experimentally controlled. But by regressing each of X and Y on to Z (see REGRESSION), an estimated contribution due to the interfering variable Z can be subtracted, and its effect artificially controlled for. The correlation between the adjusted values of X and Y is the partial correlation between X and Y controlling for Z. It should be zero, or much reduced, if Z is the cause of the correlation between X and Y. It would also be zero if Z were a causal intermediary between X and Y. But if a number of variables are considered together, and a fair amount of information supplied as to the causal ordering of the variables, it can be possible to distinguish between different causal models — patterns of asymmetric causal links — over the same set of variables by examining the behaviour of the partial correlations. In general, the aim is to reproduce the overall matrix of correlations from a simplified model assuming that certain causal links are absent. By contrast, in evaluating a multiple regression equation, the amount of variance explained in the dependent variable is the chief criterion.

Multiple regression methods are used to estimate the necessary parameters in causal modelling, and a number of assumptions are required. Influences external to the system of variables under consideration must generally be assumed to be independent, one of another and over time, and to be normally distributed. The structural equations expressing the causal links must generally be assumed linear and with effects that simply add up. Variables must generally be measurable at interval level (see MEASUREMENT), and the system must not be so interconnected with feedback cycles that it is impossible to separate out the individual effects of the variables — the identification problem. If explanatory variables are too highly intercorrelated, even where it is possible to identify the effects separately, the estimates become highly unreliable (multicollinearity).

In sociology, causal modelling is attractive because it gives a means of expressing theory in highly readable causal diagrams, united with a methodology for actually estimating the parameters of the models. In recent years, estimation techniques have become sophisticated and there has been an emphasis on qualitative variables (measurement at below the interval level, which forms the bulk of sociological variables) to extend causal inferences to these more usual cases. Causal modelling has almost reached the status of a PARADIGM in certain sectors of American sociology, such as survey analysis. However, the nature of the causal links in the models is of a peculiar kind: it is an asymmetric relationship between attributes of the individual units at one particular time, not a relationship between events ordered in time. There is disagreement as to whether the causal links of the model constitute an explanation of the observed correlation, or whether they constitute a further level of regularities to be explained in terms of social processes generating them. If the variables are related to variable values at earlier times, a time-lag unit must be introduced. While the tax year, or the month, for example, may be natural time-lags in causal links in econometrics, no such natural time periods have been established in sociology (except perhaps a generation, which is too long for most modelling purposes). Critics suggest the use of models which are more dynamic in nature and take account of time directly, such as STOCHASTIC PROCESS models or differential equation models, but these too have the problem of a time unit. In many cases, particularly as the statistical assumptions are often questionable, it is best to take a causal model as a compact, visualizable summary of the mass of data underlying a correlation matrix.

*Path Analysis.* A closely related approach with similar assumptions , widely used in the study of SOCIAL STRATIFICATION and SOCIAL MOBILITY.It uses standardized multiple RE-GRESSION equations to compare a model of direct and indirect relationships which are presumed to hold between several variables specified in the model, with observed data as measured by path coefficients. The model is assumed to be a closed system, in that all relevant variables are included. The theoretical time-order of occurrence of variables is known and specified, the variables being shown diagrammatically linked by single-headed arrows indicating the paths of direction of influence.

*Log-linear Analysis.* An entirely different technique developed by L. Goodman, this is a statistical method for analysing CROSS-TABULATIONS which depends on fitting models and estimating the parameters of the models. The analyst sets out assumptions which are believed to hold between VARI-ABLES, then uses log-linear models to derive quantitative estimates of their effects. The technique may be used with complex multi-dimensional tables unsuited to elaboration, and permits the estimation of INTERACTION effects.

Causal modelling using such techniques has in common a rigorous hypothetico-deductive approach to theory testing, unlike inductive, data-dredging techniques such as FACTOR ANALYSIS.

See H.M.Blalock Jr., *Causal Inference in Non-Experimental Research* (1964).

MB, JL

**cause.** A state of affairs which brings about another state of affairs. EMPIRICIST philosophers, following HUME, held that all we experience is constant conjunctions of events, and that we have no grounds for asserting more than this. REALIST philosophers of science, by contrast, deny that constant conjunctions are even necessary for the existence of a causal relation, which they analyse in terms of latent structures and mechanisms (which if not impeded by countervailing forces, will bring about what we perceive as 'effects'). The claim that all events are caused (denied in special circumstances by quantum theories in physics) has sometimes been seen as incompatible with free will, if human actions are determined along with other events. Whether or not our 'reasons' for acting should be analysed as causes is a continuing source of controversy in the social sciences. Some sociologists insist they are concerned to understand actions (see PHENOMENOLOGY; SYMBOLIC INTER-ACTIONISM), rather than to provide causal EX-PLANATIONS. Others, like WEBER, hold that the two go together.

See also COUNTERFACTUAL CONDITIONAL.

See M. Weber, *The Methodology of the Social Sciences* (1949).

WO

**Census.** A collection of social data by means of a complete enumeration of the total population of a country, carried out by the government on a fixed date simultaneously throughout the territory. The first US Census was conducted in 1790, the first British Census in 1801. Censuses are usually conducted at ten-year intervals, in the UK most recently in 1971 and 1981. Census data are gathered by means of a schedule of compulsory questions on demographic, economic and social issues which is completed by the head of each household on behalf of all members of the household. Topics covered include age and sex, household composition, employment, education, housing, journey to work and (in the USA and Canada) income. Census data are published in the form of aggregate statistics, providing the most complete source of information on a territory down to small geographical areas. By contrast with SOCIAL SURVEYS, Censuses suffer from the limited amount of basic information which they can collect and the use of relatively untrained staff as enumerators, affecting the data quality.

See also DEMOGRAPHY; HISTORICAL DEMOGRAPHY.

See C. Hakim, *Secondary Analysis in Social Research* (1982).

MB

**Census classes.** From around the beginning of this century national Censuses began to seek a measure of the hierarchical position of citizens, knowing already that this would be CORRELATED with such social problems as health and mortality rates, birth rates and crime (see HISTORICAL DEMOGRAPHY). In the UK the General Register Office (since 1969 the Office of Population Censuses and Surveys), like most others, arrived at a measure which is a classification of occupations. For each CENSUS, a *Classification of Occupations* is published. The 1970 edition listed more than 20,000 occupational titles in 223 unit groups; it also differentiated seven employment statuses, two of self-employed and five of employees. Occupations are also allocated to five classes (see CLASS AS CATEGORY AND SCALE) according to 'the general standing within the community of the occupations concerned'. In practice, additions and revisions are made to a basic classification devised by Stevenson from the

1921 Census returns in connection with work on mortality, fertility and morbidity rates. The five classes, with examples of occupations in each, are as follows: (1) Professional etc occupations: doctor, accountant, production engineer. (2) Intermediate occupations: manager, senior government official, nurse. (3) Skilled occupation. (N) non-manual: draughtsman, shop assistant, clerk; (M) manual: miner, sheet metal worker, bricklayer. (4) Partly skilled occupations: agricultural worker, machine sewer, postman. (5) Unskilled occupation: labourer, porter, office cleaner.

The division of Class 3 into N and M dates from the 1970 *Classification* when the mixture of non-manual and manual occupations and the preponderant size of the class (49 per cent of the economically active population in the 1971 Census) were held to limit its usefulness for analytical and statistical purposes. Partly skilled and unskilled non-manual are deemed not to exist.

Since 1951 the Census has supplemented this with a classification into 'socio-economic groups', groups of occupations 'whose social, cultural and recreational standards and behaviour are similar ... the allocation of occupied persons to socio-economic groups is determined by considering their employment status and occupation...' (1970 *Classification*). There are now 17 of these. They are somewhat heterogeneous and less hierarchical than the 'social classes'.

Neither the allocation of social classes according to social standing nor the allocation to socio-economic groups according to style of life (standards and behaviour) is based on any known research.

In many studies which use Census classifications, the unit of analysis is not the individual but the household or family. In assigning a household to a single social class or socio-economic group, researchers typically attend only to the occupation of the head of the household, taken to be the husband and father whenever present, or the principal earner, who usually happens to be male. For a comment on this sexist assumption see SOCIAL STRATIFICATION and GENDER.

The classifications of the Department of Employment's *Classification of Occupations and Directory of Occupational Titles*

(CODOT) are different from those of the Registrar General.

See also CLASS; OCCUPATIONAL PRESTIGE; STATUS.

CGAB

centre-periphery. A term periodically used by sociologists in both a social and a geographic sense to refer to the relations between the power and cultural core of a society and its peripheral regions (e.g. E. Shils, *Centre and Periphery*, 1975). At present, used widely in the sociology of development after Raoul Prebisch, first Secretary-General of the United Nations Conference on Trade and Development. In *Towards a New Trade Policy for Development* (1964) Prebisch argued that the free market world economy is divided into centre countries — the highly developed industrial countries of Western Europe, the USA and Japan — and the periphery — the countries on the Asian and African continents and the Latin and Central American subcontinents. As a result of the outdated INTERNATIONAL DIVISION OF LABOUR imposed by the centre countries upon the world economy in the 19th century, the peripheral countries continue to trade primary products (agriculture foodstuffs and raw materials) in exchange for manufactured goods from the centre. Technical progress which permits increases in productivity is the key to economic development. In the centre this technical progress has arisen spontaneously and continues at a high rate because of the industrial nature of the economy. But in the peripheral countries technical progress is slow, externally induced, and limited to those sectors engaged in production for export.

This model turned into a political ideology uniting the developing countries and articulating their common frustrations *vis-à-vis* the centre and the 'unfair' system of international trade. Prebisch demonstrated that as a result of the existing international division of labour and the associated system of international trade, the benefits of technical progress were unevenly distributed between centre and peripheral countries. The empirical evidence was a series of statistical tables which showed a long-term deterioration of the terms of trade for the peripheral countries. Between 1870 and 1930 the prices of goods from peripheral countries had declined by 36.5 per cent compared with the prices of goods exported by the centre countries.

This struck at the heart of classical and neo-classical theories of international trade, which had maintained that international specialization and trade were beneficial for all parties concerned and, if anything, would in the long run favour the exporters of primary products. Against this, Prebisch argued that a historical distortion in international markets had made factor and commodity markets at the centre of the world economy more monopolistic and oligopolistic than those in the periphery. Unionization and labour emancipation had kept wages (and hence the prices of manufactures) high, even in periods of recession. This was not so in the periphery, which during recessions suffered from income reductions amplified by the rigidities in the centre. To these politico-economic reasons for the deterioration of the terms of trade for the peripheral countries Prebisch added three technical factors: (1) primary products are subject to substitution by synthetics; (2) agricultural commodities are typically income-inelastic (ENGELS's Law); (3) technological progress makes for an increasingly unfavourable ratio of raw material inputs in manufacturing production. These three technical variables, separately and together, in the long run depress the demand for primary products from the periphery in relation to the demand for manufactures, which is forever increasing.

Prebisch's analysis indicated the kind of international reforms and development strategies needed. In joint protests, peripheral countries began to demand interventions in their favour in international markets taking the form of (1) various measures to improve or stabilize markets and prices for primary commodities; (2) preferential access to the domestic markets in the advanced countries for manufactured exports from the peripheral countries. The latter tied in with the development strategy which logically flowed from Prebisch's analysis: that peripheral countries must themselves industrialize in order to achieve objectives of economic development.

*Semi-Periphery.* In more recent years, the centre-periphery distinction seems to have lost some of its usefulness. A number of developing countries are rapidly industrializing (e.g. Brazil, Mexico, South Korea, Taiwan, Singapore, Hong Kong) and are variously referred to as semi-industrialized, newly industrializing or semi-peripheral. However, the term semi-peripheral was first used by I. Wallerstein (*The Capitalist World Economy*, 1979) with a rather more precise meaning, to refer not only to a specified location in the international economic hierarchy but also to a specific function: seeking trade with both centre and periphery, exchanging different kinds of products with each, and achieving intermediate wage levels and profit margins. Today, semi-peripheral countries import advanced technology from the centre countries and export semi-processed products to them, obtaining raw materials and exporting finished manufactures to the periphery. Semi-peripheral countries also have a politically mediating role as 'go-between' nations (see Galtung, *Journal of Peace Research*, 1971). Their function, similar to that of the middle classes within national stratification systems, is a stabilizing one, because they see themselves primarily as better off than the lower sector, if rather worse off then the upper sector. Thus they help avoid rebellions that would otherwise occur in a system based on the distribution of unequal rewards (see RELATIVE DEPRIVATION)

*Metropolis-satellite.* Prebisch's centre-periphery model was a progressive liberal critique and did not criticize the system of production which had given rise to the international division of labour and trade. Marxists soon appropriated the model, the first of such writers being A.G. Frank in *Capitalism and Underdevelopment in Latin America* (1967). According to this analysis, the division into central and peripheral countries had been generated by the capitalist system of production, since centralization — and the consequent polarization of riches and poverty — is an inherent contradiction of capitalism. Through European expansion and conquest from the 16th century this contradiction was applied on a world scale, polarizing the metropolitan centre and the peripheral satellites. The imposed patterns of European trade, followed by the export of capital by metropolitan firms to the satellites, transformed the overseas economies into ancillary economies of the metropoles. Self-sufficient subsistence economies were inserted into the world market, their economic surplus extracted and their social structures deformed. In the process, the capitalist metropolis-satellite contradiction was creatd on a domestic level: as metropolitan states appropriate surplus from the satellites, so in these satellites the towns remove surplus from the hinterland, the landlords remove it from the peasants, the shopkeeper from customers and so on. Thus the metropolitan-satellite contradiction runs in chain-like fashion throughout the world capitalist system.

See also DEPENDENCY; WORLD SYSTEM.

AH

**charisma.** A property of leadership. Its usage comes from WEBER's *Economy and Society* (II, section XIV), where charismatic authority is distinguished from two other IDEAL TYPES of authority: the rational/legal and the traditional. Charismatic signifies that the authority of the leader derives from that leader's special qualities. Leaders with charisma possess the quality of being able to inspire the faith of others, whether for good or evil. The political situation produced by this emotional relationship between leader and follower is inherently unstable. However, according to Weber, charisma is also a creative force in history and a necessary antidote to bureaucratic rigidity. The concept of charisma locates the source and general nature of the leader/follower relationship. But its essence is its identification of irrationality in political behaviour. It cannot in itself define the links between leader and led. These must be sought in the immediate political, social and economic environment, in the cultural environment, and in the personality of the leader classified as charismatic. The term charisma is now often loosely applied to any personal characteristics of a leader.

See AUTHORITY; POWER.

EMM

**charity.** Giving to others in NEED. Charitable organizations are set up primarily to offer help, not necessarily financial, to the needy. Under current UK legislation they can be granted charitable status by the Charity Commissioners and this confers considerable tax benefits. Organizations with political aims are not eligible for charitable status, and some have had their status questioned because they place greater emphasis than hitherto on PRESSURE GROUP activity.

Charitable organizations played an important role in the development of social services (see WELFARE STATE). One of the most influential in the UK was the Charity Organisation Society but others, dealing with children, the blind and the handicapped for example, made a major contribution. The development of state-provided social services in the 20th century has led to a more limited role for charitable organizations. Nevertheless, they still make an important contribution especially in the personal social services.

Some see charitable provision as more flexible than state-provided services and better able to meet individual need. However, too great a reliance on charitable provision can be dangerous, because such provision may be less certain and some potential recipients feel unhappy about accepting charity because of the stigma attached to it. See GIFT.

MPJ

**Chicago School of Sociology.** The form of American interpretative sociology developed at the University of Chicago 1918-39. (This should not be confused with the 'Chicago School' of social psychology associated with G.H. MEAD nor the 'Chicago School' of modern architecture associated with Louis Sullivan and Frank Lloyd Wright, nor with the 'Chicago School' of social anthropologists influenced by RADCLIFFE-BROWN — however, all show the extraordinary creativity concentrated in that University in the inter-war period.)

The world's first university department of sociology was founded at Chicago in 1892 under the Chairmanship of Albion Small, who was influenced by the German interpretative tradition of sociology, especially SIMMEL. Small's successor was Robert PARK,

a former journalist who had studied under Simmel in Berlin. Park's theoretical contribution is known as HUMAN ECOLOGY, but he is best-remembered for introducing the technique of PARTICIPANT OBSERVATION into sociological practice. Park gathered around him a set of brilliant graduate students whose studies of Chicago in the inter-war years have become classics in the fields of urban sociology and the sociology of DEVIANCE. These constitute the Chicago School. It produced the first major American empirical study, THOMAS and F. Znaniecki's *The Polish Peasant in Europe and America* (1917); it instigated the *American Journal of Sociology* in 1895; set up the American Sociological Society in 1905; established the first (and largest) graduate department in the world; produced the seminal sociology textbook for many years — Park and Burgess's *Introduction to the Science of Sociology* (1921), the 'Green Bible'; and established one of the largest and most productive of research programmes in sociology (much of it centred on the Society for Social Research). It was closely allied to the philosophical tradition of PRAGMATISM developed in many related departments at the University of Chicago (see D. Rucker, *The Chicago Pragmatists*, 1969).

Chicago was a 'natural laboratory' for study during the 1920s and 1930s. Park was concerned to analyse the processes which underlay the social segregation of the city into separate neighbourhoods, and how SUBCULTURES were developed and maintained within each of them. The key process identified was competition for land. This led Park and Burgess to develop the CONCENTRIC ZONE HYPOTHESIS which related the spatial growth of the city to its social segmentation. But Chicago sociology was wider than urbanism; it was eclectic and wide ranging. It espoused quantitative and qualitative research: researchers like Burgess and Shaw produced LIFE HISTORIES and aggregate data. Though field work was viewed as very important, so too was the statistical compilation (largely through Ogburn) of a local community fact book. It espoused practical concerns but also progressively developed more formal theories: of crime (SUTHERLAND'S DIFFERENTIAL ASSOCIATION) and marginality (Stonequist's *Marginal Man*).

It had an abiding concern with patterns of social organization while at the same time developing through Faris and BLUMER the first properly 'social' psychology: SYMBOLIC INTERACTIONISM and MEAD's theory of first-hand empirical research on diverse areas — on race (Park); ghettoes (Wirth, *The Ghetto*, 1928); suicide (Cavan); work (Hughes, *Men and their Work*, earlier essays collected together in 1938); marriage (Burgess); slums (Zorbaugh, *The Gold Coast and the Slum*, 1929); organized crime (Landesco); homelessness (Anderson, *The Hobo*, 1923); delinquency and crime (Thrasher, *The Gang*, 1927; Shaw, *The Jack Roller*, 1930; Cressey, *The Taxi-Dance Hall*, 1932; Reckless, *The Natural History of Vice Areas in Chicago*, 1925). Other sociology departments have tried to emulate this research success but none has fully succeeded.

The department fell from dominance during the 1930s with the rise of FUNCTIONALISM under PARSONS and a more survey-oriented research tradition (see LAZARSFELD). But research continued — notably in the Yankee City series of Warner, a Durkheimian anthropologist with a strong interest in symbolism and community studies (see CLASS AS CATEGORY AND SCALE). During the 1940s a new generation was trained — GOFFMAN, Anselm Strauss, David Gold, Eliot Friedson, W.F. Whyte (see HUMAN RELATIONS) among them. Few of these scholars remained at Chicago, but they contributed greatly to the renewed interest in symbolic interactionism and qualitative research in the 1960s. David Matza in *Becoming Deviant* (1969) dubbed them the 'neo-Chicagoan' school.

See R.E.L. Faris, *Chicago Sociology 1920-1932* (1970).

HN, KP

**child care, state intervention in.** There has long been recognition of the right of public authorities to take an interest in the care of children. In the early 20th century this was partly based on the belief that public authorities had a duty to protect children: they might thus intervene to prevent cruelty. At the same time a large number of children were receiving help from Public Assistance authorities because they were judged to be in need of material support.

The public child care services in the UK were reorganized from 1948 following the report of the Curtis Committee. Child care work was concentrated in a single local authority department, under the direction of children's officers, which could receive children into care. Following the reorganization of social work at the end of the 1960s (see SEEBOHM REPORT) child care became the responsibility of unified Social Work Departments.

Child care services offered by local authorities range from arranging for accommodation in a children's home, to fostering and adoption, to providing support to enable a child to remain at home or with relatives. After World War II greater emphasis was placed on ensuring that the child remain in its own home, possibly through the provision of CASEWORK help or material assistance. The trend away from institutional care was influenced by Bowlby's work on maternal deprivation (see J. Bowlby, *Child Care and the Growth of Love*, 1953).

One important recent development has been the Children Act 1975. This placed a statutory duty on local authorities to give priority to the 'best interests of the child' which could conflict with the interests or wishes of the parents, and was a weakening of parental rights.

MPJ

**childhood.** Refers not only to the period of biological dependency on care but also to a social age. According to Aries (*Centuries of Childhood*, 1973) childhood as a social institution developed in the 18th century among the nobility and rising bourgeoisie and was intimately associated with the development of EDUCATION and schooling as a moral instruction and social segregation from the adult world. Before this period the concept of childhood was confined to pre-five-year-olds. Children above that age were integrated into the adult world through service at court, apprenticeship and other forms of domestic service. Among the urban working class children were employed in workshops, factories and mines. A succession of Factory Acts prohibited the employment of children. Instead childhood became a period of enforced economic dependence and compulsory SCHOOLING.

Infants become social beings through socialization. This involves the internalization of social norms and values, and proceeds by abstracting general rules of conduct from personalized commands of the primary caretaker (usually the mother). For PARSONS this process has cognitive, cathartic and evaluative elements. Parsons, MEAD, BERGER and LUCKMAN, although operating within different sociological traditions, all view socialization as internalization whether through differentiation of self from others (Parsons), the separation of the 'I' from the 'me' (Mead), the development of identity and everyday knowledge through interaction (Berger and Luckman), the repression of the pleasure principle or id through the development of the superego (FREUD). This theory has been criticized for providing a picture of 'oversocialized' people and failing to identify how deviant behaviour develops (see DEVIANCE).

According to the Newsons (J. and E. Newson, *Seven Years Old in the Home Environment*, 1976), working-class mothers tend to issue commands to be obeyed, whereas middle-class mothers tend to discuss and explain their wishes. BERNSTEIN related this pattern of linguistic use to future performance in school which, as a middle-class institution, operates through the elaborated code; thus working-class children, accustomed to the restricted code, are disadvantaged at school. West Indian parents also place a high value on obedience and respect for elders and this has been linked to the inappropriateness of child-centred primary education for West Indian children.

Boys and girls are treated differently and are socialized into sex-specific GENDER roles. This begins in infancy: baby girls get less food or less time for eating; are less likely to be comforted when crying, given mechanical toys or permitted to explore. Later, toys and activities reinforce sex-role stereotyping. Juliet Mitchell (*Psychoanalysis and Feminism*, 1974) has argued that social identity is a gendered identity based on an interpretation of the Freudian Oedipus complex as entry into patriarchy. Girls define themselves as lacking a penis, begin to identify with their mother and develop a desire for a baby (boy) as a substitute for the penis. Boys' fear of the father (castration) leads them to want to become like the father. Other FEMINISTS have argued that girl children reach maturity earlier because they receive less mothering and are expected to cope alone and help the mother at an early age. Boy children receive extended mothering, are excused from responsibilities and therefore mature much later. This is a critique of Freud and Mitchell, who claim that the female Oedipus complex is easier to resolve and that hence women have weaker superegos.

INCEST occurs quite often in families, in spite of the sociological notion of the incest taboo. Mother-son incest is very rare; older brother-younger sister incest is more common; father (or male caretaker)-daughter incest is common — frequently unnoticed and unreported, and when reported the girl is frequently disbelieved, a Freudian heritage of the myth that women fantasize about being raped by the father. Statistical data is hard to come by, because sexual abuse of (girl) children is the least reported crime, and conviction rates are lower still. However, Kinsey estimated that 25 per cent of American women were sexually abused by their fathers, uncles, older brothers and grandfathers. See S. Nelson, *Incest: Fact and Myth* (1982).

EG

**Chiliasm.** See MILLENARIAN MOVEMENT.

**chi-squared test.** A test widely used in statistics, with data measured at the nominal level, to see whether or not the frequencies actually observed differ significantly from those which would have been expected if the variables were both normally distributed (see MEASUREMENT). The interpretation of the values of chi-squared ($\chi^2$) depend also on the degrees of freedom in the table (calculated from the number of cells). This statistic is widely used in interpreting CROSS-TABULATIONS, to exclude the possibility that distributions shown might have occurred by chance. Its use has been controversial, critics claiming that it is used indiscriminately as a confirmatory device. There are also simple measures of ASSOCIATION between two variables based on the chi-squared test.

MB

**Chomsky, Avram Noam** (1928- ). American linguist, philosopher and liberal critic of American policy.

Born in Philadelphia, the son of a Hebrew scholar, Chomsky was brought up in a radical Jewish community, where he acquired a lifelong interest in socialist and anarchist politics. He studied mathematics and philosophy at the University of Pennsylvania, but added a course in linguistics, attracted by the political views of Professor Zellig Harris. After completing at Harvard (1951) an MA in spoken Hebrew and a PhD, Chomsky moved to the Massachusetts Institute of Technology, where he has remained.

In the 1960s Chomsky's innovative approach to the study of LANGUAGE involved him in a debate with BEHAVIOURISM which led from linguistics into general social science and philosophy. Mathematical linguistics seemed to provide a model for a rigorous but non-POSITIVIST alternative methodology for social science. These views, coupled with a radical political outlook, in particular vocal opposition to the Vietnam war, made Chomsky a hero for the youth and student culture of the late 1960s, and his name, along with those of McLuhan and LÉVI-STRAUSS, acquired a sort of universal currency. Since then he has divided his time between political concerns, freedom and human rights, and the academic consequences of his view of language.

Instead of looking at the 'performance' aspects of language — that is, the use of actual speech utterances — Chomsky examined the linguistic 'competence' of a person — that is, his/her mastery of a system of rules by which an infinite number of sentences can be understood and grammatical mistakes recognized. How can persons understand and utter a potentially infinite set of utterances? The general models that Chomsky proposed for this syntactic process, 'generative grammars', arose from an interest in the foundations of logic and mathematics, and were only later applied to actual languages. The 'surface structure' of an utterance — that is, the string of words/sounds we speak and hear — is generated and understood by the successive application of a finite set of mental 'rewrite rules' belonging to a much more abstract 'deep structure'. This is assumed to contain the semantic content (i.e. the meaning) of the utterance. Many different surface structures may have related meanings, represented by a shared underlying deep structure. Deep structures are themselves generated by 'base rules' common to several, or even all, languages. Formally, the type of language produced depends on the restrictions placed on the rewrite rules; human natural language seems to require the most complex type of grammar, 'transformational grammar', in which syntactic structures may be completely rearranged, not just added to serially; for example, any human seems to have the capacity to immediately transform an active sentence into a passive one.

Human beings normally learn a language from finite exposure to it. Yet even an infinite set of utterances cannot specify the grammar producing them. Some sort of pre-programming appears necessary, as to the form of linguistic rules which may be encountered. Such general grammatical ability is inherent. Humanity possesses a general structural aptitude, different and more complex than that of other animals, inherent yet actuated by learning, rule-governed yet innovative. This model provides an attractive model for the study of CULTURE in general, an alternative to a model of humanity as responding to external circumstances through CAUSAL LAWS. Methodologically, Chomsky's approach is anti-EMPIRICIST: it postulates underlying relationships (deep structure) and mechanisms (generative grammars) not accessible simply through empirical generalization about observable behaviour, but which once postulated make sense of that behaviour. The effect of Chomsky's linguistics on social science is due more to this general theoretical and methodological position than to any success in the actual construction of generative grammars for particular languages or cultural practices. His formal concepts have only been used in an analogical way in sociology.

See LANGUAGE; STRUCTURALISM.

JL

**church.** The concept forms part of the socio-logical classification of types of religious organization, which include SECT, CULT, DE-NOMINATION and religious order. WEBER characterized the church as an inclusive body which seeks to incorporate all members of the society (rather than being exclusive, as is the sect), where membership is an ascribed characteristic resulting from being born into a community (rather than being achieved by the voluntary attachment of the sect convert).

TROELTSCH identified the church as one institutional form through which the Christian tradition could be expressed. It stresses the themes of redemption and forgiveness, and accepts and collaborates. with the state, regarding the wider society as having relative worth. It is hierarchical in character, expecting its professionals to maintain a higher level of purity and devotion, but making few demands on ordinary members. In its religious orders it will possess a location for containing the religious enthusiast. The church tends to be conservative in character and to identify its interests with those of the comfortable classes rather than with the poor and deprived.

The church is contrasted with the sect as above, and in terms of its respectability compared with the sect's deviance. The church is normally large while the sect is usually thought of as small (although sects such as Jehovah's Witnesses number in the hundreds of thousands in various societies). However, in the modern world the denomination has also arisen as a major type of religious organization. The church is similar to the denomination in being large and respectable, but the church (like the sect) is authoritarian in its definition of the truth and the path to salvation, whereas the denomination (like the cult) is more indi-vidualistic, a form of delegated democracy. Hence the term church, applied in popular speech to a very wide range of religious organizations, is used in a more restricted way as a sociological concept, to apply principally to large, monopolistic agencies of salvation such as the historic Catholic Church.

RW

**citizenship.** Full participating membership of a territorial STATE. The term implies a universal basis: either all adults or some general category of them (e.g. males or property-holders) are citizens. It is a pre-dominantly Western concept, originating in Greece and Rome, current in small city-states in medieval Europe, then expanding enormously in capitalist societies of the 19th and 20th centuries.

Given a central place by the British sociologist T.H. Marshall (1893-1980) in *Citizenship and Social Class* (1950), an analysis of the development of class conflict in modern states, which is a combination of Marxian and Weberian insights. CAPITALISM increased the pervasiveness of class conflict in modern societies; citizenship in the territorial state represented not its elimina-tion, but its INSTITUTIONALIZATION, and the conversion of national into NATION-STATES. In Britain this occurred in three stages: (1) in the 18th century, civil citizen-ship: equality before the law, personal liberty, freedom of speech, thought and religion, the right to own property and make contracts; (2) in the 19th century, political citizenship: electoral and office-holding rights; (3) in the 20th century, social citizenship: a basic level of economic and social welfare, the WELFARE STATE, and full participation in national culture. Subsequent research has supported the general applicability of the model to advanced capitalist nation-states, though with many particular qualifications (see Rokkan *et al, Citizens, Elections, Parties,* 1970). Bendix (*Nation-Building and Citizenship,* 1964) attempted to apply the model to THIRD WORLD countries, though this was less successful, probably because of his relative neglect of class analysis.

See also NATIONALISM, MILITARISM.

MM

**city.** A large and important town; socio-logists use the term to encompass the built environment within which the urban population dwells. URBAN SOCIETY, URBAN-ISM and URBANIZATION refer to the social life of cities. Sociological interest in the city emerged during the 19th century under the impact of extensive urbanization in Western

Europe. However, a distinctive sociology of the city was first established in the USA at the turn of the century under the aegis of the CHICAGO SCHOOL, and was founded upon three premises: (1) The city offered an autonomous frame of reference for sociological analysis; it contained a capacity for generating its own quite distinctive and separate ways of life and socio-cultural changes. (2) There existed a dualism between the country and the city such that they contained radically different cultures. This was later incorporated in the notion of a RURAL-URBAN CONTINUUM. (3) Such was the impact of the urban environment upon individual urban experience that not only could the city be analysed in its own terms, but it also came ultimately to determine the culture of the entire population, both urban and rural, in a society characterized by extensive urbanization.

In recent years each of these premises has been severely criticized, and none is now regarded as completely acceptable.

See J.R. Mellor, *Urban Sociology in an Urbanised Society* (1977); P. Saunders, *Social Theory and the Urban Question* (1982).

HN

**civic culture.** See POLITICAL CULTURE.

**civilization.** May refer simply to the presence of some established social order as opposed to its absence, as for instance in the pairing of civilization and barbarism common in early sociology (see FERGUSON). More generally applied with some qualification to a particular historical epoch or type of society, as in 'Greek civilization' or 'industrial civilization'. Used in this sense, it borders on and merges with the concept of CULTURE; the main difference lies in the tendency for the term civilization to give greater emphasis to socio-political structure and historical process.

ML

**civil religion.** Defined most explicitly by Robert Bellah as 'that religious dimension, found in the life of every people, through which it interprets its historical experience in the light of transcendent reality'. The idea derives from DURKHEIM: that society in its cohesion and integration possesses a sacred character, evoking sentiments of awe and devotion from its members. Even in religiously plural or relatively secularized societies, there will exist, quite independent of the churches, a form of religion manifest in symbolic expressions and acts which represents that society to itself in an ideal image. It provides a transcendental framework for the civil and political affairs of the nation and a set of common values and commitments around which the members of the society are unified.

Bellah found evidence for the existence of civil religion in such events as American Presidential inaugurations. Inaugural Addresses tend to be couched in a religious idiom, referring to God in general terms and to the travails of America as a modern Israel led out of Egypt. This stylized rhetoric indicates a purported commitment on the part of participants to symbols and values which unify and integrate the community and provide sacred legitimations for its affairs. Other more frequent ceremonials such as Thanksgiving Day and Memorial Day are similarly held to integrate families into the civil religion, or to unify the community around its values.

Civil religion is a FUNCTIONALIST response to the dilemma that in many advanced industrial societies religion does not appear to provide a basis for social integration either because such societies have become secularized or because remaining religious forms have become more differentiated and diversified, offering little obvious source of common values, commitments and solidarity. Civil religion resolves this problem. Beneath diversity and apparent secularity lies a hidden religion firmly tied to the nation's history and institutions, and providing the essential integration around sacred things. But civil ceremonials may not have the alleged functions, nor, when social integration is jeopardized, may the system operate to increase ritual and thereby restore equilibrium. Moreover, Bellah's interpretation of Inaugural Addresses and the like has little more support than a plausible alternative such as that American Presidents as much as any other politicians are wont to dignify their self-interested desire for office by whatever traditionally respectable rhetoric lies to hand. NATIONALISM seems to be the obvious home of 'the sacred' in modern society, but further research would be needed to establish this.

See R.Bellah, 'Civil Religion in America', *Daedelus*, 1967.

RW

**civil society.** In English this term dates back at least to 1594 to refer to men dwelling in a community. It later took on two more specific meanings, one in 18th-century Scotland and the other in 19th-century Germany. In Scottish theory, civil society meant a civilized society with a non-despotic state and polished manners, in contrast to a rude or barbaric society (see SCOTTISH ENLIGHTENMENT, FERGUSON). In 19th-century Germany, especially in the political writings of HEGEL, the term acquired a more specialized meaning, one still related to but now distinct from the concept of the STATE.

Hegel described civil society as part of Ethical Life, which was made up of three elements, the family, civil society and the state. Civil society was the intermediate phase between the close-knit, immediate dependency of the family bond, and the universal interest and perspective of the state. It referred to the sphere of social life where individuals pursue their own self-interest within universally recognized bounds. The protection of private property, the recognition of the public authority of the law and police, together with other necessary provisions for the safety of individuals were preconditions for this pursuit of self-interest. Civil society encompassed both economic and legal institutions, and arose from a system of human physical and social needs. It thus entailed a bond of 'unity through necessity' between interdependent individuals, 'a system of complete interdependence, wherein the livelihood, happiness and legal status of one man is interwoven with the livelihood, happiness and rights of all', reminiscent of SMITH's Invisible Hand, and transcended the egoism of civil society, rising above the realm of the individual's particular interests through the universal perspective of the common good.

MARX criticized Hegel's conception of civil society. Hegel derived his scheme from the particular bourgeois social and economic order of his day and failed to realize that the political institutions of civil society were instruments for the domination of one class over another and the tools for the particular interests competing in civil society. Nevertheless, because of Marx's influence within sociology, Hegel's rather than the Scottish usage predominates today. Civil society normally refers to socio-economic life as distinct from the state.

BJB

**clan.** A group of AGNATES (see KINSHIP) tracing descent from a common ANCESTOR. The term clan is more general than that of LINEAGE. Membership of a clan tends to remain constant, whereas lineage membership can be negotiable.

JE

**class.** A form of SOCIAL STRATIFICATION in which allocation to, membership of, and relationships between classes are governed by economic considerations rather than law (as in ESTATES) or religion and ritual pollution (as in CASTE). Roman census-takers introduced the term *classis* when differentiating the population on the basis of wealth for purposes of military service obligation. But its use in English for classes in society (as distinct from classes in schools or classes as part of a classification of plants etc) is associated with the beginning of the INDUSTRIAL REVOLUTION in the 18th century. Since then sociologists have generally used class in connection with the emergence, development and supersession of what is called, according to the theory adopted, capitalist or industrial society. There are two basic uses of class within sociology. Both have in common a view of classes as hierarchically arranged economic groupings in an overall system, in that classes are not single entities but are defined in relation to each other.

(1) Classes as formations playing an actual role in developments in society and history, whose existence is more or less perfectly understood by the individuals or households who compose them. This involves a degree of CLASS CONSCIOUSNESS, class action and class conflict. The two main approaches are those of MARX and WEBER,

and will be discussed below first. They have influenced almost all subsequent writing and led to the distinctively neo-Marxist and Weberian approaches discussed later.

(2) Classes as CATEGORIES which sociologists or social statisticians distinguish by applying economic criteria (e.g. level of income) or procedures (e.g. the grouping and grading of occupations) but which are not thereby presumed to have potential for class consciousness or action. Sometimes called socio-economic classes or groups, or loosely referred to as social classes, and aggregated into SCALES of one or many dimensions which are said to represent the class hierarchy.

These two basic approaches have led to rather separate traditions of class theory which will be discussed in turn. However, the two have sometimes been merged, particularly in theories of INDUSTRIAL SO-CIETY emanating from SAINT-SIMON.

See See also entries under individual classes: BOURGEOISIE; COMPRADOR; LUMPENPROLE-TARIAT; MIDDLE CLASS; NOBILITY; PEASANT; UNDERCLASS; WORKING CLASS and also PRO-FESSIONS.

See A. Giddens, *The Class Structure of the Advanced Societies* (1973); F. Parkin, *Class Inequality and Political Order* (1971).

CGAB

I CLASSES AS HISTORICAL AND SOCIAL FORMA-TIONS. 1. Class, Marx on. 2. Class, Weber on. 3. Class: Neo-Marxist theories. 4. Class: Weberian theories.

II CLASS AS CATEGORY AND SCALE.

### I CLASSES AS HISTORICAL AND SOCIAL FORMATIONS

*1. Class, Marx on.* MARX's conception centres on RELATIONS OF PRODUCTION; a class is a group of people similarly related to the means of production, more particularly to the way in which surplus labour is extracted from the direct producers. It is integral to an analysis of CAPITALISM which focuses upon EXPLOITATION, production for exchange and capital accumulation, and assumes a basic division between the BOURGEOISIE, or capitalist class, who own the means of production, and the proletariat, or WORKING CLASS, who have only their labour power to sell. It equates the production of surplus

value with productive work and insists that workers alone produce all value. Those similarly related to the means of production do not constitute a class proper until they recognize the identity of their class interest (CLASS CONSCIOUSNESS) and organize politically for action to promote it through class struggle or conflict. The transformation of a class-in-itself to a class-for-itself is helped by the socialization of production — the concentration of workers necessitated by factory production — and by the growth of industrial cities and towns. In polemical writings, Marx simplifies the concept in the interests of the formation of working class ideology. In analytical writings, he recognizes the complicating presence both of divisions within the bourgeoisie and proletariat and of other classes besides them. *The Communist Manifesto* (written with ENGELS in 1848) concentrates on the bourgeoisie and proletariat, on increasing polarization between them, and on an eventual proletarian REVOLUTION leading to COMMUNISM. *Capital III* (prepared by Engels for publication in 1894) announces on its last completed page that 'The owners merely of labour-power, owners of capital, and land-owners, whose respective sources of income are wages, profit and ground-rent, in other words, wage-labourers, capitalists and land-owners constitute, then, three big classes of modern society based upon the capitalist mode of production.' This was similar to the definition of SMITH and the classical political economists. It seems that Marx was attempting to go beyond it when death intervened. Other writings introduce further classes, including the PEASANTRY and the LUMPENPROLETARIAT; some acknowledge the difficulties of specifying the class position of groups such as state officials, industrial managers and members of the liberal PROFES-SIONS. The drafts for the *Theories of Surplus Value* (prepared by Kautsky for publication 1905-10) accept that the rise of new MIDDLE CLASSES obstructs the class polarization of bourgeoisie and proletariat expected earlier. Marx also referred briefly to the existence of classes in pre-capitalist MODES OF PRODUC-TION, but therein lie problems dealt with more explicitly by his later followers (see CLASS: *Neo-Marxist theories*). No theory has been as powerful in its theoretical and political influence. Whatever its difficulties, Marx's class theory is still crucial to sociological analysis.

See D. McLellan, *The Thought of Karl Marx* (1971); D. McLellan (ed.), *Karl Marx: Selected Writings* (1977); A. Giddens, *The Class Structure of the Advanced Societies* (1973).

CGAB

*2. Class, Weber on.* Where MARX discusses classes in connection with production, WEBER emphasizes the market, distribution and consumption. In addition, he regards class as only one of three phenomena of the distribution of POWER within a COMMUNITY, the others being STATUS GROUP and party. For Weber, classes are not necessarily communities (i.e. groups whose members feel they belong together) though they represent possible and frequent bases for social action. In *Economy and Society*, Part II (published posthumously in 1922), he contends 'We may speak of a class when (1) a number of people have in common a specific component of their life chances, insofar as (2) this component is represented exclusively by economic interests in the possession of goods and opportunities for income, and (3) is represented under the conditions of the commodity or labour markets', that is, where such people share a common class situation. Weber states 'property' and 'lack of property' are ... 'the basic categories of class situations' but then complicates matters by adding that within these categories class situations are further differentiated according to the kind of property concerned and the income it yields (in particular the property of the class of rentiers is distinguishable from that of the class of entrepreneurs) and the kind of services that can be offered in the market. Thus class situation is determined by the market situation. *Economy and Society*, Part I (in a section written after that cited above), distinguishes three overlapping types of classes: property classes, determined by property differences; commercial (some translators prefer 'acquisition') classes, determined by the marketability of goods, services and skills; and social classes, composed of those constellations of class situations between which individual and generational mobility (i.e. intra and inter-

generational SOCIAL MOBILITY) is typical and easy. Of the three, social classes are most likely to be communities; they often also constitute status groups, that is, communities based upon positive or negative honour and distinguished by a particular style of life. Weber lists four social classes: the working class as a whole, the PETITE BOURGEOISIE, the propertyless intelligentsia and specialists (technicians, white-collar employees, civil servants etc), and 'classes privileged through property and education'.

Class interests generate action by individuals in pursuit of those interests ('social action' in Weber's sense) but this only assumes the form of class action and struggle under certain conditions. CLASS CONSCIOUS organization succeeds most easily (1) against immediate economic opponents (e.g. workers against entrepreneurs, i.e. owner-managers and managers, rather than against shareholders); (2) where large numbers share the same class situation; (3) where it is technically easy to organize (e.g. where workers are concentrated in a workplace) and (4) where workers, or others, are led towards readily understandable goals 'imposed or interpreted by men outside their class (intelligentsia)'. The expression of class interests is complicated by the existence of status groups; both class and status interests may be represented by parties.

Differential power, not economic EXPLOITATION, is the point of origin of Weber's analysis of class. Though his account of rational bourgeois CAPITALISM resembles Marx's in its emphasis upon commodity production and capital accumulation, the absence of exploitation gives it a different, less critical, character. Furthermore, Weber's analysis points up internal differences of property, qualification and skill which, mediated by the market, yield different life chances. Different groups of workers have different class situations and class interests, so that it is often inappropriate to speak of the working class in the singular. Similarly, Weber identifies middle classes (in the plural) including PEASANTS, craftsmen, public and private officials, members of the liberal PROFESSIONS and workers with exceptional qualifications. His analysis of class (and status group and party) is more complicated than Marx's and is attractive to those who oppose the thesis of class polarization.

See also CLASS: *Neo-Weberian theories*; HOUSING CLASS.

See M. Weber, *Economy and Society* (1922) Part I, chapter 4; Part II, chapter 9; A. Giddens, *The Class Structure of the Advanced Societies* (1973).

CGAB

*3. Class: Neo-Marxist theories.* The resurgence of western Marxism in the 1960s and 1970s involved a re-examination of the theory of class. The separation of ownership and control of the means of production (see MANAGERIAL REVOLUTION), the decreasing ratio of managers to workers, the increasing internal differentiation of capital and labour, and the great expansion of the tertiary sector of the occupational structure necessitated reconsideration of the thesis of class polarization. The economic logic of the antagonism between capital and labour may be as compelling as ever, but it has become harder to specify who constitute the bourgeoisie and who the proletariat, and to disregard 'intermediate classes'. F. Parkin (*Marxism and Class Theory : a Bourgeois Critique*, 1979) has distinguished three basic Marxist responses:

(1) The minimalist theory of the proletariat as in Poulantzas's theory (influenced by ALTHUSSER) of the structural determination of class. This theory holds that class position is a matter of objective location in structures of political and ideological domination and subordination as well as structures of economic EXPLOITATION. The WORKING CLASS consists of only those wage labourers who engage in productive work (i.e. who produce surplus value) and who play no part in MARX's 'superintendence of labour' (i.e. the discharge of supervisory and disciplinary functions). The shrunken working class, so constituted, is demarcated from the swollen new PETITE BOURGEOISIE which comprises unproductive workers, supervisors (who contribute to the political domination of the working class even as they themselves are subordinated to the BOURGEOISIE) and all mental workers (who possess 'secret knowledge' of the productive process, contribute to ideological domination of workers and the extraction of surplus value from them, but are themselves fragmented

and dominated by the bourgeoisie). The bourgeoisie comprises those who discharge the functions of capital (i.e. allocation of the means of production to a given use, direction of the labour process and disposal of the product) including managers and the heads of STATE apparatuses who, in the capitalist state, 'manage the state functions in the service of the capital'.

(2) The maximalist theory hinges on the distinction between those social groups peculiar to capitalism and those which will also make a contribution to socialism. Thus landlords, rentiers, property speculators etc are irretrievably bourgeois and their activities will be expunged from a socialist society. Many other social groups, including the new middle class, have a different long-run political interest; their future in a socialist society is assured. In this vein Baran (*The Political Economy of Growth*, 1957) has redefined unproductive labour as that which results 'in the output of goods and services the demand for which is attributable to the specific conditions and relationships of the capitalist system, and which would be absent in a rationally ordered society'. Its generation of a large acceptable class, albeit a compound of workers and petits bourgeois, and its exclusion of social groups who do not contribute to a rational society make the maximalist theory a descendent of SAINT-SIMON's distinction between workers and idlers. The maximalist approach inevitably encourages concern for the internal differentiation of the working class. Thus technicians — petits bourgeois to some theorists — join skilled workers in technologically advanced industries to form, according to others, the new working class.

(3) Intermediate theories concentrate on divisions within the new petite bourgeoisie. They distinguish administrative labour, white-collar professions, necessary to the social co-ordination of labour, from the managerial class necessary only to the circulation of capital. Alternatively, H. Braverman (*Labour and Monopoly Capital*, 1974) stresses the contradiction that the petite bourgeoisie as a whole receives 'its petty share in the prerogatives and rewards of capital' but also 'bears the marks of the proletarian condition'. E.O. Wright (*American Sociological Review*, 1977)

refers to the 'contradictory class location' of the new middle class. Similarly, G. Carchedi (*On the Identification of Social Class*, 1977) argues that class opposition turns on the conflict between the global functions of capital (technical supervision and control of the exploitation process) and the collective worker (the generation of surplus value) and that all sections of the new middle class perform both functions to varying degrees (and are thus exploiters and exploited), although some more closely approximate the collective worker and are moving towards white-collar proletarianization.

These theoretical variations are not merely scholastic, as these classes have political responsibilities. Nor are they entirely new. The discussion of intermediate classes recalls the work of OSSOWSKI in Poland in the early 1950s and the emphasis upon political domination and super-ordination in class formation has a parallel, in the work of DAHRENDORF, a liberal conflict theorist. The attempt to distinguish higher from lower white-collar groups in terms of different life chances and market dependencies is reminiscent of WEBER.

CGAB

*Class in different modes of production.* Marx had occasionally identified classes in earlier historical periods and his overall model requires that all exploitative systems (i.e. where some appropriate the labour of others) contain classes (see MODES OF PRODUCTION). But he had also noted that only in capitalism is surplus labour appropriated primarily by economic means. Perhaps, then, in pre-capitalist modes classes were not largely economically based. Later Marxists have worried over this dilemma: for example, P. Anderson (*Lineages of the Absolutist State*, 1974) argues that before capitalism, political and economic criteria intervened in defining classes, thereby implicitly replacing economic classes with groupings like ESTATES, STATUS-GROUPS etc, as in WEBER's discussion of pre-capitalist societies. It can be also noted that such blurring between economic and political criteria arises in mid-20th-century capitalism: some theories assign the NATION-STATE (also a political entity) a specific relation to the INTERNATIONAL DIVISION OF LABOUR (e.g. UNEQUAL EXCHANGE and DEPENDENCY theorists). Perhaps, then, Marx's whole emphasis on the autonomy and primacy of economic classes is appropriate only to the 19th and early 20th centuries.

MM

*4. Class: Western theories.* A much-abused label, often little more than residual after the possibility of a neo-Marxist class theory (see above) or a FUNCTIONALIST THEORY OF SOCIAL STRATIFICATION has been discounted. Alternatively, it is applied to studies which analyse SOCIAL STRATIFICATION in terms of a number of DIMENSIONS (such as CLASS, STATUS and party of POWER), forgetting that WEBER presented his class, status and party as three phenomena of the distribution of power within a COMMUNITY (see STATUS COMPOSITION).

However, some studies are neo-Weberian. These include (1) works consistent with Weber's central emphasis upon the interpretative understanding of social action in their characterization of strata in terms meaningful to the actors concerned; (2) studies that present forms of stratification as so many variations of domination and subordination or (3) discuss class in connection with market and distributive relations; (4) studies that accept the possibility of working classes and middle classes and their consequence — a fragmentary class structure.

See also DAHRENDORF.

CGAB

II CLASS AS CATEGORY AND SCALE

These definitions have little basis in class theory but are widely used in producing a practical instrument for measuring the broad economic hierarchy of modern societies and distributing the population upon it. As this is a central feature of modern social experience, quite crude definitions based on mode of payment, amount of payment, manual or non-manual occupations, scope of working responsibility, educational level, house ownership, subjective assessments or occupational prestige etc, discriminate quite well for many analytical purposes. Thus many chronic illnesses, length of life, diet, type of newspaper read, chance of conviction for an offence, possession of consumer durables (the list is endless) are associated with class defined as the possession of one or more of the above attributes.

It is also relatively simple to construct a class system based on these variables. Occupations are most frequently grouped and graded to produce classes of this type (see CENSUS CLASSES; SOCIAL MOBILITY). All these schemes fail if over-generalized beyond their original distributional purpose, and few cope adequately even in this purpose with the problem of GENDER STRATIFICA-TION. Other schemes favour identifying, weighting and combining a number of factors in an overall scale of class, including occupational group, level of income, level of education, type of housing and aspects of style of life. Whereas MARX justified dichotomous models of class (exploiters and exploited, dominators and subordinates etc) this approach yields multi-gradational and multi-dimensional schemes — often with the additional implication that there is no great obstacle to SOCIAL MOBILITY between classes. These schemes, while often empirically quite complex, lack adequate theoretical grounding.

One variation of the approach attempts to close the gap between the somewhat arbitrary 'objective' nature of the scale approach and subjective understandings of class. Following the example of Lloyd Warner (1898-1970) — an anthropologist influenced by RADCLIFFE-BROWN, who brought to the study of 'Yankee City' (Newburyport, Mass.) fieldwork techniques previously employed among Australian aborigines (see Warner and Lunt, *The Social Life of a Modern Community*, 1941) — others have bridged the gap by basing scales of local COMMUNITY class structures upon the principles of class allocations used by locals themselves. Yet 'Yankee City' showed that even in local communities value CONSENSUS does not exist: different principles of class allocation co-exist among different sections of the population. Warner's six-class model appears to reproduce subjective class; in reality it is a social scientist's composite of a number of different, simpler notions acknowledged by the inhabitants.

See Reid, *Social Class Differences in Britain* (1977).

CGAB, RD, MM

**class consciousness.** Elements of beliefs, values and norms which arise by virtue of a group's identity, real or potential, as a CLASS (in the first sense defined in the entry for that concept), and in this broader sense similar to WEBER's notion of class as COMMUNITY. But 'class consciousness' is usually limited to a further purposive sense derived from MARX: consciousness which seeks to further class interests in opposition to those of another class. Marx distinguished between a class-in-itself and a class-for-itself, often incorrectly taken as a distinction between OBJECTIVE and subjective aspects of class. Marx never distinguished social life in this way. Rather, a class-for-itself has additional quasi-objective organizational features (economic interdependence, collective organization) which enable it to develop purposive class consciousness, act for itself, and so change history.

Much subsequent sociology has attempted to operationalize class consciousness. For example, Mann's four-dimensional approach (*Consciousness and Action in the Western Working Class*, 1973), distinguishes class identity, opposition (to another class), totality (generalizing it to life as a whole) and alternative (only for an exploited class, attempting to establish an alternative form of society). Most of this research tradition worries over why the WORKING CLASS shows far less consciousness than Marx anticipated — and also less than the BOURGEOISIE normally shows. The working class has instead in varying degrees sought sectional advantages, adhered to religion, fought for higher wages as an end in itself, pursued NATIONALISM, RACIALISM or FASCISM, joined pseudo-left parties, or adopted parliamentarianism and piecemeal reform as a mechanism of structural change. For Marxists these are either (1) false explanations of real material problems — religion and nationalism; (2) propounded to advance threatened PETITE BOURGEOIS interests — racism and fascism; or (3) partial accounts of real problems which, because they lack totality, reinforce a tendency to sectionalism amongst the workers — trade unionism and piecemeal reformism.

There have been two main types of explanation for all this. (1) Many modern Marxists argue that the working class is ideologically dominated by the bourgeoisie. Lenin wrote that workers independently achieved only TRADE UNION CONSCIOUSNESS. GRAMSCI, adapting the idea advanced by Marx that the ruling ideas of an era are the ideas of ruling classes, advanced the concept of HEGEMONY. Subsequently, Marxists have accepted the FUNCTIONALIST premise that value CONSENSUS exists in modern society, but have argued that it is bourgeois hegemony. This tends curiously towards IDEALISM and FALSE CONSCIOUSNESS, and away from Marx's historical materialism. For Marx, a class could not be prevented from attaining consciousness merely by (superstructural) ideologies.

(2) If ideas are not merely or predominantly the possession of a class ('bourgeois ideology', 'working class ideology') the problem more or less dissolves itself. People then behave and think because of the logic of their situation, because they occupy more complex roles determining actions, because they endured a particular socialization pattern etc. Though workers show elements of class consciousness, these co-exist with other beliefs, values and norms derived from other roles, identities and socialization processes they have internalized. Consciousness is here often seen as contradictory, fragmentary or pragmatic. Alternatively, workers form coherent, normative and evaluative attachments upon alternative (usually narrower) groupings, REFERENCE GROUPS (see also RELATIVE DEPRIVATION).

RD, MM

**classroom.** Since the establishment of formal SCHOOLING special buildings have been set aside for teaching pupils with rooms for this purpose. Though initially many pupils were taught in the same room, either together or in several separate groups or classes, by the mid-19th century a separate room had become usual for each class, often numbering 60-70 pupils. By the mid-20th century schools tended to be built to include a series of separate classrooms in which one teacher in a primary or elementary school

taught all school subjects to one class of about 30-40 pupils of the same age, or in a secondary school taught one or two specialist subjects to a series of differently aged classes, numbering 20-30. Recently there has been some move towards schools built in a more open style. The traditional classroom is a private area, marked by strong boundaries, within which teacher and pupils interact together to establish a specific social system characterized not only by what the actors import from outside these boundaries, but also by whatever initiatives are made by either teacher or pupils within the classroom itself. Much research, using both quantitative and qualitative techniques, has investigated the nature and determinants of interaction in classrooms of various types and has made comparisons according to various characteristics of teachers and pupils, usually with the aim of linking academic or moral outcomes to specific teacher or pupil inputs.

PWM

**cleavage.** Vertical, as opposed to horizontal (stratified) differences in society. Cleavage denotes not only the existence of social categories such as ethnic, regional, language and religious groupings, but also implies that these socially based differences have political consequences, that the differences are reflected in political organizations which pursue their own interests, and that political conflict results. Cleavage has thus come to indicate inherent and perhaps politically insoluble differences within a polity. Writers in the American PLURALIST tradition suggest that cross-cutting cleavages (where political, social and economic allegiances do not unite in their political goals) produce political stability. See PILLARIZATION.

EMM

**cline.** A gradient of change in a measurable genetic character (see GENE). For example, people in Northern Europe, America and Asia tend to have a relatively pale complexion; the closer one moves towards the Equator, the darker the native people, due to the presence of melanin in their skin. A graph showing the presence of melanin will rise steadily upwards as it moves towards the Equator and then fall. The physical differentiation of humans is mostly a gradual or continuous differentiation influenced by social patterns, notably mating. Social patterns also distort the perception of physical variation, notably by beliefs about the nature of RACE. These are challenged by the argument that 'there are no races, there are only clines'.                                    MPB

cluster analysis. A family of mathematical and computational techniques for the empirical grouping of observations into a series of hierarchically arranged classes or clusters on the basis not of single characteristics alone but of numerous characteristics considered simultaneously. Each clustering technique consists of (1) a measure of similarity to express the closeness of two profiles over the set of chosen characteristics and (2) a criterion for forming clusters of profiles at different similarity levels. As the similarity level decreases, clusters join together, and then the clusters of clusters amalgamate, forming a tree-like diagram of connections (dendrogram) expressing the hierarchy of clusters detected in the data. Both FACTOR ANALYSIS and MULTI-DIMENSIONAL SCALING can also be used to group data.

Clustering techniques were first used in psychology by Zubin in 1938 to classify individuals by like-mindedness, and in anthropology by Driver and KROEBER in 1932 to quantitatively express cultural affinities. The advent of computerization in the 1950s aided clustering because the number of computations rises rapidly with the number of observations, as does the number of possible cluster configurations to be evaluated. Cluster analysis has been used in many social science fields, and was introduced to sociology in the late 1960s as an empirical technique for simplifying the structure of large sets of data. It has no theoretical base within sociology, and the statistical and sampling properties of clustering techniques are poorly understood. Many do not have a well-defined result, and may be profoundly altered by small changes in the initial data. The strength of clustering procedures lies in the way they take account of the whole pattern of characteristics associated with an individual observation.

The problem of clustering observation profiles is important theoretically. It is closely related to the problem of pattern recognition, for example, allocating individually variable sound patterns to the class of the sentence which they represent.
                                                   JL

cognitive consistency theory. A term referring to post-war American theoretical approaches in social psychology which emphasize the meaningful organization of thought, feeling and behaviour within the individual as a central process of the individual personality. Inconsistency is viewed as an uncomfortable psychological state, motivating a move toward consistency through change in attitude or belief, through action such as avoidance, or through selective perception of potentially inconsistent features. The great strength of the concept of consistency is that it can approach both rational and irrational aspects of psychology, for the desire for consistency is in itself rational, but rationalization or even irrationality may be the means of achieving consistency.

The concept is widely used. In psychology it expresses the unity of the individual personality. In the mid-1950s, however, a number of more specific concepts were formulated to understand the organization of an individual's ATTITUDE, notably in the context of 'forced-compliance' studies, where attitudes to other individuals seemed to induce in the subject changes in attitude to objects of the environment. Leon FESTINGER has been influential in promoting a programme of empirical research on 'cognitive dissonance' and attitude change, although Heider had been the first to initiate this line of work (1946). Heider considered an individual, P, and his attitude toward another person, O, and an environmental object, C. These attitudes were said to be 'balanced' essentially if a positive attitude towards O was coupled with agreement between P and O on their attitudes towards X, and a negative attitude toward O with disagreement on X. If X is a third person, the concept of balance extends out into small-group relations, and Cartwright and Henry used GRAPH THEORY to work out the consequences of a simultaneous desire for balance on the part of all the members of a group. If relations are restricted to positive and negative this implies one solidary group with all intra-group relations positive, or two solidary groups with all negative relations between them. A number of writers have continued to examine the consequences of cognitive balance for group relations, structural balance theory, and elegant results linking cognitive balance with the theory of elementary KINSHIP systems have been established by Harrison White (1963) and J.P. Boyd (1969).

Newcomb (1953) recast Heider's approach in terms of the concept of symmetry, and postulated a 'strain toward symmetry' of attitudes in a positive inter-personal relationship. He carried out empirical demonstrations of this effect in 1954 in a specially set-up residential house at the University of Michigan. Osgood and Tannenbaum (1955) used the concept of congruity in attempting to understand the direction of attitude-change toward a person before and after declaring their attitude toward some third significant object, the prediction being that attitudes will change toward maximum simplicity of structure.

Cognitive dissonance is employed by FESTINGER to mean a situation where 'considering' two cognitive elements in isolation, the obverse of one element follows from the other. If dissonance is postulated as psychologically uncomfortable, cognitive dissonance theory can be stated formally and a large number of specific consequences follow, which have been the object of further empirical research. Some support has been found for some of these consequences, but in general there has been difficulty in defining attitudes as positive and negative in other than the simplest of situations, and in predicting or explaining which of the many routes toward the reduction of dissonance will be pursued. Much more complex formal models of belief-systems are required. Even in artificial intelligence and the theory of computing very little progress has been made in simulating the peculiar combination of RA-TIONALITY and irrationality that seems to characterize human thought.

See F. Heider, *The Psychology of Interpersonal Relations* (1959); H. White, *An Anatomy of Kinship* (1963); L. Festinger, *A Theory of Cognitive Dissonance* (1962).    JL

**cognitive dissonance.** See COGNITIVE CON-SISTENCY THEORY.

**cohort and period analysis.** Two distinct types of analysis applied in DEMOGRAPHY, and thence in sociology, to data on populations over time. A cohort, derived from the term for the tenth part of a Roman legion, denotes a set of people to whom some event, such as birth or marriage, occurs in the same time period. Cohort analysis divides the population into such groups and studies their composition and vital rates. In period or secular analysis composition and rates are calculated for particular years or time periods. Period rates form a continuous summary as cohorts move on, die out and are replaced by new ones.

Cohort analysis has the great advantage that it reflects the experiences of a real set of individuals, such as a generation as it ages, whereas period analysis characterizes an aggregate whose underlying composition varies from year to year. Demographic rates frequently depend on the time elapsed since an event: thus mortality depends upon age, and fertility upon time since marriage. Age has a genuinely dynamic character in cohort analysis, whereas when cross-sectional period data are used age is a static variable in that it characterizes that time period only. Except in France, data adequate for constructing cohort rates are a recent phenomenon and cohort analysis counts as one of the chief advances in modern demography.

In sociology, cohort analysis is particularly important. Not only does a cohort carry forward a characteristic demographic make-up, but it has similar experiences and conditions as it progresses through the educational and occupational systems, adapting to them and changing social structure as it goes. The cohort is the locus of social change, which can often be detected in particular cohorts before it is manifested in overall rates. Change in the cohort composition of the population may itself constitute an important social change.

Identifying the separate effects of the ageing of a cohort from those of the passing of historical time can be statistically difficult, as age and date are perfectly CORRELATED. Synthetic cohorts can be constructed from the period rates (see LIFE TABLES), but these will not approximate any real cohort. However, given rates for each cohort for each year of elapsed time, and the initial size of the cohorts, the period rates can be reconstructed.

JL

**collective conscience.** See DURKHEIM.

**collective consumption.** A term coined by the Spanish Marxist sociologist Manuel Castells in the late 1960s, defined as 'consumption processes whose organization and management cannot be other than collective given the nature and size of the problem' (*The Urban Question*, 1977). His examples include housing, social facilities and leisure provisions.

In urban sociology, the concept has been developed as part of the attempt to provide a sociologically valid definition of 'the urban'. The recognition that 'the urban' as a spatial unit does not coincide with either URBANISM as a cultural unit or with the CITY as a political unit has led to a reformulation of 'the urban question' and a search for the correct scientific object of study for urban sociology. Castells argues that the only candidate — one in which the social and the spatial coincide — is the collective consumption unit, which is socially organized and provided within the context of a spatially bounded system.

However, Castells's meaning is by no means clear, and it undergoes a number of shifts in different parts of his work. Other urban sociologists, such as R.E. Pahl, have argued that what is referred to is collective provision rather than collective consumption.

See R.E. Pahl, *Whose City* (1975); M. Haroe (ed.), *Captive Cities* (1977).

HN

**collectivization.** The process of amalgamating privately owned farms and/or estates under state supervision and management, forcibly and ruthlessly carried out by Stalin in the Soviet Union in the 1930s and a common feature of the reorganization of STATE SOCIALIST agriculture in a number of Eastern European states.

HN

**colonialism.** See IMPERIALISM; NEO-COLONIALISM.

**common religion.** In many societies, religion extends beyond the confines of social institutions such as the churches. The term 'common religion' refers to beliefs and practices, relating to supernatural or super-empirical beings or powers, existing independently of formal religious institutions. In Christian societies ideas concerning luck, chance, fate, astrological influence and the like normally form no part of the theory and practice of the conventional religious institutions. However, they form part of the conceptual apparatus by which many people make sense of their circumstances, and provide comfort and reassurance in the face of life's vicissitudes. Formal religious institutions may in time come to absorb aspects of common religion, in the way that many folk festivals and rites were fitted into the Catholic ritual calendar as it came to dominate. 'Official' religion and 'common' religion may exist side by side, either providing a recourse for different members of the society, or for the same members at different times. A more characteristic pattern is that whereas some social groups are associated with each, for example in industrial societies the middle classes with 'official' religion, the working classes with 'common' religion, each has recourse to the other form of religion under identifiable circumstances. The middle classes may turn to the 'common' religion at times of stress, uncertainty or illness while the working classes may turn to the 'official' religious institutions for authenticating ritual at important points of status passage such as birth, marriage, and death.

Some argue that the existence of common religion rebuts the SECULARIZATION thesis since the latter derives from a decline in church-related religious beliefs and practice and not of religion in all forms.

RW

**communication.** Social interaction is dependent upon the passing of messages between actors. Such communication points to an initiative to be taken, a recipient, a mode, content and an effect. This perspective is summarized in a question put in the late 1940s by the American political scientist Lasswell: Who says What in Which Channel to Whom with What Effect? Interpersonal interaction focuses around communication of two types: verbal and non-verbal. Verbal communication may be oral or written; spoken communication is usually accompanied by non-verbal CUES which must be taken into account in a full interpretation of the message. Such non-verbal communication, sometimes called para-communication, may also be used alone — for example, a wink, scowl or cordial handshake. Non-verbal cues may be conscious or unconscious, and if un-conscious the communication made by an actor may differ from intent. Messages are also increasingly passed under conditions of mass communication through the mass media. In this case the context (one initiator addressing a large number of anonymous recipients) differs not only from that of interpersonal interaction, but also from that in a crowd, for example a political meeting. Hence the processes involved and the outcomes achieved will be of a very different order from those achieved in small-scale situations. The seeming face-to-face relationship between listener or viewer and performer in the case of the mass media has been termed a para-social relationship. It can be analysed in both sociological and psychological terms; in this latter respect subliminal communication may be important.

See CONVERSATION ANALYSIS, CRITICAL THEORY, HABERMAS, LANGUAGE, MEDIA STUDIES.                                                PWM

**communication (in industry).** See HUMAN RELATIONS MOVEMENT.

**communism.** The doctrine that all property should be owned collectively and its proceeds held in common. MARX trans-formed it from a UTOPIAN hope to an actual future stage of post-capitalist society. He envisaged it developing in different stages: a lower one (sometimes called SOCIALISM) where the social product would be distributed according to the amount of work each individual contributed; a higher state, in which the division of labour would be transcended, production would be experienced as a creative activity and the principle of distribution would be 'from each according to his ability, to each according to his needs'. 'Communist' was the term chosen by the Bolsheviks after World War I to distinguish the parties of the newly formed Third International from the Social Democratic parties of the Second. Membership of the International came to mean subordination to the interests of Moscow and to the Bolshevik model of revolution. The Russian Revolution of 1917 not only destroyed the Czarist regime and installed the Bolsheviks in power, but also provided the first large-scale example of a modern state committed to Marxist-Communist principles. The death of LENIN in 1924 and the rise of STALIN strengthened the theory of 'socialism in one country' in which many of the original domestic and international aims of the revolution were subjugated to the primary goal of building up the industrial and military might of the Soviet Union. This strategy contributed to the defeat of the Nazis in World War II but its brutality and political paranoia, both in its own country and in its satellite countries, continues to provoke a torrent of criticism and organizational opposition from those who might otherwise have been expected to support the Soviet project.

According to Khruschev, communism would arrive in the USSR by 1980. It was that state of society, guided by the Communist Party, in which 'fair and reasonable' consumer demands would be satisfied by the state planning bodies. Although this was derided as 'goulash communism' Khruschev did agree with ENGELS that under communism the state would 'wither away'. Since the death of Stalin, many national parties have shown increasing independence of Moscow, especially recently the Euro-communists, who define communism as involving a mixed economy plus democratic rights and freedoms. In China, the victory of the Communists, completed in 1949, installed a second major power, committed to slightly different principles of communism (see MAO), and with historic border disputes and Far Eastern rivalry with Russia. An open split developed 1960-3. Since then there has been no effective world communist movement outside the rival foreign policies of the Soviet and Chinese states. A further irony is that though communism as an ideal contains the withering away of the state, modern states generally referred to as communist are extremely powerful. Indeed in the context of UNDERDEVELOPMENT, such regimes as Cuba or North Vietnam achieve their very successes through a high level of state mobilization of economic and social life.

'Communist' is also sometimes used as a term of abuse to denigrate social reformers by associating them with the USSR and its 1930s purges.

See LENIN, TROTSKY, SOCIAL DEMOCRACY, STATE CAPITALISM, STATE SOCIALISM.

DB, LS, MM, BT

**community.** A set of social relationships which takes place wholly, or mostly, within a bounded local territory. The term is used in the study of non-tribal societies, particularly within Western national states: as an organizing principle, community takes the place given to KINSHIP in the study of tribal groups. Community studies tend to concentrate on rural areas or on localized urban groups. In either case there is a strong spatial component in the definition of community, but no agreement as to how this should be arrived at. A distinctive feature of social studies in these settings is an interest in customs as interrelated sets which form cultural patterns. Community is often opposed to large structures, such as the STATE. In classical formulations, which follows TÖNNIES and WEBER on CLASS, communities are IDEAL TYPES in a continuum which stretches between two poles. These may be implicit and descriptive — such as the contrast between rural and urban society (see RURAL-URBAN CONTINUUM), or tradition and modernity — or they may emphasize particular types of social relationship. Thus 'close' ties of kinship and status in a community are opposed to 'loose' contractual relationships between individuals who experience no other type of relationship within settings characterized by a high DIVISION OF LABOUR.

The concept of community is usually value-laden, often referring generally to a form of social organization the writer values. More particularly, traditional, rural, close-knit communities are visualized as representing a past way of life and social behaviour that has been lost in the process of industrialization. The warmth and closeness of family ties are implicitly preferred to contractual relationships and the resulting studies tend to be backward-looking and stress such aspects as the supposed conservatism of peasants in rural areas. The genre of community studies also tends to stress the typicality of a particular community for a whole group or area. Thus the community, however defined, becomes a sample of a general CULTURE, acquiring a theoretical rather than a concrete existence.

There are three main sub-approaches to community. (1) As locality — a geographical expression denoting a human settlement located within a particular local territory. This is not a sociological definition in that there is no consideration of the inhabitants or their interactions. (2) As a local social system — a set of social relationships that take place wholly or mostly within a locality. This is a more sociological usage, since it refers to a network of interrelationships between people living in the same locality; however, this definition refers to the structure of these relationships, not their content. (3) As a type of relationship — that is, as a sense of identity between individuals, having no geographical (local) referent at all since this sense of identity may exist between geographically dispersed individuals. This notion of community, with its overtones of common identity, is best termed 'communion' since this more clearly conveys the sense of meaningful identity and shared experience.

Unfortunately there is a tendency to elide these three definitions. Indeed, there has been a largely unexamined assumption by writers such as SIMMEL, Wirth and those associated with the rural-urban continuum that life in particular geographical localities promotes a structure of relationships which results in the presence or absence of communion; detailed empirical investigation shows this assumption to be false.

See also GEMEINSCHAFT.

See C. Bell and H. Newby, *Community Studies* (1971).

JE, HN

**community care.** The provision of social services in the community, rather than in an institution. The popularity of community care as a way of dealing with problems facing the personal social services has increased in recent years. This is partly based on the recognition of the undesirable effects of institutionalization, highlighted by writers like GOFFMAN, partly on the belief that community care is intrinsically desirable both because it leads to a wider appreciation of social problems and because care in the community may help the recipient to return to a normal role in society.

There is a fear, however, that much of its recent popularity is due to the belief that it could be a cheaper way of providing social services. This may be misleading. Community care of a high standard may be just as expensive as care in an institution. The provision of support services, special buildings and dwellings to allow people who would otherwise be institutionalized to remain in the community can be costly. In some cases where community care has been introduced to save money, the service has been unsatisfactory, and arguably less satisfactory than institutional care.

See also WOMEN AND THE LABOUR MARKET; WOMEN AND THE WELFARE STATE.

See I. Goffman, *Asylums* (1968).

MPJ

**community control.** An approach advocating radical, POPULIST or liberal arguments about the role and function of policing organizations. Identified particularly with the politics of social control in the USA, it alludes to the decentralization of policing and the assumption of authority by the 'local community'. A proposal rather than a concrete achievement, it reflects anxiety about the allegedly class-based character of justice and law enforcement. In this context, 'community' usually refers to homogeneous neighbourhoods of the working class or ethnically disadvantaged strata. 'Control' conveys some combination of vigilance associations, informal discipline, and citizen representation on police forces.

PR

**comparative methods.** Any method that compares the similarities and differences between phenomena or classes of phenomena within one society or among many with a view to explaining them, may be described as comparative. In the most general sense, comparative methods are the methods of scientific sociology, and just as there are several versions of scientific sociology there are several main comparative methods, usually linked to the names of the classic writers.

*Evolutionary functionalism.* First elaborated in DURKHEIM's *Rules of Sociological Method* (1895) this combined the DARWINIAN notion of mankind's general progress with a sociological analysis of the FUNCTIONS of social institutions in this progress. By comparing legal systems and the division of labour, and types of social solidarity and suicide, Durkheim endeavoured to establish sociology on a scientific footing. Although many of his particular conclusions have been discredited his method is still widely used. For example, the NEO-EVOLUTIONIST school of PARSONS (see his *Societies: Evolutionary and Comparative Perspective*, 1966, and R. Marsh, *Comparative Sociology*, 1967) and much of the work of those who use the Human Relations Area Files (a quantitative compilation of the properties of social structures in a large number of primitive societies) are influenced by Durkheim's method.

*Historical comparison.* One of the major problems of early sociology was to distinguish itself from history. WEBER introduced the concept of IDEAL TYPES to help explain the vital differences between societies which also had similarities (e.g. his studies of world religions and of economic systems in the East and West). It has been argued that Weber's ideal types, especially those of BUREAUCRACY and the legitimations of AUTHORITY and his types of ACTION constitute theories rather than methodological aids; subsequent developments support this view. However, Weber's methods of historical comparison have had a substantial impact on many modern sociologists: see for example BENDIX, *Kings or People?* (1978); EISENSTADT, *The Political System of Empires* (1967); P. Blau and R. Scott, *Formal Organizations* (1963).

MARX and ENGELS applied the theory of MODES OF PRODUCTION to comparative sociology. Marx used comparative methods extensively, and in this respect has much in common with Weber (see I. Zeitlin, *Ideology and Development of Sociological Theory*, 1968). An outstanding work in this genre is Barrington MOORE's *Social Origins of Dictatorship and Democracy* (1969), a wide-ranging analysis of the roads of the major nation-states to parliamentary democracy, fascism and communism, combining a Marx-inspired emphasis on the landlords' expropriation of the peasants' agricultural surplus with a Weberian political sociology. The success of this book and the many studies that have followed in its wake testify to the desire of most sociologists to reconcile Marx and Weber for the benefit of historical sociology. However, as some Marxists (e.g. MARCUSE) and some Weberians (e.g. DAHRENDORF) have indicated, this may be an impossible project.

*Multivariate Analysis.* The development of statistical and mathematical techniques in the social sciences has combined with the continual increase in information about every conceivable human practice to promote the use of non-historical methods to correlate variables in one setting with those in another. Hobhouse, Wheeler and Ginsberg in *Material Culture and Social Institutions of the Simpler Peoples* (1915) tried to establish a connection between modes of subsistence and social institutions using the evidence of a variety of practices; about 50 years later Gouldner and Peterson (*Technology and the Moral Order*, 1962) were continuing the task with many more variables and techniques. Comparisons of variables both within a society (e.g. studies of the relations between occupation and education) and between societies (e.g. studies of economic development and communications systems) by multivariate analysis in one form or another now absorbs more expenditure of time and money than any other form of contemporary social research. Even greater expenditure, combined with statistical advances, has

recently introduced a historical dimension into this research.

There is no such thing as *the* comparative method, since all sociology is more or less comparative, whether consciously or unconsciously. Several comparative methods are frequently used in the same piece of research, often producing conceptual or empirical confusion. As sociologists are normally unable to set up experiments to test their theories, comparative methods operate by setting up a 'quasi-experimental situation' (see EXPERIMENT).                    LS

**compensatory education.** The aims of teachers are rarely fully achieved, often because of the social background and characteristics of their pupils. Many children of parents who are of low social class, black/coloured or immigrants, fail by academic criteria early in the primary school. Measures to compensate for such failure take several forms. For example, more resources may be directed towards schools where such pupils are numerous or extra tuition may be given to these children either before or after they enter formal schooling. Such measures are termed compensatory education. They are based on a definition of EQUALITY in education which focuses not upon equal chances or equal inputs for each child, but upon equal outcomes. They build upon work on social justice by Rawls, who enunciated the 'difference principle' whereby socially valued goods and services, such as education, 'are to be distributed equally unless an equal distribution is to the disadvantage of the least favoured' (*A Theory of Justice*, 1971). This has been the rationale behind such large-scale schemes of compensatory education as Operation Headstart in the USA in the 1960s and the Educational Priority Areas (EPAs) in the UK in the 1960s and 1970s. Though recent re-analysis of relevant data may force a reappraisal, such purely educational schemes seem to have failed to overcome the social causes of disadvantage, probably because educational measures alone cannot offset disadvantage structured into the larger society outside the school, particularly when the pupils concerned ultimately return to the social setting that caused the initial educational problem.

PWM

**competence.** See CHOMSKY.

**competition (economic).** See MARKET STRUCTURE; MARKET SYSTEM.

**competition (social).** See PARK.

**comprador, comprador class.** [Portuguese: 'buyer']. The early mercantile activities of European traders in far away countries with strange customs, tongues and institutions encouraged enterprising natives to fulfil the role of comprador or agent for a foreign enterprise. In 400 years of European expansion, colonial rule and neo-colonial intervention, the word has obtained a more sociological meaning, referring to an individual or a whole class who act as a social structural mediator between the metropolitan and satellite countries. Their Western tastes and life-styles, economic interests and political needs reflect the links that join the economic structure of the satellite to that of the metropolis. In radical development literature, where it is freely used, 'comprador' has become synonymous with 'deputy-imperialist'.

AH

**compulsion.** See MENTAL ILLNESS.

**Comte, Auguste** (1798-1857).The founder of the POSITIVIST and EMPIRICIST sociological traditions, Comte invented the terms 'positive philosophy' and 'sociology'. Born into an aristocratic family in Montpellier, Comte attended the progressive Ecole Polytechnique in Paris during the aftermath of the French Revolution. As secretary to SAINT-SIMON, he collaborated closely in the development of utopian socialism. Withdrawing embittered from this relationship, he turned to teaching mathematics for a living. In 1848 he established the Positivist Society. His philosophy, largely concerned with elaboration of the positivist aspects of Saint-Simonian thought, was developed during a period of acute political instability in France. Comte opposed those philosophies (egalitarianism, individualism, political sovereignty) which he considered responsible for the revolution.

From Turgot, Burdin and Saint-Simon, Comte drew his law of the three stages. Society and human thought progress through theological, metaphysical and positive stages (like other writers of the period, he used the word 'positive' as a synonym for 'scientific'). Theological thought explains phenomena with reference to actions of capricious supernatural beings, passing from anthropomorphism in the early period of fetishism ro polytheism, and then monotheism. Metaphysical thought attributes causation to abstract, less capricious forces. Positivist thought seeks scientific explanations in terms of universal laws. Metaphysical and theological thought are incompatible with the positive method of the natural sciences, which demystifies the world through empirical testing of its theories. (He followed Kantian philosophy, Hume and British empiricism in rejecting metaphysics.) In the positive stage of society, social evolution will culminate in the unity of the human mind and of the human race.

Comte's unilinear, deterministic theory of social development initially assumed that there could be only one mode of thought in each stage of social evolution. He soon modified his EVOLUTIONISM: the dominant mode of thought which distinguishes a specific state of social evolution may co-exist with other modes of thought. Positivist explanation occurs even within the theological state of society. All branches of knowledge pass through the three stages, but not simultaneously. The positivist spirit first develops in areas most removed from human control. Comte based his hierarchy of the sciences upon this principle. The higher disciplines enter the positive stage later because they are more complex and depend upon the lower sciences which lay the groundwork for their development. Astronomy and physics develop first, then chemistry and biology, and finally sociology. Chemistry and the lower sciences seek laws regulating atomistic occurrences and constitute ANALYTIC sciences. Biology and sociology share a HOLISTIC approach in dealing with organic entities and so are synthetic sciences. Positivist sociology would stand at the head of the hierarchy of sciences.

Comte stressed the importance to sociology of observation, comparison, experimentation, and historical analysis. Within sociology he distinguished between the study of statics (laws governing social order) and the study of dynamics (evolutionary laws governing social change). Statics proceeds from analysis of social institutions to a search for essential principles, and is concerned with the original and social nature of man. Under statics Comte studies the social functions of work, the FAMILY, PROPERTY, LANGUAGE and the STATE, and their contributions to social solidarity. Thus religion unifies through appealing to three basic elements in human nature (emotions, will, intelligence). His (highly sexist) analysis of the family describes it as a medium for socialization into the four types of sentiment (paternal, filial, fraternal, conjugal) which extend through all social relationships, promoting social order.

Comte's early sociology was preoccupied with evolutionary progress. His later work (1817-22) subordinated this interest to the search for essential principles of social order, producing a sophisticated analysis of SOCIAL CHANGE. It expresses the tension in Comte's work between contemporary conservatism (opposition to science, revolution, reform) and radicalism (acclaim of a new golden age of science and industry). Comte became increasingly appreciative of the conservatives' conception of social order as a system of common values. Accepting their belief that a decline in traditional and religious values had created a social crisis in Europe, he sought, through positivism, moral and intellectual reform as a prerequisite to social reform and the reconstruction of CONSENSUS. This partial shift in emphasis has been wrongly interpreted as a radical transition from an objective conception of positivism and society to a subjective emphasis upon reformism, humanitarianism, and religion, a misconception based upon the mistaken equation of Comte's positivism with 'scientism'. Comte's positivism cannot be reduced to mere empiricism.

Comte provided one of the first critiques of classical economics, alleging sterile abstraction, metaphysical thinking, and the unwarranted isolation of economic facts. Comtean thought influenced Lévy-Bruhl, DURKHEIM, Alain and Mauras in France; SPENCER, J.S. MILL, Lecky and Morley in England; the German historians Mommsen and Grote, and intellectual thought in Spain, Portugal and South America. Comte's emphasis upon social statics was a substantial influence upon the growth of FUNCTIONALIST concepts and his concept of method has, through Durkheim's work, had a fundamental influence upon contemporary sociology and anthropology. Comte contributed to that strand of sociological thought that would attribute greater power to 'men of knowledge' and shared with Saint-Simon the image of a new age in which the principal conflicts and divisions in society will be eliminated. His philosophy thus has some affinity with 'the end of ideology' and modern technocratic theories (see POST-INDUSTRIAL SOCIETY). Until 1914 Comte and Spencer were the mainstays of American sociology. Comtean positivism shares historical and intellectual links with the logical positivism of the VIENNA CIRCLE and with operationalism and conventionalism in the philosophy of scientific method. His positivism has had a wider-ranging impact upon both sociology and philosophy in its rejection of metaphysics and crude empiricism and its emphasis upon the unity of the natural and social sciences. It promoted the conception of a natural science of society and the view of philosophy as parasitic upon scientific knowledge. 'Positivism' has become a label open to much misuse. For Comte it had a systematic and moral meaning which was soon replaced within positivistic sociology by an atomistic conception emphasizing the importance of quantification for a scientific sociology. Comtean positivism sought to establish scientific social laws (see LAW, SOCIAL).

Major works: *Positive Philosophy*, 6 vols. (1830-42); *Systems of Positive Polity*, 4 vols. (1848-54). Volumes 2 and 3 of the latter work (*Social Statics* and *Social Dynamics*) contain his principal sociological writing.

JW

**conation.** A psychological concept which has its origins in philosophy, where it denotes the faculty of mind concerned with desiring and willing, with striving for action, as distinct from the faculties of cognition and AFFECT. In modern psychology, the trio of terms conation, cognition and affect are retained not as naming faculties, but as conceptually distinct aspects of any psychological process. In this context, conation refers to an actual force or impulse toward behaviour, an impulse that may be a conscious volition or merely a lack of equilibrium or a tendency to change.

JL

**concentration.** A measure of market concentration describes the extent to which a small number of firms account for a large proportion of an industry's output, sales or employment. This information is usually expressed in terms of a concentration ratio. A typical ratio measures the percentage of an industry's output that is produced by its four largest firms, or the number of firms that account for 80 per cent of the industry's total output. Monopoly and oligopoly markets are characterized by high degrees of concentration, as such markets are dominated by a small number of firms. Conversely, perfect competition has a low level of concentration as there are a large number of firms each of which accounts for only a small proportion of total market output. Estimates of the level of concentration in manufacturing industry in most countries suggest that this has increased throughout the 20th century and that the rate of increase of concentration has accelerated since World War II. Concern about increases in concentration arises because of growth of monopoly power, the lack of competition and a tendency towards economic inefficiency (see EFFICIENCY; MARKET SYSTEM). At a more general level there is also concern about the concentration of economic power and its implications for the political process (see ELITISM).

RR

**concentric zone hypothesis.** Proposed by Robert PARK and Ernest Burgess, members of the CHICAGO SCHOOL, in *The City* (1925), this relates the spatial growth of the city to its social segmentation. Developed from the theory of HUMAN ECOLOGY, it suggests the key process in understanding the social and spatial development of the city is com-petition for land. The 'principle of domination' (analogous to the DARWINIAN principle of 'the survival of the fittest') ensures that the most powerful groups obtain the land they require first (usually the 'central business district' acquired by commercial, financial and industrial businesses) with successively less powerful and less wealthy groups acquiring land according to their ability to compete in the market. The outcome is the spatial organization of the city in a series of concentric rings outwards from the centre, each zone characterized by a broad social category, but in turn sub-divided into 'natural areas' divided along ethnic, racial and subcultural lines. The rings were super-imposed upon maps of actual cities.

The hypothesis was offered as a universal model, but the pattern is very much dependent upon Chicago's history as a city built around the confluence of railroad lines. Nevertheless these ideas have recently been revived to account for the creation of ghetto-like concentrations of particular ethnic groups in areas of British cities since the 1950s, associated with the concept of HOUS-ING CLASS.

HN

**concept.** A notion or idea. Sociologists differ on how concepts should be defined, and on the relative importance of descriptive adequacy as against their incorporation into explanatory theories. The term 'concept formation' is generally used in a broad sense to refer both to the construction of individual concepts and to their incorporation into a theoretical framework. It is also used by psychologists to describe a process of cognitive development.

See W. Outhwaite, *Concept Formation in Social Science* (1983).

WO

**Condorcet effect.** The situation where a social group, such as an assembly, acts as if it had an inconsistent, cyclical order of preferences about a set of possible courses of action, despite the individual members having consistent, linear preference orderings and the use of straightforward voting procedures to establish collective preferences. The outcome of voting on a set of proposals may vary according to which proposals are voted on together, and the order in which motions are taken may also affect the result. Condorcet's effect is of basic importance as a limiting case in the theory of group decision-making. That there is no simple way of establishing group desires from those of members is a fundamental feature of the relationship between individuals and social groups.

It is named after the Marquis de Condorcet (1743-94), French mathematician, philosopher and politician, one of the last Encyclopaedists, and one of the first writers to use the theory of probability, developed for games of chance, in analysing social phenomena.

See also ARROW'S THEOREM.

JL

**conflict theory.** Emphasizes the role of conflict in society. In the late 1950s and 1960s, writers such as DAHRENDORF, David Lockwood, John Rex and Lewis Coser reacted against the then-dominant school of Talcott PARSONS which, by blending FUNCTIONALISM with an emphasis on social CONSENSUS, had greatly understated the significance of conflict in social life. Coser's *Functions of Social Conflict* (1956) drew directly on the writings of SIMMEL. Still working within an essentially functionalist framework, Coser sought to show that though conflict can be destructive of social order, it can in some circumstances serve to preserve order. Conflict frequently takes place within a matrix of wider agreement, and may function as a safety-valve or a source of creative tension that may actually strengthen a social organization. Like Simmel, Coser discussed how 'a web of group affiliations' — in which a person belongs to many groups so that his opponents in one conflict may be his allies in another — serves to moderate the depth and bitterness of conflicts. In social anthropology, Max Gluckman (1911-75) argued along similar lines, moving away from the structural functionalism of EVANS-PRITCHARD.

Other conflict theorists, notably Dahrendorf in *Class and Class Conflict in Industrial Society* (1969) were more influenced by Marxism. Dahrendorf argued that Marx had been wrong in predicting that the division between those who owned the means of production and those who did not was the dominant axis of conflict in capitalist societies. The 'decomposition of capital' (the separation of ownership and control), the 'decomposition of labour' (the differentiation of the labour force into numerous specialized groups rather than the homogenization Marx foresaw) and social mobility would tend to make the patterns of conflict in industrial societies much more complicated (see MANAGERIAL REVOLUTION).

Although there have been more recent studies, such as Randal Collins's *Conflict Sociology* (1975), conflict theory no longer exists as a distinct school of thought. Its original argument is now accepted: all sociological theories must have something to say about the ubiquity of conflict in social life.

See CAPITALISM; CLASS; GAME THEORY; INDUSTRIAL CONFLICT; JURISPRUDENCE, SOCIOLOGICAL; LAW, *sociology of*; PARK.

SJM

**consensus.** This term means agreement, and in sociology is used to denote agreement between two or more people on the general principles which should regulate their behaviour towards each other. In political philosophy, the idea that some degree of consensus is a necessary, though possibly not a sufficient, condition of order in society is an old one. In modern sociology, PARSONS and his FUNCTIONALIST followers — sometimes described as 'consensus theorists' — placed particular emphasis on the necessity for widespread agreement on the central political and religious arrangements within a society (see especially E. Shils, *Centre and Periphery*, 1975). Curiously, this argument also became widespread among Marxists. The old radical notion of 'false consciousness' was revived in MARCUSE's *One-Dimensional Man*, in CRITICAL THEORY, in a popular interpretation of GRAMSCI's notion of HEGEMONY, and in ALTHUSSER's emphasis on ideology and ideological state apparatuses. The reason the working class did not revolt was that it was indoctrinated with and accepted the norms and values of capitalist society.

In the 1970s both versions came under attack from empirical studies showing that no such general consensus existed and arguing from a broad CONFLICT THEORY perspective. Acceptance of the *status quo* was realistic or pragmatic rather than normative, based on power asymmetry between classes (e.g. Mann, *American Sociological Review*, 1970). However, none of these writers doubted that some shared norms are necessary for social life. Their precise extent and causation is still unclear.

See also CLASS CONSCIOUSNESS; RECIPROCITY.

SJM, MM

**Conservative Party.** The origins of the British Conservative Party lie in the pre-democratic era. Its lineal ancestors were the Tories, a parliamentary coterie representing, broadly, Church and landowning interests in the 18th century. During the 19th century the Tories responded to successive extensions of the franchise by transforming themselves into a modern party with a mass membership and full range of extra-parliamentary organizations. The party succeeded in broadening its electoral base, gaining not only the support of a substantial section of the newly enfranchised classes but an increasingly large part of the Whig and entrepreneurial elements traditionally attached to the Liberal Party. In the 20th century the Conservatives have been a 'catch-all' party, gaining support from all sectors of society and, in general, maintaining a flexible, pragmatic approach to policy.

Conservative doctrine is not easy to define, partly because of this flexibility but also because CONSERVATISM rejects the notion of a political doctrine in favour of pragmatism. However, the underlying elements of Conservative thought include the notion that society is an integrated, organic unit — hence the rejection of class conflict and the acceptance of hierarchical social structure; attachment to individual freedom — hence a suspicion of interventionist government; reliance on past experience as a guide to present and future

actions — hence a cautious attitude to change. Thus Conservative Governments have not only accepted most changes effected by their radical opponents (e.g. the WELFARE STATE and the nationalization of key industries) but have frequently taken the lead in effecting reforms (e.g. extensions of the suffrage and the promotion of state education).

Given the strong class appeal of Labour to the numerically dominant working class, the Conservatives' electoral success during the present century is remarkable: they have formed governments or been the dominant partner in coalitions in 1900-5, 1916-23, 1924-9, 1931-45, 1951-64, 1970-74 and since 1979. The party has consistently gained at least 80 per cent of the expanding middle-class vote while also attracting 30-40 per cent of the working-class vote, particularly from amongst the non-unionized, the skilled and the status-conscious. The party also benefits from its image as a 'natural' party of government, whose leaders possess an inherited and taught capacity to rule (see DEFERENCE). Its major regions of electoral strength are rural areas, small and middle-sized non-industrial towns and middle-class suburbs of larger cities: predominantly in southern England, with smaller but important pockets in non-industrial areas of northern England and Scotland.

The party is now undergoing an unusually ideological phase, representing a break with tradition. Key elements of this phase are an attachment to monetarist economic and fiscal doctrine, a strong antipathy to what is seen as the excessive power of trade unions, and an outright commitment to the promotion of business interests even at the expense of other sectors of society. Some unease is felt by many leading elements in the party at these developments.

JP

**conservatism.** A view about the desirable scope of policy and of constitutional change, rather than a commitment to any particular set of policies or institutions. It eschews policies which, to secure certain ends, aim to order large sectors of social life. It rejects fundamental alterations in existing institutions, holding that projects involving radical departures from prevailing arrangements fail to take account of human frailty, imperfect knowledge, and the inherently unmeasurable complexity of human affairs. This is attributed to an exaggerated RATIONALIST belief, on the part of radical reformers, in (1) the capacity of persons to allow general principles (rather than self-interest or unreflective prejudice) to govern their conduct; (2) the capacity of scientific thinking to generate models capable of capturing the multiformity of social life so as to yield reliable predictions for successful policy-design. The variety and uncertainty of human conduct are said to warrant only a pragmatic attitude to desirable political change, an attitude informed by the limits of the possible discovered through practice and example — rather than theory — and thus vouchsafed to those whose experience of governing has imbued them with an appreciation of the time-tested and intricately interwoven traditions upon which the survival of a political community allegedly depends.

HIS

**constitution.** A term used especially in NEO-KANTIANISM and PHENOMENOLOGY to denote the 'construction' by the mind of an object of thought or inquiry. This 'object-constitution' has been variously conceived as anything from structuring or giving meaning to independently existing objects to the more radical thesis that we actually 'create' the world which we perceive. In social theory, the term is extensively used by SCHUTZ, in phenomenology and ETHNOMETHODOLOGY. Here, 'constitution' is more than a purely theoretical activity, since it is held that social reality, unlike natural reality, is partly or, for some writers, entirely created by our interpretations of it. This comes close to an IDEALIST variant of the ONTOLOGICAL sense of constitution found in parts of the Marxist tradition, in which people make their world through social practice. This sense is often combined by Marxists with the more familiar theoretical one, especially by those with affinities to neo-Kantianism, such as Max Adler and Alfred Schmidt, or to STRUCTURALISM. The other main use of the term is in CRITICAL THEORY. HABERMAS argues that

the world of experience is constituted in two different ways: as objects of instrumental action and as persons with whom we can communicate. He agrees with phenomenologists that the social world given to the social theorist is partly constituted by communicative action in everyday life. Recent French structuralists have also used the term to describe the construction of human subjectivity, a process which they see as taking place essentially in language.

See William Outhwaite, *Concept Formation in Social Science* (1983).

WO

**constraints.** Most economic decision-making involves choosing an optimum strategy subject to the limits imposed upon the decision maker. These limits are referred to as constraints. Examples include the overall expenditure (i.e. budget) constraint faced by the individual UTILITY-maximizing CONSUMER or public spending agency; cost constraints faced by firms aiming to maximize sales, growth or market shares; and, more generally, the political constraints which often dictate the range of choices open to the decision maker concerned with public sector project appraisal.

See COST-BENEFIT ANALYSIS.

RR

**consumers.** A categorization of individuals which focuses upon their role as the final users of the goods and services produced within an economy. Consumers are usually assumed to have a set of tastes or preferences which, together with their incomes, are the main determinants of their DEMAND for particular goods. Conventional economic theory postulates that production takes place in response to these demands and is subject to consumer sovereignty. Similarly, the output objectives of public sector, non-charging organizations are often formulated in terms of meeting consumer preferences. This view of consumer sovereignty has been criticized for its assumption that individuals' preferences simply exist, instead of recognizing that producers may themselves determine demand through advertising and other marketing activities. The premise that consumers are the best judges of their own welfare, and that production should respond to their tastes and preferences, has been questioned by those who doubt the existence of a universal capacity for the rational pursuit of self interest (see MERIT GOODS). More generally, it is argued that consumer demand does not reflect actual NEEDS. Demand is expressed within the CONSTRAINTS of existing MARKET arrangements.

Consumption is the act of deriving UTIL-ITY through the current use of a good or service. At the aggregate level, the term consumption or consumers' expenditure, which appears in National Income Accounts, refers to the value of total goods and services produced in an economy within a given time period (usually a quarter or a year) which are bought by consumers. In recent years this item has represented about 60 per cent of National Expenditure in the UK. The consumption function is the relationship between consumers' expenditure and consumers' income: this plays a central part in the KEYNESIAN model of national income determination.

RR

**contamination.** A term used to refer to the presence in the MULTI-VARIATE ANALYSIS of statistical data of 'noise', in the form of effects on observed relationships of external factors, which influence the interpretation of results. Various techniques are available to reduce these effects, such as STANDARDIZA-TION.

MB

**content analysis.** A kind of documentary research, a research technique for the objective, systematic and quantitative description of the manifest content of communication through the printed word, film, radio, television etc. The researcher first constructs a set of mutually exclusive and exhaustive categories that can be used to analyse documents, and then records the frequency with which each of these categories is observed in the documents studied. The unit of analysis may be a single word, the theme of the document, a sentence or paragraph, an item or an individual person. The system of enumeration may count whether an item appears or not, its frequency, the amount of space given to it, or the strength or intensity of the statement. Most extensively used in MEDIA STUDIES, as in the work of Berelson and Holsti.

See O.R. Holsti, *Content Analysis for the Social Sciences and Humanities* (1969).

MB

**contradiction.** See DIALECTIC.

**conventionalism.** The view that scientific statements are grounded in conventions among scientists to choose one theory or description rather than another. These conventions cannot be given an ultimate rational justification (see POSITIVISM).

WO

**conversation analysis.** Not all sciences, at least in their initial stages, develop by means of experimentation; rather, they develop by careful observation and description of phenomena. In botany and zoology, careful descriptions of plants and species in terms of their structure helped produce the foundations of later discoveries and developments. In a similar fashion conversation analysis takes as its goal the description and analysis of the structure of human interaction. To this end audio and video recordings of naturally occurring behaviour are subjected to rigorous analysis, producing accounts of the structures of talk and 'non-verbal' behaviour.

Conversation analysis was initiated by Harvey Sacks, a student of GARFINKEL and GOFFMAN in the early 1960s, who collaborated with Emmanuel Schegloff and students Gail Jefferson and Anita Pomerantz in producing a series of studies examining the details of the organization of conversation. Jefferson developed a particular method of transcribing talk using the set of letters and symbols available on an ordinary typewriter. To date, unfortunately, no parallel method of transcription is available for 'non-verbal' behaviour.

ETHNOMETHODOLOGY has an interest in the glossing practices which people use in producing sensible and coherent interaction from indexical items, talk, gestures etc. Similarly, conversation analysis seeks to demonstrate and describe such things as the conversational organization through which people demonstrate an understanding of their talk. For example, the categories people use in referring to 'objects' varies. A person might be variously referred to as 'John', 'a guy I know', 'Mary's husband' etc. All of these ways of referring to the person are 'correct' but their interactional usages differ according to such matters as who is being talked to and the topic at hand. Later work by Sacks and his colleagues examined the close-ordering of talk. Thus work has been done on 'turn-taking' in talk, 'turn-taking' being the way in which the transition from one person's talking to another's is achieved.

As conversation analysis has progressed it has become more detailed in its analysis. In the early stages of botany it was possible for almost anybody to go into the garden and look at different plants and point to their gross structural features, but further progress soon moves away from phenomena available to the untrained eye. Certainly, no one would claim that the structure of the cell is unimportant for botanical considerations. There is now evidence to demonstrate the sociological importance of what some would consider the minutiae of interaction.

See also COMMUNICATION; ETHNOMETHODO-LOGY; LANGUAGE; PHENOMENOLOGY.

DBn

**conversionism.** A particular type of religious SECT. Bryan Wilson has identified a number of such types (see THAUMATURGY, INTRO-VERSIONISM, MANIPULATIONISM, REVOLU-TIONISM). Conversionism is of relatively recent origin. It is distinguished by the extent to which its doctrine and practice centre on evangelism. Typically, conversionist sects are fundamentalist, taking the Bible as the literal revealed word of God. Membership is dependent upon undergoing a conversion experience and acceptance of Jesus as a personal saviour.

The principal figure in the growth of conversionist sectarianism was John Wesley, whose Methodists were the first major exemplars of the type. The radical enthusiasm of the revival-converted often makes them difficult to assimilate into established churches, leading to the formation of new sects. However, conversionist sects are particularly prone to the process of denominationalization (see DE-NOMINATION). As each wave of conversionist sectarianism becomes staid and respectable, new movements emerge to encourage ardour and freedom of expression, and take the message of salvation to the unredeemed. After Methodism came the Holiness movement, which stressed the 'second blessing' subsequent to the conversion experience, which would give assurance of cleansing from sin. Later came Pentecostalism, which taught that the 'second blessing' was marked by signs of the presence of the Holy Spirit and the gifts of the Holy Ghost, such as GLOSSO-LALIA. Conversionism has been particularly attractive to migrants such as rural-urban migrants in the British Industrial Revolution, migrants from the rural American South to the urban industrial North, peasant migrants to the cities of Latin America, and West Indian migrants to Britain. For strangers in an alien world the conversionist movement legitimizes the cathartic expression of intense feeling in the face of life's frustrations. The loneliness and impersonality of city life is mitigated by the closer personal presence of God, Jesus as a personal saviour, and the warmth and friendliness of social relations in the sect. Its norms and values promise that the marginal individual can become assimilated into the respectable strata of society through thrift, abstemiousness, hard work, and the other virtues of the PROTESTANT ETHIC.

See B. Wilson, *Sects and Society* (1961), *Patterns of Sectarianism* (1967), *Religious Sects: a Sociological Study* (1976).

RW

**Cooley, Charles Horton** (1864-1929). Early American sociologist. Born in Ann Arbor, Michigan, Cooley spent most of his life there — both studying and later teaching at the University of Michigan where his father, Thomas McIntyre Cooley, was a renowned legal scholar and professor in the law school. Cooley suffered from much ill-health as a child and developed into a 'brooding' and 'introspective' young man — characteristics that were to be carried into adulthood and for which his sociological work is noted and often criticized. Although he was trained as an engineer, he later shunned such 'hard sciences' and turned to sociology, where he advocated an extreme mentalistic stance: sociologists should 'imagine imagination'. He is remembered principally for two conceptual innovations. The first was the Looking-Glass Self: one derives a sense of oneself as mirrored in the judgements and evaluations of others. This was an anticipation of, and an influence upon, the concept of the SELF advanced by G.H. MEAD and the SYMBOLIC INTERAC-TIONISTS. The second was his distinction between primary groups characterized by intimate, face-to-face association and co-operation, and secondary groups. His sociology tended to emphasize the primary group, thus drawing the criticism that his is 'a small-town doctrine of human nature'. Major works: *Human Nature and the Social Order* (1902); *Social Organization* (1909); *Social Process* (1918); *Sociological Theory and Social Research* (1930).

KP, MM

**coping.** See HEALTH, SOCIOLOGY OF; STRESS.

**corporatism.** A term that derives from the theory of the corporate state of Italian FASC-ISM. It is now used rather differently in relation to current trends in advanced Western countries to describe a system of government in which major interest groups bargain and trade off their demands in close association with state agencies in a capitalist society. Economically, a corporatist system preserves capitalist institutions, especially private productive wealth, while abandoning liberal ideas such as *laissez-faire* in favour of (some) planning, and accepting the collective organization of labour (which Fascism rejected). The unifying assumption of corporatist hypotheses is of a general growth in collectivism in capitalist societies, where the interests of individuals (whether as citizens, workers or employers) are seen to be increasingly mediated through asso-ciations, federations etc. which themselves aggregate lower-level organizations of which individuals are members. Specific theories vary a great deal, but versions focusing upon the growth of tri-partite interactions between state, employers and labour usually involve

such themes as a stress on economic 'success' (mainly growth), national cohesiveness, planning, and industrial discipline. Accounts of the inter-war and post-war history of industrial relations resorting to explanations in terms of growing corporatism have gained in popularity. In certain respects, these theories are reminiscent of some Marxist analyses of late capitalism, though utilizing a different vocabulary and predicting different outcomes. But the context is always the internal power structures of the NATION-STATE. No-one has argued, and it would be implausible to do so, that the international and TRANSNATIONAL aspects of capitalism are becoming more corporatist.

MR

**correlation.** A statistical technique for examining the degree of ASSOCIATION between two VARIABLES, where these are expressed in interval or ratio-level MEASURE-MENT. In examining the relationship of two variables, an answer is often needed to the question: to what extent does an increase of a certain number of units in one variable lead to an increase in a certain number of units in the other variable? If each variable is plotted on one axis of the two on a graph or chart, a scatter diagram can be produced to permit the search for a perfect relationship between the variables. If there is a perfect relation-ship, then a straight line can be drawn through all the points. The correlation co-efficient is a statistical means (varying in value from -1.0 through zero to +1.0) of giving expression to the pattern of the relationship. The nearer the value of the coefficient to 1, the stronger the association, but as the values of one variable increase, the values of the other variable decrease.

The correlation matrix is a means of showing correlations between a large number of different pairs of items. Partial correlation and multiple correlation are extensions of the procedure to permit MULTI-VARIATE ANALYSIS.

Correlation analysis is a powerful tech-nique, provided that interval-level data is available (though Spearman's *rho* can be used with ordinal level measures). However, great care must be exercised in interpreting the results, especially in inferring causation. Correlation analysis does not permit one to make inferences about direction of influence of two factors on one another, nor about the possible effects of other variables. Correlation does not equal causation.

See also ECOLOGICAL FALLACY; REGRESSION.

See H.J. Loether and D.J. McTavish, *Descriptive Statistics for Sociologists* (1974).

MB

**cost-benefit analysis.** A technique for assessing the desirability of a proposed project which takes into account the total social COSTS and benefits expected to arise over its lifetime, that is, private plus external costs and benefits (see also DISCOUNTING; INVESTMENT). It is usually applied to public sector projects where there is no pricing system which can be used to indicate the benefits to be derived by the CONSUMERS of a good or service, and/or where the existence of substantial externalities means that private benefits/costs do not reflect full social benefits/costs. Thus it has been used extensively in the appraisal of transport projects where the benefits and costs take the form of unpriced items such as savings in travel time, reductions in injuries and losses of life, changes in noise levels etc. To enable the incorporation of these diverse items within a single balance sheet, a monetary value is attached to each cost and benefit. This establishes the valuations the individuals who will use or will be affected by the project place upon the costs and benefits which affect them (see EFFICIENCY; WELFARE ECONOMICS). Probably the most ambitious application of cost-benefit techniques in Britain was the study carried out by the research team of the Roskill Commission on the siting of the proposed Third London Airport in 1969.

RR

**costs.** The value of the resources of land, labour and capital used in the production of a good or service are its costs of production. Because there are never sufficient resources to produce all the goods and services which would be necessary to satisfy CONSUMERS' wants completely, a series of choices have to be made about the composition of output. The choices necessitated by this scarcity of resources mean that it is possible to express

the costs of producing any given good in terms of the output which otherwise could have been produced using the same quantity of resources. As costs are being expressed in terms of the forgone opportunity to produce alternative goods, they are referred to as opportunity costs. In many instances, the money price which is paid for a resource may be taken to measure its opportunity cost, but this is not always the case: a worker who otherwise would be unemployed will have a zero opportunity cost (for he/she would have a zero alternative output) although his/her wage rate will no doubt be positive.

The costs of production incurred by firms in the form of wage and salary bills, interest charges, property rents etc are its private costs; any costs which arise because of the firms' activities, but for which it is not required to make any payment, are known as external costs (see EXTERNALITY). Environmental pollution resulting from industrial activity is a major source of external costs. Concern over the incidence of external costs has led to the increased use of appraisal techniques which take into account the social costs, that is, private and external costs, of public sector projects (COST-BENEFIT ANALYSIS). Cost functions or curves indicate the costs of production for different quantities of output of a good or service (see ECONOMIES OF SCALE). The increase in total cost resulting from a small increase in output is known as its marginal cost. This concept is of particular importance in economic decision-making as policy-makers are frequently concerned with the costs associated with a marginal increase or decrease in output.

RR

**counterfactual conditional.** The CAUSAL relation 'A caused B' can be formally distinguished from the mere conjunction 'A and then B' by saying that if A had not been present, B would not have occurred. An EXPERIMENT actually tests this by varying A to see whether B then also varies. But in historical explanation this is obviously not possible. Any attempt to vary A becomes purely hypothetical, and is called a 'counterfactual conditional'. Social scientists often make statements of this form, for example, 'if Hitler had not been born, the Second World

War would not have happened'. Some historians see such statements as empty speculations, but it can be argued that they are an essential part of any assessment of, in this case, the causal importance of Hitler in relation to World War II. To reach a judgement in the present example will require careful examination of the circumstances and also, no doubt, some general theory about the importance or unimportance of individuals in affecting historical events.

See J. Elster, *Logic and Society* (1978).

WO

**coup.** The capturing of state power by a sudden blow, most frequently in recent years by the armed forces. 'Palace' coups usually involve a change in governing personnel while leaving basic institutions untouched, and replace elections or defeat in the assembly in Latin America. Revolutionary coups involve a change both in personnel and subsequently in institutions. Counter-coups usually prevent revolutionary change, but can also simply reverse the verdict of the immediately preceding coup. Other types — defined by the rank that dominates the overthrowing forces — include generals' coups, which tend to be reactionary; colonels' coups, which tend to be technocratic and relatively progressive; captains' coups for more pay and sergeants' coups against a sectional elite.

BT

**crime.** The simplest conception of crime holds that it is activity defined as harmful to the public welfare; usually intended by one who could have done otherwise; banned by a specifically criminal law and open to prosecution by representatives of the state. Crime tends to supersede the idea of a private wrong, which is of concern only to individuals, their families or their immediate connections. The initiative for its control passes away from the victim to delegated officers. Thus crime generally entails the existence of a centralized government, the idea of a communal or abstract victim, and the work of specialized enforcement agencies.

The precise definition has been complicated by a number of petty difficulties of theory and practice which most sociologists discount. A theoretical example has been provided by anthropologists, who argue that particular pre-literate societies such as the Barotse possess the functional and formal equivalents of crime and justice despite the absence of written law and a fully institutionalized state. Justice may then be dispensed formally and in a routine fashion but without a developed bureaucracy. It is uncertain how important a prerequisite is the centralized state. A few criminologists have been reluctant to accept legal definitions of crime, asserting that they are lay constructions which lack scientific rigour and usefulness. Sellin (*Law Quarterly Review*, 1951) proposed the more precise conception of 'conduct norm': a rule supported by sanctions which reflect the value attached to the norm by the normative group. Other criminologists reject the criminal law as ideologically laden and oppressive. They define crime as that which *they* dislike. Practical complexity has been introduced by the tendency of certain states to supplement codified and enacted law by a class of unspecified analogical crimes which are taken to be substantially similar to actions which are expressly banned. For example, Article 79 of the Criminal Code of The People's Republic of China recites 'A crime not specifically prescribed under the special provisions of the present law, may be confirmed a crime and sentence rendered in light of the most analogous article under the special provisions of the present law.' Nazi Germany and Soviet Russia have had similar stipulations. In the main, however, sociologists do not regard crime as an especially ambiguous or contested entity, although they may disagree about its explanation.

See CRIMINOLOGY; DELINQUENCY; SOCIAL CONTROL.

PR

**crime, organized.** All crime is orderly enough to merit the adjective 'organized', but organized crime signifies more than patterned illegality. The meaning varies from author to author, being an object of some dispute. If the existence of organized crime is conceded, there may be a rudimentary agreement that such crime is the creature of societies with sophisticated MARKETS, an elaborate DIVISION OF LABOUR and BUREAU-CRATIC rationality. There is less agreement about the timing of the first appearance of organized crime, its dependence upon CAPI-TALISM or its precise structure. Dissent probably mirrors larger theoretical divergencies and considerable methodological problems. Organized crime is not laid bare for scholarly inspection, but concealed and misrepresented with zeal. Sociologists manage to gain no more than limited access and information, they tend to capitalize on scarce resources, and so distort and exaggerate partial perspectives. Seemingly warring definitions may be unwittingly complementary. Current descriptions revolve around the scale and rationality of structure; political consequence in neutralizing law enforcement; syndication and permanence of staff; a dependence on kinship networks; the structural function of providing effective intercession; a systematic fusion with capitalist political economy; the systematic subversion of capitalism; the systematic support of capitalism; the stabilization of disorganized markets and areas of political disorder; an entrepreneurial role in the management of illicit services; and a collective response to DIFF-ERENTIAL OPPORTUNITY STRUCTURES.

PR

**crime, white-collar.** Largely intended by SUTHERLAND ( *White Collar Crime*, 1961) to refer to crimes committed by managers, administrators and others in the routine pursuit of corporate business objectives, the term is occasionally used to describe any crimes of the middle class. Sutherland sought to reform the focus of criminology by indicating the presence of offences, offenders and enforcement procedures which had hitherto been ignored. Theory had been fundamentally deformed by its insistent concentration on solitary and usually working-class subjects. White-collar crime was defined as a normal part of business practice, massively costly and highly organized. Its constituent offences include breaches of antitrust legislation, safety regulations, controls on adulteration and pollution, and pricing regulations.

Sutherland's analysis of the recorded criminality of the largest American corporations disclosed that they were all law-breakers, some repeatedly so. Carson has achieved similar results for England. The direct implication is that there is frequent, concerted and widespread crime committed by the more powerful groupings in industry and commerce.

Sutherland made it difficult to identify crime with poverty, social disorganization or the more conventional conceptions of social pathology. Criminality is also linked with respectability, wealth and power. Sutherland also made it difficult to retain certain assumptions about the distribution of criminality: lawbreaking is diffuse although there are unresolved arguments about the character of its diffusion. While almost all members of British, American and other societies appear to have committed at least one crime or delinquency in their lifetime, they commit very different offences and with different frequencies.

PR

**criminalization.** The process of transforming lawful behaviour into crime by legal enactment. Its analysis has sometimes been joined with a discussion of secondary deviation (see DEVIANCE), it being asserted that criminalization has characteristic and predictable consequences for the social meanings, organization and experience of behaviour. There may be a tacit or overt assumption that criminalization exacerbates a problem it was intended to solve: for example, if petty drug consumption is made a crime, users are forced to consort with professional criminals to obtain supplies, increasing the power of the latter. The political remedy for such alleged amplification has been labelled 'decriminalization' as in 'decriminalize marijuana use'.

PR

**criminology.** According to Bonger, the word 'criminology' was first employed by the French anthropologist Topinard in the 1870s; it seems to have entered English in 1890. The discipline emerged from the earlier penological concerns of the 18th and 19th centuries, and was defined by a common problem — crime — rather than a common approach or method. From the beginning, it has been pursued by statisticians, lawyers, medical specialists, psychiatrists, psychologists and sociologists. A fragile unity has been secured by the publication of special journals of criminology, co-operative work between members of different disciplines, the attempt to achieve a distinct science of criminology with its own procedures and training, and the expectation that 'criminologists' would know the writings of more than one discipline.

Criminology is as varied as its component authors and writings, but is characterized by a preoccupation with the causes and origins of crime, the behaviour of criminals, the adequacy of information about crime, and the formulation of policies of prevention and treatment. Sociologists of the 1960s and early 1970s proclaimed themselves sociologists of DEVIANCE to remove themselves from the eclectic and practical discipline of criminology. Of late, radical sociologists of crime have declared themselves radical criminologists, stressing their defection from the sociology of deviance. The term 'criminology' has thus acquired an occasional political colouring.

*Radical criminology.* Blurring into the 'new', 'critical' or 'Marxist' criminology, radical criminology was heralded by the writings of Bonger, Rusche and Kirchheimer and came into its own in the 1970s. Its creators are diverse representatives of the larger radical movement within sociology. They embrace POPULISM, CONFLICT THEORY, ANARCHISM and a number of expressions of Marxism. Lent cohesion by a common opposition to 'bourgeois' or otherwise uncongenial criminology, radical criminology lacks consensus about its own principles. In the main, there would be agreement that crime should be analysed within a framework of political economy; that it should be appreciated as an integral constituent of general historical processes; that crime is defined by the (usually capitalist) state and the criminal tends to be opposed to some features of the (usually capitalist) state; criminology is accordingly a political description of the social relations of power and the only useful, worthwhile and tested

form of criminology is one that has been translated into political practice; see Taylor, Walton and Young, *The New Criminology* (1973). Actual attempts to experiment with such PRAXIS have been uncommon and it is difficult to establish how they have been employed to modify theory. Perhaps the major example is T. Mathiesen's *Politics of Abolition* (1974).

PR

**critical theory.** An approach to the human sciences and philosophy originally developed in the 1930s and early 1940s by leading members of the Frankfurt Institute for Social Research (Frankfurt School). Founded in 1923, the Institute was forced into exile during the Hitler years, and returned to Germany in the 1950s. A full list of all those associated with the Institute during this period would include many of the leading exponents of Western Marxism, but the development of critical theory was restricted to a much smaller inner circle. This included HORKHEIMER (Director, 1931-58), the sociologist and musicologist ADORNO, and the philosopher MARCUSE. Other figures, less central but greatly influential, included the essayist Walter Benjamin; the economist Friedrich Pollock; and the psychoanalyst Erich Fromm. Following Adorno's death in 1969 the Institute itself was dissolved, but critical theory continues in a rather different form, with a new generation of theorists, the most notable of whom is HABERMAS. There are many different emphases amongst these writers, and the views of some of them, especially Horkheimer and Adorno, evolved significantly over the years.

Critical theory is an interdisciplinary approach to the social sciences, drawing especially on the work of early MARX and late FREUD. It aims to criticize as well as analyse society, and so is essentially evaluative, and therefore opposed to doctrines such as POSITIVISM, which argues that the social sciences should be value-free. In opposition to positivism's account of 'what is', critical theory counterposes an ideal of 'what ought to be'.

Critical theorists stress the Hegelian dimension of Marx's thought. They refute the 'economistic' model of Marxism which sees the cultural, ideological, and political 'superstructures' as being determined by the workings of the economic 'base'. Critical theory (as with most modern, Western Marxism) shifts the focus of analysis away from the base to the superstructures. Under the influence of the early LUKÁCS, critical theory contributed to the development of 'ideology-critique', and the analysis of 'the culture industry'. Because of the failure of revolutionary movements in the West, however, and more particularly because of the rise of Fascism, these studies increasingly took on pessimistic overtones. Critical theorists abandoned faith in the revolutionary potential of the proletariat, and their conception of 'mass culture' tended to stress its negative effect on working-class consciousness (see CLASS CONSCIOUSNESS). In their *Dialectic of Enlightenment* (1947), Horkheimer and Adorno argued that the whole progress of reason since the Enlightenment has been a degeneration into positivistic modes of thought, which serve to enslave rather than liberate. Thus, both 'high' and 'popular' CULTURE were seen as serving the same ideological function (see CONSENSUS).

In Germany, as elsewhere, the 1960s witnessed a revival of Marxism that engendered both a renewed interest in earlier critical theory, and the advent of a new generation of critical theorists, including Adorno's one-time research assistant, Habermas. Like his mentors', Habermas's perspective remains evaluative and emancipatory, but without much clear indication of where, in contemporary society, the forces of emancipation are located. Where the earlier generation saw liberation as freedom from ALIENATION, and later, as freedom from submission to authority, including the authority of reason, Habermas sees freedom in an 'ideal speech situation', in which consensus is genuinely and freely arrived at. All DISCOURSE which falls short of this is subject to 'systematically distorted communication', which arises from power inequalities between the participants, and which may be analysed in the same fashion in which Freud analysed the distorted messages of dreams. The potential for freedom lies in the very nature of language itself, but the attainment of an 'ideal speech situation' depends on the elimination of distortions and constraints not only from language, but also from life.

AM

**cross-cultural comparison.** A method widely used in sociology, political science and other social sciences to co-relate and/or explain the presence or absence of one or more traits in a society with reference to their presence or absence in another. It is important to be clear about the traits being compared, for example whether they are aspects of individual personalities, of aggregates of similarly situated people, of social institutions or of national societies. Such comparisons may be carried out quantitatively (as in the Human Relations Area Files; see COMPARATIVE METHOD) or qualitatively (as in WEBER'S comparative sociology of world religions) or some combination of the two (see J. Goody, *Production and Reproduction*, 1976, on the organization of the domestic economy). Whatever the case, the discovery of a correlation between two or more traits, often termed VARIABLES, can never in itself constitute an explanation of any phenomenon, and such comparisons must be logically integrated into a theoretical framework for this purpose.

See also COMPARATIVE METHOD.

LS

**cross-tabulation.** The use of TABLES to examine relationships between VARIABLES, to search for patterns in data to provide EXPLANATIONS of social phenomena. The basic idea is to relate one variable to another to see if they are associated, then, if they are, to introduce further variables into the relationship to see if these affect the initial relationship. If, for example, social class and party preference are associated, how is this relationship affected by other variables such as sex, education, region, parental party preference etc? The method of analysing social survey data in tables was first developed by LAZARSFELD and codified by M. Rosenberg. Such elaboration is complex and time-consuming, despite the virtues of using a method of presenting the data which is readily intelligible.

See M. Rosenberg, *The Logic of Survey Analysis* (1968).

MB

**cue.** A socially recognized signal, made by one actor to another to communicate some message, often of an affective nature. Cues may be verbal, usually oral though possibly written, or non-verbal. Examples of the latter category are facial expressions or bodily sets such as scowls or hugs, noises such as hisses or growls, and the wearing of certain clothes that are intended to indicate some personality trait that an individual wishes to express, such as sobriety or homosexuality. Cues may be open or hidden, and known to all relevant actors or, as with secret handshakes, only to a few. Cues may be made with conscious intent or may be entirely unconscious, as when an actor betrays colour prejudice when trying to interact in a friendly way with a coloured person. Furthermore, cues may be misinterpreted by other actors, usually due to lack of experience or to ignorance of the system of cues used in another culture. Much social interaction is governed by non-verbal cues and this is particularly the case in educational settings, where teachers may indicate to children that they are good or bad pupils by the use of such non-verbal cues as a change in voice or a glance. This tendency has been found in some studies to be so persistent that the target pupils come to see themselves and are labelled by their peers according to the cues used by their teachers.

See COMMUNICATION; CONVERSATION ANALYSIS.

PWM

**cult.** A form of religious organization (see also CHURCH, DENOMINATION, SECT).

(1) Recent American usage views the cult primarily in terms of its deviance, that is, drawing its inspiration from outside the dominant traditions of the culture and espousing a highly unconventional conception of religion, politics, economics, or medicine. In this definition the cult differs from the SECT in that it is not merely a schismatic variant of the dominant tradition in one of these areas.

(2) The other form of definition derives from TROELTSCH's delineation of mysticism as one of the three main expressions of the Christian tradition (CHURCH and sect being the others). Troeltsch identified mysticism as a particularly individualistic form of religion. Howard P. Becker (*Systematic Sociology*, 1932) stressed the private, personal character of cult belief and the 'amorphous, loose-textured, uncondensed' nature of its organization: it lacks a developed mechanism of social control or clear criteria of membership.

The definition in terms of deviance is the most frequently employed in recent literature but it seems the less analytically fruitful of the two. The criterion of deviance does not distinguish between widely differing organizational structures, and whether a movement's ideology draws its inspiration from beyond the dominant culture or tradition, or is a schismatic variant of that tradition is not readily determinable for many movements such as the Mormons, Christian Science or the Unification Church.

The virtue of Troeltsch's definition is that it depends not upon a difference in the content of belief but upon the mode of belief (i.e. its individualistic character) and thus links belief to social organization (amorphous, loose-textured etc). The cult is epistemologically individualistic: i.e. each member is the ultimate authority as to what constitutes the truth or the good. Both cult and sect are deviant compared with the prevailing indifference, agnosticism or denominational Christian orthodoxy of modern Western societies. What distinguishes them is that the sect (like the church) is viewed by its adherents as the only significant means of access to the truth or salvation (i.e. as uniquely legitimate) while the cult (like the denomination) is viewed by its followers or members as one of a variety of paths to the truth or salvation (i.e. as pluralistically legitimate).

Cults emerge out of a cultural underground of deviant and marginal ideas and institutions (the CULTIC MILIEU) as fragile associations of 'seekers' gathered around some common interest or revelation. Their beliefs are syntheses of ideas and practices available in the cultic milieu, supplemented or adapted through the founders' insights.

Having no source of ultimate authority beyond the individual, the cult also has no basis for attributing heresy. It cannot sharply define the boundaries of its membership or belief system. As the cult is only one of many paths to salvation, any particular instance is unable to command the loyalty of members. Members typically move between groups adopting elements of beliefs and practices to fit their own personal synthesis. Overlapping membership and beliefs encourage tolerance, but render the cult precarious. It is constantly liable to sink back into the milieu from which it is barely differentiated; to suffer schism and secession as teachers or practitioners develop their own synthesis in competition; or to face indifference or passivity among its members, who have alternative resources available for attaining truth or salvation in other cults. The cult therefore tends to be short-lived, either disappearing or negotiating the transition to sect as a strategy for survival.

RW

**cultic milieu.** This term, introduced by Colin Campbell (*Towards a Sociology of Irreligion*, 1971), refers to the cultural underground from which CULTS arise. It comprises the socio-cultural context for deviant belief-systems and the practices associated with them in the fields of religion, the occult, medicine, psychology, philosophy, politics and economics. Its structure is formed by the overlapping networks of individual seekers, collectivities (such as flying saucer groups, the Theosophical Society or metaphysical study groups), media of communication, and commercial enterprises such as specialist bookshops or the Festival of Mind, Body and Spirit. Out of this milieu new cults and sects frequently emerge as syntheses of existing ideas developed and adapted by their founders.

RW

**cultural anthropology.** The study of the material life of, in practice, small-scale, non-industrial societies (see CULTURE). Within this broad range, anthropologists focus on artefacts, their design and techniques of manufacture. Given the archaeological possibilities afforded by many non-literate societies which otherwise offer little contemporary data for their historical development, cultural anthropology was at one time as central to the discipline as social anthropology is now. Collections of artefacts from different historical eras and geographical locations supplied raw material and became the battlegrounds for disputes of wide theoretical significance. For instance, the distribution of agricultural technologies (deep ploughing, surface ploughing, hoe, digging stick, slash-and-burn) was an important element in early 20th-century attempts to classify societal types, while sequences of household implements were used as evidence to support EVOLUTIONIST or DIFFUSIONIST theories of cultural change as a whole. Accounts of general material culture, usual in anthropologists' fieldwork reports until the 1940s, have largely — and regrettably — disappeared. In their place subfields concerned with single subjects have developed, notably ethnomusicology (the study of the musical theory and practice of traditional societies) and ethnobotany (the study of the relationship between simple societies and plants, including cultivation techniques and botanical knowledge). Save in the trivial form of market research the characteristics of the material culture of advanced societies have attracted virtually no attention.

ML

**culture.** Beneath an enormous variety of usage there are two basic senses in which the term is employed in the social sciences.

(1) At the most abstract level, as in the classic opposing pair, Nature-Culture (see LÉVI-STRAUSS), it connotes all human activity which is not the pure expression of biological characteristics of the species *Homo*. It is applied as a totalizing abstraction to embrace the ideas, practices, and material and symbolic artefacts of specific human groups of all types, and is thus equally used of large, differentiated groups extended in space and time (e.g. Mayan culture) and small undifferentiated groups sharply limited in space and time (e.g. the culture of Left Bank Paris in the post-war period). When applied to certain large-scale groups the term may be virtually interchangeable with CIVILIZATION (as in Greek culture and Greek civilization).

There is a growing tendency among sociologists to restrict this usage to what are believed to be autonomous groups possessing maximal states (e.g. French culture), epochs (e.g. 17th-century culture, Sixties culture), ethnic character (e.g. black culture), social institutions (civic culture, the culture of the city) or social categories (working-class culture, mass culture). Which, if any, of these dimensions to emphasize and how, if at all, they interrelate is a vexed question allowing no satisfactory or orthodox answer. Too often the expression in practice means no more than a general residuary predisposition for a particular population to think or act in certain rather ill-defined ways and is invoked to explain anything left unexplained by other, more precisely defined, variables. In such contexts it is idle to look for consistency or rigor.

Where the problem has been faced directly there have been two, opposed models. The FUNCTIONALIST approach resolves possible contradictions by positing a core culture more or less shared by the members of a society (i.e. CONSENSUS), generally conceived of as a nation-state. Sometimes it is argued that the creation of a core culture — a coherent, embracing, ubiquitous mode of apprehending and understanding, universally held within defined geo-political boundaries — is distinctive to the modern nation-states. Subordinate secondary cultures add to or elaborate the core but in no way fundamentally modify it. The expression SUB-CULTURE is applied to the distinctive traits of specialized or minority groupings occurring within the over-arching core culture, with the implication that differences and singularities are of relative insignificance in comparison with similarities.

In recent years the alternative model, CONFLICT THEORY, has gained ground. This emphasizes the different understandings of the world possessed by the various groups sharing some common institutional matrix. In particular the influence of Marxist theorizing has given rise to a concern with CLASS-CONSCIOUS cultures. Socio-economic position is seen as playing the decisive part in determining patterns of meaning, so that societally shared cognitions and beliefs are secondary to disagreements and contradictions between meaning systems. From this point of view societies or other social institutions, unless homogeneous in class terms, possess no core culture but are composed of a variety of (sub-) cultures held together in essentially conflictual relations.

Culture shock describes the cognitive and psychological crisis which can arise with the encounter of two (or more) groups or societies such that new ways of ordering reality and rendering it intelligible are suddenly imposed on a people or otherwise disrupt its accustomed patterns of thinking. In particular it describes the reaction of traditional societies to the imposition of the ways of thinking and behaving of advanced industrial societies.

(2) Social scientists also use the term culture in a sense close to its common lay application: the product of intellectual and especially artistic activity. This meaning is found in the opposition of Culture and Society. Rather than embracing all distinctively human products it is restricted to the symbolic realm — literature, the visual arts, music and formally constructed bodies of knowledge. More restrictive still is its use in Anglo-American society to refer exclusively to literary and artistic products. Thus some writers have talked of the two cultures, one literary-artistic, the other natural scientific.

This sense is rendered complex by questions of aesthetic evaluation. Lay usage is more likely than social scientific to apply the word 'culture' only to a sub-set of all the formal SYMBOLIC products of a group or society, limiting itself to those conventionally regarded as of enduring world-historic value. In lay terms a Beethoven symphony or a play by Shakespeare will count unequivocally as culture, whilst the entitlement of a popular song or a television soap opera to belong in the category is open to question. Although such distinctions are inappropriate for the social scientist, it is convenient to classify an extremely large, and heterogeneous class of activities in complex societies. Hence the term 'high culture' refers to artistic and literary products seen as of great and enduring aesthetic merit, though the expression often also implies an association with elite socio-economic strata. It is complemented by 'popular culture' or 'mass culture', though the precise connotation of these terms varies. Of the two, popular culture carries weaker evaluative implications, referring more to the scale of its audience than to the aesthetic merits of its material. Mass culture is commonly used with pejorative connotations, implying commercial products of little or no aesthetic worth. Systematic variation between groups in their access to and consumption of formal symbolic goods is often referred to as 'cultural stratification' (see also CRITICAL THEORY).

The fact that there has been relatively little systematic study of culture (in either sense) by sociologists makes it necessary to draw on other disciplinary fields, notably the history of ideas and *Kulturgeschichte* or *Geistesgeschichte* (cultural history). The former (typified by A.O. Lovejoy, *The Great Chain of Being*, 1936) discusses concepts or items of belief whose applications or connotations are pursued through their historical career and developments. The latter (typified by Jacob Burckhardt, *The Civilization of the Renaissance in Italy*, 1929) discusses specific historical moments and seeks to uncover unities of idea and sentiment lying behind and informing the diversity of arts, letters and styles of life. See LANGUAGE.

ML

**culture of poverty.** Originally put forward by Oscar Lewis in 1959 and later developed through studies on Mexican and Puerto Rican families. Lewis identified differences between the life of the poor and the NORMS of the rest of society. The poor had different family and sexual practices, failed to participate in the major institutions of the larger society and seemed resigned to their position with a lack of motivation to change. These traits had developed as ways of coping with poverty and had become so inbred and extensive as to be described as a culture (*see* CULTURE sense 1). This was passed on from parents to children so that children were taught how to accept poverty rather than how to develop skills to escape it. See O. Lewis, *Life in a Mexican Village* (1951),

*Children of Sanchez* (1961), *La Vida* (1966).

The thesis has been influential in many countries. In the USA it influenced the War on Poverty; in Britain it influenced Sir Keith Joseph's views on the CYCLE OF DEPRIVATION. It has also found support from other researchers and has been linked to Riessman's work on educational achievement.

The thesis has also been criticized. Some have attacked the methodology: for example, the small sample of families used by Lewis to develop his theory. Another line of criticism has suggested that the differences between the poor and the rest of society that Lewis pointed to were questionable: a number of studies suggested that the unemployed poor retain the desire to obtain work. It has been argued that the thesis ignores the importance of economic factors: poverty is a result of low income rather than the culture of the poor. See POVERTY; PROBLEM FAMILY.

MPJ

**curriculum.** The purposeful organization of learning experiences by formal educational institutions such as schools. These experiences may occur within the educational institution that plans them or outside it (e.g. homework or visits to a museum). The curriculum consists of that selection from the culture of their society that those planning it see as important enough to transmit to the next GENERATION. Educational institutions tend to give most open attention to their academic curriculum, usually expressed in terms of subjects based on recognized disciplines and presented with an attendant syllabus of selected material and PEDAGOGY. Chosen subjects are often seen in a stratified hierarchy so that, for example, in the 19th-century English 'public' (i.e. private) school Classics were seen as more important and of higher status than science or foreign languages, and today art and music tend to be given a lowly place in many schools. Particularly in British schools, some attention is given to the moral curriculum, namely, formal and informal instruction in behaviour seen by those in charge of the school or of the educational system as relevant to the normal way of treating others.

Moral lessons may be taught through the organization of the school (e.g. the prefect system) rather than through formal lessons in the classroom. In British schools games have been given high status because they are seen as ways of teaching such desired character traits as being a good loser, obedience to rules, or acting as a loyal member of a team under a leader.

The term 'hidden curriculum' has also come into use; sometimes this refers to lessons that the planners of the curriculum intend to be learned, but which the learners themselves do not recognize as such, as was usually the case when pupils played team-games in British schools. However, sometimes the term refers to the unintended lessons of a given curriculum, as where the learning of material ostensibly to pass an examination may be said to teach competitiveness. Both analytical concepts have social reality, but the latter meaning may better be described by the term 'unanticipated curriculum'.

See also WOMEN AND EDUCATION.

PWM

**cybernetics.** The study of communication and control systems in machines and living creatures. The word was introduced just after World War II by the mathematician Norbert Wiener, who had begun to develop his ideas while working on a device for automatically controlling the fire of anti-aircraft guns. The central concept is feedback. The most familiar example of a feedback mechanism is a simple thermostat controlling a central-heating boiler: the boiler heats the house to the temperature at which the thermostat breaks the circuit and cuts out the boiler; the temperature then falls until the thermostat switches the boiler on again. Thus the results of one phase of the process feed back so as to control the next phase, and the temperature of the house fluctuates within a few degrees of the desired temperature at which the thermostat has been set. Analogous processes, known as homeostatic systems, exist within living organisms, controlling among other things body temperature, the level of sugar in the blood and the rate at which the heart beats.

The thermostat illustrates how feedback mechanisms simulate purposeful behaviour — the same pattern of control could be achieved by a person looking at a thermometer and manually switching the boiler on and off. Indeed, the human capacity for purposeful behaviour may be said to exist because the mind can anticipate the likely effects of an action, and modify later actions in the light of actual results. Cybernetics has been applied to the study of mental processes; it has also played a large part in the development of the artificial intelligence of computers.

In sociology, cybernetic ideas and jargon were fashionable in the late 1950s and 1960s. They appealed to protagonists of FUNCTIONALISM who sought to escape the charge of illegitimate TELEOLOGY by arguing that SOCIAL SYSTEMS contained cybernetic or feedback mechanisms which enabled them to behave in a self-maintaining or goal-directed manner (see EVOLUTIONISM).

SJM

**cycle of deprivation.** A term first used by Sir Keith Joseph, then Secretary of State for Health and Social Security, in 1972 to explain why, despite long periods of full employment and relative prosperity and a major increase in the provision of welfare services, deprivation and maladjustment continued on an important scale. His answer was that in a proportion of cases the social problems affecting one generation were reproduced in the next: deprivation was transmitted through the family. This had much in common with earlier discussions on the PROBLEM FAMILY and the CULTURE OF POVERTY.

Joseph's views were attacked from a number of different standpoints. Many social problems, like mental illness and alcoholism, were not concentrated in the lowest social classes as he had suggested. Amongst those families that suffer severe deprivation there are striking discontinuities from generation to generation in the extent to which problems occur. The most consistent criticism was that he ignored the economic causes of deprivation and sought to deflect attention from the need to redistribute resources.

One of Joseph's most controversial comments (October 1974) was that a high proportion of children were born into families least fitted to bringing them up. The implications of these comments for population control were strenuously challenged and led to a minor political controversy recalling much earlier debates concerning Social DARWINISM.

See also DEPRIVATION; POVERTY.

MPJ

# D

Dahrendorf, Ralf (1929- ). German socio-logist whose career has combined academic sociology, politics and academic admini-stration. Born in Hamburg, the son of a Social Democratic politician, Dahrendorf was imprisoned in a concentration camp from 1944-5. He studied philosophy and classical philology at Hamburg (1947-52) and sociology at LSE (1952-4). His Hamburg doctorate was published as *Marx in Perspektive* (1953); his London PhD, 'Unskilled Labour in British Industry' (1956) has not been published but contains the germ of his arguments in *Class and Conflict in Industrial Society* (1957; English edn. 1959). At LSE he was influenced by Popper, and in 1957-8, when a fellow at the Center for Advanced Study in the Behavioral Sciences, Palo Alto, came to admire the work of another liberal, Milton Friedman. Between 1957 and 1969 he taught at the universities of Saarland, Hamburg, Tübingen and Constance. Prompted by the concerns of his *Society and Democracy in Germany* (1965, English edn. 1968) and his opposition to the formation of the CDU-SDP Grand Coalition in 1966, he increas-ingly turned to politics, and was a Free Democratic member of the Landtag of Baden-Württemberg (1968-70) and the Bundestag (1969-70). In 1969 he was appointed Parliamentary State Secretary for Foreign Affairs, and in 1970 a member of the EEC Commission, where he held first the External Relations and then the Education and Science portfolio. In 1974 he took up his current position of Director of the London

School of Economics and also gave the Reith Lectures (*The New Liberty*, 1975). He was awarded an honorary knighthood in 1982.

Dahrendorf's academic work has con-cerned four themes: (1) CLASS and CONFLICT THEORY, (2) ROLE theory, (3) society and democracy in Germany, with particular emphasis on education and the possibilities of reform in higher education and (4) modernization as a global process, in which recent work is notable for greater recognition of its social costs.

*Class and Conflict* (1957) presents a revised theory of class which retains the idea of class conflict as the lever of social change but which substitutes participation in, and exclusion from, the exercise of AUTHORITY for ownership and non-ownership of the means of production. (A later formulation announced that 'the dialectic of POWER and resistance is the motive force of history'). The theory is applied to all imperatively co-ordinated associations (see WEBER) from the state to a village football club, although the relations between such associations and the extent of superimposed lines of cleavage are not examined systematically. Dahrendorf uses the theory to reject the utopian belief that all conflicts can be resolved (as distinct from regulated) and to endorse a liberal political philosophy — conflict is endemic because those subject to authority have an ineliminable interest in challenging the justice of their subordination. In a sub-sequent revision to the theory of class (*Conflict After Class*, 1967) he argues that 'individual competition and collective action are in principal mutually convertible': both 'are basically equivalent expressions of the same great social force "contest"', the determination to impose one's will upon others. Contest crystallizes as class conflict only when individuals cannot realize their interests by individual endeavour; conversely, class conflict may dissolve into individual competition when opportunities for individual advancement improve. Moreover, 'modern market-rational societies typically offer such chances of individual advance'.

His approach owes much to MARX, and even more to WEBER, and so he helped to articulate the CONFLICT THEORY offered as an alternative to the structural-FUNCTIONALISM and CONSENSUS theory of the 1950s and 1960s. Where PARSONS and others analysed societies in terms of stability, the integration of elements, the functional contribution of elements to system maintenance, and value consensus, Dahrendorf countered that analysis was equally possible in terms of change, conflict, the contribution of elements to system disintegration, and coercion. Later he claimed that conflict theory is logically prior, rather than just an alternative, to integration theory.

*Homo Sociologicus* (1958; English edn. 1968) proposes a model of sociological man, which is as much an abstraction as that of economic man. It locates him at the intersection of the individual and society and discusses him entirely in terms of incumbency of social positions and his response to the role expectations which attach to them. These expectations are derived from the NORMS and sanctions of each REFERENCE GROUP to which a position is necessarily related; thus the teacher numbers among his or her reference groups the employing education authority, superiors in the school, colleagues, the union, parents and pupils. The theory has generated controversy in Germany for its separation of (empirical) sociology from philosophical anthropology and its assumption that the individual has a personality, or SELF, which is at least partially 'free of all ties to society' and therefore free from sociological inquiry. In the Anglo-American context, Dahrendorf treats the determination of role expectations as an empirical question, though not (in contrast to Gross, Mason and McEachern) one that can be answered by interviewing, because respondents' subjective opinions are deemed different from objective social norms.

In *Role Distance* (1961) GOFFMAN constructed a role theory along lines almost totally contrary to Dahrendorf's. Dahrendorf's theory pertains to a field of social relations, Goffman's to focused face-to-face interaction; Dahrendorf discusses gratifications from role compliance, Goffman concentrates on role distance; Dahrendorf cherishes the individual personality which eludes sociology, Goffman attacks the idea of a self safe from sociological inquiry etc. This striking contrast has failed to elicit systematic comment.

*Society and Democracy in Germany* asks why so few Germans embraced the principle of liberal democracy. Dahrendorf examines four preconditions of liberal democracy that were not met in the Imperial, Weimar and Nazi past, and are imperfectly met now: (1) the supersession of the subject by the citizen; (2) the recognition of social conflict as endemic and its rational regulation; (3) the establishment of a political diverse elite; (4) the predominance of public virtues which facilitate social relations over private virtues which favour ideals of self perfection in isolation from society. This book aroused controversy when first published in German because Dahrendorf argued that by destroying many of the traditional and particularistic structures of Wilhelmine society, the Nazi episode had the effect of laying more stable foundations for democracy in post-war Germany.

For all his disquiet, Dahrendorf pointed to many encouraging developments in the Federal Republic. In addition he has participated in the reform of higher education, with a view to making the universities less authoritarian in structure and more accessible to working-class students.

In the 1970s Dahrendorf speculated on a cluster of grand topics including MODERNIZATION, the energy crisis and the future of the developing world. His *Life Chances* (1979) recognizes that opportunities ('options') and social bonds ('ligatures') are both commonly valued; it is hard to enhance the one without reducing the other.

CGAB

**Darwin, Social Darwinism.** Charles Darwin (1809-82), English naturalist, formulated the theory of natural selection which explained the process of evolution. Three aspects of his work are of interest to sociologists: (1) the structure of the Darwinian revolution is important to the sociology of science; (2) the evolutionary understanding of physical variation is important to the study of RACE RELATIONS; (3) the attempt to create a sociology upon supposedly Darwinian principles constituted a significant phase in its history. This entry will concentrate on the second of these; the first and third are considered in the entry on EVOLUTIONISM.

The first half of the 19th century saw the construction of a theory of racial typology (see RACISM), according to which there was a limited number of permanent racial types, each suited to a particular habitat. Darwin's *Origin of Species* (1859) destroyed this theory by showing that all species were constantly changing as they adapted to changes in their environment. A physically distinct group which migrated to a new region would not necessarily retain its distinctive features. Where the typologists had presented human races as permanently distinct species, Darwin showed that their distinctive characters derived from geographical isolation and that since cross-racial mating produced fertile offspring they were properly classified as sub-species. This overthrew the approach based upon LINNAEAN classification and caused a scientific revolution (see RACE).

Darwin's central argument was that the variations which arise in living forms are transmitted by heredity while subject to processes of selection, both sexual and natural. In the struggle for life, fitness was a question of leaving more offspring in order to transmit particular qualities. Other writers attempted to interpret social affairs in terms of this theory, notably Walter Bagehot, GUMPLOWICZ, Otto Ammon, Georges Victor de Lapouge and William Graham SUMNER. Sir Arthur Keith, for example, contended that evolution is assisted if interbreeding populations are kept separate so that they can develop their special capacities; racial prejudice serves this function and therefore plays a part in the improvement of mankind. It has been customary to classify these authors, including marginal figures like Herbert SPENCER, as representatives of a social Darwinist school of thought within sociology. But apart from those who formed part of the Eugenics movement it is difficult to identify a core of writers subscribing to a common doctrine. For several decades much of social thought was suffused with ideas which owed something to Darwin's discoveries and appealed to them as a source of authority.

See Halliday, 'Social Darwinism: a Definition', *Victorian Studies*, 1971.

MPB

**decarceration.** A term devised by Scull (*Decarceration*, 1977) to refer to the social movement and practices associated with the partial or total closure of reformatories, asylums and prisons in the USA and elsewhere. Decarceration has been prompted by a combination of ideological, practical and political arguments, and is in some measure a response to the failure of institutional treatment to rehabilitate the offender (see GOFFMAN), It extols COMMUNITY CARE, and in the USA is also an answer to court decisions and budgetary recommendations which present decarceration as a means of saving money.

PR

**decision-making.** The process whereby decisions are arrived at over questions of general policy in an organization or over the practical implementation of an established policy. For sociologists, the main focus of interest is the degree to which different groups with an interest in the outcome of the decision are able to participate in and influence the process. Decision-making has long been used, especially in the PLURALIST tradition, as a measure of where POWER lies. Critics of pluralism argue that this usage fails to include the power to remove issues from the decision-making agenda (i.e. 'non-decisions').

See also INDUSTRIAL DEMOCRACY; ORGANIZATIONS.

MR

**deep structure, surface structure.** See CHOMSKY.

**defence mechanisms.** In Freudian theory, the techniques used by the Ego when faced with conflict. Their purpose is to protect the Ego against instinctual demands of the Id, and they consequently play a crucial role in accounting for the relation between instinctual impulses and overt behaviour and, therefore, in symptom formation (see FREUD; PSYCHOANALYSIS). POSITIVIST critics of psychoanalysis have singled out some of the defence mechanisms as epitomizing the unscientific nature of psychoanalytic thought, but the concepts of defence have had a profound impact on popular and professional psychology and are used even by those who reject many other components of psychoanalysis.

The defensive process to which Freud paid most attention was repression, a term first used in his 'Preliminary Communication' on hysteria (1893), where the terms defence and repression were used interchangeably. The essence of repression lies in the simple function of rejecting and keeping something out of consciousness. More specifically, the drives of the Id had to be repressed. Some repression was essential to the development of the normal adult, but in neuroses there was excessive repression. In *Inhibitions, Symptoms and Anxiety* (1925) Freud clarified the relation between repression and defence, and argued that repression was only one mechanism of defence. He suggested, however, that repression played some part in all neurotic mechanisms, although other defences might come into operation as well.

Precisely which other psychic mechanisms are part of the defensive process is a matter of debate. Other important mechanisms commonly listed by psychoanalysts include regression, reaction formation, projection, and denial.

Regression involves a retreat to the personality organization and conflicts of an earlier phase of development; Freud considered it an important defence mechanism in compulsion and obsessions (see MENTAL ILLNESS) which involved regression to a sadistic anal phase of development as a result of fear of castration (see PSYCHOANALYSIS).

Reaction formation is a defensive process in which the repressed impulse finds expression through an exaggeration of the opposite tendencies to those contained within the unconscious. If, for instance, the instinctual impulse involves a desire to kill the father, this desire may be manifest by the process of reaction formation in over-zealous care and solicitousness for the father. Since the mechanism suggests that our overt behaviour may be the opposite of our underlying desire the concept has been a typical locus of attack for critics, since even if observed behaviour is quite opposed to what might be predicted it can be interpreted as reaction formation.

Projection is the process whereby the ego. In denial the Ego asserts the opposite desires, seeing in other people what are the Id's own wishes and impulses. By contrast, in introjection the demands and attitudes of other people, especially the parents, are incorporated by the individual as his or her own. Hence introjection is one mechanism underlying the development of the Super-ego. In denial the Ego asserts the opposite of what the Id's libidinal impulses desire: murderous impulses towards the father, instead of finding expression in solicitousness to the father as in reaction formation, lead to verbal assertions and protestations of love and concern.

JB

**deference.** The form of social interaction which occurs in situations that involve the exercise of TRADITIONAL authority; subscribing to a moral order which endorses the individual's own material, political and social subordination.

The simplest version regards deference as merely a type of behaviour — bowing, curtseying, touching the forelock etc. The difficulty here is to distinguish between powerlessness, or dependence, and deference, for a great deal of supposedly deferential behaviour is the product of dependence and the necessary pose of the powerless. Deference means more than subservience or powerlessness: it indicates some underlying commitment by the actor to such behaviour. An alternative is to regard deference as a set of attitudes, but this can lead to an over-statement of the degree of fixity and coherence which characterize the attitudes of individuals (see CONSENSUS). It also ignores the social content within which attitudes are formed and acted upon. The attitudinal definition of deference is still widely used, but the concept should be considered not as an ideological attribute of individuals but as typifying certain relationships into which they enter. Thus its relational aspect is more apparent, and account is taken not only of the 'deferential' individual but of who possesses traditional authority, how it is maintained, how it may change over time, the range of this authority and the extent to which it is accepted by those in subordinate positions.

See H. Newby, *The Deferential Worker* (1977).

HN

*Deference in politics.* The term deference was first used in a politically significant sense by Bagehot in *The English Constitution* (1867). Given the near certainty that eventually the majority — necessarily the poor and ill-educated — would be voters, how could Britain remain stable and property remain inviolate? In 1824 James Millar, in the *Encyclopaedia Britannica*, had argued that most people would follow the political lead of their social and intellectual superiors and would not form a separate and majority interest. Bagehot explained that people were not fully rational and calculating but preferred to live in circumstances they were accustomed to and with which they felt comfortable. An extension of the franchise entailed no danger of revolutionary or dramatic change provided some of the 'mystery' remained in British politics so that people would hesitate to tinker. The mystery was provided by a political system which was a combination of the efficient and the dignified: pomp and pageant intermingled with the rational and the aristocratic, the experienced with the plebeian or the inexperienced. The latter deferred to the former — the social lower to the social higher and both to the constitutionally mysterious.

Latterly the term deference has been much used to account for the failure of the British working class in Britain to vote for the Labour Party: this is explained by the psychological reward of symbolically associating themselves with their Conservative-voting betters by themselves voting Conservative (see CONSERVATIVE PARTY).

Some analysts combine this view with a Bagehot-type account of deference to institutions. Others see the middle class or fractions of the middle class as being deferrent. The term has also been used to account for working-class militancy, which is seen as an expression of deference to trade union leaders by rank and file members. But others express considerable scepticism: (1) some people vote Conservative because they believe that party has policies which suit them best; (2) it is not a matter of deference but that some workers perceive themselves as middle class because of structured ties with middle-class people; (3) there is no natural affiliation of the working class to socialism or social democratic parties, so there is nothing to explain.

See also CLASS CONSCIOUSNESS; REFERENCE GROUP.

RED

**definition.** A word, or phrase or process which gives the MEANING of another word or phrase. Definitions may be verbal or ostensive; the latter involve pointing at an example of the thing to be defined (definiendum). Descriptive definitions report on established usage, while prescriptive, stipulative or persuasive definitions attempt to introduce a new usage. A distinction is often drawn between nominal definitions, which simply report on verbal usage, and real definitions which purport to say something about the nature of the definiendum (e.g. defining a substance in terms of its molecular structure). Real definitions were out of fashion during the heyday of logical positivism, when they were widely seen as essentialist and metaphysical. Their use is now being revived by RATIONALISTS and REALISTS.

See William Outhwaite, *Concept Formation in Social Science* (1983).

WO

**definition of the situation.** A concept mentioned by W.I. THOMAS in *The Polish Peasant in Europe and America* (1918) and developed in *The Unadjusted Girl* (1923); subsequently influential in the CHICAGO SCHOOL OF SOCIOLOGY. The definition of the situation is one of three components of a total situation, the others being objective conditions and the pre-existing attitudes of individuals and groups. It stresses that in sociological work the way people subjectively interpret their situation should always be considered. This subjective, personal meaning may be at odds with objective conditions, but since it is real for the person who defines the world that way it has a definite impact on the situation. Thomas put this epigrammatically in his classic statement 'If men define situations as real, they are real in their consequences', later dubbed, 'the Thomas theorem' and 'the self-fulfilling prophecy' by MERTON.

KP

**de-industrialization.** See INDUSTRIALIZATION.

**delinquency.** Strictly, a fault, misdeed or failure in obligation, neither discriminating between lawful and unlawful activity nor pointing to the misbehaviour of any age group. However, it has come to acquire a colloquial meaning in sociology and criminology: sometimes coupled with the adjective 'juvenile', it commonly refers to the criminality and misconduct of the young.

English criminal law has conferred a peculiar status on the doings of youth. For over a thousand years, it denied children full moral responsibility, inflicted special punishments and imposed special proscriptions. Youthful deviance was given an even greater prominence at the end of the 19th century in both England and America with renewed concern over the danger of moral contamination by adults, the importance of classification and segregation, the differentiation of treatment and the developmental properties of behaviour. Adult criminality was held to be the mature phase of a process which might be arrested in its earlier stages. Children were thought to display symptoms or signs which could be professionally diagnosed; appropriate and timely intervention could prevent later crime, and the establishment of new courts and reformatories would enable the proper management of wayward or vulnerable children. Otherwise minor acts attained major diagnostic significance. Adjudication was paternalistic, conducted in the child's best interests and lacking many conventional legal defences and procedures. In the USA, Canada, Britain, Scandinavia and elsewhere, juvenile delinquents were radically redefined. Their qualities became immanent, reflecting not only what children were but what they might become.

The age of delinquency has varied from time to time and between jurisdictions. However, sociological analysis has not borrowed its formal definitions from law but has tended to describe all youthful misbehaviour as delinquency. It has insistently dwelt on a restricted range of people and activities. 'Delinquency' has generally been employed to examine the crimes of the young, urban, working-class male.

The explanation of delinquent conduct has echoed the irregular development of sociology itself. Arguments reveal the diversity of sociological theories, of delinquent forms and contexts, and of the problems and purposes set by delinquency. Thus allusion has been made both to excessive and to deficient social control, some announcing that youth is over-disciplined, others that youth is under-disciplined.

The principal theories are as follows: (1) Thrasher and other members of the CHICAGO SCHOOL in the 1920s and 1930s represented delinquency as the natural playfulness of the streets, a playfulness displayed in public view, transmitted from generation to generation, concentrated in particular neighbourhoods, and liable to deformation and corruption by inappropriate LABELLING (see F. Thrasher, *The Gang*, 1927; C. Shaw and McKay, *Juvenile Delinquency and Urban Areas*, 1942). (2) ANOMIE theorists portrayed delinquency as the state achieved by those whose aspirations were balked: blocked careers in the legitimate world engendered a STATUS FRUSTRATION which supplied the motives for deviation (see MERTON; see also R. Cloward and Ohlin, *Delinquency and Opportunity*, 1961). (3) Matza resurrected the ideas of Thrasher, recast the delinquent as the miscast, playful hedonist enmeshed in the workings of formal social control, and referred to DEVIANCE as drift undergone by one whose will was prey to techniques of NEUTRALIZATION (see D. Matza, *Delinquency and Drift*, 1964; *Becoming Deviant*, 1969). (4) Members and affiliates of the Birmingham Centre for Contemporary Cultural Studies married the cultural analysis of MARX and GRAMSCI with an emerging radical criminology (see CRIMINOLOGY). The fruit of that union was an emphasis upon the recurrent problems faced by working-class youth, the phrasing of these problems in a cultural vocabulary provided by capitalist HEGEMONY, and the manufacture of an inapposite symbolic response which is necessarily precarious. Delinquency becomes a misconceived form of cultural resistance (see P. Cohen in *Journal of Cultural Studies*, 1972, and P. Willis, *Learning to Labour*, 1978). (5) Control theorists shift attention to the work of social control in the inhibition of deviance. H. Wilson (*Parents and Children in the Inner City*, 1978) argued that delinquents could be distinguished from the non-delinquent by their lack of exposure to parental 'chaperonage', chaperonage being supervision, surveillance and companionship.

See also SUBCULTURE.

PR

**delusion.** See MENTAL ILLNESS.

**demand.** The amount of a good or service for which a CONSUMER is able and willing to pay. (Its dependency upon ability to pay distinguishes demand from the concept of NEED.) The total quantity of a good demanded by all consumers is its market demand. The demand for any good will depend upon, *inter alia*, its price, the price of substitute and complementary goods, consumers' tastes and their incomes. Demand refers to the quantity of a good consumers wish to buy at given prices etc, not the quantity actually bought; for a good may not be supplied (see SUPPLY) at this particular price. The amount by which the quantity demanded changes when any one of these determinants changes is referred to as its elasticity of demand, measured as the percentage change in demand divided by the percentage change in the determining variable in question. If demand changes more than proportionately, it is elastic; if less, it is inelastic. This measure is necessary to forecast the consequences of numerous policy decisions such as the demand for drugs following a change in prescription charges, the effect on total revenue of an increase in rail fares, or the

quantity of resources likely to be devoted to housing as incomes increase through time.

A demand curve or schedule is a diagrammatic representation of the relationship between demand and the price of a good, on the assumption that all other factors remain unchanged. It is usually depicted on a two-dimensional chart with price measured on the vertical axis and demand on the horizontal: the curve slopes downwards from left to right embodying the theoretical expectation that, for most goods, demand will increase as price falls. If a supply curve is imposed upon the same diagram, the point of intersection of the two curves indicates the equilibrium price and quantity of the good.

The total demand for all goods and services within an economy is known as aggregate demand. In their efforts to control the rates of INFLATION and UNEMPLOYMENT, governments employ demand management policies, involving TAXATION and monetary instruments (see MONETARISM), to try to ensure that aggregate demand is equated with the productive potential of the economy.

RR

**democracy.** Popular rule, from the Greek *demos*, 'people'; the collective determination of law and policy by a people, equal in CITIZENSHIP rights, who reach decisions after public debate by a procedure of majority vote. Disagreements about the definition of democracy usually turn out to be disagreements about how much of it is desirable or realizable, not about what it means. In representative democracies people surrender their rights to determine law and policy to elected representatives, to whom the government is directly answerable. In such systems, popular rules comes down in practice to a question of the accountability and reponsiveness of a government to the people via both their formal representatives and other informal channels of public opinion — interest groups, the media etc. Even in this more restricted sense democracy presupposes the following: free and fair elections on the basis of universal suffrage; guaranteed freedoms of association and expression, independent of governmental control; openness of government action to public scrutiny; an effective jury system;

equality of access for citizens to the means of influencing public decision-making. The so-called 'people's democracies' of Eastern Europe fail to meet most of these criteria; the 'liberal democracies' of the West usually meet the first four (though in differing degrees), but fail to meet the fifth. They meet the democratic requirement of open government more effectively than its requirement of political equality. Political sociologists of liberal persuasion correspondingly emphasize social PLURALISM as a necessary precondition for democratic institutions, where Marxists emphasize economic EQUALITY (see COMMUNISM). Whether a society is possible in which both are realized is still an open question.

See also TOCQUEVILLE.

DB

**demographic transition.** A way of conceptualizing the changes in population which accompanied INDUSTRIALIZATION, seeing in these changes a transformation from a system with high birth rates balanced by high death rates to one with low death rates balanced by low birth rates. In the stage of transition there is a surplus of births over deaths and a rapid growth of population. In a stronger form, demographic transition constitutes a theory of population change in currently developing societies, and contains elements of a general theory of population growth (see POPULATION THEORY). The idea of demographic transition, introduced by Warren S. Thompson (*American Journal of Sociology*, 1929) and developed by F.W. Notestein, has been the central theoretical focus of post-war demography, although there has been disagreement as to the level at which the model applies and hence as to what it predicts.

The pre-industrial system is characterized as having a high and stable birth rate, of the order of 40/1000, a high and fluctuating death rate of 30-50/1000, with a long-term tendency to slow but highly irregular growth. Technological improvements lead to a fall in death rates through increased production, public health and perhaps medicine. The birth rate, determined more by social and cultural patterns, remains high and there is a 'population explosion'. The essentially

modern characteristic is for approximate equilibrium to be restored by a fall in birth rate through rational social and cultural change to control fertility, rather than by a resurgence of high death rates. The post-transition population system has low, stable death rates of only 10-20/1000, and a fluctuating birth rate which acts as the main determinant of population increase. The system is largely hypothetical, as even the most advanced industrial countries have only just begun to enter upon this stage, the modern use of birth control technology having only spread in the 1920s.

As a general theory, demographic transition proposes that populations are normally roughly in equilibrium, and that growth occurs in brief cycles of transition from one equilibrium to the next, corresponding to qualitative advances in technology and the consequent quantitative increases in production and standard of living. In this form the theory is an elaboration of Malthus.

As a description of the demographic history of modern industrial societies, the generalizations that make up the model have been widely criticized. Some writers argue that modern population growth began not with a fall in death rates but with a lowering of the age of marriage and/or a rise in birth rates. Others have argued that an intermediate stage of medium vital rates must be introduced to describe countries like the USA, Canada, Australia and New Zealand. Vital rates do not correlate well with measures of modernization, but demographic transition was not intended to give a cross-sectional classification of societies but rather a dynamic model of change within them. The post-transition system has been criticized on empirical grounds: birth rates have undergone systematic changes not predicted by the simple theory of a gradual fall to equilibrium. If a central aspect of the modern demographic transition is a rational control of fertility, models of economic rationality ought to be able to explain some of these changes. Correlatively, it has been questioned whether the birth rates for pre-industrial societies are consonant with a lack of systematic birth control or a biological determination of fertility, attenuated only by social custom and psychology.

Demographic transition is accompanied by important changes in population structure and social composition, especially during the transitional period, although these changes can be complex and difficult to predict. A fall in mortality initially makes for a younger population with a higher SEX RATIO, but as time goes on increasing life expectancy, coupled with falling birth rates, leads to a relatively ageing and female population. Declining birth rates tend at first to selectively affect cosmopolitan, mobile, well-educated groups; coupled with the URBANIZATION that accompanies technological development, wide differences in social patterns arise between urban and rural areas during transition. Programmes of birth control attempt to reach this rural population in developing countries and hasten the decline in birth rates through deliberate fertility control which, according to transition theory, is the remedy for explosive population growth. Such programmes have experienced considerable difficulties when they have preceded the economic modernization and changes in the relation of production associated with technological development. See POPULATION TURN-AROUND.

JL

**demography.** The numerical study of human populations, their size, distribution and composition, and their changes through birth, death, MIGRATION and SOCIAL MOBILITY. The term was first used by Guillard in 1855, and the discipline is to be distinguished from the more general area of POPULATION THEORY by its history and characteristic methods. See BIRTH-AND-DEATH PROCESS; COHORT AND PERIOD ANALYSIS; LIFE TABLES; MORTALITY; NUPTIALITY.

The central concern of demography is to establish reliable estimates of total population numbers, and of the vital rates of birth, marriage and death. For most of history, and for much of the world today, such estimates are highly problematic. The most reliable data, from CENSUSES and the registration of births, marriages and deaths, extends back about 200 years. Even where the data exist, variations in questions asked and registration procedures can make interpretation difficult, especially in economically underdeveloped

areas or where bureaucracies are inefficient. The estimation of demographic trends requires data that are reliable and long-term (about 150 years given the length of human generations) and so methods which extend data series backwards in time are of great value (see HISTORICAL DEMOGRAPHY).

Crude birth, death and migration rates are too highly aggregated to allow conclusions about population changes, as a given crude rate may be made up in many different ways from the sub-populations within the populations. The age-and-sex composition (see POPULATION PYRAMID) and the age-and-sex specific vital rates are the most important factors required, although further breakdowns by class, race, residence, parity (number of children born to a woman) and birth interval may be necessary for an adequate picture, especially for sociological purposes. In modern societies, census and registration data are supplemented by employment statistics, sample surveys, medical records, shipping and air-travel records etc.

While demographic factors form a base for sociology (see SOCIAL DEMOGRAPHY), demography grew up largely separately, fostered by governments interested in 'political arithmetic' — the size of the tax base, the supply of labour and soldiers, numbers of voters, supplies of food etc — and by the actuarial profession. The first demographic study in modern form was that undertaken by the Englishman John Graunt (1620-74), who used the Bills of Mortality showing weekly numbers of deaths in an area and their causes to construct life tables, estimate the population of London and the countryside and study fertility, migration and housing. The astronomer Edmund Halley (1656-1742) took advantage of data from Breslau to construct a life table, and a wider general interest in population arose, divided by profound disagreements between the participants as to the merits of their local sets of data. MALTHUS's pessimistic view of an increasing population eating up all foreseeable supplies of food was an influential argument about the relation between population and poverty in the 18th century, but provoked much disagreement, especially from MARX and other socialists, who saw surplus population as the result of underproduction (see POPULATION THEORY), and remediable by changing social and economic relations.

Records improved in 19th-century Europe and North America, and investigators like William Farr (1807-83), who worked for the British Registrar-General, drew attention to problems of infant mortality, hazardous occupations and insanitary conditions. A fall in birth rate, particularly in the upper social strata, led to fears of both population and genetic depletion, and a science of human breeding, eugenics, was started by Francis Galton. Mathematical models of stable populations, first used by Leonard Euler (1760), were pioneered by Alfred Lotka in the early 20th century, and Verhulst's S-shaped logistic curve of population growth (1838) was incorporated into population projections. After World War I, the League of Nations, and then the United Nations, co-ordinated and standardized demographic work; population projections emphasizing a world population explosion (see DEMOGRAPHIC TRANSITION) have characterized the post-war period. Simulations by computer of the world ecological system have been attempted (see WORLD SYSTEM) but unrealistic economic and political assumptions and the absence of social factors have led to widespread criticism.

JL

**dendrogram.** See CLUSTER ANALYSIS.

**denomination.** A form of religious collectivity, sometimes a development from an earlier phase as a SECT. Membership is achieved by voluntary attachment, normally without any severe test of merit or worth. The denomination is inclusive, accepting all who wish to belong and only very rarely excluding a member for heresy, moral turpitude or non-conformity. It is doctrinally tolerant, viewing itself as only one among a number of equally valid paths to salvation. It imposes no dogmatic statement of belief upon members and is prepared to co-operate with other similar non-dogmatic collectivities in the pursuit of shared goals in respect of evangelism, welfare, education etc. It is relatively undemanding of its members, accepting prevailing standards of morality and cultural

values. Congregations are normally supervised by a professional ministry, assisted by laymen. The denomination is the most recent of the major forms of religious collectivity (see also CHURCH, SECT, CULT). It can only exist in a society where religious toleration is established. Earlier social circumstances where powerful religious bodies commanded a monopoly (except for small oppositional sects) were not conducive to the emergence of large, tolerant competitors. The denomination is only a significant social formation from the 18th century, and is a product of social differentiation and the emergence of distinctive strata and social groupings which feel comfortable with a particular religious style. Though in principle open to all, in practice it draws its support predominantly from a single sector of society.

RW

**denominationalization.** A process identified by H. Richard Niebuhr in *The Social Sources of Denominationalism* (1929). The WEBER-TROELTSCH distinction between CHURCH and SECT did not do justice to many contemporary religious collectivities, particularly in the USA, where there had been no national church, but where over the course of time inclusive, tolerant and relatively undemanding denominations had developed from radical enthusiastic sects. Niebuhr adopted Troeltsch's view that sectarianism was a response from within the ranks of the 'disinherited' to the tendency for the Christian message to become compromised over the course of time, reflecting the interests and style of the socially privileged. New sects emerge filled with enthusiasm for a radical interpretation of the Christian message. They actively proselytize, often in the face of opposition, drawing the newly converted into the warmth and spontaneity of their close fellowship. They adopt an ascetic attitude which distances them from the pleasures of the world, and stress the equality of all believers. However, Niebuhr believed that sectarian fervour tended to be undermined within a generation. Children born to existing members become the focus of educational effort designed to commit them to the faith but their conviction, not having been 'fashioned ... in the heat of conflict and at the risk of martyrdom' is likely to be less zealous than that of their parents. Moreover, the ascetic doctrine will have led members to rise in the world, so that their children are less likely to feel themselves 'disinherited'. They aspire to enjoy some of the advantages their increased wealth and social standing make available, to receive respect appropriate to their new rank, and to abandon more constricting aspects of moral doctrine and more idiosyncratic aspects of their religion. So the fervour of the movement declines, its evangelistic zeal attenuates, services become more formal, and the need for a trained professional clergy is felt. The sect moves towards a denomination, abandoning any substantial test of merit upon entry and viewing itself as one expression of the Christian tradition with no monopoly over access to salvation.

Niebuhr argued that not all would prosper at the same rate. The poor and 'disinherited' would again begin to feel ill at ease, to feel that the movement had compromised with its radical early message, and break away to establish a new enthusiastic sect. Denominationalization is a continuous development and accommodation to the world, provoking schism, followed by the development and accommodation of the new sect in turn.

Subsequent commentators such as Bryan Wilson have noted that although this model fits the history of many conversionist SECTS, others of a millennialist and introversionist character are more able to resist this process and arrest the rapprochement with society over many generations.

RW

**dependency.** The theory of dependency arose as a neo-Marxist critique of theories of MODERNIZATION and development. The dependency school argued that contemporary manifestations of development and underdevelopment were not different stages in the evolution of mankind, but two aspects of the same historical process. This began in the 16th century with the emergence of capitalism in Western Europe, from where it spread through mercantile expansion and then direct colonial rule over the entire globe. This did not spread the benefits of capitalism evenly; it was characterized by international relations of dominance and subjugation in which the Western capitalist countries reorganized the structure of society and economy of the overseas lands to suit their own needs.

Paul Baran in *The Political Economy of Growth* (1957) argued that 'development and underdevelopment' is a two-way street: the advanced capitalist countries developed by expropriating economic surplus from overseas countries with whom they traded and which they later colonized, while the overseas countries became underdeveloped in aiding the ascendancy of the West. Interaction with the industrializing capitalist countries left the overseas countries with a narrowly specialized, export-orientated primary production structure which found its handmaiden in a frozen internal class structure dominated by a small, mercantile COMPRADOR elite. The imposed specialization of production and the continued coincidence of interests between the imperialist states and the ex-colonial elites even after political independence blocked any attempt at industrialization and internal social transformation (e.g. a bourgeois revolution). Overall economic stagnation and pauperization of the masses resulted. In contrast to MARX's optimism regarding the historically progressive role of capitalism everywhere, Baran led neo-Marxists in demonstrating the impotence of the imported variety.

A.G. Frank's *Capitalism and Underdevelopment in Latin America* (1967) expanded and formalized this into a theory of dependency and underdevelopment, postulating three laws of motion of the process of development and underdevelopment, coining the concept of metropolis-satellite to characterize the nature of imperialist worldwide economic relations (see CENTRE-PERIPHERY). He became the best-known dependency theorist.

The Baran-Frank dependency theories advocated a 'radical break' with world capitalism as a requisite for the development of the now underdeveloped countries. Recently, Latin American scholars (sometimes called 'Dependistas') reformulated dependency theory in the light of economic development which has taken place there within international capitalism. Recognizing that domestic industrialization and sustained economic growth have occurred under an imperial alliance between foreign multi-national companies and the national state, they have concentrated on pairing apparent economic success with social failures such as rising social inequalities, increasing MARGIN-ALIZATION of substantive sectors of the population, deepening class conflict and mounting repression by authoritarian regimes. Early dependency models regarded the internal class structure as a lifeless victim of external domination, but the new dependency theory is more optimistic about the potential for internal class struggle, reform and even transitions to socialism without a prior radical break with the world capitalist system being necessary (e.g. Cardoso and Faletto, *Dependency and Development in Latin America*, 1979).

In Latin American economies today a new dependency has been created by foreign penetration and control over the industrial producer-goods sector. This has increasingly to rely on an alliance with the state as direct producer in the public sector. In Brazil, Chile, Colombia, Peru, Mexico and Venezuela the public sector contributes more than 50 per cent to the annual formation of capital, the remainder contributed by private national and foreign enterprise. The counterpart is the expulsion of more sectors of the national bourgeoise as well as the working classes from the process of national economic development. The state is thus becoming more divorced from the nation, from civil society. Yet the very expansion of industrial dependent capitalism needs the members of civil society as producers and consumers. At present, so the new dependency theorists claim, there is greater scope than ever for various social and political movements to develop and to improve both dependency links (i.e. better deals with the multinational companies) and the nature of the regime (e.g. a change towards greater democracy).

AH

**depression.** See MENTAL ILLNESS.

**deprivation.** Linked to but wider than the concept of POVERTY, deprivation is not restricted to consideration of income but includes other social factors such as housing, education and employment. Studies have shown that inequalities in access to a variety of social factors mirror inequalities in income, and that in many cases inequalities in access to non-income factors also overlap: poor housing is often associated with poor health, poor education with unemployment, and so on. Some writers note the tendency of deprivations to cluster (multiple deprivation) so that individuals may be judged to be deprived not simply on one or two indices, but on a whole range. Social deprivation is often concentrated in certain geographical areas, particularly those close to the centres of large cities. This may exacerbate the problems faced and has led policy-makers to devise special efforts to help such areas.

See CYCLE OF DEPRIVATION; RELATIVE DEPRIVATION.

MPJ

**Descartes, René** (1591-1650). French philosopher and mathematician. Descartes aimed to reconstruct the whole of philosophy, reduced by his method of systematic doubt to the sole indubitable proposition that I am thinking, therefore I exist (*cogito ergo sum*). His stress on EPISTEMOLOGY rather than ONTOLOGY and his highly individualistic starting-point, sometimes known as 'Cartesian privacy', had a lasting influence on philosophy, as did his stress on the primacy of mathematical knowledge. The effects of this conception can still be seen in POSITIVIST conceptions of the social sciences. His doctrine of 'innate ideas' has been recently revived in linguistics, especially in the work of CHOMSKY. His clear distinction between mental and physical processes (generally referred to as 'mind/body dualism') has had a lasting influence on the way many modern societies treat health (see MEDICAL MODEL). Major work: *Discourse on Method* (1637).

See A. Kenney, *Descartes: a Study of his Philosophy* (1968); W. Doney (ed.), *Descartes: a Collection of Critical Essays* (1967).

WO

**descent.** The structural principle of genealogical connection by which attachment to a particular ancestral group is attained.

Descent rules specify the relative importance of maternal or paternal filiation for social purposes, such as inheritance of property or status or kinship rights and obligations.

See also ANCESTOR; KINSHIP; LINEAGE.

JE

**de-skilling.** See SKILL.

**deviance.** A word without a single agreed meaning, though most uses centre on deviation from social rules or norms which carries disrepute, stigma or disapproval and which, therefore, evokes attempted social control over it. Deviance is therefore broader than CRIME. More specific definitions abound, reflecting more specific theoretical leanings: for example, deviance is the ambiguous and disturbing quality of phenomena which cannot be neatly classified (Scott); an attribute bestowed on the powerless by the powerful (Davis); conduct which arises from or contributes to strains in the social system (PARSONS); a property of the vanquished in social conflict (Lofland); an area of symbolic disorder or meaninglessness (BERGER); an accompaniment and manifestation of absurdity in everyday life (Douglas); that which is censured by the community (Bastide); statistically uncommon behaviour (Wilkins); a quality of the socially unsuccessful (Douglas); creative innovation which is as yet unestablished (Parsons, Coser); the antithesis of that which is lauded or valued (Schafer); an educative process which underscores rectitude (Erikson); the commonly unrecognized and stigmatized buttress of general or particular social order (Bell, Davis, MERTON); that which confers organization in areas ill-regulated by legally constituted institutions (Merton, Whyte); and simply that which Everyman identifies as deviant (Becker). So confused and contradictory are definitions that some have proposed the abandonment of the study of deviance (Phillipson); others emphasize confusion and contradictoriness as intrinsic to the phenomenon (Matza); others display indifference to accurate and authoritative naming (Becker); while others strive to achieve the mastery of their own term. Limited prominence should be given to

(1) Lemert, whose *Social Pathology* (1951) revitalized the study of deviance in the 1950s and 1960s. Lemert presented deviance as conduct which evoked a hostile reaction from society. In a later work and following DURKHEIM, he claimed that it was the hostile reaction which generated deviance. (2) Becker, whose *Outsiders* (1963) is one of the two most commonly cited works in American criminology. In a much-quoted statement he asserted 'deviance is *not* a quality of the act the person commits, but rather a consequence of the application by others of rules and sanctions to an "offender". The deviant is one to whom that label has successfully been applied; deviant behavior is behavior that people so label.'

Two principal reasons are usually advanced to justify the sociological concentration on deviance.

Compared with CRIMINOLOGY, the sociology of deviance is expressly sociological, an enterprise free of alleged entanglements with eclecticism and the making of policy. Since the 1960s, it has tended to signify a certain set of intellectual attachments rather than the peculiar properties of the thing studied. The definition of deviance is less important than the analytic stance or methodology adopted: usually SYMBOLIC INTERACTIONISM, PHENOMENOLOGY or RADICAL SOCIOLOGY (see also NATIONAL DEVIANCY CONFERENCE).

Compared with crime, deviance is sometimes held to be more fertile as a topic. The category apparently excludes little. Mental illness, bestiality, voyeurism, lying, stripping, homosexuality, blackmail, sectarianism, blindness, radicalism, stuttering, prostitution, murder and physical illness and all been identified as deviant by sociologists. See also SICK ROLE.

*Deviance amplification.* First tendered by Leslie Wilkins in *Social Deviance* (1964), it joins items from sociology, statistics and cybernetics in one model of the development of deviant processes. Deviation is represented as a statistically uncommon event whose very infrequency has significant social effects. In mass society, the information acquired by the majority about a minority is necessarily mediated, distorted and sparse. The doings of deviants are accordingly ignored or misreported. When misreported, they may invite a response which produces yet further misreported conduct. That conduct, in turn, may receive a reply which moves the process on to another phase. Amplification refers to the distorting of knowledge, the exaggeration of social reaction and the deviants' countering actions. It may lead to a real or assumed increase in the numbers of deviants; in the quality, content or intensity of deviation; in the public moral reputation of an individual or group; or in some combination of the three.

Initially only tentatively formulated, the concept lacked rigor. Little work has been done on the selection and presentation of candidates for deviance amplification, the duration and character of amplification cycles, the conditions under which amplification does not take place, and the occurrence of 'de-amplification' (J. Ditton, *Contrology*, 1979). Instead, 'deviance amplification' has been grafted on to other models. Thought to have an affinity with arguments dwelling on LABELLING, SOCIETAL REACTION and DEVIANT CAREERS, it has been sponsored by a number of sociologists who have little stake in Wilkins's original cybernetic and statistical framework. Amplification encouraged the re-emergence of a sociology of the mass media, crime waves, SUBCULTURES and that supposedly ill-founded alarm called 'MORAL PANIC' (S. Cohen, *Folk Devils and Moral Panics*, 1972). It was largely absorbed in those concerns, giving way to an analysis which alludes to it less and less often (S. Hall *et al*, *Policing the Crisis*, 1978).

*Deviant Career.* Anticipated by other terms virtually identical in meaning: 'moral career', 'delinquent career' and 'natural history'. Their common stress is the extension and development of phenomena in time. Deviation is defined as 'emergent' or 'becoming', a process whose significance becomes apparent only as it unfolds. The career is a sequence of stages strung together and moving towards a discernible goal; the stages recognized by the deviant, by people about him/her, by the sociologist or by a grouping of the three. Passage through the career may be accompanied by transformations of identity and moral worth (see GOFFMAN). Though subject to criticism as mechanical and deterministic, the deviant career is most frequently described as a series of opportunities and constraints which can be resisted or modified. Its organization and clarity are shaped by repetitiveness, centrality to formal institutions and processes, diffusion of practical knowledge about deviance (see BECKER), and the bargaining positions of those involved.

In one sense, sociologists maintain that all deviant episodes have orderly and describable histories. In another sense, the various groups involved in the production of deviance tend to create patterned sets of experiences for those who break rules: drug-takers learn how to become deviant; homosexuals learn how to become homosexual; police learn how to manage drug-takers and drug-takers the police. Those experiences are typically staggered in time. Underpinning their analysis is a special conception of causality, 'sequential causation', which stresses that causes will exercise different effects at different points in a career. See also CAREER; CAUSE.

*Deviation, Primary and Secondary.* Wishing to emphasize the significance of social reaction, Lemert proposed a distinction. Primary deviation is an initial act of rule-breaking. Secondary deviation occurs when the rule-breaker is required to manage the response elicited by his/her transgression. It may entail a new organization of the self, perspectives and motives. Its chief effect is to direct analysis at the interplay between act and audience and away from first causes. Publicly identified deviance is held to be *sui generis*: primary deviation can occur without secondary, and secondary deviation can take place without primary.

See E. Lemert, *Social Pathology* (1951) and *Human Deviance, Social Problems and Social Control* (1967).                                        PR

**Deviancy, National Conference on.** See NATIONAL DEVIANCY CONFERENCE.

**Dewey, John** (1859-1952). American philosopher, psychologist and educational theorist. One of the main exponents of PRAG-MATISM, and an important influence on G.H. MEAD and SYMBOLIC INTERACTIONISM.

WO

**diachronic** [opposite: synchronic]. Terms used in STRUCTURALISM but rejected by some structuralists. Diachrony involves (the study of) a process over time, while synchrony denotes (the study of) the state of a system at a particular moment. LANGUAGE, for example, can be studied historically or in terms of the structured relations which compose it.

WO

**dialectic.** Used by the Greeks in a general way to refer to processes of argument and reasoning. The modern sense of the word derives mainly from the IDEALIST philosophy of HEGEL, in which thought (and therefore, in Hegel's view, reality) develops by means of contradictions and the reconciliation of contradictions in a more adequate synthesis. This idea was adopted in an ambiguous way by MARX and vulgarized by ENGELS and others in dialectical MATERIALISM, in which all material processes are governed by dialectical laws. 'Dialectical' is often used loosely to indicate approval that a person or text shows some sensitivity to the contradiction and complexities of reality.

See Roy Bhaskar, *Dialectics, Materialism and Human Emancipation* (1983).

WO

**differential association.** This theory translated some of the arguments and implications of the urban sociology of the CHICAGO SCHOOL into a system of formal propositions. It was first described by SUTHERLAND in 1934, and later promoted by Sutherland, Cressey and Glaser. It was advanced as a general explanation of CRIME, matched against a succession of empirical examples of criminality, and progressively modified until it applied to every instance inspected. It involved a number of propositions. Criminal behaviour is learned in interaction with other persons, especially within intimate personal groups, in a process of communication. Learning includes tech-niques of committing the crime (which are sometimes complicated, sometimes simple) and the specific direction of motives, drives, rationalizations, attitudes and definitions of legal codes. A person becomes deviant because of an excess of definitions favour-able to violation of law over definitions unfavourable to violation of law. Differential association may vary in frequency, duration, priority and intensity. The process of learning criminal behaviour by association with criminal and anti-criminal patterns involves all of the mechanisms that are involved in other learning. Though criminal behaviour is an expression of general needs and values, it is not explained by those general needs and values, since non-criminal behaviour is an expression of the same needs and values. See B. Sutherland and D. Cressey, *Principles of Criminology* (1966).

This theory had significant effects on the evolution of the sociology of crime. It resisted the description of law-breaking as a pathological consequence of pathological conditions, thereby averting entanglement with the fallacy that 'like' must always cause 'like'. It explained crime by common social processes within the general province of sociology, so that criminology remained firmly attached to the broad movements of sociology proper. It sustained the earlier emphasis of Chicago sociology upon the learned character of conduct and motiva-tion, providing a foundation for the later erection of SUBCULTURAL theory. It attended to the processes and workings of the intimate personal group, anticipating the renaissance of the ethnographic deviance studies of SYM-BOLIC INTERACTIONISM (see also DEVIANCE).

There is a critical ambiguity in its weak version, where argument alludes to criminal patterns. It is possible to associate with criminal patterns which are broadcast by films, novels and people but avoid con-sorting with criminals themselves. Almost every person is so exposed and the theory loses some of its capacity to predict and discriminate. In its strong form, the argument talks of association with criminals. It is most telling in an analysis of professional crime which is reproduced by apprentice-ship. But, as numerous criminologists assert, the theory is false when applied to 'naive' or isolated criminal acts; see Lemert, *Human*

*Deviance, Social Problems and Social Control* (1967).

PR

**differential opportunity structure.** ANOMIE in MERTON's sense turns on the social strains which flow from the conflict between an alleged universal desire for material success and the unequal distribution of life-chances. SOCIAL STRATIFICATION is mirrored in the ease or difficulty with which people attain access to conventional and unconventional CAREERS, and may be presented as a graded series of obstructions which pose characteristic problems for different sections of a population. The organization of the whole is a differential opportunity structure (see Merton, Cloward and Ohlin, *Delinquency and Opportunity*, 1960). Attempts to cope with obstacles can arise from and produce a frustration which is dependent on the scale of ambition and the extent of blockage. In turn, the character, direction and fate of those attempts will supply the motives and content of various forms of DEVIANCE.

See also MERTON.

PR

**diffusion.** A term introduced by E. Tylor (*Primitive Culture*, 1871) to describe the spread of culture traits by any means apart from independent invention. In its extreme form it has been argued that a particular society (ancient Egypt in one version) was the source for all subsequent socio-cultural development. Controversies between diffusionists and local EVOLUTIONISTS (who assert that the development of a particular society was indigenous) are widespread among scholars of early civilizations. Diffusionist enthusiasts have sailed across oceans in boats made of reeds to prove that one people could have influenced another over distances of thousands of miles.

With the explosion of European global power in the early modern period, diffusionism has tended to predominate in modern societies.

LS, MM

**Dilthey,** Wilhelm (1833-1911). German philosopher and historian of ideas. Influenced by KANT and increasingly by HEGEL, Dilthey aimed to provide a 'critique of historical reason' which would establish the foundations of the human sciences. These are based on a partial identity of subject and object, the fact that historians are themselves historical entities; historical research occurs in a nexus of experiences, the expressions to which these experiences give rise, and the understanding (*Verstehen*) of these expressions. Dilthey's anti-NATURALISM is based on the idea that the content of the human sciences is essentially different from that of the natural sciences; the former are concerned with the experiences of human minds and therefore with questions of psychology and HERMENEUTICS. His theories influenced WEBER.

WO

**dimension.** A measurable attribute, independent of, but analogous to, other attributes of the same overall phenomenon. These attributes can be plotted spatially, each on a separate dimension. Thus objects of study are not approached as totalities but as collections of individual attributes. Dimensions define a space in which the objects lie, in the same way as the three dimensions of physical space serve to uniquely define the position of a physical object. Normally the attributes, to qualify as dimensions, should be uncorrelated one with another, that is, at 'right angles' to each other in a geometrical sense. Modern Weberian theories argue that class, status and power are three dimensions of SOCIAL STRATIFICATION systems so that all persons can be assigned to a particular point in three-dimensional space; see CLASS: *Weberian theories.* Usually implies that the quality in question is in principle measurable at least at the interval level (see MEASUREMENT). The objects of study can thus be defined relative to one another by their scores on the several dimensions. Critics see it as impossible to define most social science entities simply by a collection of scores, insisting they have to be approached holistically, by a method defined by the overall nature of the object of study in question. Thus stratification systems cannot be decomposed. They are totalities, whose overall structure influences the particular nature of class, status and party.

See CLASS; MULTI-DIMENSIONAL SCALING; PERSONALITY; RELIGIOSITY; TRAIT.

JL, MM

**discounting.** In economics, the current value attached to COSTS and benefits which accrue in the future will depend upon the precise time period in which they occur: those which accrue at more distant dates will have lower present-day values than those which accrue in the near future. The method which adjusts future values so that they can be expressed in present-day equivalents is known as discounting. The discount rate (e.g. 5 per cent, 10 per cent) determines the extent to which a future value will be discounted: as the rate increases so the present value of future costs and benefits falls. Time preference and the fact that current assets may be invested to produce returns in the future, provide the rationale for valuing future returns less highly than those accruing at the present.

RR

**discourse.** A concept widely used in modern French thought with the multiple purpose of distancing oneself from the philosophy, ideology or scientific specialism under discussion, leaving its status open, while at the same time emphasizing the relative independence of thought and language from the world and the need to analyse systems of thought in terms of the language in which they are expressed. Discourse analysis became fashionable in the late 1970s; see SEMIOLOGY.

See Michel Foucault, *The Archaeology of Knowledge* (1969).

WO

**discretion.** In many areas of social policy the providers of the service are given firm guidance on what kind of assistance, and how much assistance, is to be offered. The guidance is likely to be tighter in organizations based on the BUREAUCRATIC than the PROFESSIONAL model. However in all areas the providers of the service retain some freedom to make decisions of their own or exercise discretion. It would be impossible to foresee all the issues that are likely to arise

and to issue an instruction to cover them, and in many instances it is felt desirable that the service should not simply be the same for everyone, but should take some account of individual circumstances.

The term administrative discretion is frequently used in situations where an official is required to exercise his/her own judgement, even if only within limited bounds. This is contrasted to maladministration, where an official has exceeded his/her discretion or exercised his/her own judgement in an area where pre-established rules should be followed.

Discretion in social assistance services has caused considerable debate. The way in which officers have used discretion, the values that they have brought to bear, and the extent to which discretion has been used consistently have been the source of controversy. This has in part been about the use of such discretion as the officers have been required to apply, and in part about maladministration.

MPJ

**discrimination.** The differential treatment of people ascribed to particular social CATEGORIES. To establish that an action is discriminatory it is necessary to show that someone is treated differently because he or she is thought to belong to such a category; it therefore entails a comparison of a particular action with others. British legislation (which has followed North American precedents) penalizes discrimination based on sex, colour, RACE, ETHNICITY and national origins. Whether the victim properly belongs to the category in question is irrelevant so long as he or she has been treated less favourably on that ground. To establish this it may be necessary to examine the account which the alleged discriminator gives of his or her activities, or to collect evidence about any differences in the pattern of his or her behaviour when dealing with those who may be presumed to belong to one of those categories.

The form of racial discrimination which has received most attention is that based on a desire to avoid association with members of a minority. This desire can often be interpreted as a form of PREJUDICE: in economic analyses it is said to spring from a taste for discrimination. Another form of discrimination suffered by members of racial minorities but particularly relevant to the analysis of inequalities associated with sex, is called statistical discrimination. A woman may be denied a job not because she is a woman but because she is thought to be more likely than a man to acquire family responsibilities that will prevent her working overtime, require her to take time off, or result in her leaving (see WOMEN AND THE LABOUR MARKET). There may be factual evidence to indicate that in particular occupations female workers have job-relevant characteristics different from male workers of the same age. Statistical discrimination may therefore be economically rational behaviour. It may be defined as the unfavourable treatment of persons which arises from a belief that people in particular categories are more or less likely to possess particular undesired or desired attributes. The behaviour that characterizes categorical and statistical discrimination may at times appear similar, and so may the consequences, but the motivations are different and strategies effective against the former may be ineffective against the latter.

The British Race Relations Act of 1976 introduced a distinction between direct and indirect discrimination, derived from the American case of *Griggs v. Duke Power Co.* of 1971. Indirect discrimination has occurred if a person has applied 'a requirement or condition ... (i) which is such that the proportion of persons of the same racial group as that other [the victim] who can comply with it is considerably smaller ... and (ii) which he cannot show to be justifiable ... and (iii) which is to the detriment of that other'. In the case of *Hurley v. Mustoe* (1981) a woman had been refused employment as a waitress in a small restaurant because she was the mother of small children. As the employer did not ascertain whether male applicants for employment had small children he was held to have practised direct discrimination. In the case of *Price v. The Civil Service Commission* (1978) the condition that applicants for appointment as Executive officers must be no older than 28 years was held to discriminate indirectly against women, many of whom might have been unable to apply

earlier because of family responsibilities. From a comparison of the judgements in these two cases it would appear that the legal definition of indirect discrimination will cover the practice of statistical discrimination.

Policies providing more favourable treatment for members of social categories are known as positive discrimination or reverse discrimination; this is a form of categorical discrimination in which any inclination to discriminate against members of the minority is counterbalanced by sanctions which induce people to discriminate against members of the majority.

See also EQUALITY.

See M. Banton, 'Categorical and Statistical Discrimination' in *Ethnic and Racial Studies*, 1983, 6 (3).　MPB

**dispersion, measure of.** A descriptive STATISTIC which summarizes information about the spread of values in a distribution around the central value. There are three common measures of dispersion, corresponding to three common measures of LOCATION. The range (linked to the mode) is the difference between the highest and lowest values in a distribution. The interquartile range (linked to the median) includes the central 50 per cent of cases in a distribution, defined as the distance between the first and third quartiles. The standard deviation (linked to the mean) is based on the square of the deviation between each score and the arithmetic mean. The standard deviation is of particular importance because of its applicability in a wide variety of statistical contexts, and its use as a standard measure of the area under the curve of a normal distribution (see SAMPLING).　MB

**divination.** A social process in which the divine is brought into play in order to allocate blame and suggest remedies in cases of illness or other affliction. Blame may be apportioned to sorcery by some living person, the activities of a ghost, or the agency of non-human spirits. The divinatory rite is one way of not only allocating blame but also seeking justice, in societies or situations without a legal code. By mystical means it first finds the category of agent responsible for the affliction and then which individual agent within that category is responsible. Unlike legal systems, divinatory institutions are more concerned with restoring harmony than with exacting retribution or punishment.

The divination may be spontaneous, initiated by clients or part of a tribal court. The means used can be objective or subjective. In the former case, the diviner may use mechanical methods, casting objects such as shells or sticks, and freely translating the configuration in which they fall in terms of local knowledge of the situation. Alternatively, the diviner may make an exposition of the problem and its causes either by observing the behaviour of animate creatures, like an insect crawling up a twig, or by examining the entrails of a dead animal, such as the chicken oracle which EVANS-PRITCHARD vividly described among the Azande. Subjective divination takes place by spirit mediumship, when the diviner is possessed by a spirit and consultation takes the form of a seance.

The diviner is not so much responsible for eliciting the facts as for discovering the mystical causes. Since all the facts are known in a small-scale society and there are a limited number of possible and recurrent causes of a situation, it is possible to reduce the crisis situation to a number of principles and factors from which the diviner can reach a decision which accords with the views of the majority of persons present at the divination. This is achieved not only through the diviner's own experience but also through the experience of society incorporated in SYMBOLS. Such symbols are likely to be multireferential rather than the more usual condensed symbols used in other rituals. They represent configurations of social relationships.

See MAGIC, WITCHCRAFT.

JE

**division of labour.** Originally a term used by economists to mean the process by which people come to perform more and more specialized tasks in social life. Under names such as 'role differentiation', the process is familiar in many non-economic contexts, but most obvious in the growth of more and more complex occupational structures. Division of labour is one of several interconnected long-term social processes — urbanization, state-formation, bureaucratization, population growth and, of course, industrialization — which led to the emergence of the large-scale industrial state-societies of the modern world.

Division of labour is inevitably bound up with questions of POWER. It spins a growing web of interdependence through society: a person's or a group's position within the division of labour makes others dependent on them, and simultaneously makes them dependent on others. Everyone who performs some specialized task on which others depend has some degree of power over them, but this may be far outweighed by the power others have over him/her. In societies with a complex division of labour, scarcely anyone produces more than a fraction of his/her own needs, so that even the most powerful are dependent on countless others.

A classic discussion is Adam SMITH's *Wealth of Nations* (1776). Smith describes a small pin-making factory — an example borrowed from the French *Encyclopédie* — where ten men, each specializing in one stage of making a pin, could make about 240 times as many pins in a day than if each worked separately and performed all the operations himself. Later economists, including John Stuart MILL, developed this to demonstrate by means of the 'law of comparative advantage' the advantages of international trade between countries specializing in different types of production (see INTERNATIONAL DIVISION OF LABOUR).

MARX recognized these wealth-creating effects, but also pointed to the unequal balances of power thus engendered between different classes in an emerging capitalist society. Specialization also prevented work being a means of human self-fulfilment, and therefore was a cause of ALIENATION.

DURKHEIM's *Division of Labour in Society* (1893) distinguishes mechanical and organic solidarity. 'Mechanical' solidarity, in small-scale societies with a low division of labour, stems from people performing together a relatively small number of similar social roles; 'organic' solidarity in more complex societies is the interdependence of people playing many dissimilar roles.

Durkheim was not very successful in explaining the process of the division of labour, the transition from low to high specialization. He criticized SPENCER who, like the economists, had stressed the incentives to specialize provided by increased productivity. Durkheim argued that social order and solidarity preceded specialization: before people could enter into contracts to perform specialized services they had to have confidence in each other's capacity and willingness to fulfil the contract, and to know that 'society' would punish those who failed to do so. There is some truth in both Spencer's and Durkheim's views, but it is a circular, chicken-and-egg, argument. Durkheim was right that 'all that is in the contract is not contractual'. But a moral order encompassing a whole society is not essential for the division of labour to proceed: if ten men see the advantage and agree amongst themselves to divide their labour in the manufacture of pins, they will set up a compelling trend which forces others to follow their example, whether they like it or not, or go out of the pin-making business. Such trends initially created an industrial labour force and continue to transform it.

SJM

Industrial sociologists have further developed the concept of division of labour along three lines.

(1) The economic principle, largely sound from a narrow 'productivist' viewpoint, whereby a complex operation is decomposed into smaller elements, each of these being regarded as a distinct task (e.g. Adam SMITH's pin manufacture example, described above). Specialization reduces the time required to perform each unit operation and therefore the time to produce a unit of output — provided the flow of semi-finished articles from operative to operative is correctly articulated. (As part of redesign, superfluous actions may be elimited; see SCIENTIFIC MANAGEMENT). A further gain in productivity may be obtained by devising specialist tools to apply in unit operations. But unless strict labour discipline can be imposed, an ensuing loss in motivation on the part of workers confronted by fragmented tasks may seriously offset gains in overall productivity.

(2) The structure of detail tasks in a given LABOUR PROCESS. This structure may result from the decomposition of a traditional handicraft, in line with the foregoing logic. Commonly, since the mechanization of industry, it has been unstable, altering with the invention of new tools or machinery (themselves often devised with the express aim of increasing the specialization of operations), the cost and supply of high quality labour, the level of production engineering expertise and other factors, including the relative ability of some worker groups to resist 'rationalization'.

(3) The occupational composition of an economy as a whole. Official listings of occupations enumerate many thousands of occupational labels, especially for semi-skilled manual work. This range actually dramatizes the extent of narrow specialization in modern industry: from the point of view of inherent difference, the apparent variety is a statistician's mirage. There is little technical, sociological or economic sense in recognizing more than a few dozen (at most) distinct semi-skilled or unskilled manual occupations. Much the same goes for routine white-collar work. Yet the number of reasonably distinct occupations has grown somewhat since industrialization. Diversification mainly affects highly trained or educated persons; at the foot of the scale there is a spurious heterogeneity. Occupations are usually aggregated into a few CENSUS CLASS groupings, normally established with little reference to sociological theory. All three notions are linked via the idea of specialization. With growing reaction against scientific management strategies of work design and signs of worker resistance to fragmented detail tasks, some steps have been taken to 'enrich' routine work either by adding new elements to a fragmented operation (job enlargement) or by permitting operatives to perform, successively, a series of fragmented operations (job rotation). The number of such programmes, no less than their individual scope, leave much to be desired.

See INTERNATIONAL DIVISION OF LABOUR; PLURAL SOCIETY; UNANTICIPATED CONSEQUENCES.

See C. Sabel, *Work and Politics* (1982).

MR

**divorce.** The legal term denoting a broken marriage contract. Today divorce is fairly easy to obtain but this has not always been so; indeed, before 1857 it was only available by a very costly private act of Parliament. This is because the major British religions (Church of England and Roman Catholicism in particular) have traditionally regarded marriage as a contractual arrangement sanctioned by God and subject to His will. With few exceptions marriages were dissolved by His will only in the event of death. Today religion has no direct influence on matrimonial legislation but it has played an important part since the mid-19th century in shaping successive reforms in the law. The only remaining effective sanction is the refusal of the Christian marriage service to divorced brides and grooms.

The process of divorce law reform in Britain has involved a move away from ecclesiastical to civil jurisdiction, growing equalization of access to divorce for women, the provision of financial legal aid, and more latterly the abandonment of the principle of matrimonial offence and with it the acceptance of the individual's right to decide whether or not the marriage is workable. The situation today contrasts starkly with what prevailed in the first half of the 19th century where the separated or divorced woman might forfeit all rights to property, maintenance and even access to the children. Since 1969 the irretrievable breakdown of marriage has been the sole cause of divorce, and both partners enjoy (potential) enforceable rights to a share of conjugal property as well as to alimony and child maintenance payments. In practice, the courts almost invariably award the custody of children to the divorced mother and impose an obligation on the divorced father to maintain his estranged family. Many of the rights and obligations of the married at separation and divorce also apply to common law spouses. In the USA a new concept, palimony, has emerged for the unmarried partner's rights to property and maintenance.

During the 20th century successive changes in the law have been associated with a growing incidence of divorce and a falling of incidence of legal separation, combining to produce an overall increase in broken marriage. In the early 1980s more than one in three marriages is likely to end in divorce. The rate is proportionately higher for younger brides and grooms, the formerly married, and the lower social classes. When the duration of marriage is standardized the divorce rate appears to be unaffected by fertility and family size.

Among the petitioners for divorce there are twice as many women as men. This sex difference is largely an artefact of the legal aid system, which provides assistance only for the unemployed or the very poor. Before 1969, the prohibitive costs of a contested divorce meant that in the large number of undefended cases men were, by default, declared guilty of a matrimonial offence. They simply could not afford to clear their reputation. In these circumstances the statistical data of court proceedings present a very skewed picture of causes and casualties of divorce. Another reason for women being predominantly the protagonists in the courts is to be found in the prevailing conjugal DIVISION OF LABOUR and household resources which renders the female the economically vulnerable partner. After separation and divorce alimony is invariably paid out of the male's wage or salary and ex-wives use the courts to secure their continuing rights over their ex-husband's earning-power. However, given low average incomes in the UK and the reluctance of many men to support households of which they are no longer a part, a very large proportion of single-parent families created out of rising divorce rates fall into the state social security net. Remarriage rates are high and an estimated three-quarters of the divorced are recruited back into the conjugal state. More men than women remarry and the rate also falls off with age.

The rising divorce rate has provided ammunition for two opposed views of the state of marriage and family life and contemporary society. While some have perceived in the trends a sign of weakness, others interpret them as signifying the overriding importance of the institutions to the individual who is unprepared to tolerate a less than wholly successful conjugal relationship. The latter view is backed up by high remarriage rates (one in three marriages is a remarriage for at least one partner).

Divorce has been used by sociologists

as an indicator of social disorganization, revealing the impact of normative structure (legal NORMS) on social behaviour. DURK-HEIM pointed to the association between divorce and suicide rates, arguing that it was an example of normlessness or ANOMIE. Much subsequent research has focused on the divorced person, who in sociological eyes has been a woman, as a problem status in the social structure. William Goode's well known study *Women in Divorce* (1956) analyses the problems of divorced women as ROLE conflict stemming from a lack of normative acceptance and regulation. British researchers have found divorce more interesting as a social problem and have focused on the social and economic diffi-culties of single parents (see D. Marsden, *Mothers Alone*, 1969). From the SYMBOLIC INTERACTIONIST perspective, the problems of the divorced appear in a more processual form. As a critical life event, divorce involves the negotiation of a status passage (see RITES OF PASSAGE) in which the subject must con-struct a new social reality and display a reper-toire of coping skills. The emphasis here is on problems of *becoming* rather than *being* the incumbent of a deviant social role (see N. Hart, *When Marriage Ends*, 1976).

In the sociology of divorce it is men rather than women who are the invisible social actors. Most research has concentrated on women probably because it has been implicitly assumed that they are the principal victims of the process. This view is made explicit by feminist writers for whom divorce gives evidence of the oppression of women in a PATRIARCHAL society. Ironically, the record of empirical research supports their case only because sociological researchers, caught in the wider cultural web of gender stereotypes, have produced a skewed or blinkered vision of divorce as an almost totally female experience.

NH

**documentary research.** See CONTENT ANALYSIS; HISTORICAL METHODS; PERSONAL DOCUMENTS.

**dole.** Originally the corn distribution (*dole*) made by the Roman state to the poor population of major cities. In modern times, a term for charitable assistance, usually

sparingly given. Since Unemployment Insurance was introduced in the UK in 1911 the term has been specifically associated with unemployment benefit; its links with earlier use have also been maintained, for the term usually indicates that aid is grudgingly given.

MPJ

**domestic labour debate.** See HOUSEWORK.

**domestic mode of production.** See HOUSE-WORK.

**dramaturgy.** A major metaphor which views society as if it was a theatre and all its members as if actors and actresses playing parts. Such a view has a long history — the Greeks are often cited, and Shakespeare's Jaques in *As You Like It* is a classic allusion — but it is in the writings of Kenneth Burke (*A Grammar of Motives*, 1945; *A Rhetoric of Motives*, 1969) that the metaphor was most effectively introduced into social science. The approach was ingeniously developed by GOFFMAN in his earlier work, where he considered how individuals present themselves to others in careful ways so as to control the impressions made and thereby the outcomes. Goffman's first major book, *The Presentation of Self in Everyday Life*, provides a manual of such skills: players work in 'teams' or singly give 'perform-ances', use 'props', control their 'scripts', enter 'settings' and move between 'front-stage' and 'back-stage' (hidden from others). Later works study particular settings (*Behaviour in Public Places*, 1963; *Asylums*, 1961), particular theatrical problems (managing 'STIGMA', coping with embarrass-ment), particular strategies employed (game moves, face work) and a host of theatrical rituals.

Dramaturgy has proved a very fruitful metaphor but it remains unclear whether it is to be used simply as an analytical tool, like systems theory, which aims to show how society works, or whether it is an actual description of consciousness — that indi-viduals self-consciously present themselves. If the latter position is taken, the drama-turgical metaphor may come to view 'the players' as cynical, opportunistic mani-pulators of social life.

See ROLE.

See D. Brissett and C. Edgley (eds.), *Life as Theatre* (1975).                                   KP

**dualism.** Probably the first theoretical concept invented to characterize the social and economic structure of underdeveloped areas. It originated in the 1930s with Boeke's analyses of the Dutch East Indies (now Indonesia); see J. Boeke, *Economics and Economic Policy of Dual Societies* (revised edn. 1953). Social dualism was the clashing of an imported social system with an indigenous social system of another style. Underdeveloped societies of South and East Asia had a modern, capitalistic export sector and a traditional, pre-capitalistic, subsistence sector, with little direct contact between the two. The former was an 'enclave' in an Eastern land, 'not touching native life at any point'. Neither the capital nor the labour employed was indigenous, the land was waste land, the product was exported, and even the necessities of life for the workers were brought in from elsewhere. The reason was that Western and Eastern economic activity were different and could not be reconciled: the former was spurred on by unlimited needs, the latter immobilized by the limitation of wants and needs; the former sought profits, the 'Oriental' avoided risks, disliked investing capital and offered his labour only long enough to meet immediate needs. This resulted in the puzzling phenomenon of the backward-sloping supply curve of labour: the higher the wage, the fewer hours the 'Oriental' would choose to present himself for work. Boeke concluded that Western marginal productivity theory was inapplicable to dualistic economies. Any policy attempting to superimpose Western economic markets, techniques of production, and organization of industry on Eastern society would fail and cause retrogression and decay.

Notwithstanding Boeke's pessimism and lack of confidence in Western economic theory, dualism inspired several generations of Western economic development experts, until Frank's critique of the concept cooled their enthusiasm in 1967 (see DEPENDENCY). Abandoning Boeke's explanation, they turned dualism from a dependent into an independent variable to explain the slow economic growth of underdeveloped countries. The arguments derived from marginal productivity theory. A dual economy has different marginal efficiencies of identical factors in different parts of the economy. Returns for labour and capital differ in the 'modern' and 'traditional' sectors. This paralyses national economic development rather than stimulating it. People queue up for the few well-paid jobs in the modern sector rather than work for low wages to improve conditions in the traditional sector; they prefer to invest and consume in the modern sector. Massive rural-urban migration results, further undermining the vitality of the traditional sector. Where the gap in marginal efficiencies in the dual parts of the economy is too wide, the traditional sector thus becomes a drag on the modern sector, pulling the whole economy down (see B. Higgins, *The Dualistic Theory of Underdeveloped Areas*, 1956). The theory was later criticized by Frank (see DEPENDENCY).

AH

**Durkheim,** Emile (1858-1917). French sociologist, one of the great names of modern sociology. The son of a rabbi, Durkheim was born in Alsace, one of the departments lost by France in the Franco-Prussian War of 1870. The national trauma of this defeat, and the ensuing political and social instability of the early years of the Third Republic, helped to give Durkheim the concern with social solidarity which runs through all his work. Durkheim's other great theme, the establishment of sociology as an autonomous discipline, also reflects his practical concern with social problems; following COMTE in the tradition of POSITIVISM, he saw sociological knowledge as capable of quite direct application to social reform.

Durkheim's career did much to further the cause of sociology in France. A student at the Ecole Normale Supérieure, he taught at Bordeaux (1887-1902) until he was recalled to Paris to a chair of education and then, in 1913, appointed to the first titular chair of sociology in France. Durkheim published four major books. The first was *The Division of Labour in Society* (1893) (see DIVISION OF LABOUR). Discussing this already well-worn subject, Durkheim introduced the notions of *mechanical solidarity,* found in small-scale societies with a low division of labour, and *organic solidarity*, found in larger-scale societies with a complex division of labour. Durkheim differed from previous writers such as TÖNNIES (in his discussion of GEMEINSCHAFT and GESELLSCHAFT) in using the term 'organic' in connection with an advanced rather than a restricted level of specialization. He held that an advanced division of labour bound people together 'organically' through their interdependent specializations. In smaller-scale societies, on the other hand, people following very similar ways of life developed a *conscience collective*. Later, Durkheim argued that conscience collective was also found in complex societies, or should be there if they were functioning well. Another concept in this first book is ANOMIE — in an anomic division of labour people's specialist activities are ill co-ordinated. Durkheim also describes as a 'pathological' form what he calls the 'forced division of labour', by which he means approximately that situation which Marxists regard as normal in capitalist society (see CAPITALISM).

The distinction between normal and pathological social forms is also prominent in *The Rules of Sociological Method* (1895). Durkheim's development of the biological analogy, inherited from earlier writers, makes him a founder of modern FUNCTION-ALISM, though in the fifth chapter of the *Rules* he also enters important reservations often ignored by later functionalists. The *Rules* is a forthright statement of a POSITIVIST methodology, containing the famous injunction to treat 'social facts' as 'things', to be explained causally by reference solely to other social facts. The distinguishing characteristics of social facts are that they are external to any particular individual and that they constrain people's behaviour.

What this means in practice is seen clearly in *Suicide* (1897). Using official statistics in an original and sophisticated way, Durkheim shows that suicide rates vary from country to country and from one social category to another in a relatively stable manner, and that this variation cannot be explained by an appeal to individualistic psychology. Eliminating all non-sociological explanations, Durkheim distinguished three principal

kinds of suicide — altruistic, egoistic and anomic — for each of which he provided an explanation in terms of the social situation in which it occurred, rather than in terms of the individual suicide's motivation (see ANOMIE; ECOLOGICAL FALLACY).

The *Elementary Forms of Religious Life* (1912) is a study (from written reports, not observation in the field) of the beliefs of Australian aborigines. Durkheim's views on social solidarity and the conscience collective are further worked out. He defines religion as the sacred, 'things set apart' from material interests. It is created by society as a kind of metaphor for the necessity and sacredness of its own normative solidarity (see CONSENSUS).

Durkheim also published many essays, particularly in the journal *L'Année Socio-logique*, which he founded; one of the most important, written with Marcel Mauss, is 'Primitive Classification', which was to prove a major influence on STRUCTURALISM. After his death, various courses of lectures were also published, including *Moral Education* (1925, English edn. 1961), *Professional Ethics and Civic Morals* (1950, English edn. 1957) and the unfinished *Socialism and Saint-Simon* (1928, English edn. 1958). In several of these he expressed his concern for the restabilization of French society, advocating the setting up of occupational associations or guilds. Because of the faint resemblance to the corporate state (see COR-PORATISM), Durkheim has occasionally been accused of being an intellectual precursor of FASCISM, but his political record and his friendship with the great French socialist Jean Jaurès suggest that he is better seen as a not-quite-fully-committed sympathizer with guild socialism.

Durkheim was the centre of an intellectual circle known as the *Année Sociologique* group, which included the sociologists Mauss and Maurice Halbwachs, the anthropologist Lucien Lévy-Bruhl and the sinologist Marcel Granet. This group remained powerful in French academic life long after his death. Outside sociology and anthropology, its influence can be seen in the work of members of the ANNALES SCHOOL of historians, notably Lucien Febvre. Through RADCLIFFE-BROWN, Durkheim was a decisive influence on British social anthropology and, through PARSONS, his influence permeated functionalism in sociology after World War II.

See also CIVIL RELIGION; FUNCTIONAL THEO-RIES OF RELIGION; RELIGION.

See S. Lukes, *Emile Durkheim* (1973).

SJM

# E

**ecological fallacy.** The statistical fallacy of taking ecological correlations as estimates of individual correlations. The individual correlation denotes the correlation between two attributes of individuals using those individuals as the units of analysis. If these individuals are aggregated into groups, and the proportions of individuals with particular attribute values are correlated, the result is an ecological correlation, using the aggregates as units. This ecological correlation may bear no relation to the individual correlation; it may even be of opposite sign: that is, one may be a positive correlation and the other negative. Thus, for example, if a number of urban areas are scored on percentage Jewish and percentage anti-semitic and show a strong positive correlation, it does not follow that anti-semitism and being Jewish will correlate at the individual level. Extra information about the distribution within and between areas is needed to say whether it is the same people who are both anti-semitic and Jewish. The ecological correlation is no guide to the individual correlation, but it remains valid in its own right as a fact about the urban areas themselves considered as social entities.

The accusation has been levelled most famously at DURKHEIM's study of suicide rates of aggregate populations from which he claimed to explain the causes of individual suicides. The fallacy is particularly likely in sociology where frequently data on both individual persons and social groups are encountered together. Aggregate data are often used as a substitute for individual data, either because the latter are not available, or because they seem less reliable than data on large collections. The level of analysis must be clearly defined by theory if ecological fallacies are to be avoided.

JL

**economic activity rates.** The proportion of the population employed or seeking employment. Exact definitions vary between countries: some include members of the armed forces, seasonal workers and those seeking their first job as economically active, others do not. Most definitions exclude students, women solely occupied in domestic duties, retired people and people living on their own means.

In most Western nations, male economic activity rates have declined in recent years whereas female economic activity rates have increased. However towards the end of the 1970s, although the decline in male economic rates continued, the rise in female economic activity rates was reversed. One possible reason for the change in the female trend was the increase in the level of unemployment. Those people, especially women, who see no prospect of work may decide it is not worthwhile looking for employment and may be removed from the classification of those who are economically active.

MPJ

**economies of scale.** These occur when an increase in the productive capacity of an industry or firm results in a smaller proportionate increase in total COSTS than in output. Accordingly, costs per unit output decrease. A major source of economies of scale is the existence of sophisticated plant and machinery that can only be operated efficiently at large volumes of output. Conversely the management problems associated with large-scale organizations are sometimes a cause of diseconomies of scale. Considerable debates occur over whether trends towards greater CONCENTRATION are the result of economies of scale.

RR

**education.** In its widest sense, education refers to the whole process of bringing persons up and is usually, though not necessarily, used in respect of the young. In this meaning all parts of the social structure, such as political activity or family life, can have an educational influence. However, the term has been both widened and narrowed. More widely, it refers to the education of persons at all stages of the LIFE CYCLE; more narrowly, to refer to that part of bringing-up that occurs in formal institutions, and is more accurately termed SCHOOLING. The term is also often used in relation to the standards of achieved or perceived learning. Thus 'the educated' refers to those meeting a given, usually high, standard of education, while 'over-' and 'under-educated' are similarly used, as is also 'uneducated', although strictly very few social actors are uneducated, since most have been brought into the NORMS of behaviour and knowledge accepted in their society. Since norms vary through time and space, standards of education vary empirically by cultures. All adjectives associated with the term education are culturally relative rather than absolute. As formal education has become more common its organization has grown more complex so that it has been divided into stages to cater for different ages of pupils. The usual division is into primary, secondary and tertiary, with the breaks respectively at about eleven or twelve and seventeen to nineteen years of age. Functional divisions also exist, covering, for example, technical or special education for the disabled or extremely precocious.

See WOMEN AND EDUCATION.

PWM

**Education Act (UK) (1944).** The formal educational system of the UK has since 1870 been subject to a number of Education Acts, the most important of which were passed in 1870, 1902 and 1944. These Acts officially covered only England and Wales; similar legislation relating to Scotland was passed subsequently in each case. At present the educational system operates under the 1944 (1945 Scotland) Act as subsequently amended. In outline this Act provides that (1) there shall be a Minister of Education; (2) there shall be three stages of education, primary, secondary and tertiary, the first two of which shall be free to all; (3) the school leaving age shall be 15, subsequently amended to 16; (4) independent schools may exist, but administrative mechanisms shall exist for their control and inspection; (5) religious instruction shall be compulsory under a system of locally agreed syllabuses, though individuals are able to opt out of this teaching; (6) the detailed running of the primary, secondary and lower status tertiary institutions shall be undertaken by some 140 local education authorities (LEAs), a fundamental part of the system of local government.

PWM

**efficiency.** A technically efficient production technique is one that maximizes output from a given quantity of factor inputs; or, put alternatively, produces a given output with the minimum quantity of inputs. Economic efficiency takes into account the prices of the factor inputs; thus an economically efficient production technique is one which maximizes output subject to a given cost CONSTRAINT, or minimizes the cost subject to a given output constraint. These conditions are prerequisites of a more general state of PARETO efficiency, whereby it is impossible to make any person better off without simultaneously making someone else worse off. The Pareto criterion states that one allocation of resources is superior to another if it is possible to make at least one person better off without making anyone else worse off. The concept of Pareto efficiency is used extensively in the area of WELFARE ECONOMICS. Its use in actual policy options is restricted because it avoids making interpersonal comparisons of UTILITY: a change which makes some people better off and others worse off cannot be assessed in terms of the Pareto criterion. To overcome this, applied welfare economists often use the potential Pareto or Hicks-Kaldor criterion; this states that a policy change constitutes a welfare improvement if the gainers would be able to compensate the losers and still remain better off. This is used extensively in COST-BENEFIT ANALYSIS.

RR

**effort bargain.** A process, sometimes open but largely tacit, in which there is reference to some convention regulating the quantity and quality of output produced by workers in return for a given reward. Employers, supervisors and operatives may, on rare occasions, share identical views on what should constitute an appropriate effort; the content of the bargain can embody customary notions of a 'fair day's work', take account of the state of the labour market, and be subject to other economic and social influences. Yet even when initial perceptions and expectations are roughly congruent, they frequently diverge later. All industry is subject to a quest for productivity, the spur to this under CAPITALISM being that of profitability. Here the lack of symmetry in the employment contract becomes important. I may accept an employer's offer to pay me a specific sum for every hour I work. But this contract does not specify how hard or effectively I must work — though unspoken understandings may govern this matter. If the standard of performance expected of me is subsequently raised unilaterally by the employer I have no redress, except by pleading a breach of good faith. The employer is not likely to agree, and may point out that I am free to leave this employment to find other work. This illustrates the mainly Marxian notion of EXPLOITATION. Wage-payments never exactly equal the value added by operatives through their work; in the employer's view, wages compensate the operative for allowing the employer to make the best use he can of the operative's capacity to work during an agreed period. This need not imply that the employer possesses some satanic impulse always to push his operatives to the limits of endurance. Indeed the analytical value of the concept of exploitation is clouded by such emotive imagery: for even highly paid operatives with excellent security and working conditions can be exploited in the technical sense. A further paradox is tha employees may recognize the realities of their situation and accept the employer's attempts to raise his profits by raising efficiency, their hope being to share in the gains through productivity deals. Orthodox Marxists maintain that state ownership of industry automatically eradicates exploitation, but others insist that it must remain wherever wage payments and distinct enterprises exist (as they do in, for example, the USSR). In any dynamic socio-economic system workers as a whole can never be awarded the 'full fruits of their labours', because a proportion of total output must always be used to renew equipment, or to achieve a net addition to the stock of capital, thereby securing economic growth. It is possible to conceive of a society where decisions about such matters, and about the relative rewards allocated for differing work operations, would be decided more openly and democratically than under capitalism. Sceptics point out that intellectuals who have such visions are unsuccessful in persuading workers of their viability, and that novel forms of control — analogous to the spur of capitalist profit, or the quotas and norms of Soviet planning — would be required for the economy to function reliably.

See W. Baldamus, *Efficiency and Effort* (1961).

MR

**ego.** See PSYCHOANALYSIS.

**Eisenstadt, Shlomo N.** (1923- ). Israeli comparative sociologist. Born in Warsaw, Eisenstadt was educated at LSE and the Hebrew University in Jerusalem, where he has taught in the sociology department since 1948. A prolific writer, he has contributed to three main areas of comparative sociology. *Absorption of Immigrants* (1954), *From Generation to Generation* (1964) and *Israeli Society* (1967) addressed problems of the development of Israeli society. Influenced by both PARSONS's FUNCTIONALISM and the political sociology of WEBER, he has produced numerous studies on the MODERNIZATION process which include *Modern-*

*ization, Protest and Change* (1966), *Tradition, Change and Modernization* (1973) and *Revolution and the Transformation of Societies* (1978). His best-known work is the monumental *Political System of Empires* (1967), produced with a team of researchers at the Hebrew University, one of the landmarks of 20th-century historical sociology. While the theoretical framework of this book has suffered in the general critique of functionalism, it remains an unrivalled survey of the political sociology of the pre-industrial non-tribal world. Its central argument is that the power of imperial regimes depended on (1) their ability to generate universal 'free-floating resources', both material and cultural, relatively independent of the particularisms of locality and lineage; but (2) on the support of local lineage elites (nobility and gentry) against the masses. These are contradictory, and so empires are essentially dynamic.

See also BENDIX; FEUDALISM; PATRIMONIAL-ISM.                                                    LS

**elections.** One of several ways in which a larger group provides itself with a smaller group of leaders; alternative methods include inheritance of office, purchase of office and bestowal of office. Generally speaking, a society is thought of as DEMO-CRATIC when at least the major POLITICAL decisions are made by elected representatives. However, few societies elect all politically important people: there is usually bestowal of some political offices upon those considered to meet some relevant criterion or criteria. For example, expertise, age, sex, experience, religion or ethnic identity have been regarded as qualifications for holding particular offices, yet elections cannot be guaranteed to yield people holding these qualifications.

Elections are generally justified with one or both of two arguments: (1) participation in political life is a good thing and a value in itself; (2) without elections leaders would be controlled only remotely, by conscience or fear of violence: elections make leaders responsive to the will of the electorate. In modern liberal democratic states (2) is generally more widely regarded and was the ideological underpinning of the more or less

rapid granting of the franchise to all adults. The rate at which adults were admitted to the franchise, and what constitutes adulthood, varied widely, but today there are few countries in which adults from between 18 to 21 years and upward are not enfranchised. Many of these are, however, one-party states where voters may at most choose from a slate of candidates all drawn from the same party. Western political scientists do not generally regard these as 'genuine' elections.

However, even where competitive elections are genuine, such 'representative democracy' is far removed from 'direct democracy', rule by the people themselves. ACTIVISM is low. Around one-third of franchised persons do not even vote at national elections and two-thirds at local elections. Even voting itself is a trivial and infrequent act. Milbrath (*Political Participation*, 1965) suggests that in the USA only 7-9 per cent of the population attend a political meeting or make a voluntary contribution to a party, while only 1-3 per cent ever stand for any office themselves. UK estimates would not be dissimilar. Theoretical interpretations of this vary. One school interprets low popular participation as satisfaction that current political representatives act broadly in the people's interests. Others argue that participation is low because people take a realistic view of their own very limited power capacities in an unequal society. In this view, inequalities in the electoral process are caused by broader power inequalities.

Broadly, studies have concentrated on (1) the factors which lie behind a personal, class, or group voting preference; (2) the significance for systemic stability of regular elections; (3) the relationship, if any, between election outcomes and trade cycles, weather, size of constituency, type of electioneering and party system etc.

Early studies of elections in the USA and Britain revealed that VOTERS were greatly less rationally calculating, informed and interested in politics than had been suggested by politicians and theorists who demanded a popular franchise; see Campbell, Gurin and Miller, *The Voter Decides* (1954); Benney, Gray and Pear, *How People Vote* (1956). Factors such as parental vote, class location, education and age were seen to account for voting behaviour. Later work has modified these findings, especially comparatively: for instance, religion and regional affiliations, generational shifts and increasingly volatile electorates are important features of electoral behaviour in Europe and the UK; see for example Butler and Stokes, *Political Change in Britain* (1971); I. Crewe and B. Sarlvik, *Decade of De-Alignment* (1983).

The older, rather naive picture of the calculating voter has gone permanently. Today debate is over questions like would it be rational to calculate the odds against affecting electoral outcomes; is the working-class person who votes Conservative behaving oddly; are male and female voters likely to respond to different electoral cues? Additionally, interest centres upon processes of class socialization which are thought to affect voting behaviour. Current interest is shown in systemic stability as affected by elections, conceptualized as one of the transmission belts which carry to leaders the wishes and preferences of people.

Traditionally, discussion revolved around whether an elected goverment should regard itself as the implementer of the popular will or the guardian of the nation's long-term interest — that is, responsive or responsible government. Current debate is about the role of electoral politics in causing governments in most industrial societies to become 'overloaded' with both electoral promises and executive powers. In this view overload results from competitive electoral bidding by rival parties and the increasing power of the elected government to carry them out. Thus democratic societies have to be protected from majorities (usually defined as transient) by, for example, Bills of Rights, powerful second chambers, revived local government, and a withdrawal of the state from large sectors of the economy. Opponents claim that the broad distribution of wealth in industrial democracies has hardly changed except during major wars, and that elections are only one factor amongst others in causing the interventionist state, others being pressure from industry and agriculture for support, the growth of the welfare state, development of pressure groups, institutionalization of an interventionist bureaucracy and the imperatives of international economic competition (see CORPORATISM).    RD

**Elias, Norbert** (1897- ). German/British sociologist. After studying at Breslau and Heidelberg, Elias was MANNHEIM's assistant at Frankfurt until the Nazis took power. He emigrated first to Paris, then to Britain, where after the war he taught at Leicester University. In the 1970s he returned to live mainly in Germany and Holland, where he was recognized as a major intellectual figure and leader of the 'figurational' school of sociology. His major works, published or republished in German in the late 1960s and 1970s, slowly became available in English. In *The Civilising Process* (2 vols, 1939; English edn. 1978 and 1981) he presents a detailed theory of state-formation in Western Europe and shows how over the centuries long-term processes of development in social structure brought about changes in individual personality structure. People acquired a greater capacity for self-control, and their behaviour became more 'civilized'. The theory has served as a PARADIGM for research by others. Elias himself has worked out its implications in many essays, especially in the sociology of knowledge and science. His other books include *The Established and the Outsiders* (1965), *Die Höfische Gesellschaft* (1969) and *What is Sociology?* (1978).

SJM

**elitism.** The rule of the many by the few. Three different types of elitism can be distinguished, one normative and two empirical.

(1) Normative arguments are as old as social theory itself. The control of society's affairs ought to be the preserve of a special group of individuals, selected according to their distinctive qualities, to be accorded privileges commensurate with or necessary to their special function. Theories differ on the precise character of the qualities necessary for the elite (birth, intelligence, special knowledge, energy etc) and the social values their performance guarantees (order, progress, economic or military supremacy etc). All such theories agree that if the elite are not accorded sufficient power and privilege, social evil will result. It is in the interest of the masses themselves to accept their subordinate position, though they may on occasion aspire for their children to enter the elite under carefully monitored conditions. Elit-

ism in this sense constitutes the most basic and recurrent form of the legitimation of power (see LEGITIMACY).

(2) 'Elite theory', an empirical, and rather cynical, argument developed in the second half of the 19th century in reaction to the spread of DEMOCRACY. It was sociological in form. Writers like MOSCA and PARETO argued that elites were not so much advantageous as inevitable, democracy not so much undesirable as impossible. This was a 'scientific' law. It had two main sub-types:

(a) Psychological: elite power stems from particular psychological qualities that fit their members for leadership roles. For Pareto, elites are composed of two psychological types — 'foxes' (skilful, manipulative, inventive) and 'lions' (strong, incorruptible, conservative). The composition of elites varies according to a cyclical pattern (the 'circulation of elites') with 'lions' being recruited in increasing numbers by the 'foxes' to the point when the 'lions' predominate, causing the elite to become rigid, exclusive and conservative. At this point a counter-elite of 'foxes' is formed, which displaces the 'lion'-dominated elite, and thus the cycle begins afresh. Such processes are often referred to as the 'circulation of elites': elites are continually renewed by vigorous elements from below.

(b) Organizational: elite power stems from superior organization and the possession of functional skills by certain members of society. For Mosca, the organized few can rule over the unorganized masses. This explains the emergence of such diverse elites as priestly control over the Nile waters in ancient Egypt and the bourgeois control over the means of production in industrial societies. For MICHELS, the key factor is the emergency of BUREAUCRACY, which he sees as a necessary concomitant of modern complex organizations; and bureaucracies, he argues, are inherently oligarchic and exclusive because only they can manage the organizational needs of a society. In both sub-types, the advent of democracy did not bring power to the masses, but represented merely the rise of a new kind of elite and a new method for selecting its membership. Marxism also was the ideology of a new elite rising to power on the backs of the proletariat.

(3) Pluralist theory (see also PLURALISM). This more recent empirical theory seeks to reconcile the existence of elites with the norms of democracy. Schumpeter for example argues that organizationally determined elites emerge but are fragmented and set in competitive relationships by the need for democratic legitimation and self-defence. Thus democracy can be 'rescued' if it is redefined as a system of free competition between rival elites for popular endorsement.

This diversity of arguments reflects the rather chequered history of elite theories and the inability of any single one to command widespread acceptance. However, there are loose connections between them. One reason advanced for the inevitability of elites is their social necessity, and if they are inevitable, the question of their quality becomes of crucial social concern. The first two types of argument share a simplistic distinction between the 'elite' and the rest of society, a derisory view of the 'masses', an emphasis on conspiracy, and confusion as to whether the supposedly elite capacities are innate or socially acquired. The third is often special pleading for existing liberal-democratic regimes.

DB, JP

**embourgeoisement.** The process of incorporation into the BOURGEOISIE of elements of other classes, the case most discussed being that of affluent workers. Similarly, proletarianization is the process of incorporation into the WORKING CLASS of elements of other classes, the most discussed case being that of lower white-collar employees (see MIDDLE CLASS; PETITE BOURGEOISIE).

The embourgeoisement thesis was discussed by Sombart and MICHELS in Germany early this century, and was taken up, especially in Britain, in the late 1950s and the 1960s, usually by journalists and political commentators rather than sociologists. It was tested by Goldthorpe, Lockwood, Bechhofer and Platt in their study of Luton factories, *The Affluent Worker* (1968-9). They identified a normative convergence between affluent workers and white-collar employees, particularly convergence on an instrumental orientation to unions; but concluded that the affluent workers pursued neither a traditional working-class nor a middle-class way of life but rather that of a new type of privatized worker.

Students of working-class embourgeoisement and white-collar proletarianization inquire whether a section of one class is merging into a section of another. They frequently conclude that no such merger is taking place; instead, the men and women concerned constitute something new, either within the working or middle class or between them. Such class fractions and intermediate classes generate the appearance of a fragmentary class structure. Whether the appearance is deceptive or anything new is much disputed.

See CAPITALISM; CLASS: *Neo-Marxist theories*; WORKING CLASS.

CGAB

**emergence.** This term has two crucial and associated meanings in sociology.

(1) Social institutions, once created, have distinctive 'emergent' properties which mean that their subsequent behaviour cannot be given a REDUCTIONIST explanation in terms of their original causes (see e.g. STATE). Associated particularly with DURKHEIM'S attack on UTILITARIANISM and an essential part of sociology's attack upon biological and individualistic theories of society (e.g. SOCIOBIOLOGY, models of 'economic, rational man' etc) which CAPITALISM seems continuously to spawn. This view may reify SOCIAL STRUCTURE, and hence a second view has developed, especially in SYMBOLIC INTERACTONISM.

(2) Social life is a creative, precarious, open-ended process, rather than a stable, determined structure. In examining biographies, encounters or total societies, the idea highlights the view that humans have to work at, negotiate or construct what is taking place and outcomes can never be wholly known in advance: linear patterns of order may be imposed retrospectively and stable lines of activity may be agreed upon, but at any present moment they are always in a process of 'becoming'. This view, forcefully presented in the work of Herbert Blumer and in Anselm Strauss's *Mirrors and Masks,* is not reductionist. It concerns not timeless individuals, but actors involved in social processes.

The central theoretical dilemma of modern sociology is to steer a way between or among these two views of emergence. Either 'social facts' or 'social processes', or some combination of the two, constitutes the subject-matter of sociology.

MM, KP

**empiricism.** Philosophy which stresses the importance of experience for our knowledge, as against *a priori* categories or logical reasoning. Logical POSITIVISM or logical empiricism, the most influential 20th-century variant, holds that statements must be grounded either in logical relations between propositions or in (actual or possible) experience of the states of affairs to which they refer. Thus a statement which appears to be about a matter of fact but cannot be VERIFIED by experience is meaningless. See HOBBES; HUME; LOCKE.

In social science, the term 'empiricist' is extended to cover authors and texts committed (or suspected of being committed) to this philosophy. It is often used in a pejorative sense to connote the absence of theoretical reflection, an excessively narrow focus on a specific problem etc. 'Empirical research' is often used to distinguish 'field' research based on first-hand information from that based on written records.

See Peter Halfpenny, *Positivism and Sociology* (1982).

WO

**encapsulation** [incapsulation]. A process whereby a minority ETHNIC GROUP isolates itself within a larger society in order to maintain its cultural distinctiveness (compare SECT).

MPB

**endogamy** [endogamous]. The practice of seeking MARRIAGE partners within the group. Endogamy may entail a preference to marry within a particular LINEAGE or, more broadly, can apply to social sanctions that prevent or deter marriage between members of different CASTES or ETHNIC GROUPS.

See also EXOGAMY; INCEST.

JE

**Engels, Friedrich** (1820-95). Mainly remembered as the life-long friend and collaborator of MARX, Engels made notable personal contributions in a great variety of fields. A skilled journalist, social historian, military specialist and businessman, Engels supported Marx both financially and intellectually until the latter's death in 1883. Thereafter, by his work on the two un-completed volumes of *Capital*, by his systematization and popularization of 'historical materialism', and his political work with the German Social Democratic Party, it was to a great extent Engels who assured both the fact and the form of the widespread dissemination of Marxism.

Born in Barmen in the German Rhine-land, Engels was the son of a textile manu-facturer with interests in both Barmen and Manchester. His mother came from a family of Dutch schoolteachers. Despite his literary interests, he was set to work in the family firm at an early age, and it was during his commercial training that he published essays on social issues, and came into contact with the group of Left Hegelians with which Marx was also associated. From 1844, they became firm friends and Engels's work on political economy at this time had a decisive influence on the future development of Marx's thought.

In 1845, Engels published *The Condition of the Working-Class in England*, which drew vividly on his personal observations of conditions in Manchester. Between 1845 and 1846, he and Marx collaborated on *The German Ideology* (which remained un-published during their lifetimes), in which they criticized the ideas of their former Young Hegelian colleagues, and established the foundations of their mature world-view. In 1848 they jointly published *The Com-munist Manifesto* (Engels preparing the first draft). After the failure of the con-tinental revolutions they fled to exile in England. In 1850 Engels returned to the family firm in Manchester, where he remained for the next 20 years, helping Marx both financially and by writing articles under Marx's name for the *New York Daily Tribune*.

After his retirement from business and return to London in 1870, Engels devoted himself to the philosophical and historical studies which were his chief contribution to Marxist theory and which before 1914 had a greater influence amongst Marxists than the works of Marx himself. Engels's *Anti-Dühring* (1878), especially the excerpt published separately in 1880 as *Socialism: Utopian and Scientific*, became the popular textbook of Marxism. In this work, and in *Ludwig Feuerbach and the end of Classical German Philosophy* (1888), Engels produced a systematization of historical materialism. He revived Hegelian 'laws' of dialectical change (see HEGEL), and assimilated Marxism to the then-prevailing POSITIVISM and Darwinian EVOLUTIONISM. This 'scientistic' understanding of Marxism was subsequently transformed into official Soviet dogma. Since the 1920s, dissenting Marxists have blamed Engels for an over-deterministic and over-scientific view of the Marxist theory of historical change. Engels was greatly interested in the natural sciences, and in the posthumously published *Dia-lectics of Nature* (1925), he extended the laws of dialectical change to the natural sciences. This has never commanded much support outside Soviet orthodoxy.

Engels's evolutionism is also visible in his famous *Origins of the Family, Private Property and the State* (1884). He postulated a development of marriage forms through different stages of human development, from savagery, through barbarism, to civilization. Matriarchal forms enjoyed chronological priority, men being relatively unimportant prior to the advent of agri-culture. Although still regarded as an important early socialist feminist text, it is now generally agreed that Engels relied heavily on the dubious historico-anthropo-logical speculations of Lewis Morgan's *Ancient Society* (1877).

During the last decade of his life, Engels continued his work on Marx's unpublished manuscripts. The second volume of *Capital* appeared in 1885, the third in 1894. He gave constant encouragement and advice to Marxists in the international labour movement, and especially in the German SPD, which adopted a thoroughgoing Marxist programme at the Erfurt Congress of 1891.

AM

**environmentalism.** A set of ideas based upon ecology; a social movement which promotes harmony with the natural environment; a 'back-to-nature' philosophy. Ecological or scientific environmentalism stresses the importance of sustaining a viable physical or biological environment. Humanistic environmentalism stresses the incompatibility of modern scientific and technological developments with humanistic principles.

See AGRARIANISM; TECHNOLOGICAL SOCIETY.

HN

**epidemiology.** The study of the distribution of clinically defined disease within and across populations. The variables of GENDER, CLASS, occupation, RACE and ETHNICITY are searched for clues of the organic disease mechanisms which are the primary focus of the MEDICAL MODEL, from which it takes its frameworks of analysis, definitions of problems and modes of interpretation. Epidemiology differs from the sociology of health which credits sociologically defined variables with a direct causal significance.

See also HEALTH, SOCIOLOGY OF; MEDICAL MODEL; STRESS.

NH

**epistemology.** Branch of philosophy conerned with the theory of knowledge (Greek: *episteme*). The important contrast is with ONTOLOGY, the study of the nature of things. The relative primacy of ontology and epistemology is an ongoing debate in the history of philosophy, since the nature of things presumably determines our ability to know them, while on the other hand they can exist for us only through our knowledge of them. EMPIRICISTS are generally sceptical of ontology, while HEGEL, for example, attacked epistemological attempts to guide the process of knowledge as being like wanting to swim without getting into the water. One method, whose validity is still contested, of getting from epistemology to ontology is by the use of transcendental arguments, which ask what things must be like for us to have the kind of knowledge of them that we do. It can be argued that MARX's *Capital* takes this form, asking what the nature of a capitalist economy must be

for it to appear as it does to common sense and to classical political economy.

Within epistemology, there is a traditional opposition between empiricists, who stress the role of experience in our knowledge, and RATIONALISTS, who stress the importance of *a priori* categories of thought and our processes of reasoning.

In French, *épistémologie* does not mean philosophical theories of knowledge in general, but rather the philosophy (often combined with historical and social study) of scientific knowledge.

See Roy Bhaskar, *A Realist Theory of Science* (1975).

WO

**equality, social.** There are three main types of equality. (1) Equality of opportunity. The provision of equality of access to institutions and social positions among relevant social groups, such as equality of entry to university for students of both sexes, and all class origins. (2) Equality of condition. Equality in the conditions of life for all relevant social groups, such as equality of incomes. It is impossible to maximize equality of opportunity without attending also to equality of condition. Proponents of equality of opportunity who relish the differential benefits obtained by persons of different abilities ignore the material and cultural advantages which one generation of the successful is able to transmit to the next. Inequalities of condition obstruct equality of opportunity; all do not start from the same point. (3) Equality of result or outcome. The application of different policies or processes to different social groups in order to transform inequalities at the beginning into equalities at the end. Positive discrimination in favour of women or blacks or the inner city poor in educational and occupational selection, for example, is meant to compensate for inequalities of condition which would otherwise make nonsense of equality of opportunity (see COMPENSATORY EDUCATION).

Social equality is not synonymous with classlessness. Definitions of CLASS vary, but they all allow that the elimination of class does not of itself remove all social inequalities.

See FUNCTIONAL THEORIES OF STRATIFICA-
TION; SOCIAL MOBILITY; STATUS COMPOSI-
TION.

CGAB

**error.** All sociological data are subject to
error, an expression of imperfection and of
incompleteness in description. Errors may
be either SAMPLING errors, arising from the
fact that a sample is drawn from a population, or non-sampling errors arising from
other sources. Sampling errors are calculable
if random sampling is used, but non-
sampling errors are not calculable and can
only be reduced by precautions at all stages
of the research process. Total error is a
function of both, and cannot be substantially
reduced unless both types are controlled.

There are various methods of controlling
non-sampling errors. Grosser forms of bias
— for example, in asking leading questions or
allowing interviewers to influence the results
of surveys — can be controlled by careful
question design and interviewer training.
Response errors, arising from the respondent's poor memory, misunderstanding or
failure to give the correct answer for other
reasons, can be a major source of difficulty,
particularly in investigating complex or
sensitive subjects. Record checks, consistency checks and re-interviewing can
control and estimate the extent of response
error.

MB

**estate.** A type of social stratum (see SOCIAL
STRATIFICATION) defined in law in respect of
its composition, its political rights and duties
and its capacities and incapacities. Main
examples are the NOBILITY, clergy, burghers
or citizens, and serfs or free PEASANTS of
post-feudal Europe. Estates can be understood 'economically' in terms of their respective contributions to a broad division of
labour in society, socially in terms of their
combination in a system of social stratification and, above all, politically in terms of
their rights of both self-government and
assembly for treaty with the territorial ruler.
Thus estates are communities, collectivities
with a consciousness of their own, organized
for a purpose. Though they have figured in
varying degrees throughout European history from the Roman Empire to the 19th
century, their *locus classicus* is not feudal

societies (precisely because they are COMMU-
NITIES whereas feudal social relations depend
primarily on personal bonds of vassalage; see
FEUDALISM) but post-feudal society, especially the *Ständestaat*, the 'estate-state'
which succeeded the feudal state over most
of continental Europe.

As corporate groups with legal rights of
self-government, estates or estate-like
(*ständisch*) groups were numerous. As
estates of the realm (constituents of a
corporate state) they were few. Thus in early
17th-century Prussia before the rise of the
ABSOLUTISM of the Hohenzollern dynasty,
there were three estates, the nobility
(Junkers), the burghers (and other
permanent residents of towns) and the serfs.
The first two assembled at intervals in Diets to
deliberate on those matters about which the
local princeling was obliged to consult them
(foreign and fiscal policy, the raising of
armies etc) because they constituted the sole
means of judicial, public and fiscal
administration.

In France until 1614 — and then finally in
1789 at the beginning of the Revolution —
the three estates of clergy, nobility and
burghers met in the States-General. This is
also the name of the Dutch parliament to this
day. The British Houses of Lords and
Commons also derive from estates. Such
anachronisms apart, references to estates in
advanced industrial societies are still
sometimes made where institutions display
some of the characteristics of a state within a
state (e.g. the military with its regulations
and courts martial and the church with its
canon law), or where their rights of self-
government, whether from fear or envy,
attract the complaint that they have become
a law unto themselves (e.g. universities or
established PROFESSIONS like medicine). See
STATUS.

CGAB

**estimation.** The statistical inference of likely
population values from sample data.
Provided random SAMPLING has been used,
probability theory may be used to make
inferences from the sample to the population
from which it was drawn. This is often useful
in descriptive SOCIAL SURVEY research,
where one wants to establish population
values on the basis of sample data.

Estimation indicates the degree of confidence which one can attach to particular values. Point estimates provide a single figure, based on the sample mean. Interval estimates (which are preferable) indicate the range of values around the sample mean within which the true population mean may lie, at a given level of probability (e.g. 95%, 90%). This is called a confidence interval. In choosing the probability level, there is a trade-off between precision and certainty; both cannot be maximized.

MB

**ethnic colony.** A group or community of persons of common ETHNICITY who have settled in another country but take many of their cultural standards from their country of origin and may plan to return there. This is close to the original significance of the word 'colony' which has been overlaid in the 20th century by its association with IMPERIALISM to indicate colonialism.

MPB

**ethnicity, ethnic group.** The first recorded use of the word 'ethnicity', the character or quality of an ethnic group, dates from 1953. It generalizes one of the elements in the family of words deriving from the Greek *ethnos*, a people. In anthropology, 'ethnic group' is sometimes used to designate a culturally distinctive, autonomous group, but the more general application is to a distinct CATEGORY of the population also sharing common cultural features and social institutions as a group. An ethnic group often overlaps with a political group and it may be thought racially distinct. Nationalist movements have often appealed to ethnic sentiment and used evidence of ethnic distinctiveness as a justification for political claims. In Soviet ethnography, the word ethnos is in current use, as is ethnogenesis — the process whereby a sense of people-hood is generated. There is much concern with the classification of different kinds of ethnic community. Ethnic communities, having often been physically as well as culturally distinctive, used frequently to be referred to as races, suggesting that their cultural attributes were determined by their physical ones. It was partly to avoid this error that,

since the 1930s, the designation ethnic group has been more generally employed, though in recent times this usage has been found to have additional advantages (see RACE RELATIONS).

Much of the sociological interest in ethnicity has derived from the study of processes associated with immigration and the persistence of cultural distinctiveness among immigrant ethnic groups; it has also been reinforced by demands for political autonomy made by representatives of ethnic minorities. Initially, sociologists expected immigrant ethnic groups to adopt the culture of the majority society (see PARK; HANSEN'S LAW) but in circumstances such as those of the Northeastern USA ethnic groups became interest groups as well. A political party putting forward three candidates for election might seek to have one Irish, one Italian and one Jewish name on its list, and ethnicity became a basis for political organization. Similar factors, but on a larger scale, have seemed to underlie conflicts between English- and French-speaking Canadians, Dutch- and French-speaking Belgians, Protestants and Catholics in Northern Ireland, Greeks and Turks in Cyprus, Malays and Chinese in Malaysia, and so on. Some social scientists conclude that ethnicity is a primordial affinity, part of a person's basic group identity that asserts itself whenever social or political organization runs counter to the ways in which people have been programmed. Others infer that ethnic sentiment is a variable and that its intensity and significance is determined by circumstance. In some situations people choose to seek their ends by organizing on an ethnic basis, in others on a class basis; in yet others religious organization may serve similar functions. In some societies, Nigeria for example, everyone is expected to have an ethnic identity and ethnic organization is regarded as legitimate in many areas of social life; in other countries the population is ethnically homogeneous and less inclined to regard the ethnic distinctiveness of immigrants as relevant to the conduct expected of people in public life.

MPB

**ethnic relations.** See RACE RELATIONS.

**ethnocentrism.** The tendency to evaluate matters by reference to the values shared in the subject's own ethnic group as if that group were the centre of everything. This concept was borrowed, without acknowledgement, by SUMNER from GUMPLOWICZ.

See also AUTHORITARIAN PERSONALITY.

MPB

**ethnomethodology.** Coined by GARFINKEL to refer to ideas arrived at in the course of a study of jurors. He had found that the jurors, in order to make 'rational' and 'reasonable' decisions, referred to their knowledge of the way in which society worked and to the 'methods' or procedures by which they had obtained that knowledge. Thus they were concerned with being legal while recognizing that they were not lawyers; they were dealing with matters of motivation while not being psychologists, and so on. In addition, while they were doing this they were constructing the setting in which they deliberated as a 'jury'. 'The deliberations-of-a-jury' were produced by the persons in that setting and were derived from nowhere else.

These ideas were then extended to cover all occasions and settings. Any co-ordinated interaction is taken as being an 'achievement' or 'accomplishment' of the parties to that interaction, by means of whatever knowledge and procedures they use to represent to each other the 'rational', 'coherent' and 'planful' nature of the interaction. Ethnomethodology is the study of the 'folk methods' by which people come to understand and produce the features of co-ordinated interaction and social organization. However, ethnomethodology does not stand in contrast with some putative 'scientific' knowledge about such matters. For such a 'science of society' is itself at pains to distinguish fact from fancy and demonstrate its rational, coherent and planful nature. It has to rely on 'what everybody knows' in order to demonstrate the 'reasoned' and reasonable nature of its procedures and findings. Thus sociology is yet another area for study, no different from the study of the practices of witchcraft, water divination and alchemy, or of physics, chemistry and cell biology.

The similarity between sociology and, say, alchemy does not mean that sociology is merely another form of alchemy. But in any practical enquiry, be it the interviewing of a person to discover his or her attitudes towards family planning, or the following of a recipe to produce gold by chemistry, certain features are always encountered. These features relate to the 'indexical' properties of language, that is, the 'sense', 'meaning', or 'truth value' of an utterance, rule, description, instruction etc, which varies across time, place and personnel. The instruction might be 'heat for 15 minutes', but if the materials had achieved the 'right consistency' after five minutes this would not be 'reasonable'. Similarly, there are expressions 'whose sense cannot be decided by an auditor without his necessarily knowing or assuming something about the biography and purposes of the user of the expression, the circumstances of the utterance, the previous course of discourse, or the particular relationship of actual or potential interaction that exists between the auditor and the user' (Garfinkel and Sachs). Thus, on all occasions of enquiry, be it following a recipe or conducting an experiment, people have a concern with 'remedying' indexicals in order to make sense in the here and now. For ethnomethodology, this constitutes the basis of its phenomena.

However, most ethnomethodologists do not write abstract theory. First, they analyse the unfolding and self-revealing nature of a social setting and the course of actions which comprise it. Second, they provide descriptions of those courses of action to reveal the structures of interaction. Thus there have been studies of queueing, of court rooms, official records and their various uses, and of the structure of talk. As one would expect, all of these studies differ not only in the content and structure revealed but also in the manner in which the enquiry was conducted.

There is no single ethnomethodological method. Ethnomethodology is not a theory with a consistent coherent set of interrelated concepts, and its products in terms of research vary amongst its practitioners and amongst the topics studied. For instance, Aaron Cicourel, unlike other ethnomethodologists, attempts to match the scientific observer's view of the world with that of the actor, through a process of indefinite TRIANGULATION. To date the most productive area studied by people with ethnomethodological concerns has been CONVERSATION ANALYSIS.

DBn

Most sociologists accept to some degree the insights of ethnomethodology derived from PHENOMENOLOGY. They also accept that the 'small change' of everyday life may reveal much about underlying social processes. But they might reject the claim that society consists merely of the sum of the creative achievements of individuals in the present. They argue that the sociological tradition has established a large number of general processes — socialization, ROLE, INSTITU-TIONALIZATION etc — by which actors confront macro-social and historical structures which have endured and are relatively obdurate. Individuals act as members of a GENDER, of CLASSES, NATIONS, RELIGIONS, age-cohorts etc. Moreover, most socio-logists also explain creativity and change in terms that are largely structural and historical (e.g. ANOMIE, DEVIANCE, CLASS conflict, REVOLUTION etc). Many processes of both stability and change are observable in 'trivial' everyday experience, but many are quite hidden, deducible only by adding a general understanding of macro-structures (e.g. Adam SMITH's 'invisible hand'). Many others result from the everyday understand-ing of a minority, but because of their power are imposed from outside on the understand-ings of the majority: for example, the onset of war or unemployment. It is not clear whether ethnomethodologists are aiming only at unearthing universals of human experience. If so, these are likely to be limited. How can they go on to examine social varia-tions without accepting social-structural concepts like those mentioned above? To these criticisms ethnomethodologists have responded indirectly, with analogies drawn from other disciplines and with a research programme into more and more minute details (see CONVERSATION ANALYSIS). Sociology awaits their discovery of the 'structure of the social cell' referred to in that entry with considerable scepticism.

MM

**evaluation research.** A type of ACTION RESEARCH in which applied research at-tempts to measure the effects of some oper-ating programme or policy. It may attempt to measure the effectiveness of a total pro-gramme, or of some specific part of a pro-gramme. It does so against a standard of the desirable and undesirable consequences of an action that has been taken in order to advance some goal that society values. Most highly developed in the USA, it employs vigorous scientific RESEARCH DESIGNS, often of an EXPERIMENTAL kind.

See L. Saxe and M. Fine, *Social Experiments: Methods for Design and Evaluation* (1981).

MB

**Evans-Pritchard, Sir Edward Evan** (1902-73). British anthropologist. Born in Sussex, the son of a clergyman, his background and later conversion to Catholicism (1940) are often cited as influencing his emphasis on religion as central to social experience. He studied modern history at Oxford, taking his BA in 1924, and retained an interest in history which led him to stress the place of anthropology in the humanities rather than the sciences, in contrast to the empiricist, functionalist traditions associated especially with RADCLIFFE-BROWN. He studied anthropology under MALINOWSKI at the LSE, and taught there from 1926 to 1936. His extensive fieldwork in Africa included studies of the Azande of the Southern Sudan, the Nuer, the Amak and the Luo in the 1930s, as well as collecting data among the Sanusi of Cyrenaica in Libya. He was Profes-sor of Sociology at the Fuad I University, Cairo (1932-4) and Research Lecturer in African societies at Oxford (1935-40). In 1945 he taught briefly at Cambridge until he succeeded Radcliffe-Brown as Professor of Social Anthropology at Oxford, where he remained until his retirement in 1970. He was knighted in 1971.

Evans-Pritchard was engaged in debates regarding political systems and kinship with FORTES at the LSE in the 1930s, but the main focus of his work was RELIGION, MAGIC and oral tradition. He emphasized the internal logic of systems of magic and religion, particularly in studies of the Azande and the Nuer. His publications include a wide variety of ethnographic data as well as theoretical contributions. He also disseminated social anthropological ideas in the mass media, principally through radio lectures. Major works: *Witchcraft, Oracles and Magic among the Azande* (1937); *The Nuer* (1940); with M. Fortes (eds.), *African Political Systems* (1940); *Kinship and Marriage among the Nuer* (1951); *Essays on Social Anthropology* (1964); *The Position of Women in Primitive Society and Other Essays* (1965); *The Azande* (1971); *Man and Woman among the Azande* (1974).

JE

**evolutionary theories of religion.** A number of the major theories of RELIGION have been evolutionary in character, that is, they argue that religion began at some point in time and then underwent a process of change involving a series of stages. Different societies have arrived at different stages. DURKHEIM argued that the least developed form of society was likely to display the least developed form of religion — that is, that form most closely approximating to its original state. The prominence of EVOLUTIONISM in late 19th-century thought led many to view religion in these terms. While most theorists argued that the evolution of religion had taken a progressive form, a few argued that it had degenerated. Wilhelm Schmidt (1868-1954) and others believed that the current state of religion to be found among many pre-literate peoples, with a multitude of gods and spirits, marked a degeneration from an earlier stage when only one god had been worshipped. The degenerationists were often missionaries who wished to rescue the benighted savage from the depths.

The majority of evolutionary theories, however, view change as progressive. They fall into two main schools of thought: the rationalist or intellectualist, and the irrationalist or emotionalist. Tylor, SPENCER, and FRAZER were the leading rationalists. They argued that religion had originated in the attempt of early people to make sense of the world in which they lived and their own biological processes: the transition from day to night, life to death; the experience of dreams and visions; the relationships of causation between events.

Tylor believed that an idea of the soul developed from an appreciation of the differences between life and death, an awakened state and one of sleep etc. Primitive man came to believe that the soul could separate from the body and, surviving after death, retained power to protect its family. Religion evolved through ancestor worship into a stage of polytheism. Deities become ranked in terms of importance. The minor gods recede and disappear, leading to the stage of monotheism.

Frazer believed mankind passes, sooner or later, through three stages of intellectual development: MAGIC, religion and science. In the magical stage man believes the world operates by lawlike means. Possession of the right formula permits him to manipulate events in the world. In time, however, the more intelligent realize that magic does not work. Man is not so powerful as he assumed, and consequently other powerful beings must lie behind events. Their favour could be gained by worship and supplication. Later, the more intelligent again realize that supplication does not produce the desired effects but discover that empirical means can do so. So gradually one form of thought dominates and replaces earlier modes, although two or more modes of thought may co-exist at any time in a society.

The emotionalist or irrationalist evolutionists do not call on the advance of human reason as the dynamic of change. Marrett, for example, saw religion as more a feeling than a theory and argued that it developed from a reaction of awe, fear, wonder, respect etc to the power of nature. Religion evolved out of belief in an impersonal power (*animatism*) which later became embodied in personalized deities. FREUD in *Future of an Illusion* offers the best-known emotionalist evolutionary account. Man, helpless against nature, endows natural forces with personality and this enables him to feel at home in the cosmos. He feels and acts toward these spiritual beings in the way he did when helpless as a child, endowing them with the characteristics of the father whom he tried to appease but looked to for protection. Belief in god is born of the projection into a cosmic setting of ambivalent feelings toward the father. As man matured Freud hoped and believed that he would learn to live without the need for this 'infantile obsessional neurosis' and rest his faith on science. Emotional maturation replaces the advance of human reason as the basis of change.

Robert Bellah (*Beyond Belief*, 1970) is one of the few modern sociological theorists to employ an evolutionary approach to the development of religion. He defines evolution as a process of increasing differentiation and complexity of organization that endows the unit in question with greater capacity to adapt to its environment and render it more autonomous of it. Bellah argues that religion passes through five stages: (1) *Primitive*, in which mythical and real world overlap closely, and no separate religious organization and roles exist. (2) *Archaic*, in which mythical beings became more objectified and external to the human world. Specialized religious roles emerge. The gap between gods and men is mediated by worship and sacrifice. (3) *Historic*, in which a dual cosmology becomes formalized, this world is conceived as inferior, and religious action is directed toward salvation in the other world. Religious collectivities become clearly differentiated, the CHURCH becomes distinct from and partially independent of the state. (4) *Early modern*, in which the hierarchy of this world and another transcendental world collapses and salvation is found in the midst of worldly activities. The individual has a direct relationship to transcendent reality, and abandons a hierarchy of religious professionals. (5) *Modern* is the most vaguely described of Bellah's five stages and is an attempt to characterize the proliferation of personal, highly individualistic forms of belief and 'religious' action in North America. Bellah regards religious evolution as related to more general social evolution, but provides no account of this relationship and hence no explanation for the transition from one stage to the next. Moreover it is not always clear — for example, for the last two stages — whether the process indicates increasing differentiation and complexity or autonomy from the environment.

RW

**evolutionism.** A characteristic common to most of the great social thinkers of the 19th century was their concern with how human societies had evolved from relatively small-scale and simple forms of organization to large-scale and complex ones. Sharing the confidence in human progress of the Victorian age, such writers as Lewis Henry Morgan, Edward B. Tylor, L.T. Hobhouse, L.F. WARD and, most notably, Herbert SPENCER, conceived of societies as having developed through a sequence of stages from 'primitive' and 'savage' to the pinnacle of their own contemporary industrial society. Such rigid and unilinear ladders of development are inadequate to understanding the immense variety of patterns of social organization which exist now or have existed in the past. Nevertheless, the analogy between social development and biological evolution remains an issue of lively interest.

The impact of DARWIN's *Origin of Species* (1859) was immense. Darwin offended religious susceptibilities by his demonstration that the innumerable species of plants and animals had not been created all at once by divine will, as depicted in Genesis, but had gradually evolved over millions of years. But he was not the first to propound a theory of evolution: it was current among writers such as Erasmus Darwin (1731-1802) and Jean-Baptiste Lamarck (1744-1829), and Spencer claimed with some justice to have anticipated several of the key ideas of the younger Darwin. Darwin acknowledged that his thinking had been decisively influenced by the theory of competition and social conflict advanced by MALTHUS. But Darwin contributed a particularly cogent account of the mechanism of biological evolution, *natural selection*. This involves an interaction between the species and its environment. For example, certain species of formerly light-coloured British moths have been observed to be becoming darker in sootier industrial areas of the country. It is an advantage in the new conditions to be darker, but they cannot become darker by an act of will. Darwin had none of the modern knowledge of genetics, but suggested that by some random, unplanned mechanism species always produce a small number of mutations. A proportion of darker moths must always have been bred; but in a light-coloured environment they would tend to stand out more than the lighter majority, be more vulnerable to the birds and in consequence breed less (and thus fail to pass on their genetically determined darkness), so the species remained predominantly light. In the new darker environment, the darker moths survive better, breed more and in time the species as a whole becomes darker. Spencer designated this 'the survival of the fittest'. Darwin suggested that where members of what was originally one species exist in separate and different environments they can evolve into two or more separate species. Over millions of years, this was how the enormous number of extant and extinct plant and animal species had evolved into different and increasingly complex forms.

In Darwinian natural selection changes in the environment do not cause mutations or innovations in the biological organism. The mutations arise by quite independent mechanisms, but are then selected or not selected according to their advantages or disadvantages in the particular environment. There is causal feedback (see CYBERNETICS) through the interaction of organism and environment, but genetic mutation and changes in the selection conditions are causally independent or 'uncoupled'. This contrasts to the earlier theory of evolution proposed by Lamarck, who had suggested that changes in the environment cause the organism to adapt, and that the organism is then capable of transmitting to its progeny the adaptations it has made in its lifetime. For Lamarck, the 'inheritance of acquired characteristics' was possible, and there was causal 'coupling' between changes in the environment and in the organism. Darwin denied this; though there are dissenters, his view has prevailed among biologists.

Do the origination and adoption of innovations in social evolution most resemble the Darwinian or the Lamarckian theory of biological evolution? A Darwinian view has the advantage of emphasizing the unplanned nature of social processes (see UNANTICIPATED CONSEQUENCES), and it is easy to find examples which fit the model: for example, the formal organizational structures which prove successful in industrial forms vary according to the kind of technology, product and market conditions involved. Some studies have suggested that the structures have not been carefully thought out in relation to the particular needs of each form, but hit upon largely by chance. Then market forces (the economic equivalent of environmental 'selection conditions') have ensured that those forms with the most appropriate organization have prospered and the inappropriate ones failed. But humans, unlike most lower animals and all plants, have acquired the mental equipment to think about the problems they encounter, to try out solutions, and to learn from mistakes and successes. Changes in their natural or social 'environment' are likely to provide a stimulus to conscious innovation. And with the capacity to use language and the device of written communication, the successful innovations of one generation are passed on to the next. Thus in human society something analogous to the inheritance of acquired characteristics is possible. Social changes proceed through the accumulation of CULTURE far faster than biological evolution. The biological constitution of the species *Homo sapiens* has remained unchanged since palaeolithic times, while forms of social organization have changed and evolved with increasing rapidity. Rom Harré (*Social Being*, 1979) suggests that early mankind hit upon crucial social innovations more nearly at random, but that with the growth of increasingly complex societies, the 'causal coupling' between selection conditions and innovations greatly increased. In historic societies, Lamarck provides a model more closely analogous to social development than does Darwin.

Evolutionism went out of fashion among social scientists in the early 20th century. FUNCTIONALISM represented a partial rejection of evolutionism. Anthropologists like RADCLIFFE-BROWN and MALINOWSKI rejected Tylor's notion of 'survivals': institutional patterns in tribal societies (like the famous JOKING RELATIONSHIP) which did not seem to make much sense to the observer had often been interpreted as irrational survivals from earlier stages of social evolution. Functionalists wished to interpret them in terms of their function or contribution to the society as it currently existed. But functionalists remained fundamentally evolutionist in their outlook, because the doctrine that institutions could always be understood in terms of their contribution to current social structure (the doctrine of 'universal functionalism') implies that any institution which exists has been 'selected' as an appropriate adaptation to its wider structural context.

A revival of interest in evolutionary theory among social scientists became evident in the 1960s and 1970s, largely as a consequence of renewed debates on the subject among biologists and revived interest in problems of long-term social development among sociologists themselves.

SJM

The original theories of the social evolutionists still also survive: for example in the impact of COMTE's views on the development of the human mind on our conceptions of the history of the sciences; in the notion of differentiation elaborated by SPENCER and developed as an important COMPARATIVE METHOD by contemporary evolutionary functionalists such as PARSONS; and in the useful distinction of the anthropologists Sahlins and Service (*Evolution and Culture*, 1960) between the general evolution of whole cultures and the specific evolution of particular forms within these.

See also NEO-EVOLUTIONISM.

LS

**exchange theories.** Sociologists view a wide variety of non-economic relationships as exchange relationships. This is done in three main ways: extending the economic analysis to cover a wider range of activities; using a mixture of BEHAVIOURAL psychology and economics; and viewing exchanges as expressions of underlying social relationships. The first two approaches focus on the individual, the third on the collective.

The high status of economics led Blau (*Exchange and Power in Social Life*, 1964) to analyse almost all human relationships as exchanges. Though people cannot negotiate about love, friendship or esteem without transforming them, Blau argues that they can be analysed as if they are exchanges of goods and services. People's choices in the MARRIAGE market result in ending up with somebody who has roughly the same quantity of

social assets as they possess themselves. Power is seen as the result of a situation in which A has something that B values highly and in which B has nothing A wants. To get A to enter into a relationship where B is getting from A what B wants, B must agree to give A power. Although seeing people behaving as if they calculate the benefits of their actions does provide some insights into human activity, exchange theory plays down the effects of people's pasts and discounts history.

Homans (*Social Behaviour: Its Elementary Forms*, 1961) presents people as providing each other with rewards which have costs to them but that also elicit behaviour that they find rewarding. Viewing people as exchanging rewards provides the basis of an attempt to combine behavioural psychology with economics. The attempt is unsuccessful, for behavioural psychology explains people's present actions in terms of the past pattern of reinforcement, while economics explains people's present actions in terms of future expected benefits.

LÉVI-STRAUSS (*Elementary Structure of Kinship*, 1947) sees exchanges as expressing already formed social relationships. Instead of seeing exchanges leading to the formation of relationships, he sees social relationships being expressed and cemented by exchanges. His primary concern is the exchange of women as brides among several primitive groups. This generalized exchange involves univocal RECIPROCITY, reciprocation involving at least three people where each person does not benefit the other directly. Generalized exchange as opposed to restricted exchange (two person) with univocal reciprocity precludes direct negotiation and thus is possible only if social bonds have already been formed. While the calculative element that tends to enter into exchanges may undermine social cohesion, exchanges may also be expressions of social cohesion.

KM

**existentialism.** A broad philosophical movement stressing individual existence and resulting problems of freedom, choice, decision and 'authenticity'. Man is what he makes himself on the basis of (ideally) autonomous choices; to abdicate or ignore this duty to choose is to live inauthentically or in 'bad faith'. Existentialism is generally held to originate with Søran Kierkegaard (1813-55) and NIETZSCHE and to include at least Karl Jaspers (1883-1969), Gabriel Marcel (1889-1973), HEIDEGGER, SARTRE and MERLEAU-PONTY. Heidegger has been influential in Germany and, more indirectly, in France, where existentialism enjoyed considerable popular success in the 20 years after World War II.

WO

**exogamy** [exogamous]. The practice of seeking MARRIAGE partners outside the social group, defined by rules stating the categories of suitable marriage partners. Exogamy arises from the need to form alliances through exchange of women between groups, and is particularly associated with exchange of sisters between men of opposing subsections of a society. In such cases it is also related to INCEST rules and prohibitions. However, the term may be more loosely applied to denote marriage ouside a group, LINEAGE, CASTE, RACE or SOCIETY.

See also ENDOGAMY.

JE

**experiment.** A type of RESEARCH DESIGN which attempts to maximize control over the relationship between VARIABLES being investigated. Classically, the subjects of scientific research are randomly assigned to two different experimental and control groups, both of which are observed. Then the experimental group is exposed to the assumed causal factor (independent variable), the control group is not, and the two groups are observed again to find out the difference which the causal factor made (if any). In this way, three conditions for inferring CAUSE are satisfied: (1) ASSOCIATION between two or more variables is observed; (2) the time-order of the effect of the independent variable is controlled; (3) the effects of other confounding variables are eliminated by random assignment to the experimental or control groups.

Experimental designs are more common in social psychology and in applied policy research than in sociology, due to serious theoretical, practical and ethical problems concerning the manipulation of human behaviour. Many social variables (e.g. social CLASS, occupation, RACE) are not manipulable; even if manipulation is possible, random assignment of individuals to experimental or control groups for research is practically and ethically objectionable in many cases (e.g. to receive different types of education; different types of custodial treatment).

*Laboratory experiments* are most characteristic of psychology. Phenomena are studied in an artificial environment created by and under the control of the investigator. Control over the variables examined is greater, but the unnatural environment may influence the behaviour of subjects. *Field experiments*, such as the New Jersey Negative Income Tax experiment, are carried out in real life situations where experimental and control groups can be formed and only one group exposed to a certain stimulus. Control over the research situation is less, but the environment is not an artificial one. *Natural experiments* make use of events occurring in the world to make a comparative study of two or more groups, one of which has been exposed to an independent stimulus while the other(s) have not.

*Quasi-experiments*, common in policy research, resemble true experiments except that random assignment to experimental and control groups is not possible. Comparisons between groups therefore may be affected by other factors, the effects of which are controlled statistically. Given the difficulties which there are in carrying out the true experiments in social science, this type of research is often more feasible, as D.T. Campbell has shown.

A major problem of all social science experimentation is the realism of the experimental situation, and the effects which being part of an experimental research situation may have on the subjects of it. In science this is well-recognized and medical experiments, for instance, make use of placebos and double-blind procedures to minimize it. In many social science experiments such procedures are not feasible; experimenter effect (an important type of ERROR) may then come into play and confound the results. Despite these difficulties, the experiment remains important, both as the most powerful type of research design available, and as a model for the logic of EX-PLANATION in social science, a logic followed by other types of research (e.g. SOCIAL SURVEY) even when the design cannot be experimental.

See D.T. Campbell and J.C. Stanley, *Experimental and Quasi-Experimental Designs for Research* (1963).

MB

**explanation.** To explain something is to show how or why it happened. EMPIRICIST philosophers in recent decades have argued that this is done by subsuming the event to be explained (sometimes called the explanandum) under a general LAW to the effect that events of this kind always occur, given a set of initial conditions which obtain in the case to be explained. REALIST philosophers of science argue that this is merely a redescription of the explanandum; a proper explanation is one which isolates (e.g. by experimentation) the structures and mechanisms which produced it. The empiricist 'covering law' account, now dominant for some time, creates problems for historical explanation, since it is difficult to specify the initial conditions in such a way that the covering law is not either false or trivial. If, for example, we wish to explain why King Charles I's head was cut off, we cannot say that all kings have their heads cut off, nor that anyone who acted just like Charles I in identical circumstances would have his head cut off. A realist, by contrast, would probably argue that the execution was the product of a set of CAUSAL tendencies — some common to revolutions in general, some peculiar to the circumstances of the English Civil War — which together made it likely that events would take the form they did. A further problem is whether the intentions, purposes and 'reasons for acting' of those concerned should be treated as causes, or whether they involve some other notion of TELEOLOGICAL explanation which one might prefer to call understanding (*Verstehen*). Realist philosophers differ on this point.

Explanation is often distinguished from description, but this is problematic. As we have seen, the 'covering law' account looks like a re-description of the explanandum, while on the other hand it may be argued that an informative description, for instance of a piece of behaviour as a religious ritual, is at least a partial explanation of it. Descriptions of this kind, sometimes called 'thick descriptions', are relevant both to the work of sociologists and anthropologists and to narrative explanations in history. (See also CAUSE, TELEOLOGY, VERSTEHEN.)

See C.G. Hempel, *Aspects of Scientific Explanation* (1965); W.G. Runciman, 'Describing', *Mind*, 1972; C. Geertz, *The Interpretation of Cultures* (1965).

WO

**exploitation.** In sociology, generally used in an economic sense: the taking of economic value from direct producers without adequately rewarding them. For MARX only labour, by definition, produces value. Where labourers do not own or control the means of production, they will always receive less value (in wages etc) than they produce, and so be exploited. In Marx's economics, the level of payment is sometimes stated to be that necessary to keep the worker alive, productive and reproductive. Thus the rate of exploitation is in principle measurable: the difference between the level of payment made and the value added by the worker's labour. In practice, however, the latter is almost impossible to calculate. Most sociologists use the term less widely but more evaluatively to refer to an unusual degree of worker subjection.

See CAPITALISM; EFFORT BARGAIN; HOUSE-WORK; LABOUR PROCESS.

MM

**externality.** This occurs when the amount of benefit (UTILITY) a CONSUMER receives, or the COSTS of production a firm incurs, are affected by the actions of another consumer or firm without there being any mechanism for charging for benefits or paying compensation for costs. A chemical plant which pollutes a river may impose external costs on consumers who use the river for recreational purposes and on firms downstream who use river water in a cleansing process. Similarly, an individual vaccinated against an infectious disease bestows an external benefit on those unvaccinated individuals with whom he/she comes into contact. Externalities arise because of the absence of property rights over common resources: in the above examples no-one owns the river or controls access to themselves in public places. Hence they cannot control activities involving the common resource which affect their costs and benefits. Thus a private market system is unlikely to produce an EFFICIENT allocation of resources. For, as no payment is made for benefits or compensation paid for costs, individual decision-makers who engage in externality-generating activities cannot be relied upon to take them into account. Accordingly, there will tend to be over-production of external cost-generating goods and services, and underproduction of external benefit-generating activities. Governments who seek to control these market failures may levy TAXES on producers imposing external costs, subsidize those who produce external benefits or use direct regulation such as pollution standards or public health legislation.

RR

**extraversion-introversion.** A pair of op-posed personality TRAITS used by JUNG to describe the degree to which libido or psychic energy is oriented to the outer world of the physical and social environment — extraversion — as opposed to the inner world of thought and feeling — introversion. For Jung, both personality traits exist in opposition, and the balance of psychic energy between the two may alter through life as well as vary between individuals. When combined with the distinction between the rational functions of thought and feeling, and the irrational ones of sensation and intuition, the extraversion-introversion polarity forms the basis for Jung's psychological types.

Outside the context of Jung's theories, extraversion-introversion refers to the degree to which an individual is in general sociable, gregarious and active as opposed to isolated and reflective. The terms are also used psychometrically by EYSENCK to label one of the chief dimensions of PERSONALITY identified by FACTOR ANALYSIS from a multitude of personality scores on numerous individuals (see MMPI).

JB

**Eysenck, Hans Jurgen** (1916- ). BEHAV-IOURIST psychologist, prolific writer and publicist, well-known for his controversial views on a range of topics including the scientific inadequacies of PSYCHOANALYSIS as theory and its ineffectiveness as therapy; the importance of genetic factors in INTELLI-GENCE and criminality; the need for a divorce in PSYCHIATRY between its strictly medical and its psychological parts, in addition to his efforts to develop measures of PERSONALITY and intelligence; see also EXTRAVERSION-INTROVERSION.

Born in Berlin, he lived in Germany until 1934, witnessing Hitler's rapid rise to power. He moved first to study at Dijon, then to Exeter University, obtaining his PhD at the University of London in 1941. He was appointed a research psychologist at the Mill Hill Emergency Hospital in 1942. At the end of the war he moved to a post as a psychologist at the Maudsley Hospital in London, and in 1950 was appointed a Reader of the University of London and Director of the Psychology Department of the Institute of Psychiatry at the Maudsley. He became a professor in 1955. By then Eysenck was already beginning to write for wider audiences as well as producing academic texts. His early work on person-ality — *Dimensions of Personality* (1947), *Scientific Study of Personality* (1952), *Structure of Human Personality* (1953) — was followed by the first of three more general books, *Uses and Abuses of Psycho-logy* (1953), (*Sense and Nonsense in Psychology* appeared in 1955, *Fact and Fiction in Psychology* in 1965) and a range of books on selected aspects of personality and intelligence. These dealt variously with political ATTITUDES (*Psychology of Politics*, 1954; see also AUTHORITARIAN PERSONAL-ITY); with various forms of what Eysenck, following behaviourist principles, prefers to call not MENTAL ILLNESS but abnormal behaviour (*Dynamics of Anxiety and Hysteria*, 1957; *Behaviour Therapy and the Neuroses*, 1960; *The Effects of Psycho-therapy*, 1966), with criminal behaviour (*Crime and Personality*, 1964), and with RACIAL differences (*Race, Intelligence and*

*Education*, 1971). Numerous other books, both popular and academic, cover similar and related topics.

Eysenck's overriding commitment is to scientific (that is, behaviourist) psychology, both theoretically and methodologically, built on POSITIVIST foundations. The distinctiveness and importance of his work comes in large part from his attempts, as a psychologist working in the applied field, to use and adapt the principles of his type of scientific psychology to the issues and concerns of those working in educational and clinical settings. Many behaviourists have focused on developing general principles of learning but Eysenck concentrates on areas such as personality and intelligence,

neurosis and criminality, where individual variation is the concern, areas that are less amenable to the sort of scientific analysis he values. In his effort to subject individual variation to scientific analysis, he has attached more importance to genetic factors than many behaviourists and, in line with his behaviourist principles, has ignored the detailed exploration of subjective experience and meaning on which clinicians have so often relied. For many, it is just these features that make much of his corpus unacceptable. His work generates, it is argued, an oversimple and inaccurate human psychology, that cannot in practice conform to the behaviourist principles on which it is supposedly based.                                    JB

# F

**factor analysis.** A statistical technique for MULTIVARIATE ANALYSIS, originally developed by the psychologist L.L. Thurstone to look at interrelationships among scores on different sorts of PERSONALITY or INTELLIGENCE TESTS. If a large number of items or indicators are inter-correlated, these interrelationships may be due to the existence of one or more underlying VARIABLES or factors (e.g. a general factor of 'intelligence'). Factors are identified by producing CORRELATION matrices for the variables in the study and analysing these using matrix algebra to extract the principal explanatory factors. The technique requires large sample sizes and interval-level MEASUREMENT of the variables included. Since neither condition is frequently satisfied in sociology, the technique is used rarely. Moreover, as an INDUCTIVE, data-dredging procedure it is no substitute for careful theoretical thinking.

For further examples, see EXTRAVERSION; MMPI; SEMANTIC DIFFERENTIAL.

See H. Harman, *Modern Factor Analysis* (1960).

MB

**false consciousness.** The discrepancy between the views or ideology held by a person, group or class, and what would be in accord with that person or group's 'objective' social and economic position. On the basis of MARX's theory that consciousness is determined by position in the social relations of production, such discrepancies need to be explained, although the theory has been criticized because it is impossible to work out a satisfactory criterion of objective interest. False consciousness is frequently a denigratory term, especially as applied to working-class individuals or groups who do not have a revolutionary consciousness (e.g. working-class conservatives). Marx himself did not use the term, but it was employed by ENGELS with reference to the middle class.

See also CLASS CONSCIOUSNESS; TRADE UNION CONSCIOUSNESS.

MMG, MM

**falsification** [falsifiability]. See POPPER; VERIFICATION.

**family, the.** Universality has been claimed for the family, and this has been located either in the biologically created mother-child dyad or in the socially constructed mother-father-child triad. There are many different family forms: the extended family (both across and within generations), the stem family (groups of brothers with their wives, and perhaps parents), and the nuclear family (parents and children). Each family goes through a LIFE CYCLE — people are born into their family of origin, marry and start their own family of procreation, become grandparents when their own children start families. Family ROLES change as the individual moves through the life cycle of the family.

Traditionally, the family has been viewed as a unit with several functions, notably legitimate sexual outlet for the partners, procreation, socialization of children, and in some cases, production. PARSONS argued that industrialization brought about two significant changes: the predominance of the geographically mobile neo-local nuclear family, and the erosion of functions since much of health-care, education and production was removed from the home and located within the public sphere. He argued that within the nuclear family women perform the expressive nurturant roles and men the instrumental work roles (see Parsons and Bales, *Family: Socialization and Interaction Process*, 1956). Conjugal roles have been viewed as reciprocal, rather than unequal, and perhaps tending towards greater equality — this is the symmetrical family, where men 'help'. Segregated conjugal roles associated with extended network of kin are said to be disappearing because of urban renewal, and joint conjugal roles are developing instead.

Parsons has been criticized for historical inaccuracy. Laslett has shown that nuclear family units were the norm in rural England and Young and Willmott argued that extended kinship networks exist in working-class areas, sustained by mother-daughter friendships. Help from the family of origin and other kin is also common among middle-class families, but frequently disguised as wedding or birthday gifts.

The normality of the nuclear family has also been questioned by those who demonstrate that only a minority of households conform to the ideal. Single-parent, especially fatherless, families are now increasingly common; as divorce rates rise many families either go through this state before the single parent remarries, or remain in that form.

Feminists have criticized this view of the family, arguing that the family is an unequal institution in terms of income distribution, the power to make decisions, the giving and receiving of services. They have located the structural origins of women's oppression in the family by pointing to male control of female sexuality, male rights to female servicing and the non-enforcement of male responsibility to provide financially for the family. Even in dual-career families childcare and housework still remain the wife's duty.

The family is not the cosy haven it is sometimes depicted to be. According to the Frankfurt School it tends to produce AUTHORITARIAN PERSONALITIES which tend towards FASCISM; according to LAING and the anti-psychiatrists it produces schizophrenia; and feminists have shown that violence is prevalent in the family, in the form of wife-battering and sexual abuse of children. Marxists see it as integral to capitalism in its role of socializing future generations of docile workers. Feminists have also criticized the notion of the family-work split which occurred with the development of the factory system. They argue that while the family may represent leisure for men, for women it constitutes hard labour.

Black women have criticized white feminists for assuming a universal right to the family. In the UK, immigration policies result in a long wait before families are united; some family members are not permitted to reside in Britain (e.g. grandparents or children over 16).

See also KINSHIP; MARRIAGE; WOMEN AND CRIME; WOMEN AND EDUCATION; WOMEN AND THE LABOUR MARKET; WOMEN AND MADNESS; WOMEN AND POLITICS; WOMEN AND THE WELFARE STATE.

See M. Anderson (ed.), *Sociology of the Family* (1975); S. Friedman and E. Sarah (eds.), *On the Problem of Men* (1982).

EG

**family allowances.** A cash benefit provided for families with children. Introduced in the UK in 1946 following a lengthy, though not intensive, campaign that dated back to the beginning of the 20th century. Its introduction had been recommended in the BEVERIDGE Report.

At first, family allowances only applied to families with two or more children, the rate was low and was only infrequently adjusted to take account of rises in the cost of living. However, they were additional to tax allowances for children (although the benefit itself was subject to tax) and without a MEANS TEST. Throughout the 1960s the system of financial help for families with children was extensively criticized, especially by the Child Poverty Action Group: it was argued that family allowances should be increased as a replacement for tax allowances for children. The rationale was that this would give more help to the poorest sections of society.

The Labour Government of 1974 moved in this direction by introducing child benefits at a significantly higher level than family allowances, to apply to first as well as subsequent children and replace tax allowances for children. The scheme was delayed, partly because of trade union resistance to the elimination of tax allowances during a period of wage restraint, but eventually introduced in 1977.

MPJ

**Family Income Supplement.** A benefit introduced in the UK in 1971, providing cash help to families whose income is below a defined level. The benefit is equivalent to half the difference between the income of the family and the defined level, up to a maximum. The scheme introduced a number of novel features. (1) A cash benefit to families in full-time employment, the opposite of the normal social assistance condition that recipients must not be working. (2) Although based on a MEANS TEST, assessment relies less on detailed personal investigation and is reviewed less frequently than is normal with social assistance schemes. (3) It is linked to entitlement for other means-tested benefits so that, for example, recipients are entitled to exemption from prescriptions and other health service charges without further assessment.

The scheme was viewed by some as an inadequate response to the problems of family poverty on the grounds that higher FAMILY ALLOWANCE rates would have been a more appropriate policy. It was also opposed because it is a means-tested benefit, though it has had a relatively high take-up rate.

MPJ

**family reconstitution.** A technique in HISTORICAL DEMOGRAPHY in which parish registers are used to collect together all the demographic events relevant to each family appearing, in order to estimate MORTALITY, fertility and NUPTIALITY rates. Aggregate rates are insufficient for estimating age-and-sex specific rates, and even age at death is often unrecorded. The technique was introduced in France in the late 1950s, and was then taken up elsewhere (see HISTORICAL DEMOGRAPHY). Family reconstitution data have their own hazards, such as the difficulty of correctly piecing together the elements of a specific family and in assessing the representativeness of those families which can be reconstructed.

JL

**fascism.** Derived from the Latin *fasces*, a bundle of bound rods with an axe in the centre carried by magistrates in ancient Rome, the term was first used to describe the Fascist Party founded by Mussolini in Italy in 1919. It quickly became a generic term and has been so used ever since, though there are significant differences between fascism in different countries. It is important to distinguish between fascism as a movement, a state form and an ideology.

(1) Fascist movements are characterized by violent hostility to the organizations of the WORKING CLASS and, to a lesser degree, of big business; by MILITARISM and extreme NATIONALIST and/or RACIALIST propaganda; by their mixed composition of PETITS BOURGEOIS strata and disaffected elements from all classes. Initially a product of the backwash caused by World War I, fascist movements can gain support whenever there is an extended period of capitalist crisis, particularly among those unprotected from economic distress by trade union organization. Not all fascist movements achieve state power; this depends upon the economic crisis generating an acute political crisis, in which parliamentary legitimacy is undermined, and after other, more acceptable, forms of 'exceptional' regime have been tried and have failed.

(2) As a form of state, fascism is distinguished from other forms of dictatorship by the combination of legal means and extra-legal mass violence used to seize power and destroy the organizations of the working class. Among its first tasks the fascist state guarantees 'order' for large capital by the suppression of the socially radical (often SOCIALIST) elements among its own supporters. This heralds the incorporation of independent social institutions into the fascist system, and the 'purification' of society of all those elements which stand in the way of national regeneration. Italian fascists sometimes claimed that this would lead to a 'corporate state' in which vertically organized interest groups like industries and

professions would act as representative bodies, but this was never implemented (see also CORPORATISM).

(3) Fascist ideology is often held to be a rag-bag of ideas, promising contradictory things to different social groups. Yet it is impossible to understand the sheer destructive dynamic of Nazism without taking its racialist programme and its cult of the leader seriously. Fascism in general is consistent in its outright opposition to the major political values of post-Enlightenment Europe: LIBERTY, EQUALITY, DEMOCRACY and SOCIALISM. In this it distinguishes itself from traditional CONSERVATIVE doctrines by its emphasis on a new heroic elite of the will, and its belief that the supreme human values can only be realized in war.

DB

*Explanations of Fascism.* S.G. Payne (*Fascism: Comparison and Definition,* 1980) distinguishes nine such explanations. Marxists have seen fascism as a violent, dictatorial agent of bourgeois CAPITALISM. Cultural historians see it as the product of cultural or moral breakdown, Freudians as proceeding from neurotic or pathological psychosocial impulses. There are MASS-SOCIETY approaches, exemplified by Arendt or Kornhauser. Fascism has also been seen as the consequence of a particular stage of economic growth or national development, as one aspect of 20th-century TOTALI-TARIANISM, as a manifestation of resistance to modernization and as a unique radicalism developed by the MIDDLE CLASS. Finally, some writers deny that there is any common set of characteristics to fascist movements.

Empirical research shows that before taking over a country, fascist movements are subject to sudden surges of membership, with periods of stagnation or decline. After taking power, established social forces will flock to its banner. Although the Nazi Party had a high level of non-proletarian membership, P.H. Merkl (*Political Violence under the Swastika,* 1975) warns that all political movements tend to have a lower middle-class membership, and there are difficulties in identifying which occupational groups belong to the lower middle class.

Nazi Party members yended to be younger than in other parties, except the Communist Party. Working-class membership varied from 57.3 per cent of the French PPF to 17.5 per cent in Austria. White-collar and civil service membership varied from 15 to 29 per cent and exceeded the percentage of these groups in the population. The old middle classes of business, handicraft and the professions frequently approached half of total membership. In rural areas, farmer membership was high. Veterans, ex-officers and students were also an important group. Merkl classifies fascist movements into six groups on the basis of occupational profile, ranging from Left (e.g. French PPF) through Left-Centre (e.g. Falange), Centre (e.g. Nasjonal Senties), Centre-Right (e.g. Irish Blue-Shirts), Left-Right (e.g. Iron Guard), to Right (e.g. Heimwehr). Left and Left-Centre groups tend to predominate in the West and South, while centrist and centre-right groupings are typical of Central and Northern Europe. Merkl argues that this relates fascism directly to the consequences of World War I, which uprooted many Europeans and exacerbated ethnic conflicts.

The record of Fascists in office is ambivalent. They achieved high levels of employment, control over the trade union movement and centralization of industry, all of which added up to economic growth and raising of living standards. But this was at the expense of high levels of prison and concentration camp populations. They also seemed incapable of avoiding foreign adventurism and war, with the exception of Franco, who only achieved growth through American investment in the 1960s. Some argue that by concentrating on scapegoats, fascists must end up with a war. They come to power by blaming identifiable minorities, either racial or left-wing and imprison these minorities. Society's ills continue. Since they have established the principle that particular people are responsible for society's problems, it must now be people from other countries that are causing the problems.

Neo-fascist parties continue to spring up. The MSI in Italy and associated terrorist groups like New Order and Black Order have created problems for Italian society and gained a significant percentage of the vote. The UK has the more extreme offshoots of the National Front, such as the New National Front, the British Movement and the British

Resistance agitating over the issue of race. West Germany had troubles with the NDP in the period of the Grand Coalition, but mainly as an electoral threat. In Spain, Francoite groups wait in the wings to exploit any failure by the democratic parties. Reports from Latin America frequently attribute fascist aspects, including anti-semitism, to various military governments.

See also AUTHORITARIAN PERSONALITY; POL-ITICAL VIOLENCE; ROKEACH.

BT

**feminism.** A social movement of women whose aim is to abolish PATRIARCHY. The multi-faceted nature of patriarchy is reflected in the variety of issues, campaigns and types of feminism. Feminist movements differ in how they view patriarchy and how they organize to combat it.

The history of feminism can never be written fully. Known feminist history begins with the first wave of feminism inspired originally by the ideals of the French Revolu-tion and women's participation in it. In Britain the publication in 1792 of Mary Wollstonecraft's *A Vindication of the Rights of Women* (repr. 1979) ushers in this first wave. She was concerned with women's right to equal education and many 19th-century feminists fought for this, opening up schools and colleges for women, gaining entry into men's colleges and male professions, such as medicine.

Legal reforms which altered the legal status of married women from being their husbands' property to becoming legal individuals who could be awarded custody rights, own property and sue for divorce, were all victories partly attributable to feminist pressure.

Feminists were also concerned with SEX-UALITY. They campaigned successfully to abolish the Contagious Diseases Acts which permitted policemen to forcibly examine and lock up any woman suspected of being a 'common prostitute'. They petitioned successfully to raise the age of consent to protect young girls from the White Slave Trade. Feminists were divided over contra-ception: some supported women's rights to enjoy sex and control their own fertility, others, notably working-class women, feared the overt MALTHUSIAN and eugenicist

elements in the birth control movement; others distrusted the 'normality and joy of married heterosexuality' movement on grounds of the undesirability of MARRIAGE.

The suffrage campaign is probably the best-known movement, but the popular focus tends to be on the Suffragettes of the Women's Social and Political Union (1903-14) who adopted militant tactics and went on hunger strike inside Holloway prison. The suffrage campaign, dedicated to using legal means, began long before the birth of the WSPU, and was also crucial to the winning of the vote in 1918 on restricted terms and in 1926 on equal terms with men.

Feminism continued in the inter-war years, but largely within existing political parties, especially the Labour and Com-munist Parties. It became less of a mass movement and more of a parliamentary reform movement; as a political vision it became subsumed under socialist doctrines.

The birth of the second wave of feminism is associated with Betty Friedan's *Feminine Mystique* (1963) in which allegedly happy, upper middle-class full-time housewives and mothers speak about their misery and frus-tration. This was the 'problem with no name', the unconceptualized dissatisfaction of women with their lives in spite of having faithfully followed patriarchal prescriptions for female happiness. Feminism in Britain and the United States also grew out of the revolt of women in the New Left against their treatment by male comrades. In the UK, there were also equal pay strikes — revolts by employed women.

The Women's Liberation Movement is one of the main forces within the second wave. It is not a hierarchical, structured-membership organization but loosely struc-tured, encompassing many groups, political theories and campaigns, defined by com-mitment to the Seven Demands. There are two discernible strands within the Women's Liberation Movement: socialist or Marxist feminism and radical and revolutionary feminism.

Marxist feminism is primarily concerned with the interrelationship between capital-ism and patriarchy. Its intellectual roots lie in ENGELS's theory that patriarchy originated with the development of private property; its political roots lie in the socialist movement.

Bebel, LENIN and TROTSKY wrote on 'the woman question', Klara Zetkin organized a women's section of the German SDP, and Alexandra Kollontai worked for women's rights in marriage and the family in post-revolutionary Russia.

The orthodox Marxist view is that women's oppression is a function of capitalism. Engels argued that women's emancipation depended on women going 'out to work', becoming proletarians and struggling for socialism, which would also free women. Lenin argued that housework was demeaning drudgery and that socialized services (staffed by women!) should supplant it.

Second-wave Marxist feminists criticized this view for being economistic, REDUCTIONIST and biologistic. Women's oppression is seen as predominantly economic and capitalist in origin and the result of natural biological differences. But the same class/gender problematic remains. The domestic labour debate (see HOUSEWORK) and the reserve army of labour theory both attempted to demonstrate the necessity of patriarchy to capitalism. Capitalist patriarchy is another variant which sees capitalist social relations and the sexual division of labour as mutually reinforcing forms of oppression. Other Marxist feminists, following STRUCTURALIST interpretations of Marx and Freud, view the two systems as relatively autonomous, with patriarchy structuring the ideological level and capitalism the economic. The relative autonomy lies in the determination by the economy in the last instance only (see ALTHUSSER).

Radical and revolutionary feminists are concerned with sex-class theories. They criticize Marxist feminists for subordinating patriarchy to capitalism, if only in the last instance, and argue for the primacy of patriarchal relations. A small number of radical feminists situate women's oppression in biological inequality but most view it as socially structured, pre-existing capitalism and possibly even the source of all other systems of domination like CLASS and RACE, identifying POWER and control as its fundamental elements. Women are viewed in the economic sense, in the domestic labour debate, and in the political sense, as a sex-class controlled by actual or threatened violence. Theories of male violence led to the growth of revolutionary feminism, which is primarily concerned with compulsory heterosexuality as the mechanism for controlling women's reproductive power. This control operates through ideological means such as romantic ideology and through violence, as in wife-battering, rape, pornography and so on (see MARRIAGE).

Radical and revolutionary feminists have been criticized for treating men and women as biologically determined. As a counter-argument one can say that patriarchy operates through notions of natural differences, and that we therefore tend to conflate arguments about women, especially when these treat all women as the same in some profound way, with statements about biological females.

The second wave of feminism has also given rise to Women's Studies, which originated in the political practice of consciousness-raising — learning about women's oppression from discussions of personal experiences. Initially, Women's Studies were defined as redressing the balance in sociology to include women, who had been left out of all areas and confined to the family to perform biological functions. From there feminists began to question the reasons behind this virtual absence of women.

All knowledge is socially constructed, in that it is selected and ordered. As a social construct it reflects patriarchal concerns in these processes. All knowledge handed down in educational institutions is patriarchal in form (hierarchy, competition) and content (disciplines and their boundaries). On this view women's studies is a new discipline which embraces the feminist principle of women's oppression and attempts to analyse how patriarchy is structured.

See also WOMEN AND POLITICS.

See Banks, *Faces of Feminism* (1981); Feminist Anthropology Collective, *No Turning Back: Writings from the Women's Liberation Movement, 1975-80* (1981); Gamarnikow *et al.*, *Public and Private* (1983); Oakley, *Subject Women* (1981); Strachey, *The Cause* (1928, repr. 1978); Wandor, *The Body Politic: Writings from the Women's Liberation Movement, 1969-1972* (1972).

EG

**Ferguson, Adam** (1723-1816). Philosopher of the SCOTTISH ENLIGHTENMENT, whose overriding concern was to show the inter-relations between human beings and social institutions. Today he would be considered a historical sociologist.

Born at Logierait, Perthshire, Ferguson was the son of a Presbyterian minister. He took his MA at the University of St Andrews in 1742. He began to study for the ministry and in 1745 was appointed chaplain to the Black Watch, the famous Highland regiment. (Ferguson was the only member of the Scottish Enlightenment who spoke Gaelic, the language of the Highlands.) He became Professor of Natural Philosophy at Edinburgh in 1759, and was Professor of Moral Philosophy from 1764 to 1785. During these years he visited the Continent and the American Colonies.

His writings covered Roman history, ethics, politics and essays on refinement. *An Essay on Civil Society* (1767) traced the progression in human history from the rude stages of savagery and barbarism to the polished civilized society of his day. In Ferguson's vocabulary, civil society was a broad concept, and referred to political and social refinement, non-despotic government, and civilized or cultivated moral sentiments. Instead of locating the mode of subsistence as the crucial feature of each state of development, as did Adam SMITH, Ferguson distinguished the savage from the barbaric stage by the ownership of private property. Commercial society presupposed private property, and certain corruptions in commerce and manners could result, leading potentially to despotic government. In commercial society, Ferguson observed the tendency to judge individuals increasingly by what they owned rather than by their moral character. The self-interested pursuit of wealth and material improvement produced self-centred and egoistic individuals. A stable, efficient government which protected the individual and achieved the rule of law could encourage this 'moral corruption' by enabling people to pursue solely their self-interest; they could become politically indifferent, and the social bonds between them could weaken. Encouraging a martial spirit was one way to strengthen fundamental human bonds and overcome the individual-ism of commercial society.

In his moral works, Ferguson denounced the selfish system of ethics put forth by HOBBES and Mandeville, and presented a doctrine of ethics based on the principle of moral approbation. He distinguished two types of morality: that which could be enforced by laws, and the sort that relied on individual duty and free will. He treated the social bond and the qualities of moral approbation as basically unproblematic, and assumed the objectivity of both with the same confidence.

BJB

**Festinger, Leon** (1919- ). American psychologist, Professor of Psychology at the New School for Social Research, New York, mainly known in sociology for the development of COGNITIVE DISSONANCE theory. Festinger was born in New York and educated at City College, New York, and the State University of Iowa, where he was a student of LEWIN. From 1943 to 1945 he was a statistician employed in the selection of pilots. After the war he worked at MIT, home of Lewin's Research Center for Group Dynamics. When the Research Center moved to the University of Michigan on Lewin's death in 1947, Festinger moved with it. In 1951 he took a chair in psychology at the University of Minnesota, moving to Stanford in 1955 and to the New School for Social Research in 1968.

His original interest was in ATTITUDE change. In the mid-1950s he evolved the concept of cognitive dissonance to express the 'non-fitting relation among cognitions' which, amongst other things, may lead to attitude change through processes described as conflict, decision and dissonance; see *A Theory of Cognitive Dissonance* (1957). Selective cognition, however, may simply avoid or reinterpret dissonant elements, as happened in the case of a MILLENARIAN sect when its central belief was disconfirmed; see Festinger *et al, When Prophecy Fails* (1956).

JL

**feudalism.** Used in a general sense to characterize the aristocratic, militaristic and theological social order thought to have dominated Europe from the Dark Ages to early modern times. Since the 19th century there has been considerable controversy over .the use of the concept, arising from whether feudalism is seen principally as a political system, an economic system or a legal system.

*Political system.* WEBER argued that feudalism is a system of government 'whose basis is a ruling class dedicated to war or royal service and supported by privileged land holdings, rents or labour services of a dependent, unarmed population'. This ruling class was relatively autonomous, for the hallmark of the feudal state, as opposed to PATRIMONIALISM, was its decentralization of power and authority. Against this view, BLOCH in *Feudal Society* argued that there were strong and weak monarchs in feudal societies and that the extent of central power did not affect the fundamental institutions of feudal society. These fundamental institutions, about which there is general agreement, are the fief, vassalage, and the manor. Roughly, a lord could reward the services of a vassal (a dependent who bore arms and could command his own followers) with the grant of accommodation in the lord's household or by endowing him with a piece of land and the products of those who worked it. This property right in the land was known as the fief (or benefice). In the course of time fiefs came to be hereditary and, particularly in periods of weak monarchs, provided the basis of the local autonomy that Weber considered so important. The lord's own subjects inhabited the manor. The serfs or peasants worked the land of the lord (called demesne land) and handed over to him in taxes a large part of the surplus from the land they worked for themselves (called tenements), financing the power of the lord against his own vassals. The system was complicated by the fact that small lords were vassals of great lords, that big vassals were lords to small vassals, and that networks of cross-cutting rights and duties were established with each new feudal tie. Bloch quotes the example of a 13th-century German baron who was an enfeoffed vassal of 43 lords. The whole system rested economically on the servile peasantry and small artisans who were responsible for all productive labour. This has led some writers to con-

centrate more on the economic rather than the political-military aspects of feudalism.

*Economic system.* Stressed by Marxists who use the concept of the feudal MODE OF PRODUCTION to analyse the dynamics of the system. This involves an emphasis on serfdom and the class struggle of the feudal peasantry against the exploitation of vassals, lords and the feudal state in general. M. Dobb (*Studies in the Development of Capitalism*, 1946) propounded the influential thesis that feudalism is best understood in terms of the efforts of the landlords to expropriate the agricultural surpluses from the serfs and the variety of ways in which the serfs resisted this. Thus relations between the different orders of landlords is of secondary importance. This thesis is controversial.

*Legal system.* Feudalism is defined in a legal-normative sense by many writers, such as F. Ganshof (*Feudalism*, 1947), who sees it as a 'body of institutions creating and regulating the obligations of obedience and service'. While this approach is not necessarily incompatible with the others it emphasizes the fundamentals in different ways.

No one denies that feudalism, however defined, is primarily a European phenomenon. Nevertheless, some scholars have found something like it practically all over the world. The clearest non-European case is Japan, where a well-developed feudalism endured for many centuries. This and other cases are discussed in R. Coulborn (ed.), *Feudalism in History* (1956), a useful collection of articles limited only by its assumption that feudalism is exclusively a governmental-political system.

LS

**Feyerabend, Paul** (1924- ). Philosopher of science. Professor of Philosophy at Berkeley since 1958. Main works: *Against Method* (1975); *Science in a Free Society* (1978). Starting from a position close to that of POPPER, Feyerabend has drawn increasingly radical conclusions. He accepts much of Kuhn's account of the history of science, while violently objecting to his implied conservatism. The consequence to be drawn from the 'sloppiness' of science — for example, the rarity of conclusive falsifications — is that scientists should be tolerant of alternative theories and indeed should try to invent as many as possible. In his later work, this principle is affirmed with increasing shrillness as 'anarchism', 'dadaism' or 'anything goes'. Science must be demystified and subordinated to other purposes of life — not least, the freedom to choose what we believe in.                                    WO

**field theory.** A holistic psychological theory or, more accurately, meta-theory, associated with the German-American psychologist LEWIN, which asserts that individual behaviour is determined by the totality of the particular concrete situation, and not by general laws acting on certain abstract TRAITS of the individual or situation. The totality of events or facts determining an individual's behaviour at a given time is termed the 'psychological life space'. The principle of concreteness limits admissible events or facts to those that are concrete, that is, those which constitute individual facts at a specific moment in time. Causation is argued to be contemporaneous, because 'since neither the past nor the future exists at the present moment it cannot have effects at the present'. History only acts through its embodiment at a specific moment in the life space of an individual.

Field theory is committed to an inter-disciplinary approach, for all aspects of a situation must be considered, not just those within certain disciplinary boundaries. This should not be done by simply importing theoretical constructs from other disciplines, such as physiology or physics, but by concepts tailor-made for psychology and capable of describing behaviour in all its related aspects. Mathematical techniques are necessary to express the totality of the structure of the life space, but topological methods rather than those of normal Euclidean space are appropriate.

In sociology, field theory directs attention to the interaction of all the specific detail of social situations as the explanation of individual social behaviour, rather than the operation of general sociological laws upon abstract qualities. Methodologically, this view reinforces detailed fieldwork or case studies as opposed to the sample survey

methods needed to generate lawlike relationships between abstract variables.
                                    JL

**filiation.** See LINEAGE.

**fixation.** See PSYCHOANALYSIS.

**folk society.** A model of TRADITIONAL society developed by Robert REDFIELD ('The Folk Society', *American Journal of Sociology*, 1947) and characterized as small, isolated, non-literate and homogeneous, with a strong sense of group solidarity. Behaviour is traditional, spontaneous, uncritical and personal; there is no legislation or habit of experiment and reflection for intellectual ends. KINSHIP, its relations and institutions, are the typical categories of experience and the familial group is the unit of action. The sacred prevails over the secular; the economy is one of STATUS rather than the MARKET.

Redfield developed this as an abstract model of pre-industrial communities, but it is clearly based upon his classic studies of Mesuins peasant society in the 1930s. There are close affinities with the concept of GEMEINSCHAFT developed by TÖNNIES.
                                    HN

**folk-urban continuum.** A typology of COMMUNITY according to five criteria: size, degree of isolation, degree of social homogeneity, literacy and sense of group solidarity. It is a refinement of the RURAL-URBAN CONTINUUM which attempts to avoid ecological determinism.
                                    HN

**formalism.** (1) In general terms, an approach to intellectual enquiry in which emphasis is laid on the form of a phenomenon rather than its substantive nature or content. Formalism implies both a theoretical principle, that explanation is to be sought in regularities associated with a given form, and a methodological prescription, to categorize and study phenomena according to similarities of form irrespective of context. In 19th- and early 20th-century logic and mathematics, formalist methods achieved great success by being restricted to specifications as to how certain terms were to be combined, despite difficulties of substantive comprehension, for example as to the nature of infinite numbers or non-Euclidean geometry.

Sociological critics argue that by taking objects out of context, formalism substitutes relations of an abstract and artificial character for real, dynamic social processes. Marxists add that this is characteristic of tendencies of bourgeois science.

(2) The formal school of sociology refers to the approach associated with SIMMEL, a pioneer of the study across different societies of given social forms such as the dyad, the triad, co-operation and conflict. Leopold von Wiese took these ideas to the USA, where they influenced Howard Becker Snr. (1899-1960) and became a strand in American sociology.

(3) Russian formalism refers to a school of literary criticism in Moscow and Leningrad in the 1920s, later suppressed. Its members included Viktor Shklovsky and Roman Jakobson, and were concerned with the operations of LANGUAGE in literature, particularly poetry, in a manner similar to structural linguistics. In poetry, language seemed to be used in special ways, as both signifier and signified, in creating meaning. In the analysis of prose, concern lay chiefly at the level of the structure of the narrative plot, and V.I. Propp's analysis of folk tales, deriving from this school, is an early classic of structural analysis. The label 'formalist' was applied by their critics.

See FORMAL MODEL; STRUCTURE.

JL

**formal model.** An ideal-type representation of a phenomenon in terms of a system of mathematical or verbal statements, including certain essential features of the phenomenon but not others, and set up as an aid to understanding and reasoning. A formal model is not a theory. Reality is not made up of the units of the model, and the model does not constitute an explanation of the phenomenon: it is a possible reconstruction of it in a comprehensible form. The origins of such an approach in sociology can be traced back to WEBER's IDEAL TYPES and SIMMEL's formal sociology, such as his analysis of the dyad and the triad. However, most of the

models themselves have been imported from statistics, economics and mathematical psychology.

The criteria for judging a formal model are not those for assessing the truth of a theory, although a sufficiently well-developed and interpreted model would be indistinguishable from a theory. The criteria for a good formal model include: (1) it should reflect the essential features of the phenomenon; (2) it should produce an interesting class of deviations for empirical examination; (3) it should allow the generation of fruitful hypotheses and incisive questions about the empirical phenomenon. Equally, a bad model can be most damaging and, as it cannot be directly falsified, can become persistent.

The most commonly used formal model in sociology is the general linear model, which consists of a set of interval variables (see MEASUREMENT) linked by linear, additive relationships and perturbed from without only by normally distributed error terms. STOCHASTIC PROCESSES, computer programmes, systems theory, GRAPH THEORY, formal logic and axiomatic systems have also been used as formal models of social phenomena.

See also MATHEMATICAL SOCIOLOGY.

JL

**Fortes, Meyer** (1906-83). British social anthropologist. Born in South Africa to immigrant Jewish parents. His PhD at University College, London, was a cross-cultural study of intelligence. He joined MALINOWSKI's anthropology seminar at LSE and undertook fieldwork in Africa, studying the Tallensi and Ashanti. Professor of Social Anthropology at Cambridge University 1955-73.

Major works: (with Evans-Pritchard, eds.) *African Political Systems* (1940); *The Dynamics of Clanship among the Tallensi* (1945); Introduction to J. Goody (ed.), *The Developmental Cycle in Domestic Groups* (1958); *Oedipus and Job in West African Religion* (1959); *Kinship and the Social Order* (1969); *Time and Social Structure and Other Essays* (1970).

The field experience of Fortes and EVANS-PRITCHARD in Africa influenced the development of British social anthropology in much the same way as that of BOAS in North America affected the course of cultural anthropology there. The theories they developed retained the flavour and structure of the tribal societies they studied. They refined kinship in relationship to a political order, which was expressed in kinship terms. Fortes explored the meaning of kinship and inheritance through a consideration of the social consequences of certain psychological imperatives. His examination of the social importance of inter-generational relationships, which expresses psychological crises such as the Oedipal conflict in social terms, may be his most lasting contribution to anthropological theory.

His empirical, inductive and atheoretical approach has been criticized, notably by Leach, and studies in other areas have not confirmed his emphasis on unilineal inheritance in kinship theory. Nevertheless, the political concepts and kinship terminology which Fortes, Evans-Pritchard and others elaborated in the late 1930s established the categories of FUNCTIONALIST social anthropology for 20 years, and their influence has persisted despite criticism.

See also ANCESTOR; KINSHIP.

JE

**Foucault, Michel** (1926- ). French historian specializing in the history of the human sciences, of penal and medical institutions and of sexuality. Main works: *A History of Madness in the Age of Reason* (1961), *Birth of the Clinic* (1962), *The Order of Things* (1966), *The Archaeology of Knowledge* (1969). Although he rejects the title, Foucault is generally considered a STRUCTURALIST: what he calls epistemes (in *The Order of Things*) are fundamental modes of thought which are historically discrete. In *The Archaeology of Knowledge* this conception is abandoned in favour of an even more radical division between DISCOURSE and reality.

WO

**Fourth World.** A concept which first gained currency in the early 1970s when it became apparent that THIRD WORLD countries

differed remarkably in their economic development performance (see MARGINALIZATION). Official UN Resolutions began to speak of Least Developed countries, while the World Bank introduced the classification middle-income versus low-income countries in its literature. The official UN classificatory criteria for the Least Developed group are: (1) per capita income of 100 dollars or less (in 1970); (2) share of manufacturing in total gross domestic output 10 per cent or less; (3) literacy rates 20 per cent or less. The World Bank's classification of low-income group adds the criterium of annual per capita growth rates of 2 per cent or less over the past two decades. Reference to the Fourth World, which is not an officially designated group of countries, usually mixes these two definitions, and includes most countries of sub-Saharan Africa and some of the more populated countries of Asia, namely Bangladesh, Sri Lanka, Pakistan and (arguably) India.

AH

**Frankfurt School.** See CRITICAL THEORY.

**Frazer, Sir James George** (1854-1941). Scottish classicist and 'armchair' anthropologist. Born in Glasgow, studied at Glasgow University 1869-74. In 1874 he moved to Trinity College, Cambridge, where he became a fellow in 1879 and remained for the rest of his life, except for 1907-8 when he was Professor of Social Anthropology at Liverpool, the first person to hold a chair with that title. Major works: *The Golden Bough* (1900); *Totemism and Exogeny* (1910); *Psyche's Task* (1920); *Garnered Sheaves* (1931); *Anthologia Anthropologica* (1938-9).

The main influences on Frazer's work were 19th-century folklorists and ethnographers like Tylor and Morgan, who were collecting data on other cultures and attempting to construct universal theories of human societies and institutions. Although Frazer did not himself perform fieldwork, he carried out an intense correspondence over many years with educators, administrators and missionaries in other countries, often giving detailed instructions regarding the type of material they should collect. His most famous work, *The Golden Bough,* is an immense collation of worldwide examples of myths and divine kinship. Legend has it that reading *The Golden Bough* converted MALINOWSKI from natural sciences to anthropology. But Frazer's anthropology was firmly rooted in a tradition of classicism and idealism from which Malinowski and the empirical tradition of British social anthropologists later broke away. Frazer's theories of magic and religion have been heavily criticized in social anthropology and have not been influential in the discipline since the 1920s, but his influence upon literature is evident in the work of Kipling, T.S. Eliot, Ezra Pound, D.H. Lawrence and many others, and thus his theories have become part of popular culture.

JE

**free riders.** See PUBLIC GOODS.

**Freud, Sigmund** (1856-1939). Practising physician, specialist in nervous diseases, and founder of PSYCHOANALYSIS. The impact of his ideas on psychiatric practice in Western countries, especially in relation to the treatment and theorizing of neurotic conditions (see MENTAL ILLNESS), has been profound, as has their influence on everyday and, to a more limited extent, academic psychology. Although his ideas have been widely attacked by POSITIVISTS for their lack of scientific foundation, Freud provided almost the only comprehensive general theory of individual psychology. His concepts have been of special value to psychoanalysts, counsellors, social workers and educationalists who deal on a day-to-day basis with individuals and their problems. Consequently, more practitioners and professionals than academic psychologists have turned to his ideas for guidance in dealing with the complexities of understanding an individual's mental life. Freudian ideas, with their focus on symbols and meaning, have also had an important influence on intellectual ideas about cultural life — art, literature and the cinema. However, Freud's theorizing about society, unlike his individual psychology, has never gained widespread acceptance.

Freud was born in Freiberg, Moravia,

then part of the Austrian Empire, of Jewish parents. His father, a wool-merchant, was 41 when he was born and already had two children by his first marriage. Freud's mother was 21 when Sigmund, her first child, was born, and he felt himself her indisputable favourite. When he was four, following the collapse of his father's business, the family moved to Vienna, where he was to live until 1938. Freud began to study medicine at the University of Vienna in 1874. He was attracted to the natural sciences, involving himself more in academic research than in clinical medicine, and did not take his degree in medicine until 1881. His research in anatomy and physiology continued when in 1882, due to financial pressure, he took up a post as a hospital resident at the Vienna General Hospital. He worked on cerebral anatomy and did some research on the organic diseases of the nervous system. In 1885 he was appointed lecturer in neuropathology and won a travelling scholarship to Paris, where he studied with Charcot and arranged to translate his lectures. From Charcot Freud acquired an interest in hysteria, a diagnosis he later applied to himself, and contact with hypnosis as a method of treatment. Charcot rejected the idea that hysteria had its origins in an irritation of the womb and was specific to women, but his focus was still largely on the organic processes underlying the disease.

On his return to Vienna in 1886 Freud took the decisive step of setting up in private practice, specializing in nervous diseases, in order to make it financially possible to marry Martha Bernays, to whom he had been engaged for several years. Their first child was born the following year. Anna, their fifth and last child, who was herself to make a substantial contribution to psychoanalysis, was born in 1895. Freud's shift to clinical practice was decisive. He focused attention on treatment and finding a method of therapy that would provide an adequate living for his family. He initially tried electrotherapy and hypnosis, but though the latter produced some dramatic success the difficulties he encountered with both methods, together with observations made by a friend, Joseph Breuer, led him to try new techniques such as free association and to develop new ideas about the origins of hysteria. He formulated a theory of a traumatic seduction in childhood, the memory of which had been repressed and was unconscious, and developed a cathartic method of treatment. These ideas were first published in 1893 in a 'preliminary communication' with Breuer and were developed in their book *Studies in Hysteria* (1895). Within two years Freud came to realize that the supposed seductions had not occurred, but were a fantasy of the patient. His ideas then developed in two directions: (1) studies of the role of fantasy, repressed desires, and the unconscious and an analysis of symbols, their meaning and interpretation; he identified dreams as the means of access to the unconscious and developed dream analysis as a new technique of therapy (*The Interpretation of Dreams*, 1900); (2) the amplification of his ideas about infantile sexuality, emphasizing sexual drives (or instincts); his approach was more biological and natural scientific than his work on dreams. In *Three Essays on the Theory of Sexuality* (1905) he delineated the phases of psycho-sexual development from birth to adulthood.

Freud's work was now attracting attention, and though he was attacked for his ideas about infantile sexuality he had followers and admirers. A group that included Adler began to meet regularly in 1902 and became the Vienna Psychoanalytic Society in 1908. The International Psychoanalytic Society was founded in 1910, with JUNG as its first president. In 1909 Freud, Jung and other psychoanalysts went on a lecture tour to Clark University in the USA and aroused considerable interest in psychoanalytic ideas, especially amongst the expanding number of specialists in nervous diseases working privately in non-custodial settings, and it was in America that Freud's work was to have perhaps its greatest impact. However, rivalries and frictions developed within the new psychoanalytic circle: Freud broke with Adler in 1911 and with Jung in 1913. Freud continued to develop his ideas about the dynamics of PERSONALITY. He introduced the concepts of the id and the ego as components of the personality, (*The Ego and the Id*, 1923) and added a third component, the superego, in relation to his broadening concern with society as a whole (*Civilization and Its Discontents*, 1929).

*Totem and Taboo* (1913) and *The Future of an Illusion* (1927) on the topic of religion had already dealt with some of these wider concerns (see TOTEMISM). He had also begun to apply his psychoanalytic concepts to individual biographies as in *Leonardo* (1910), developing a new genre of psycho-biography. In 1938 Freud and his family moved to London in the face of Nazi persecution. He died in 1939 from cancer of the jaw, first diagnosed in 1923. By the time of his death Freud was well known, and his ideas were beginning to be fashionable in intellectual and professional circles.

Freudian ideas have been criticized and rejected by the BEHAVIOURIST tradition of academic psychology with its POSITIVIST foundations, and more recently by a number of FEMINIST writers on grounds of their sexist assumptions (see PSYCHOANALYSIS). Many who have followed Freud have attempted to modify and develop his ideas. Within the psychoanalytic tradition the Neo-Freudians, a group including Erich Fromm, Karen Horney, Henry Stack Sullivan and Erik Erikson, as well as Alfred Adler, provide one example. Their basic point of divergence with orthodox Freudians has been over the role and importance of libido and of biological drives; neo-Freudians attach far greater importance to interpersonal relations and to the social and cultural factors in an individual's life. They are sometimes referred to as ego psychologists, a term also applied to more orthodox Freudians who, while continuing to emphasize biological drives, have developed Freud's ideas about ego functioning. Both developments have been especially influential in the USA where many of the neo-Freudians and ego psychologists have worked.                                    JB

**Friedmann, Georges** (1902-77). French critic of SCIENTIFIC MANAGEMENT in both the West and the USSR. He promoted industrial sociological investigations in post-war France (his best-known pupil was TOURAINE), focusing on the impact of technical advance on traditional crafts and skilled worker groups. The approach in *Problèmes humaines du Machinisme* (1947) [trs. *Industrial Society*] and *Le Travail en Miettes* (1956) [trs. *The Anatomy* *of Work*] antedates views that became widespread in English-speaking countries two decades later, with its concern for the issue of 'de-skilling' (see SKILL) and a somewhat starry-eyed view of work before industrialism. Friedmann was a follower of Proudhon rather than Marx on the question of the LABOUR PROCESS and its desirable evolution. Far from being transcended, work should remain at the centre of social life, even when automation might appear to promise its widespread abolition, for Friedmann shared Proudhon's belief that the acquisition of craft knowledge produced a qualititative moral alteration in the human individual. Advanced technical change risked destruction of what was most human and the course of accelerated industrialism in France after 1950 rendered him increasingly pessimistic.

See also SOCIOLOGIE DU TRAVAIL.

MR

**function.** A term used in mathematics, biology and social science to denote properties of interdependence between parts of a system. In mathematics, it refers to a VARIABLE considered in relation to one or more other variables on the value of which its own value depends. It is used in this sense in talking about ASSOCIATION between variables: for example, birth rates are a function of economic status. In biology, function refers to the contribution which different parts of an organism make to the maintenance of that organism, for instance the part played by the heart, liver and kidneys in maintaining human life. In sociology, by analogy, the term was introduced by RADCLIFFE-BROWN and MALINOWSKI to suggest that different parts of society met different societal needs, and that society could be conceptualized as made up of interdependent parts in reciprocal relation with each other.

See FUNCTIONALISM.

MB

**functionalism.** A theory based on an organic analogy: society is a bounded, self-maintaining system that maintains its equilibrium in the face of a hostile environment. To ensure a society's survival, its various social processes must mesh smoothly together to meet the system's needs. Functionalism's basic question is 'How does society meet its needs?' Each process, institution and practice is seen as performing a function that meets a societal need and thereby helps to maintain the society's structure or equilibrium. Social processes and institutions are understood in terms of their contribution to an ongoing social whole, not in terms of what people in the system think they are doing. A function is manifest when known to people and latent if they are unaware of its true role in the system.

Thus social practices must be understood in terms of their present contribution to a society. Whatever the origins of a practice, it will only be maintained if it continues to play a vital role in the society. This was stressed by MALINOWSKI and RADCLIFFE-BROWN: strange customs made sense when their total context was understood. In anthropology functionalism proved popular. The total context is available through the fieldwork method, but the history of pre-literate societies is more difficult to obtain. In sociology, the insistence of DURKHEIM on 'social facts' led to an emphasis on seeing social practices in relation to other social practices rather than in relationship to biological or individual psychological factors.

The basic functionalist explanation starts by identifying a problematic activity — one which seen in isolation appears to make no sense. Then this activity is placed in a wider social context and shown to be meeting some social need(s). Identifying the function constitutes the explanation of the activity. For instance, a Hopi Indian rain-dance appears to make no sense as it does not produce rain. However, it brings people together and reaffirms their faith in the collectivity, and thus the rain dance has the function of promoting social solidarity that will help the society cope with the drought. Some functionalist explanations go a step further and try to identify functional prerequisites — needs which any society must meet to survive. The best-known list of these is PARSONS's: adaption, goal attainment, integration and pattern-maintenance.

Functionalists explain change in a system

as a response to changes in the environment. The system, in order to remain adapted to its environment, is forced to change. Frequently this change takes the form of functional differentiation — one structural component will split into two new components that will perform more specialized functions more efficiently than the original single component (see DIVISION OF LABOUR).

One criticism is that functionalism is TELEOLOGICAL: it explains a cause (the function) by its effect (meeting a system need and thereby contributing to the system's stability). While this is sometimes a valid objection, functionalists can reverse their argument so that it is presented as partial explanation of system stability. When all institutions are functional each is maintained as part of an ongoing system by all the other institutions. This is not teleological. However, it assumes that everything in society is supportive of everything else. This postulate of functional unity is not accepted by most sociologists. Functionalism gives too integrated and harmonious a view of society. It tends to ignore the use of power to advance the interests of one group at the expense of other groups (see CONFLICT THEORY; CONSENSUS).

MERTON, in *Social Theory and Social Structure* (1949), makes functionalism more flexible by relaxing its basic assumptions. Social practices may be functional or dysfunctional (failing to support the social structure). In addition, for some given function there might be several functional alternatives. The price that is paid for this flexibility is that functionalism then ceases to be a useful theoretical approach. One knows only after analysis whether something is functional or not. In addition, no functionalist explanation of a dysfunction can be given, so that admitting dysfunctions undermines the basic functionalist approach. However, functionalism will always be a temptation when sociologists isolate social practices from their current context. That activities must be seen in relationship to the whole system in which they occur is functionalism's major contribution to society.

See also FUNCTIONAL THEORY OF STRATIFICATION; SOCIAL SYSTEM.

KM

**functional theories of religion.** Theories which consider religion primarily in terms of what it does for the individual, community or society (see RELIGION). MALINOWSKI saw religion and magic as assisting the individual to cope with situations of stress or anxiety. Religious ritual may enable the bereaved to reassert their collective solidarity, to express their common norms and values upon which the proper functioning of the community depends. Religion can also supplement practical, empirical knowledge, offering some sense of understanding and control in areas to which such knowledge does not extend.

A more influential tradition of functionalist thought on religion derives from DURKHEIM, whose *Elementary Forms of the Religious Life* presents a theory of religion which identifies religion with social cohesion: religious beliefs and rituals are understood in terms of the role they play in promoting and maintaining social solidarity. RADCLIFFE-BROWN argued that religious ceremonial, for example in the form of communal dancing, promoted unity and harmony and functioned to enhance social solidarity and the survival of the society. Religious beliefs contained in myths and legends express the social values of the different objects which have a major influence on social life, such as food, weapons, day and night etc. They form the value CONSENSUS around which society is integrated.

Recent functionalism has rejected Durkheim's view that religious beliefs are merely symbolic representations of society, while retaining his notion that religion has a central role in maintaining social solidarity. Kingsley Davis argues that religious beliefs form the basis for socially valued goals and a justification of them. Religion provides a common focus for identity and an unlimited source of rewards and punishments for behaviour.

Functionalist theories of religion face a problem in the apparent decline in religious belief and participation. What is viewed as SECULARIZATION in other theories is seen as simply religious change in functionalist terms. Functionalist theorists argue that religion takes different forms in apparently secular societies: it is more individualized, less tied to religious institutions. The character of modern industrial capitalist society, particularly its rampant individualism is thus seen to be expressed in the differentiated character of religion in a society like the USA. Although seemingly having little basis for integration, the celebration of individualism is itself an integrating feature of such diverse religious forms. Moreover, new and distinctive forms of religion may perform latent functions for the system by deflecting adherents from critical appraisal of their society and its distribution of rewards.

In anti-religious societies such as some Communist states this argument cannot hold, but here it is claimed that functional alternatives to traditional religion operate. Other systems of belief, such as communism itself, fulfil the same role as religion elsewhere. National ceremonial, ritual celebration of communist victories, heroes etc meet the same need for collective rites which reaffirm common sentiments and promote enhanced commitment to common goals.

Finally, even in highly secularized Western societies CIVIL RELIGION exists. This consists in abstract beliefs and rituals which relate a society to ultimate things and provide a rationale for national history, a transcendental basis for national goals and purposes.

Functional theories of religion suffer all the problems of FUNCTIONALISM generally. There is no consensus as to what social goals, if any, religion serves. There is also little evidence that if what are held to be such goals are not achieved society generates increased religious ritual, or some functionally equivalent substitute for it, or that its survival is fundamentally jeopardized by its failure so to do.

RW

**functional theory of stratification.** A number of functional theorists (see FUNCTIONALISM) have written on SOCIAL STRATIFICATION, including PARSONS. A prolonged debate arose from an article by Davis and Moore (*American Sociological Review*, 1945) arguing that 'social inequality is ... an unconsciously evolved device by which soci-

eties ensure that the most important positions are conscientiously filled by the most qualified persons.' This view combines a theory of occupational placement with a theory of motivation: 'In general', it suggests, 'those positions convey the best reward, and hence have the highest rank, which (a) have the greatest importance for the society and (b) require the greatest training or talent.' Inducements or rewards contribute to 'sustenance and comfort', 'humour and diversion' and 'self-respect and ego expansion'. Positions are not necessarily rewarded in proportion to their differential functional importance, but they should be rewarded sufficiently to attract competent people. Thus a second factor also determines reward — the differential scarcity of personnel with the requisite talents and training. Some positions demand rare and highly rewarded talents. 'In many cases, however, talent is fairly abundant in the population but the training process is so long, costly and elaborate that relatively few can quality. Modern medicine, for example, is within the mental capacity of most individuals, but a medical education is so burdensome and expensive that virtually none would undertake it if the position of the MD did not carry a reward commensurate with the sacrifice.'    There are many difficulties in accepting this theory. (1) It treats stratification as a universal, yet also speaks of stratification as an evolved device. This opens up the possibility of a prestratified society. Davis and Moore might have done better to present stratification as an example of what Parsons later called an evolutionary universal, that is, a structure which all societies adopt sooner or later in the course of their evolution. (2) It fails to consider alternative mechanisms of occupational placement and motivation consistent with an egalitarian society (see EQUALITY). (3) It is hard to make the concept of functional importance work. Davis and Moore offer two 'clues'. One concerns the uniqueness of a position, the degree to which no other position can perform the same function satisfactorily; the other is about dependence, the degree to which other positions are dependent upon the one in question. But uniqueness implies (horizontal) interdependence and, within the terms of the theory, may just as easily justify equality of reward. Is the hospital boilerman less functionally important than the consultant? And (vertical) dependence involves a tautology. The theory avers that stratification is composed of 'unequal rights and perquisites', necessary to ensure that the most important positions are filled by those best fitted; it then offers as one clue to functional importance dependence, which is defined in terms of super and subordination, an hierarchical structure of unequal rights (of command). (4) It treats stratification as facilitating a society's adaption to the conditions of its existence, where these conditions refer to both its physical environment and the relations and exchanges with other societies which it has evolved. When the conditions are changing, however, stratification may be more of a hindrance than a help insofar as it embodies the means by which the privileged perpetuate themselves from one generation to the next. Critics complain that in the USA and the UK stratification has obstructed the realization of the talents of subordinate groups to the detriment of society as a whole, whether the basis of disadvantage be economic (workers), racial (blacks) or sexual (women). Davis and Moore concede that inheritance and succession interfere with the filling of positions by the best qualified, but they try to save the theory by locating inheritance and succession in the KINSHIP system which then impedes the operation of the stratification system proper, as if the unit of stratification analysis is never the family or household, and the transmission of material and cultural advantage through the family has nothing to do with stratification. (5) The idea that training is a sacrifice has been criticized in that earnings foregone are typically recovered relatively quickly thereafter. Moreover student life is usually an agreeable experience in itself. (6) The theory is part of a general functional analysis which assumes that all societies enjoy a basic value CONSENSUS. In such a context it seems natural that differential rewards should follow from the differential evaluation of positions. But the argument can be reversed to say that dominant values are the product of dominant strata. Instead of deriving stratification from the differential importance of positions, the reverse argument proposes that dominant strata generate dominant conceptions of the relative importance of positions.

CGAB

# G

**Gadamer, Hans-Georg** (1900- ). German philosopher and historian of ideas. Main work: *Truth and Method* (1960). His PHENO-MENOLOGICAL HERMENEUTICS draws heavily on HEIDEGGER, and emphasizes the active commitment or engagement which is at work when we confront a historical text. The 'prejudices' we bring to the text are not something to be brushed aside but are a crucial part of the tradition which mediates our relationship to the text. The 'truth' of a historical interpretation is therefore a more complicated and even subjective matter than appears in the OBJECTIVISTIC 'methods' of traditional hermeneutics.

WO

**game theory.** This term can be used in two rather different senses: more generally it refers to the analysis of social interaction using the everyday concept of a game as a guiding analogy; more specifically it refers to a mathematical theory of rational behaviour in the face of action by others in situations of conflict and co-operation.

As a model of social interaction, the everyday concept of a game draws attention to interaction as divisible into episodes within which a well-defined set of players makes moves from a limited permissible set according to rules, and which have a clearly marked end when social value is redistributed according to the succession of moves made. RATIONALITY is preserved as long as moves make sense within the rules. As a mathematical concept, a game consists of two or more players, a limited set of possible strategies for each, and a function

assigning to each combination of strategies a UTILITY value to each player of the outcome of that combination of strategies. Game theory seeks an extension of classical utility-maximizing economic rationality to situations with more than one player.

Leibnitz (1710) saw the need for a theory of games of strategy as well as those of chance, but mathematical game theory began when John Von Neumann in 1928 proved its fundamental result, that all two-person games of pure conflict have optimal strategies for each player. This result was elaborated to analyse games of more than two players as well as economic phenomena in Von Neumann and Morgenstern's *Theory of Games and Economic Behaviour* (1947). They term situations of pure conflict zero-sum games, for what one player loses, another gains. Non-zero-sum games have an element other than pure conflict; an extra player can be added to make the game zero-sum, and the gains and losses accruing may be interpreted as benefits to the community or something similar. In n-person games, attention focuses on theories of coalition-formation between players with similar interests.

As a theory of rational social action, mathematical game theory makes heavy demands in terms of the measurement of the utility values required, the availability of information to each player about the others, and the time required for making complex reasonings. Very few social situations conform to these requirements, but some do, such as the international arms race (analysed for example by Anatol Rapoport) and

142

competition between firms or the media of communication. But in many such cases the situation is complicated by the explicit use of game-theoretic methods by the players themselves.

However, game theory has also been used to illuminate the structure of certain widely recurring situations of co-operation and conflict. Much work has been done on a situation termed 'prisoners dilemma'. A and B have jointly committed a crime, observed by no one. They are arrested, but provided both keep quiet, they will be discharged. However, each is individually offered a reduction in sentence for informing on the other, and an intermediate sentence if both inform. Should A or B do so, to avoid the worst possible outcome, the maximum sentence, if the other informs? Minimizing the worst possible outcome, a minimax strategy, both A and B inform, leading to them both serving the medium term, despite the existence of a better outcome for both if neither informs. So what does rational behaviour consist of here? Co-operation has advantages for both, but pursuing individual interests leads to a contradiction. This mixture of co-operation and conflict can be seen in many social situations of interaction and exchange, where NORMS of trust must be generated to ensure that the co-operative strategy dominates. The effects of different social-psychological and sociological assumptions upon the outcome can be investigated both in theory and by experiment.

This example illustrates the strengths of game theory in analysing the structure of interests in social situations, but it also illustrates its weakness. It can only deal with the lowest common denominator of social relations, and can tell us little about their diversity of form. Game theory is inadequate alone, but by stressing interaction between rational actors, individuals or groups it presents social reality in a more recognizable form than many more mechanistic models.

See CONFLICT THEORY.

See M. Shubik, *Game Theory and Related Approaches to Social Behaviour* (1964).

JL

**gamma.** See ASSOCIATION, COEFFICIENTS OF.

**Garfinkel, Harold** (1917- ). The founder of ETHNOMETHODOLOGY, though himself reluctant to be seen as the leader of any group. Born in Newark, New Jersey. A student of PARSONS, he completed his doctoral thesis, 'The Perception of the Other', in 1952. Strongly influenced by SCHUTZ and other PHENOMENOLOGISTS such as Aaron Gurwitz and HUSSERL, Garfinkel became interested in the analysis of the structure of the everyday world. He gathered colleagues and students around him at UCLA. In 1967 he published *Studies in Ethnomethodology*, papers designed to show the scope of ethnomethodology interest. Because of its dense prose style the book was initially greeted with some hostility and bafflement, and controversy still surrounds ethnomethodology. However, his work has subsequently attracted a number of adherents and a degree of general interest within sociology.

DBn

**Gemeinschaft.** A concept developed by TÖNNIES, usually translated as COMMUNITY. However, it refers strictly to a type of social relationship — one that is intimate, enduring and based upon a clear understanding of each individual's position in society. Culturally, societies characterized by Gemeinschaft are relatively homogeneous since their culture is enforced quite rigidly by well-recognized moral custodians — the church and the family. *Gemeinschaftien* sentiments place a high premium on the sanctity of KINSHIP and territoriality, and are also characterized by greater emotional cohesion, sentiment, continuity and authenticity. They may be contrasted with GESELLS-CHAFT.

HN

**gender and biological sex.** Sex refers to biological males and females distinguished by reproductive organs. Gender refers to feminine and masculine attributes and social ROLES. The central issue is whether gender, the social construction of sex, is in any way biologically determined.

There is a strong tradition which argues for biological difference and/or inferiority to explain women's subordination to men. In the 19th century women were viewed as totally controlled by their ovaries and the ebb and flow of the menstrual cycle. Women's passivity was derived from the passive, or 'anabolic', features of the ovum, and contrasted with the 'katabolic' or active nature of sperm, and hence men. In the 20th century women's 'natural' roles of wife and mother are viewed as genetically pre-programmed (in sociobiology), and male AGGRESSION and female passivity as hormonally produced.

Sex difference studies attempt to prove innate biological differences on the basis of performance on INTELLIGENCE tests. These studies show that women score higher in verbal ability and men in spatial ability. Girls do better on IQ tests until puberty when boys get higher scores. In school boys perform better at science and maths. All this is used as evidence for innate biological sex-differences. These studies have been criticized for ignoring similarities, for being biased in favour of tests which prove male superiority, for ignoring the effects of socialization and sex-role stereotyping and for incorrect inference of biological causality from socially (test-) produced differences.

The proponents of gender point to children attributed to the wrong biological sex at birth who cannot be resocialized into the correct gender when the classification is rectified. Transsexuals also constitute a problem, since they are usually biological males who strongly feel that they are women trapped in a male body. Other important pro-gender evidence comes from studies of mother-infant interaction, which indicate that mothers unknowingly respond differently to boys and girls. Girls are fed more quickly, left to cry more often and for longer periods, not played with as frequently, discouraged from exploring, and their behaviour is interpreted in stereotyped ways — all before the age of six months. Thus sex difference studies merely measure at a much later age behaviour which was learned in infancy.

Cross-cultural studies also furnish evidence for the gender hypothesis. Margaret MEAD, for instance, found that although societies embody some form of gender differentiation and the sexual DIVISION OF LABOUR, the actual tasks performed by men and women vary widely. Women's role in one society is men's in another. A powerful constant is the lower status

attributed to tasks if they are considered the province of women, and the higher if that of men.

Support for theories of innate difference would seem to imply impossibility of change, whereas support for gender theories de-naturalizes PATRIARCHY and thus makes social change possible. Another viewpoint is to argue that there probably are biological differences, but that until equality does away with socially constructed differences we cannot measure the biological ones. And do differences necessarily imply a hierarchy? Classification does not necessarily entail ranking. Most feminists would argue that gender differences are socially constructed. Psychoanalytic feminists have imposed a STRUCTURALIST interpretation on FREUD, arguing that his statements about women lacking a penis, being incomplete men, suffering from penis envy etc, do not refer to bodies and biological lacks but to the patri-archal symbolic order represented by the phallus as the signifier of that order. Radical and revolutionary feminists emphasize that the term sex-class refers to social relations and not to biological persons.

See also SEXUALITY.

See A. Oakley, *Sex, Gender and Society* (1972); J. Sayers, *Biological Politics* (1982).

EG

**gender stratification.** In the 1970s the Women's Movement (see FEMINISM), inside and outside sociology, drew attention to massive evidence of inequalities in the life chances of males and females, and of male domination in relations between them. This posed problems relating to SOCIAL STRATIFI-CATION which have not yet been satisfactorily resolved. The FAMILY has usually been taken as their unit of analysis and the occupation of the head of household (the male if present) or the principle earner (again usually the male) as the chief determinant of class position. They concentrated on the family because class material and cultural advantages and disadvantages are inherited, and on the occupation of the male, no doubt because of implicit sexism and because they feared any other procedure would render impossible the allocation of each household to a single class.

Feminists object that this fails to give women's work its proper due and fails to see that housewives are houseworkers (who daily reproduce, according to Marxists, the labour power of those members of the household working outside it, and who bear and raise, and thereby reproduce, the next generation of workers); see HOUSEWORK. Stratification theory and research practice should connect the generation, maintenance and transformation of structures of class and status outside the household with both material and cultural inequalities between households and relational inequalities within them. Class allocation by occupation will have to be abandoned in favour of approaches which are more sensitive to changes in the organization of domestic life and the composition of the labour force. Without reform the sociology of stratification in the 1980s could all too easily produce little more than a distorted analysis of the male half of the adult population only.

See also PATRIARCHY.

See A. Oakley, *Subject Women* (1981).

CGAB

**gene.** A nucleoprotein molecule within a chromosome which controls the chemistry of the cell and thereby influences the structure and properties of the organism. The underlying genetic constitution of an organism with respect to a particular trait or traits is called the genotype and can be contrasted with the phenotype, which is the organism's visible or measurable appearance with reference to the same trait or traits. Thus skin colour and eye colour are phenotypical traits controlled by the genotype. Differences of colour, hair and facial features have often been referred to as racial but they are better classified as forms of phenotypical variation. While groups conventionally classified as races have distinctive genetic profiles there are many important inter-group similarities and intra-group variations of a genetic character which are not outwardly visible (see CLINE). Differences in the genetic profiles of human groups arise from mutations (caused by changes in the chemistry of a gene); from natural selection (see DARWIN); and from genetic drift, a chance

factor arising from the formation of particular communities, as by migration.

MPB

**general linear model.** See FORMAL MODEL.

**generation.** In any society an aggregate of persons who are of more or less the same age may be termed a generation. This concept, like that of social class, allows the analysis of the influences at work on those occupying a similar social position, in this case of age. Thus there is the possibility of uncovering the social aspects of the biological process of ageing. The concept may be used narrowly in relation to those born at different times of the same parents within a family unit, or broadly in relation to those born within a period, usually about thirty years, within one society. Each generation, by virtue of the different collection of experiences it has undergone, will perceive historical events from a different perspective. The young and the old see the past and present differently, conflict can easily result over interpretation of social events and differences can result over the future courses to be worked for. Such differences between the generations form one source of social change and for this reason theorists, or reformers interested in change, give great importance to the younger generation. The process is more complex because within any one generation those experiencing reality similarly because they occupy the same social positions (e.g. within one social class) can form what MANNHEIM (*Essays in the Sociology of Knowledge,* 1952) called 'generation units', so that intra- as well as inter-generational conflict is also possible.

See ADOLESCENCE; CHILDHOOD; LIFE CYCLE.

PWM

**generative grammar.** See CHOMSKY.

**Gesellschaft.** A concept developed by TÖNNIES, usually translated as 'society', 'organization' or 'association'. However, it refers strictly to a type of social relationship — one that is impersonal, contractual and calculative; such relationships are increasing due to the growth of urban, industrial society, with a consequent decline of GEMEINSCHAFT.

HN

**gesture.** In G.H. MEAD's social philosophy, the gesture is that part of an ACT which came first, is overt, and epitomizes the full act to come (e.g. a dog growling). It is a cue for an appropriate response by others but does not carry any conscious meaning or intent in itself (e.g. another dog may growl back but does not interpret). This non-linguistic communication is referred to as a 'conversation of gestures'. In contrast, a significant gesture is one where the act has meaning both to the actor and to the other toward whom the actor gestures. As Mead says: 'If a gesture calls out a like gesture in the other individual and calls out a similar idea, then it becomes a significant gesture. It stands for the ideas in the minds of both of them.' (*Mind, Self and Society*, 1934).

See also CONVERSATION ANALYSIS.

KP

**Giddings, Franklin H.** (1855-1931). American sociologist. Born in Sherman, Connecticut, the son of a Congregational minister, Giddings studied engineering and then became a journalist. From 1888 he taught sociology and political science at Bryn Mawr College and in 1894 he became the first full time professor of sociology in the USA, at Columbia University.

Giddings fused SPENCERIAN EVOLUTIONISM with COMTEAN POSITIVISM. In his early work he expanded WARD's psychological evolutionism, subsequently developing an interest in the new psychological BEHAVIOURISM and quantification. Giddings diverged from Spencer in believing society to be a primarily psychic phenomen. Sociology as the psychology of society should be concerned with the integration of subjective and objective processes in the formation of social life. Rejecting a rigid evolutionary determinism, Giddings's Social DARWINISM differs from SUMNER's in stressing the conscious, volitional nature of choice. He believed that nature will reject harmful choices through natural selection. Social evolution is progressive as the 'survival of the fittest' promotes moral and intellectual attributes.

Giddings's *Principles of Sociology* (1896) and *Elements of Sociology* (1898) are strongly influenced by Spencerian evolutionism and borrow from Ward the concepts of 'genesis' and 'telesis' and the distinction between 'social statics' (structure) and 'social dynamics' (change, evolution). His interest centres on the interaction between psychic laws and physical laws of natural selection and survival. His central concept 'consciousness of kind' suggests the influence of DURKHEIM. Social groups arise through natural selection and psychological and physiological activities, and group members share a common social mind based upon mutual recognition of being of like kind. In his subsequent shift towards behaviourism Giddings attributed this process to 'pluralistic behaviour' (the like response to the same stimulus). He distinguished four stages of social evolutionism (zoogeny, anthropogeny, ethnogeny, demogeny) and three types of society (military-religious, liberal-legal, economic-ethical). Believing that classes based on moral, mental and physical differences were more significant than economic class divisions, he outlined four such classes: social (the elite), nonsocial (the masses), pseudosocial (those dependent upon others' assistance), anti-social (the criminals).

Giddings favoured comparative historical methodology. *Inductive Sociology* (1901) discussed the use of statistics in furthering this end. His main works were *Studies in the Theory of Human Society* (1922) and *The Scientific Study of Human Society* (1924). Giddings failed to draw upon contemporary developments in psychology and anthropology and created a widespread misunderstanding of Spencer's evolutionism through publication of an outline of Spencer's ideas exclusively concerned with the transition from military to industrial society. He paved the way for neo-positivism and quantitative analysis.

JW

**gift relationship.** Traditionally associated in social anthropology with the theories of Marcel Mauss; for this usage, see RECIPROCITY. The concept was revised and changed in the field of social policy by TITMUSS during a study of blood donors (*The Gift Relationship*, 1970). Donorship was a 'sensitive universal social indicator' or 'an index of the cultural values and quality of human relationships prevalent in a particular society'. In the USA blood donors were paid and were not typical of the population: they were more likely to be members of low-income and racial minority groups. The need to offer payment to blood donors showed the importance of cash incentives and their incompatibility with a sense of COMMUNITY in American society. In Britain, donors are not paid and are more a cross-section of the whole community (some over-representation of CENSUS SOCIAL CLASSES 1 and 2 is probably the result of a number of variables other than the level of interest among the people concerned). Titmuss argued that in Britain people volunteered for a variety of reasons ranging from pure altruism to awareness of the value of the blood transfusion service, but that such people felt integrated into the community. The British system only worked because of the existence of a social climate quite different to that noted in the USA. Titmuss also noted that in the USSR blood donors were offered incentives through longer holidays, free public transport, time off work, free meals and cash payments. This showed that, as in the USA, the service of community must be low.

While Titmuss's study has been recognized as important it has provoked criticism. The selection of blood donorship as the basis for the construction of a general argument was unwise; though no monetary reward is offered in the UK, donors are not aware that they are giving something for which reward could be sought. If other areas of social policy had been examined, Titmuss's conclusion about the nature of the social climate in Britain might have been different.

MPJ

**glossolalia.** Speaking in tongues, derived from the Greek root for 'tongue' and 'language' and used to refer to vocal utterances possessing language-like properties in terms of rudimentary phonological differentiation and syntactical arrangement, but lacking systematic semantic structuring. Glossolalia is vocalization believed by the speaker to be some natural or supernatural language but unintelligible to the normal hearer. It is usually produced in a religious context and may be employed as a form of praise or prayer, expressive of diffuse feelings and sentiments of the worshipper. Alternatively, the utterances may be believed to contain some message of hope, admonition or prophecy, 'interpretable' by the speaker or by a listener possessing the 'gift of interpretation'. In the Christian tradition 'speaking in tongues' as one of the charismatic gifts of the Holy Spirit dates from the Day of Pentecost after Christ's death when the disciples were gathered together 'And there appeared unto them cloven tongues like as of fire, and it sat upon each of them. And they were filled with the Holy Ghost, and began to speak with other tongues, as the Spirit gave them utterance.' (Acts 2:3-4) Speaking in strange tongues accompanied many of the great Revivals of the 18th and 19th centuries, but these were largely sporadic occurrences until the emergence of Pentecostalism at the end of the 19th century. Pentecostal SECTS found their main support among the poor and among migrants, for example poor American blacks from the Southern States who moved to the Northern cities, West Indian immigrants to Britain, and rural Indian and *mestizo* migrants to the cities of South America.

Glossolalia and other 'Gifts of the Spirit' heightened the emotional atmosphere of Pentecostal services, providing occasions for emotional release. They gave assurance of inward power to the powerless, the presence of supernatural comfort to the isolated and lonely, and of expressive lucidity to the ill-educated and those who were ill at ease in a culture and perhaps a language to which they were not native. Since the 1960s glossalalia has emerged as a regular aspect of worship within many major churches and denominations, including the Catholic Church. These neo-Pentecostals remain part of their existing denomination but where the congregation is not entirely favourable they hold services and meetings in addition to those normally scheduled and at these allow the Gifts of the Spirit to manifest themselves. The neo-Pentecostals are overwhelmingly middle class in composition and glossolalia

## 148   goals

provides a means of reinvigorating religious practices that have become increasingly formal and intellectual, providing an experiential reassurance of faith.

See W.J. Samarin, *Tongues of Men and Angels* (1972).
RW

**goals.** Intended outcomes from given social actions. The term may cover informal interpersonal actions or the more formal social behaviour that occurs within formal organizations. In this latter case goals are often specified in written form for specific organizations. Such goals are put into operation by actors who interpret the goals subjectively. Under such human interpretations the stated goals of an organization may mislead because those in power may be steering their organization towards a different set of goals. Even if those running organizations succeed in meeting the written goals or their own goals, the functions fulfilled by the organization in relation to interlocking social institutions may be other than anticipated or intended. A similar variation in goal and function may also occur in the case of informal interpersonal behaviour. For example, a formal examination system established to select persons competent by academic criteria may succeed, but may also act dysfunctionally by discouraging entrants or by reducing personal initiative in answering examination questions. However, much sociological analysis has been in terms of intentional action and as a result has examined various ways of relating ends or goals to means. In contemporary Western societies particularly attention has been given to various forms of RATIONALITY in this respect.

See ORGANIZATIONS; UNANTICIPATED CONSEQUENCES.
PWM

**Goffman, Erving** (1922-82). Famous both within sociology, and outside that discipline, for his analyses of the style of interpersonal relations. Born in 1922 in Manville, Canada, he gained his first degree at the University of Toronto in 1945 and subsequent degrees at the University of Chicago (MA 1949, PhD 1953). He conducted field research in the Shetland Islands between 1949 and 1951 and this emerged as his first, and possibly most central, book *The Presentation of Self in Everyday Life* (1956). Subsequently he worked on several projects in Chicago under the direction of E. Shils and E.C. Banfield before embarking on research into psychiatric wards in Bethesda and Washington between 1954 and 1957 (published as *Asylums* in 1961). Moving to a professorship at Berkeley, his distinctive sociological style of writing and theorizing was widely recognized and he became a central figure in American sociology, serving as President of the American Sociological Association in 1981. Although he is frequently identified with DRAMATURGY and DEVIANCE he moved well beyond these in his later works, *Frame Analysis* (1974) and *Forms of Talk* (1981), but his abiding life-time concern was with patterns of human communication. In 1968 he became Benjamin Franklin Professor of Anthropology and Sociology at the University of Pennsylvania.

See DRAMATURGY; ROLE; STIGMA; TOTAL INSTITUTION.
KP

**Gramsci, Antonio** (1891-1937). Italian Marxist theorist. Born in Sardinia, Gramsci became a member of the Italian Socialist Party when at Turin University. From 1919 he was a member of the editorial group of *L'Ordine Nuovo*, active in the factory council movement and a leading figure in the factory occupations in northern Italy in 1920. He was on the Central Committee of the Italian Communist Party (PCI) from its foundation in 1921, and replaced Bordiga as General Secretary in 1924, the year he was also elected to parliament. In 1926 he was arrested, deprived of his parliamentary seat, and condemned by the Fascist government to 20 years imprisonment, the privations of which led to his death.

Gramsci's writings up to 1926 were mainly journalistic, while those from his prison period are unsystematic, elliptical (often to evade the prison censor) and subject to varying interpretations. But Gramsci is agreed to have made a major contribution to the development of post-war Marxism. A central feature is his rejection of the base-superstructure dichotomy and his insistence on the pervasive importance of culture and ideology both for ruling class domination and as the terrain for contesting its supremacy (see HEGEMONY). A political revolution could only be successful where the working classes had already won the struggle of ideas in civil society. This gave special importance to the role of intellectuals, though never as the bearers of a scientific truth that was unavailable to the masses. Scientific interpretations of Marxism as a system of economic and social laws were incompatible with any genuine popular self-activity. In the same vein Gramsci never abandoned the spirit of the Workers' Council Movement even when he advocated a more decisive role for the party after 1921.

Gramsci's ideas, and the more 'open' conception of Marxism they represent, have won increasing influence since the 1950s, not least among Communists seeking an alternative to official Soviet orthodoxy. His exploration of distinctively Italian cultural and historical themes and his insistence that the revolutionary movement must assume a national character if it is to win widespread support, have contributed to this influence, both in Italy and elsewhere.

See LAW, *Marxist Theory of.*

DB

**graph theory.** A branch of mathematics that does not deal with graphs in the normal sense of charts plotting variables against each other but with graphs in a specialized sense. A graph in this sense consists of a set of points or vertices, represented geometrically as points, and a set of line-segments connecting them, representing, by directed or undirected arrows, relations between the point-set. The theory is concerned, for example, with the way the lines connect up the points (connectivity), with the existence of cycles, the way the lines impinge on and depart from the points, and the ways the graph can be decomposed into sub-graphs. The theory is of the utmost generality, and while almost anything can be represented as a graph, the points are usually individuals or groups, and the lines represent the network of social relations of different sorts between them.

In the 1950s graph theory arose in sociology in the context of the related areas of

SOCIOMETRY, and the organization of interpersonal attitudes (see COGNITIVE CONSISTENCY THEORY). In sociometry, individuals are typically asked to make choices of other individuals from their group, and the pattern of these choices tabulated in a sociomatrix or represented as a graph. Graph-theoretic concepts such as symmetry and transitivity were used to discuss the way the choices fitted together and the way they formed cycles or linear orders, and random graphs were constructed for purposes of comparison. Interest also focused on the identification of closely connected subgroups (cliques) although these lacked coherent theoretical interpretation. Mostly concern was not with structural properties of the graph but with the distribution of choices given or received for characterizing the individuals.

In the field of interpersonal attitudes, Cartwright and Harary (*Psychological Review*, 1956) represented positive and negative attitudes between people as a graph, and used graph theory to work out the consequences for the graph of theories of the cognitive organization of attitudes (the bipartition theorem). Structural balance theory developed from this beginning, and although no new fundamental results were developed after the bipartition theorem, numerous hypotheses were proposed as to the consequences for the individual and the group of different types of imbalance, and as to the general principles governing movement toward balance. Indices were constructed to measure imbalance for individuals and graphs as a whole, but these turned out to be of little use in understanding social behaviour, although at the intuitive level the idea of a social network or graph provided an alternative concept to that of the institutionalized group for picturing informal social organization.

Boyd (1969), using abstract algebraic methods, formalized the result that structural balance theory was a special case of a more general set of consistency conditions in social networks (Group Partition theorem), seen most importantly in the prescriptive marriage systems analysed earlier by Whyte in *Anatomy of Kinship* (1963). Other social systems are able to tolerate possible inconsistencies in social and kinship networks, for the theorem has proved of limited applicability.

Graph theory and related methods have also been used to analyse the structure of formal organizations. In social network applications, a range of computer programme packages is available for analysis, and these tend to limit the production of new techniques. A major difficulty has been the lack of a sampling theory for graphs: how are inferences about structural properties of a whole graph to be made from a sample subgraph? Without such a theory graph methods can be very cumbersome. However, Harrison White's unit at Harvard has made consistent attempts to produce programmes that will simplify structure by grouping individuals into categories on the basis of the total set of connections obtaining in the network, and thereby to replace concepts like ROLE, CLASS and STATUS — which tend to be treated as individual attributes — with counterparts that, in the graph-theoretic sense, are genuinely structural.

JL

**Green Revolution.** High-yielding varieties of wheat and rice, a result of an ingenious invention by Norman Borlaugh in 1953. Until then the use of fertilizers, pesticides and other important agricultural techniques had normally resulted in plants growing taller rather than yielding more grain. In wind and rain these plants would topple, reducing productivity. Borlaugh bred dwarfing genes into disease-resistant plants. Instead of growing taller when fertilized they grew larger heads of grain, thus increasing yields up to 100 per cent. The Green Revolution has been a mixed blessing for the hungry people of the world. The application of its technology is expensive, and requires large-scale holdings and an abundant water supply to be economically viable. This excludes small peasants and tenant farmers from its benefits. Unless accompanied by co-operative or socialist forms of land reform, the introduction of Green Revolution techniques exacerbates social inequalities in the rural areas of the THIRD WORLD.

AH

**guild.** An organization set up, usually in conjunction with local political rulers, to control entry to and the practices of trades and professions in urban settlements. Guilds are to be found in one form or another in most societies with a complex DIVISION OF LABOUR but they reached their zenith of economic, social and political power in the medieval cities of Western Europe. The most interesting sociological analysis of their role as the first real organizers of free labour and the crucial part they played in sustaining the autonomy of the city in feudal society is to be found in WEBER's *The City.*

LS

**Gumplowicz, Ludwig** (1838-1909). Of Polish-Jewish parentage, Gumplowicz was Professor of Public Law at the University of Graz, Austria, from 1875 until his death. Principal works: *Rasse und Staat* (1875), *Der Rassenkampf* (1883), *Grundriss der Soziologie* (1885), translated as *Foundations of Sociology* or *Outlines of Sociology.* Gumplowicz was a Social DARWINIST believing in EVOLUTION as the survival of the fittest, and a MATERIALIST who nevertheless asserted the primacy of MILITARISM in society. Men pursue economic goals but are unable to expropriate the possessions or exploit the labour of other members of their own, broadly egalitarian, kin-group. But as ETHNOCENTRISM (a term he coined) is original to the human group, they attempt to kill outsiders and expropriate their possessions. The 'fittest' achieve this. When they turn from Extermination to the EXPLOITATION of labour, they found the STATE as a set of permanent legal and political institutions. In time, these conquest relations (called 'super stratification' by later militarist theorists, such as Rustow) settle down into SOCIAL STRATIFICATION. The different CLASSES come to gradually regard each other as members of the same human group — 'society'. In this way, societies became larger and more complex through the historical process.

Though the theory was over-generalized, parts of it were more germane than 20th-century sociology has acknowledged. The emphasis on conflict and process had an influence on Albion Small and through him on PARK and the CHICAGO SCHOOL. But the

Social Darwinist and, especially, the late 19th-century RACIST aspects were not acceptable. These popularized the theory among FASCISTS and discredited it among Fascism's victorious conservative, liberal and Marxist opponents. As a result the important role of militarism in societies has been neglected by contemporary sociology.

MM

# H

**Habermas, Jürgen** (1929- ). German philosopher and sociologist who taught philosophy and sociology in Frankfurt 1964-71 and is currently working at the Max Planck Institut, Starnberg. Main works: *Structural Change in the Public Sphere* (1962), *Theory and Practice* (1963), *Knowledge and Human Interests* (1968), *The Logic of the Social Sciences* (1970), *Legitimation Crisis* (1973), *The Reconstruction of Historical Materialism* (1976). The leading figure in the second generation of the Frankfurt School of CRITICAL THEORY, Habermas ranges over the contemporary human sciences in a unique way, tracing connections between speech-act theory and the ideologies of late capitalist societies, developmental psychology and the historical growth of normative structures, the philosophy of science and technocratic politics. His central theme is the possibility of a rational political commitment to socialism in societies in which science and technology are dominant. This is the broader context of his critique of POSITIVISM in *Knowledge and Human Interests*.

See also KNOWLEDGE, SOCIOLOGY OF.

WO

**Halévy thesis.** The name given to a range of ideas presented by Elie Halévy (1870-1937) concerning the role of Methodism in the development of English society in the late 18th and 19th centuries. Halévy argued that England's stability during a period of revolutionary upheaval through Europe could not be accounted for adequately in terms of British political institutions or economic circumstances: the Industrial Revolution created massive economic hardship unmitigated by a corrupt oligarchic system of government. Methodist preachers, though ousted from Anglican pulpits for their irregular, improvised style of preaching and radical message of justification by faith through grace, promulgated a socially conservative ideology which stressed individual rather than collective salvation and personal rather than political change. In a situation of widespread popular discontent Methodism replaced incipient political revolt by religious enthusiasm. Through their demand for methodical religious observance and moral conformity the Methodists carried to the lower classes the values and aspirations of a respectable bourgeoisie, and thus facilitated the social mobility of their adherents, bridging the gap between the labouring classes and the Anglican establishment. Rising from humble origins a man might join the Methodists as a part of his striving for a more respectable style of life. Should he, or his children, continue to rise in the world, they might in due course join the Established Church. Wesley himself identified this tendency.

Halévy also believed that Methodism, by winning the attachment of the aspiring middle classes, denied discontented bourgeois leadership to incipient popular revolt. Though pushed out of the Anglican Church Methodism infected the Church, inspiring some Anglican clergy to adopt its methods and doctrine. Evangelicalism infiltrated the middle and upper classes, substantially changing the moral ethos of England in the 19th century from an earlier aristocratic to a more bourgeois code of conduct. This also narrowed the cultural gap between the social classes and inspired the charitable and reform endeavours of the Victorian Evangelicals, who sought to assimilate the poor and reprobate to a middle-class standard of behaviour and morality.

Halévy's thesis has received support from social historians such as E.P. Thompson (*The Making of the English Working Class*, 1963), for whom Methodism was one of the ideological factors aiding in the subordination of the work force to the discipline of factory production. Influenced by Marx, Thompson stresses the compensatory character of religious enthusiasm, its role as an 'opiate' in conditions leading to despair. One of the leading critics of the Halévy thesis is Eric Hobsbawm, who rejects the notion that religious enthusiasm is an alternative to political protest (*Labouring Men*, 1964). He argues that political radicalism and Methodism spread simultaneously in some areas, the latter providing leaders in many of the struggles for the rights of working people that took place in the late 19th century and beyond.

See also PROTESTANT ETHIC.

RW

**hallucination.** See MENTAL ILLNESS.

**Hansen's Law.** Marcus Lee Hansen (1892-1938), historian of Swedish immigration into the United States, formulated the 'principle of third-generation interest' concerning differences in the attitudes of successive generations towards the culture of the country from which they originated. It was briefly expressed as 'what the son wishes to forget, the grandson wishes to remember'. Second-generation immigrants experienced a pressure to conform to the ways of the majority; the third generation, feeling secure in their society, had more freedom to identify themselves with their ancestors.

MB

**hardware.** See SOFTWARE.

**Hawthorne Studies.** A series of field experi-

ments, observations of working groups and depth interviews with employees undertaken in the Hawthorne plant, Chicago, of the Western Electric Company, between 1924 and 1939. Initiated through the Personnel Department of the company, the programme became associated with the Harvard University Business School and with MAYO. The results constituted the main evidence used by the HUMAN RELATIONS MOVEMENT to create theories of industrial behaviour stressing social influences, as well as providing a great impetus to the growth of modern personnel management. Perennially controversial, these studies remain a focal point in Industrial Sociology and Organization Theory.

MR

**health, sociology of.** A counterpart to MEDICAL MODELS of explanation which concentrate on organic disease mechanisms, sociological explanation redirects attention to social relationships as powerful determinants of changing health experience. Drawing on EPIDEMIOLOGICAL knowledge and technique to reveal the distinctive social distribution of medically defined conditions in a population, attention is focused on variables like GENDER and CLASS as possible direct influences in the AETIOLOGICAL process. A related concern is the development of new concepts of health and ill-health from non-medical perspectives.

In the analysis of individual experience, the onset of illness is conceptualized as a process characterized by a complex sequence of interactions between physiological, psychological and social factors. Social variables appear either as mediating mechanisms determining the individual's capacity to cope with the negotiation of critical life events such as bereavement, DIVORCE, and unemployment, which are seen as the underlying or prior causes of disease onset, or they are themselves accredited an independent causal role.

The subject matter of the sociology of health overlaps with the sociology of medicine, medical sociology, and EPIDEMIOLOGY. See also MEDICAL MODEL; MEDICINE, SOCIOLOGY OF; STRESS.

See E. Mishler *et al.*, *Social Contexts of Health, Illness, and Patient Care* (1981).

NH

**Hegel, Georg Wilhelm Friedrich** (1770-1831). The central figure of German IDEAL-ISM and of 19th-century philosophy in general. Major works: *Philosophy of Right, Phenomenology of Mind, Philosophy of History.* Hegel's idealism is distinctive in its historical emphasis. The mind comes to know itself by externalizing or alienating itself in the 'outside world' (see ALIENATION). He argued that reason and reality can be subsumed under what he called the 'absolute spirit'. This manifests itself in history through the DIALECTICAL cancelling out of conflicting tendencies (thesis and antithesis) resulting in a synthesis at a higher level of reason and freedom. Every event in history can be located in this movement. Great historical figures may believe themselves to be acting autonomously but they are really uncon-scious tools of the 'cunning of Reason'. The spirit will finally reach its highest stage in an eternal state which can alone guarantee freedom and justice. It is morally superior to the individual and is indeed the force which makes humans truly moral. Hegel came increasingly to believe that constitutional monarchy, and the Prussian monarchy in particular, could be such a state. Its bureau-crats could, therefore, become a 'universal class', capable of acting in the interests of humanity as a whole.

It can thus be seen that Hegel's system covers the whole spectrum of philosophy, including the philosophy of history and political philosophy. Though these theories were very widely accepted in the 19th century, they have lost most of their appeal in the 20th. For sociology, Hegel's importance is to have influenced later writers, especially MARX. The concepts of alienation, PRAXIS, the dialectic and the universal class (for Marx, the proletariat) were given a mate-rialist twist by Marx, who indeed claimed to be standing Hegel 'on his feet' again. Hegel's concept of 'objective mind', expressing itself in the cultural life of an epoch, was also a dominant theme of later HISTORICISM.

WO, MM

**hegemony.** A term which was in use in the 19th century with the sense of one state or ruler having political predominance over another. In the 20th century its use has been extended, following the Italian Marxist GRAMSCI (see *Selections from the Prison Notebooks,* 1971) to relationships of domination between social classes, as in the phrase, 'bourgeois hegemony'. It is now commonly used to indicate a state of con-sensual predominance of the powerful group or class in a society or social system over the ruled. It covers the whole range of NORMS and values, not just the political, involved in the ruling group's view of the world. A ruling class or group to which legitimacy is given has achieved hegemony; its rule is accepted without question and alternatives are not mooted. A hegemonic class imposes its own views on society as a whole. It may be contrasted with another of Gramsci's concepts, a corporate class which pursues its view of society within a structure determined outside its own control. Hegemony is rare, though groups in power seek constantly to attain it. Although power may be achieved by force, hegemony ultimately rests upon agreement with a specific set of norms and values. Hence, the formal educational system is important in achieving hegemony. Some analysis of education has been carried out in terms of attempts to reach, impose and preserve a state of hegemony. Such analysis directs attention to the relations of the cultures of the classes or groups in any society, and to the success or otherwise of the hegemonic class in imposing its culture upon other classes or groups.

See CONSENSUS, CLASS CONSCIOUSNESS.

PWM

**Heidegger, Martin** (1889-1976). German philosopher. Main work: *Being and Time* (1927). Heidegger used HUSSERL'S PHENO-MENOLOGY to create a philosophy which is generally considered (though not by Heidegger himself) to be EXISTENTIALIST, since its central concept is *Dasein*, human being in the world. His existentialism and his later reflections on philosophy and language powerfully influenced French philosophy; some ETHNOMETHODOLOGISTS in the Anglo-Saxon countries have also drawn on his later work.

WO

**hermeneutics.** The art of interpretation. Initially applied to the understanding of classical and biblical texts, the term was extended to the field of the human sciences (cf. VERSTEHEN). It is also used within EXISTENTIALISM in the more speculative sense of an inquiry into the meaning of human existence.

Two major controversies exist in hermeneutic theory. The first is between OBJECTIVIST theories which search for a 'correct' meaning of texts, human actions and institutions, and subjectivist theories which stress the interaction between interpreter and text and the importance of what the text means 'for us'. The second controversy concerns the scope of hermeneutics in relation to other modes of human inquiry such as sociological and psychological theories concerned with providing causal explanations. This question was the subject of an extended exchange between GADAMER and HABERMAS. There is also a tension within hermeneutics, stressed particularly by Paul Ricoeur, between a 'debunking' tradition represented by MARX, NIETZSCHE and FREUD and a more conciliatory or eclectic approach which examines a variety of texts for the elements of truth they may contain.

WO

**historical demography.** A recent and growing area of DEMOGRAPHY concerned with the numerical study of past populations, sometimes distinguished from demographic history, the study of the history of population changes and their causes. Demographic facts about historical societies are important to demography in that they extend backwards the data upon which the understanding of current population processes is predicated. In history and sociology estimates of such facts can help (1) to fill the gaps in the assumptions of theories of DEMOGRAPHIC TRANSITION from pre-industrial to industrial society and (2) to elaborate over-simple theories of the relationship between population, family structure, mode of production and technology. Changes in social structure tend to be important when comparisons of demographic rates over long time-periods are made. From the point of view of demography, it is difficult to control for these social factors; from the point of view of sociology historical demography provides the best chance to study the intimate relationship

between demographic and social development.

Graunt's early work (1662) contains historical material (see DEMOGRAPHY), and Rickman, who organized the first British CENSUS of 1801, extended data series back to 1570. But the first systematic modern work in this area is that of Louis Henry and the French Institut d'Etudes Démographiques in the 1950s. Parish registers were extensively used and a collection of procedures, such as FAMILY RECONSTITUTION, were developed for making use of this source on the *ancien régime*. E.A. Wrigley applied these methods to Colyton in Devon over the period 1538-1837, and the Cambridge Group for the History of Population and Social Structure was formed to carry on work on parish registers. The output has been used by the Group's Director, Peter Laslett, amongst others, to evaluate models of Western marriage (suggested by Hajnal) and family structure as enduring patterns and to study rates of legitimate and illegitimate births. Interest has been stimulated by historical demography in the related areas of sexual behaviour and the concept and history of childhood.

Historical demography, even more than demography in general, is vitally dependent on the nature and quality of its sources, and it is the co-ordinated exploitation of every scrap of information that has marked post-war developments. Apart from census and registration data, sources that are available include bills of mortality, ecclesiastical records, fiscal and military records, property lists, wills, marriage settlements, genealogies, tombstones, the founding of new towns, colonization, price trends and archaeological remains. These sources are of widely varying quality, and even census and registration data can be difficult to interpret due to differences in procedure over time.

JL

**historical methods.** Sociologists have shown increasing interest in using the methods and materials of the historian. Two distinct uses of historical data have been made by sociologists.

(1) As secondary sources. Extensive reliance has been placed upon published historical work as a basis for further socio-

logical investigation and analysis. In this mode of research, historical monographs form the raw materials which are then analysed within a broader theoretical and comparative framework, as in the work of Barrington MOORE (*Social Origins of Dictatorship and Democracy*, 1966), P. Anderson (*From Antiquity to Feudalism* and *Lineages of the Absolutist State*, both 1974) and I. Wallerstein (*The Modern World System*, 1974). Broader theories of social development may be illuminated in this way, although critics point to the selective use of evidence and the tendency to illustrate rather than demonstrate propositions. The scope and power of theories is achieved at the expense of a firm empirical grounding, giving macro-theoretical historical sociology a somewhat speculative character.

(2) As primary sources. There are many cases in which sociologists have adopted the methods of the historian, selecting original research data from surviving documentary material. This brings problems, familiar to historians, of the selective survival of materials and of judging the REPRESENTA-TIVENESS and RELIABILITY of the source. TRI-ANGULATION is often important in checking historical data. The actual sources used include all types of documentary record, both official and unofficial (see HISTORICAL DEMOGRAPHY).

Another valuable method for the recent past is oral history, the systematic collection of recollections about the past to throw light on particular problems and provide an archive for future social historians. P. Thompson's work on the Edwardian period (*The Edwardians*, 1975) is seminal here.

Historical sociology often differs from historical research in its more explicit use of theory and more abstract concepts, although relying on the same basic research techniques. However, the line between the methods of the historical sociologist and the sociological historian is increasingly difficult to draw.

See R.F. Berkhofer, *A Behavioural Approach to Historical Analysis* (1969); P. Abrams, *Historical Sociology* (1982).

MB

**historicism.** The words *Historismus* and *Historizismus* came into frequent usage in Germany between the Wars, but the central idea — the radical importance of history as an explanatory principle — goes back to the end of the 18th century and the beginnings of German romanticism. 'Historicism' has been used in a pejorative sense by NIETZSCHE and HUSSERL. Historicists argue the positive thesis that historical epochs are radically distinct from one another and that historical phenomena must therefore be studied and evaluated 'in their own terms'. This principle thus contradicts the tendency of 18th-century thought to assume that human nature and social institutions are relatively unchanging. The 'historical school' of law, for example, attacked the idea of a constant law; economists like Gustav Schmoller opposed the construction of deductive theories of general application.

Various alleged implications of this principle are stressed by different writers. DILTHEY emphasized the concept of VERSTE-HEN. RICKERT and Friedrich Meinecke (1862-1954) stressed the need to focus on individual historical phenomena. TRO-ELTSCH attacked historicism for its relativist implications, Karl MANNHEIM argued for a qualified RELATIVISM which he calls relationism. For Schmoller, economic laws can only be laws of economic development. This developmental theme is also the basis of POP-PER's use of 'historicism': for Popper, historicism is the philosophically wrong and polit-ically pernicious doctrine that the social sciences can predict long-term historical trends, a doctrine that leads to fascism and communism. Despite its very tenuous con-nection with earlier senses of historicism (which Popper calls historism) his usage, though perhaps not his polemic, has been widely adopted in the English-speaking world.                                          WO

**Hobbes, Thomas** (1588-1679). English philosopher and political theorist, author of *Leviathan* (1651). This argues that man must submit to the state so as to escape the 'war of every man against every man' which would exist in a state of nature. This is the 'problem of order' or the 'Hobbesian problem' invoked by PARSONS and other sociologists. Hobbes is also the first modern exponent of MATERIALISM, drawing analogies between his social theory and the mechanical universe of Galilean physics. His criticism of the METAPHYSICAL abuse of language foreshadows that of the Logical POSITIVISTS.

See SOCIAL CONTRACT.

WO

**holism** [wholism]. See METHODOLOGICAL INDIVIDUALISM.

**homelessness.** Literally, anyone without accommodation is homeless, but this definition says nothing about the standard of accommodation and to discover the extent of housing problems the definition should be extended to include those without adequate accommodation. In 1977 the British Government placed responsibility on local authorities to provide accommodation for homeless persons in 'priority' groups (these included families with children or elderly persons and the sick), though this was not to apply if the family had become homeless intentionally. The application of this legislation has been uneven, but the 1977 Act resolved previous uncertainty about responsibility for homelessness, making it clear that it was a housing rather than a social work problem. Previous uncertainty had often led to the Social Services Department taking responsibility and dealing with the problem by providing temporary, often bed-and-breakfast, accommodation, sometimes splitting families up in the process.

MPJ

**homeostasis.** The process whereby a system is maintained in a stable condition of equilibrium, returning automatically to it by adjusting to any outside disturbance. The concept was part of FUNCTIONALIST theory, but it is now usually doubted whether societies are so perfectly self-regulating.

MM

**Horkheimer, Max** (1895-1973). German philosopher and sociologist. Director of the Institute for Social Research in Frankfurt (see CRITICAL THEORY) from 1930 to 1958 and Rector of the University of Frankfurt from 1951. Co-author with ADORNO of *Dialectic of Enlightenment* (1947); author

of *Eclipse of Reason* (1947); editor of *Studien über Autorität und Familie* (1936).

WO

**housework.** Until recently housework was not considered by sociologists to be work. The reasons for this lie in sociological sexism — the fact that for male sociologists housework is not work, but a service to which they, as husbands, have a right, and that sociological theories developed to explain the male public sphere of economy, industry and the state. The home was equated with nurture, confined to the non-social, and housewives defined as 'economically non-active'. In Britain, Ann Oakley's study of housework and housewives (*The Sociology of Housework*, 1974) demonstrated that women define housework as work, find it to be as monotonous and fragmentary as men experience assembly-line work, and that women work far longer hours than men. The average working week of the housewife is 77 hours. The average male working week is about 48 hours.

Housework is women's responsibility in MARRIAGE, and becomes virtually exclusively her domain after she becomes a MOTHER. Some husbands 'help', but this is regarded as a gift and women are still responsible, even if they supervise and direct their husbands. Housework is a service women perform for men as a result of marriage. This is the result of the sexual DIVISION OF LABOUR within the FAMILY. Although the content of housework varies cross-culturally, the flow of services from women to men seems to hold true for all PATRIARCHAL societies.

Although some household tasks have been automated, no appliance has proved to be a 'labour-saving' device. Evidence shows that technological innovation brings about a rise in standards of cleanliness, thus intensifying the domestic LABOUR PROCESS. Another way of analysing this change in the content of housework is to say that whereas in pre-industrial society women produced most of the food, clothing and so on, and thus housework was truly an integral part of the work of the household, today women simply consume. This notion of housework as consumption has been criticized by FEMINISTS from a Marxist and Radical Feminist perspective.

Marxist feminists in the 'domestic labour debate' attempted to demonstrate that housework is work by using Marxist categories to determine whether domestic labour is necessary to CAPITALISM, whether, that is, it produces surplus value. In Marxism production under capitalism is socialized, that is, takes place within the public sphere where labour power is sold to the capitalist for a wage and set to work in combination with other labour powers, subject to the capitalist division of labour. The wage relationship is EXPLOITATIVE in that the wage is equivalent only to the value of the commodities bought in the market place needed to reproduce that labour power. All production over and above the value of labour power, surplus value, is appropriated by capital. The question is whether housework is necessary in some way to capitalism. Its necessity would be demonstrated by its contribution to surplus value. Some argued that housework is necessary to capitalism because one wage secured two labour powers, one bought, the other free, for capital. Others argued that domestic labour reduces the value of the wage and this increases surplus value, because the wage covers the cost of commodities as raw materials. Housewives do not buy dinners — they buy food and transform that food into dinners. It is argued that if wage labourers had to buy not only the commodities but also cooking, cleaning, laundry and similar services, wages would have to rise and hence surplus value fall. However, a problem with this line of argument is that some domestic services have been socialized, and the extent of socialization in fact grows in times of economic prosperity. Others have asserted that it is impossible to prejudge whether it is better for capitalism to keep wages down through reliance on domestic labour, or whether the family impedes the expansion of capitalist production and reduces the accumulation of capital by defining certain services as unsocializable and hence not a potential source of wage labour and exploitation. The debate was largely inconclusive. It was later criticized by Marxist feminists for being FUNCTIONALIST, that is, seeking to derive the 'necessity' of domestic labour from the 'systemic needs' of the capitalist mode of production. Radical feminists criticized the debate for not addressing the central issue, which is why housework is women's work.

Theories of the domestic mode of production developed out of this radical feminist critique. Here Delphy (*The Main Enemy*, 1977) argued that marriage is a labour contract by which men appropriate women's labour power in exchange for upkeep. This constitutes exploitation because wives do housework for themselves and the husband and, like wage labourers, they receive only the value of their own upkeep, not the total value of their housework services. Its relative autonomy as a MODE OF PRODUCTION lies in the nature of the male-female relation by which it is structured. All husbands have rights over their wives' housework; wives must give housework to men for 'free'; all women who marry become housewives; and all women are affected by it because they are treated as potential or existing housewives. It is husbands who exploit the labour of their wives. The asymmetry of this relationship can be seen when wives are employed. In addition to their third, paid job, women still carry the responsibility for housework, or for providing for substitutes, notably buying alternative childcare. Empirical evidence can be found in the sheer disparity of hours worked by women and men.

The housework debate spawned two different theoretical pursuits in feminism. Marxist feminists began to consider whether the importance of housework should be located in the role of housewives as a reserve army of labour (see WOMEN AND THE LABOUR MARKET). Radical feminists began to question why women get married, and once married, why they remain there. This led to an examination of reproduction, marriage and compulsory heterosexuality.

See A. Oakley, *The Sociology of Housework* (1974); E. Kaluzynska, 'Wiping the floor with theory: a survey of writings on housework', *Feminist Review*, 1980.

EG

**housing class.** A concept developed by Rex and Moore (*Race, Community and Conflict*, 1967). It takes elements from the Chicago School's CONCENTRIC ZONE HYPOTHESIS and allies them to the approach to social class advocated by Weber (see CLASS: *Weber on*). The basic process underlying urban social interaction is seen to be competition for scarce and desired types of housing. Individuals are distinguished by their strength in the housing market or, more generally, the system of housing allocation. Rex and Moore modify Weber's notion of differential placement in a market situation to include differential placement with regard to a system of bureaucratic allocation, and from this arrive at the concept of housing class. Seven classes are distinguished: the outright owners of whole houses; mortgage payers who own whole houses; council tenants in council-built houses; council tenants in short-life property awaiting demolition; tenants of private house-owners; house-owners who take in lodgers; lodgers in rooms. These are arranged in a hierarchy of status and have a definite ecological position in the city. Competition for housing takes the form of a 'housing class struggle' and many of the conflicts which typify urban politics can be analysed in these terms.

The concept of housing class has been heavily criticized, but remains a useful tool for understanding the morphology of urban housing and the character of the socio-spatial structure of the city.

HN

**human capital.** A concept based on the recognition that expenditure on education and training represents an INVESTMENT in human beings which can be expected to increase their productivity, and hence lead to a stream of benefits in the future, in much the same way as investment in physical plant and machinery operates. Used extensively in the evaluation of different types of education. A typical project includes a forecast of the additional COSTS and benefits expected to accrue over the lifetimes of a group of individuals who undertake a particular course of education or training. These are then DISCOUNTED to establish whether the programme will offer positive net benefits.

See INVESTMENT; LABOUR MARKET.

RR

**human ecology.** The theory of human organization developed by PARK and the CHICAGO SCHOOL in the 1920s and 1930s. Until the recent interest in SOCIOBIOLOGY it

was the last example of a NATURALISTIC theory of society in American sociology.

Human ecology was influenced by a number of European theories: the evolutionary theories of SPENCER, the interactionism of SIMMEL, and the sociological positivism of DURKHEIM but most of all by Social DARWINISM and the British Victorian empirical tradition of social investigators like BOOTH. It made the fundamental assumption that societies are characterized by two levels of organization — the biotic and the social. The biotic level is not unique to human societies but is found wherever living things share a common habitat. Its most significant feature is close-knit patterns of interdependence between its cohabitants. It is essentially communal. Because this level of organization is viewed as common to all forms of life, one of the basic aims of human ecology is to determine the applicability of the principles of plant and animal ecology to the study of human communities. The social order is regarded as unique to human societies and involves relationships which only humans are capable of creating and sustaining.

The biotic order is not the product of deliberate and rational human activity — rather its organizational pattern is automatically determined as numerous individuals congregate in a limited territory, such as the CITY. The forces giving a COMMUNITY its shape and structure are impersonal and subsocial, a product of natural instinctive processes of which the individual is unaware. Relations at the biotic level are symbiotic — that is, they consist of impersonal patterns of coexistence and interdependence. Thus, although they may not be aware of it, the inhabitants of a given community are just as dependent upon each other for their existence as plants or animals found in any given territorial area. Paradoxically, the biotic order is also typified by competition, which in the long run selects and distributes the populations and institutions of an area in a manner akin to Darwinian natural selection.

In contrast, the social order consists of a network of interpersonal relationships held together by a shared culture and forms of communication. The social order is inherently CONSENSUAL.

In analysing the city, human ecology

notes how the territory of the city is distributed via a process of intense competition for land. This sorts and segregates the urban population into NATURAL AREAS (neighbourhoods) each of which is internally socially homogeneous and supports a distinctive SUBCULTURE. From this Park and Burgess developed their CONCENTRIC ZONE HYPOTHESIS of urban growth.

See R.E. Park, *Human Communities* (1952).

HN

**human factor tradition.** An approach to the study of industrial behaviour associated with the British psychologist C.S. Myers and investigators of the Industrial Health Research Board (IHRB), a British government agency founded in 1918; also, to a lesser extent, with the National Institute of Industrial Psychology (founded 1921). Growing out of emergency studies of absenteeism, accidents etc, amongst munitions workers in World War I, the IHRB's approach to worker behaviour was at first strongly BEHAVIOURIST. Behaviour was conceived as a response to the physical environment (temperature, illumination, noise) of the workplace or to the physical exertion and mental strain of industrial tasks. Adjustment of the working environment and of working hours would improve productivity and worker satisfaction. Through the notion of 'industrial fatigue' the IHRB investigators counterposed a more complex model of the (manual) worker to that utilized by the SCIENTIFIC MANAGEMENT movement. Turning from the problems of physical exertion to those of boredom and monotony in work, the IHRB stressed individual psychology as an intervening variable. By the early 1930s some of its researchers had suggested that some bio-psychological aspects of worker response to the work situation were themselves in part influenced by social factors. Largely neglected in Britain, the IHRB's work achieved modest renown in the USA, where MAYO became interested in it. Now largely superseded by Ergonomics and Industrial Sociology, the tradition is maintained only in popularized forms, as in advertisements for industrial ventilation which suggest that overheated workshops are a major cause of strikes.

See M. Rose, *Industrial Behaviour* (1975).

MR

**Human Relations Movement.** A social movement which has left a deep historical imprint on Western capitalist societies, particularly English-speaking ones, and has even affected thinking on personnel questions in STATE SOCIALIST countries. It has had prophets, serious scholars and dedicated practitioners, as well as its intellectual charlatans, opportunist exponents and dupes. Nor is it dead, though its message, methods, and scope have been greatly modified since around 1960.

*Origins.* Elton MAYO interpreted the early results from the HAWTHORNE STUDIES as evidence of rootlessness and ANOMIE suffered by workers under industrialism. Poor output performance and resistance to supervision indicated a frustrated human need for social collaboration and social integration. The latter could be achieved by making the plant a focal social unit, this task being entrusted to a managerial elite trained in social science. The results from the Hawthorne Studies can be interpreted in different ways, and, to some extent, were so interpreted by those in charge of the work (F.J. Roethlisberger and W.J. Dickson), though they shared Mayo's prejudice against giving economic factors weight in the explanation of workplace behaviour. By the 1940s, 'social man' thus replaced the cash-fixated individualist projected by SCIENTIFIC MANAGEMENT.

*Elaboration.* The CHICAGO SCHOOL of Human Relations continued the anthropologically orientated elements in the Hawthorne research programme, stressing the 'non-logical' aspects of worker behaviour, and the opportunities (rather than the obligations) this presented to managers. The elite were entitled to manipulate the 'aborigines' through social engineering to achieve harmonious social relations, which would guarantee economic efficiency. Gradually, one member of this 'applied anthropology' group, W.F. Whyte, developed a less cynical and ideological approach through his sensitive field studies of conflict and the operation of incentive systems. Whyte's work helped created the SOCIO-

TECHNICAL SYSTEM concept by stressing the influence of technical factors at an early age. (Such factors had already been recognized by Roethlisberger and Dickson; Mayo appears never to have sensed their significance.) A second elaboration was undertaken mainly by applied social psychologists, especially those influenced by the approach of LEWIN with its stress on interpersonal influence and group dynamics. A multitude of experiments, many undertaken by the Survey Research Center of the University of Michigan, were conducted in the 1950s on the relationship between leadership styles, 'performance' (i.e. productivity), expressed job satisfaction and degree of group integration. Though now treated more sceptically, the results were widely accepted at the time as indicating that successful supervision equated largely with skilful 'democratic' leadership, and that the successful leader was, above all, a good 'communicator'. Whyte's work had also come to stress communication, though it also recognized the organizational and technical constraints on achieving it. 'Neo-human relations' theory, appearing around 1960, stressed a need to alter total organization structures to achieve successful human relations practice.

*Applications.* Assimilation of Human Relations doctrine into managerial technique was uneven and selective. Results were variable, as an increasing number of appraisal studies indicated the superficiality of much human relations training (e.g. for supervisors) and its impracticability in industrial situations where conflict was structured into the relations of managers and managed. Ideologically, its overall message was welcomed, and the social unity of the corporation (and, by derivation, the identity of economic interests of its component strata) became a favourite theme in managerial utterances. This 'big happy family' rhetoric was distant from Mayo's own social philosophy of industrial life, though his name was perpetually invoked. For him, the manager's elite status was one of *noblesse oblige*: the goal of social harmony preceded (though it never excluded) those of compliance and productivity.

*Eclipse.* Human Relations attracted criticism from different quarters. Political

radicals attacked its anti-union bias (why should unions not be a focus for a new social integration?). Liberals (including those who were economic conservatives) condemned its anti-individualism and its distrust for economic explanations of work behaviour. Sociologists pointed out that 'Industrial Sociology' (between 1940 and 1965 largely equated with Human Relations research and doctrine) had abandoned concern with social structural explanations of industry, its scientific credibility having already been crippled by its commitment to managerial aims. Practitioners themselves recognized that manipulatory social engineering often did not work. More subtle varieties of personnel practice were sought, especially whilst rapid economic growth, creating labour scarcity, was shifting power towards the shop-floor. Present economic conditions of recession help ensure worker co-operativeness through more traditional means; but the managerial search for methods of securing positive worker commitment remains active. There are some signs of a revival in the human relations outlook in the notion of 'quality circles', informal groupings of lower managers and workers to discuss and implement productivity schemes. The continuing relevance of human relations to any valid sociology of industry resides principally in the permanent effects on personnel administration and managerial thought.

See M. Rose, *Industrial Behaviour* (1975).

MR

**human rights.** See RIGHTS.

**Hume, David** (1711-76). Scottish philosopher and historian, central to the SCOTTISH ENLIGHTENMENT. Main works: *A Treatise of Human Nature, An Inquiry Concerning Human Understanding* and *A History of England.* Hume's approach was consistently sceptical, whether discussing EPISTEMOLOGY, CAUSALITY, morality or religion. He argued that what we call a causal relation between two events is nothing more than a constant conjunction embellished by our own imaginations. There is no basis for our belief that the future will resemble the past (Hume's problem of INDUCTION). Morality, too, is a matter of subjective approval or disapproval, not a property of the object itself. In a formula which became a principal theme of logical POSITIVISM, Hume rejected any statements which were neither ANALYTIC nor empirical. It was this denial of the possibility of METAPHYSICS which woke KANT, as he himself put it, from his 'dogmatic slumber'.

WO

**hunter-gatherer.** Subsistence based on the hunting of animals or fishing and the gathering of wild fruits, seeds etc, without the agricultural cultivation of plants or domestication of animals or the import of such foodstuffs from other societies, constitutes at least 90 per cent of the prehistory of human beings on earth. There are few such societies in existence, although several combine hunting and gathering with other economic activities, such as settled agriculture. The Mbuti pygmies of the Central African rain forest and the San (Bushmen) of the Kalahari Desert follow a hunting and gathering way of life, while the Inuit (Eskimo), certain Amazonian tribes and Australian aborigines gain the bulk of their subsistence in this manner.

The prerequisite of a hunting and gathering economy is a limited population which can make extensive use of available resources, usually by following a nomadic way of life. Such societies exhibit varied forms of social structure, but tend to be flexible and non-authoritarian. Political organization and group size can vary according to immediate needs and daily or seasonal conditions. Because of this flexibility and frequent changes of locale, as well as the relative absence of technology, members of these societies have very little private property. The American anthropologist Marshall Sahlins (*Stone Age Economics*, 1972) has called them 'the original affluent societies' because their wants are few and easily satisfied by only a few hours' daily labour.

Traditionally, anthropologists often held a sexist and quasi-militarist view of such societies, centred on the notion of 'Man the Hunter'. After World War II, however, the economic and calorific contribution of gathering rather than hunting began to be emphasized. FEMINISTS added considerable pressure to this revisionism.

JE, MM

**Husserl, Edmund** (1859-1938). German philosopher, founder of PHENOMENOLOGY. Main works: *Logical Investigations* (1900,1901), *Ideas for a Pure Phenomenology and Phenomenological Philosophy* (1913), *The Crisis of the European Sciences and Transcendental Phenomenology* (1936).

WP

**hysteria.** See MENTAL ILLNESS.

# I

**iatrogenesis.** A term used by Ivan Illich in *Medical Nemesis* (1976) to denote the risks to human health and wellbeing of the power of medicine as professional practice and as social ideology in contemporary society. Iatrogenesis takes three forms. Clinical iatrogenesis refers to the risks associated directly with medical therapy itself. In questioning the material benefits of medicine, Illich goes well beyond the documentation of evidence revealing the very minor contribution of specifically medical measures in the historical decline in MORTALITY and to its relative impotence in the face of contemporary epidemics. He asserts that doctors actually cause disease and suffering, either directly through the aggressive and impersonal resort to technological treatments, or indirectly as the side effects and accidents associated with unnecessary surgery and drugs.

But clinical iatrogenesis is only one dimension of the problem; even more significant are the social and structural forms of doctor-induced suffering, disease and disability. These are respectively the result of the medicalization of life brought about by both the spread of medical ideology and treatment to all spheres of life, and the destruction of pre-existing cultural modes of coping with pain, suffering and death, through the imposition of a common medical culture which aims to anaesthetize all sensation and feeling.

In this Illich challenges the role of medicine as an agency of social control and of doctors as MORAL ENTREPRENEURS, on the grounds that their power and influence are achieved through the suppression and subordination of individual autonomy and integrity. Doctors induce a new form of disability by eroding people's capacity to make decisions about and care for their own bodies and minds, and claiming these rights for themselves.

The critique is part of a much wider reaction to the monolithic power wielded by centralized, bureaucratically organized corporate institutions of which medicine is only one, albeit a pre-eminent, example. It is also at the heart of the anti-industrialization, 'small is beautiful' thesis (see TECHNO-LOGICAL SOCIETY).

See also MEDICAL MODEL; MEDICAL PROFESSION; SICK ROLE.

NH

**id.** See PSYCHOANALYSIS.

**idealism.** The philosophical theory contrasted with MATERIALISM that the 'external world' is in some way created by the human mind. The most influential form of idealism was probably the philosophy of HEGEL, but the term has also been applied to HUSSERL's later work in PHENOMENOLOGY. In social theory, the term has been loosely applied, following MARX, to theories which are thought to exaggerate the role of ideas in social life.

See M. Mann, 'Idealism and Materialism in Sociological Theory' in J.W. Freiberg (ed.), *Critical Sociology* (1979).

WO

**ideal type.** The classification of phenomena into types is common in science 'and, as SCHUTZ emphasized, in everyday life as well. Many scientific concepts involve an element of idealization, as when we speak of a perfect vacuum or a perfectly competitive market. (This is not of course a moral conception of the ideal.) The concept of the ideal type, most explicitly discussed by WEBER, involves the further element that the types of action, ideology or economic system which concern the social scientist tend to be constructed on the basis of a variety of criteria. The defining characteristics of a type will be 'more or less present and occasionally absent' in particular cases. An ideal type is an 'exaggeration' of certain features which tend to be present in reality; once the type is constructed, a concrete situation can be understood by means of comparison with the ideal type. At their most general, these may be types of action of the sort discussed in micro-economics and in GAME THEORY and decision theory. But they may also be relatively concrete, such as the ideal type of the medieval city or the Protestant ethic.

Ideal types, Weber insists, are not HYPO-THESES; they are not falsified if they are not fully instantiated in a particular case or even at all. They are heuristic aids in the construction of hypotheses. Critics object that ideal types are essentially arbitrary; the only check on their use is what Weber sometimes called the 'tact' of the historian or sociologist: they involve a CONVENTIONALIST philosophy of science. Weber saw Marx's *Capital*, for example, as the description of an ideal type, but it can be argued that Marx intended it as something more ambitious: a description of the fundamental structures and mechanisms of the capitalist MODE OF PRODUCTION. (One might choose to call this a 'real type', but this expression is very rarely used.) Despite these controversies, the construction of types remains common in sociology; the growing importance of STRUCTURALISM has perhaps encouraged this.

See M. Weber, *The Methodology of the Social Sciences* (1949).

WO

**identification problem.** See CAUSAL MODEL-LING.

**ideology.** When first coined at the end of the 18th century by Destutt de Tracy (1755-1836) the word meant simply the science of ideas (contrasted with 'metaphysics') but it rapidly came to take on a distinctly pejorative sense, implying false or mistaken notions, especially in social and political contexts. In the work of MARX and ENGELS, where the term is frequently used and of major theoretical importance, both the evaluatively neutral and evaluatively negative senses are to be found. In *The German Ideology* (and elsewhere) it denotes an essentially wrong apprehension of reality, and is virtually interchangeable with the expression FALSE CONSCIOUSNESS. It denotes ways of thinking about the world and explanations of behaviour which are radically defective in that they fail to take account of fundamental material circumstances and constraints. But Marx and Engels also use the term in a sense far closer to its original significance, as denoting the transformation of real experience into the realm of ideas, without any implication that such a transformation has distorted or misrepresented the experience.

These two senses continue to coexist in contemporary usage. The pejorative connotations are strongest when the word is employed in popular, non-specialist discourse, though they are also to be found in conservative social theorists and commentators, of left and right alike (as witness ALTHUSSER's radical antithesis of 'science' and 'ideology'). In such contexts the term denotes social and political ideals, strongly (not to say fanatically) held, together with the implication that they are quite impractical and have no foundation in mundane reality. By contrast, professional social scientific usage normally endows the word with no such negative implications. It generally refers to those ideas defining fundamental conceptions of natural, psychological or social reality. Moreover, the term implies that such ideas are both systematically interrelated and widely extensive in their application, though specific areas of thought or activity may be indicated by expressions such as 'political ideology', 'economic ideology' and so on. When used without such adjectival qualification 'ideology' is distinguished from other, similar terms (for instance, 'beliefs') (1)by the range of phenomena to which it applies; (2) by the fact that it is rarely, if ever, articulate. It is an attribute to be inferred rather than observed. Whether the origin of any given ideology is to be explained in material, cultural or individual terms depends upon the theoretical persuasion of the would-be explainer. Thus, Marxists tend to see ideological positions as a function of CLASS position, whilst for Weberians it springs from STATUS identity and other cultural factors. Comparable difficulties are raised by the question of ideology's social impact. On the one hand MATERIALISTS see it as no more than a reflection or *post hoc* construction serving to order and render intelligible actions, events and experiences, but possessed of no motive capacity of its own. On the other hand, and equally extreme, some IDEALIST social theorists have argued that, in the last resort, human social actions are generated by ideas and oriented towards ideal goals. MANNHEIM used the term in a quite distinctive sense: ideologies justify the status quo, unlike UTOPIAN ideas, which justify social change.

ML

**idiographic.** The distinction between idiographic and nomothetic methods was first drawn by the German philosopher Wilhelm Windelband (1848-1915). An idiographic approach is concerned with individual phenomena, as in biography and much of history, while a nomothetic approach aims to formulate general propositions or 'laws' [Greek: *nomos*]. These approaches are generally presented as IDEAL TYPES; thus evolutionary biology, for example, is at least partly idiographic. Windelband and RICKERT argued that history is essentially idiographic, and distinguished it from the 'natural sciences' which they took to include economics and sociology. The defence of an idiographic approach to economics was the principle theme of the 'Historical School' of economists in 19th-century Germany.

See HISTORICISM; WEBER.

WO

**imperialism.** The practice of one state extending its sovereignty over others, usually by force of arms and for the purpose of economic exploitation and national glorification. Colonialism is a specific form of imperialism in which a sharp distinction is made between the territories of the conquering nation and its 'colonies', and where the inhabitants of the colonies have inferior political and legal rights. Imperialism and SLAVERY went hand in hand in the ancient world, but conquered territories were normally integrated and did not remain colonies. From the early days of CAPITALISM, Western European imperialism began to embrace most of the globe, and generally adopted a colonial form (especially in the case of the British and Dutch empires). At one time or another most of the peoples of the world have been the victims (rarely the beneficiaries) of imperialist or colonialist rule (see NEO-COLONIALISM).

In the 1890s imperialism became a major political issue in Britain. This led to a number of works on imperialism, of which J.A. Hobson's *Imperialism* (1902) was the most seminal. He influenced LENIN's *Imperialism, the Highest Stage of Capitalism* (1915). Since Lenin, Marxists have developed theories of imperialism based on capitalism's need to expand abroad as the profit rate falls domestically. This is sometimes specifically based on a need to export capital. This remains controversial and tends to neglect other aspects of imperialism: NATIONALISM, RACISM, and the far older historical process of state aggrandisement. Since the Soviet military presence in Eastern Europe at the end of World War II, Western imperialist powers have accused the Soviet Union of Russian imperialism in Europe and elsewhere. This has been developed theoretically, particularly in the Chinese concept of social imperialism, to relate internal economic, political and ideological conditions in the Soviet Union to its foreign policy.

The concept of imperialism plays an important part in contemporary sociology of development and less so in political sociology. Many writers prefer the term *neo-imperialism* to describe the economic exploitation of poor countries by rich countries without direct military intervention. Guides to the debates and literature around the subject are to be found in T. Kemp, *Theories of Imperialism* (1967); R. Owen and B. Sutcliffe, *Studies in the Theory of Imperialism* (1972); D.K. Fieldhouse, *Economics and Empire* (1973).

See also DEPENDENCY; MILITARISM; UNEQUAL EXCHANGE.

LS, MM

**import-substitutive industrialization.** The home replacement of an existing market for final consumer goods. It is a strategy of INDUSTRIALIZATION which seeks to stimulate domestic infant industries through policies of tariff protection and tax concessions, and became a favoured development strategy of poor countries in the 1950s and 1960s when it was realized that competition in finished manufactures from already industrialized countries discouraged local entrepreneurs from investing in local industry. Yet industrialization was seen as necessary to the development of poor countries because of what was thought to be the prevailing patterns of unequal world trade between rich and poor countries. Import substitution has been criticized: (1) protection raises domestic costs, discouraging these industries from building up a competitive position in the unprotected export market; (2) it has led to even more liberal importation of producer goods, thus establishing a new, more costly, form of DEPENDENCY upon the advanced countries; (3) it has encouraged the spread of multinational corporations, since — in order to protect future markets — multinationals would 'jump' the tariff barriers and set up local subsidiaries even if this meant operating locally at a loss over a sustained period.

AH

**incapsulation.** See ENCAPSULATION.

**incentive payments.** Generic term for an array of 'payment by results' (PBR) schemes, usually for manual production workers in manufacturing industry. The classic form is the piece-rate method, where individuals (sometimes WORK GROUPS) are paid a set price for each article or given unit of output they produce. This might seem to remove the scope for 'exploitation' that exists under fixed time-rate wages (*see* EFFORT BARGAIN).

Rather, it converts the surplus value received by the employer upon each output unit into a constant. Its merits are to motivate workers and thus dispense with costly managerial control systems. The set price is determined beforehand, in rate-setting, usually with the aid of work-study (SCIENTIFIC MANAGEMENT). Moreover, rates may be frequently altered, because of changes in the market (for products or labour), technical change or redesign of the product, or because work-study has been defective. This gives scope for employers to vary the effort bargain in their favour, and for workers to resist. Piece-work is notorious for the number of disputes it can generate. Also the supposed motivational potency of piece-work is reduced by the establishment of output norms within workgroups, that is, an agreed 'reasonable' daily output, with a voluntary restriction of output on the part of well-integrated group members — imposed on recalcitrant 'speed kings' or 'rate-busters' with the aid of informal sanctions. In some establishments, junior management may also become implicated in ingenious 'fiddles' that frustrate the intended aim of PBR. Even where initially successful for an employer, PBR schemes tend towards distortion and 'senescence' (i.e. the fade in appeal of the incentive). Piece-work payment has been falling out of favour, but remains common in the construction industry, usually in looser forms, without work study, merging into subcontracting.

See W.F. Whyte, *Money and Motivation* (1955).

MR

**incest.** All societies have rules which prohibit marriage and/or sexual relations between particular categories of individuals. The study of incest is often confused by an ethnocentric bias which assumes that particular sexual relationships between close kin (e.g. mother and son) are universally prohibited. This is not so: the categories vary between societies and in some cases include people who are not connected by blood ties. Nevertheless there are biologically based theories which claim that these prohibitions function to prevent inbreeding, which would, over time, cause physical and mental degeneration in societies. Tyler, the 19th-century ethnologist, was particularly interested in the genetic implications. Similarly, DURKHEIM in *Incest: the Nature and Origins of the Taboo* (1896) emphasized the importance of blood relations and FREUD in *Totem and Taboo* (1913) assumed a universal psychic ambivalence in parent-child relationships.

Some theories of incest prohibitions claim that they function to preserve the integrity of the family and regulate access to women. But nearly all theories aim to discover the origin of these prohibitions and to find the extent to which this origin is natural or social. For LÉVI-STRAUSS the origin of incest taboos, whatever their form, is also the locus of the origin between the natural and the cultural. He agrees with Freud that the social can only be defined for its members through the intervention of incest rules. Lévi-Strauss's theory is of reciprocal exchange between groups of males, forming an alliance between two groups (see RECIPROCITY), and is linked to his theories of language and myth (see SYMBOL, MYTH). As words and myths are signs to be exchanged in the communication systems of social life, so women are also signs. But whereas words and myths are the common property of public life, women have a value because they belong to a particular social group, and can be exchanged with other social groups according to marriage rules. Thus systems of marriage are essentially systems of exchange and alliance (see KINSHIP). Incest rules are not prohibitions on marriage but represent a command to exchange women. Lévi-Strauss is therefore adhering to the idea of Mauss and MALINOWSKI that reciprocity is a universal type of human social behaviour; it is in culture. But because incest and mariage rules are concerned with sexuality as well as reciprocity, they lie also in the biological, in nature. Thus incest prohibitions are at the threshold between nature and culture, and at the origin of social life.

See also CHILDHOOD; WOMEN AND CRIME

JE

**income.** The increase in purchasing power over a given period of time. In a MARKET SYSTEM income is obtained by selling the services of the factors of production which an individual owns. Thus those who sell the services of their labour receive income in the form of wages and salaries, while those who own capital receive income from its use in the forms of interest, profits and dividends. Those groups who are unable to sell the services of factors of production (e.g. the retired, unemployed and sick) receive transfer incomes from the government in the form of pensions, unemployment and sickness benefits, which are financed from TAX revenues. Income may be used for consumption expenditure (see CONSUMERS) or saved in the latter case it constitutes an addition to the individual's WEALTH.

The distribution of income measures the way in which a society divides its total income between its members. The functional distribution measures the way in which it is divided between the owners of factors of production, such as labour (wages and salaries) and capital (interest, profits and dividends), whereas the size distribution measures the share of total income which is received by groups with different levels of income, irrespective of the sources of their income. The size distribution is often expressed in terms of a Gini coefficient or Lorenz curve which indicates the degree of inequality in income distribution.

National income is the total flow of income produced within an economy within a given time period. It includes all household incomes in the form of wages and salaries; rents, interest and dividends, referred to above (but not transfer incomes) plus any retained earnings held by firms. National Expenditure and National Product are alternative measures of National Income.

RR

**indicator.** The empirical researcher faces the problem of representing or measuring sociological concepts, which are often complex and highly abstract. This is done by using indicators — items with specific reference which stand for the more abstract concept and permit empirical data to be collected which relate to that concept. Thus, in research on social CLASS, a commonly used indicator is occupation, a more specific item of information which can be gathered as part of a questionnaire and then used to infer a person's social class.

Devising indicators can be problematical. Terms such as ALIENATION carry philosophical and evaluative overtones which makes the identification of more specific items which can be used to OPERATIONALIZE the concept difficult. Bridging the gap between concept and indicator is necessary if sociological theory and empirical research are to be fused.

See P.F. Lazarsfeld, 'Evidence and Inference in Social Research', *Daedalus*, 1958.

MB

**individualism.** An approach to normative political theorizing that assigns significance solely to the interests and/or freedom of individual persons, and treats these as the only criteria for defining the conditions of JUSTICE, POLITICAL OBLIGATION and the satisfaction of the public interest. Individualistic political theories repudiate accounts of these conditions that refer to the circumstances of collectivities (e.g. classes, nations, races, the human species) and are not reducible to statements about the circumstances of persons. Though historically associated with LIBERALISM (see also NATURAL RIGHTS), such theories bear only a contingent connection to it (see HOBBES; UTILITARIANISM). They specify the proper scope of STATE activity — which may be minimal or extensive — in terms of what is required to secure the LIBERTY or maximum wellbeing of individuals.                                      HIS

**Indscal.** See MULTI-DIMENSIONAL SCALING.

**induction.** The process by which a general principle or LAW is 'inferred' from a certain number of what are taken to be instances of that law. Contrasted with deductive reasoning, which merely brings out what is implicit in its premises. Frances Bacon stressed the importance of induction for science, but HUME later argued that inductive inference is invalid: we cannot be sure that the future will resemble the past in the relevant respect. Three attempted solutions of Hume's problem may be mentioned. (1) Inductive inference itself has worked reliably in the past and should therefore be trusted. (2) Induction is indeed invalid but science proceeds by the deduction of HYPOTHESES from THEORIES, and the subsequent testing of the theories (see VERIFICATION). (3) REALISTS argue that Hume's problem derives from his mistaken analysis of the CAUSAL relation. We expect the sun to arise in the morning, not because it always has done so in the past, but because of well-supported theories about the structure of our planetary system. See ANALYTIC.

See K. Popper, *The Logic of Scientific Discovery* (1935); R. Bhaskar, *A Realist Theory of Science* (1975).                                      WO

**industrial conflict.** Dramatized in strikes, worker occupations and lockouts, conflict in economic organizations can take a multiplicity of other forms, some deliberate and co-ordinated (e.g. working to rule, overtime bans), others spontaneous and largely individual (sabotage, restriction of output). In many industrialized countries expressions of conflict have been extended amongst professionals (e.g. teachers), service personnel (e.g. bank workers), civil servants and even groups representing the force of the state (e.g. the police). Determining the causes of such conflicts is seldom easy; often an immediate cause of a strike (e.g. a quarrel over bonus payments) masks a longer term, quite distinct grievance (e.g. fears of redundancy). In industry the vast bulk of conflict reflects disagreements between employers (or their managerial representatives) and operatives over the effort expended by the latter in performing their tasks. This holds true for formal pay demands as well as for individual restriction of output. Some writers distinguish sharply between conflicts over 'control' issues and those with 'economistic' bases; but at shop-floor level such categories can be artificial. Similarly, links between industrial conflict and politically mobilized CLASS conflict often require intricate specification, in which a distinction between the 'raw' conflict consciousness of worker groups and the authentic class consciousness of political militants may be helpful.

See also EFFORT BARGAIN; LABOUR PROCESS; RELATIONS OF PRODUCTION.

MR

**industrial democracy.** Orthodox and radical analysts disagree sharply both over defining industrial democracy, and over strategies for increasing it. The most common variant of orthodoxy maintains that recognized TRADE UNIONS can act as an effective check on employer autocracy, protect legitimate individual worker rights, provide channels of effective liaison and consultation with management, reduce costly evasions of efficiency like labour turnover and go-slows, and in general constitute a legitimate source of countervailing power in industry — providing they use this power 'responsibly'. The furtherance of industrial democracy is seen as a question of ensuring that employers recognize trade unions as legitimate bargaining partners, and that trade unions behave 'responsibly'. Such a relationship has been compared to that of elected governments and loyal oppositions in a parliament. Critics protest that this analogy is misleading, since a loyal opposition expects to form a government itself, unlike a union. Moreover, the concept of 'responsibility' implies a collaborative relationship with employers that compromises the responsibilities of union leaders to their own rank-and-file members. Radicals raise the fundamental character of capitalist RELATIONS OF PRODUCTION: without the abolition of private ownership of industrial wealth, relations between employer and employee must remain unequal and prone to conflict. Radicals (especially Trotskyites and Anarcho-Syndicalists) therefore demand some form of worker control. For SYNDICALISTS, this is based upon existing branches of industry: hence their stress upon industrial unionism to provide the organizational skeleton of socialist society — itself to be produced somewhat apocalyptically through a General Strike. Syndicalism as a serious movement was wiped out in the USA with the violent suppression of the 'Wobblies' in the inter-war years. In Britain it was supplanted by the Guild Socialist programme of 'encroaching control', whereby coalitions of worker groups would gradually establish controlling councils for each industry, in association with the state (which would protect consumers). Trotskyite proposals initially focus more closely on the enterprise, and some give as much stress to worker general assemblies, worker councils and similar organs of 'direct democracy' as anarchists. Though somewhat utopian when stated baldly, programmes of worker control have been regaining their appeal over the last two decades, drawing sustenance from the unconvincing record of the more statist regimes of Eastern Europe as industrial democratizers, from continental theories of the new working class, and from the general growth of anti-authoritarian social currents in the West. This has coincided with intense capitalist industrial CONCENTRATION, for which contemporary culture does not provide ideological support. Proposals of a more realistic nature have begun to be debated. Interest has focused on the system of self-management in Yugoslav enterprises. Full-blooded worker control theorists complain that Yugoslav 'market socialism' limits the development of these institutions. Less impatient observers regard them as an instructive experiment.

Governments in advanced capitalist countries have been obliged to take account of these stirrings. Offical concern to increase worker 'participation' in running industry has been expressed frequently in many Western European countries in the last decade. In Britain, the offical Bullock Report (1977) recommended a system warmly welcomed by numerous trade unionists but which managerial critics regarded as intolerably radical. Many of those professional managers who regard themselves as progressive would no doubt welcome a system of co-determination on the West German pattern. To most British trade union leaders, this in unacceptable; to radicals it is anathema.

There can be no technical proposals acceptable to all for solving such a conspicuously political problem.

See also DEMOCRACY; TRADE UNION.

See P. Brannen, *Wage Slaves or Citizens* (1983).

MR

**Industrial Health Research Board (IHRB).** See HUMAN FACTOR TRADITION.

**industrialization.** Most narrowly, a process of transformation of a predominantly agricultural economy into one where the manufacture of goods increasingly contributes to overall output and exports. As a corollary, the percentage share of people employed in agriculture declines and that in industry increases.

Careful examination of historical INDUSTRIAL REVOLUTIONS, especially that of Great Britain, reveals other changes in the economic and social organization of production and distribution which are necessary accompaniments of industrialization: a high degree of DIVISION OF LABOUR and specialization, and the use of mechanical, chemical and power-driven as well as intellectual aids in production. The systematic application of science and technology in the organization of production points to the essence of industrialization, which is a method of organizing production to reduce the real cost per unit of producing goods and services.

Industrialization in this wider sense has less to do with the transition from agriculture activities to manufacturing activities, than with a more general process called MODERNIZATION. For example, in development literature it is common to include the commercialization and modernization of agriculture in the definition of industrialization. Modernization of agriculture involves scientifically developed techniques to increase the fertility of the soil, protect crops from insects, and introduce higher-yielding varieties of seeds as well as tractors and combine harvesters. New Zealand, which derives 77 per cent of its export earnings· from agriculture products, is an 'industrialized' country in this sense.

The term *de-industrialization* reverts back to the restricted definition of industrialization: the focus is once more on the percentage share of manufacturing output in total output, the percentage share of people engaged in manufacturing industry, and the international competitiveness of a nation's manufactured goods.

AH

**industrial revolution.** From the second half of the 18th century through the first half of the 19th century, Britain experienced a series of economic, technological, social and organizational changes which transformed it from a predominantly agrarian and small-manufacturing society to the world's first factory-based machino-facturing society. Although there is considerable controversy surrounding many aspects of the industrial revolution, it is generally agreed that it was first fuelled by demand for improved clothing and household metal implements among a prospering class of farmers, and this gave impetus to the textiles, iron and coal industries. Ensuing ingredients were the growth of steam power to operate the factories, the building of roads and railways to move goods and raw materials, capital investment on a large scale particularly in textiles, coal mining and metal industries, and cities to house the wage labourers who worked in the factories. The revolution created a largely urban society, enormous population growth, and large organized MIDDLE and WORKING CLASSES. In the following centuries many other countries went through their own industrial revolutions, and the processes of INDUSTRIALIZATION in these countries differed in some important respects from those in Britain, whose first place gave certain disadvantages (such as ageing machines and obsolete technology). One generalization which still stands up well is that the later a country's industrialization, the greater the degree of STATE involvement and encouragement of it. The term 'Second Industrial Revolution' is sometimes used to refer to a phase of growth between $c$1880 and 1910, especially in Germany and the USA (rather than Britain), led by large joint-stock corporations applying 'big' science and mass production and marketing methods. Accounts can be found in E. Hobsbawm, *Industry and Empire* (1968); D. Landes, *Unbound Prometheus* (1969); E. Gerschenkron, *Economic Backwardness in Historical Perspective* (1962).

LS, MM

**industrial society.** Coined by SAINT-SIMON to denote a society dominated by industrial production, and frequently used in this very general sense. But it may also indicate adherence to three particular theses about modern society which also emanate from Saint-Simon: (1) industrial, not CAPITALIST, production relations are decisive; (2) CLASSES are not to be viewed as property-based groups but as occupational groups deriving from the DIVISION OF LABOUR; (3) conflict between such groups is not dichotomous but multiple (and usually conducted within an overall CONSENSUS). Indeed in this tradition, stretching through COMTE, SPENCER, DURKHEIM and TÖNNIES to PARSONS and much of contemporary American sociology, the term class is often replaced by 'strata', 'socio-economic group' or some other less conflict-ridden term. The tradition sometimes regards these as organized, conscious 'formations', sometimes as 'categories' (see CLASS) but, in any case, its consensual model downplays the importance of any separate CLASS CONSCIOUSNESS which might arise. In the 20th century two further theses have been added: (4) ostensibly capitalist and STATE SOCIALIST societies are converging into a single industrial mould, technocractic, meritocratic and managerial; (5) the further development of the division of labour is leading both capitalism and state socialism to a new stage, POST-INDUSTRIAL SOCIETY.

Both its general and particular uses imply a loose MATERIALISM: that the structure of industry broadly shapes the structure of modern society as a whole: SECULARIZING its religion, transforming its FAMILY STRUCTURE, moving it from GEMEINSCHAFT to GESSELLSCHAFT, making it TRANSNATIONAL etc. In all these respects it is more similar to its principal rival, capitalist society, than is generally recognized.

See R. Aron, *Eighteen Lectures on Industrial Society* (1962); C. Kerr *et al.*, *Industrialism and Industrial Man* (1960).

MM

**inflation.** A continuing increase in the general level of prices. Inflation has become a major policy concern of the Governments of most Western advanced industrial nations in recent years. Domestically, inflation is generally held to be undesirable because it redistributes INCOME in unintended ways. For example, those groups unable to increase their money incomes at the same rate as prices increase experience a fall in their real incomes, whereas those with strong bargaining power are able to increase their real incomes. Similarly, unanticipated inflation may discourage saving by redistributing

income from lenders to borrowers: when a loan of a fixed money sum is repaid it is worth less in real terms than when it was borrowed. Internationally, a country experiencing a domestic rate of inflation above that of its competitors will suffer a decline in its export competitiveness. Theories of the causes of inflation may be divided into two general categories: demand-pull theories and cost-push theories. Demand-pull theories point to the role of aggregate demand (see DEMAND): when this exceeds the capacity of the economy to produce the required quantity of goods and services, prices will be bid or 'pulled' up. While KEYNESIANS would expect a variety of expenditure items to be possible sources of this excess demand, MONETARISTS emphasize the effect of increases in the supply of money. They also point to the part played by inflationary expectations in sustaining inflationary pressures — through, for example, wage and salary demands which include an element designed to protect workers from the erosion of their real incomes that would otherwise result from expected inflation. Cost-push theories maintain that it is increases in the COSTS of production, which are not associated with the level of aggregate demand, that are the initiating cause of inflation. Powerful unions that obtain excessive wage increases or sudden increases in raw material prices (e.g. oil) are cost-push pressures that have been cited in recent years. Policy instruments that are available for controlling inflation include fiscal policy, monetary policy and PRICES AND INCOMES POLICY. Both fiscal policy (i.e. increasing TAXES and reducing public expenditure) and monetary policy may be used to reduce aggregate demand. Prices and incomes policy may be used to restrain cost-push pressures, and has the added advantage that the consequences in terms of UNEMPLOYMENT are less severe.

RR

Sociologists have also responded to recent inflationary spirals. Those influenced by MARX concentrate on the vicious circle produced by economistic class conflicts, arguing that a CORPORATIST state is increasingly required to manage them. Goldthorpe, with a perspective derived more from DURKHEIM, has argued that wage-led inflation demonstrates ANOMIE, the lack of a 'moral economy'.

MM

**institution, institutionalization.** Although sociologists have long and frequently spoken of 'social institutions', the term has no precise and uniform usage. It is generally applied to aspects of social behaviour regulated by well-established, easily recognized and relatively stable NORMS, values and laws. Indeed some sociologists have used it to designate the complexes of norms, values or laws rather than the patterns of actual behaviour. Sometimes it has been argued that all societies can be analysed into a handful of major institutional spheres, such as FAMILY and KINSHIP, economic, political and cultural institutions, and SOCIAL STRATIFICATION, each of which regulate important aspects of social life. (In this case, the idea of institution is linked to that of functional prerequisites of a society; see FUNCTIONALISM.) But the word 'institution' is also often used by sociologists in the looser, everyday sense of a variety of patterns of social organization found in society.

Institutionalization as a process means the gradual growth and crystallization of rules of behaviour in various social and organizational settings. Examples of institutionalization include the routinization of CHARISMA and the gradual emergence of rational-legal administration, both described by WEBER, or the process of state-formation and associated civilizing processes described by ELIAS, or the institutionalization of class struggle in modern societies through regulated union-management bargaining and the competition of mass democratic political parties.

SJM

**institution, total.** Term used by GOFFMAN to refer to residential establishments where individuals carry out their daily activities of sleep, work and play, with the same people, and under the same authority, which co-ordinates and plans the activities of the organization. Total institutions are, therefore, bureaucratically organized establishments (see BUREAUCRACY) that are more encompassing than usual. Consequently they offer those who run them special powers and opportunities for the manipulation of members in accordance with their own designs and interests.

KP

**intellectuals.** Though use of the adjective 'intellectual', in the sense of having to do with things of the mind, is to be found at least from the end of the 16th century onwards, the noun is no older than the last century, nor is the application of the adjective to types of work and social roles. Contemporary usage recognizes both a broad and a narrow application of the expression. In its wider signification intellectual work, work with the brain, is opposed to manual work: some Marxist-influenced states thus categorize their labour forces into 'workers, peasants and intellectuals'. Such a broad definition of the intellectual category is, however, less common than definitions in terms of some sub-set of non-manual occupations rather than all of them. The great difficulty lies in knowing where the line within the non-manual hierarchy is or should be drawn. The matter is further complicated by the fact that definitions which do not include all those who work with mental and not manual skills almost invariably draw on non-occupational criteria of one kind or another. In the end the distinguishing mark of intellectuals is not merely their possession of a certain kind of job skill, but also their readiness to make more than a circumscribed, job-centred use of that skill allied to a vision extending beyond the immediate work task and horizon.

At the core of all restrictive definitions of 'intellectuals' lies some notion of their engagement with and/or their commitment to speculative thought and its expression. Such criteria inevitably raise acute doubts as to whether all members of any occupational group, no matter how educationally qualified or socially esteemed, qualify to be defined as intellectuals. Nonetheless, the DIVISION OF LABOUR in advanced industrial societies (1) provides, in the training and qualifying phase for certain occupational positions, markedly advantageous access to the skills of symbol manipulation which intellectual activity properly so-called requires and (2) differentially facilitates and rewards intellectual work according to occupational position.

Hence a very high proportion of intellectuals tends to be drawn from a limited range of occupations associated with education, the media and the arts. This does not preclude either many, perhaps the majority, engaged in those same occupations having only a professional or technical rather than an intellectual orientation to their exercise of symbolic skills, nor the occasional intellectual's emerging elsewhere — a proletarian artist, bank-clerk poet or working-class autodidact writer, for instance. Cross-nation comparisons suggest that particular socio-economic structural factors may lead to the emergence of intellectuals from a variety of social positions other than those typical in the advanced industrial societies of the West — engineers, the church, the military, among others.

The existence of an intellectual group of some kind has characterized all large-scale literate societies — the scholar gentry of classical China, the learned priests of India and their Mayan equivalents, the philosophers of the Greek city states, the clerics of feudal Europe. In all cases there have been endemic problems in resolving the contradiction between speculative thought, the very badge of the intellectual, and the risks that such thought entails for the stability of the existing distribution of power and resources. The relation of intellectuals — individually and, even more, collectively — to their environing social world is as much a problem for the inhabitants of that social world, generally speaking, as it is for sociologists. Certainly, since the Renaissance varying but always significant fractions of the intelligentsia (the collective noun for intellectuals as a social category) have taken up a critical or even an oppositional position to the existing social order. This has been particularly true since the beginning of the last century, and coincides with the convergence of previously craft groups (the plastic arts) and the socially marginal (performers) with the various scholar and writer strata. By the second half of the century artistic-intellectual activities and life-styles had been hypostasized as Bohemianism, a term whose primary connotation is one of marginality, defining artists as living outside the structure of normal society. Around the turn of the

present century, splits within the intelligentsia gave special prominence to one fraction, known as the *avant-garde*, which was committed to experiment and innovation. The term *avant-garde* implies both that thought and the arts are in a state of continuous, progressive change and that changes which are revolutionary on their first appearance will, in the end, be accepted as belonging to the orthodox mainstream of ideas. *Avant-garde* intellectuals are commonly regarded as standing in an oppositional relations to conventionally accepted notions of CULTURE and, by extension, as standing in an oppositional relation to conventional society.

Among social scientists, the social position of intellectuals has been extensively and inconclusively debated. Their social origins (the majority have been born in relatively wealthy and socially esteemed families), the nature of the work they do, and the occupational positions they hold have led to their being identified as part of or allied with ruling strata. However, their frequent critical and oppositional observations, their commitment to speculative thought and their isolation, *qua* intellectuals, from economic resources have equally often been argued as evidence of their identity with the ruled.

ML

intelligence. The relating capacity of the mind, especially in the context of meeting and adapting to new circumstances. More particularly this relating process involves the manipulation of symbolic material. Although some psychologists believe that a general factor is common to the whole activity of intelligence, most hold the view that there is not a uniting factor but that the general factor works in combination with sub-factors such as those specifically concerned with verbal or spatial relationships. The general and specific factors of intelligence are measured by various written and oral tests, the former often given to groups of respondents and the latter to individuals. Such tests are normed (i.e. scored in relation to the average) for specific age groups in the society for which they are intended. The results of many of these tests, particularly those measuring verbal intelligence, are converted into scores called

Intelligence Quotients (IQ). The IQ of any respondent is reached by dividing his Mental Age as indicated in the test by his Chronological Age and multiplying by one hundred. An average IQ is thus 100. There is considerable disagreement about whether results, even if the test is reliable and valid, measure an innate capacity or the present learned, operational capacity of the respondent. One of the main suspected sources of invalidity and bias in the past has been that tests are produced by members of the white middle class or for the ruling group and are, often unconsciously, based upon their cultural NORMS. Sociologists tend to interpret IQ scores as measures of operational capacity, thereby allowing for the influence of the present and previous social environment upon the respondent. Tests of verbal intelligence have been important in many educational systems since they have been used to allocate pupils between schools with more or less of an academic bias and, hence, have assumed a major place in discussions about such questions of social policy as the reorganization of secondary education, equality of educational opportunity at the tertiary level and the consequent effects of such issues upon elite formation.

See also GENDER.

PWM

**interaction, statistical.** A statistical term used to refer to the effect of two or more independent VARIABLES which explain more of the variation in a dependent variable when present together than the independent variables do by themselves. This effect is due to the mutual influence of the two independent (or independent and control) variables upon each other, strengthening their influence upon the dependent variable.

MB

**intermediate treatment.** The Children and Young Persons Act 1969 gave juvenile courts the power to issue an intermediate treatment order along with a supervision order. Treatment could be provided which fell in between custodial care and supervision at home. The precise form can vary from attendance on a residential course, to outdoor activities, to participation in a series

of discussion meetings. Intermediate treatment is normally seen as a move towards a 'child care' view of delinquency. Prevention and rehabilitation are stressed rather than punishment. The framers of the recommendations for the policy initiative were strongly influenced by a 'social work orientation'.

In practice, intermediate treatment has developed relatively slowly. It took four years for the first Regional Scheme to be introduced, and although more progress has been made lvels of expenditure and provision remain limited. There are a number of possible explanations for this slow development: intermediate treatment was not clearly defined in terms of detailed provisions, and the underlying philosophy was not shared by all who had an influence on its development.

MPJ

**internalization.** See PSYCHOANALYSIS.

**international division of labour.** In a regional or global economy countries may specialize in different kinds of economic activity and so be interdependent — just as occupations are in the DIVISION OF LABOUR. In the modern WORLD SYSTEM countries are also, either in actuality or in pretensions, cohesive NATION-STATES, raising the possibility that within the international division of labour each may be a CLASS. This is a widespread popular assumption — as in the phrase 'the national (economic) interest' — and also an implicit assumption of much writing in international political economy. Theoretical discussion has been largely confined to THIRD WORLD countries (see CENTRE-PERIPHERY; DEPENDENCY; UNEQUAL EXCHANGE). This is curious since they are less cohesive, more subject to TRANSNATIONAL power influences, than are advanced countries. In many of the latter, control of domestic economic resources is largely indigenous, the state redistributes domestically about half of gross national product (GNP), and the state has an active policy-making role in the international division of labour. In these respects nation-states are collective economic actors. This raises an important mid-20th-century problem for class theory: what is the relation between international versus transnational aspects of class?

See TRANSNATIONAL.

MM

**introjection.** See DEFENCE MECHANISMS.

**introversionism.** The label given by Bryan Wilson (*Sects and Society*, 1961) to one of the several types of SECT he has identified (see also REVOLUTIONISM, CONVERSIONISM, MANIPULATIONISM, THAUMATURGY) to describe a religious response which construes the surrounding world as evil and thus seeks salvation and the preservation of the purity of the faithful by withdrawal from the world. Introversionist sectarians such as the Amish, the Doukhobors or the Hutterites often emerge as revolutionist or millennialist movements which expect an imminent and radical transformation of the world. When this fails to occur the movement postpones and transcendentalizes its hopes and expectations. The radical transformation will occur at some more distant date, or perhaps in another realm rather than on earth. The members therefore patiently await the day, isolated from the surrounding society as far as possible by barriers of dress and speech, geographical segregation, and bans on association or marriage outside the sect. They view themselves as an elect or a collective remnant of the faithful, and have little interest in recruiting new members from outside; rather they renew themselves and expand on the basis of their own offspring.

Introversionist sects often follow an agrarian way of life and may implement varying degrees of communalism, usually the consequences of the circumstances of their persecution and migration. The object of hostility in the societies in which they originally emerged (dominated by a monopolistic church), they were forced to migrate toward frontier areas away from a hostile state and disapproving neighbours. Farming became the obvious basis for their economy and communalism a means of securing economies of scale and of maximizing available labour power in a new environment (for example on migration to North America), given few other resources to invest.

Introversionist sects display considerable capacity for survival over many generations, but nonetheless exhibit little tendency to undergo the process of DENOMINATIONALIZATION.

RW

**investment.** Expenditure on capital equipment (i.e. plant and machinery) which yields a flow of productive services in the future. Thus current investment expenditure increases the quantity of goods and services available for consumption (see CONSUMERS) in the future. There are various investment appraisal techniques which indicate the desirability of alternative projects by estimating their respective future costs and benefits, and DISCOUNTING them to take account of their time profiles (e.g. discounted cash flow and net present value methods). COST-BENEFIT ANALYSIS is an investment appraisal technique used widely in the public sector.

RR

**invisible religion.** Thomas Luckmann (*The Invisible Religion*, 1967) argues that religion should not be identified merely with religious institutions, but that the human animal is essentially religious in its transcendence of biological nature. Such transcendence is possible through the creation of a meaningful sense of SELF, a process which usually takes place in the context of a world-view that gives everyday life its ultimate significance. In modern societies, Luckmann claims that a new social form for religion is emerging based on consumer preference, and possessing a more differentiated character than in the traditional world. The themes which figure in this 'invisible religion' are elaborations of individualism: the pursuit and celebration of individual autonomy through various forms of self-expression and self-realization, most notably in social mobility and achievement, in sexuality, and in the privatized family as a buttress to personal identity. These and numerous subordinate themes constitute a 'sacred cosmos' from which the individual can construct a sense of self and endow his everyday life with meaning. On Luckmann's account, SECULARIZATION cannot be simply inferred from declining commitment to, or involvement in, institutional religion. What appears as religious decline is merely a shift from one social form of religion appropriate to a particular phase of social development to another more consonant with a highly differentiated world. See also COMMON RELIGION.                                RW

# J

**job creation.** Literally, virtually any attempt to increase the level of employment in a community but currently applied in a more limited sense to special programmes introduced by governments or official bodies to encourage new employment opportunities. These programmes may involve private enterprise, though typically they are based on public or non-profit making organizations.

The public works programmes of the inter-war years were job creation programmes but most governments would argue that current programmes have little in common with earlier endeavours: they are much more refined, emphasizing the value of the product and improving the employment prospects of participants. The forerunner of current programmes are the measures introduced in the USA in the 1960s under the Manpower Development and Training Act and the Economic Opportunity Act. Job creation programmes have since been introduced in most Western nations. In the UK, the Job Creation and Work Experience programmes were started 1975 and 1976. The major programmes in the early 1980s are the Youth Opportunities Programme and the Special Temporary Employment Programme (the latter was replaced by the Community Enterprise Programme in 1981). Between them they covered over half a million people.

Job creation programmes have been attractive to many governments because they appear a relatively quick and cheap way of reducing high levels of unemployment with less inflationary consequences than many other alternatives. However, most aim to provide only temporary employment opportunities. When first developed, this appeared a reasonable basis on which to organize schemes because many believed that high levels of unemployment were temporary. The growing realization that high unemployment is likely to persist has led many to be more critical of the role of job creation programmes.

See KEYNESIAN ECONOMICS.

MPJ

**joking relationship.** A formulation derived from RADCLIFFE-BROWN'S observations regarding the type of social interaction often seen between mother's brother and sister's son in a matrilineal society. In some cases, the sister's son, who will inherit from his maternal uncle, indulges in ritual stealing or verbal and practical jokes against him. This joking relationship is a social mechanism by which the tensions inherent in a relationship are not only socially recognized but also released through the symbolic use of particular joking formulae. The idea has been extended to include other situations of social tension. 'Mother-in-law' jokes are a well-known example. But this mechanism is not universal in such situations. It is also common for relationships between mother-in-law and son-in-law, or mother's brother and sister's son, to be marked by RITUAL avoidance, which prevent social interaction between two possible protagonists.

JE

**judges.** Responsible for the processing of cases through courts (see LAW: *Legal Institutions*), judges in so doing exercise considerable influence on the meaning and application of legal rules (see LAW) by interpreting the meaning of rules which appear relevant to the case and deciding how those rules apply, given the facts of the case. In certain important cases, they create new law. Notwithstanding these powers, the tradition of the independence of judiciary which exists in many countries ensures that the role and authority of judges is to a considerable degree immune from public criticism and accountability. Indeed, it is often argued that judges can only perform their tasks if their decisions are not subject to constant critical scrutiny.

*Appointment.* Because of the power inherent in judicial office, it has been argued that some control of that power could be exercised through the method of their appointment. A number of models of appointment exist. In Europe, judges are appointed by the State and trained from a relatively early age to perform judicial tasks. In the USA many judges are elected, though the most powerful judges, those of the Supreme Court, are appointed directly by the President. In the UK judges emerge from the ranks of the practising legal profession (and are almost exclusively barristers); formally, they are appointed by the Lord Chancellor.

*Judge-made law.* In common law jurisdictions (see LAW, *classifications of*), for example, the UK, the USA or Canada, much law is based on principles of law created by the judges themselves. For a long time it was asserted, especially by judges, that they did not create law, but merely revealed principles of law that already existed. This declaratory theory of common law is no longer tenable. In deciding individual cases, particularly those heard on appeal, judges establish precedents that are said to have mandatory authority. They must be 'followed', that is, their principles adhered to, in subsequent cases. However, the mandatory character of precedents is much diminished by the practice which allows judges to 'distinguish' between and within lines of precedents. This practice gives rise to the technicality and complexity of the precedent system.

In the UK judges have been particularly active in defining such broad principles as what counts as a contract, as negligence, and as criminal intent (*mens rea*). TRADE UNION rights and responsibilities have also been defined by judges as well as Parliament; for instance, the Taff Vale judgement of 1901 made union financially liable for losses sustained by employers attributable to strikes, but was then reversed by Parliament in 1906. Such judgements have been important milestones in labour history. However, in the UK the doctrine of parliamentary sovereignty means that legislation can always over-rule precedent law. This is not so in the USA, where the Constitution is, in principal, supreme, and its final interpreter is the judicial system culminating in the Supreme Court.

Four points of significance arise from the role of judges in both countries. (1) Legal concepts, like the contract, are conceptual pigeonholes into which problems as defined by lawyers may be placed. They may be quite different from the conceptual framework used by non-lawyers. Much legal procedure (particularly at the pre-trial stage) is designed to afford opportunities for lawyers to reconstruct the realities of other people's experiences in a legal framework. (2) The creation of these fundamental principles of law is, to a large extent, the result of judicial activity. They manifest the power of the judicial role. (3) Important questions are now being raised by socio-legal historians about the interaction of the development of those legal concepts and the broader social and economic developments that occurred at around the same period. This leads to consideration of the importance of law and the legal system in supporting and enhancing the political ideology of a country (see LAW, *theories of*). (4) In addition to a general concern that is sometimes expressed in relation to the power of the judiciary, a more specific case has been made that the British judiciary are biased in their administration and application of such areas of the law as industrial relations and the law of the welfare state. It is argued that the class background and education of judges prevents them from understanding, and therefore applying sympathetically, such laws (see Griffith, *The Politics of the Judiciary*, 1981). No satisfactory empirical study has been conducted in Britain which tests this hypothesis, but the fact that many people believe it to be true may, of itself, be of considerable social importance. In the USA this trend of work is much more developed. The American Legal Realists emphasized the part played by differential 'judicial attitudes' in deciding cases. More recently, judicial behaviouralism and jurimetrics have sought to develop predictive models incorporating variation in judicial attitudes.

MP

**Jung, Carl Gustav** (1875-1961). Swiss PSYCHIATRIST who became an early member of FREUD's circle. Following his break with Freud in 1913, Jung developed his own ideas into a distinctive school of PSYCHOANALYSIS termed Analytical Psychology, considered metaphysical and antiscientific by many academic psychologists and psychiatrists. His contribution came from his conceptualization of the personality types of introversion and EXTRAVERSION (see PERSONALITY), from his use of the term 'complex' to describe a constellation of emotionally oriented ideas, and from his introduction of the Word Association Test, a simple form of PROJECTIVE TEST used for diagnostic purposes. His ideas about symbols, archetypes, and the collective unconscious have interested those concerned with cultural history and mythology.

Born in rural Switzerland, Jung's father was a pastor in the Swiss Reformed Church and religion was an important preoccupation throughout his life. Jung described his father as kind, liberal and rather weak. His mother he considered the more powerful and dynamic. From the age of 11 Jung was educated in Basel, studying medicine at the University since archaeology, his first choice, was not available there. He obtained his medical degree in 1900, then specialized in psychiatry due to the scope it offered for reconciling the subjective and objective approaches that already interested him. As assistant at a mental hospital in Zurich he worked under Eugen Bleuler, whose study of dementia preacox (see MENTAL ILLNESS) had

won international repute. He also studied with Janet in Paris. Much of his work, unlike Freud's, was with psychotic patients. Having read Freud's *Interpretation of Dreams* he began to apply psychoanalytic ideas to the study of dementia praecox, publishing a book on the topic in 1906. He sent a copy to Freud and they began to correspond, meeting for the first time in Vienna in 1907. A lively exchange of ideas between the two developed a close and emotional friendship. They travelled together to lecture at Clark University in 1909 along with other psychoanalysts, and in 1910 Freud proposed Jung as the first President of the International Psychoanalytic Society, despite opposition from his Viennese supporters. By 1912 differences in their ideas were becoming more apparent, and personal animosities, some over Jung's handling of the presidency, emerged. At the beginning of 1913 Freud broke off personal relations with Jung, who resigned from the International Psychoanalytic Society the following year.

The immediate source of the intellectual disagreement between Freud and Jung was over the nature of libido. Jung viewed it as a creative, future-oriented, indestructible life force, not specifically sexual in character, striving towards wholeness and individuation, capable of being channelled in different directions. He distinguished two general directions or attitudes present in all individuals, but with a tendency for one to be dominant. One is outwards, towards the external world of objects and people (the more objective); the other is inwards, towards the inner world of the individual (the more subjective). These two general attitudes underlie respectively the two personality types of introversion and extraversion. Jung postulated four basic functions of personality: sensation and intuition (modes of apprehension) and feeling and thinking (modes of judgement). Ideally these should work in harmony, but one of each pair is likely to dominate. Genetically, Jung distinguished only three phases of development: an initial stage lasting until the third or fourth year; a prepubertal stage roughly corresponding to Freud's latency period; and a final stage following puberty when the individual has the potential for psychological maturity.

Jung called the external, visible and conscious aspect of the personality, the persona. Beneath this layer was the personal unconscious, the anima or animus, which he conceived as largely compensatory in function. What is strong in the conscious will be weak in the unconscious: in men the unconscious is likely to be feminine, in women, masculine. Finally, there is at a deeper level, the collective unconscious: the collective beliefs and myths of the race to which the individual belongs, termed archetypes. At the deepest level some of these will be universal archetypes common to all humans. Neurosis arises not as in Freud's schema from a conflict of libido with the demands of the real, social world, but from unequal development of different aspects of the personality. A particular personality adaption, for instance, the dominance of intuition over sensation, may be inadequate to deal with the individual's situation. This may lead to regression that allows the individual to call up resources to cope with the situation (a more positive view of regression than Freud's). If no solution is found then the individual will continue to follow infantile patterns of behaviour and neurosis exists. Present difficulties rather than past repressions produce pathology. Therapy should focus on the present and the future rather than the past. This is not a matter of a practical adjustment of the individual to the situation but of getting in touch with the healing properties of the collective unconscious. As with Freud, dreams serve as a major means of access to the unconscious, but for Jung the analysis of the symbolic content of dreams moves from the particular (the specific detail of the dream) to the general (the archetypes they represent), rather than from the general to the particular (the symbols of the dream to its personal meaning for the individual).

JB

**jurisprudence, sociological.** A field of study that emerged at the beginning of the 20th century, deriving from the conscious attempt to integrate certain elements of sociological theory, in particular SOCIAL CONTROL, and insisting on understanding the role and function of law within the wider social totality. Sociological jurisprudence was thus a reaction against the narrow internal focus of legal positivism or analytical jurisprudence (see LAW: *Trends in Legal Theory*) which was dominant during the 19th century, particularly in Britain and America. Its strongest influence was in the USA, particularly through Roscoe Pound (1870-1964): see R. Pound, *Jurisprudence* (1959).

Law is conceived of as the most specialized agency of social control. Human needs and claims, in the form of 'interests', press for legal recognition, and courts of law are thus continuously involved in policy decisions giving effect and recognition to some interests rather than others. The function of legal process is to provide a mechanism of reconciling conflicting interests; Pound proposed that all claims, advanced as competing individual interests, should be weighed and evaluated in the form of social interests (e.g. an individual claim for repayment of a debt should be evaluated in terms of the social interest in the security of the debtor-creditor relationship as a necessary component of capitalist economic relations).

Sociological jurisprudence has stressed the historical and evolutionary character of law. Pound's typology of stages of law drew heavily on Sir Henry Maine's thesis concerning the modern transition from law based on STATUS to law based on (SOCIAL) CONTRACT. Pound proposed a contemporary stage of the socialization of law. This recognized the increasing range of social classes and interests pressing demands on the legal system. Modern law is capable of functioning as a mechanism of social engineering, directed towards minimizing waste and friction and maximizing conflict resolution and the satisfaction of human claims. A naive optimism underlay these PLURALIST and conflict-resolution functions.

See CONFLICT THEORY; SUMNER.

AH

**justice.** Classically defined as 'giving each person his or her due' and as 'treating equals equally (and unequals proportionately unequally)'. These injunctions to impartiality can be given either a purely procedural interpretation (i.e. in adjudicating between conflicting claims) or also a substantive one (i.e. in determining what entitlements each person has). Interpreted substantively, justice is a distributive principle prescribing a certain dispersion (of liberties, benefits) over a population, rather than an aggregative principle prescribing the maximization of such goods over a population (see UTILITARIANISM). Theories differ over the appropriate criterion for this allocation — over what counts as a person's 'due' or as 'equals and unequals'. Persons' just entitlements (sometimes termed NATURAL RIGHTS) have been variously construed as determined by need, productivity, social rank, contractual undertakings or as simply equality. Injustice consists in the deprivation of one's just entitlements and occurs in the form of either forcible expropriation or EXPLOITATION. More recent accounts of justice (e.g. J. Rawls, *A Theory of Justice*, 1971) have attempted to overcome the problem of competing criteria by deriving its distributive implications from the premise of personal inviolability. See EQUALITY.

HIS

The concept of justice is inextricably bound up with conceptions of LAW. It is the primary means through which attempts have been made to specify the ends or objectives not only of law but more widely of human conduct, and the concept has been central not only to legal theory but to moral and political philosophy. Justice is a relational concept which seeks to provide a means of evaluating the impact of human action, whether by an individual or by a legal system, upon another individual or group. 'Justice' invites or requires the specification of criteria of evaluation; thus criteria of 'fairness' or 'EQUALITY' have often been closely associated with the concept of justice.

Recent debates in legal theory have been much preoccupied by two related themes. (1) The relationship between formal or procedural justice (treating like cases alike) and substantive or substantial justice focusing on the results and consequences of the content of a legal process. (2) The tension between individual and social/collective/communal justice. While the former is consistent with an emphasis on procedural justice, the latter focuses on the structural location of groups (e.g. ethnic minorities, women, the poor) and highlights the impact of the content of law and regulation upon the category. The increasingly important issue of positive DISCRIMINATION or affirmative action embodies this concern with social justice.

AH

# K

**Kant, Immanuel** (1724-1804). German philosopher. Main works: *Critique of Pure Reason* (1781), *Critique of Practical Reason* (1788), *Critique of Judgement* (1790). Kant accepted the EMPIRICISTS' denial of innate ideas prior to experience, but insisted that knowledge is not derived merely from experience but formed by the mind. His 'Copernican revolution' involved supposing not that our knowledge must conform to objects but that objects must conform to our knowledge of them. Some of the properties we ascribe to objects may be a function of our own perceptual apparatus. This does not threaten, indeed it guarantees, the certainty of our knowledge, but it means that our knowledge cannot go beyond experience. We can only know phenomena, not 'things in themselves'. This conclusion was resisted by later IDEALISTS.

Kant's second *Critique* introduces a notion which has recurred in philosophy and the social sciences. The grounds for moral action must be a matter of pure practical reason, independently of any causal influence such as the dictates of our interests. This idea that free action in some way transcends causal determinations has recurred in NEO-KANTIANISM and in post-war ANALYTIC philosophy, as a key element of the anti-NATURALIST case.                    WO

**Kelly, George Alexander** (1905-67). American psychologist, a pioneer in clinical psychology and clinical training. Born in Perth, Kansas, where his parents were farmers. His father had trained as a Presbyterian minister, and both parents were religious fundamentalists. Kelly's early education was irregular. He graduated in mathematics and physics, but his interests shifted towards social problems. While working at various teaching jobs in Labour Colleges and teaching immigrants, he took an MA in Sociology at the Unversity of Kansas. In 1929 a fellowship took him to the University of Edinburgh, where he completed a degree in education and his interests focused on psychology.

Kelly's first academic post was at Kansas State College (1931-43), where the Depression pressured him away from his chosen interest, physiological psychology, toward clinical psychology, for which there seemed to be a need. He developed a clinical service for the Public School System and for College students, and was forced to innovate by virtue of his lack of background in psycho-analytic techniques. In this clinical experience with non-pathological, intelligent, articulate subjects, Kelly developed PERSONAL CONSTRUCT THEORY with its emphasis on the cognitive aspects of personality. The way people act depends crucially on the way they conceive the world around them in terms of individually constructed categories. The task is to investigate the organization of these personal constructs, the way they change over time, and the way they structure the individual's perceived possibilities for action. To this end, Kelly developed a family of methods, the REPERTORY GRID TECHNIQUE, starting with the Role-Construct Repertory Test designed to measure how individuals saw their own close personal contacts.

From 1946 until his death Kelly was Professor of Psychology at Ohio State University. *The Psychology of Personal Constructs* was published in two volumes in 1957, the first volume detailing the formal theory of personal constructs and the second covering clinical diagnosis and psychotherapy. These ideas, apart from their direct contribution to social psychology, have had some interest for MATHEMATICAL SOCIOLOGY, both through the analysis of the matrices produced by the Repertory Grid Technique, and through the development of a formal theory of subjective categories.

JL

**Keynesian economics.** A general description of the school of economic thought which derives from the work of the Cambridge economist J.M. Keynes (1883-1946). In his seminal work, *The General Theory of Employment, Interest and Money* (1936), Keynes challenged the prevailing classical economists' claim that an unregulated economy will move automatically to a position of full employment. He argued that under certain conditions it was possible for equilibrium to be established at less than full employment. Any government wishing to pursue a policy of full employment should stimulate aggregate expenditure to increase national output and thereby reduce UN-EMPLOYMENT. This recommendation for governments to assume responsibility for stabilization policies became part of the accepted orthodoxy in all Western economies for most of the post World War II period. In times of recession governments would endeavour to increase aggregate expenditure and — more importantly in recent times — when faced with near full employment and INFLATION they would seek to reduce aggregate demand. Both fiscal (i.e. changes in TAXES and government expenditure) and monetary (i.e. variations in interest rates and the supply of credit) policy were used in the pursuit of full employment and stable prices. Towards the end of the 1960s the simultaneous emergence of high rates of inflation and high levels of unemployment, and the apparent failure of conventional policies to control them, led to disenchantment with Keynesian diagnosis and remedies. In particular the work of the

Chicago economist, Milton Friedman (1912- ) and his associates emphasized the role of the money supply by reformulating the pre-Keynesian quantity theory of money (see MONETARISM). At the present time debates between neo-Keynesians and monetarists constitute a major source of disagreement on how governments should formulate their macro-economic policies.

See also JOB CREATION; UNANTICIPATED CONSEQUENCES.

RR

**kindred.** A category of non-corporate groups of kin reckoned in both female and male lines by a particular individual, so that no two groups of kindred are exactly alike.

JE

**kinship.** The study of kinship is often taken as central to the discipline of social anthropology, which has elaborated the social relevance of biological relationships or fictional, but socially recognized, blood ties within different societies. Such ties entail systems of rights and obligations. The central components of kinship studies are the question of social paternity for the purpose of inheritance, the nature of MARRIAGE and the varying social forms and behaviours of three biological pairs: parent/child, husband/wife, and brother/sister (although relationships formed through marriage are often discussed as AFFINAL, rather than kinship, relations). These three have been examined particularly through the study of genealogy, of classificatory kinship terminology, of marriage preference and inter-generational cycles of social reproduction.

All types of kinship theory depend on the hypothesis that kinship and affinal relationships constitute coherent social institutions with related NORMS and behaviours. The parent/child couple determines inheritance and inter-generational rules as well as politico-jural units and societal models (see ANCESTOR). The husband/wife couple influences relationships between groups as well as various types of rights in women's labour, sexuality and reproductive powers. The sibling link can also be associated with these and, like the parent/child relationship, is critical to the formulation of INCEST rules.

Kinship theories tend to be grouped through their relative adherence to the principles of descent or alliance, that is, their emphasis on either parent/child or marriage bonds, with disagreement on the role of sibling bonds. Descent theories, particularly associated with RADCLIFFE-BROWN and FORTES, suggest that kinship systems function to ensure the inter-generational continuity of lineage groups by the maintenance of descent links through either or both parents (see LINEAGE). They stress inheritance and succession. In alliance theory (e.g. LÉVI-STRAUSS) the vital unit of kinship is a son's relationship to his maternal uncle (mother's brother) because it is the latter who released his sister for formation of an alliance, through marriage exchange, with a man from another group. Alliance theorists tend to study marriage and incest rules, and regard kinship systems as existing not so much to allocate rights and duties as to generate marriage possibilities or impossibilities. Although the controversy has been heated, some later theorists have claimed that the difference between the two schools has been exaggerated. Goody suggests that descent theorists use examples involving homogeneous transmission of property, while alliance theorists concentrate upon divergent distribution of property after death. The difference lies partly in levels of theory. Descent theory is usually associated with the study of concrete systems, while alliance theory is concerned with the derivation of societal models of kinship.

Within alliance theories of kinship, particularly in work derived from the work of LÉVI-STRAUSS, it is common to talk of *structures of kinship* as elementary or complex. In elementary systems the spouse is selected according to the social structure, while in complex systems a suitable spouse is not defined in structural terms but rather chosen individually. Though the terms are often associated respectively with simple (traditional) and complex (modern) societies, the terms are heuristic devices. All systems have an elementary core to define INCEST prohibition, and all have a complex aspect which allows for choice.

Anthropologists distinguish *kin terms* from *kinship terminology*. Kin terms are descriptive names such as 'uncle', 'brother', 'mother', used in a society to designate not only specific biological relationships, but also the distribution of particular rights and duties associated with them. They can classify political and economic relations as well as marriageable and non-marriageable categories. Kinship terminology attempts to create an IDEAL TYPE classification of particular societies.

For kinship terminology, see also AFFINAL; DESCENT; ENDOGAMY; EXOGAMY; FILIATION; KINDRED; LINEAGE.                    JE

**Klein, Melanie** (1882-1960). Psychoanalyst whose theories and therapy focused on childhood development. After moving to London in 1926 she was at the forefront of PSYCHOANALYSIS in Britain and her ideas are still dominant in British psychoanalysis. Kleinian psychoanalysis is more biological and more individualistic than its counterpart in the USA and these features are the focus of much of the criticism of the approach.

Born Melanie Reizes of Jewish parents in Vienna, Klein was the last child of her father's second marriage and her mother's fourth child. Her father had qualified as a doctor but eventually went into dental practice. Her mother, with whom her relationship was closer, kept a shop selling plants and animals. Klein studied medicine at Vienna University but, to her subsequent regret, changed to humanities when she became engaged since her husband's work meant they would not remain in Vienna. She married at 21 and lived in small towns in Slovakia and Silesia where her first two children were born, before settling in Budapest in 1910, where she had a third child. In Budapest she read some of FREUD's work and, as a result, sought analysis with Ferenczi, a friend and follower of Freud and a central figure in the International Psychoanalytic Association. With his support she began to analyse children. Separating from her husband in 1919, she moved to Berlin, where she began a second analysis with Karl Abraham, another of Freud's early disciples. This ended with his death nine months later, but nevertheless, Klein regarded herself as Abraham's pupil and was influenced by his ideas, for instance on melancholia. In 1925, at the invitation of Ernest Jones, a central figure in British psychoanalysis, she lectured in England, and in 1926 moved there permanently.

Freud himself had discussed analysing children, but had done so only once in the case of Little Hans. As well as moral problems concerning bringing a child's unconscious sexual feelings into consciousness, there seemed to be technical difficulties relating to access to the unconscious and to transference. Klein developed a technique of play analysis, contending that play was not, as Freud has suggested, only a symptomatic act, but a major route to the unconscious. She claimed that transference was possible in young children: in contrast to Freud she held that many key dynamics of the Oedipus complex and superego development, considered necessary for transference, occur in the first year of life.

Unlike the majority of post-Freudians, Klein developed Freud's idea of the death instinct, focusing on the child's early feelings of aggression and the inner world of fantasy that surrounds its relations to the environment. She conceptualized the child's environment in terms of objects such as the breast, faeces and penis, to which the child relates primarily through fantasy, attaching particular importance to the DEFENCE MECHANISMS of introjection and projection. The term 'object relations theory' has been used to refer to Klein's work, but this designation now refers less to Kleinian theory than to the ideas of British Freudians such as Fairbairn, Winnicott and Balint who have moved away from Freud's drive theory.

According to Klein the first important object to which the child relates is the mother's breast. This becomes not only an object of pleasure-seeking and love but also of aggression, and Klein emphasizes the oral-sadism of the young child. Good and bad feelings towards the breast (mother) create tension, conflict and anxiety that may be handled by splitting — the tendency for an object to be viewed not as a single object but as two part-objects. The child's instinctual feelings and the fantasies to which they give rise are compounded by the child's introjection of parental prohibitions, and the projection of aggression and hostility on to external objects, initially the breast. The projection of hostile feelings in the early months of life is such that Klein talks of this as the first of two phases or complexes of the first year — the paranoid position. Later the child recognizes the breast as a whole object and the hostile feelings, now no longer projected on to the breast (the bad mother) are directed against the self, producing depression. In this depressive position the conflict between good and bad is internalized. Klein's formulation of the paranoid and depressive positions provides a theoretical framework that facilitates the therapy of psychotic conditions (see MENTAL ILLNESS), often considered beyond the reach of psychoanalysis.                     JB

**knowledge, sociology of.** The study of the social origins and effects of ideas. In a general sense, this is an important theme throughout the history of sociology, most notably in MARX's theory of IDEOLOGY and in DURKHEIM's studies of fundamental categories of human thought in *The Elementary Forms of the Religious Life* (1912) and in *Primitive Classification* (1903). The sociology of knowledge may be more narrowly defined as a specialism which flourished in the German-speaking countries between the wars; the prevalent atmosphere of doubt and self-questioning no doubt contributed to its popularity.

The PHENOMENOLOGIST Max Scheler provided the first systematic account of the sociology of knowledge in his introduction to a collective work he edited, *Versuche zu einer Soziologie des Wissens* (1924). Scheler distinguished three types of knowledge: knowledge for work or domination, cultural knowledge and knowledge of salvation (this later influenced HABERMAS's trichotomy of knowledge-guiding interests). To the central question of the mechanism by which knowledge emerges from its social base, Scheler's answer was that systems of ideas have an internal logic of their own, but that 'real factors' in the outside world determine the rate of development and the influence of these ideas — they 'open and close the *sluices* of the spiritual stream'.

The other central figure is MANNHEIM, whose essays on the sociology of knowledge and his major work *Ideology and Utopia* (1929) returned again and again to the relationship between ideas, especially philosophical and political ideas, and their social base, and to the possibly RELATIVISTIC implications of this relationship. This emphasis on relatively formalized systems of ideas and the philosophical issues raised by the attempt to analyse them has remained characteristic of the sociology of knowledge, though Peter BERGER and Thomas LUCK-MANN in *The Social Construction of Reality* (1967) attempt to deal with everyday knowledge in a more or less PHENOMENOLOGICAL manner. The sociology of knowledge has recently been extended into the realm of the natural sciences (which Mannheim excluded on the grounds that they were largely independent of social influences); this new body of empirical material has led to a considerable revival of the sociology of knowledge itself.

See J.E. Curtis and Petras (eds.), *The Sociology of Knowledge: a Reader* (1970); G. Remmling (ed.), *Towards the Sociology of Knowledge* (1973); S. Lukes, 'The Social Determination of Truth' in R. Horton and Finnegan (eds.), *Modes of Thought* (1973).

WO

**Kroeber, Alfred Lewis** (1876-1960). American anthropologist. Born in New York of German parents, Kroeber studied at Columbia College from 1892, obtaining his doctorate in 1901. In 1897 he was appointed as an assistant in Rhetoric, but he was already showing an interest in psychology and coming under the influence of BOAS. In 1899 he was awarded a Columbia fellowship in anthropology and two years later went to California to take up an appointment as Curator of Anthropology at the California Academy of Science. Based in California for the rest of his life, he carried out intensive ethnography on its native peoples, publishing the *Handbook of the Indians of California* in 1925. He was Director of the Anthropological Museum at the University of California until his retirement in 1946.

Like Boas and the students they both influenced such as BENEDICT and MEAD, Kroeber was interested in studying CULTURES in their entirety. Besides working with the Californian Indians he carried out field research on other North American Indians as well as in India, Southeast Asia, China, Korea, Japan and Indonesia. He was among the first to suggest the concept of a geographical culture area, within which particular cultural configurations are to be found. Partly because of his background in the humanities, Kroeber placed more emphasis on the historical dimensions than did Boas. His work was as much a philosophy of history as anthropology, with cultural development as the focus. Major work: *Configurations of Culture Growth* (1944).

JE

**Kula ring.** See RECIPROCITY.

**L**

**labelling.** Although 'labelling' has come to be associated with specific authors and arguments in the sociology of DEVIANCE, it is not really the basis of a discrete school or intellectual position. Some sociologists welcome the identification, others do not.

The principal context of the evolution of labelling theory was the framework of assumptions provided by the social psychology of William James and G.H. MEAD, the philosophy John DEWEY and Charles Peirce, and the sociology of W.I. THOMAS and C.H. COOLEY. It was claimed that people plan projects around their conception of SELF and SOCIAL STRUCTURE. That conception is itself built upon acts of naming that organize and give significance to the world. Names are important facts in their own right, offering stimuli and serving as an environment of meaning. Society is transformed into a symbolic construction which is maintained by conversation. Removed to the study of deciation, those assumptions led to the assertion that rule-breaking is reshaped and produced by naming.

Such a perspective achieved prominence during the 1950s and 1960s through the work of the Society for the Study of Social Problems in the USA and its house journal, *Social Problems*, and the NATIONAL DEVIANCY CONFERENCE in the UK. The tradition criticized established POSITIVIST traditions in criminology for an exaggerated interest in the deviant as a type of person, for a marked value bias that remained uncritical of the status quo's definition of deviance, and for an overly deterministic view of what causes deviance. In its place, labelling argued for a shift in emphasis — to study the processes by which groups identified deviance rather than the deviant *per se*. It was seen as a radical perspective because in asking about the societal reaction to deviance it challenged what earlier theories had taken for granted, and shifted from a position of absolutism to one of relativism. Although not endemic in the tradition, it tended to have sympathies with the deviant, and in its heyday during the late 1960s it was strongly identified with the counter-culture and liberation movements (prisoners, mental patients, gays) who were fighting back against being defined in dehumanizing ways (see G. Pearson, *The Deviant Imagination*, 1975).

The perspective is often assumed to argue that it is labels which make deviants, but this is too simple. In essence, it is concerned with tracing the natural history of STIGMA categories and showing their impact upon human experience. Thus after examining how a particular label evolves historically (such as the evolution of the notion of 'a DELINQUENT' in the 19th century, it analyses the processes by which agents of SOCIAL CONTROL recognize, identify and select people to fit that label (and how some people may label themselves), before finally examining the way such a label may transform, amplify — and sometimes even generate — problem behaviour and new features such as guilt and identity crises. It is not peculiar to deviance, to formal organizations or to critical turning points. People continuously explore the significance of their own and others' acts; deviance is a salient

187

part of such exploration, and the imputation of deviance need not be consequential. Labelling is therefore directed at the self by the self, by insignificant others, by significant others, by those vested with authority and by those who are impotent. It can take place in an abundance of settings, some fateful and some not (GOFFMAN). Moreover, behaviour is frequently ambiguous and open to multiple interpretations. It may be covered by any one of a number of competing labels, and the application of a label may be provisional, contingent and negotiable. Labelling can confirm common-sense classification, displace it, or create new classifications. But its importance is usually defined as situational and circumstantial rather than absolute.

Although well-established and productive, the perspective has many critics. Positivists argue that it does not hold up to scientific testing; Marxists argue that it is a liberal social psychology that neglects the economic order; conservative criminologists see the sympathies of labelling theorists as subversive and even anarchistic.

The approach has built up a mass of new concepts and findings from field work. See DECRIMINALIZATION; DEVIANCE; MORAL ENTERPRISE; STIGMA.

See E. Lemert, *Social Pathology* (1951); H. Becker, *Outsiders* (1963); E. Schur, *Interpreting Deviance* (1979).                    KP, PR

**labour aristocracy.** A popular descriptive term by the 1840s, referring to the artisanal elites and, later, the high wage earners. It was first used as an analytical tool by MARX in his explanation of the 'failure' of Chartism: such groups accepted reformist political and industrial forms of action, abandoning the Chartist mass movement. Thus the notion that a 'labour aristocracy' constrained the development and actions of the working class (by monopolizing the trade union movement, for example) took shape.

ENGELS developed the use of the concept more coherently, arguing that this 'working class aristocracy' made material gains through Britain's trade monopoly. LENIN elaborated this, maintaining that when the trade monopoly was broken, Britain's position as an Imperialist power sustained the 'upper stratum' of labour (see IMPERIALISM). Both argued that these gains were largely made at the expense of the interests of the mass of the working class. Indeed, the interests of the 'labour aristocracy' were deemed to be more compatible with those of the 'capitalist class'.

Resurgence of interest in labour history during the 1960s heralded a renewed controversy over the 'labour aristocracy' to which a simple 'Marxist versus non-Marxist' division is inapplicable. Central to the debate is the question of the validity and usefulness of the concept in explaining the peculiar development of British labour history. While there is some general agreement that the term might have some use as a descriptive tool, though perhaps only of specific industries, there is disagreement in varying degrees and on different points, as to the existence of any 'theory' of the 'labour aristocracy'.

The term is still often popularly used to describe any group of highly paid workers.

DS

In Development Studies the term is also used to refer to labour employed by foreign-induced and controlled capitalist industrialization in many parts of the THIRD WORLD, especially Africa, involving (1) capital intensive techniques requiring relatively little labour input; (2) a bias towards investment in consumer goods industry which favours the employment of semi-skilled and high-level manpower (professional and clerical workers) over unskilled and skilled labour; (3) willingness by the international firms to pay sufficiently high wages to stabilize a section of the labour force, and keep it committed to the firm. The contrast between the lucky few — the wage workers who find employment in the foreign-dominated capitalist sector — and the masses of peasants, rural workers and unemployed LUMPENPROLETARIAT in the towns, is responsible for the use of the term 'labour aristocracy'.

AH

**labour markets, theories of.** Orthodox economic doctrine assumes that labour markets operate rationally, that is to say, primarily as a smooth reflection of the largely economic calculations of workers and employers. Disturbance of the process by 'institutional' factors, for example a customary allocation to different tasks on the basis of race or sex, is generally discounted. Exponents of an ACTION APPROACH to industrial behaviour have argued that a highly instrumental or 'economistic' orientation is possessed only by distinct groups of workers, while others place greater stress on non-economic rewards (e.g. a pleasing work task, agreeable work companions). This can be easily fitted into orthodox economic theory. Research evidence is complex, and the notion of orientations has been subject to damaging criticism. Even in a situation of full employment the range of jobs and tasks available to the vast majority of manual workers (especially) is very restricted, and workers' own knowledge of market opportunities can be very limited. In recent economics and industrial sociology, the orthodoxy has come under severe attack by theories of segmented labour markets, which take one of two forms: (1) Dual labour market theory stresses the possible division between 'primary' and 'secondary' employment sectors, the first dominated by large enterprises which offer stable employment to favoured sections of the labour force, the latter consisting of small firms recruiting labour mostly among oppressed, marginal or disadvantaged groups such as immigrants, women, semi-literates etc (see DISCRIMINATION). The clearest segmentation in all countries (save perhaps South Africa) is between men and women. In Britain, apart from this, there is less evidence of such a pronounced dichotomy than there is for the USA. (2) Internal labour market theory (put forward most vocally by radical or Marxist economists) stresses the variety of types of status and reward within firms, portraying this as an attempt by employers not so much to secure the supply of the scarcer skills or abilities as to introduce or reinforce divisions between workers as a whole. This segmentation prevents effective political mobilization of the working class.

Dispute surrounds both these theories, whose empirical validation remains inadequate. If employers do court certain categories of worker, their motivation seems to be to procure reliable and compliant work behaviour, rather than segmentation *per se.* Exceptions to this rule no doubt exist: 'fighting bosses' employing segmentalizing personnel tactics are much more common on the European continent, notably in France and Italy. Other factors (including job security legislation) may render internal labour markets more important in the future. Labour markets are far less orderly than any available theory suggests.

See also HUMAN CAPITAL; LABOUR PROCESS; WOMEN AND THE LABOUR MARKET.

See R. Blackburn and M. Mann, *The Working Class in the Labour Market* (1979).

MR

**Labour Party.** Formed in 1906 from a merger of several TRADE UNION and SOCIAL-IST organizations. Support grew steadily during the interwar period and reached a peak in early 1950s of 14 million voters and one million individual members. During this period, Labour's support was drawn overwhelmingly from the urban working class, over 60 per cent of whom identified with the party, and who accounted for some 85 per cent of the total Labour vote. Geographically, the Labour vote was concentrated in the industrial regions of inner London, South Wales, the Midlands, Northern England and Central Scotland. Since then Labour support has declined, especially among the WORKING CLASS, only about half of which now identifies with Labour. This is somewhat offset by an increase in middle-class support, especially among the public sector, INTEL-LECTUALS and those of working-class origins.

Apart from two brief periods of minority government (1924 and 1929-31), Labour was first elected to power in the landslide victory of 1945. Between 1945 and 1951 the Government implemented a sweeping programme of socialist-type reforms, including nationalization of many basic industries and public utilities, establishment of a national health scheme, an ambitious housing programme, and a redistributive fiscal and taxation policy aimed at eroding inequality (see WELFARE STATE).

Labour was re-elected to power 1964-1970 and 1974-79. The difficult economic circumstances of this period, coupled with the cautious attitude adopted by leading cabinet ministers, markedly diluted the government's socialist commitment. This led to continuing friction with the party's militant activists who, after the 1979 defeat, succeeded in forcing a number of constitutional reforms designed to increase the constituency party's control over its parliamentary wing. This was seen by many party moderates as posing a serious threat to Labour's electoral prospects, and some resigned to form a new centre-left (Social Democratic) party.

A noteworthy feature of the Party is the complete integration of affiliated trade unions at all levels of party organization. This provides the bulk of the party's income and forms a powerful, often decisive, voting bloc at the annual party conference which — at least in theory — determines party policy.

JP

**labour process.** Any organized system of activity whereby the human capacity to produce results in a useful product or service. It is usually understood that such production is the specific aim of whoever establishes the system (thus 'creative play' is excluded), and that production requires collaboration. Derived from Marxian vocabulary, the concept goes some way to removing the ambiguities of the term 'work' as an instrument of technical analysis.

According to the Marxian analysis, any labour process comprises three distinguishable abstract types of concrete phenomena: (1) the physical actions of those performing tasks; (2) the raw materials upon which these 'labourers' work to transform them into a finished product or 'value'; (3) tools and equipment, which extend the range of operations performed on raw material and reduce the time and effort required to produce a given unit of output. There is also a significant intellectual element linking the interactions between a producer, his tools, and the raw material: because activity is systematic, the possibility exists of analysing and communicating the 'programme' of operations that has been applied. Activity, likewise, is purposeful, stemming from the human need to ensure survival and subsis-

tence, and from the human inclination to improve the material quality of existence.

Below these realms of abstraction any specific labour process is shaped by powerful conditioning factors reflecting the social and historic environment in which it is embedded. The relative technological and technical competence of a culture is important; so is the nature of its fundamental socio-economic relations. Indeed, the technological and socio-economic spheres may be seen as linked, though the nature of this interdependence should never be conceived as one of simple determinacy. The most common fault is to regard technology or the direct labour process itself as the determinant of social structure. The existence of markets — especially in a money economy — is critical for the nature of the labour process since the act of production may progressively become less directed towards the aim of creating goods for the producer's own consumption ('use value') and more towards the aim of producing at least some that will be sold ('exchange values', commodities). This accentuates specialization and so tends to increase overall productivity. As it rises above subsistence level, the motivation to produce 'surplus values' amongst the producers of such a society will grow, which may encourage technical inventiveness in traditional crafts and the creation of yet more specialisms. But such technical and economic tendencies may be severely checked by traditional political, social and ideological structures (*see* FEUDALISM).

For the labour process, the historical importance of CAPITALISM has been decisive, through the predominance of commodity production and treatment of labour ('labour power' or 'labour capacity') itself as a commodity. With these changes there also appeared powerful incentives to technical innovation and the constant revision (and later, systematic 'rationalization') of all aspects of the labour process. A capitalist employer bought through payment of a wage the right to utilize a labourer's capacity to produce (EFFORT BARGAIN), and therefore a right to organize and supervise the activity of production to realize a profit on the product. (In Marxian language, EXPLOITATION with the object of 'valorization'.) Efforts by workers to resist the extent of exploitation resulted in increasingly elaborate control systems, and at least some technical innovation was directed towards solving problems of industrial discipline.

In industrial sociology, lively debate has arisen in recent years about three main aspects of the labour process under capitalism.

(1) To what degree has capitalism dehumanized or 'degraded' human labour through eradicating traditional SKILLS? Writers like H. Braverman (*Labour and Monopoly Capital*, 1974) argue that capitalism has done this in a wholesale manner. But others have believed that the system offsets this tendency by creating numerous new highly skilled or responsible work tasks, and contest the prevalence of genuinely skilled work in the past. And some note that though jobs may be deskilled, workers are not: degraded jobs, such as lower clerical jobs, are predominantly filled by persons from lower-graded jobs or from outside the labour force (e.g. married women). Empirical studies demonstrate that the vast majority of manual tasks, and many lower-level nonmanual tasks, are fragmentary and lacking in responsibility, making fewer demands on the operative than other operations he performs daily, such as driving to work.

(2) Has the tightness with which employers can control work performance been exaggerated? Through informal resistance, as well as TRADE UNION power, some groups of workers are able to evade some forms of control and limit the extent of effective exploitation — though firms may be developing more subtle methods of control as their need for reliable performance increases (see LABOUR MARKETS). Furthermore, all advanced countries are experiencing increasing resistance to fragmented work operations and blatantly hierarchical forms of control.

(3) To what extent is the contemporary labour process generic, not merely to capitalism, but to all industrialized economies? Empirical evidence from STATE SOCIALIST societies is less than encouraging here, especially since the apparent change of options in the People's Republic of China since MAO. Would a primary commitment to 'humane' organization of the labour process

entail a serious loss of overall productivity? It is possible to envisage alternatives to prevailing modes of organizing the labour process, but the scale of socio-economic change demanded does not (as yet?) arouse the degree of popular commitment sufficient to realize it over the short historical term.

MR

**Lacan, Jacques** (1901- ). French psychoanalyst and doctor of medicine. He trained at the Paris Medical Faculty, of which he became Chef de clinique in 1932, and later taught at the St Anne Hospital. In 1963 he became Chargé de Conférences at the Ecole Pratique des Hautes Etudes and founded the Ecole Freudienne de Paris. During the 1960s and early 1970s his seminars became a major focus of Parisian intellectual life. Lacan is associated with the movement of STRUCTURALISM and is notable for attempts to revivify the thought of Freud through the use of structuralist concepts derived from the linguistics of SAUSSURE and Jakobson. 'The unconscious', he maintains, 'is structured like a language.'

Lacan's best-known contribution to psychoanalytic theory concerns the 'mirrorphase' of infant development. He argues that the child first develops a concept of its own ego when it can perceive itself in a mirror, but that this leads to a quite false belief in the wholeness and stability of the ego, which Lacan prefers to see as a dynamic, continually restructured, process.

Lacan has had little influence on British or American psychoanalysis, although his influence has been felt in literary criticism. Like many other contemporary French structuralists, he eschews clarity of expression; his wilfully obscure punning and convoluted style, along with his use of an eccentric mathematics, has led to charges of charlatanism.

See also FREUD; PATRIARCHY; PSYCHO-ANALYSIS.

AM

**Laing, R.D.** (1927- ). Psychiatrist and psychoanalyst who became one of the best-known critics of psychiatry of the 1960s, earning himself and others the label of anti-psychiatrist. His dominant theme has been the need to understand and make intelligible the experience — the thoughts, feelings and behaviour — of the person who is said to be mentally disturbed. His commitments to the validity of that experience led him to a radical critique of psychiatric ideas and practice, although he has subsequently renounced much of his more radical work.

Born in Glasgow, Laing was the only child of lower middle-class parents who lived on the edge of the Gorbals slum district. A strong presbyterian religious influence at home gave him familiarity with religious texts and a rather narrow and strict moral upbringing. Educated at local primary and grammar schools, where he received a classical education, he obtained his medical qualification at Glasgow University in 1951. Having decided to specialize in psychiatry, he spent six months in a neurosurgical unit before he was called up for military service and was for two years a psychiatrist in the British Army. On his return to Glasgow, he took a post at the Royal Mental Hospital, and was also attached to the University. During his years on the wards of a public mental hospital Laing became involved in trying to make intelligible the apparently irrational thoughts, feelings and action of psychotic patients (see MENTAL ILLNESS), and in attempting to rehabilitate them.

In 1957 Laing moved from the custodial milieu of the public mental hospital with its long-stay patients and their psychotic and organic conditions, to the psychoanalytically oriented Tavistock Clinic in London, which provided outpatient services, including marital and family counselling, to those whose complaints were, in psychiatric terms, mostly neurotic. He had an analysis with Charles Rycroft. His first book, *The Divided Self* (1960), begun in Glasgow, built on a diverse range of intellectual currents including EXISTENTIALISM and PSYCHO-ANALYSIS and dealt with the subjective experience of a particular group of his former psychotic patients, those with schizophrenia. From this analysis of individual experience, Laing moved to a concern with interpersonal perception and experience, attempting to understand individual experience within its immediate interpersonal context, particularly that of the FAMILY. *The Self and Others* (1961) and his study with Aaron

Esterson, *Sanity, Madness and The Family* (1964) are the main products of this development. The latter work drew on the ideas of American social scientists suggesting that schizophrenia is a response to disturbed relationships within the family. Laing rejected the causal relationship between family processes and schizophrenia; instead, in line with his PHENOMENOLOGICAL perspective, he asserted the necessity for a distinctive science of persons in which the causal laws of POSITIVISM could have no part. He sought to make comprehensible the behaviour of the schizophrenic patient in relation to his or her situation.

Laing's stress on the intelligibility of behaviour that has been identified as pathological led him to question the value neutrality of judgements of madness and sanity. He went on to reject values that judge people to be sane or insane and the institutions, like the family, that constrain them. Schizophrenia, he contended (*The Politics of Experience and the Bird of Paradise*, 1967), was a voyage of discovery in which individuals could find themselves through a natural process of healing. He became involved in establishing private communities where this healing could occur. Elements of radicalism and mysticism in Laing's ideas led to alignment with left-wing radicals and to prominence as a near folk-hero of the later 1960s. However, though Laing's work directed attention to social processes and he began to use a number of Marxist concepts, his theorizing of the social was limited. In the 1970s his more radical ideas, like those of SZASZ, were largely superseded by a more politically and sociologically informed analysis of mental illness and psychiatry that emphasized its similarities to, rather than its differences from, the rest of medical practice.

See also PSYCHIATRY; PSYCHOANALYSIS.

JB

**Lambda.** See ASSOCIATION, COEFFICIENTS OF.

**language.** The concept of language is used in many different ways to refer to different aspects of the use of arbitrary symbols in potentially endless combinations as a form of communicative behaviour in humans, animals or machines such as computers. Human natural language in the form of speech is the paradigm, though written language, important in the accumulation and development of culture, is not always derivative in the sense of being a phonetic representation of speech (e.g. Chinese ideograms, Mayan glyphs).

Language as a general category occupies an ambivalent position in relation to CUL-TURE, being sometimes treated as a part of culture and sometimes as a separate entity within which culture is articulated and expressed. Particular languages are difficult to define in pure form. Linguistic change predominates and typically, even within a defined community at a given time, a formalized literary language coexists with a vernacular spoken form, merging at the extremities into a collection of dialects. Linguistically, boundaries relate to particular usages; sociologically, they may be barriers to comprehension. The tendency for people to mark linguistic boundaries as part of the reinforcement of cultural identity provides the analyst with provisional units.

Formally, the minimal complete unit within a language can be seen as the sentence, a STRUCTURE of words, each of which may possibly have a use on its own. In turn, words are constructed from a small, finite set of discrete, meaningless sounds (phonemes), a dual structure characteristic of human speech. The rules of association between sound and meaning can be formally analysed into a syntactic component, producing from an underlying deep structure, which feeds into the semantic component, concerned with meaning, a surface structure from which the phonological component produces the sound utterance.

Formal analysis, following CHOMSKY, concentrates on the syntactic component, partly because the others are poorly understood, partly because syntax seems more central than semantics in defining permissible speech acts, as it seems possible to have acceptable but meaningless utterances.

In real language use, situational factors, as well as expectations, prior knowledge etc, enter into the production and comprehension of utterances. Chomskian formal analysis does not exclude these, but separates out a certain purely linguistic competence. However, in some contexts semantic considerations are used to help reduce ambiguity in syntactical structure, and other theorists propose an interaction between syntactic and semantic analysis which negates the privileged position of syntax in linguistic competence.

Within everyday social interaction, complete sentential structures are rare, Meaning is seen by many modern sociologists as negotiated in an interchange so completely welded to the accompanying gestures, background situation and taken-for-granted knowledge as to be inseparable from them. In terms of WITTGENSTEIN's 'linguistic' philosophy, meaning in language relates to mode of use within a given 'form of life' (see also CONVERSATION ANALYSIS).

The mutual relationship between the semantics of a language and the categories of a people's culture is a question of debate. The American tradition of anthropological structural linguistics, deriving from BOAS, studied pre-literate Indian languages and connected these with the differing world-views of their speakers. The so-called Sapir-Whorf hypothesis holds that while language and other aspects of culture arise as a whole, language has the greater influence on world-view. But others argue that semantic distinctions merely reflect or encode distinctions of material culture and social structure.

Within a given social or linguistic community, variations in use of language have been related to underlying social differences, in CLASS (see BERNSTEIN), status, EDUCA-TION, RELIGION, SUBCULTURE etc. To what extent non-linguistic behaviour can be predicted from linguistic behaviour remains the subject of debate.                          JL

**latency.** See PSYCHOANALYSIS.

**law.** *General.* Law has a self-evident institutionalized existence epitomized in the practice of *legal institutions*, in the *legal profession*, in a more or less systemized system of legal rules (statutes, and precedents) and in the activities of varieties of enforcement agencies (police, prisons, bailiffs etc). Yet the literature, in particular that of legal theory, is marked by long-standing controversies concerning the definition of law. Within the Anglo-American tradition this is an aspect of the opposition between natural law and legal positivism.

The central controversy revolves around the adequacy of a definition of law as 'a specialized system of rules backed by sanctions'. This definition, arising from the tradition of legal positivism, emphasizes: (1) the notion of 'valid rules', focusing on the constitutional requirements of the creation and identification of rules as legal rules; (2) the universality of legal rules in contrast to the particularistic or optional character of non-legal rules; (3) the necessary relationship between legal rules and the sanctions imposed by and through legal institutions. Within this framework most lawyers argue that legal rules have very specific functions: to prescribe procedures for certain transactions; to provide rules for the regulation of disputes; to give constitutional authority to the activities of government officials; to lay down standards.

But this equation of law and rules is often criticized as being unsociological. It produces a model of law as an internalized and isolated system preoccupied with the internal, logical interrelationship of rules and procedures. It excludes or minimizes the role played by principles and policies that are not reducible to rules in constituting law. It thus fails to articulate a concept of law which focuses attention upon its relationship to the wider society within which it is formed and operates.

The authority of legal as opposed to non-legal rules derives partly from the mode of their creation, reflecting in turn the structure and organization of political power in any given society. Legal rules may always in the last resort be enforced by law-enforcement agencies such as the police, bailiffs, prisons.

Analyses of legal rules based on this more sociological view focus more on their ideological function; for example, questions have been posed relating to the extent to which law should be and can be understood as a means for giving legitimacy to the interests of powerful groups within society (see JURISPRUDENCE, SOCIOLOGICAL; LAW, *sociology of*; LAW, *Marxist theory of*).

This second position is less concerned with advancing a verbal definition of law than with emphasizing the non-reducibility of law to a set of rules or orders with a conception of law located within the wider social system. See R. Brown, *Rules and Laws in Sociology* (1973).

AJH

I TRENDS IN LEGAL THEORY. 1. Legal Positivism. 2. Natural Law theory. 3. American Legal Realism. 4. Sociology of Law. 5. Marxist Theory of Law. 6. Neo-conservative and neo-liberal theories.
II CLASSIFICATIONS OF LAW.
III LEGAL INSTITUTIONS. 1. Courts. 2. Tribunals. 3. Ombudsmen and other investigatory bodies. 4. The Legal Profession.
IV LEGAL SERVICES. 1. Legal Aid/Judicare. 2. Public-interest Law. 3. Law Centres.

I TRENDS IN LEGAL THEORY

The term legal theory is broadly interchangeable with 'jurisprudence' and 'philosophy of law'. Its history, particularly in Anglo-American tradition, has been characterized by a long-standing opposition between legal positivism and natural law theory.

1. *Legal Positivism* adopts a strict separation between fact and value. Its focus is upon the identification and operation of legal 'rules' as social facts, and its central preoccupation the identification of 'valid' rules. It thus involved a search for a sharper differentiation between the legal and the non-legal, and so embodied a complacent and unproblematic conception of law which, by virtue of its status as law, was the object of obedience. Thus POSITIVISM moved increasingly towards a concern with the internal functioning of law as a system of rules. This is manifest, for instance, in Hans Kelsen's *The Pure Theory of Law* (1911, English edition 1967), whose theory is 'pure' in that it sought to be uncontaminated by metaphysics or sociology. Legal norms were hierarchically organized in a logico-deductive process founded on a fundamental NORM (*Grundnorm*), the only norm not logically derived from other legal norms. A different aspect of this trend is found in H.L.A. Hart who, dissatisfied with Austin's imperative/command theory, focused on the different types of legal rules that fulfil different functions within the legal system. Hart advanced a distinction between primary and secondary rules, one directed to

legal subjects, the other to legal officials and judges ( *The Concept of Law*, 1961).

The long ascendency of legal positivism encouraged an isolationist conception of law as an arena to be understood through the special properties of judicial logic and the definitional analysis of legal concepts. English legal positivism was also influenced by Jeremy Bentham, whose UTILITARIANISM focused on both the efficacy and the efficiency of legal rules and institutions. Aside from the writings of Bentham, much of whose juristic writings did not become available until fairly recently, utilitarianism never developed a strong theory of jurisprudence, being influential through its reformist associations and application, for example in Fabianism. The reaction against formalism, epitomized by sociological JURISPRUDENCE, also broke with the individualist calculus of Bentham's version of utilitarianism to advance a social utilitarianism.

2. *Natural law theory* adopts criteria external to the positive law against which the latter could be evaluated. The invocation of divine law as a basis for comparison with human positive law characterized theological versions of natural law. The close association of natural law theory with Catholicism accounted in part for the ascendancy of legal positivism in the Protestant Anglo-American tradition. This association has been less pronounced in more recent literature. Natural law is increasingly rationalist, seeking to identify criteria and principles against which legal institutions and rules may be evaluated. The most influential are varieties of SOCIAL CONTRACT theory, from ROUSSEAU to Rawls, which seek the basis of the social obligation to obey law. In its rationalist version the opposition between legal positivism and natural law recedes, and indeed in fundamental respects the title natural law itself becomes redundant. Hence more recently there have been signs of a fusion of concerns between the two traditions; see, for example, the exchange between H.L.A. Hart, *Law, Liberty and Morality* (1963) and Lon Fuller, *The Morality of Law* (1969).

Legal positivism was undermined by its inability to respond adequately to external political developments: it could not avoid granting formal recognition to Nazi law since it met the criteria of formal validity. Many jurists sought a theory that concerned itself with the content as well as the form of law. Hence there has been a strong re-emergence of more rationalistic natural law theories in the 20th century. Debates in legal theory since World War II remained located within a series of ritual encounters between positivism and natural law in such a way as to mark a continuing predominance of an essentially positivist problematic. Some of the more important jurisprudential discussions, such as those involving H.L.A. Hart, Lon Fuller and Ronald Dworkin ( *The Philosophy of Law*, 1977), have only slowly broken through the positivism-natural law opposition.

The broader field of legal theory has shifted to issues around *legal rights* (e.g. Dworkin, *Taking Rights Seriously*, 1979) and JUSTICE (e.g. J. Rawls, *A Theory of Justice*, 1971). These evaluate the substantive content of legal rules and the effectiveness of law as a mechanism of social regulation and control. In this shift the coherence of jurisprudence, long under the dominance of legal positivism, has been disrupted. In the present period it is much intermixed with theories of the STATE and politics, and with the *sociology of law* (see below).

3. *American Legal Realism*. A school of legal theory whose influential figures were Oliver Wendell Holmes, Karl Llewellyn and Jerome Frank. They adopted a PRAGMATIST stance to focus on law as it really is, emphasizing the contrast between law in books and law in action, and were less concerned than (SOCIOLOGICAL) JURISPRUDENCE with the overall place of law within the social system. They denied ideal models of legal process and described what courts of law actually do. Their approach was much influenced by the needs of practising lawyers to be able to predict the likely outcome of legal disputes.

The legal realists incorporated in an eclectic fashion elements of psychology, sociology and economics. In particular, they insisted that JUDGES are not neutral rule-applying robots but necessarily give effect to subjective attitudes and prejudices in arriving at decisions. This has given rise to the recent American trend of jurimetrics which makes use of complex attitudinal inventories to predict patterns of judicial decision-making (see JUDGES).

They also stress the indeterminacy of the facts upon which legal cases are decided and emphasize the element of choice and selection, influenced by judicial attitudes, involved in determining the facts before the court.

Their focus reveals a faith in the perfectability of law and legal process. This reformist orientation led many legal realists to play an active part in the legislative process of Roosevelt's New Deal in the 1930s. Concern with legal reform and a focus on the judicial process has had a marked impact on the subsequent development of American *sociology of law*, in which links with the Realist tradition remain pronounced.

Realism has had only limited impact in the UK. The predominant influence of the *legal profession* on legal education in Britain has perpetuated a traditionalism and formalism which results in an almost exclusive emphasis upon knowledge of legal rules as the proper content of legal education. The political and legal theorist Harold Laski was the only significant contemporary British figure to be influenced by American Realism. A realist influence arrived much later through the growth of the sociology of law, and had a limited impact on legal education.

4. *Sociology of law.* The specialist area of study describing itself variously as sociology of law, legal sociology and socio-legal studies has had a complex lineage. Unlike other subdivisions of sociology, the intellectual origins of the sociology of law have not been an outgrowth from general sociology: the major moving force has been from within the field of legal studies and legal theory. The development of the sociology of law can be traced to a reaction against the narrowness of legal positivism and as part of a wider 'revolt against formalism'. Sociology of law at the most general and pervasive level insists upon law being viewed and studied within its wider social context. In the main it has developed in law schools rather than in sociology departments. However, a considerable

impetus to the growth of a theory in the sociology of law was provided by DURKHEIM and WEBER, who wrote extensively on problems of law, crime and punishment. Particular varieties of sociology of law were advanced in the first half of this century by such writers as Eugen Ehrlich, Georges Gurvitch and N.S. Timasheff.

Sociology of law began to develop coherence after World War II, particularly in the USA. American sociology of law revealed a close connection with the major tradition in inter-war legal theory, *legal realism* (see above). The general frame of reference was explicitly a reform orientation to explore the gap between legal ideas and legal reality, paralleling the gap between 'law in books' and 'law in action'. These concerns developed within general acceptance of the dominant normative integration perspective within American sociology (see CONSENSUS). The emphasis was upon law as an imperfect but improvable mechanism of conflict resolution. This orientation has remained the most pervasive within sociology of law.

With the emergence of CONFLICT THEORY during the 1970s a substantial literature emerged emphasizing the conflict-institutionalizing role of law, the subservience of legal processes to dominant economic interests, and the ideological role of central legal ideals and practices. One significant feature of this trend was that it cut across subdisciplinary boundaries; it became difficult and unnecessary to distinguish between radical deviancy theory (see DEVIANCE), radical CRIMINOLOGY and radical sociology of law. This merging of fields did, however, shift the concerns of radical sociology of law towards the criminal justice system.

Later in the 1970s radical sociology of law became influenced by the *Marxist theory of law* either as an embodiment of a conflict perspective or, increasingly, as a theory going beyond the limited opposition between conflict and consensus theoretical paradigms. This resulted in a dominance of theoretical controversies. But by the end of the 1970s a trend emerged towards Marxist empirically centred studies that have been historical in method, concentrating on 19th- and 20th-century legal developments.

Since then, mainstream sociology of law has become increasingly micro-empirical, and quantification has strengthened the trend towards behavioural analysis. In addition, the techniques of micro-economics have been borrowed and the economic analysis of legal regulation has expanded. In British sociology of law opposing views are expressed through the very names 'socio-legal studies' and 'sociology of law'. The former designates a stronger commitment to empirical concerns and to 'borrowing' from other disciplines in order to advance the study of legal phenomena; thus the Socio-Legal Centre at Oxford brings together economists, psychologists, sociologists etc to study and research law. 'Sociology of law' denotes greater concern with the theoretical base of legal phenomena, empirical studies being seen as expressions of concern rather than ends in themselves.

5. *Marxist theory of law.* This arose entirely outside the file of jurisprudence. Legal theory texts had ignored or denigrated Marxism as having no relevance to juris-prudence. The Marxist theory of law was an outgrowth of the expansion of western Marxism taken up within critical crimino-logy, DEVIANCY theory and *the sociology of law.*

Marxism was first harnessed to CONFLICT THEORY to emphasize the coercive or repressive character of law and legal insti-tutions. There was much emphasis upon the relationship between law and the STATE, often neglected in non-Marxist theories of law, but there was a tendency to reduce both law and state to a one-dimensional role of repression. The expansion of Marxist scholarship within the Anglo-American tradition led to both a re-examination of the classical texts of MARX and ENGELS and the rediscovery of earlier Marxist texts on law. While neither Marx or Engels produced a text in which law was the primary object of enquiry, it became clear that both indivi-dually and together they had written much that related, both directly and indirectly, to law. These writings could not be assembled to provide a single or developed theory of law, but a number of major issues were high-lighted, such as the relationship between legal form and capitalist RELATIONS OF PRODUCTION, the legitimation of law, the role of law in political action etc.

The rediscovery of early texts underlined the diversity of strands within the Marxist tradition. Karl Renner, an Austrian Social Democrat, emphasized the functional continuity of legal regulation. Rushe and Kirschheimer provided an economistic account of the relationship between forms of punishment and the development of capitalist economies. Evgeny Pashukanis (an early left-Bolshevik jurist) focused attention on the homologous relationship between legal form and the commodity relationship.

The development of Western Marxism gave rise to a range of work focusing on the structural location of law, with particular reference to the relation between law and the state. The GRAMSCIAN tradition has been particularly influential; its focus has been upon the part played by law in reproducing legitimation and HEGEMONY within civil society by elaborating Gramsci's notion of the educative role of law. This marks an important shift of emphasis. It does not deny the repressive, coercive role of law, but explores the contribution made by law in the production of social and political consent. The shift is towards an emphasis upon the contradictory character of law, not simply imposed upon subordinate classes but able to protect and advance the interest of sub-ordinate classes while binding them within existing political and ideological structures.

In the most recent Marxist literature there has emerged a sharper controversy about the relationship between law and the transition to SOCIALISM. At one pole is the position which draws heavily on Pashu-kanis's theorization of the 'withering away of law' as socialism is a 'non-legal social order'. At the other pole stands E.P. Thompson's insistence that a radical libertarian tradition is embodied within law. The protection of civil liberties and the principles of the rules of law is being abandoned by the bourgeoisie, and it is the historical task of the socialist movement to bring this to fruition (see LAW, RULE OF).

Marxist studies are now moving away from general theorizations towards increas-ingly concrete and empirical concerns. This is most pronounced in the growth of his-torical studies which stress both the generation and impact of specific, parti-cularly legislative, legal developments.

These have focused particularly upon the 19th century, upon contemporary legal history, and upon studies of specific aspects of legal regulation embodying its contradictory functions.

6. *Neo-conservative or neo-liberal theories.* These have arisen alongside radical and Marxist theories. They are most explicit in F.A. Hayek's *Law, Legislation and Liberty* (3 vols., 1973-9). This challenges the central assumption, which he sees as common to logical jurisprudence, that law can be a logical jurisprudence, tha law can be a conscious agency of social change. In its place Hayek insists upon the limits of law and the primacy of liberty (over for example fairness and EQUALITY). See also MONTES-QUIEU.                                  AJH

II  CLASSIFICATIONS OF LAW

There are a number of ways in which law and legal systems may be classified.

(1) *Civil and common law systems.* Civil law is found in countries which have adopted or modified principles of Roman law, in which the main areas of law are brought together into codes (e.g. a Criminal Code, Civil Code). Common law is found in countries which have developed judicial law-making (see JUDGES).

(2) *Common law and equity.* England is the primary model of a common law system. Its principles, developed in courts of common law, became subject to extremely rigid procedures. Unless a case could be encompassed within a recognized form of action, the common law courts refused jurisdiction over a case. Petition could be made to the Lord Chancellor requesting him to 'do justice' in the particular case. This jurisdiction, originally personal, eventually developed in the Courts of Chancery. The principles of law applied in the Courts of Chancery became know as 'equity'. Since 1875, all courts in Britain have had power to apply principles of both common law and equity.

(3) *Case and statute law.* Although the foundations of the common law are found in judicial case law, the role of the state has developed considerably, particularly over the last 150 years. Laws enacted through Parliament at the instigation of politicians and governments are known, generally, as statute law.

(4) *Public and private law.* Broadly speaking, private law provides the basis for the regulation of disputes between private individuals (e.g. those which may arise from breach of contract, or damage caused by an accident). Public law regulates the activities of government and the relationship of the individual to the State. In many countries, particularly those with civil law systems, the distinction is fundamental in that different courts take jurisdiction in relation to each category. Though the distinction is important in English law it is not embodied in an institutional specialization of courts (see *Legal Institutions*).

(5) *Constitutional law.* Most developed countries have a written constitution and many have a special constitutional court with jurisdiction to resolve issues relating to the legality of the exercise of powers by the legislative and executive arms of government under the terms of the constitution. Such disputes frequently arise in federal states where there are conflicts concerning the legitimate scope of the central and provincial (state) brances of government. In many countries, including the USA, constitutions also contain Bills of Rights (see RIGHTS, HUMAN) which have been the basis of major legal cases relating to civil liberties and fundamental freedoms.

(6) *Civil and criminal law.* A distinction was drawn above between systems of civil and common law; this reflects the different kinds of legal systems found in different countries. In any given legal system, a more specific distinction can be drawn between civil law and criminal law. Broadly, civil law relates to the resolution of disputes between individuals in a society: its remedies will typically be for monetary compensation (damages) to compensate for injury or breach of contract, or for some court order (e.g. an injunction) ordering one party to the action to do or not to do some particular act. Criminal law results in the imposition of a sanction by the state (e.g. a term of imprisonment, or a fine, or the death penalty) on those who have been proved to have infringed the criminal law. Any given situation may give rise both to civil and criminal proceedings: for example, the driver of a car may be

prosecuted for the criminal offence of dangerous driving and/or may be sued by an injured party for damages for personal injury (see CRIME).

MP

III LEGAL INSTITUTIONS

Social anthropologists have long demonstrated that all kinds of society require formal means for the resolution of disputes. They argue that no hard-and-fast distinction can be drawn between institutions that those living modern industrialized societies might regard as 'legal' and other formal procedures (see Roberts, *Order and Dispute*, 1979). This entry, however, concentrates on the institutions of modern society.

1. *Courts.* The primary model for the resolution of disputes in a modern society. Courts tend to be organized on a hierarchial basis. Decisions of 'higher' courts which may hear appeals from lower courts are authoritative and binding upon 'lower courts', and the scope of a court's powers depends on its position in the hierarchy: the lower courts deal with more trivial cases.

A sharp distinction is drawn, particularly in the lower courts, between those dealing with criminal and civil cases. In many countries (though not in Britain) there are also separate constitutional courts, empowered to resolve issues that arise over the interpretation and application of a country's constitutional documents.

Court procedures tend to be formalized and rigid. Whether countries adopt an 'inquisitorial' process (where the judge takes an active role) or an 'adversary' process (in which the judge adopts a more passive role in proceedings dominated by rival advocates), the moment at which each party is allowed to present their part of the case is relatively well-defined. This formalized process has given rise to a number of analyses of court process as RITUAL or drama. Drama is often heightened by the formal architecture and other trappings of the court (e.g. robes and wigs and other special clothes). Though detailed aspects of court process often change, legal institutions frequently appear to be of great antiquity, further enhancing the sense of ritual and drama. One consequence is that the dispute that is the subject

matter of the proceedings will, to an extent, be transformed or reconstituted into a form that is susceptible of legal analysis.

While this rigidity and formality may in principle be regarded as an attempt to ensure that the parties to a case receive a fair hearing, it also makes courts daunting, an alien forum where representation by practising lawyers becomes an important element. This ensures that litigation before the courts becomes expensive, indeed increasingly so. What are the most effective means of ensuring that all those, including the poor, who have disputes which are resolvable in a court forum, have access to the courts? In recent years, 'access to justice' has become a slogan for many reformist critiques of the work of the courts and the *legal profession.* A number of measures have been advocated to improve such access: legal aid/judicare or other forms of legal service (see *Legal Services*); alternative dispute resolution forums (see *Tribunals*) and 'delegalization', the resolution of disputes by informal non-judicial processes.

In popular imagination, the show-piece trial is often regarded as the stereotype for resolving disputes. But in practice the courts deal only with the tip of the iceberg, most disputes being resolved by other means: the negotiation, the bargain, the fight. The typical dispute does not go to court; indeed some aspects of court procedure, particularly on the civil side, are designed to encourage settlement out of court.

2. *Tribunals.* A major 20th-century development in many countries has been the creation of large numbers of specialist tribunals with specialized powers to deal with disputes arising in particular from the law of the WELFARE STATE, management of the economy and the regulation of business. The number of cases dealt with by tribunals frequently rivals that of the ordinary courts. Their stated purpose is to offer a cheaper, speedier, more informal and more technically knowledgeable means for the resolution of disputes. Experience suggests that those objectives are by no means always satisfied. While tribunals are cheap, at least for those who appear before them, many operate with substantial delays; however informal those who sit on tribunals may think

they are, they are perceived as formal institutions by those who appear before them; and the quality of decision-taking is often criticized.

The alleged success of these tribunals, combined with criticism of the more formal courts, has also led in many countries to demands for the creation of special courts to deal with other issues currently dealt with before the ordinary courts. Among the most frequent demands are for specialist small claims courts, housing courts, and juvenile and family courts.

Although such tribunal-courts may be quicker and cheaper, lack of representation may result in an imbalance of advantage for those appearing before them: the first-time litigant is likely to be at a disadvantage compared with the frequent litigant (see Galanter, 'Why the "Haves" Come out Ahead', *Law and Society Review*, 1974).

3. *Ombudsmen and other investigatory bodies.* Another more recent development has been the extension to many countries of the Scandinavian-based concept of the Ombudsman. It has been increasingly conceded that court processes are an inadequate means of detecting and combating official maladminstration. In the UK, Ombudsmen exist in relation to central and local government and the Health Service. Increasing demands are being heard for an effective means of dealing with complaints against the police. In addition, agencies with powers to combat DISCRIMINATION, on grounds both of sex and race, have been created in many countries. So too have officers to deal with matters such as consumer complaints, environmental health, and health and safety at work. Such bodies are procedurally much less formal and more inquisitorial in approach than the ordinary courts.

4. *The Legal Profession.* Once societies rely on formal law as one of the principal means of maintaining social order (see LAW, *General*), groups of persons learned in the law emerge to administer that law, give legal advice and act as advocates. The earliest evidence of the emergence of a group of lawyers in England is from the 12th century. However, professional organization, as currently understood, is a more modern

phenomenon, reflecting an increasingly sophisticated DIVISION OF LABOUR in society. The essential feature of professional organization, found in many if not all PROFESSIONS, is the successful assertion by its members of control over numbers and standards of admission and the education of members of the profession who breach its self-defined rules of conduct. More generally, professions assert their independence and claim to act in the public interest. All these attributes may be seen to apply to the legal profession, particularly in Western liberal democratic societies.

While many of these self-defined attributes may provide a means of ensuring that those who utilize the services of members of the legal profession receive a good standard of service, their effect is, in many respects, to place members of the profession beyond public scrutiny and accountability. In the context of all professions, increasing debate has been directed to the question of how to increase public accountability.

Professions in general and the legal profession in particular need constantly to assert their claims to be acting in the public interest. Many functions that lawyers perform will not easily be performed by those not trained in the law. Indeed, in many countries the legal system itself recognizes the monopoly of lawyers over advocacy in the courts or the power to draft certain kinds of documents or the conduct of certain kinds of legal business.

Since monopoly power always affords to its holder the opportunity for abuse, legal professions have been adept at emphasizing the primacy of the public interest in the work they perform. Attacks on the power of the legal profession are frequently defused by claims that the legal profession is an essential element in the preservation of freedom and the rule of law in society. One particularly strong claim asserted by the legal profession is to be regarded as independent: lawyers must remain free to act in the interests of their clients without any direction or interference by the state. The concept of the fearless independent lawyer, representing the underdog and confronting the might of powerful groups in society, is frequently found in literature and the mass media. To a degree, this popular stereotype is justified in the practical world. However, another consequence of the successful claim to independence is that lawyers themselves decide what legal services to offer, and where they will offer them. For example, there are now about 40,000 solicitors in private practice in England and Wales. Studies show that their distribution is very uneven, with considerably more in property-owning areas such as Bournemouth than in poorer areas such as Bootle. The legal profession operate where those who can afford to pay for their services are to be found (see also *Legal Services*). There are also many respects in which the role of legal practitioners is confused; for example, lawyers who appear as advocates in the criminal courts may face conflicting pressures: many wish to act on behalf of their client, but they will also see themselves as, in part, officers of the court. They will be made to realize that if their case goes on too long, other cases may be delayed. Recent studies on plea-bargaining have highlighted the existence of these conflicts.

In many, though not all, countries whose legal system is based on the English system of common law, there is a divided legal profession. In England and Wales, the division is between solicitors and barristers. Barristers are primarily responsible for acting as advocates, particularly in the higher courts, while solicitors' primary responsibility is to deal directly with clients and, where necessary, prepare cases for court. Only solicitors may be instructed by members of the public; barristers are instructed indirectly through solicitors.

Critics argue that this sustains restrictive practices in the public interest. It is also claimed that these divisions keep the cost of legal services high and that clients are in some cases obliged to hire additional lawyers they neither want nor need (M. Zander, *Lawyers and the Public Interest*, 1968). Advocates of the divided profession argue that only by keeping the profession divided can an adequate supply of specialist advocates be supported and kept available for all those who need their services. The powerful representative bodies of the legal profession believe that, on balance, division is desirable. This view has, so far, prevailed in England (see Royal Commission on Legal Services, 1979).

Arrangements for controlling lawyers vary considerably. In England, the solicitors' branch of the legal profession is controlled by the Law Society, responsible for internal discipline, rules of professional etiquette, professional education etc. The Law Society also administers the civil *legal aid* scheme on behalf of the Government (see *Legal Services*) which, in itself, raises difficult problems of independence. On the barristers' side, internal discipline, and rules of professional etiquette are governed by the Senate of the Inns of Court. Limited recognition of the problem of lawyers judging lawyers has led both sides of the legal profession to incorporate a limited 'lay' element in their disciplinary process.

See also MEDICAL PROFESSION; PROFESSION.

MP

IV  LEGAL SERVICES

*The provision of legal services.* Little research has been conducted into the exact nature and scope of the legal services provided by the *legal profession* (see above). Official statistics give some idea of the number of cases processed through the principal *legal institutions*, but lawyers will not necessarily be involved in all such cases. Such data give no indication of the amount of non-contentious business (not leading to litigation) which lawyers undertake. A number of studies in various jurisdictions indicate that legal services are provided much more extensively for those who own property, than for those who do not.

1. *Legal Aid/Judicare.* The expense of using law has led to attempts to ensure that the poor have access to law in many countries. A number of models have been developed, of which the most common is legal aid (UK) or judicare (USA). Under this system, all or part of the expenses incurred by ordinary lawyers working in private practice is paid from public funds. The level of subsidy usually depends on a MEANS TEST based on the client's income and capital resources. In the UK, where the scheme has existed since 1950, legal aid has been used predominantly for matters arising out of criminal cases, matrimonial breakdown and personal injuries; legal aid has not been available for

representation of cases heard by tribunals (see *Legal Institutions*).

It has recently been argued that there is a considerable additional unmet need for legal services in other areas of law. Many legal rights contained in legislation enacted particularly since the end of World War II relating to the protection of tenants, or the provision of social security payments, or mental health, inter alia, go by default because ordinary people do not have access to lawyers. More lawyers should be provided in various localities, funded by increased government subsidies, so that more people can take advantage of legal services. It is argued that this would be an unqualified benefit to society since such services would result in greater social justice.

Critics argue that: (1) The need for any social service can never be conclusively defined; the concept of 'unmet need' is thus meaningless. (2) Much of the case for more extensive legal services derives from lawyers anxious to develop new forms of profitable work. (3) To concentratee on legal rights may ignore many fundamental political issues relating the the distribution of resources in society. Social justice is not primarily a question for courts of law, but a reflection of the particular social and economic structure of society. Notwithstanding those criticisms, a number of alternative models for the provision of legal services have developed, such as Law Centres (see below), suggestions for new forms of dispute resolution (see *Legal Institutions*), and the public interest law firm.

2. *Public interest law.* A development in the USA which has received considerable discussion elsewhere. The concept is based on the proposition that in a pluralist society there are a number of interest groups (e.g. environmentalists, consumers) whose claims tend to go unheard. Since social order depends on satisfying the demands of conflicting interest groups, those groups who lack representation should be represented more positively, not only in the courts but also in the legislative and executive branches of government. Lawyers working in public interest law firms offer such a representative service.

3. *Law Centres.* Created in a number of juris-

dictions, including the UK, in recent years, law centres issue a number of challenges to existing *legal professions.* In the British context, solicitors and barristers have found that they can operate together in the same office. Those working there have been dedicated to developing expertise in areas of law largely neglected by the private legal profession (e.g. housing, social security). They have also challenged a traditional view of the legal profession that all cases should be dealt with on an individual basis; some law centres argue that it is also important for collective action to be taken. All centres attempt to run educational programmes to inform residents of their legal rights and how to assert them: the poor are, at best, lacking in power, and only by combining will they develop sufficient strength to challenge accepted power structures. This approach has been challenged by more traditional lawyers who argue that it is no function of lawyers to become involved in political struggles. This fails to acknowledge that merely asserting political neutrality may be as political an act as actively engaging in political struggle.

MP

**law, rule of.** A powerful symbol in legal discourse. It carries no single or one-dimensional definition; rather it embodies a number of interrelated ideas which combine to express a commitment to government by and through legal authority as distinguished from tyranny or anarchy, and provide a basis or rationale for the citizen's obligation to obey LAW.

More concretely, the concept expresses a commitment to procedural regularity ('due process of law') and also to the universality of legal jurisdiction such that all, including both rulers and ruled, are subject to law, to the same rules of law, and to the same legal institutions. Thus not only is the citizen subject to law but there is also a notion of a check upon or limitation upon the activity of rulers. It is dependent upon the concept of the separation of powers (see MONTES-QUIEU) since it presumes a judiciary autonomous from legislature and executive. The British and American judiciary see themselves as defenders of the individual citizen against the incursions of the leviathan state (see JUDGES).

Discussions on the rule of law involve controversy as to the degree to which any particular legal system realizes the complexity of the rule of law in practice. In addition, important disputes occur around the significance of the ideological content and significance of the slogan (e.g. E.P. Thompson's call for a socialist commitment to the rule of law; see LAW: *Trends in legal theory* (*Marxist theory of law*).

AJH

**law, social.** General propositions which state invariant and necessary relations between properties in a social scientific theory. Social laws, modelled on natural laws developed in physics, chemistry, astronomy etc, are intended to state relations which cannot be broken and which hold in all circumstances, to provide an explanation of the phenomena observed. Laws are theoretical terms whose truth or falsity is established by empirical verification. A hypothesis is a tentative law-like statement whose universal truth has not been satisfactorily established.

Social laws have an important place in the logic of social explanation, for example in the hypothetico-deductive method, where they provide the base from which explanations are constructed. In practice, there are very few convincing social laws (as distinct from empirical generalizations), due to the complexity of explaining human behaviour and the gulf which often divides sociological theory and empirical research. See EXPLANATION.

See R. Brown, *Explanation in Social Science* (1963).

MB

Only in the 17th century did the concept of law of nature lose its prescriptive meaning as, for example, a principle laid down by God which things were morally obliged to follow. However, 'laws of nature' in the sense of the principles governing the relations between things are still thought to involve a more than accidental regularity. Despite criticisms by POSITIVISTS and EMPIRISTS of the idea of 'natural necessity', it is generally agreed, for example, that laws sustain COUNTERFACTUAL CONDITIONALS, whereas 'accidental' empirical generalizations do not.

WO

**Lazarsfeld, Paul F.** (1901-76). Austrian-American sociologist. Born in Vienna, he obtained a PhD in mathematics. He became interested in social psychology, and at the Buhlers Institute at the University of Vienna carried out a class study of unemployment in the town of Marienthal (1933) with M. Jahoda and H. Zeisl. In 1933 he left Austria for the USA, where he became involved in mass media research, first at the University of Newark, then at Princeton, and from 1940 at Columbia University, where he taught in the Sociology Department until his retirement in 1969. In the early 1940s he established the Bureau of Applied Social Research at Columbia, the first successful institutionalization of the SOCIAL SURVEY in a university context. This provided his research base, an instrument for methodological innovation, and a training ground for a whole generation of younger quantitative researchers.

Lazarsfeld has been the most important single influence upon quantitative research methodology in sociology in the 20th century. He organized and developed social survey research, making particularly notable contributions to indicator-construction and the logic of the analysis of data using CROSS TABULATIONS. He also made major contributions to MATHEMATICAL SOCIOLOGY, the study of mass communications, political sociology and applied sociology, and wrote many important monographs. But it is as a fertile and enormously inventive methodologist that his influence has been greatest, and has extended all over the world.

While at Columbia he formed a fruitful partnership with MERTON, and came under attack from MILLS for practising 'abstracted empiricism', a charge which was hardly fair, since Lazarsfeld was particularly aware of the need to bridge the gulf between sociological theory and empirical research.

See R.K. Merton *et al, Qualitative and Quantitative Social Research* (1979).

MB

**leadership.** See HUMAN RELATIONS MOVEMENT.

**legal institutions, legal profession, legal services, legal theory.** See LAW.

**legitimacy.** All systems of power and privilege seek to establish themselves as legitimate, that is, morally justifiable, in the eyes of the subordinate and disadvantaged (see WEBER on POWER). Legitimating beliefs secure the latter's consent to the exercise of power, promote stability and minimize the costs of coercion. They are really self-conscious fabrications: the first who need to be convinced of their system's legitimacy are the advantaged and powerful themselves. Their justifications are typically formulated in terms of an existing stock of ideas. The powerful are well placed to disseminate their own beliefs among the subordinate through their preferential access to the means of influencing opinion, and in this sense Marx's dictum that the ruling ideas of a society are those of its ruling class is just. Yet in any society there are divergent individuals and social groups who do not accept the dominant culture, and for whom actual or threatened coercion constitutes the main reason for obedience.

Legitimating ideas not only reinforce but set limits to systems of power: power-holders cannot do just as they please. Furthermore, most justifications for power incorporate claims to promote the wellbeing of the subordinate. If these claims repeatedly fail to be realized, a progressive loss of legitimacy will result, though in the absence of an alternative source of legitimacy power structures can survive for a long time. There comes a point, however, when they can only be preserved by the widespread use of coercion. Even the most repressive systems require legitimacy in the eyes of their own administrative and coercive apparatus; if this also fails, disintegration is the inevitable result.

See AUTHORITY; POWER; REVOLUTION; STATE.

DB

**Lenin, Vladimir Ilyich** (1870-1924). As moving spirit of the Bolshevik revolution and leader of the first Soviet government, Lenin's historical stature is unquestioned. His contribution to the political theory of Marxism was closely related to this achievement, concerning itself primarily with the questions of what kind of REVOLUTION was possible in a backward society like Russia and what form the revolutionary organization should take.

(1) On the first of these questions, Lenin contested the Menshevik view that the revolution against Tsarist autocracy should be carried out under the leadership of the BOURGEOISIE; it was too weak to make its own revolution, and DEMOCRACY would have to be established by an alliance of the proletariat and PEASANTRY. By 1917 he had come to accept TROTSKY's idea that this revolution could pass straight over into a second, socialist revolution. This was more likely in a backward country, owing to its accumulation of social contradictions and the existence of a proletariat uncomprised by the spoils of IMPERIALISM (*Imperialism, the Highest Stage of Capitalism*, 1916).

(2) On the question of party organization, Lenin formulated in *What is to be Done* (1902) and other writings from this period a number of distinct emphases: the proletariat on its own was only able to achieve a TRADE UNION economistic, or bourgeois, consciousness (see CLASS CONSCIOUSNESS); the party was the sole repository of the scientific socialist doctrine which had to be brought to the proletariat, and it should be organized as a cadre party of committed revolutionaries, not as a mass movement. The last emphasis was partly a product of the conditions of the period, which made party activity illegal; in any case, Lenin saw revolutionary organization always as a complement to, not a substitute for, the mass activity of the proletariat. The limitations on party democracy during the Civil War and after, which paved the way for STALINISM, were more a surrender to the exigencies of the time than the product of a consistent ELITISM, as writing such as *State and Revolution* (1917) indicate. Lenin's tendency to elevate tactical requirements of the moment to the status of universal principles makes the interpretation of his work a matter of continuing controversy.

See COMMUNISM; SOCIALISM; STATE SOCIALISM.

DB

**less eligibility.** See POOR LAW.

Lévi-Strauss, Claude (1908- ). French social anthropologist, a major figure within STRUCTURALISM. Born in Brussels (though the family soon moved quickly back to their home in Paris) of a Jewish family. Despite there being several rabbis within the family, neither Claude, his father (a painter) nor his mother were religious believers. He studied law and philosophy at the Sorbonne and was at this time an active member of the Socialist party. After military service and two years as a schoolteacher he was appointed lecturer in sociology at Sao Paulo University, Brazil, in 1934. There he engaged in fieldwork among the Bororo Indians, a great formative experience. Called up into the army in 1939, he left France soon after the German occupation. In New York he joined the Free French forces and made friends with the linguist Roman Jakobson (see STRUCTURALISM). The two continued to influence one another deeply. In 1945 Lévi-Strauss published a 'manifesto' for structuralism (later republished in 1958 as Chapter 2 of *Structural Anthropology*, English edition 1968). Since 1945 he has worked in Paris, first as assistant director of the Musée de l'Homme; in 1950 he moved to a chair at the Ecole Pratique des Hautes Etudes; and in 1959 a special chair in social anthropology was created for him at the prestigious Collège de France.

His other major works to date are *The Elementary Structures of Kinship* (1949, English edn. 1969); *Tristes Tropiques* (1955, English edition under the title *World on the Wane*, 1968); *The Savage Mind* (1962, English edn. 1969); *Totemism* (1962, English edn. 1963); the four-volume *Mythologiques* comprising *The Raw and the Cooked* (1964, English edn. 1969); *From Honey to Ashes* (1967, English edn. 1973), *The Origin of Table Manners* (1968, English edn. 1978) and *L'Homme Nu* (1971); and *Structural Anthropology*, Vol. 2 (1973, English edn. 1977).

Lévi-Strauss has been strongly influenced by aspects of FREUD and MARX, both of whom, he claimed, embodied the structuralist method of advancing understanding by reducing surface reality to a deeper, structural level. But Lévi-Strauss also developed his own distinctive and on the whole consistent approach. Underlying

observable everyday customs — kinship, cooking, table manners etc — are universal rules, much like syntax and semantic structures in linguistics (see LANGUAGE). These can be mapped out by studying systematically compatibilities and incompatibilities: what goes with what, and what are considered binary opposites and even taboo. Even the most trivial of practices turns out to be a symbolic mediation between opposites such as nature and culture, heaven and earth, man and woman. All cultures embody the same basic structural transformations, reflecting the essential characteristics of the human brain, operating according to binary classificatory principles.

Lévi-Strauss's striking formulations and grandeur of conception had wide cultural resonance in the 1970s. Among sociologists and social anthropologists he has influenced many, yet converted relatively few. Most sociologists remain sceptical, committed to the comparative method, studying variations not universals. For a short appreciation from the standpoint of sympathetic criticism, see E. Leach, *Lévi-Strauss* (1970).

See also CHOMSKY; EXCHANGE THEORY; KINSHIP; RECIPROCITY; STRUCTURALISM.

MM

Lewin, Kurt (1890-1947). German-American psychologist, widely known as an advocate of a type of holistic approach to psychology described variously as FIELD THEORY or topological psychology. (For holism, see METHODOLOGICAL INDIVIDUALISM).

Born in Mogilno, Prussia, Lewin was educated at the Universities of Freiburg, Munich and Berlin. He taught at Berlin from 1921 until 1933 when, like many other German intellectuals, he moved to the USA. From 1935 to 1945 he was Professor of Child Psychology at the Child Welfare Research Station of the State University of Iowa. In 1945 he founded the Research Centre for Group Dynamics at MIT, a Centre which after his death moved to the University of Michigan.

Lewin's interests altered through his life. Field theory, developed in the context of the study of cognitive processes of learning and perception and the social influences upon them, held that an individual's behaviour was determined by his or her total situation, the 'psychological life space'. However, interpersonal facts, and then group facts, had increasingly to be separated out as constituting a social space, more than just facts in the individual life space, and Lewin's interests shifted to group phenomena such as leadership and to the nature of social restraints.

Lewin's ideas have been developed in the mathematical direction by, among others, Dorwin Cartwright, using qualitative techniques such as GRAPH THEORY. Other students include Leon FESTINGER, the social psychologists Thibaut and Kelley, and Alex Bavelas, who in the areas of belief systems, interpersonal relations and group phenomena have carried on Lewin's holistic, relational approach.

JL

**liberalism.** Although liberalism tends to be characterized by INDIVIDUALISM — society is seen as a collective of individuals having rights — it is not a single doctrine. 'Liberal' as a political term became established during the first quarter of the 19th century, though it looked back to a political tradition exemplified by LOCKE; it referred to political movements or parties advocating LIBERTY, conceived in individualistic terms: specifically, the establishment or preservation of constitutional regimes which legally guaranteed to their subjects various rights and freedoms such as security of person and possessions (no deprivation of life, liberty or property without due process of law), legal standing (the right of access to the courts of law) and liberty of opinion, association and the press.

Classical liberalism (see LOCKE, MILL) adopts a negative conception of liberty, and assigns to the STATE only the functions of protecting life, limb and property, leaving individuals otherwise legally unobstructed to do as they wish. This involved sweeping away monopolies and corporations guaranteed by the early modern state as restraints on individual (usually economic) activities. The constitution of the state is of secondary importance, since there are no necessary reasons why an autocrat would pursue a more interventionist course than would a democratic assembly.

A more recent form of liberalism, espoused by 19th-century English IDEALISTS and arguably traceable to ROUSSEAU, attributes primary significance to the state's being democratically constituted, and is less concerned to restrict its intervention in spheres of private choice. This is because political participation is either a more important kind of (negative) liberty than others — which may therefore be subordinated to it — or because it is a necessary condition of a person's enjoying (positive) liberty. This often also involves establishing rights of welfare (universal education, health services, benefits for sickness, old age and unemployment, housing, family support etc). Contemporary liberalism includes proponents of free-market, laissez-faire views (now typical of continental European liberalism) but also denominates other advocating a WELFARE STATE and even SOCIAL DEMOCRACY (e.g. in the USA). Often the term refers to whatever doctrines are held by a particular Liberal Party.

See CITIZENSHIP; LIBERTY.

MMG, HIS

**Liberal Party.** Despite its 18th-century Whig origins, the British Liberal Party remains essentially the creation of 19th-century social and economic forces. In opposition to the hierarchical, landed, Anglican orientation of the Conservatives, the Liberals offered the combination of free trade, social reform and religious toleration, a combination that secured the allegiance during the second half of 19th century of newly enfranchised entrepreneurs, artisans and skilled workers of the expanding industrial sector, plus the subcultural and religious minorities found especially in the 'Celtic fringe' of Britain. This alliance of socio-economic peripheries kept the Liberals in the forefront of politics despite two serious splits until the emergence of CLASS as the dominant political cleavage in the early decades of 20th century and the emergence of the LABOUR PARTY. Increasingly unable to straddle this cleavage, the Liberals gradually dwindled to lesser party status, attracting 5 to 20 per cent of the vote and a far smaller proportion of seats. So far, revivals of party fortunes have been due to short-term defections of discontented major-party identifiers.

JP

**liberty.** Differences over the meaning of liberty are amongst the most fertile sources of controversy in political theory (see LIBER-ALISM). The wide variety of definitions offered can be classified as negative and positive conceptions. A person is negatively free to do an action if no one constrains him or her from doing it (HOBBES, LOCKE, MILL). Proponents of the positive conception add a further condition for being free to do an action: the action is morally permissible or rational or in the real interest of the actor (ROUSSEAU, HEGEL). These differing conceptions underwrite different and opposed views of what sorts of social relation and institutional arrangement can count as constraining or coercive. On the negative definition, a person's lack of the ability or resources to pursue an activity does not imply his or her unfreedom to do so. Correspondingly, a person whom others forcibly prevent from doing something which is wrong, irrational or self-damaging, is not thereby rendered positively unfree. Being unimpeded by others from doing such acts is, on this view, license and not liberty.

HIS

**libido.** See PSYCHOANALYSIS.

**lie detection.** Scientific attempts at detecting lies through the interpretation of involuntary physiological responses date from World War I, a time of great interest in psycho-physical measurements. The ancient Chinese knew that the fear associated with conscious deception caused a drying-up of the saliva, the basis for the rice-chewing test. In recent times, the first experiments on lie detection were carried out by Marston in the Harvard Psychological Laboratory in 1917. He found a positive correlation between judgements based on the systolic blood pressure of the accused and jury decisions. Early methods were used in the Army and (in 1918) for the detection of theft among the black employees of a Washington agency.

Many physiological methods have been tried, including JUNG's reaction-time test with word-association; blood-volume and pulse; and the psycho-galvanic skin response (a lowering of the electrical resistance across the skin of hands and feet in response to certain arousal states), as well as the administration of scopolamine injections, first used as a 'truth drug' by House, a Texas obstetrician, in 1921. The psycho-galvanic skin response seemed too sensitive to broader emotional states than lies, but it became usable in 1936 when Father Walter Summers, a Jesuit at Fordham University, devised a control scheme for repeating the questions.

The modern polygraph technique, based on multiple physiological measures (blood pressure, pulse, respiration, PGR), was introduced in 1921 by John A. Larson at the California Police Laboratory. Lie-detector evidence was first admitted into court in Indianapolis in 1924, but the evidence of innocence in a murder case had earlier been excluded in Washington DC in 1922. Larson tested hundreds of people in California during the 1930s, but the legal status of lie-detection evidence remained, and remains, variable. Sometimes it has been admitted as expert testimony in the USA, but in general the courts have allowed no right to a lie detector test.

Lie detection is of interest in sociology in two ways. (1) It represents the most concrete form of the belief that intention can be inferred from measurable physiological changes alone. While this belief seems less plausible in sociology, the idea of an objective mind-reading technique has exercised great sway over the public imagination, and sets a limiting goal for some forms of psychology. (2) Lie detection forms a test case of social attitudes to the power and uses of science. Courts of law, while recognizing expert testimony, have been slow to recognize scientific truth, or even scientific agreement, as legal truth. Scientists have not been in agreement on lie detection, but it is not the scientific status of lie detector tests that has been considered when deciding on their admissibility.

JL

**life cycle.** In any society there are a number of social groups based on biological age. These are known as age grades and the succession of age grades through which

individuals move from birth to death constitutes the life cycle. This succession varies
through time and by society, as each defines
and redefines biological age in different
ways. The age grade of childhood has grown
longer in recent centuries in advanced
societies and the new grade of ADOLESCENCE
was differentiated out in many European
societies during the 18th century. In most
contemporary western societies the life cycle
includes the following age grades: baby,
child, adolescent, young adult, married
person/adult, old person, who may be a
widow (er). A set of behaviour is expected of
those filling each of these grades so that a
description of the life cycle in any society can
give an account of the effects of many
important socialization processes, particularly those relating to the FAMILY. In the past,
movement between age grades was usually
marked by some form of ritual or RITE OF
PASSAGE, particularly the movement from
childhood into adult status; today only the
marriage and funeral ceremonies remain in
general use.

See DELINQUENCY; RITES OF PASSAGE; STRESS.

PWM

**life events.** See HEALTH, SOCIOLOGY OF;
STRESS.

**life expectancy.** A quantity in DEMOGRAPHY
expressing the average number of complete
years lived after a given age, or from birth if
no age is specified. Life expectancy cannot
directly measure the probable life-span in the
future of any real individual. For a given birth
COHORT, its actual MORTALITY experience
and hence its expectation of life can only be
revealed after it has disappeared. Estimates
must be based either on current age-specific
rates, or on the experience of past completed
cohorts. The life expectancy is thus less
useful for characterizing mortality in a
population than the age-and-sex specific
mortality rates.

For a LIFE TABLE showing $l_x$ lives remaining at age $x$, the expectancy of life at age $x$ is
given by dividing the total number of years
lived after age $x$, by those reaching age $x$,
divided by the number reaching age $x$,

$$(\sum_{t=1}^{\infty} l_{x+t})/l_x.$$

For most of history and for much of the
underdeveloped world until recently, the
best estimates show life expectancy at birth
of the order of 30 years, rising to perhaps 40
upon surviving infancy. Using the death rates
for Britain in 1841, life expectancy at birth
was 40 for men, and 42 for women; by 1961
rates, the figures had risen to 68 for men and
74 for women, and a life expectancy of
around 70 years characterizes modern
societies (see DEMOGRAPHIC TRANSITION).
The increase in life expectancy associated
with INDUSTRIALIZATION has mostly been
gradual, but there have been sudden leaps in
some countries, such as that consequent
upon the eradication of malaria.

JL

**life history.** See PERSONAL DOCUMENTS.

**life table.** A basic concept of DEMOGRAPHY,
a life table is a chart showing the numbers
living and dying at each age out of an initial
population. It represents the MORTALITY
experience of a real COHORT, or more often
of a fictitious one formed by applying known
mortality rates progressively to a hypothetical initial generation. A family of
associated life-table functions forms an
important class of demographic techniques.
The life table and its methods may be
extended to analyse progressive decrements
in any sort of population.

The earliest life table known is probably
that produced by Ulpian in 225 AD for
calculating the capital value of annuities for
inheritance purposes. This table was in use in
Northern Italy until the 18th century. In
England, John Graunt produced a life table
in 1662 using the improved christening and
death lists associated with the plague period,
and since then there has been a continuous
sequence of up-dated and specialized tables.
Mathematical techniques for modelling life
tables were investigated from as early as
1570, and the 20th century has produced a
variety of techniques for abridging life tables
by five- or ten-year periods.

See also MORTALITY.

JL

**lineage.** A group of people who claim a
genealogical connection of descent through

male or female lines. Genealogical connection is only the basis of a lineage system, in which lineages also act as corporate political units for specific purposes. Lineages may or may not be associated with particular territories or localities, and they may or may not be EXOGAMOUS units.

Unilineal descent groups are those where descent is claimed through real or fictional blood ties to a particular group through the father (patrilineal) or mother (matrilineal) from a common ANCESTOR or ancestress, through known genealogical links. In societies with bilateral or double-descent groups, such as the Yako of Nigeria, lineages are traced through both maternal and paternal lines. In principle, patrilineal systems depend upon the passing of status and property from father to legitimate son. In such systems, it is important to ensure the legitimacy of the son, through control over access to reproductive females, and it is more usual for women to be exchanged between domestic groups. In matrilineal systems inheritance is traced from the maternal uncle (mother's brother) to nephew (sister's son), and the tendency is to try to ensure the corporate identity of sibling groups. The techniques take several forms in which rights over women's labour, sexuality and reproductive powers are differentially distributed between husbands and brothers.

Unilineal descent groups are the basis of particular types of SOCIAL STRUCTURE, such as those found in ACEPHALOUS societies, in which they are corporate groups with political autonomy. They are generally regarded as typical of societies with rudimentary technology and relatively little durable property, and as tending to break down within economically complex societies with a high DIVISION OF LABOUR. Where unilineal descent groups are found, KINSHIP will be likely to provide the definition, sanction and framework for the individual's social relationships.

In descent groups, the principle of filiation or parenthood ensures the individual's membership of a group, through being acknowledged to be the legitimate child of a particular known parent. In patrilineal and matrilineal systems this is the father or the mother respectively. But although relationship to one parent may be stressed within the

system, the tie with the remaining parent can also be socially important, a process which anthropologists call complementary filiation. This is not the same as double or bilateral descent, which allocates different social roles to matri- and patrilineages. Nor should it be confused with cognatic descent groups, which are corporate, but overlapping, groups which recognize descent through both male (agnatic) and female (uterine) lines. Double or bilateral systems tend to focus on the descent group as an entity, while corporate systems emphasize the individual's ability to claim descent and thus membership of more than one group, depending on the purpose.

See also ANCESTOR; CLAN; DESCENT; KINSHIP.

JE

**linguistic analysis.** See ANALYTIC.

**Linnaeus, Linnaean.** The 18th-century Swedish botanist Linnaeus — Karl von Linne (1707-78) — introduced a comprehensive system for classifying living forms. It is known as the binomial system since it used the last two names as identifiers (e.g. *Homo sapiens, Homo* being the genus and *sapiens* the species). 19th-century race theorists inherited the assumption that different human forms represented separately created species. In place of a static conception of permanent differences, the DARWINIAN revolution introduced a view of all living forms as subject to constant change through natural selection.

MPB

**literacy.** A word invented in the 19th century to cover the ability to read and write to a socially defined acceptable level of skill. Its counterpart was illiteracy, which since the 18th century had indicated absolute inability to read and write. Today both terms are interpreted in a more relative way. Persons who can read and write a little, but are ignorant of much that many people consider the general knowledge necessary to operate in their society, will be called illiterate, while there are frequent disagreements about how skilled and knowledgeable a person must be to be called literate. For this reason considerable disagreement exists on the measurement of lack of literacy, or illiteracy. Since the mid-20th century a new set of terms relating to numeracy has come into general usage, extending to mathematical skills and knowledge the ideas underlying the concept of literacy. These two domains, literacy and numeracy, formerly called the 3 Rs (i.e. reading, 'riting and 'rithmetic) are often seen as the core of the school CURRI-CULUM and are sometimes referred to as 'the basics'. This last version demonstrates the culturally based nature of the concept, since the skills and knowledge concerned must be basic to some social function, such as the economic, political or leisure processes of the social structure. This complexity is often forgotten when attempting to measure levels of literacy. Tests based on writing a letter and simple arithmetic, for example, are basic to the economy in most societies, but are not necessarily a valid measure of political literacy.

PWM

Literacy is also important in historical socio-logy because its invention and spread had major consequences. According to Goody and Watt (*Literacy in Traditional Societies*) it enabled CULTURE and RELIGION to be stabilized across time and space for the first time. Restricted or craft literacy has existed since it first developed in various ancient civilizations and more recent semi-primitive societies. Majority literacy developed first in classical Athens (*c*7th-6th centuries BC) and was an important ingredient in Greek political DEMOCRACY. Then it receded somewhat in Europe until the 18th-20th centuries when it also became crucial to political movements, especially NATIONAL-ISM. In the EVOLUTIONISM of PARSONS such trends became a generalized IDEALISM: large-scale societies develop, held together and given purpose by common cultural values (see CONSENSUS) led first by a literate ELITE; then in Greek and in modern times a universal democratic culture emerges.

MM

**local government autonomy.** Although local government in Britain has never had the degree of freedom allowed (and in some cases guaranteed) in many federal systems, it has been given responsibility for the provi-sion of rented accommodation, personal social services, and education. Local govern-ment has not been the only agency respons-ible for the provision of these services, nor has it been entirely free to decide policy, but in these and other areas local authorities have had a degree of freedom to decide the nature of the service that should be provided.

The justification for local autonomy has been that the kind and sometimes the level of service provided should be allowed to vary from area to area to reflect differences in NEED and political preference. In practice, variations in provision often reflect not differences in need but the ability of an area to finance a certain level of provision. However, local authority autonomy permits areas to make choices, and even if this is constrained and does not follow assessed need, it may reflect local preferences between different methods of provision or priorities.

The extent of autonomy has always been limited by both parliamentary sovereignty and the reliance of local government on central government for a great deal of its finance. Autonomy has been further reduced in recent years by the decisions of central government to try to control local govern-ment expenditure as part of its more general attempt to control public expenditure.

MPJ

**location, measure of.** A summary descrip-tive STATISTIC (also known as a measure of central tendency) to show which value is most typical of a numerical distribution. There are three common measures of loca-tion: the mode (the most commonly occurring value); the median (the middle value in the distribution going from highest to lowest), and the arithmetic mean (the sum of all the values divided by the number of observations). The arithmetic mean is the most important because of the part it plays in the logic of other statistical procedures, but it requires interval level MEASUREMENT.

See also DISPERSION, MEASURE OF.

MB

**Locke, John** (1632-1704). English philos-opher; leading exponent of British EMPIRIC-ISM and of LIBERALISM. Main works: *Essay*

*Concerning Human Understanding, Two Treatises of Government* (both 1690). The *Essay* criticizes the concept of innate ideas and attempts to demonstrate the empirical origin of all ideas. The *Treatises* attack the doctrine of the divine right of kings and uphold a theory of SOCIAL CONTRACT and natural rights. Each person is endowed with NATURAL RIGHTS to life, liberty and property, and the AUTHORITY of the STATE is confined to protecting these. All persons, being morally equal, are each the legitimate owners of themselves and any unowned objects upon which they expend their labour. As such, they have a right to buy and sell their goods and services. Over time, this commerce has resulted in the accumulation of unequal property holdings. In the absence of government, each person has a right to defend himself and his property and to exact compensation from offenders. It is through each person's consent to relinquish this enforcement right to a common agency that the state receives authority which is thereby limited to that function. The failure of the state to protect persons' rights implies its loss of that authority and the consequent lapse of individuals' POLITICAL OBLIGATION.

See also SOCIAL CONTRACT.

WO, HIS

**logical positivism.** See POSITIVISM; VIENNA CIRCLE.

**log linear models.** See CAUSAL MODELLING.

**lumpenproletariat.** Literally, ragged or trash proletariat. Marx wrote of 'the *lumpenproletariat*, which in all big towns forms a mass sharply differentiated from the industrial proletariat, a recruiting group for thieves and criminals of all kinds, living on the crumbs of society, people without a definite trade, vagabonds ...' (*Class Struggles in France*, 1850), which can always be bought by the forces of reaction and counter-revolution. The term is not now generally used of advanced countries, but is found in THIRD WORLD countries where the same contrast now exists between relatively secure, skilled workers and a mass of unemployed and casual labour.

See LABOUR ARISTOCRACY; WORKING CLASS.

CGAB

**Luxemburg, Rosa** (1871-1919). German revolutionary socialist. Born in Poland, Rosa Luxemburg spent most of her life in Germany, where she became a leader of the left wing of the Social Democratic Party. A committed revolutionary socialist and internationalist, opponent of both the reformist and centrist tendencies within the party, she was imprisoned 1915 for her opposition to the war. She was murdered by Prussian troops during the Spartakus rising in Berlin in 1919. Her brilliantly polemical writing was distinguished for its consistent advocacy of democracy within the revolutionary movement, and her belief in the creative energy of the revolutionary masses. Her main works were: *Reform or Revolution* (1899), a critique of Bernstein and revisionism; *Organizational Questions of Russian Social Democracy* (1904), a critique of LENIN's centrist model of party organization; *The Mass Strike* (1906), a celebration of the 'living political school' of revolutionary struggle. *The Accumulation of Capital* (1912), her major economic work, argued that the expansive dynamic of capitalism depended on the existence of noncapitalist markets, whose incorporation into the capitalist system would bring about its demise. This was based on the assumption, so far false, that CAPITALISM's markets had fixed limits. The *Junius Pamphlet* (1916) was a bitter denunciation of the SPD's surrender to MILITARISM and *The Russian Revolution* (posth., 1922) defended the Bolshevik revolution, though with substantial reservations about its nondemocratic tendencies. Luxemburg has been criticized for overlooking organizational questions and for extending her internationalism into an opposition to movements of national liberation, as in her native Poland. Her work proved an embarrassment to orthodox COMMUNISTS for decades, but it has an assured place in the revolutionary socialist canon.

DB

# M

**magic.** Magic and RELIGION occupy the realm of supernatural or supra-empirical beliefs and practices and thus occupy a similar situation in relation to empirical science. They are distinct not in that their beliefs have not all been empirically proven (since that is true of science also), but in that their beliefs are not normally susceptible to disproof. If a magical ritual does not work it is not because the ritual is inefficacious and the beliefs upon which it is predicated are false, but because of the countervailing spell of an enemy, a failure to recite the formula accurately, or some other of a myriad protective justifications.

Magic and religion share the same relation to science in this respect but religion differs from magic and science in being oriented primarily to supernatural beings which are propitiated or worshipped by a community, while magic and science are primarily concerned with the manipulation or control of impersonal forces; in the case of magic, largely for the immediate and concrete ends of an individual. Magic involves an instrumental orientation toward the supernatural.

MALINOWSKI argued that people living at a low level of technology possess a fund of empirical knowledge which they employ to good effect, but that certain features of their environment remain beyond effective empirical control. At these points, non-empirical ritual means will be invented to allay anxiety. Malinowski over-emphasized the degree of conscious intent and awareness possessed by the actors as to which of the practices they employ are empirical and technical, and which are supernatural. The growth of such awareness is probably itself a consequence of the development of means for, and interest in, testing whether or not beliefs are empirically founded — that is, of the growth of science — and demands a world more differentiated into distinctive spheres than is characteristic of many pre-literate peoples. Hence the distinction between natural and supernatural, between technical, empirical knowledge, and magical belief, will not be drawn by many actors to whom it is applied. They do not see them-selves doing anything different when they engage in technical or ritual activity, and explanations for magical acts that construe them as different from technical acts have to explain them in ways that are quite independent of what the actors think they are doing. Malinowski argued that they were really bolstering their confidence when they used magic, while RADCLIFFE-BROWN argued that magic performed a collective function, facilitating the passage of a community through a situation of crisis and reinforcing the collective identity of members by solemnizing the event. The difficulty with such approaches is that they distinguish magic from technology or science on the grounds that its acts are inefficacious and its beliefs false. However, that is also true of much technology and science in the past (e.g. the history of medicine before the late 19th century), yet Malinowski and Radcliffe-Brown would not offer the same explanations for the use of leeches, purgings and calomel in the days of 'heroic' medicine.

It is more satisfactory to treat magic as an

essentially loose descriptive term rather than the cornerstone of a theoretical argument. Magical behaviour should be explained in the same terms as technical behaviour. Both are performed because they are believed to work, and that belief is confirmed by the actors' interpretations of the evidence, not because they are held to be psychologically or socially useful. When actors find their magic rituals ineffective, they typically do not retain them for their social or psychological uses, but try something else if it is available and appears to meet their needs.

In well-differentiated, technologically developed societies, magic seems largely to have disappeared except in more rural or less educated subcultures, but the change is, to some extent, one of idiom. Beliefs and practices directed to controlling some aspect of the world but not supported by science will, nonetheless, be presented as 'scientific' by their adherents. The forces and powers allegedly manipulated are sometimes amenable to exploration by scientific means, though a 'reactionary scientific establishment' ignores them. Alternatively, they are presented as possessing capacities too subtle to be registered by any conventional scientific apparatus. In the advanced industrial world, much magic is naturalized, metamorphosed into deviant (or 'pseudo') science.                                    RW

**Malinowski, Bronislaw Kaspar** (1884-1942). British anthropologist, one of the founders of FUNCTIONALISM. Born in Cracow, Poland (then part of the Austro-Hungarian empire) Malinowski was the son of a Slavic philogist and spoke Polish, Russian, German, French, English, Italian and Spanish. His initial training at the Jagellonian University of Cracow was in physics and mathematics, in which he obtained a PhD in 1908. He is reputed to have read FRAZER's *Golden Bough* during a period of ill-health and been impressed by it. During a brief time at Leipzig he was influenced by Wundt and Bucher, who were conducting important studies of language and folklore. In 1910 he entered LSE to carry out research on the culture of Australian Aborigines. The main influence in his research at this time was the work of Haddon, Rivers and Seligman, who had all

done fieldwork rather than relying on the reports of missionaries, administrators and other travellers. Through Seligman, Malinowski obtained funds to carry out extensive fieldwork in the Mailu in the West Pacific (1914-15) and the Trobriand Islands (1915-16 and 1917-18). He had lectured briefly at LSE in 1913 and returned to teach there throughout the 1920s. He was elected to a readership, and in 1927 was appointed to the first chair in anthropology in London. In 1938 he went to the USA on sabbatical leave and taught at Yale from 1939 until his death.

During his years at LSE Malinowski taught fieldwork method and anthropological theory to a whole generation of anthropologists including Meyer FORTES, Raymond Firth and Edmund Leach. The publication of his first Trobriand researches, *Argonauts of the Western Pacific*, in 1922 is usually taken as a turning point in social anthropology, for it broke with the classicist, speculative tradition of Frazer, and crystallized the methodological approach of intensive fieldwork advocated by Haddon, Rivers, Seligman and others. None of these, nor Malinowski's contemporary RADCLIFFE-BROWN, had specified the object of social anthropology as separate from history and evolutionary ideas. Malinowski's concentration upon the importance of institutions and the way they function within extant societies enabled him not only to formulate the methodology of ethnographic data-collection but also the organization of the data in monograph form. His teaching of ethnographic theory and practice developed into an exposition of the method of 'statistical documentation of concrete evidence'. He advocated the preparation of detailed charts and tables, genealogies and censuses, a detailed diary noting normal events and deviations from the norm, and a self-critical account of the ethnographer's progress. He thus laid the foundations for the way anthropological fieldwork is still carried out. Although associated with functionalism, he did not develop a rigid theory like Radcliffe-Brown's structural functionalism, and constantly modified his idea of 'function'. It is partly because of this theoretical difference that the rivalry between the two has frequently been emphasized.

At times a controversial figure, Malinowski was a brilliant popular writer and his work caught the public imagination, particularly through his books on sexuality in the Trobriand Islands, which were in fact part of a lengthy debate with the psychoanalyst Ernest Jones, a pupil of FREUD, regarding the possible form of the Oedipus complex in matrilineal societies (see LINEAGE). Later, particularly during his time in the USA, he became interested in CULTURE and began to develop an EVOLUTIONARY perspective reminiscent of the speculative and historical ideas of Frazer and Rivers.

Major works: *Argonauts of the Western Pacific* (1922); *Crime and Custom in Savage Society* (1926); *Sex and Repression in Savage Society* (1927); *The Sexual Life of Savages* (1929); *Coral Gardens and their Magic* (1935); *A Scientific Theory of Culture and Other Essays* (1944); *Magic, Science and Religion and Other Essays* (1948); *A Diary in the Strict Sense of the Term* (1967).

See also RECIPROCITY.

JE

**Malthus, Thomas Robert** (1766-1834). English political economist, whose famous *Essay on Population* (1798) argued that population tends to a geometric rate of growth outstripping any arithmetic growth of the means of subsistence. Population remains proportional to the available supplies of necessities through the operation of the positive checks of death and disease or the preventive checks of fertility control (moral restraint).

Born near Dorking, Surrey, the son of a prosperous middle-class family, Malthus was educated at home under the guidance of his father, a follower of ROUSSEAU and a friend of HUME. He attended Jesus College, Cambridge, where he became a Fellow in 1793 and took Holy Orders in 1797. He was interested in contemporary problems of poverty and saw the increases in population of his time not as a sign of economic well-being, but as contributing to ever-present deprivation. The *Essay on Population* uses these ideas to introduce a limiting factor to economic optimism and to the ideals of a free, rationally ordered society current in the

18th century. The first edition, published anonymously, was almost entirely theoretical; only in the second edition 1803 was empirical material collected on travels in Europe introduced. In 1805 he became Professor of History and Political Economy at the East India Company's College at Haileybury, Hertfordshire, the first post to use the term 'political economy'. He became friendly with the economist David Ricardo, and among his proposals was one to promote luxury expenditure rather than saving as a cure for economic distress — a precursor to KEYNESIAN theory. In 1834 he became a co-founder of the Royal Statistical Society.

None of his later work attracted the interest of his early ideas of population. The *Essay on Population* provoked great contemporary controversy and attracted widespread hostility. MARX later attacked the Malthusian theory of population, arguing that CAPITALISM produces a poverty-striken surplus population independent of demographic trends. Malthus's theory justified an inevitable fall of wages towards subsistence whatever the form of social organization, and his reputation remains bad in many STATE SOCIALIST countries. However, Malthusian principles have been retained in modern population models which stress the fixity of world resources such as land and fossil fuels, and in many accounts of population trends in periods preceding Malthus's own times.

See also POPULATION THEORY.

JL

**management.** A category used ambiguously in industrial and organizational studies. Besides referring to the activity of managers (co-ordinating, planning, controlling etc) the term management is also used frequently (especially in industrial relations) where 'employers' would be more exact. Sometimes it denotes merely the executive managers of manufacturing industry, excluding such supervisory groups as foreman and chargehands at the lower level, and directors at the higher; at other times it refers to all such groups in every branch of economic activity (and even in public administration) as well as all employers. Some writers add qualifiers such as 'higher' or 'middle', which remove some of the vagueness. 'Line management' refers to executives concerned mainly with organizing the work of other people; 'staff management' to experts (economists, statisticians, market researchers etc) who advise executives and directors. This imprecision, which also occurs in other languages, has been responsible for misapprehensions and confusion in theoretical debate. The most worrying example is that concerning 'managerialism', that is, the hypothesis that 'managers' have been superseding capitalist proprietors as the effective controllers of the modern corporation (and in some versions, effective controllers of the state apparatus), which they may operate less according to narrow criteria of profitability and more in line with some 'social' ethic. If such writers identify management inclusively on one page and narrowly on the next, how can we evaluate their theses properly?

MR

**managerial revolution.** The transition from pre-industrial to INDUSTRIAL SOCIETY was marked by the rise of the entrepreneur as a socio-economic type. The entrepreneur established a business, hired labour, and managed its affairs. As organizations expanded, the entrepreneur was often obliged to share his power to make strategic business decisions with investors who had purchased large shares in his company, or lent him money to expand; at the same time, he had increasingly to entrust his administrative, technical, and supervisory powers to a growing corps of specialists, technicians and general managers. MARX claimed that joint stock companies and the spread of managerial personnel were already beginning to 'socialize' the capitalist MODE OF PRODUCTION in the second half of the 19th century.

Fifty years later, Berle and Means (*The Modern Corporation and Private Property*, 1933), influenced by Thorstein VEBLEN, theorist of the 'leisure class', were able to present evidence which seemed to show that most large American corporations would rapidly pass into managerial hands. (Veblen had argued that modern society should be technocratic and value 'the instinct of workmanship', but was being increasingly stifled by the dominance of a leisure class.) Soon after, James Burham (*The Managerial Revolution*, 1941) asserted that not only industrial establishments but every significant organization of modern society, including state agencies, would soon be dominated by managerial professionals. Berle and Means had predicted that managers — unlike capitalists — would not use their power for private (or 'sectional') ends, but Burham claimed that the 'managerial revolution' would occur precisely because managers had sectionalist ambitions.

Over the last four decades debate has continued on nearly all aspects of the thesis. Marxist writers either deny that managers have usurped power from capitalists, or maintain that even if they have done so, they nevertheless will behave similarly to capitalists because they operate in a market economy and have 'inherited' predominantly capitalist social and political institutions, as well as a capitalist mentality.

'Managerialists' divide into: (1) 'sectionalists' who believe the managerial stratum will, as Burham predicted, behave rather like a new ruling class but with values and aims dissimilar to those of old-fashioned capitalists; (2) 'non-sectionalists' who assert, in the Berle and Means tradition, that 'the managers' will favour a consensual, corporatist set of goals and institutions in government, and seek to render the work organization a humane (or, as Berle once put it, a 'soulful') environment even at the expense of short-term profitability.

Evaluating these arguments is difficult, not only because of the complexity of such evidence as does exist, but also because much of what would count as decisive evidence (e.g. how and why top managers make decisions) is lacking and seems unlikely to become available in the immediate future.

See also BUREAUCRACY; CORPORATISM; TECHNOCRACY.

See W.A.T. Nichols, *Ownership, Control and Ideology* (1969).

MR

**manipulationism.** One of the types of SECT identified by Bryan Wilson (*Religious Sects,*

1970). Unlike the other types of sect which, in varying degrees, reject the world as evil, the manipulationist sect largely accepts the structure and values of the world. It offers esoteric means for securing the valued goals of this world, for securing health, wealth, 'self-realization', psychological stability or reassurance, or improved status, power and social relationships. Such sects possess a theory concerning the sources of human suffering, disability or dissatisfaction, and a set of techniques or practices for remedying the difficulties experienced by individuals.

Manipulationist sects have few collective activities, being primarily oriented towards individuals, and are thus largely organized on a professional-client basis, with a fixed fee for service. In corporate structure they are as often modelled on the large-scale business firm as the traditional church. They address themselves to an educated and affluent urban constituency, satisfied with the advanced industrial world but more desirous of its benefits. Two of the principal examples are Christian Science and Scientology. They straddle the boundary between religion and psychology and many of the most recent examples would view themselves as secular rather than spiritual (e.g. the Encounter movement and much of the Human Potential Movement), while others (e.g. Transcendental Meditation) shift between presenting themselves as religious or secular depending upon the particular advantages to be gained from the state or in marketing their services, at any particular point in time.

See also CONVERSIONISM; INTROVERSIONISM; REVOLUTIONISM; THAUMATURGY.

RW

**Mannheim, Karl** (1893-1947). Hungarian sociologist. He participated in a Budapest discussion group organized by Georg LUKÁCS. In 1920 he emigrated to Heidelberg and later became Professor of Sociology in Frankfurt. Dismissed by the Nazis in 1933, he taught at LSE and London University Institute of Education until his death. Mannheim's main achievement was in the sociology of knowledge but he also wrote on political subjects, especially democratic planning, and on education. Main works: *Ideology and Utopia* (1929); three volumes

of essays on sociology, social psychology and the sociology of knowledge and culture (1952, 1953, 1956); *Man and Society* (1940); *Freedom, Power and Democratic Planning* (1950). Mannheim's work in the sociology of knowledge represents an imaginative, if not entirely coherent, fusion of the two influences of German HISTORICISM and Marxism. His political proposals too are marked by the attempt to combine liberal democracy with socialist planning.

See also KNOWLEDGE (SOCIOLOGY OF).

WO

**Mao Ze-Dong** (1893-1976). Although Mao's achievements as organizer of peasant revolutions and unchallenged leader of the Chinese Communist Party are unquestioned, his standing as a political theorist is more debatable. The main themes of Maoism are the importance of the PEASANTRY as an independent revolutionary force; the necessity of continuous struggle and renewal if the revolution is not to stagnate after the achievement of power; the erosion of the divisions between intellectual and manual labour and between town and country; the 'primacy of practice' and the 'mass line'. Maoism has had considerable influence in the THIRD WORLD as offering an alternative model of development to that of the Soviet Union, though how far its alternative is really distinctive, successful or replicable elsewhere is controversial.

DB

**Marcuse, Herbert** (1898-1979). German-American Marxist philosopher, early member of the Frankfurt School and exponent of critical sociology (see CRITICAL THEORY). Born in Berlin, the son of a Jewish businessman, Marcuse studied under HEIDEGGER before joining the Frankfurt Institute for Social Research. He fled from Hitler's Germany, first to Geneva, then to New York, where he taught at Columbia University. During World War II and for a time afterwards he worked in Intelligence and for the State Department. Between 1951 and 1970 he held academic appointments at Columbia, Harvard, Brandeis and the University of California at San Diego. After a relatively orthodox career, Marcuse came to prominence late in life, when his radicalization of FREUD and his analysis of contemporary capitalism became the intellectual inspiration for the hippies and student revolutionaries of the 1960s.

Marcuse's analysis of the repressive dimension of social relations led to an exploration of their emancipatory potential. His work can be seen as a synthesis of HEGEL, MARX and Freud through a radical reinterpretation of their ideas. His early interpretation of Hegel (1932) pointed to the revolutionary character of the Hegelian DIALECTIC. His account of Marx argued that the idea of human essence or species being in the early Paris Manuscripts was central for understanding Marx's theory of history (see ALIENATION). He later modified the Marxian conception of human nature to embrace Freudian elements, while also subjecting Freud's categories to a historical reinterpretation. Marcuse's concept of 'surplus repression' pointed to the way in which the necessary denial of instinctual gratification in the interests of economic production was intensified and perpetuated by repressive social structures far beyond what was required by existing technical possibilities (*Eros and Civilization*, 1955). This perspective was drawn on in his critical analyses of both Soviet and Western societies in the 1960s. His popular work *One Dimensional Man* (1964) identified the source of repression in the POSITIVIST tradition of Western science and technology, and its capacity to blunt opposition by stimulating and satisfying a host of artificial or false needs. The WORKING CLASS, incorporated into the system and developing FALSE CONSCIOUSNESS, was unable to act as the agent of general emancipation, a role that, Marcuse argued tentatively, had passed to students and socially marginal elements.

In the late 1960s Marcuse produced more optimistic assessments of the possibilities for liberation in the light of growing unrest among Blacks and students, and the developing campaign against the Vietnam war. His essays 'Repressive Tolerance' (1965) and *An Essay on Liberation* (1969) greatly influenced New Left thought, both in America and Europe, and he became something of a cult figure. His work has subsequently been subjected to critical reappraisal by Marxists and non-Marxists alike.

See also CONSENSUS.

DB

**marginal costs.** See COSTS.

**marginalization.** In many successfully developing countries, national economic progress is accompanied by the exclusion of large sections of the population from economic life. This is because the path of industrialization and economic development typically involves heavy reliance on imported capital-intensive techniques and the neglect of staple food production. Both the urban poor and the rural poor are 'marginalized' in relation to national economic development and condemned to an existence of absolute POVERTY because the lack of social and welfare provisions makes a decent human existence contingent upon gainful employment.

The concept of marginalization thus defined was first used to describe the appalling social failures of the Brazilian 'economic miracle'. The achievement of enviable rates of economic growth and industrialization had resulted in a net loss of industrial employment, increased the percentage share of total domestic income accruing to the top 10 per cent of the population, and led to an increase of the absolute numbers of people living below the poverty line. Marxist writers argue that marginalization is not just a consequence of capitalist penetration in THIRD WORLD countries, but is also functional to capitalist production there because it creates an industrial reserve army which permits the suppression of wages and demobilizes the WORKING CLASS within the capitalist sector.

The concept of marginalization is also, though less commonly, applied on an international level to describe the gradual exclusion of whole nations from world economic arrangements. Certain countries in the THIRD WORLD (more usually called FOURTH WORLD) are unable to overcome their (colonially imposed) dependence on the exports of one or two cashcrops for which demand and/or prices in world markets have steadily declined. While their participation in world trade diminished over a long period, their impoverished economies were also shunted by international capital. Having neither the resources nor the potential domestic markets to attract foreign investors, this Fourth World can no longer meaningfully participate in world economic arrangements and can be said to have become marginalized.

AH

**market structure.** A description of the market conditions under which particular goods and services are supplied. A market in which there is perfect competition has a large number of buyers and sellers so that no firm or individual is large enough to influence the market price; all firms sell identical products and there is perfect freedom of entry to the market so that new firms may enter and thereby ensure that abnormal profits are not made by existing firms restricting output. If certain conditions are met, a perfectly competitive system will produce an EFFI-CIENT allocation of resources (but see EXTERNALITY and PUBLIC GOODS). It is this feature which provides the theoretical basis of the case for the MARKET SYSTEM. Monopolistic or imperfect competition occurs when there are a large number of firms in a market, as in perfect competition, but where each firm has succeeded in differentiating its product from those of its competitors by techniques such as advertising, establishing brand loyalty etc. This reduces the price elasticity of DEMAND for its products and leads to lower output and higher prices than would exist if the market was perfectly competitive. A *monopoly* exists when there is a single seller within a market. As there is no close substitute for the firm's goods, the demand curve facing the firm will be more inelastic than in a monopolistic market. Unlike the firm in perfect competition, the monopolist has control over product price; this leads to the theoretical prediction that a profit-maximizing monopolistic will choose a higher price, and hence a lower output, than would exist if the market was perfectly competitive. In the UK, the Monopolies Commission investigates possible abuses of monopoly power in specified industries upon receipt of a reference from the government.

The Commission also investigates oligopoly markets. These occur when there is a high degree of market concentration; that is, when a small number of large firms account for a large proportion of market output. Oligopoly is the most widespread form of market structure in most advanced capitalist countries today. It is characterized by a high degree of interdependence between firms' decisions and may lead to collusion.

RR

**market system.** A decentralized system of economic organization in which the actions of individual buyers and sellers are co-ordinated through their common response to price 'signals'. Decisions about what is produced, how it should be produced, and to whom it should be distributed are made through the interaction of DEMAND and SUPPLY in factor (i.e. land, labour and capital) and goods markets. Changes in price indicate whether the quantities of particular goods should be increased or decreased, and bring about these changes in output automatically. In the words of Adam SMITH, the father of modern economics, there is an 'invisible hand' at work. This contrasts with a planned economy where decisions about production are usually made by centralized bureaucratic edict, although a number of planned economies are experimenting with the use of SHADOW PRICES in an effort to improve their systems of resource allocation. Subject to certain conditions, a free market system will establish an efficient allocation of resources. In practice these conditions are often not met: EXTERNALITIES and the problems posed by PUBLIC GOODS represent two sources of market failure. A free market system may fail to achieve the objective of equity or social justice that a society is likely to set itself in connection with the distribution of INCOME. A market system is based upon the private ownership of the factors of production (see CAPITALISM); the distribution of these factors is a major determinant of the distribution of income. Income distribution produced by a market system is highly unequal, but in advanced capitalist societies some form of government intervention redistributes income and reduces inequality.

RR

**Markov process.** A STOCHASTIC PROCESS in which knowledge of the history of the process gives no extra information as to its next state over-and-above that supplied by knowledge of its current state alone. The concept is named after the Russian mathematician A.A. Markov (1856-1922) and was introduced in 1907. It is one of the most important classes of stochastic process, both in probability theory and in social science, and many processes that are not Markov at first sight can be made so by redefining the states of the process to include relevant information about its history.

A Markov process is specified by an exhaustive set of possible states for the system, by a set of probabilities of transition from one state to another (the transition matrix), and by an initial starting position. Then if the process is Markov, the probability of a given chain of moves from a given initial position is simply the product of the transition probabilities. The transition probabilities may be fixed (stationarity) or vary over time, and the time-scale may be continuous or discrete, although most sociological applications have used discrete-time, stationary models. The process may have absorbing states which once entered are never left, and the probability of entering each of these states, and the expected waiting-time to absorption can be calculated. That distribution over the states of the process which is unaltered by the operation of the transition probabilities is a characteristic vector of the transition matrix, and under certain general conditions — if all sequences of states are possible — the process will tend to this characteristic distribution in the long term, independent of starting position.

Markov processes have been used in sociology to model the mobility of populations between states defined in terms of social class, status, occupation, area etc. In the field of inter-generational SOCIAL MOBILITY, the inheritance of occupation and status can be represented by transition probabilities and the consequences of changes projected by the Markov assumption. In this case, stationarity is empirically unlikely over such long time-periods, and very long-run data would be needed for testing. If the model is applied between generations, the distribution over the states of the process cannot be equated with the distribution at any particular time-period, since generation-length varies in the population. Analysis would have to be by generation cohorts, whereas data is normally cross-sectional (see COHORT AND PERIOD ANALYSIS).

In the study of intra-generational social mobility, states are mostly defined by broad status groupings, and the attempt is to model individual careers toward a final status, starting at a status defined by one or both parents. Total mobility can be conceptually decomposed into that brought about by the pull of overall changes in occupational distribution, such as a secular decline in farm-work, that brought about by exchange between categories, and that brought about by the push of individual career decisions. Models seek to account for this pattern of mobility, as well as to construct measures of overall mobility appropriate for comparisons between societies at different times and places.

The Markov assumption in intra-generational social mobility suffers two related problems. (1) It supports the idea that final position is independent of starting position if the process goes on long enough, an ideological assumption of meritocracy that is not empirically supported. (2) The numbers moving over several time-periods tends to be lower than expected from the transition rates for a single time-period. The Markov assumption can be saved by dividing the population into sub-populations (e.g. 'movers' and 'stayers'), each governed by a Markov process with different transition rates, for the aggregate of such processes will not itself be Markov. Final position will then depend on the distribution of the sub-populations across the starting categories. Another approach has been to focus on chains of interdependent moves in the occupational structure, and by assuming that vacancies move in a Markov manner a process is generated in which the counter-flow of people does not move in a Markov way.

JL

**marriage.** Firstly, a RITE OF PASSAGE whereby an unrelated man and woman leave their

FAMILY of origin and begin their own family of procreation; secondly, a relationship that is normally expected to last beyond the time necessary for procreation. It is also a legal contract, which when amplified in judge-made law (see JUDGES), normally involves an assumption in Britain today that it is the wife's duty to perform housework and childcare and the husband's duty to support the family financially. In modern Western societies, marriage is the end result of a process of heterosexual dating, courtship and engagement.

For LÉVI-STRAUSS, marriage represents the unity of groups of men through the exchange of women. For Delphy (*The Main Enemy*, 1977), marriage represents a labour contract whereby women's labour power is exploited by the husband.

In Britain and most Western countries marriages are love marriages subsumed under the IDEOLOGY of romantic love: a woman and man meet, fall in love, get engaged and then marry. The ideology stipulates that there is one 'right' person for each of us. In arranged marriages, for example among Muslims and Hindus, the match is organized by parents. It is primarily a relationship between families rather than between individuals. This need not preclude love, however: here young people marry and then fall in love. The degree of acquaintance between marriage partners and the level of their involvement in the arrangement can vary from marrying total strangers to strongly influencing parental choice. The end result in both cases is homogany — marriage within classes and among people who lie in close geographical proximity.

Marriage can be monogamous, in which each partner has only one spouse, or polygamous, in which one partner has more than one spouse. Polygyny, whereby one man has more than one wife, is a more common form of polygamy than polyandry, whereby one woman has more than one husband (often brothers). Most marriages are hypergamous, that is, husbands are older than wives. In Britain, the USA and other Western countries, cohabitation, common-law marriages, or living together without a wedding ceremony is becoming a more accepted social practice. The majority of common-law marriages are viewed as trial marriages and frequently end in a proper marriage.

Most marriages in Britain are neolocal, whereby the couple set up in their own household. In most societies which are patrilineal residence is patrilocal; in matrilineal societies it is frequently matrilocal. Neolocality in Western urbanized societies, however, depends on the availability of housing. Where there is a shortage of housing young people may marry in order to leave home and to establish legitimate claims on their own residence.

Marriage is centred on the couple. The sexual DIVISION OF LABOUR generally prevails, although conjugal roles can be segregated (with each partner having her/his own duties and networks of friends and relatives) or joint, whereby the couple forms a social unit. Marriage also entails sexual exclusivity, although FEMINISTS have argued that this applies more to women, whose adultery is more severely censured. In surveys of sexual activity from the Kinsey Report onwards, males will openly admit to greater activity than females. According to the Hite Report on male sexuality, 60 per cent of husbands have had an extra-marital affair. Both 19th- and 20th-century feminists have claimed that prostitution, the selling of sexual services by women to men, forms the underbelly of marriage in PATRIARCHAL or male-dominated societies.

The principal motives of marriage are to engage in a legitimate, affective and sexual relationship, to 'start a family' and to have children. Only marriage can bestow legitimacy on children. Thus feminists have argued that, since men do not have direct access to children, the male need for legitimate heirs has resulted in the male control of women through marriage. Female adultery would be a serious infringement of male rights to pass on PROPERTY to their own children. This has led feminists to argue that marriage is a form of compulsory heterosexuality, an institution whose main aim is to control women's sexuality by tying it irrevocably to that of the husband — the biological and social father. It is this, together with men's control over women's labour in HOUSEWORK which is said by feminists to constitute marriage as the central source of women's oppression under patriarchy.

Feminists have also argued that marriage is dangerous to women: the more intimate a woman's relationship to a man, the more likely she is to experience violence from him. Rape in marriage is not a crime, since a woman's marriage vows are interpreted to constitute open consent to all her husband's sexual advances. It has been estimated that violence by husbands towards wives occurs in at least 30% of marriages. This ranges from emotional violence to severe physical assault. Feminists claim that marriage divides women into assaultable wives and rapable non-wives. Although wife-battering was technically outlawed in 1829 in Britain, the police are reluctant to intervene in crimes which they call 'domestic disputes'. Instead they urge the wife to take out an injunction against the husband or institute divorce proceedings — while living with her husband. Theories of female masochism, sanctioned by FREUD and his followers, lay the blame on the victim. Women are urged to put up with wife-assault in the interests of the children to keep the family together. Victim blaming, lack of alternative accommodation, unsympathetic attitudes among police and social workers and the ideology of romantic love, often trap women in marriages which are a danger to their emotional and physical wellbeing.

See also DIVORCE.

See M. Anderson (ed.), *Sociology of the Family* (1975); S. Friedman and E. Sarah, *On the Problem of Men* (1982); R.E. and R. Dobash, *Violence against Wives* (1980).

EG

**Marx, Karl** (1818-83). German philosopher, sociologist, economist and socialist revolutionary. Born in Trier, in the Prussian Rhineland, of a prominent local lawyer and a Dutch mother. Both his parents were descended from distinguished lines of rabbis, but converted to Christianity to preserve his father's occupation. In his youth, Marx was influenced by his father's 18th-century rationalism and by the Romanticism of his father's associate, the Baron von Westphalen, whose daughter Jenny he later married.

Educated at the universities of Bonn and Berlin, Marx gained his doctorate in 1841,

but his association with the radical group of Young Hegelians barred him from his intended academic career. He turned to journalism, and in 1842 was made editor of the liberal *Rheinische Zeitung*, suppressed the following year. He then went to Paris as co-editor of the short-lived *Deutsch-französische Jahrbücher*, and in 1844 wrote fragments published in the 1930s as the *Paris Manuscripts* in which he first set out his views on alienated labour (see ALIENATION). At this time began his life-long collaboration with Friedrich ENGELS, and together they wrote *The Holy Family* and *The German Ideology*, in which they criticized their former colleagues in the Young Hegelians. Now based in Brussels, Marx wrote *The Poverty of Philosophy* (1847), criticizing Proudhon, and with Engels prepared the *Communist Manifesto*, which appeared at the time of the 1848 revolutions. In 1848 Marx moved back to Paris, and then to Cologne as editor of the *Neue Rheinische Zeitung*. When this was finally suppressed, he fled into exile, first to Paris, and then London, where he remained for the rest of his life.

During the next twenty years, Marx engaged on the studies in political economy for which he was to become famous. For many years, until legacies and a regular annuity from Engels eased the burden, the family lived in dire poverty (greatly worsened by Marx's chronic financial mismanagement), and three of his children died in infancy. Throughout this period, Marx's output multiplied, although he published relatively little. In 1857, impelled by what he perceived as the increasing likelihood of capitalist crisis, he wrote the massive *Grundrisse* in a mere six months, although the text remained unpublished in his lifetime. In 1859, he managed to publish the preliminary *Contribution to the Critique of Political Economy*, whose short Preface was for long taken as the definitive summary of Marx's method. In 1867 the first volume of *Capital* appeared, the second and third volumes being published under Engels's editorship after Marx's death.

In 1864 Marx helped to found the International Workingmen's Association (First International), and the affairs of this loose association of organizations and individuals subsequently took up much of his time. In 1870-2 he engaged in a serious dispute in the International with the followers of Bakunin, and in 1872 effectively wound up the organization by transferring it to New York.

Although his financial situation improved during the 1870s, Marx suffered from ill-health and appeared to lose much of his creative impulse. After his death, much of his work was brought to publication by others.

*Marxism.* In the century since his death, Marx's thought has assumed a variety of forms, both political and academic. In the years before World War I a strongly determinist version of Marx's theory became the doctrine of much of the European working class movement. Marx's followers believed he had discovered the 'laws of motion' of the capitalist economies, and that these laws revealed the inevitable breakdown of CAPITALISM and the equal inevitability of REVOLUTION. Under the pressure of disputes about the War, the Russian Revolution, and the necessity or otherwise of 'revising' Marx's doctrine, the European movements split into two broad sections: the 'revisionist' SOCIALISTS, and the more radical COMMUNISTS. Eventually the socialists were virtually to abandon Marxism, and as in the course of the 20th century a variety of Marxist regimes emerged in Eastern Europe, Asia, and the Caribbean, further doctrinal splits developed in the communist movement itself.

Academically, Marxism has always maintained an uneasy relationship with the rest of the social sciences, especially sociology. The tension between Marxism's claim to scientific status and its aim to represent the world-view of the revolutionary working class has proved a constant barrier to full assimilation into those social sciences which attempt to be 'value-free'. Nonetheless, Marxism has proved a ready pool of key concepts and insights, especially in the study of CLASS and CLASS CONFLICT. It is by no means only the sociology of WEBER which has been characterized as 'a debate with the ghost of Marx'. If sociologists have been suspicious of the pretensions of Marxists, however, the reverse has equally been true, especially since the 1920s, when both the

failure of revolutionary movements in the 'advanced' Western European economies, and the successful revolution in 'backward' Russia, led many Marxists to abandon the notion of pre-determined 'laws' of historical development, and to be equally critical of other 'POSITIVIST' and 'scientific' approaches in social science.

In the period before the Russian Revolution, in keeping with the then dominant view of Marxism, it was Marx's economic interpretation of history that had the most impact in other work in the social sciences. In the 1880s and 1890s the work of TÖNNIES, Sombart and others showed the influence of Marx's belief that the characteristics of social structure could be explained in terms of those of the society's economic system, and the class relationships thus produced. From early in the century, however, Marxism and academic sociology steadily diverged, and the impact of the Russian Revolution wrought considerable changes in Marxism itself. In the East, Marxism-Leninism became an official, and relatively unchanging, State dogma (see LENIN). In the West, Marxist thought went through a dramatic change of focus. Where previously Marxists had concentrated on the economic 'base' of society, they now turned their attention to the ideological 'superstructures'. Faith in the inevitability of economic collapse was replaced by a strategic attention to the factors which promoted or hindered CLASS CONSCIOUSNESS. The work of LUKÁCS, Karl Korsch and GRAMSCI, along with the later rediscovery of Marx's early writings, and the studies in CRITICAL THEORY of the Frankfurt School, all combined to produce a 'Hegelian', 'humanist', even EXISTENTIALIST Western Marxism that provided a sharp contrast to official Soviet orthodoxy.

Since the student upheavals of the later 1960s Marxism has become a more sharply defined presence in Western intellectual life, particularly in the social sciences. Initially the original Western Marxism of Lukács, Gramsci, and especially MARCUSE predominated but Marxist intellectuals have been increasingly influenced by STRUCTURALISM and the anti-humanist, anti-Hegelian Marxism of ALTHUSSER. Although Althusser's influence now seems to be on the wane, Marxism will continue as an important and distinctive perspective in the social sciences. Marx's status as a 'founding father' of those sciences is secure.

See also ALIENATION; CLASS; MATERIALISM; MODES OF PRODUCTION.

AM

**mass society.** The notion of mass society has a lineage stretching from the early Greek social theorists through TOCQUEVILLE, MARX, MANNHEIM and, latterly, Hannah Arendt, C.W. MILLS and MARCUSE. Largely conservative in inspiration, the term denotes a shapeless and unstructured social order in which traditional sources of attachment, such as FAMILY, COMMUNITY, SUBCULTURES, CLASS, STATUS groups are severely attenuated. The 'rootless mass' of 'atomized individuals' thus formed is prone to manipulation by anti-democratic forces.

Various factors have been held responsible for the creation of a mass society, including excessive egalitarianism, cultural decay, the growth of the mass media, domination by elites armed with sophisticated instruments of control, and so forth: all, in various ways, seen as the culmination of the logic of INDUSTRIALIZATION. Though the mass society tradition is both long and varied it is firmly tied to conservative social thought and, as such, constitutes a reaction against the rise of modern industrial society.

See also FASCISM.

JH

**materialism.** The philosophical theory according to which whatever exists is matter or at least is entirely dependent on matter for its existence, contrasted with IDEALISM. Human minds, for example, are seen as a property of the matter of the brain. MARXISM has been divided by some into historical materialism, a theory of history and society, and DIALECTICAL materialism, a more contentious theory of matter in general which owes more to ENGELS than to Marx. Dialectical materialism holds that the basic processes governing the behaviour of matter are those of contradiction and the reconciliation of contradiction. Historical materialism concerns itself with the sphere of human history, claiming that the most basic

historical processes and contradictions are those of economic production and that these influence other sorts of social phenomena (e.g. political and ideological). Social theories are sometimes loosely called materialist or idealist according to the emphasis they place on 'material' relations of domination, economic exploitation etc, or on ideas, values, and norms. (*Compare* ONTOLOGY.)

See M. Mann, 'Idealism and Materialism in Sociological Theory' in J.W. Freiberg (ed.), *Critical Sociology* (1979).

WO

**mathematical sociology.** A collection of topics and approaches where mathematical or formal methods have been used, rather than a coherent body of mathematical theory of society. The application of exact mechanistic mathematical laws to social phenomena has been condemned as a limited 'social physics'. Most uses of mathematics have adopted alternative strategies for dealing with the complex and uncertain nature of social life.

In STOCHASTIC PROCESS models the variability of social phenomena is treated as the outcome of the operation of probabilistic processes whose overall behaviour can be analysed mathematically. GAME THEORY deals with the rational core of co-operation and conflict situations. SYSTEMS THEORY and structural methods use mathematics to model the total pattern of connections in a complex phenomenon, as opposed to the detail of its parts. In METHODOLOGY, mathematics has been used to criticize and refine procedures for making inferences from evidence, and in analysis to construct techniques for overcoming the special problems of the MEASUREMENT and simplification of social data (see CAUSAL MODELLING; CLUSTER ANALYSIS; ECOLOGICAL FALLACY; FACTOR ANALYSIS; MDS). Where analytical mathematical solutions are not available, COMPUTER SIMULATION may be used to define and investigate the behaviour of a complex process over time by representing it as a computer programme, (e.g. 'world models' as deployed in the Club of Rome's *Limits to Growth* study; see WORLD SYSTEM).

Mathematical sociology is largely a post-war American phenomenon, encouraged by a deliberate policy of mathematical education amongst social scientists fostered by the American Social Science Research Council based on examples of mathematical work in psychology and economics. Early influences included Herbert Simon, whose *Models of Man* (1957) showed a variety of approaches, from a causal interpretation of spurious correlation to theories of rational decision-making and small-group dynamics, and contemporary work on the analysis of processes of conflict using economic and game-theoretic methods (Richardson, Boulding, Rapoport), and in methodology (see LAZARSFELD).

In the 1960s mathematical sociology enjoyed its largest expansion. H. Blalock's *Causal Inferences in Non-experimental Research* (1961) codified causal modelling for an expanding clientele, which extended quickly into the mainstream of American sociology. J. Coleman's textbook *An Introduction to Mathematical Sociology* (1964) became available for university courses, although his ability to use simple equilibrium models and processes such as the Poisson and its relatives in an illuminating way has proved difficult to imitate. Harrison White's innovative use of abstract algebraic methods to analyse KINSHIP systems with prescriptive marriage rules ('elementary structures of kinship') demonstrated structural methods and showed that mathematical sociology did not have to follow in the footsteps of quantitative methods. In a similar spirit GRAPH THEORY was applied to the analysis of social networks, and to group structure in structural balance theory (see COGNITIVE CONSISTENCY THEORY). The use of topological methods was proposed, including catastrophe theory, a mathematical theory of discontinuous processes where quantitative changes may become qualitative ones.

In the 1970s, despite being a target of anti-POSITIVIST criticism, particularly in Europe, causal modelling and data analysis continued to be foci of interest, with particular emphasis on the development of qualitative methods. Harrison White maintains a tradition of algebraic, structural work on social networks at Harvard, where he and his students have added a range of computer programmes to those available for network

data. There is a continuing tradition of stochastic process models particularly in the analysis of social mobility and population processes (see MARKOV PROCESS).

See also SOCIOMETRY.

See P. Doreian, *Mathematics and the Study of Social Relations* (1970).

JL

**matriarchy.** (1) A form of social organization in which the mother is the head of the family and descent and relationship is reckoned through her. (2) By extension, a society in which mothers hold the main power positions. Anthropologists acknowledge that (1) often exists. But (2), the more general usage, is controversial and speculative. It is not certain whether or not such matriarchies have even existed. ENGELS (*Origins of the Family, Private Property and the State*, 1884) argued that the earliest societies were HUNTER-GATHERER matriarchal societies, and that PATRIARCHY originated in male control of cattle or wealth, with the development of sedentary agriculture. He based his discussion on Bachoffen, who argued that societies pass from a Mother-right stage in which women hold power, to Father-right, or patriarchy.

This EVOLUTIONIST perspective was at first criticized and abandoned by 20th-century anthropology, which claimed that individual societies must be viewed as unique cultural entities rather than exemplifications of an evolutionary, progressive scale, or hierarchy. More recently, however, various writers have resurrected some of these ideas, arguing that the most primitive societies contained rough gender equality, and that patriarchy emerged with agricultural settlement and with the rise of some combination of warfare and the heavy work involved in clearing and ploughing land. In turn, FEMINISTS have criticized some of these notions and reinterpreted archaeological data, finding female mummies and skeletons of warriors wrongly classified as males, artefacts (and hence skills) falsely attributed to men, and inconsistent explanations or social structures. The present state of knowledge seems to indicate greater variability of gender relations in primitive societies than sweeping theories of either matriarchy or patriarchy suggest.

Nevertheless, some feminists also maintain that matriarchies existed. They claim to have found evidence in the existence of goddess religions in the Middle East and North Africa, and in the persistence of goddess worship among witches. They argue that goddess-worship is not possible in societies which glorify men; they view it as evidence for societies in which women's fertility was revered and where the male role in conception was unknown or socially unrecognized. Patriarchy was imposed on these societies through conquest. Marriage and the family have their origins in male access to children through controlling women. The period of patriarchal conquests coincides with the substitution of the goddess by male gods or god. Evidence for this is located in the Greek myths, which male scholars also use as proto-historical evidence, and in biblical accounts of the monotheistic patriarchal assaults of the Israelites on goddess-worshipping communities.

The argument is influenced by an ideological desire to show that male domination has not been universal and/or biologically rooted. We have no means of knowing whether it is true. However, myths of matriarchies exist in a number of societies. They are frequently alluded to in ideological justifications of the patriarchal *status quo* as better than the chaotic women-controlled past. Some societies also have Amazon myths which, feminists argue, express male fears of women. These myths are important in that they point to how the social categories of man and woman are ideologically represented. What the individual sociologist reads into these myths is, to some extent, a matter of political choice.

Many feminists who argue for the existence of matriarchies do not regard them as the mirror-image of patriarchy. The goddess represents female 'powerfulness' rather than female power over men. In this usage matriarchy represents equality, lack of hierarchy, and living in harmony with the environment. For many feminists it is a powerful UTOPIAN vision contrasted with male control of women and children, war

and competition, and destructive mastery of nature.

See E. Reed, *Women's Evolution* (1975); E.G. Davis, *The First Sex* (1975).

EG

**matrilineal.** See LINEAGE.

**Mauss.** See RECIPROCITY.

**Mayo, Elton** (1880-1949). Australian-American social anthropologist who greatly influenced managerial practices. Born in Australia, the son of a doctor, Mayo soon abandoned plans for a medical career and studied psychology at the University of Queensland (1905), where he later gained a teaching post. During World War I he successfully treated shell-shocked soldiers. He emigrated to the USA in 1922 and became a researcher in the Business School of the University of Pennsylvania, applying the psychiatric notions of (especially) Janet to problems of industrial discipline. Moving to Harvard Business School in 1926, he was introduced by the biologist Laurence Henderson to the sociology of PARETO and DURKHEIM, and the FUNCTIONALIST social anthropology of MALINOWSKI and RADCLIFFE-BROWN. He seems also to have become acquainted with HUMAN FACTOR industrial studies in the mid-1920s. In 1927 he became consultant to the Western Electric Company's Personnel Division, and was closely connected — both as adviser and publicist — with the HAWTHORNE STUDIES then in progress. As a popularizer of the Hawthorne programme Mayo achieved considerable public acclaim in the 1930s, and he led research concerned with productivity in the American arms industry during World War II. He was retained by the Labour Government in Britain to advise on human problems in British industry after 1945, and died in England in 1949.

Largely because he has, mistakenly, been regarded as the 'leader' of the HUMAN RELATIONS movement, Mayo's reputation is a storm-centre of controversy over the nature of workers' motivation and behaviour, the role of modern management, and the moral character of industrialized society, as well as more earthy matters such as the control (for many, the manipulation) of employees through sophisticated personnel policies. He is credited with having counterposed the 'social' model of the industrial worker to the economic man of SCIENTIFIC MANAGEMENT, this being linked to a social philosophy of industrialized societies that stresses the disintegrative forces in modern life. But it is necessary to distinguish Mayo's personal contribution from that of Human Relations as a whole, to note that his own analytical stance evolved in important ways during his professional life, and to remember that many managers (not necessarily employers) had become receptive to Mayoite ideas thanks to socio-economic developments.

The core of Mayo's thought is to be found in *Human Problems of an Industrial Civilization* (1932) and *Social Problems of an Industrial Civilization* (1949). Stated bluntly, ignoring loose ends and inconsistencies, their message is as follows: industrial problems, notably industrial conflict, reflect an excessive reliance by managers upon economic controls, and the transmission to the work situation of individual neuroses created by the rootlessness and ANOMIE of urban industrialized society. At work, unknown to themselves, workers are fundamentally seeking to satisfy non-logical drives towards the co-operation and sociability denied them in their out-plant existence in mass society. Professional managers have a duty to use social science to gain insight into these processes, and devise personnel methods that will supply the worker with a primary sense of attachment to, and community within, the plant.

Critics accuse Mayo of cynicism: was not this message mere propaganda to elevate the status and enhance the power of the professional managers who adulated him, while enabling them to solve their problems of authority, compliance and productivity in the enterprise? But critics often overlook the fact that Mayo, like most effective ideologues, was thoroughly sincere. Criticism has been directed against Mayo from all points of the political compass, Marxists radicals accusing him of crypto-fascist and corporatist aims, liberals accusing him of anti-individualism, others perceiving in his 'programme' a socialistic assault on the

institutional bases of capitalism. Irritated vilification of Mayo by his scientific critics, and uncritical veneration by his managerial admirers, has given way in recent years to more measured evaluations of his contribution, which raises issues of continuing urgency in societies where economic dynamism remains a more important goal than social harmony for its own sake.

See M. Rose, *Industrial Behaviour* (1975).

MR

**Mead, George Herbert** (1863-1931). American social psychologist, a founder of SYMBOLIC INTERACTIONISM. Born in South Hadley, Massachussetts, where his father was a Congregational minister. His mother became President of Mount Holyoke College (1890-1900). Mead studied at Oberlin College (1879-83) and at Harvard, Leipzig and Berlin (1887-91). After teaching at Michigan (1891-4), where he came under the influence of DEWEY and COOLEY, he moved to the philosophy department at the University of Chicago, where he taught for the rest of his life. He became one of the prime movers of the new school of philosophy known as PRAGMATISM, and attacked the psychological BEHAVIOURISM of Watson in favour of a SOCIAL BEHAVIOURISM. Mead's social psychology centred around his theory of the mind, the SELF, the nature of communication and the social ACT, but he also taught courses on 19th-century thought and the philosophy of science. His major works *Mind, Self and Society, Movements of Thought in the Nineteenth Century* and *The Philosophy of the Act* were posthumously published in 1934-8. In sociology, his major impact is through BLUMER's translation of his ideas as a basis for symbolic interactionism.

See D.L. Miller, *George Herbert Mead: Self, Language and the World* (1973).

KP

**Mead, Margaret** (1901-78). American anthropologist. According to her autobiography *Blackberry Winter* (1972), Margaret Mead was born into a relatively comfortable Philadelphia family, the daughter of an economist father and a schoolteacher mother. Educated largely at home, she graduated in 1923 from Barnard College where she took a course with BOAS and also met BENEDICT, who was working there as a teaching assistant. Mead completed an MA in psychology at Columbia in 1924 before turning to anthropology. She carried out field research among the Samoans, Manus, Arapesh, Mundugumors, Tchambuli, Balinese, Iatmul and the Americans. She was of major importance in the foundation of the 'culture and personality' schools of American anthropology alongside Boas, Benedict and KROEBER. Her lasting intellectual contribution lay in the symbolic interpretation of CULTURE, her ideas being later elaborated by anthropologists such as Victor Turner and Clifford Geertz. Her early comparative approach to child-rearing practices was influential upon American ideas of childhood and attitudes to SEXUALITY. Her easy, jargon-free writing style gave her ideas a wide, popular dissemination. Mead did not have a conventional academic career. Her income came largely from her own writing, though she was connected to the American Museum of Natural History from 1925, where she became Curator Emeritus of Ethnology in 1969. In 1944 she established the Institute for Intercultural Studies, a non-profit-making body for research into the behavioural sciences financed partly from her own earnings, and she became the director of the Columbia University Research in Contemporary Cultures after the death of Ruth Benedict in 1948. Mead was the author of 44 published books (18 co-authored), of which these are the best-known or most representative: *Coming of Age in Samoa* (1928); *Growing up in New Guinea* (1930); *Sex and Temperament in Three Primitive Societies* (1935); *Male and Female* (1949); (with Martha Wolfenstein) *Childhood in Contemporary Cultures* (1955); *Culture and Commitment* (1970).

See also GENDER.

JE

**meaning.** Many sociologists believe that we can and must understand the actions and social relations of human beings (and the higher animals) in a different way from that in which we understand the behaviour of inanimate objects. The understanding of meaning, or VERSTEHEN, characteristically refers to (1) the conventional nature of many human actions, such as religious rituals, and (2) the purposes and intentions with which such actions are performed. There is a close analogy with the meaning of linguistic expressions, which may also be analysed both in terms of the conventions of a given language and in terms of the speaker's intentions. Where 'meanings' are quite complex, as in WEBER'S account of the 'meaning' of economic activity for Protestant entrepreneurs and workers, the system of these beliefs and attitudes may be described as a meaning-complex (in this case, the PROTESTANT ETHIC).

See W. Outhwaite, *Understanding Social Life* (1975).

WO

**means test.** The provision of a service or benefit only after an assessment of income and wealth. The range of services and benefits so provided (e.g. social assistance benefits) are only available if a means test shows NEED; items like prescriptions may be available free if a means test shows inability to pay. The advantage of a means test is to allow services and benefits to be targetted where they are most needed. Their major disadvantage is that people frequently object to detailed examination of their circumstances, believing that others will be made aware of their difficulties and that a STIGMA will be attached to the acceptance of help. As a result, many people do not claim benefits to which they are entitled. However, there are major variations in the extent to which benefits are claimed. In some cases the variations reflect the value of the benefits (it is not worthwhile claiming a very marginal benefit), while in other cases they reflect the way the benefit and means test is administered. An additional problem arises when the number of services and benefits covered by means tests increases. The introduction of new tests complicates matters and adds to administrative problems, and an extension of means-tested benefits can also lead to other problems such as the POVERTY TRAP.

See also NEGATIVE INCOME TAX.

MPJ

**measurement.** Any process by which a value is assigned to the level or state of some quality of an object of study. This value is given numerical form, and measurement therefore involves the expression of information in quantities rather than by verbal statement. It is a most powerful means of reducing qualitative data to more condensed form for manipulation, presentation and analysis. Measurement is the basic process which makes quantitative social research possible.

Four levels of measurement are distinguishable. (1) Nominal measurement simply involves using numbers to represent categories, and permit more efficient use of the data. (2) Ordinal measurement, in addition to having numbers represent categories, also permits the ranking of the categories in terms of the possession of some quality (e.g. in attitude research: strongly agree/agree/disagree/strongly disagree). (3) Interval measurement shares the characteristics of ordinal measurement, and in addition the property of a unit (or scale) by which differences in magnitude can be expressed precisely (e.g. number of years of education; a temperature scale). (4) Ratio measurement shares the characteristics of interval measurement, plus the property that the scale has a true zero (e.g. income). Nominal and ordinal measurement are non-metric; interval and ratio measurement are metric.

The level of measurement is of critical importance in STATISTICS. Different statistical tests and techniques make different assumptions about the properties of the data being analysed. Parametric statistics assume that the data are metric; to use such statistics on non-metric data is incorrect. Non-parametric statistics may be used with scores that are not exact in any sense, but are nominal or ordinal. Data for most social VARIABLES (e.g. religion, occupation, social class) are non-metric. Hence non-parametric statistics are of particular importance in sociological research.

The feasibility of measurement in sociology has been the subject of enduring controversy. Critics such as Cicourel point to the assumptions involved in expressing social behaviour and attitudes in numerical form and subjecting the resulting data to statistical manipulation. If social action is subjectively meaningful, it is argued, how can it be reduced to quantities? Those who use quantitative methods however, maintain that measurement of objective characteristics is relatively straightforward while the measurement of subjective states (e.g. using SCALES of attitudes) is feasible and produces RELIABLE results.

See R.S. Weiss, *Statistics in Social Research* (1968); A.V. Cicourel, *Method and Measurement in Sociology* (1964).

MB

**media studies.** The study of formal systems for encoding, storing and transmitting information has three distinct aspects.

*Audience Research.* Since the 1930s newspaper and magazine publishers have carried out regular programmes to discover who reads their product. Governmental concern with both the extent and nature of the impact of public information and propaganda services during the war years accelerated and broadened interest in the nature of media audiences, and the way in which readers, radio listeners and, later, television viewers were influenced by what they read, heard or watched. This focus on media influence and media audiences is quantitatively the most important among sociologists. Among topics frequently studied are the political influence of the media; whether they cause people to act violently; whether they amplify civil disorder; the extent to which readers/listeners/viewers imitate recorded behaviour (e.g. crimes or modes of suicide). Though a rather simple empiricism predominates, answering such questions requires some theoretical model. Three models have been specially influential. (1) The simple causal model (sometimes referred to as the 'hypodermic' theory) according to which people react directly to media experience (e.g. the representation of killings on television causes murders to happen or the presence of sexist material in newspapers causes men to act chauvinistically). (2) Models of mediated causality, the best known of which is the two-step flow theory. Within any community there exist opinion leaders, respected figures in key positions whose views are sought and valued. In order to respond to demand such people will be assiduous consumers of media news and views, and act as channels through which media influences and opinions are transmitted; through them the media exert force on the public at large. (3) Models which deny any independent influence to the media but instead point to processes of selective perception or opinion sets among audiences. According to this view, media audiences are not plastic or readily malleable. Readers, listeners and viewers already hold relatively firm and systematic views of the world, and they shape their consumption of media information in terms of those views; they give the greatest weight to media information which reinforces or serves to confirm positions already held and little or no weight to information which contradicts them.

Research on audiences has been in theoretical content weak, but it has been an important area for developing field research technique and has enviably (if narrowly) RELIABLE data series. The label audience research is normally given to the investigation on behalf of mass media organizations, especially those concerned with newspapers and broadcasting, of the social patterns of viewing and listening. The results are widely used by academic social researchers, despite variations in the quality of data. The practice and the techniques originated in the USA because of the commercially sponsored nature of radio and, later, television broadcasting services, to provide advertisers with information on the numbers and social characteristics of viewers and listeners. Thus audience research has been principally concerned with who listens to, or watches, or reads, what, rather than how or why. Recent research, particularly by the UK broadcasting authorities, has sought to go beyond this rudimentary question. However, although the research techniques, especially in SAMPLING, are sophisticated, doubts persist about the reliability of all save the most simple information obtained. Nonetheless, the resources devoted to it, the frequency and regularity with which the research is carried out and the size of the samples studied make its use a necessity for most academic researchers in the field.

In the UK the most frequently cited sources are the BBC research department, the Audit Bureau of Circulation, JICTAR and JICRAR. The first is self-explanatory. The second carries out regular routine surveys of newspapers and magazine readership in the UK to provide those who advertise in the press with information concerning the aggregate number of buyers and readers of periodicals and their socioeconomic characteristics. The accuracy and availability of this information makes its regular use and citation by social scientists inevitable, but it is important to bear in mind the motives for and circumstances of its collection. It is unfortunate that the intervals and classifications employed (e.g. of social CLASS) differ markedly from those in common academic use. The Joint Industry Committee for Television Audience Research and the Joint Industry Committee for Radio Audience Research carry out roughly comparable functions for the commercial broadcasting system.

*The Study of Media Organizations.* Research in this field is more recent than that of audiences and has been independent of it. The principle issues have been: (1) The relationship between personnel directly concerned with generating the content of the media itself and those performing ancillary functions, (e.g. between journalists and newspaper proprietors and managers). (2) The relation between media organizations, many of which make universalistic claims, and particular interest groups in the environing society. (3) The mechanisms by means of which media organizations choose which items of information to transmit and which to reject. Borrowing from the language of social anthropology, media organization have been described as gatekeepers, to focus on their function as critical forces in determining the constitution of CULTURE in advanced industrial societies.

*Media Content.* Given the complexity of all save the most trivial items communicated in the media, discussion of content has presented acute methodological difficulties for sociological analysis (see CONTENT ANALYSIS; SEMIOTICS; STRUCTURALISM). The central substantive question has been whether and to what extent the media represent the ruling IDEOLOGY of the environing society. The content of the mass media, especially newspapers and television, has attracted the bulk of attention.

ML

**medical model.** Used to characterize the dominant PARADIGM within medicine for the understanding and treatment of disorders of health, and referred to variously as a bio-medical, machine or engineering model of disease. Its basic assumption is caught in the idea of the human body as a machine comprises of divisible and abstractable parts. Within this mind and body are distinct entities (a legacy from DESCARTES) without implications one for the other in the process of therapy. Hence the human subject becomes a non-sentient object in process of treatment. Attention is focussed on the mechanics of observable bodily disease and the treatment specific symptoms. The orientation is towards curing diseased individuals abstracted from social environment, relationships and identity.

The narrow focus on organic disorder outside the context of the thinking, feeling subject is a legacy of the pioneering work of Pasteur and Koch in the late 19th century. By revealing disease as a process of pathogenic invasion, germ theory provided a basis for the elaboration of the doctrine of specific AETIOLOGY. This was a turning-point in medicine and thereafter the isolation of single and observable agents of disease causation became the dominant approach, made all the more sophisticated by the development of the microscope and, in the 20th century, the technology of micro-photography. It marked the beginnings of the redirection of public policy for health away from preventive measures aimed at the population at large towards curative attempts aimed at individual sufferers. In the 20th century, with the eclipse of contagious disease (the result of largely non-medical measures), the idea of toxic invasion as the explanation of aetiology rather than as a secondary outcome has been applied well beyond the bounds of infectious disorders. But as R. Dubos (*Mirage of Health*, 1961) has pointed out, germ theory has a fundamental weakness: it cannot reveal why it is that disease is so rare when infective

agents are omnipresent. The same objection can be raised against other toxic and polluting agents. The initiation of an infective or toxic process must require other conditions. It is the investigation of these other conditions which has focussed attention on the role of social and psycho-logical factors in disease onset. There is no single alternative paradigm to equal the powerful and pervasive influence of the medical model but the concept of STRESS has proved to be an attractive heuristic device in the search for a more complex understanding of the many factors which are thought to interact in the process of disease.

Despite its limitations the medical model has captured the public resources available for health care, and as an IDEOLOGY it has been accused of seeking to spread its influence to other spheres of human welfare other than health narrowly defined (the process of medicalization). In contemporary medicine, the influence of the machine metaphor is further evidenced by the growing dependence of practioners on complex technological machinery and chemical engineering as aids to diagnosis and treatment. Furthermore, the profession itself embodies the mechanistic principle of the whole, comprising divisible parts through the development of specialist practitioners for different sites in the human body, different phases of the human lifetime, and different diseases.

The social success of the medical model in contemporary society is not borne out of proven efficacy. For most major causes of premature death in adults there are no effective medical theories or treatments.

See IATROGENESIS; MEDICAL PROFESSION; STRESS.

See T. McKeown, *The Role of Medicine* (1976); E. Mishler *et al.*, *Social Contexts of Health Illness and Patient Care* (1981).

NH

**medical profession.** Medicine, perhaps more than any other professional sphere, typifies those work conditions which are seen to require special safeguards for the client and special rights for the practitioner. The work itself may be awesome, involving calculations of life and death and, for a small but visible elite, procedures which are both wondrous and terrifying for the layman. As a matter of course the doctor must routinely transgress many of the TABOOS which attach to normal social interaction. These include the invasion of the personal body space of the client and the exposure of intensely private thoughts, feelings and emotions. In these circumstances of extreme vulnerability on the part of the client, the appeal for legal regulation of practice carries a self-evident legitimacy.

The first English Act regulating the practice of medicine was issued by Henry VIII in 1508. Nine years later his personal physician, Thomas Linnacre, was granted a charter to constitute the Royal College of Physicians which enjoyed the sole privilege licensing physicians within a seven-mile radius of London. In one form or another, state regulation of the practice of medicine has continued since that date. The 1858 Medical Act, a response to the laissez-faire politics of the period, removed that restriction on the practice of medicine but left the Royal College with its monopoly right to license physicians. This, together with a clause permitting only licensed physicians to be employed by the state, effectively strengthened the profession and left it well placed to capitalize on the growing involvement of the state in the delivery of health care.

In the USA, an expanding, heterogenous and more egalitarian society resisted the professionalization of medicine until the 20th century. In the latter half of the 19th century North America was awash with healers of all descriptions and a myriad of medical training schools largely unconnected to the university system turned out a bewildering variety of 'qualified' persons. The appearance, in 1910, of the Flexner Report on Medical Education marked a turning point in the volume of choice offered to the American consumer of medical treatment. Thereafter, the curricula of a much-pruned medical school system were reorganized to provide a uniform and standardized university-based medical training which established the criteria for certifying doctors.

The ideology of medical practices embodies all of the classical traits associated with professionalism. High ethical standards are enshrined in the Hippocratic Oath, which enjoins the newly qualified to put the relief of suffering above all other considerations, and to observe absolute confidentiality about the treatment of individual clients. A systematic body of knowledge exists, requiring a prolonged period of prescribed training which qualifies the new doctor to practise free from outside interference. The doctor's right to clinical autonomy was the fighting slogan of the profession in its struggle to resist incorporation in the state salariat when the National Health Service was established in 1948 (see WELFARE STATE). The compromise the profession reached with Aneurin Bevan, Labour Minister of Health, involving salaried employment for hospital staff and fee-paid independence for general practitioners, has shown no tendency to diminish the profession's right to self control or to shift power and resources away from the privileged hospital sector to the less well-endowed system of primary care.

Sociological interest in the analysis of the medical profession and in health policy has been most in evidence in the USA. Indeed, until very recently all of the serious social scientific research on the NHS was produced by North American scholars; see for example H. Eckstein, *The English National Health Service* (1959), *Pressure Group Politics* (1960).

Talcott PARSONS drew upon his own earlier empirical field study of medical practice to illustrate the abstract model of social structure in *The Social System* (1950). This was the context in which the SICK ROLE concept was developed and undoubtedly owed much to collaboration with the physician L.J. Henderson. Modern medicine provided Parsons with an example *par excellence* of occupational specialization involving the application of scientific knowledge. Parsons clearly recognized the power of medicine as an agency of social control, but he attributed the source of the profession's influence to technical rather than ideological factors. A similar concern is revealed in his translation (assisted by Henderson) of WEBER's writings on POWER and AUTHORITY. Judging Weber to have been overconcerned with processes of domination in social life, leading to a neglect of technical expertise as a basis for the legitimate exercise of power, Parsons seeks to add a specifically technical dimension to the rational-legal IDEAL TYPE. Here again Parsons draws on the example of the physician to illustrate his case.

The weakness of Parsons's view of the foundations of professional power is highlighted by criticisms of medical practice from within the profession itself. It is well-known that many routine treatments continue to be practised in the absence of any clear evidence of their efficacy. The practitioners have been shown to be unwilling to undertake rigorous randomized controlled trials to demonstrate the validity or otherwise of therapy in common practice (see Cochrane, *Effectiveness and Efficiency: Random Reflections on the National Health Service*, 1972). But quite apart from this, technical knowledge can never provide a secure base for exercise of power because unlike RELIGION, or even LAW, it is by its nature subject to upheaval and reinterpretation on the basis of scientific research, making today's remedies tomorrow's fallacies.

Other writers have been less convinced of the significance of technical knowledge *per se* as a key to understanding the power and occupational privilege of the medical PROFESSION. Some have dissolved the analytical problem in a ruling class solution (see Navarro, *Medicine under Capitalism*, 1976). But it is Freidson's more subtle interpretation of the role of technical knowledge in the emergence and maintenance of professional power (*The Profession of Medicine*, 1970) that remains the most interesting challenge to the technocratic model. Following Hughes (*Men and their Work*, 1952), Freidson argues that scientific knowledge should be distinguished in its pure and applied forms. This distinction leads to a classification of professions as scholarly (pure knowledge) and consulting (applied knowledge). As a scholarly profession medicine depended crucially on the sponsorship of a powerful elite. As the general public came increasingly to look and draw upon the profession as a means to solve practical problems of health, medicine became a consulting profession. The consulting profession survives as much by sustaining the confidence of the lay public as

it does through political sponsorship. But because clients do not present laboratory-designed problems, the technical expertise of the practising professional will always consist in large measure of a wisdom borne out of personal experience only loosely connected to a systematic body of knowledge. The same reasoning underlies the profession's insistence on the individual practitioner's right to clinical autonomy and freedom from lay control. Having secured the confidence of the public through the demonstration of some degree of practical efficiency and effectiveness in meeting needs as defined by the client, the established profession is then able to impose its own definition of need on the public. At this point it achieves the status of MORAL ENTREPRENEUR, gaining control of a relevant sphere of ideology which bestows the authority to define what is health and what is illness in society. In securing a privileged access to the 'ear' of the general public, the profession achieves a degree of autonomy from any political elite and it is this which Freidson identifies as the essence of professional privilege in the division of labour.

Defined in these terms only a handful of real professions could be said to exist. They enjoy the power to represent their own professional interests as public interests in a form which has the appearance of technical impartiality. The successful claim to autonomy frees them from procedures of public accountability which provides a degree of immunity unmatched in the political realm. This view is echoed in the swingeing attack of Illich on the power of professions in industrial society.

Freidson's analysis employs a number of dimension of the source of professional power in a historical sequence — political sponsorship, the demonstration of practical effectiveness apparently linked to technical SKILL, and the control of IDEOLOGY. Each is a necessary ingredient of professional hegemony but their individual significance varies according to the stage of development of the profession.

See IATROGENESIS; PROFESSION; SICK ROLE.

NH

**medicine, sociology of;** medical sociology. The study of the form and influence of medicine as IDEOLOGY and of its practitioners as a powerful PROFESSIONAL organization enjoying a privileged status in the process of constructing knowledge of what constitutes health and illness in society. It overlaps with the sociologies of KNOWLEDGE, POWER and occupations. Linked primarily with medical sociology, it is a complementary adjunct to medical training and treatment focussing on the social and symbolic dimensions of illness and therapy, in particular as these are experienced within the total institutional environment represented by the modern hospital. A more subversive set of concerns, perhaps more appropriately incorporated within the sociology of health, is the development of alternative accounts of the causes, form and nature of sickness in society.

See also HEALTH, SOCIOLOGY OF; MEDICAL MODEL; STRESS.

See E. Freidson, *The Profession of Medicine* (1970).

NH

**mental illness.** A term commonly used to group conditions and illnesses whose major symptons relate to aspects of psychological rather than physical functioning. The concept is given formal meaning by psychiatrists through the specification of a series of distinct illnesses differentiated, following medical practice, largely in terms of symptoms, and, where possible, their AETIOLOGY. The mental illnesses commonly listed vary considerably in their symptoms, severity, presumed or established aetiology, onset and prognosis, and are usually classified into a number of basic types. Current psychiatric classifications have their immediate antecedents in the work of a number of European psychiatrists, especially Kraepelin, who attempted to synthesize the different approaches to classification that prevailed within psychiatry. There is, however, no universally accepted classification and particular classifications are subject to frequent modification, as are precise descriptions of particular illnesses.

A major division in many classifications is between *psychoses* and *neuroses.* Psychoses (e.g. schizophrenia and the different types of manic-depressive psychosis) are more severe — Kraepelin held them to be progressive and irreversible — and are often loosely said to involve loss of contact with reality. They roughly correspond with what was formerly called lunacy or insanity. The neuroses are less severe mental illnesses, closer to everyday experiences and feelings, said to involve an exaggerated response to reality. According to FREUD, neurosis is the result of a conflict between the Ego and the Id, whereas psychosis is the analogous outcome of a similar disturbance between the Ego and the external world (see PSYCHOANALYSIS).

The best-known psychosis is *schizophrenia* which often serves as the paradigmatic mental illness and epitome of 'real' insanity. The term schizophrenia was first used by Bleuler in 1911, but the syndrome had been identified as early as 1860. Kraepelin called the illness *dementia praecox* (precocious or early insanity) emphasizing the onset of the illness in young people and the usual progression to an irreversible state of mental deterioration. He distinguished catatonic, hebephrenic and paranoid schizophrenia. These three, along with so called 'simple' schizophrenia, have remained the most common subtypes in classifications. Schizophrenia is characterized by disorders of thought, perception, emotion and motor behaviour; the most well-known, but neither inevitable nor exclusive, symptoms are *hallucinations* (a perception in the absence of an external stimulus) and *delusions* (a false, unshakeable belief, out of keeping with the patient's cultural background). In the USA the diagnosis is more frequent than in the UK, and the category is broader.

The different types of manic-depression, often termed the affective psychoses, are characterized by severe disturbances of mood such as extreme elation, wretchedness or gloom. These may also be accompanied by disturbances of thought (such as delusions), perception and behaviour. The group includes the category *endogeneous depression,* which unlike neurotic or reactive depression has no immediate environmental cause. A diagnosis of some type of manic-depression is more common in the UK than in the USA.

The term neurosis was first used by the English physician William Cullen in the 1780s to refer to disordered nerve function. Later, the prefix psycho- was added for nervous disorders whose cause was solely psychologically (Freud makes a distinction between neuroses proper and psycho-neuroses). More recently, the term neuroses has been used to refer to only the more restricted subgroup of psychoneuroses, and the prefix has been dropped. Anxiety neurosis, hysterical neurosis, obsessive-compulsive neurosis and reactive depression all fall within this category. Medical interest in conditions that now belong to this group is long-standing, and they have come to form a more important part of psychiatric and medical work during recent decades with the spread of psychiatric outpatient services to all sections of the community.

*Anxiety neurosis* is an extreme form of anxiety involving agitation and nervousness almost amounting to panic, and often diffuse in quality. (Though the terms anxiety and fear are often used interchangeably, fear tends to have a more specific object.) *Phobias* which involve intense fear and dread in the presence of an object or situation may be regarded as a sub-type of anxiety neurosis or an alternative type of neurosis. Common phobias include a fear of open spaces (*agoraphobia*), of closed spaces (*claustrophobia*), of water, heights, certain animals etc. Fear and anxiety have a number of bodily correlates, such as raised heart beat and increased sweating that can be directly measured (*see* LIE DETECTION).

*Reactive or neurotic depression* is differentiated from endogeneous depression by the presence of some precipitating trauma and by symptom differences. In particular, the symptoms of endogeneous depression such as early morning waking, loss of weight, self-depreciation and marked retardation, are held to be absent. In *obsessive-compulsive neurosis* the main symptom is a subjective compulsion to carry out some action, to dwell on an idea, or recall an experience, which is felt to be alien to the person and thus resisted. Compulsive activities often take the form of quasi-rituals such as hand-washing.

Some forms of *hysteria* or *hysterical neurosis* still feature in most psychiatric classifications, though its status as a distinctive syndrome is questioned by some. What were considered the classic symptoms of hysteria — paralysis and disturbances of sensation and physical functioning without physical cause — are now apparently rare. A second form of the disorder is differentiated in terms of disturbances of consciousness termed dissociative states.

The psycho-neurotic distinction is not usually treated as exhaustive, and a third group of mental illnesses, sometimes loosely termed *behaviour disorders*, is distinguished. Like neuroses, these are non-psychotic illnesses, but their symptoms involve disturbances of behaviour rather than of mental processes. The group includes so-called personality disorders, such as *psychopathic* behaviour (chronic anti-social conduct), sexual deviations, drug dependence, alcoholism and special symptom disorders such as eating disturbances. *Anorexia nervosa*, where symptoms focus on weight loss, belongs to this latter category. In many of these conditions the breaking of social rules and norms of conduct explicitly feature as symptoms of the illness. Consequently, for some it is the most problematic group of mental illness, since it raises problems of distinguishing behaviour labelled wrongful from disturbed — badness from madness (see LABELLING).

Following the principle that aetiology should be the preferred means of classification, a number of psychiatric classifications make a further distinction between types of mental illness — between organic and functional mental illnesses. The organic category includes all mental illnesses with an established bodily cause involving some structural lesion or deficiency of the nervous system. Amongst these are *senile* and *pre-senile dementia*, characterized by a deterioration of intellectual functioning resulting from some brain lesion, among those of over 65 and under 65 respectively. Illnesses such as general paralysis (GPI) resulting from syphilitic infection and encephalitis also fall into this category. Substance-induced psychotic conditions, such as alcohol or drug psychoses, are often termed organic, though no structural lesion is involved. Although the organic-functional distinction was initially based on a contrast between disorders of brain structure and brain function (without structural lesion), in practice the category of functional mental illnesses tends to be residual: mental illnesses with no known or presumed bodily cause are located there. Usually this means that only neuroses and behaviour disorders are regarded as functional. Since the distinction not only embodies a dualism between mind and body but also raises problems of differentiating organic causes from organic correlates, it is regarded by some as problematic. Within British psychiatry the organic-functional distinction has generally been given primacy over the psychotic-neurotic division, and mental illnesses with an established organic aetiology are grouped separately.

As the opposition of organic and functional illnesses might suggest, it has been common during much of this century to contrast physical explanations or mental illness with psychological ones, and to debate the respective merits of biogenesis versus psychogenesis. The POSITIVISTIC development of professional medicine has helped to ensure that much pshychiatric attention has focussed on the organic aetiology of mental illnesses, including the role of heredity, as well as on physical methods of treatment. The early, occasionally successful, search for structural lesions has shifted to the study of biochemical factors. These studies have not proved especially successful, but it is likely that the biochemical basis of different mental and emotional states, both normal and pathological, will eventually be determined. Whether this will provide an adequate aetiological account of many mental illnesses is more controversial. The physical processes that underly particular mental processes may have psychological causes, and whether they do or not, the occurrence of illness will be related to social and environmental factors. SZASZ and LAING have objected to the language of mental illness and to the medical focus on organic aetiology. They hold that conceptualizing and responding to phenomena in this way represents a political position, not scientific necessity, and that such phenomena can equally be understood and dealt with in other ways. Analysis of the causes of mental illness, whether at the physical, psychological or the social level, readily becomes confused with debates about the politics of psychiatry and the mental health service.

See also PSYCHIATRY; STRESS; WOMEN AND MADNESS.

JB

**Merleau-Ponty, Maurice** (1908-61). French philosopher, specializing in the PHENOMENOLOGICAL analysis of consciousness and action. Main works: *The Structure of Behaviour* (1942), *Phenomenology of Perception* (1945), *Signes* (1960), *The Adventures of the Dialectic* (1955). Merleau-Ponty shared with SARTRE the editorship of the Marxist journal *Les Temps Modernes*, but was more openly critical of Stalinism (see *The Adventures of the Dialectic*).

WO

**merit goods.** Those goods which society deems so fundamental to an individual's welfare that it is considered necessary to ensure that everyone receives at least a minimum quantity of them irrespective of whether they would choose to do so. These goods occupy an uneasy place within economic theory because it is argued that their allocation should be based upon paternalistic judgements instead of CONSUMER preferences. Thus merit wants are not consistent with the predominant assumption that the individual is the best judge of his or her own welfare. Education is probably the most widely held example of a merit good.

RR

**Merton, Robert K.** (1910- ). American sociologist. Educated at Temple University and Harvard; after teaching briefly at Harvard and Tulane Universities, he went in 1941 to the Department of Sociology at Columbia University, where he taught until his retirement in 1979. At Columbia he was also Associate Director of the Bureau of Applied Social Research, collaborating there with LAZARSFELD and others.

Merton's books include *Science, Technology and Society in Seventeenth Century England* (1938, 1970), *Mass Persuasion* (1946), *Social Theory and Social Structure* (1949, 1957, 1968), *The Socio-*

*logy of Science* (1973) and *Sociological Ambivalence and Other Essays* (1976). He co-authored or edited numerous other important books, including *Contemporary Social Problems* (4th edn., 1976), *The Focussed Interview* (1956), *A Reader in Bureaucracy* (1952), *The Student Physician* (1957). These titles give some impression of the great range of Merton's interests, from theory to methods through a very diverse array of empirical research.

Merton's work is noted for the close connections between theoretical issues and empirical evidence. In the late 1940s he argued for 'theories of the middle-range', in contradistinction to the 'grand theory' being elaborated by his former teacher PARSONS, in whose work abstract conceptual schemes retained only tenuous connection with problems of empirical social research. *Social Theory and Social Structure* contains many of Merton's most influential essays. These include 'Manifest and Latent functions', one of the most important critiques of FUNCTIONALISM. Together with the essay on 'The Self-fulfilling Prophecy', it also represents Merton's concern with UNINTENDED CONSEQUENCES of social action, a theme which runs through much of his work, theoretical and empirical. Another famous essay in the same volume is 'Anomie and Social Structure', in which Merton presented a five-fold typology of forms of deviant behaviour derived from DURKHEIM's concept of ANOMIE; Merton's explanation of DEVIANCE has been criticized, but the essay remains important.

Merton has been described as the founder of the sociology of science in its modern form. His early work on science in 17th-century England shows his concern with general theoretical questions in relation to particular empirical research: he shows that Marxists are not wholly wrong in emphasizing the part played in scientific discovery by economic and military necessities (such as the need for better means of navigation), but starting from WEBER's thesis of the PROTESTANT ETHIC, he demonstrates that Puritan religious beliefs provided a source of motivation for many early scientists. He later wrote essays on the organization of modern science and scientific competition.

SJM

**messianic movement.** A religious movement overwhelmingly oriented to belief in a present or coming Messiah or saviour. The Judaeo-Christian tradition, in which this theme has historically been a major element, has been particularly productive of messianic movements. Norman Cohn reports on numerous individuals who believed themselves to be Christ returned or his equal during the Middle Ages, but culture heroes can also fill the role of Messiah. The figure of Charlemagne gave rise to belief in the Emperor of the Last Days who would come to vanquish evil and secure for the faithful their just reward. In the 16th century Jan Bockelson (John of Leyden) was acclaimed by the radical Anabaptists of Münster as a Messiah and King of the New Jerusalem.

Messianic movements have appeared in various Third World settings, particularly South Africa. A miracle-working visionary or healer provides protection from witchcraft, or magical remedies for disease. In a situation of relative powerlessness this supernatural figure, or living god, conveys a sense of power and hope for a better future.

Messianic movements have not disappeared in advanced industrial societies. Father Divine, an uneducated black man, was regarded by several thousand Americans in the Father Divine Peace Mission, mostly black, as god incarnate until his death in 1965.

The terms messianic movement and MILLENARIAN MOVEMENT are often used interchangeably, but should be distinguished since millenarian movements may not have messianic leaders and not all messiahs herald the onset of the millenium. Rather than proclaiming the complete transformation of the world and society in all its manifestations, many living messiahs restrict themselves to creating a 'heaven on earth' within the confines of their own movement.

See POLITICAL MESSIANISM.

RW

**metaphysics.** Used in philosophy to describe the investigation and characteristics of the fundamental nature of reality (compare ONTOLOGY). IDEALISM and MATERIALISM are prominent metaphysical theories, as are, for example, claims that reality is (fundamentally) unitary or diverse, changing or unchanging. Social theories may be loosely said to involve metaphysical assumptions in this sense, with the implication that these assumptions are not directly susceptible of VERIFICATION or FALSIFICATION.

WO

**methodological individualism.** The doctrine, found for example in HOBBES, J.S. MILL and POPPER, that explanations of complex phenomena (especially social phenomena) must be formulated as, or be reducible to, explanations of individual human beings. Although strictly speaking a prescription for explanation, it often goes along with an ONTOLOGICAL claim that only individual human beings are ultimately real, and that social structures such as armies, churches, nations and classes are in some sense fictions or heuristic devices. Methodological individualism also has affinities with liberal individualism in the political and economic sense, though Steven Lukes has shown in *Individualism* (1973) that the various senses of individualism are distinct. Their historical association, however, helps to explain the acrimony with which disputes between methodological individualists and their opponents have been conducted.

Methodological individualism involves the reduction of structural explanations in economics and sociology to explanations in terms of individuals psychology or deductive models of RATIONAL action. This is perhaps most pronounced in neo-classical economics, but it is also strong in VERSTEHENDE sociology. The extreme opposite of methodological individualism is a doctrine sometimes called methodological *holism* which claims that all explanations of individuals phenomena must be in terms of the larger wholes in which they are contained. This would amount to a methodological analogue of ontological monism. But the denial of methodological individualism does not involve a commitment to holism. One may argue, for example, that social life may be explained both by individual actions and by the structures which form and condition those individuals. This has been variously conceived in terms of a dialectic between 'individual' and 'society' and in terms of social relations both between individuals and

between groups. In both cases, socially structured individuals by their actions create (or more usually modify) social structures. There is an affinity between an emphasis on individuals and a 'voluntaristic' stress on action as against social structures, although individualism and voluntarism are logically distinct. The attempt to resolve these important tensions within social theory is the positive content of long-standing and confused discussions of methodological individualism.

WO

**metropolis-satellite relations.** See CENTRE-PERIPHERY.

**Michels, Robert** (1876-1936). German social and political theorist. Born in Germany, of cosmopolitan parentage, Michels's adult life involved a complex trajectory from revolutionary SYNDICALIST via political sociologist to being an apologist for FASCISM. His most famous work, *Political Parties* (1912), explained the loss of revolutionary impetus in the socialist movements of Western Europe by the oligarchical tendencies to which their organizations inexorably gave rise, combined with the aspirations for social advancement of their leaders. Since the socialist movements espoused democratic principles, they served as a crucial test case to prove the inevitability of oligarchy and the law of elite circulation. As a limited case study, albeit supported by a wealth of empirical evidence, Michels's work is possibly a more successful exemplar of ELITISM than the more general works of MOSCA and PARETO, which range across the whole of human history. *Political Parties* is still widely read, though Michels's other sociological writings — on sexual morality, nationalism, the rise of fascism etc — are mainly of historical interest.

See ELITISM.

DB

**middle class(es).** An imprecise term, but with great resonance in Anglo-American popular culture, equivalent to the broader usages of the term BOURGEOISIE in continental Europe. 'Middle' indicates: (1) That the class lies between the WORKING CLASS (usually conceived of as manual workers) and the upper class (conceived of either as big capital or as dominant ELITES). The small numerical size of the upper class means that surveys which distribute the whole population into classes (see CLASS AS CATEGORY AND SCALE) often use 'middle class' to indicate all non-manual persons, dichotomized from the (manual) working class. (2) An evasion of what the class is supposed to have in common, reinforced by the frequent interchanging of middle class(es) as singular or plural. The impression reflects sociological uncertainty regarding a major development in 20th-century societies: a large expansion in the middling reaches of social stratification of propertyless, employed persons. Are they actually or potentially working class, or integral allies of capitalists/ruling elites, or a distinct third major class; do they form several distinct middle classes or decompose still further into fractions of all three classes? All these possibilities have been suggested at one time or another; see CLASS: *Neo-Marxist theories*; DAHRENDORF; LABOUR PROCESS.

However, most authors prefer versions of 'decomposition' because non-manual employed experience is diversified as follows: (1) Elongated organizational hierarchies in state BUREAUCRACIES and capitalist corporations. Though clerks and top functionaries may be equally non-manual and equally divorced from ownership of the means of production, the former receive orders, the latter give orders, and a long, steep hierarchy of positions exists between them. (2) Careers. Orderly hierarchal movement during the working life is experienced by far more middle class persons than by either manual workers or capitalists, but this is differentially distributed among them. Persons working in the same occupations, some on a career track, others not, do not have the same overall class life-chances. (see CAREER.) (3) Educational qualifications. Access to further and higher education gives technical, semi-professional and professional groups distinctive entry-points, age-career patterns, and even collective monopoly controls over labour supply. At the extreme, among professionals, trade union-type collective controls give substantial autonomy from the formal employer yet without any other resemblance to the working class. (4) Gender. The expansion of relatively routine clerical and sales occupations has been accompanied by their increasing feminization. However sociology eventually copes with GENDER, the stratification experience of women is different from that of men and yet also more internally decomposed (their occupational histories are usually, though not always, broken by a child-rearing phase; they are usually, though not always, secondary wage-earners within households: their overall life chances are more determined by connections with men than vice versa; their distinctive experience of HOUSEWORK; they are usually, though not always, dominated and discriminated against). Yet this may simplify the problem in one respect: if most non-manual males have good hierarchical and career prospects, and most non-manual females do not, then only the latter are predominantly candidates for the working class.

From this flow four conclusions. (1) There is greater diversity and greater stratification within middling groups, making the collective plural label ('middle classes') more appropriate here than at either extreme of the class structure. It is rare to find behaviour that is distinctively and autonomously 'middle' class. (2) The most appropriate cutting-point in separating them from the working class is no longer (if it ever was) the manual/non-manual divide. To the extent that a dichotomous or a trichotomous class structure exists, the lower or lowest class must be defined more broadly in terms of a clear-cut separation from control of the means of production. This includes lower-level, white-collar exployees quite as much as manual workers. If such a separation is only of limited sociological significance today, that is principally because of the intervention of gender stratification, not because of supposed STATUS consciousness or antipathy to collective action among such employees. In most countries union membership density rates and voting patterns do not differ greatly between manual and lower-non-manual workers, controlling for gender. (3) Making a cutting-point above the middle classes is more difficult, partly because the higher up we go the more differentiation we find, partly because the capitalist class, unlike the working class, tends to lack collective organization (to which middling groups might or might not belong). It rules principally through a decentralized, diffused, competitive MARKET SYSTEM — Adam SMITH's 'invisible hand' — in which ownership of capital, corporations, bureaucracies and state intersect in an unplanned way. Thus (4) class structure is not symmetrical. At the bottom, the working class is collectively separated from control, and at its core, collectively organized. At the top and overall, there is a capitalist system, but not a collective, organized capitalist class. Somewhere within the middling groups these different principles of stratification pass by one another, making neat identification of class impossible there.

It may be, finally, that the most precise use of the term middle class is the popular cultural one. A capitalist mode of production has become institutionalized, and its rule is adapted to DEMOCRACY and the NATION-STATE through the broad support given by middle class (or BOURGEOIS) culture and experience, diverse as that is.

See also CAPITALISM; PETITE BOURGEOISIE; PROFESSION; WORKING CLASS.

MM

**migration.** The more-or-less permanent movement of people across a social boundary. It is to be distinguished conceptually from nomadism, seasonal migrant work, the travel of one or more workers from a fixed household in search of work and regular movements between town and country, though the distinction is often difficult empirically. International migration is the best recorded, though systematic deception of immigration officials as to the length of intended stay and illegal immigration are commonplace. Migration may be politically as well as economically motivated, but forced population movements such as those of refugees are excluded from United Nations figures. For UN purposes, residence of a year or more defines migration, though residence is defined by official rules that vary from place to place and it is difficult to allow for remigration in the available figures.

Rates of migration have been much less studied in DEMOGRAPHY than those of birth, marriage and death, partly because of the lack of data (Sweden is an exception here) and partly because of models which stress the relative insignificance of migration in determining population levels. If population tends to equilibrium in line with available resources, then migration is merely a short-term redistributive mechanism with no long-term determining effect. MALTHUS argued that potential emigrants were effectively a population surplus which would be wasted in one way or another if not by emigration. Stable population models tend to assume a population closed to migration, yet have still proved empirically useful.

The effects of migration upon social composition and FERTILITY and MORTALITY rates have been more controversial. In the first instance, emigration must deplete the population and the gross rate of increase of the population of origin, and increase that of the host population. If the emigrants then have children who remain in the host population the fertility of the population of origin should be decreased and that of the host population increased, exacerbating the effect of the initial migration. However, migration tends to be associated with social changes such as URBANIZATION and MODERNIZATION, which have the predominant effect upon fertility and mortality. In terms of social composition, migration selectively affects certain age-and-sex categories, usually young and male, altering the structure of the labour force, the SEX RATIO, and the age at marriage. The concentration of immigrants in young adulthood may lead to an appearance of disproportionate fertility in the immigrant group, and fuel fears among the host population.

The experience of migration may have psychological effects upon the individual, for example, the reinforcing of ACHIEVEMENT motivation. This may lead to a young, ambitious group in the migrant population being particularly ready to embrace and emphasize the values of the host culture. Some writers see migrants as representing those with the most initiative and intelligence in the population of origin, while in direct contrast others see them as representing those unable to compete successfully or adapt. The trajectory of immigrant groups may constitute a significant social phenomenon in its own right, as well as illuminating the social structure of the host society.

Attempts have been made to model and predict the migration within national boundaries which constitutes phenomena such as labour mobility and URBANIZATION, of great interest to governments and planners as well as to social scientists. Patterns of overall movement have proved difficult to build up from simple models which attempt to predict pair-wise mobility from one location to another in terms of basic factors such as population numbers, distance and employment opportunities. The social factors which attach people to a place are more complex, and frequently stronger, than economic rationality would predict and, once mobile, it is difficult to understand the social, economic and individual determinants of where a migrant will settle.

JL

**militarism.** The preponderance in society at large of military practices, organizations and values, especially the glorification of martial character and honour and of war itself. In 19th- and early 20th-century theory it was often considered as a (or the) key element in pre-capitalist or pre-industrial social structures (e.g. COMTE, SAINT-SIMON), and SPENCER's term for complex pre-industrial societies was MILITANT, indicating the predominance of 'coercive co-operation' regulated by a militaristic state. Such arguments were taken to extreme by writers like GUMPLOWICZ and Franz Oppenheimer (*The State*, 1908). They argued that military conquest was the initial determinant of the origins of the STATE and SOCIAL STRATIFICATION and that military structures remained predominant up to their own times. However, in common with almost all theorists, they regarded industrial capitalism (or its successor, socialism) as pacific either in its present structure or in its immediate destiny. Since then, with a few exceptions — notably Andreski, *Military Organization and Society* (1954) — sociologists have not integrated militarism or military structure into their general theories of modern society. 'The sociology of the military' has become a specialist institutional or occupational area, with a more central role only in analyses of

MILITARY INTERVENTIONS, usually in the THIRD WORLD. Recently, however, there has been a reappraisal of the reality of militarism in contemporary society on the grounds that we cannot (or should not) continue the stance of pacific neglect because: (1) The survival of the world itself is threatened by Superpowers and their allies combining a militaristic-cum-diplomatic foreign policy entirely traditional to the Great Powers of history with a wholly new and devastating armoury of nuclear and biological weapons. (2) Their militarism is as pervasive as most historical societies, though in different forms. Their cultures do not glorify personal combat and violence, but a more dispassionate, technocratic militarism is strongly rooted in a mass NATIONALISM unusual in history. Their 'military participation ratios' (Andreski's term for the proportion of the militarily utilized individuals in the total population) are also relatively high if we include the armaments-production industries and their spin-offs. Perhaps only Republican Rome has ever equalled the extent to which 20th-century societies have, on occasion, mobilized for military purposes. (3) A research tradition on 'the statistics of deadly quarrels' has shown no secular decline in the incidence of warfare. Though the 19th century was unusually peaceful (accounting perhaps for the theories of the decline of militarism) the 20th century is close to the historical norm. (4) The effects of the major 20th-century wars on social structure have been profound. They have encouraged the NATION-STATE, SOCIAL DEMOCRACY, and REVOLUTION because of the participation of the masses in victory and defeat, but more controlled forms of militaristic mobilization have also encouraged FASCISM and TOTALITARIANISM. Wars have also caused or speeded shifts in the global balance of power between NATION-STATES.

Sociological responses have as yet been varied and fragmentary. The 1950s notion of 'the military-industrial complex' associated with C. Wright MILLS has recently been revived. E.P. Thompson coined the term 'Exterminist mode of production' (*New Left Review*, 1980) to identify the essential militarism of both CAPITALISM and STATE SOCIALISM, but its precise structure and causes remain unclear. Until sociology modifies its general TRANSNATIONAL stance and theorizes nation-states more adequately, it will not deal adequately with militarism.

MM

**military intervention.** The military intervenes when it exceeds some nominal level of impact on the STATE. All military establishments have some impact on civilian rulers, ranging from influence to replacement of civilian rulers by a military regime. The analysis of military intervention concerns situations in which one or other end of the range dominates a country's experience. It implies a separate military establishment and a proper level of influence. There is no military intervention when civil and military are fused as in FEUDALISM or most TRIBAL societies. The proper influence of a separate military is a matter of speculation though most Western thought implies the subordination of military to civilian authorities. The replacement of civilian rulers is unusual in advanced CAPITALIST and STATE SOCIALIST societies, but military influence may be high enough to warrant epithets like 'military-industrial complex', 'welfare-warfare state', 'garrison state' etc. Most attention has been devoted to the THIRD WORLD, the 'seismic zone of military intervention'. Intervention here has been attributed to (1) differential INSTITUTIONALIZATION of armed forces and polity, variously attributed to length of existence of armed forces, their greater internal coherence, the better education of the officer class as a substitute for a middle class etc; and (2) on the civilian side to a general lack of attachment to political regimes, itself a consequence of 'tribalism', regionalism, uneven economic development, low literacy, low education etc. Marxists and others usually on the left ascribe intervention to class struggle: the needs of foreign capital and domestic COMPRADOR bourgeoisie to use coercion to suppress WORKING CLASS demands for wages and reform.

Military regimes are normally a consequence of military intervention, but can also follow defeat or victory in war. Most analysis concerns the implications of officers' social class, regional origins and modes of training for their behaviour as rulers. Additional foci of interest include the role of military ideology in setting administrative procedures, the military as furthering or impeding economic and political change, and the conditions for military disengagement. Generally, a ruling military of necessity enters a more or less formal coalition with the upper echelons of the civil service. This, plus the military preference for command, normally leads to an administrative ruling style of commissions, bureaucratic simplifications and attempts to ban politics.

Despite their own pretensions, military regimes probably offer no long- or even medium-term solution to the problems of Third World countries. Their failures generally lead to replacement by civilian, loosely-democratic rulers, and then sometimes to an unstable oscillation of civilian and military regimes.

See also COUPS.

See Finer, *The Man on Horseback* (1962).

RED

**Mill, John Stuart** (1806-73). English EMPIRICIST philosopher, economist and social critic. Main works: *System of Logic* (1843), *On Liberty* (1859), *Utilitarianism* (1863). Educated by his father, James Mill (1773-1836), he considerably modified the utilitarian theory developed by his father and by Jeremy Bentham into LIBERALISM. Mill retained the idea that actions and social arrangements are right or good 'in proportion as they tend to produce happiness', but criticized Bentham's crude account of happiness, which did not distinguish between 'higher' and 'lower' pleasures: those which more actively engage and develop the intellect yield greater utility. Self-development, as a means of maximizing social utility, is enhanced by democratic institutions which foster a deeper sense of personal responsibility through the increased extent of participation they permit. The same effect is to be had by allowing individuals considerable personal LIBERTY inasmuch as this encourages intellectual discovery and experimental life-styles which, even when unsuccessful, contribute to human progress by advancing our knowledge. Personal liberty may only be restricted where its exercise would harm others;

paternalistic intervention is illegitimate. Even respect for individual rights, traditionally presumed justifiable only by reference to the opposed principles of JUSTICE, is claimed by Mill to be justifiable on utilitarian grounds due to the utility yielded by the security of personal expectations that such respect engenders. Though a firm advocate of laissez-faire, Mill favoured cooperative forms of industrial organization and expressed reservations about the defensibility of private property rights in land.

His philosophy of social science, developed in Book VI of *System of Logic*, builds on his account of INDUCTION in Book III to examine methods of CAUSAL EXPLANATION in the 'moral sciences'. Both this and his politics were influenced by COMTE, though he rejected some of the more illiberal parts of the POSITIVIST programme.

HIS, WO

**millennial movement.** Sometimes referred to as 'millenarian' or 'chiliastic'. Identified in terms made familiar in the work of Norman Cohn and of Yonina Talmon as movements which imminently expect the miraculous transformation of this world by supernatural means. Believers expect salvation to occur on earth, or for heaven to come down to earth. Membership of the heavenly Kingdom (which, in traditional Christian eschatology, was to endure a thousand years) is the collective reward of the faithful alone.

Historically, millennial movements have often displayed an activist response to their rejection of the world, believing that secular insurrection and revolt were necessary accompaniments or precursors of the Battle of Armageddon or other supernatural overthrow of the present ungodly order of things. More recent movements have taken a more passive stance born of a recognition of the unlikelihood of successful revolt in modern states. They have seen their role as warning the world of the coming end and calling out the faithful rather than initiating that end by the use of violence (e.g. Jehovah's Witnesses).

Millennial movements are often faced with difficulties that result from the failure of the end to occur on the date prophesied (see FESTINGER). Some movements, such as the Millerites in 19th-century America, fragmented as the result of such a failure of prophecy. Others are able to accommodate to such failures, reinterpreting them in a way which shows the prophecy to have been essentially correct in spiritual rather than concrete physical terms, or to have been a result merely of human misinterpretation of God's message. In the long run the millennium tends to be more spiritualized and postponed to some distant, rather than imminent, date. Millennial movements tend then to turn in on themselves, concentrating on cultivating their own collective purity rather than spreading the message of the end. They thus move towards INTROVERSIONISM as their expectation of the millennium recedes.

See MESSIANIC MOVEMENT; POLITICAL MESSIANISM.

See N. Cohn, *The Pursuit of the Millennium* (rev. 1970).

RW

**Mills, C. Wright** (1916-62). American radical sociologist. Born in Waco, Texas, of middle class parents. After graduating from the University of Texas, Mills obtained his PhD in Sociology from the University of Wisconsin. He began teaching at the University of Maryland, and then moved to Columbia where he became a full Professor 1956, after a long delay due to political prejudices.

Mills's major concern was the use and especially the abuse of power. He saw the USA as ruled by a power ELITE, with a powerless mass at the bottom whose TRADE UNION leadership aims only at a larger slice of wealth. Between these groups was a middle class made powerless by bureaucratic employment. In *The Power Elite* (1956) he argues that an integrated elite of politicians, businessmen and military men, not a PLURALISTIC balance of competing interests, determines the direction of American policy. *White Collar: The American Middle Classes* (1951) traces the decline of farmers and small businessmen who formed the old middle class and had their own power base. They have been replaced by the new MIDDLE CLASS of salaried professionals, managers, office workers and sales staff, who, dependent on BUREAUCRACIES for their jobs, are powerless conformists. Throughout his life Mills sustained his indignation at this structure. He denounced it as depriving people of their independence, and as undemocratic because people do not knowledgeably participate in decisions that affect them. Mills was basically a south-western radical populist in his values and in the focus of his attacks — elites and big interests that manipulate the little person. He offered no vision of an alternative society and was not attached to any political group.

*The Sociological Imagination* (1959) attacked American sociology for being either statistical investigation of trivia or grand theory (see PARSONS). This paralleled the milder attack made by MERTON. Grand theory is so concerned with abstract features of society that it avoids dealing with the major social problems of the present. Mills's attack on the nature of most sociologists' work and his emphasis on social conflict provided a major influential critique of the CONSENSUS and FUNCTIONALIST view of society dominant in the USA during his lifetime. His clear, aggressive writings attracted a large audience and his ethically committed approach to sociology had a major influence on the American New Left.

See also CONFLICT THEORY.

KM

**minimax strategy.** See GAME THEORY.

**minimum wage controls.** Legal restrictions which specify the minimum wage rate that an employer may pay a worker. In Britain these are administered through Wages Councils which cover certain traditionally low-pay industries such as textiles, hotels and catering, and retail distribution. Critics of minimum wage controls argue that because they increase the costs of labour they tend to reduce the level of employment in the industries covered. Opponents of this view claim that this will only be true in competitive industries: in those industries where employers collude to reduce wages, minimum wage controls may increase wages without reducing employment.

See also PRICES AND INCOMES POLICY.

RR

**minority.** Literally, the smaller number or part. In sociology this usage has been overlain by a tendency to confuse the purely numerical concept of a minority with the existence of minority groups preserving distinctive attributes. For WIRTH, a group was a minority only if it was singled out for differential treatment because of its physical or cultural characteristics, and its members therefore regarded themselves as objects of collective DISCRIMINATION and tended to develop distinctive attitudes which set them further apart. Wirth classified minorities according to their orientation towards the majority society (assimilationist, pluralist, secessionistic, militant) but did not explore the significance for their social relations of the different kinds of physical and cultural characteristics that set them apart. It is more satisfactory to use the term minority in a numerical sense and specify the unit in respect of which it is a minority and the distinguishing attribute. Thus Protestants are a religious majority in Northern Ireland but a minority in Ireland. A Belfast Protestant belongs to a political majority within the Province but in relation to the United Kingdom can be seen as a member of an ethnic minority, since all Northern Ireland people share some common cultural characteristics distinguishing them from English people. These numerical entities vary in the extent to which they form self-conscious groups, whether of the majority or minority. Definitions of the kind advanced by Wirth cannot so discriminate: they represent blacks in South Africa as forming a minority even though they constitute three-quarters of the population. According to the alternative approach, black South Africans are a numerical majority and a political minority divided into ETHNIC and linguistic minorities (Zulu, Khosa, Venda etc) which may be either CATEGORIES or GROUPS.

MPB

**miscegenation.** The mating of people of different race. The word was coined by two journalists working producing covert propaganda for the Democratic Party during the campaign leading to the United States presidential election of 1864. In a book of this title they contended that such mating produced people of superior stock and that it was therefore the policy of the Republican Party to encourage it. Use of the word is to be avoided since it presupposes a pre-Darwinian conception of permanently distinctive races (see CLINE; DARWIN; GENE; RACE).

MPB

**MMPI** [Minnesota Multi-phasic Personality Inventory]. A non-projective, multi-DIMENSIONAL, pencil-and-paper personality test, developed at the University of Minnesota. The first studies by Hathaway and McKinley appeared in 1940, and it became perhaps the most widely used general personality test, particularly in the 1950s and 1960s. It has been extensively used in sociology, mainly in the USA, to investigate the social correlates of PERSONALITY.

The MMPI predicts the occurrence of current diagnostic psychiatric categories (see MENTAL ILLNESS). Its items are borrowed from other tests, and include many oriented to pathological conditions. It is a purely empirical test and is not intended to measure a theoretically based idea of personality dimensions, nor to be a general personality inventory. Nevertheless, the MMPI has frequently been taken as a standard personality measure, the amount of evidence relating to it tending to suggest, many think wrongly, that it overcomes problems of interpretation.

The MMPI invites subjects to make self evaluations by saying whether or not each of 550 statements is true of themselves. The items are arranged into 14 scales, such as depression, psychasthenia, masculinity/femininity, including 4 control scales intended to assess misleading responses. FACTOR ANALYSIS suggests three principal factors underlie test scores (the first two are sometimes identified as 'ego strength' and EXTROVERSION/INTROVERSION; the third is less readily labelled) together with second-order factors, one identified as 'emotionality'.

JL

**mobilization.** The process by which members of society are led to participate in various types of political activity involving the defence or promotion of particular ideas, values, positions, situations, persons or groups. Various factors have been associated with the ability to mobilize individuals politically: NATIONALISM or national feeling, patriotism, ETHNIC feeling and loyalties, regionalism, LEADERSHIP (especially that of a CHARISMATIC leader), a great variety of IDEOLOGIES (e.g. fascism, national socialism, pacifism, liberalism, imperialism and socialism), religion and strong moral feelings on particular issues (e.g. social reform, human rights, abortion and racial discrimination). Socialist and Marxist theorists generally agree that mobilization is a prerequisite to fundamental change in society. Studies of SOCIAL MOBILITY support this view, since in most societies this mobility tends to be limited. Research also shows that in industrialized societies the middle class is more easily mobilized than the working class, though the extent to which the industrial workforce is unionized may have a considerable impact on its receptiveness to attempts at mobilization.

MDR

**model.** A representation of something in terms of something else which it resembles and which is usually better known. Thus billiard balls, real of imagined, may provide a model for the movements of gas molecules, or a hydraulic model may represent the transactions in an economic system. An IDEAL TYPE such as 'rational economic man' may also be called a model. 'Model' is often used interchangeably with 'THEORY', especially of theories which are incomplete or uncertain. REALIST philosophers differ from POSITIVISTS over the importance of models for the development of science. For realists, models are not just aids to understanding but may also represent, by analogy, the real structures and mechanisms which produce observable effects. Viruses, for example, were once part of a hypothetical model of disease, but are now known to exist.

See Mary Hesse, *Models and Analogies in Science* (1963).

WO

**modernization.** A central concept in the sociology of development, referring to the interactive processes of economic growth and social change whereby historical and contemporary underdeveloped societies are thought to become developed. Moderniza-tion studies typically deal with the effects of economic development on TRADITIONAL social structures and values, and — con-versely — with the manner in which traditional social structures and values can either hinder or facilitate successful economic development. For instance, modernization studies examine patterns of SECULARIZATION following the introduction of cashcrops into traditional peasant communities, or the effect of INDUSTRIALIZA-TION on the prevailing family system.

Modernization has also come to stand for one particular, controversial, and exclusively Western, perspective on development and developing countries. Its critics (see DEPEND-ENCY) claim it has even become an ideo-logical apology for IMPERIALIST interference with, and EXPLOITATION of, developing countries since their independence from colonial rule. This claim is based on a critical analysis of the intellectual origins of the concept, which had two ante-cedents: (1) The practical observations of (Western) economic advisors to govern-ments of newly independent countries. In the early 1950s these experts argued that policies of economic development could only be successful if they formed a part of comprehensive planning affecting the entire social and cultural fabric into which the economic policies were injected. (2) Sociolo-gists began to underlie these practical observations with a theoretical framework consistent with mainstream sociological the-ories of society (structural FUNCTIONALISM) and of historical/social change (NEO-EVOLU-TIONISM).

The issue of this mixed parentage was modernization theory according to which (1) The general evolution of society is a process of development in stages. (2) Each stage is a characteristic combination of a certain degree of SOCIAL DIFFERENTIATION (e.g. of the DIVISION OF LABOUR) and of a certain manner of integration. At each stage the structural and cultural components of a society are mutually compatible. (3) The modern societies of Western Europe and the North Americas are the latest in the sequel of historical social evolution. (4) Contem-porary developing countries are societies in a pre-modern stage of evolution. (5) Given

that contemporary developing countries wish to adopt the economic institutions (money, markets, industrialism, etc) of modern societies, the second premise above — that of 'structural compatibility' — dictates that they adopt the social, political and cultural forms characteristic of modern societies.

This theorizing was soon criticized for equating modernization with 'Westerniza-tion'. Since Westernization as a develop-mental ideology is partisan to Western commercial interests, modernization theory was entirely rejected by radical writers on THIRD WORLD development (see DEPEND-ENCY).

AH

**modes of production.** An organizing concept developed by MARX to explain the structure and dynamics of any given society (or in his terms, SOCIAL FORMATION) and, particularly, the transition from one to another. Marxists today generally argue that this does not refer exclusively to the economy but to something broader and more complex, the structured relationships between the means of production (raw materials, land, labour, tools etc) and the RELATIONS OF PRODUCTION (the ownership of these means of production and the social relationships they entail). In the simplest expression of this concept, the Preface to *A Critique of Political Economy* (1859), Marx argues that 'the mode of production of material life conditions the social, political and intellectual life process in general', but in his other works, and those of subsequent Marxists, this straightforward thesis has been considerably modified. It is, therefore, necessary to distinguish between different conceptions of modes of production, the various modes of production to be found in actual societies, and the transition between modes of production.

*Conceptions of modes of production.* Marx's own conception, although it changed from time to time, revolved around the key idea that people produce not only linen and flax (as he said in his criticism of Proudhon in *The Poverty of Philosophy*) but in so doing also produce definite social relations. The social relations of production are the basis of the Marxist analysis of society. In *The German Ideology* (1846) the modes of production are equated with stages of development in the diversion of labour or forms of ownership, whereas in the volumes of *Capital* (1876 onwards) the capitalist mode of production is specified in great detail in relation to a wide spectrum of economic, political, and ideological factors.

In the hands of his more popularizing and/or dogmatic followers the theory was turned into something approaching a magic formula for the explanation of everything in any society. This interpretation, often labelled 'mechanical' or 'vulgar' materialism, was common in the German Social Democratic Party up to 1914, the CPSU in the 1920s and 1930s, and has not disappeared today. It was argued that events in the material base of society (its economic structure) strictly determined events in the ideological superstructure (politics, culture, religion etc). Such an absurd position, contrary to the spirit though not always the letter of Marx's sociology, led to an almost total eclipse of the theory of modes of production until its re-emergence in the 1960s.

ALTHUSSER and his colleagues (*Reading Capital*, published in France in 1966) were responsible for the current widespread use of the theory in several branches of sociology and cultural studies. Althusser's conception postulates a mode of production and the social formation for which it is primarily responsible as a 'structure-in-dominance' in which relations of production and means of production (the economic level) dominate but are locked into a structure of politics and ideology. This emphasis on the structural relationships of the components of modes of production and social formations makes more plausible the historical analysis of any given mode of production and its political and ideological (cultural) effects. But it raises further difficulties for a theory of transitions between one mode and another, and it makes obscure the ultimate causal relations between economic and political, military and ideological aspects of social life.

*Historical modes of production.* As Hobsbawm suggests in his clarifying Introduction to Marx's *Pre-capitalist Economic Formations*, there are both theoretical and empirical difficulties in identifying modes of production. On at least three (the ancient, the feudal and the capitalist) there is now general agreement. Several others, including the tribal (or clan), the slave and 'the ancient Asiatic and other ancient modes of production' (*Capital*, vol. I) were also mentioned by Marx, but there is a good deal of controversy as to the actual historical existence and/or theoretical cogency of any of these examples (see ASIATIC MODE OF PRODUCTION). The African, peasant, colonial and domestic modes of production have been invented by Marx-influenced scholars.

(1) The ancient mode of production is characterized by the emergence of private property consequent on a more complex DIVISION OF LABOUR made possible in the Iron Age by the rise of specialized animal husbandry, settled agriculture, handicrafts etc. These conditions produced social CLASSES which gave this and other modes of production an exploitative character.

A very common form of exploitation in ancient society was SLAVERY, and relations between slaves and masters and other free citizens structured the conditions of existence in the ancient mode. Greek and Roman slavery was not identical, but sufficiently similar to be usefully analysed in terms of the ancient-slave mode of production. However, the large-scale development of slavery in parts of the New World in early modern times makes the conceptual establishment of a slave mode of production *per se* a dubious venture. Apparently slavery can be inserted in very different wider production systems. The economic dynamic of the ancient mode involved a class of landowners, usually based in cities, expropriating agriculture surpluses from slaves or servile PEASANTS. These landowners ruled, and continually replaced their labour force, through the manipulation of STATE power and militaristic IMPERIALISM. The formal destruction of the Roman Empire merely signalled in dramatic terms a gradual disintegration of the ancient mode of production, the replacement of slaves by dependent peasants on the land, and the splintering of state power in favour of a local warrior NOBILITY.

(2) The feudal mode resulted (see FEUD-ALISM). The greater and lesser nobilities and their military, clerical and domestic retinues live off the surpluses produced by the enserfed small peasantry. Surpluses are extracted through RENTS, either in money, in kind, in labour, or any combination of these. As in all exploitative modes of production, the producers (the subordinate class) have their surplus product expropriated by the non-producers (the ruling class and their agents) by a mixture of economic, political, and ideological coercion. There is controversy among Marxist scholars on a whole range of issues concerning the feudal mode. These, summarized in R. Hilton (ed.) *The Transition from Feudalism to Capitalism* (1976), include the disputes between Dobb and Sweezey as to the relative salience of class struggle and the development of commerce for the fate of feudalism, the precise role of the rising bourgeoisie and the city, and the degree to which the feudal mode of production was economically progressive. Perry Anderson (*Lineages of the Absolutist State*, 1974; *Passages from Antiquity to Feudalism*, 1974) has considerably influenced and widened the scope of these debates, particularly with respect to the differences between feudal modes in Western and Eastern Europe and in Japan.

(3) The rise of ABSOLUTISM in 17th-century Europe, when monarchs built STATE power over a divided aristocracy, heralded both the end of the feudal mode and the dawn of the capitalist. Here, the capitalist class, the BOURGEOISIE, stand against the mass of landless labourers who, having been divorced from their means of subsistence in land, have only their labour power to sell. By ownership of capital and through it the means of production, the bourgeoisie accumulates more and more capital by expropriating the surplus value produced by workers in the form of profits made from exchange of commodities (e.g. factory products) in the market. Marx analysed the economic, political and ideological features of CAPITALISM in great detail throughout his works. Subsequent Marxists and anti-Marxists have written on a quite bewildering array of topics of relevance to the capitalist mode without much agreement. Marxists and anti-Marxists disagree among them-

selves as frequently as they disagree with each other.

It has been argued that the theory of modes of production adds nothing to the general economic interpretation of the origins and dynamics of any society. An unusually subtle analysis is needed to refute this argument in concrete terms. Nevertheless, the theory does identify the social character of economic relations in a manner that gives a distinctive sociological force to the concepts of slave and master, serf and lord, PROLETARIAN and capitalist, in their respective modes of production.

*Transitions between modes*: Marx was unequivocal that the ancient mode gives way to the feudal mode, the feudal to the capitalist, and the capitalist to the socialist. However, in a letter to a Russian critic, Mikhailovsky, he said this was not an iron-clad law but a general tendency that could only confirmed or disconfirmed in any actual case on the basis of historical research. The theory of modes of production is not an abstract theory of SOCIAL CHANGE but a recommendation to study history with Marxist concepts. There are many unresolved problems: for example, the relation between economic forces and class struggle, the question of REVOLUTION, the precise ways in which a dominant and a subsidiary mode of production can co-exist in the same society, and the effects of IMPERIALISM in general and the TRANS-NATIONAL modes of production in particular on national societies. This last problem has had a considerable impact on the sociology of development, through DEPENDENCY and WORLD SYSTEM theories, amongst others.

Modes of production, while not yet a commonplace among non-Marxist sociologists, is beginning to gain currency as an organizing concept in the analysis of historical and contemporary societies. Nevertheless, its adherents have in common a relative emphasis on material production factors in their total explanations, and this still divides them from those with different exphases. For an alternative view, see POLANYI.

See also HOUSEWORK.

**monetarism.** A loose description of the school of economic thought which maintains that changes in the supply of money are the major source of fluctuations in national income and the price level. This relationship was originally formulated by the Yale economist, Irving Fisher (1867-1947), and became known as the quantity theory of money. Formally, this theory may be expressed as $MV = PT$; the stock of money (M) multiplied by its velocity of circulation (V) is equal to the general price level (P) multiplied by the level of real output (T). Because it is hypothesized that the rate at which money is spent, that is, its velocity of circulation (V), remains constant, changes in the money stock (M) will either change the price level (P) or the level of real output (T). However, as the quantity theory was integrated into the classical theory of economics — in which it was maintained that national output would be determined at the full-employment level through unregulated competition in the labour market — it was argued that changes in the supply of money, unable to affect real output, would simply affect the general level of prices (*see* INFLATION). This classical view of the economic system was challenged by J.M. Keynes (see KEYNESIAN ECONOMICS) who emphasized the possibility of less than full-employment equilibrium national output. According to Keynes, governments could and should use monetary and fiscal policy (i.e. taxes and expenditures) to regulate national output and employment. In the late 1960s high rates of inflation, and the apparent failure of Keynesian remedies led to renewed interest in the original money-supply explanations of inflation. The most prominent advocate was the Chicago economist Milton Friedman (1912- ) who presented a modern reformation of the quantity theory. At the present time, monetarist economists dispute the Keynesian claim that governments should restrict their activity to letting the money supply grow steadily at the rate of growth of the economy's productive potential.

RR

**monopoly.** See MARKET STRUCTURE.

**Montesquieu, Baron Charles de** (1689-1755). Charles de Secondat, Baron de la Brède et de Montesquieu, studied law, physiology and natural history, became a legal apprentice, then a magistrate. Inheriting land and a fortune, he was taken up by the society of Regency Paris after publication of his *Persian Letters* (1721) which explored French society through the imaginary eyes of two Persians to illuminate commonly unquestioned customs and institutions as extraordinary and problematic. He was elected to the French Academy in 1728. During his travels in Europe between 1728 and 1731, he was influenced by the English Whigs. Major works: *Considerations on the Causes of the Greatness of the Romans and Their Decline* (1734); *Spirit of the Laws* (1748).

*Spirit of the Laws* consists of a disparate series of 31 books produced over 20 years. The first 13 books developed a theory of government using an analytic device later proposed by WEBER as the IDEAL TYPE. Montesquieu distinguished between the 'essential nature' (external structure) of a government, and its 'principle' (sentiments necessary to its functioning). Thus republics might be DEMOCRACIES or ARISTOCRACIES but were infused with the principle of virtue (respect for law, commitment to group welfare). Honour (respect for privileges and duties of rank) is the mainspring of monarchical regimes which rule through established laws. Absolute rule under despotism requires the creation of widespread, socially divisive fear, which indicates corruption and impending political collapse. Books 14-18 investigate the impact of physical and material factors upon societies. Montesquieu was not a strict climatic determinist, and recognized that society may be shaped by a variety of factors such as type of government, history, laws, religion and physical environment. He refused to assign *a priori* causal supremacy to any of these, as causal significance varies widely between societies. Book 19 discusses the 'general spirit' of a nation (its CULTURE). Books 20-26 examine the impact of religion, population and trade upon social and legal phenomena. Book 29 deals with the formulation of laws and the remaining books explore Roman and feudal legislation.

Montesquieu combined the search for a rational universal order with an emphasis upon the cultural diversity of social life. Materialistic elements in his thought never extended to an analysis of social stratification, systems of production, or the division of labour. His liberal exposition of the condition of LIBERTY in a free society requires the existence of conflict between competing groups: CONSENSUS is never absolute and is achieved through a balance of forces. Although he believed in the innate EQUALITY of men, Montesquieu developed his conception of social balance with reference to inegalitarian aristocratic societies and in response to ideological debates in France about the position of the aristocracy in relation to the monarchy. Under monarchies social balance requires the preservation of distinction and rank. In England the separation of the powers safeguards political liberty (see LAW, RULE OF).

In examining the connections between laws and forms of government, Montesquieu treats laws as natural regularities. He marries positive law, with its emphasis upon the search for causal laws explaining 'law-as-command', with natural law philosophy. Principles of justice ensue from the natural equality of men. Montesquieu condemns religious persecution, slavery and despotism as contrary to natural law. His sociology of law is primarily concerned with investigation of the conditions under which legal commands are uniquely suited to a particular society. The 'spirit of the laws' denotes the totality of relationships between the laws and those factors which causally influence them (see LAW: *Trends in Legal Theory*).

As a founder of social and political theory, Montesquieu was influenced by Aristotle, Machiavelli, HOBBES, KANT and Spinoza. He was the first theorist to explain political institutions and law by examining features of the societies to which they belong, founded the European conception of Asiatic despotism (see ASIATIC MODE OF PRODUCTION), and was a precursor of the sociology of law. His emphasis on culture and relative values was an important contribution to the early Enlightenment. He promoted EMPIRICIST observation in place of METAPHYSICS and rationalism. However, he failed to revise his ideal-types in the light of empirical findings or to include representation in his ideal type of democracy. Deficiencies in his

economic analysis (restricted to revolutions in trade and commerce) and a narrow definition of society in terms of political system meant that he could not offer a comprehensive analysis of SOCIAL STRUCTURE. Since he failed to appreciate the significance of technological development for the transition to industrial society, he could offer no theory of social change.

JW

**Moore, Barrington.** From the institutional base of the Russian Research Centre at Harvard University, Barrington Moore Jr has produced a series of works on historical sociology in general and Soviet society in particular. In *Soviet Politics: the Dilemma of Power* (1950) and *Terror and Progress: USSR* (1954) he successfully transcended current Cold War categories to produce the foundations of a political sociology of Soviet power. He is best known for *Social Origins of Dictatorship and Democracy* (1966), which rekindled theoretical interest in the sociology of historical processes. More recent works such as *Reflections on the Causes of Human Misery* (1973) and *Injustice* (1978) have tended to be rather more social-philosophical and have attracted less attention, though *Injustice* contains the best contemporary analysis of the rise and decline of the German labour movement in English. Moore has also written works of political theory, among which *Political Power and Social Theory* (1958), and *Critique of Pure Tolerance* (1965, with MARCUSE and Woolf), may be mentioned.

See COMPARATIVE METHODOLOGY.

LS

**moral crusade.** A form of social movement in which members protest against some alleged infraction of a moral NORM or principle held to be fundamental to the society (*see* MORALITY), and seek to create or to secure the enforcement of sanctions against such infractions. Since such movements appear to pursue an intangible goal which brings the protesters no concrete gains in power or resources, some theories have referred to such movements as symbolic crusades, concluding that since the goals pursued are symbolic the movement is more interested in the expressive activity of protest than in the instrumental achievement of its goal. Others aver that if the purpose is symbolic the actual goal pursued is merely a mask for some underlying motive, such as defending jeopardized social standing or prestige. However, many moral crusaders appear sincerely to desire the implementation of moral changes (i.e. to have a primarily instrumental purpose) and to have no ulterior motive beyond defending a form of their culture to which they are strongly attached, often for religious reasons.

RW

**moral enterprise.** Theories of moral enterprise maintain that social problems should be regarded specifically as practical achievements or constructions. A social problem is itself defined as an event, process or phenomenon which receives sufficient public recognition to be both acknowledged and consequential: something ought to be done about it. An abundance of potential issues might become the object of such a social and political response, but few mature into social problems. It is not always the intrinsic qualities of an issue but its public presentation and organization that distinguish it from others. The development of public awareness and reaction often has to be actively managed by some individual or association. Becker has called the managerial projects involved moral enterprise, and their members moral entrepreneurs (*Outsiders*, 1963). Analysed examples include the Prohibition movement, the history of narcotics legislation, and 'mugging'. 'Moral enterprise' bears an implicit connotation of mild or strong disapproval of the ends pursued: the term is rarely applied to campaigns applauded by a scholar.

See DEVIANCE; IATROGENESIS; LABELLING.

PR

**morality.** The principles that govern how members of a society or group act in situations where there are consequences for others. The concept of morality must therefore be among possible actions in interpersonal situations or at the societal level when choices over social policies (e.g. poverty programmes) are made. In socio-

logical analysis, morality must be concerned with central NORMS existing in any group(s) or society (Durkheim, *Moral Education*, 1925). A distinction has been made between primary morality relating to fundamental aims, and secondary morality relating to the means of reaching such aims (McIntyre, *Secularization and Moral Change*, 1967). Since norms vary by society, morality, even at the primary level, can be seen as a relative concept. Some moral philosophers, particularly before this century, argued for an underlying level of absolute morality, but there is much anthropological and comparative evidence to support the contrary view that morality is situational, varying between groups, societies and historical periods. For example, at the level of primary morality, murder for revenge is permissible in some societies, and at the secondary level the amount of physical or mental violence allowed in relationships with others has varied through time. The way morality changes is analysable in terms of DEVIANCE. For example, actions recently defined as immoral in familial or sexual behaviour are now accepted as normal and moral. Morality is, however, seen as central to the stability of all societies. Those with power see themselves, and are often seen by others, as agents of respectability who must defend current standards of morality. Deviance of a comparatively minor nature may provoke such agents to a MORAL PANIC (e.g. over the length of boys' hair or girls' skirts). Because of the social importance of morality, schools are often seen as an important support to the family in teaching the current morality and teachers have been seen as agents of moral respectability (see CURRICULUM).

PWM

**moral panic.** Allied to the 'pseudo-disaster' and the 'collective delusion', the 'moral panic' is a turbulent, excited or exaggerated response to DEVIANCE or a social problem. The term is intended to convey the unreasonable, unrealistic or inappropriate quality of social reaction. 'Panic' suggests that such a reaction magnifies an original incident (see, for example, S. Cohen's analysis of the Mods and Rockers in *Folk Devils and Moral Panics*, 1972), attributes a spurious identity to deviants and deviance, or produces the very phenomenon by which it is agitated. It carries an implication of social contagion and, occasionally, political fabrication.

PR

**mortality.** The rates of death in a population are one of the central studies of DEMO-GRAPHY. They are much less studied in sociology, in part because of all population processes they are least subject to human control. Mortality has been declining ever since records began, although for individual societies rates of mortality are highly stable in the short term, excluding war and epidemics. Differences in mortality between societies are largest for infants and decrease steadily toward old age. As infants are maximally dependent upon social support for life, infant mortality has been held to be the most sensitive indicator of social conditions. However, critics argue that while decreases in infant mortality are of great importance — for all societies known, deaths in the first year of life exceed those in any other year — this sanitary index is not the best guide to either the adequate functioning of social relations or to the level of technological development. In the latter, deaths in the post-neonatal period (1-11 months) and in the age-range 1-4 years have been suggested as a better discriminant, for it is here that the largest drop has been seen in advanced countries.

For comparing mortality between societies or sub-populations, the total death rates are too highly aggregated, and the age-and-sex rates do not reflect the relative importance of the different age-and-sex categories. Mortality indexes form a weighted average, using either the actual crude rates or the composition of a standardized population as weights. The CMF (Comparative Mortality Factor) takes the ratio of index values for populations of standardized composition; the SMR (Standardized Mortality Ratio) compares index values with those for a population with standardized rates. The UK Registrar General's Comparative Mortality Index uses a compromise base, the mean of the standard and actual population compositions, and Fisher's Ideal Index takes the geometric mean of the CMF and the SMR.

The type of index used depends on the type of comparison to be made: between populations of widely differing composition, or between sub-populations of the same population.

Mortality rates do not reflect deliberate action very much, although important reductions in certain age-cohorts may result from war, and overall decline in death rates in all countries has been due to medical advances — a decrease in infectious disease such as influenza, tuberculosis, and pneumonia, particularly in childhood — and the influence of environment and standard of living in resisting these factors. Rates show a corresponding increase in cancer and heart disease, the wearing out of the body, although changes in systems of death certification and in medical diagnosis make interpretation difficult. Certain events, such as marriage, have a selective effect (a term from life insurance) in distinguishing a sub-population whose death-rates are lower than an otherwise similar group, an effect that may stay with the cohort or decay over time.

Social class (see CLASS *as category and scale*) correlates inversely with death rates, although controlling for other factors can be difficult. Statistics suggest that differences are declining in industrial countries, and are largest under conditions of intermediate levels or mortality. Specific occupations with high death rates have been identified from the 19th century onwards, but interpretation is difficult since the social patterns which underlie fitting people into occupations are highly complex and may frequently have a stronger significance than the occupation itself; for example, clerical jobs may be selectively filled by the less physically robust or the old.

Changes in levels of mortality differentially affect certain groups within society, and this may be more important sociologically than overall changes. The SEX RATIO in one or more cohorts may be altered, and bulges or gaps in the population pyramid work themselves through the age distribution with effects on the ratio of producers to consumers, the composition of households, the structure of the labour force, the demand for services etc. Falling death rates tend initially to affect the young and male most, that is, those with the highest rates, thus decreasing the average age of the population and increasing the sex ratio.

See DEMOGRAPHIC TRANSITION; LIFE EXPECTANCY; LIFE TABLE; SEX RATIO.

JL

**Mosca, Gaetano** (1858-1941). Italian political theorist, one of the founders of ELITISM as a theory and often paired with PARETO as one of 'new Machiavellians'. Born in Sicily, Mosca trained as a constitutional lawyer and held posts in constitutional law at Turin university and in the history of political institutions at Rome. He was elected a deputy to the Italian Parliament in 1908 and appointed a senator 1918. He is best known for his systematic work *The Ruling Class* (1896). He argued that a political class, monopolizing power and its advantages, was a universal feature of all societies; he identified two different levels of this class and explored the various political formulae used to win the acquiescence of the governed; he distinguished between an open or closed political class in respect of its recruitment and its degree of accountability to the governed, and identified various social forces responsible for the changing composition of the political class. Mosca's manifest anti-democratic bias raises doubts about his claim to have finally established the study of politics on a scientific foundation. As a founder of elite theory he is still widely read (see ELITISM).

DB

**motherhood.** Primarily a social institution, not a biological function. Cross-cultural evidence demonstrates that childbirth and mother-child relationships are variously structured and interpreted. In Britain, most women give birth in hospital, are subject to numerous technological interventions and then return to the nuclear FAMILY home where they remain isolated with total responsibility for their child. In many societies childbirth is controlled by the mother and female assistants; in Britain it is defined by doctors as a medical or pathological event and hospitalized. In most societies childcare is not the sole responsibility of the mother, but shared to a greater or lesser extent with other women, sometimes classificatory mothers, at others, female kin, friends or neighbours.

The mother-child relationship, it has been argued, is the result of a biological maternal instinct. FREUD said that women transform their desire for the penis they lack into a wish for a child. Erikson claimed to have discovered that women have an emotional 'internal space' which must be filled by children. Others have argued that this biological instinct is created by the hormonal build-up during pregnancy, immediately after birth, and as a result of breast-feeding.

Arguments against this biological drive to maternity point to women's ability to love adopted children, to the lack of desire for a child among some women, and to the facts that women do not instinctively know how to breastfeed and care for their infant, and that the mother-child bond grows as the relationship develops.

Another argument against the biological nature of maternity lies in the linking of motherhood with MARRIAGE. A single mother is stigmatized as deviant, and in Britain may be encouraged to terminate her pregnancy or give her child up for adoption. A married woman's pregnancy is treated in a diametrically opposed fashion.

In the UK women normally have sole responsibility for childcare. Evidence shows that paternal involvement in housework decreases with the arrival of the first child. Maternity thus entails locking women into domestic and childcare duties. Mothers of pre-school children form the smallest category of female employees. Crèches, nurseries and other day-care provision remains a luxury for those who can pay; state-funded provision is rare and often cares for 'problem' families.

Motherhood and fatherhood are not symmetrical roles. Fathers express much of their commitment and responsibility through absence from the home, or employment. Mothers express it through total presence. Fathers bestow legitimacy on children through marriage to the mother; mothers cannot alone bestow legitimacy.

Paternal involvement is slowly being recognized. In Britain fathers are usually permitted to remain with women during childbirth, and a small percentage of single-parent families are motherless.

Although motherhood is technically a matter of choice, in practice women are pressured into having children by families of origin, the IDEOLOGY of maternity and family. Access to abortion is controlled by the MEDICAL PROFESSION, as is fertility control, which is often neither safe nor effective.

Most mothers combine maternity with employment. Some women do not enter the LABOUR MARKET until the youngest child is at school, and when they do so they tend to take part-time jobs which fit in with school hours. This has negative implications for women's position in the labour market (see WOMEN AND THE LABOUR MARKET).

Because women are seen as primarily responsible for childcare, they have been blamed for resulting DEVIANCE in their children. Bowlby (*Child Care and the Growth of Love*, 1953) claimed that delinquency in children was caused by 'maternal deprivation', although the children he studied were in institutions and thus experienced 'familial' or even 'paternal' deprivation (see CHILD CARE). LAING blamed mothers for causing schizophrenia, and male homosexuality and lesbianism have similarly been blamed on either too much or too little mothering. In homes where father-daughter INCEST occurs, mothers have been blamed for colluding in it by denying sexual access to their husbands.

Feminists have argued that motherhood forms a central core in women's oppression, and have claimed that we must not confuse the joy of having children with institutionalized maternity under PATRIARCHY.

The responsibilities of motherhood and fatherhood are not equally enforced. Although men earn a 'family wage', wives are not legally entitled to know how much they earn and husbands may not increase the wife's housekeeping allowance when their wages go up. Women can be penalized for not being good mothers by having their children removed.

Immigration laws tend also to discriminate against Black mothers. Black women have been sterilized without their consent during childbirth or an abortion. In parts of the USA Black women have been forced to undergo sterilization as a condition of receiving welfare payments, known as the 'Mississippi appendectomy'. Unsafe contraception, such as the Dalcon Shield IUD, banned in the USA and Britain, has been exported to THIRD WORLD countries and Black women in Britain and in the Third World have been injected with the contraceptive Depro-Provera, sometimes without their knowledge and consent, whose side effects are extremely unpleasant and potentially mortally dangerous.

See N. Chodorow, *The Reproduction of Mothering* (1978); A. Oakley, *Women Confined* (1980); A. Rich, *Of Woman Born* (1977).

EG

**motivation.** The concept of motivation covers those states of mind in which actions are mobilized towards some part of the environment and is therefore related to the term GOAL. For example, the term achievement motivation is a common one, covering mobilization, often of a competitive nature, towards completing socially acceptable tasks that enhance status, such as passing examinations (see ACHIEVEMENT). Patterns of motivations vary cross-culturally and are learned during the process of socialization, particularly, but not entirely, in the family and at school. VOCABULARIES OF MOTIVE are learned, such as 'being a gentleman'. There are problems of measuring motivation, since motives are often imputed from observed actions rather than from statements of actors, and statements may be untrue or only partially translated into action.

PWM

**multicollinearity.** See CAUSAL MODELLING.

**multi-dimensional scaling [MDS].** A term coined by Torgerson in 1958, referring to a family of mathematical and computational MEASUREMENT techniques for representing a set of observations by points in space in such a way that increasing distances between the points correspond to decreasing similarities between the observations. In metric MDS (see MEASUREMENT), numerical properties are assumed of the similarities, whereas in non-metric MDS only their rank order is significant. MDS was originally developed in psychology to account for the pattern of subjective judgements of the similarities between a set of stimuli when this could not be reflected by scoring the stimuli on a single response dimension. But more general measures of similarity (e.g. from MULTI-VARIATE ANALYSIS) could be substituted for the original judgements and the technique used to produce a multi-dimensional map of a set of observations.

Given a matrix of similarities or dissimilarities between a set of observations, multi-dimensional scaling ALGORITHMS start with an initial set of geometrical co-ordinates for the observations, compute a stress coefficient designed to measure how badly distances reflect dissimilarities, and then move the points towards a lowering of the stress coefficient. The algorithm proceeds until a minimal stress value is reached. The procedure is then repeated from a new initial position to make sure that this really is the minimal stress value overall. Configuration solutions can be produced for different numbers of dimensions, the stress value obtained increasing as the number of permissible dimensions for the solution decreases. Where there is a sudden increase in the stress value, it can be argued that the natural dimensionality underlying the observations has been reached, the number of dimensions needed to scale the basic data structure. Whether it is essential to be able to interpret these dimensions has been the subject of disagreement, some arguing that if they are not interpreted, the procedure is meaningless to social science theory, others arguing that there is no way to assign labels to the dimension in other than an *ad hoc* way.

Where a map representation is required, the solution is constrained to two or three dimensions for the purposes of visual inspection. The grouping of the points can be used to cluster the observations (*see* CLUSTER ANALYSIS), and different mappings of the same objects can be compared. Such techniques have been used in sociology to produce cognitive maps — for example, of the occupational structure — associated with individuals or groups, and a special set of techniques developed in the late 1960s at Bell Telephone Laboratories is available for handling individual differences (INDSCAL). The model produces a space for the group of individuals as a whole, from which each individual's perspective is seen as a transformation changing the degree of emphasis on the different dimensions.

MDS can be used as a specific theory of subjective perception by individuals, in which case the output must be interpreted, and the transformation of distances into similarities has theoretical significance as the model of an actual psychological process involved in making judgements. Alternatively, it can be used as a purely empirical technique of data analysis, in which case the output is in the relation of a summary to the original data, and the algorithm has no theoretical interpretation.

Non-metric MDS is most attractive in sociology because of its lack of strong assumptions as to MEASUREMENT level. Merely ordering the similarities between the observations is in theory sufficient to constrain the assignment of scores to a very narrow range, but in practice the performance of some algorithms is unreliable and ill-understood, and large amount of computer time can be used in adequately exploring the possible configurations. For ease of interpretation, configurations must often be compressed into two or three dimensions at the expense of a large stress value, largely negating the point of the technique in accurately representing observations by the use of many dimensions.

See also SCALES.

See R.N. Shepard *et al.* (eds.), *Multi-dimensional Scaling: Theory and Applications in Behavioural Science* (1972).

JL

**multi-variate analysis.** A general term referring to the analysis of relationships between VARIABLES in order to search for patterns in data to provide explanations of social phenomena. Various different procedures may be used, including CROSS-TABULATION, CORRELATION, REGRESSION, FACTOR ANALYSIS, path analysis and log-linear models, each involving different statistical procedures. See CAUSAL MODELLING.

See H.M. Blalock, *Social Statistics* (1969).

MB

**myth.** Unlike everyday language, sociology does not regard a myth as merely a false tale.

Theories regarding mythology can be divided into historical, psychological, functional and structural. In the historical tradition, particularly in the 19th century, myths are taken to be incomplete records of specific historical events, traditional tales which are acted out or remembered in ritual. At the turn of the century, there was a controversy regarding the historical priority of myth and ritual. Some classicists claimed that myths occurred in order to explain ritual, rather than vice versa. Some psychological theories of myth (e.g. JUNG) go so far as to suggest that myths are racial daydreams incorporating general elements (archetypes) which are part of the mental structure of the whole human race. FREUD also used these ideas to explain the universality of the Oedipus complex, suggesting an actual historical incident of father-killing and mother-son incest to explain not only Oedipal myths, but also the mother-son INCEST taboo. But he also pointed to the relationship between myths, which are a social product, and the individual's dreams, which he likened to myths in that they use the same symbolic devices of metaphor and metonym (see SYMBOL). Whereas the content of myth is common to people sharing the same cultural context, the elements used in dreams are drawn from the experience of an individual.

All these ideas appear in social anthropological theories of myths. MALINOWSKI proposed a FUNCTIONALIST theory, suggesting that myths legitimate elements of social life, acting as 'charters' for social rules and social structures. He criticized former theories for abstracting stories from their social context, claiming that myths are living realities with social relevance, and are distinct from legends (which are actual historical events) and folk tales (which are enjoyable stories). From his study of the myths of the Trobriand Islanders, he proposed that the living reality of myth is an expression not only of social structure but also of the values through which it is legitimated. Critics claim that this is inadequate to explain the psychological impact of myth and the origin of the myth-making faculty.

STRUCTURALIST interpretations of myth depend on theories developed within linguistics, first elaborated in social anthropology by LÉVI-STRAUSS. From linguistics and PSYCHOANALYSIS he takes the ideas that meaning is expressed in language and thought by the symbolic devices of metaphor and metonym (see SYMBOL). But he adds the insight that mythological meaning is not only to be found in isolated symbolic elements, like the archetypes suggested by Jung, but also in the means of telling the story, the narrative devices through which the elements are combined. Myths are like dreams but they are also like language, except that there are larger elements of meaning (mythemes) which operate at the sentence level, rather than at the level of individual words or phrases. The ability to form and relate to the structural devices of myth is a communicatory attribute of the human mind, comparable to language and the symbolic function. Lévi-Strauss also connects it to the tendency to form links of alliance between social groups through the development of prescriptions and prohibitions in marriage rites (see INCEST).

Both functionalist and structuralist theories of myth are current, and are not mutually exclusive. After the early 1960s there was an intense interest in structuralist studies of myth, an interest shared by various theories of literature. Critics of this approach, like critics of structuralism in general, claim that it is REDUCTIONIST: by analysing the elements of myths as if they are all transformations of a smaller number of elements, structuralist theory reduces the themes of mythology to a set of universal principles, often related, as with Freud, to incest prohibitions. Just as functionalist theory tends to ignore the common elements of all myths in its study of the particular social function of a specific myth, so structuralist theory can negate the social context in which a myth is related.

JE

# N

**narcissism.** See PSYCHO-ANALYSIS.

**National Deviancy Conference.** A loosely structured group of British sociologists of DEVIANCE active in the 1960s and 1970s. Variously described as an organisation devoted to: (1) radical action in the politics of crime and control; (2) the injection of Marxism or of critical or radical themes into the sociology of deviance; (3) the cultivation of ideas like EXISTENTIALISM or PHENOMENO-LOGY which were intellectually new but politically unencumbered.

There was an expansion, a breaking of academic traditions and an intellectual flux in the British universities of the 1960s. The newly emergent community of graduate students in the sociology of deviance was composed of those who were aware of the negotiable character of their discipline, appreciated their enhanced life-chances, sensed themselves as estranged from certain orthodoxies, and were receptive to the novel work of Becker, Lemert and others. That consciousness of difference prompted some to meet regularly at the University of York, the home university of Laurie Taylor. The original small group was based on a small, largely informal network. Its members were to explore and crystallize an original and shifting synthesis of SYMBOLIC INTERACTION-ISM, LABELLING, and allied thoughts borrowed from existentialism, ETHNO-METHODOLOGY, Marxism and phenomenology. Naming itself the York Deviancy Symposium, the group held small conferences three times a year, and received mild recognition from scholars in America and Europe.

Three principal influences shaped the evolution of the Symposium. The York meetings attained celebrity as an unofficial opposition to established criminology. They attracted large numbers, became institutionalized and lost their anchorage in the first informal network. Retitled the National Deviancy Conference, those meetings were conducted by people with university posts, with confidence and bearing and a commercial appeal to publishers. A loose cohesion was replaced by efforts to furnish more individual statements about deviance. Efforts revolved around the discrediting of a school identified as POSITIVISM. The break with positivism was declared radical, though the radicalism was itself ambiguous.

The Conference came later to be unequivocally yoked to Marxism, conducting meetings with such bodies as the Conference of Socialist Economists, and losing most of its original preoccupation with symbolic interactionist and companion works. The move was symbolized by the eschewing of Sociology of Deviance as a title and the new allegiance to radical criminology (see CRIMINOLOGY).

See S. Cohen, *Images of Deviance* (1971); P. Rock and M. McIntosh, *Deviance and Social Control* (1974); I. Taylor, P. Walton and J. Young, *The New Criminology* (1973); I. Taylor *et al., Critical Criminology* (1975).

PR

**nationalism.** The belief among a people that it comprises a distinctive community, with special characteristics that mark it off from others, and the desire to protect and promote that distinctiveness within an autonomous state. Nationalism takes many forms. The demand for self-government for the nation against alien rule is the paradigm form, though a distinction should be made between the demands of those peoples among whom a sense of national identity is already present, and those where it is not (e.g. the anti-imperialism of African countries after World War II). Once self-government is secured, nationalism may take the form of establishing a national identity out of disperate peoples comprising the state; of reaffirming an existing identity against internal or external threat; of seeking the incorporation in the state of cognate linguistic or cultural communities which lie outside it (irredentism); of securing the supremacy of the nation over supposedly inferior peoples (see IMPERIALISM).

The idea that nations constitute the only legitimate units for statehood is a product of the 19th century and the entry of the masses into the political arena. Nationalism has had three main bases: (1) a ruling ELITE with the means of securing the allegiance of the population to the new territorial and administrative unity constituted by the modern STATE; (2) a marginal, highly educated, urban BOURGEOIS group providing leadership to a nation ruled from outside; (3) a popular sense of shared identity once the local particularisms of TRADITIONAL societies had been eroded. Most Marxist writers have emphasized the first of these aspects at the expense of the others; seeing nationalism as a contrivance of the ruling classes, they have repeatedly underestimated its popular strength in comparison with the alternative claims of CLASS CONSCIOUSNESS. Economic EXPLOITATION and rivalry may provide fertile soil for nationalism to flourish, but it cannot be explained as merely a by-product of these forces.

There is a massive discrepancy between the power of nationalism as a political force and its theoretical coherence as a political doctrine. While the preservation of cultural diversity may be defensible, the idea that one nation's way of life, or the existence of its people, has greater value than that of any other lacks serious foundation. Furthermore, such an idea in a world of states armed with nuclear weapons can only lead to self-destruction (see MILITARISM).

See also ETHNICITY; ETHNOCENTRISM.

DB

**nation-state.** Supposedly found where the boundaries of state and popular NATIONALIST consciousness coincide. But this is almost never strictly found: contemporary states generally contain significant sub-national divisions more salient and divisive than mere SUBCULTURES. Thus nation-state generally has a looser meaning: states legitimating themselves in terms of rule by or for the people (DEMOCRACY in its various senses), almost exclusively 19th- and 20th-century states. The term 'multi-national states' often describes the last great federal Empires — Austria-Hungary, Tsarist Russia, the Ottoman Empire — which were supplanted by a greater number of nation-states. 'National state' often describes the immediate predecessors of nation-states, whose monarchs and aristocracies imbibed a national consciousness about 100-300 years before their peoples did.

The nation-state exists as a unit in a system of states, rather as a CLASS presupposes the existence of other classes. Its use thus has an advantage over abstract theories of the STATE, for inter-national relations are an essential part of modern social structure (see INTERNATIONAL DIVISION OF LABOUR, TRANSNATIONAL, DEPENDENCY, WORLD SYSTEM).

MM

**Nativist Churches.** See SYNCRETISM.

**natural areas.** The term used by the CHICAGO SCHOOL in the 1920s and 1930s to designate urban neighbourhoods. They were unplanned neighbourhoods segregated from each other by an internal homogeneity which marked them out in what was overall a heterogeneous urban environment. Each natural area forms the basis for a SUBCULTURE and together they constitute a complex mosaic of zones and areas which create a kaleidoscopic urban society.

HN

**naturalism.** The belief that the methods of the natural sciences and the social sciences are or should be basically the same. Some naturalists, also uphold the REDUCTIONIST view that the subject matter of the social sciences is also identical with or reducible to that of the natural sciences. Traditionally, the main stronghold of naturalism has been within the POSITIVIST tradition, and its main opponents have been writers influenced by HERMENEUTICS (see MEANING; VERSTEHEN). More recently, however, Anglo-Saxon analytic philosophy has moved from a naturalist (and broadly positivist) to an anti-naturalist position, while REALISTS have argued that the rejection of positivism makes possible a more adequate version of naturalism.

The term is also used in another sense to refer to the ethical theory that judgements of good, bad etc are grounded in facts about the things being commended or condemned. Ethical SUBJECTIVISTS call this 'the naturalistic fallacy' and deny that evaluations can be thus grounded.

A third, more general sense of naturalism is simply the denial of any supernatural realm (see RELIGION).

See Roy Bhaskar, *The Possibility of Naturalism* (1979).

WO

**natural rights.** Personal entitlements regarded as the most fundamental moral rights of the individual. Political theories embracing natural rights (see LOCKE) conceive them as the NORMATIVE foundation and framework upon and within which individuals acquire their particular entitlements to objects and the services of others. Such rights serve as a standard for moral evaluation of legal rights and function primarily as prohibitions against interference by other persons (including the STATE) with individual choice in disposing of his or her life, labour and property. A crucial element in any natural rights theory, apart from its prohibition of coercion, is its account of the rules governing the legitimate acquisition and retention of property. There is disagreement as to how claims about natural rights can be validated, with proposals ranging from that they are self-evidently true, to that they are derived from essential human nature, to that they are entailed by the common conceptual features of all the various, apparently conflicting, theories of natural rights.

See LAW: *Trends in Legal Theory;* MORALITY.

HIS

**need.** A concept widely used in social policy and social administration. A dictionary definition is 'a condition of affairs placing one in difficulty or distress; a time of difficulty or trouble ... marked by the lack or want of some necessary thing'. The term can be used in this sense in social policy to define the objectives of a service. However, to say that someone is in need or 'lacks or wants some necessary thing' is not the statement of an objective fact, but a point of view, and there is room for disagreement about the values such statements imply. For example, the point of view and values may be those of an external observer, the potential consumers of a service, the providers of a service or the controllers of resources. Such views and values are likely to differ and to be affected by the administrative and organizational contexts in which they are made.

See LAW: *Legal Services;* POVERTY.

MPJ

**needs, basic.** A concept connected with a new departure in development policies that has gained ground in organizations and negotiating forums of international development assistance. The term was first coined by a group of Latin American scholars (Herrara *et al., Catastrophe: A New Society,* 1975), in a document spelling out an alternative development strategy for the THIRD WORLD.

Since the late 1960s the rapid growth of some Third World countries has contrasted sharply not only with the stagnation and decline of others (see FOURTH WORLD) but also with the relative pauperization and MARGINALIZATION of large sections of the population within the successfully developing countries themselves. Since World War II, the number living in absolute and relative POVERTY has increased: it is estimated that today some 800 million people live in absolute poverty, while another 200 million live in relative poverty. Consequently, development assistance organizations have become increasingly concerned with the failure of conventional 'growth'-oriented economic planning.

In the early 1970s, the World Bank and suborganizations of the UN (e.g. the ILO) emphasized redistribution and employment programmes. It was argued, contrary to mainstream development economic theory, that objectives of growth and of income distribution must be pursued simultaneously. The basic needs strategy was a logical next step and a radical extension of this programme. Instead of justifying the new poverty focus as a means to national economic growth, its aims were to eradicate absolute poverty and meet the basic human survival needs of the world's poor.

Though the basic needs approach is neither a coherent theory nor a methodologically coherent development programme, a number of loosely knit themes commonly surface in the rapidly growing basic needs literature. Basic human needs are recognized as of two kinds: (1) material needs necessary for physical survival, such as food, shelter, clothing, access to water, hygiene, and health, and (2) non-material needs, such as education, fundamental human rights and 'participation', which is conceived of in the widest sense so as to include employment, political decision-making, and participation in national cultural life. Basic needs are acknowledged to vary in place and in time: as countries become richer, so the definition of minimal survival will be adjusted upwards.

Attempts to define and clarify basic needs set specific targets for particular countries, and also provide a measurement of comparative development performance more meaningful than conventional criteria of GNP per capita and growth rates. However, the problems of operationalizing basic needs in different cultures and climates are considerable. Apart from nutrition levels below which life cannot be sustained (3,000 calories and 90 grammes protein intake per day) strategists have not come up with universal targets for other material needs. For example, shelter is clearly a basic need and — arguably — can be operationalized in terms of number of rooms per person, yet variability in climate and culture undermines a 'minimum' human target of, say, one room per person. However, despite such operational difficulties, the basic needs

approach is appreciated as a tool for setting development priorities and standards.

As to the means for achieving these objectives, there is some consensus that what is required are policies of SELF-RELIANCE, selective de-linking from international production and marketing arrangements, redistribution of assets and incomes, employment-generating methods of production, and greater utilization of local resources. Possibly the weakest aspect of the basic needs approach is political: few writers spell out if and how satisfying these needs will challenge existing class and power structures.

By the late 1970s, the prevailing consensus (if not the actual practice) among donor countries and agencies was that concessionary aid should be targetted on the least developed countries, while other forms of assistance should focus on the poorest segments of the middle-income countries. Donor countries could and should use their aids flows as a lever to encourage the adoption of basic needs development programmes. This humanitarian, yet essentially interventionist, orientation of the basic needs ideology, has been a source of contention between the rich and poor countries. It accounts for the fundamentally ambivalent attitude of the developing countries towards the basic needs approach, despite the fact that the concept had originated as an authentic Third World perspective on development.

See also FOURTH WORLD: THIRD WORLD.

AH

**needs, hierarchy of.** A theory of personal MOTIVATION proposing that human NEEDS may be divided into a number of different levels, lower-level needs having to be satisfied before motivation shifts towards the satisfaction of higher-level ones. The concept of a hierarchy of needs is associated with the American psychologist Abraham Maslow (1908-70), who identified five levels: physiological needs; the need for safety; the need for love and to belong; the need for esteem; the need for self-actualization.

Maslow developed this hierarchy in an attempt to humanize psychology by providing a mediating link between the opposing positions of physiological BEHAVIOURISM and PSYCHOANALYSIS. He was influenced by the European émigré intellectuals who fled to New York in the late 1930s and 1940s, such as Fromm, Adler and Horney, and by the cultural anthropologist Ruth BENEDICT. He moved away from his earlier research on sexual behaviour in primates to study sexual behaviour in humans and finally to work on self-actualization — the goals and actions actively generated by the SELF. The hierarchy of needs links the different levels of research, allowing for both deficiency motivation (in the needs for oxygen, food and water) and growth motivation (in the striving for knowledge and personal development).

JL

**negative income tax.** The use of the TAX system to pay out benefits as well as collect money: where a person's income falls below a defined level, additions rather than reductions would be made. The scheme was widely discussed in the late 1960s and early 1970s. Its advantages were thought to be: (1) it might permit SELECTIVITY in benefits without the usual problems of take-up associated with MEANS TESTS, including STIGMA; (2) because a person may always increase his or her net income by earning more (i.e. the marginal tax rate is always less than 100 per cent) the disincentive to work represented by the POVERTY TRAP would be avoided; (3) the replacement of diverse means-tested schemes by a single integrated tax system would yield savings in administrative costs. The main disadvantages are that a negative income tax scheme which replaced a significant number of existing income-maintenance schemes would require guaranteed MINIMUM WAGE CONTROLS that would be expensive to finance, and would probably necessitate politically unacceptable increases in positive income tax rates. In the UK, the development of the system was resisted by the Inland Revenue, and proposals were shelved by the Conservative Government of 1970-74. It has also been claimed that the objects of a negative income tax could be better met by the development of an adequate system of FAMILY ALLOW-ANCES and rent and rate rebates.

MPJ, RR

**negotiation.** Originally applied mainly to the settlement of disagreements between societies, the term is now often used in analyses of interpersonal relationships and small groups. Attempts, often successful, may be made to resolve disagreement in social situations at whatever level through the discussion of differences to try to clarify the positions of the ACTORS and/or through the exchange of material goods (e.g. money) or symbolic goods (e.g. praise) to redistribute power amongst those concerned. When this process excludes the open use of power it is termed negotiation and may be carried out overtly, (e.g. in words) or covertly (e.g. using non-verbal CUES). During negotiation an actor may redefine his or her view of the position in exchange for a similar redefinition by another or other actors; the mutual benefits are perceived to cancel out and temporary postion of equilibrium is reached. Negotiation is particularly relevant to the analysis of DEVIANCE; a person LABELLING another as deviant or one who is so labelled will often try to negotiate or renogotiate this definition of the situation since the outcome will eventually govern future action.

PWM

**neo-colonialism.** Originally, a term expressing the retention and extension of economic dominance by the old metropolitan countries (such as Britain and France) over their colonies after they had surrendered formal state control. Soon the predatory interest in THIRD WORLD resources and markets on the part of new metropolitan countries (USA, Japan and West Germany) were included, even though they had never possessed formal colonies (or, in the case of Germany, very few).

After independence, the emerging nations of Africa and Asia soon realized that without economic independence their political independence meant very little. During the colonial period, the colonial economies had been reorganized to serve as ancillary economies to their mother countries. Many ex-colonies had extremely narrow production structures, dependent on the export of one or two cashcrops, the prices fixed in distant markets, often failing to keep pace with the prices of the imported manufacturers (UNEQUAL EXCHANGE). Distribution and marketing, and in most cases the production of these export commodities were in the hands of metropolitan firms. Penal tariffs and other protective measures in the advanced countries discouraged efforts by emerging nations to diversify their economies and industrialize. Moreover, when they did embark on industrialization they were dependent on capital and patented technology from the advanced countries. Their efforts to develop increased their indebtedness to the metropolitan countries and to new forms of domination. Attempts to escape by reneging on debts or nationalizing metropolitan firms met with foreign political and/or military intervention, either covert or overt. Collective awareness of this 'neo-colonial' situation crystallized at the Bandung Conference of Asian and African countries in 1955. The prolific use of the term in radical development literature dates from that conference.

Although the term neo-colonialism was coined to refer to economic domination, it does not exclude the many forms of political pressure, military support, destabilization policies and outright intervention by metropolitan countries (more especially the USA) to secure their overseas economic interests. As contradictions between metropolitan interests and the national aspirations of the Third World countries have deepened against the backdrop of the geo-politics of the Cold War, so the political and military dimensions of neo-colonialism have become more visible, sometimes obscuring the economic goals they are supposed to serve, as in the Vietnam War.

See IMPERIALISM.

AH

**neo-evolutionism.** A modification of EVOLUTIONISM which was prevalent in the USA in the middle of this century. Where earlier models conceived of human social evolution as a unilinear progression from 'primitive' to 'modern' forms, neo-evolutionary theory transcends unilinearity and the simple primitive modern dichotomy.

It distinguishes the general evolutionary process from the evolution of specific societies. The former is an overall, discontinuous, accumulation of the breakthroughs (e.g. written language, administrative bureaucracy, money-markets, formal legal systems etc.) achieved in the evolution of specific societies. Because breakthroughs may be transmitted by cultural diffusion from societies at a higher evolutionary level to lower ones, they permit the latter to 'skip stages'. This has had much influence on MODERNIZATION theories. PARSONS, in *Societies* (1966) and *The System of Modern Societies* (1971) produced the most elaborate and logically consistent version. He defines five stages in general social evolution, each stage being a characteristic combination of a level of social differentiation and a method of social integration. The modern stage, reached by the capitalist societies of Western Europe, the USA and Japan, as well as the socialist societies of the USSR and Eastern Europe, is the last station in the evolutionary voyage. No new stage of human social evolution is envisaged, only a geographical spreading of the modern society over the whole world until it is one 'modern' WORLD-SYSTEM.

While older evolutionary beliefs naively identified human social evolution with the Progress of Mankind (a notion patently shaken by the brutalizing events of two World Wars), neo-evolutionary theory tries a more objective, value-free definition of evolution. It avoids the 'moral issue' of progress altogether by defining the goal of social evolution to be the enhancement of 'general adaptive capacity of society' or of 'all round capability of Culture' (M. Sahlins and E. Service, *Evolution and Culture*, 1960). In such a definition it is possible to disassociate progress of society from a moralistic conception of human progress. Greater adaptive capacity of society is objectively assessed in terms of three interdependent criteria: (1) the embodiment of more varied and more effective means of exploiting the energy resources of a greater variety of environments; (2) relative autonomy of the society from conditioning environmental forces; (3) the ability to dominate and replace less advanced types.

AH

**neo-Kantianism.** Used to describe a number of philosophical movements in late 19th- and early 20th-century Germany which aimed to revive and continue the work of KANT. The banch of neo-Kantianism most relevant to the social sciences is the 'southwestern', 'Heidelberg' or 'Baden' school dominated by Wilhelm Windelband (1848-1915) and Heinrich Rickert (1863-1936). The ideas of this 'school' were a powerful influence on SIMMEL and WEBER.

Rickert upheld a radically anti-NATURAL-IST conception of the historical or 'cultural' sciences, which he distinguished from the 'natural sciences' (including economics and sociology). Starting from the principle that reality is too complex to be known other than by means of simplifying assumptions, he argued that there were basically two possible sorts of selective principle: a 'generalizing' approach concerned with regularities and characteristic of natural science, and an individualizing approach interested in the specific character of individual historical phenomena from the standpoint of a set of values. Weber took over from Rickert the emphasis on selection and the doctrine of value-reference, but combined it with a view of sociology as a generalizing science.

The term neo-Kantian is now sometimes used of later writers who are thought to be committed to the same principles as one or more of the neo-Kantian movements.

See A. Arato, 'The Neo-Idealist Defense of Intersubjectivity', *Telos* 1974; G. Rose, *Hegel Contra Sociology* (1981).

WO

**neo-Tylorianism.** A school of thought in anthropology which follows Sir Edward Tylor (1832-1917) in viewing statements about supernatural beings in pre-literate societies (and elsewhere) as explanatory statements, attempts to account for occurrences in the world. This view fell out of favour under the impact of structural-FUNC-TIONALISTS, who argued that since what was being asserted was so clearly false, there must be some other reason why people held beliefs so patently untrue and engaged in practices so evidently inefficacious. They therefore looked for some underlying explanation, such as that the beliefs affirmed provided a focus for the integration of the community around a set of common values, and the practices a way of reaffirming solidarity and identity as members of the community (see FUNCTIONAL THEORIES OF RELIGION). Neo-Tylorians, however, assert that no special explanation is required for believing things that turn out to be false: the history of science is a catalogue of false beliefs.

Both religious and scientific beliefs seek to describe and explain aspects of the world, although they employ different idioms to do so, and scientific beliefs are viewed as tentative knowledge which should be subjected to test while religious beliefs are regarded as absolute knowledge, accepted on faith and routinely confirmed for the believer. The Neo-Tylorian, or intellec-tualist, school thus argues that although scientific beliefs are different from religious beliefs in content (for example, they refer to impersonal entities as the underlying sources of events) and in the critical scrutiny to which they are subjected, they have the common aim of explaining the world. This is not to say that religious beliefs only have this purpose, but that it is a major one.

See also RELIGION.

RW

**neuroses.** See MENTAL ILLNESS.

**neuroticism.** Clinically refers to the condition of having a neurosis (see MENTAL ILLNESS). Neuroses are of various types, but are all characterized by excessive anxiety, lack of gross distortion of reality of PERSON-ALITY, and awareness of the condition by the subject. These characteristics, following R.B. Cattell, the American personality theorist, apply in varying degrees to all people. Neuroticism is generally used in sociology and personality theory to express the degree to which an individual partakes of these TRAITS.

For the purpose of measurement, neuroticism is broken down into constituents such as sensitivity, depressiveness, over-seriousness, submissiveness. A questionnaire is constructed from a set of SCALE items assembled to reflect these components, as, for instance, in the NSQ (Neuroticism Scale Questionnaire) and the IPAT Neurotic Personality Factor Test. Neuroticism has also been identified as a principal factor in FACTOR ANALYSIS of the results of multi-dimensional personality questionnaires.

JL

**neutralization.** In the sociology of DEVI-ANCE, this term is applied to the neutralizing of guilt and the social control emanating from guilt. Following an earlier tradition which concentrated on VOCABULARIES OF MOTIVE, Sykes and Matza ('Techniques of Neutralization', *American Sociological Review* 1957) took MOTIVATION to be a series of linguistic constructions. DELIN-QUENCY is willed behaviour which becomes possible when a conventional guilt is coun-tered by conventional techniques of extenu-ation or exculpation. The major instances of such a neutralizing vocabluary are the denial of responsibility, the denial of the victim, the condemnation of the condemners, the appeal to higher loyalties and the denial of injury.

PR

**new religions.** The religious movements that have emerged or grown to prominence in the period since World War II. Of particular importance have been the new religions which emerged in Japan after its defeat and transformation under American occupation, and the new religions which have appeared in the advanced industrial west, such as Scientology, the Krishna Consciousness Movement, the Jesus People, Divine Light Mission, the Unification Church, and the like. Although they differ greatly in belief-system, practice and style, these movements can be comprehended most readily by viewing them in terms of two analytically distinct types, world-rejecting and world-affirming.

The world-rejecting movement, though deviant in comparison to most churches and denominations, is clearly religious in character. It has a traditional conception of God as an entity distinct from humanity and imposing a clear set of moral demands upon it. It views humanity as having departed from God, rejecting religion and embracing secularism and materialism. The world-rejecting movement condemns modern urban-industrial society — its individualism, its obsession with consumption, its treatment of persons as means rather than ends — and aspires to return to a more rural, traditional way of life based on service rather than self-interest. It awaits an imminent transforma-tion of the world, the arrival of a new, simpler, more loving, humane and spiritual order of things. In the meantime, the faithful separate themselves from the world, anticipating utopia in the communal life wherein they remain uncontaminated. They break with friends and family, education and career, routinizing contact with outsiders and focusing upon the life of the community. Life within displays a high level of affectivity. Having been mandated by God through the medium of a prophet or messiah, they tend to be highly authori-tarian, imposing an extensive range of constraints and demands upon members.

The world-affirming movement presents a contrast. It exhibits few characteristics traditionally associated with RELIGION. God is referred to not as a personal deity imposing his will on man and history, but as a diffuse, amorphous and immanent force in the universe, present most particularly within oneself. The self may be the only God of which the movement takes notice. It adopts a pragmatic view of the religious label, donning it when this may produce advant-ages from the state, dropping it in the interest of marketing strategy. Modern industrial society is viewed as largely acceptable. Members seek not a new world but improved access to the valued goals of this world. The source of suffering, of disability, of un-happiness, lies within oneself rather than in the social order. The world-affirming movement is individual rather than com-munal. It offers a service or technique which can be marketed like any other commodity. Its adherents are customers rather than full-time members; they participate in their leisure time and make few changes in other routines or relationships in their lives.

The rationalization of industrial society has produced the attenuation of COMMUN-ITY; the fragmentation of life between public and private domains; an increasing stress on ACHIEVEMENT rather than ascription as the basis for status allocation and a sense of worth; and the isolation of individuals, unable to locate outside the family persons with whom they may interact in more than a role-oriented fashion. The new religious movements have developed in response to, and as attempts to grapple with, the consequences of rationalization. But the specific appeal of the two types rests on different aspects of this phenomenon.

The world-rejecting movement appeals mainly to those who feel themselves to be at the margins of society. The new religions which developed in the West in the middle and late 1960s appealed almost exclusively to the young, at first particularly to counter-cultural 'drop-outs'. The demographic fact of a post war 'baby boom', affluence and the expansion of higher education encouraged the emergence of youth culture, an idealistic belief in the attainability of perfection, and the postponement of adult constraints and responsibilities. Political protest in connection with the civil rights of black Americans, the Vietnam War, and university reform were attempts to change the prevailing social order. The hippie lifestyle, drugs and the secular commune movement attempted to create viable social and cultural alternatives. When protest was repressed, drugs produced physical and psychological disintegration and the hippie communes slid into anarchy, some turned to religion as the only remaining resource for the realization of their idealistic vision. The counter-cultural utopia of a sharing, caring society seemed to have been realized in the communalism of the Children of God, the Unification Church etc. When all else had failed only a messiah, or God acting through his prophet or guru, could transform the world.

Movements such as Scientology, est, the human potential movement and Transcendental Meditation may have gathered recruits from the collapse of the counter-culture, but these world-affirming movements had their sources in more durable features of advanced capitalist societies. Their appeal lay in the persistence of inequalities of power, status, self-confidence, personal attractiveness, and access to numerous rewards both tangible and symbolic. They offered to provide adherents with means for securing these rewards, for attaining their aspirations, for

achieving the standards of success everywhere touted as available to all yet nonetheless elusive. Alternatively they offered those of their adherents who had achieved the benefits of advanced capitalist society recipes for reconciling themselves to the discovery that life still seemed bleak and lacking.

The world-affirming movement draws upon a constituency centrally located in urban-industrial society and firmly committed to it. Through physical and mental exercises, encounter sessions, creative fantasy and self revelation the individual is released from childhood inhibitions and habits of conventional ritual, given relief from strains or tension, or provided with enhanced self-confidence. By casting off constraints and restrictions on his physical, mental and spiritual functioning, the individual will discover self.

Between the two poles lies a middle ground of movements such as the Divine Light Mission or the followers of Meher Baba. They combine elements of both types. They adopt a communal life-style while also encouraging followers to take 'respectable' jobs or to complete their education. While their religious beliefs are culturally deviant, they usually discourage premarital sex and drug use. Such movements occupied a strategic position between conventional culture and counter-culture in the late 1960s and early 1970s, providing a kind of 'halfway house' through which former drop-outs and radicals could become reintegrated in the prevailing social order. Many Jesus People groups provided a way station back from drugs and the hippie life to the world of their parents. These groups possessed sufficient continuity with the counter-culture to be attractive to those for whom secular social experiments had proven unsuccessful, but their norms and values encouraged behaviour less stigmatized and less evocative of hostility from parents and dominant institutions.

In the changed economic and social climate of the late 1970s and early 1980s the world-rejecting movements experienced sharp contraction. Their former constituency disappeared in the face of economic recession. Some have begun to accommodate to the prevailing social order, rejecting it less fiercely. World-affirming movements, having less historically specific sources, may weather the recession more easily, although as luxury goods they too may be affected in time by the contraction in surplus income available for disposal on non-essentials.

See R. Wallis, *The Elementary Forms of the New Religious Life* to be published (1984).

RW

**Niebuhr, H. Richard** (1894-1962). American theologian. Born in Wright City, Missouri, the son of a German immigrant, Niebuhr followed his father and elder brother Reinhold into the ministry of the German Evangelical Church. Educated at Elmhurst College and Eden Theological Seminary (1908-15), he worked for three years as a Pastor in St Louis while studying for a Masters degree in History at Washington University, and then spent three years teaching at Eden. He attended Yale Divinity School 1922-4 and took a BD and PhD. After six years of teaching at Elmhurst and Eden, he moved to Yale in 1931 and taught there for 31 years, ending his career as Sterling Professor of Theology and Christian Ethics.

Niebuhr's doctoral thesis had been on TROELTSCH's philosophy of religion, and he made many contributions to modern Christian thought, particularly by combining liberal political views with the conservative theology of Barth's 'neo-orthodoxy'. Niebuhr is best known to sociologists for his *Social Sources of Denominationalism* (1929) in which he related divisions within Protestantism to differences of a socio-historical kind (e.g. CLASS, STATUS, RACE and NATIONALITY) rather than to differences of a doctrinal kind. In his work he developed the ideas of Troeltsch and WEBER on the CHURCH and SECT dichotomy in a way appropriate to the nature and development of religious collectivities in the USA. He sought to explain the process of accommodation and loss of enthusiasm as a sect becomes a DENOMINATION in terms of the different degrees and kinds of commitment held by different sorts of members (see DENOMINATIONALIZATION).

RW

**Nietzsche, Friedrich** (1844-1900). German philosopher. Professor of Philology in Basle from 1869 until 1879, when ill-health forced him to resign. The rest of his life was spent in France, Italy and Switzerland. Main works: *The Birth of Tragedy* (1872), *The Gay Science* (1882), *Thus Spoke Zarathustra* (1883-92), *Beyond Good and Evil* (1886), *The Genealogy of Morals* (1887) and *The Antichrist* (1895). His notebooks were posthumously published as *The Will to Power* (1901).

Nietzsche criticized academic philosophy and history as well as religion and morality in the name of an ideal of aristocratic individualism and self-reliance expressed in his concept of the superman (*Ubermensch*). Christian morality made people soft, as did an excessive respect for rationality and truth. Nietzsche's philosophy has analogies with PRAGMATISM and EXISTENTIALISM, and he was a powerful influence on HEIDEGGER. Much contemporary French philosophy is concerned with a critique of philisophy drawn partly from Nietzsche and Heidegger. His cultural criticism and his critique of EPISTEMOLOGY influenced the Frankfurt School (see CRITICAL THEORY), but he was also selectively appropriated by Nazism. His contemporary influence was considerable, and his emphasis on individual choice and decision is a central theme in WEBER's work.

WO

**nobility.** A class inheriting its titles and privileges, usually deriving its wealth from land, in European feudal and post-feudal society (which stretched from the decline of FEUDALISM in the 14th and 15th centuries until the rise of industrialism in the 18th and 19th centuries). The nobility was divided into a number of ranks, with dukes at the top; at the lower end, the nobility shaded into the gentry. Remnants of the nobility have persisted as the upper class in some advanced industrial societies. ARISTOCRACY is not a strict synonym for nobility, but a reference to the nobility as a ruling class.

CGAB

**non-parametric.** See MEASUREMENT.

**non-response.** See SAMPLING.

**norm.** Groups of people interacting over a period are likely to evolve common rules governing their behaviour, often described as norms. A famous example is in the Hawthorne 'Bank-wiring Group' (see HAWTHORNE STUDIES) described in F.J. Roethlisberger and W.J. Dickson, *Management and the Worker* (1939), where norms limiting the rate of work and the maximum output developed among the group workers. A norm is more than an average; it is an ideal standard of behaviour to which people conform to a greater or lesser extent. There are various possible reasons for conformity. PARSONS and other FUNCTIONALIST/CONSENSUS writers emphasized that people come to feel moral commitment to the norms which define the rights and obligations of various ROLES within their social group. But this understates the influence of fear of the consequences of not conforming, especially when some people or some roles are more powerful than others. A norm is not found within the PERSONALITY of an individual, but can only be observed as a regularity in the behaviour of two or more people together.

SJM

**normal distribution.** A symmetrical distribution with a single mode (coinciding with the mean and the median), tailing off indefinitely towards its extremities. 68 per cent of observations, on average, lie within one standard deviation of the mean, and 95 per cent within two standard deviations. The normal distribution was first discovered by the French mathematician Abraham De Moivre in 1753, and was revived by the German mathematician Carl Gauss (1777-1855) as a theory of the distribution of errors of observation. It is the most widely used statistical distribution in sociology.

The normal distribution is in theory the limiting form for a VARIABLE which is determined by numerous small factors, and this is the justification for its use in many sociological contexts. However, in both the natural and social worlds the normal distribution has proved to be a less useful description of empirical distributions than was at first imagined, and the paramount importance of the distribution lies in its central position in statistical theory.

Several variables may be jointly normally distributed — a multivariate normal distribution — and in this case the shape of the distribution is determined by the COEFFICIENTS OF CORRELATION between the variables. In sociology, the assumption of multivariate normal distribution underlies REGRESSION, much of CAUSAL MODELLING, and many tests of SIGNIFICANCE, although it is seldom possible to test this assumption directly.

JL

**nuptiality.** The rates of MARRIAGE in a population are important quantities in DEMOGRAPHY because of their relation to FERTILITY and are also important in sociology because of the nature of marriage as a fundamental social relation and the basis of family structure. Gross rates measure the number ever married at a certain age as a proportion of those aged 16; net rates attenuate these according to mortality. In most Western countries rates of marriage have been stable for the last century despite a decline in age at first marriage, but tend to be lower than those outside Western countries. Where statistics are available they show a rise in DIVORCE rates, but a fall in the proportion of long-term widows and widowers.

Variations in the social definition of marriage are widespread and can make statistics difficult to obtain. Institutionalized marriages with formal registration are relatively easy to count, but even within such a system purely religious or customary procedures may remain. In the Caribbean and Latin America, a woman with her children may form a series of relationships with men that in all respects except formal registration resembles marriage. The occurrence in Islamic societies of polygyny, and in some societies of polyandry, further complicates quantification.

The SEX RATIO forms a basic constraint on nuptiality, and the further it departs from 1, the lower the proportion who can marry. Restrictions on marriage partners due to KINSHIP, CASTE, CLASS, religion or locality exacerbate this effect, while increases in geographical and SOCIAL MOBILITY tend to offset it. War losses and emigration initially decrease the numbers of young men and produce more unmarried women than men;

immigration produces the opposite effect. In Ireland, extensive emigration over a sustained period has contributed to low marriage rates for both men and women, and to a high age at marriage.

In Islamic societies, the demographic effect of polygyny is severely limited by the supply of women and by a typical pattern where an extra wife is only added late on in the first marriage. The proportion of women never married is very low in polygynous systems, and first marriages for women tend to be at a very young age. The pre-industrial Western European pattern, by contrast, seems to have involved relatively late marriage, and commonly a stage of domestic or other service in a non-kin household prior to marriage. Schofield and Wrigley have recently suggested that a lowering of the age of marriage in 18th-century England was the principal factor in the modern rise of population (see DEMOGRAPHIC TRANSITION).

JL

# O

**objective, objectivism.** 'Objectivity' is usually defined negatively as the relative freedom from subjective biases which might distort the accuracy of a report. If, however, objective knowledge is specified more positively as 'presupposition-less' or as a direct 'reproduction' of reality, this ideal involves an EMPIRICIST conception of the knowledge-process. The term objectivism is sometimes applied (especially by HUSSERL and HABERMAS) to the view that science furnishes the only possible description of reality; such a view neglects the fact that scientists, like non-scientific observers, must construct their descriptions and that the 'same' reality can be known in a variety of ways. WEBER had earlier expressed a similar criticism of the idea of a presupposition-free description of reality. He held that social reality can only be described from a variety of essentially arbitrary value-standpoints, but that this does not make scientific objectivity impossible. Objectivism in ethics is the view that what is good or bad is so independently of our own or anyone else's subjective opinions.

Sociologists of knowledge suggest that a person's social origins are relevant to an evaluation of his or her thought, but this claim too is contested. Various relatively recent solutions to problems of objectivity in sociology have been proposed, by MANN-HEIM, G. Myrdal, POPPER and E. Nagel among others. One general aim of sociological methodology is to produce REPRE-SENTATIVE, RELIABLE and VALID empirical knowledge which has the status of objective knowledge.

See M. Weber, *The Methodology of the Social Sciences* (1949); E. Husserl, *The Crisis of the European Sciences and Transcendental Phenomenology* (1936).

WO, MB

**obsession.** See MENTAL ILLNESS.

**occupational prestige.** Studies of SOCIAL MOBILITY and STATUS COMPOSITION involve estimates of the relative standing of different occupations. Survey researchers have tried to order these relative standings into occupational prestige hierarchies by asking respondents to rank or classify a selection of occupations. However, (1) it is not always clear whether respondents have indicated how they believe selected occupations are ranked or how they believe they should be; (2) the aggregation of responses to generate a single hierarchy can conceal variations, especially in the middle of the hierarchy, according to the occupational group of the respondent; and (3) the conceptualization of occupational prestige is often unclear. Prestige ought to refer to STATUS (social honour, respect of the community etc) as distinct from CLASS or POWER. In practice it usually refers to a composite of all the factors that make some jobs better than others, including income, perquisites, education required, location in structures of authority etc, as well as status. It is therefore better to speak of the social grading of occupations unless the intention is to isolate the components of prestige or

268

status from all other factors involved.

See CENSUS CLASS; CLASS (AS CATEGORY AND SCALE).

CGAB

**Oedipus complex.** See PSYCHOANALYSIS.

**official statistics.** Statistical data compiled by official, i.e. governmental sources, and available to the public. There are four main types: (1) registration data on births, marriages and deaths; (2) data on a variety of social topics from the CENSUS, published in aggregate form; (3) aggregate data derived from administrative records and compiled as a statistical by-product of administrative functions; (4) aggregate and individualized data derived from government social surveys, both continuous surveys (like the UK General Household Survey and Family Expenditure Survey) and specific surveys on particular subjects.

Most such data is published in special reports and synthesized in collections such as *Social Trends*. In Britain, individualized data from government (and other) social surveys, together with census small area statistics, are held in the Social Science Research Council's Survey Archive at the University of Essex.

Official statistics have notable virtues and defects for sociological research. In terms of coverage and REPRESENTATIVENESS they are unrivalled. Census and registration data provide complete coverage of the population, while government sample surveys have larger sample sizes than comparable academic surveys. Their defects lie in being collected in terms of official, not sociological, categories, which may or may not be useful for sociological research. The sociologist has no control over how the data was gathered. As Morgenstern has shown, various kinds of ERROR may have crept into the data. Particularly well-known problems of RELIABILITY and VALIDITY arise in the study of suicide and social DEVIANCE. Official data on such subjects are more a reflection of what the authorities define as deviance than of its actual occurrence. For example, the 'dark figure' of crime represents the gap between crimes reported to the police and crimes actually occurring (as

reported in research surveys of the general public).

Criticism of official statistics tended to be exaggerated in the 1970s, and their usefulness was consequently underestimated.

See CENSUS CLASS; DEMOGRAPHY; HISTORICAL DEMOGRAPHY.

See C. Hakim, *Secondary Analysis in Social Research* (1982); O. Morgenstern, *On the Accuracy of Economic Observations* (1963).

MB

**oligopoly.** See MARKET STRUCTURE.

**OLS estimators.** See REGRESSION.

**ontology.** A branch of METAPHYSICS concerned with the nature of existence, with what kinds of thing may be said to exist and in what ways. Largely rejected by EMPIRICIST and KANTIAN philosophy in favour of EPISTEMOLOGY, it has continued to be an important theme of some continental philosophy, notably that of HEIDEGGER. REALIST philosophies of science have also re-established the centrality of ontological questions concerning the entities presupposed by scientific theories. Such questions may be identified in the social sciences in discussions of the nature of social reality. DURKHEIM'S conception of social facts, for example, is radically opposed to WEBER'S insistence that structural concepts must be reducible to the actions of individuals. Some theories portray social reality as made up of relatively fixed structures, systems, roles and institutions, while others see it as something much flimsier, sustained by ongoing processes of interpretation and negotiation. Many sociologists, however, still uphold the view, developed within logical POSITIVISM, that the choice of an ontological framework is basically nothing more than a choice of language, and that what counts is the result of an investigation.

See R. Bhaskar, *The Possibility of Naturalism* (1979).

WO

**operationalize.** The process by which hypotheses and concepts are translated into a form in which RELIABLE and VALID empirical observations may be made in terms of them.

The means of bridging the gap between concepts and INDICATORS, involves devising satisfactory empirical classifications by which to attempt to measure more abstract theoretical entities. Thus, for example, social class is operationalized by gathering data on occupation, and using these data as a basis for social class classification (see CLASS AS CATEGORY AND SCALE). The original connotations of the term related to direct physical measurement, and the term is still most commonly used in quantitative research. Critics such as Blumer argue that it portrays too mechanical and rigid a view of research and too fixed a view of sociological concepts.

MB

**opportunity cost.** See COSTS.

**oral history.** See HISTORICAL METHODS.

**organization.** Sometimes referred to as 'formal' or 'complex organizations', these are deliberately created devices for co-ordinating human effort, marshalling solidarity or focussing sentiment, and are manifested in a great variety of forms — as business corporations, government agencies, armies, churches, trade unions, political parties, schools, hospitals, charitable bodies, clubs etc. Four main features distinguish such entities from primary social groupings such as the family, the friendship clique, or the informal group of work-mates: (1) they were consciously established to marshall social power; (2) they possess relatively explicit aims or goals; (3) they are composed of functional positions and roles that are distinct from the individuals occupying them; (4) explicit rules govern the relations between roles.

Within sociology, research and theory on organizations has frequently become enmeshed with that on BUREAUCRACY, often stultifyingly. This becomes evident in the long-standing problem of classifying organizations. Some authors give the impression that there can be only two types of organization: bureaucracies and 'non-bureaucracies'. This approach leaves a vast number of different organizations in the 'non-bureaucracy' class, it being a residual category and not part of a genuine dichot-

omy. However, an occasional virtue of such approaches is that they retain an element of the Weberian effort to characterize global tendencies in industrialized societies, by assessing the degree to which roles and norms governed by organizational rules have penetrated — or even permeated — the world as experienced by social actors. An extension of such analyses are those in which individual psychological or moral effects of alleged 'bureaucratization' are traced in (commonly pessimistic) essays on the nature of 'organization man'.

Investigators and theorists dispensing with the (often treacherous) notion of bureaucracy have, however, often dispensed also with true sociological analysis. Albeit unwittingly, many 'analytical' studies of organizations adopt a prescriptive approach: their typologies of organizations may derive from an effort to establish which organizational structures and practices enhance 'effectiveness' or 'efficiency'. Such questions should interest sociological analysts: definitions of 'effectiveness' held in society are sociological data, as are such matters as who holds what sort of definition of 'effectiveness', and how much power or authority groups have to impose these criteria upon other organizational participants holding conflicting views. But once a sociologist concentrates upon disclosing the organizational conditions of effective operation he/she is likely to view organizational goals as aims held by all participants, when in fact they are often merely those held or claimed by its controllers.

Care should therefore be taken in evaluating notions like that of goal displacement, that is, the process whereby the formally stated goal of an organization becomes, in practice, subordinate to some other aim, or at least appears to. A fine line divides the use of such notions, on the one hand, merely as a reflection of the view of things held by organizational controllers, and, on the other, as the starting point for a fruitful exploration of organizational dynamics.

Because some analysts and investigators have been deeply involved in organizational consultancy (almost invariably on behalf of organizational controllers), much of the literature on organizations must be assessed and interpreted with care. Studies establishing empirical associations between factors such as technology (in particular) and certain organizational properties of enterprises co-exist with more enigmatic material claiming to offer grounded theories of an ambitious kind about the interdependence of organizations and their 'environment'. Likewise, elaborate comparative empirical data, after sophisticated statistical treatment, have shown that organizational structure varies systematically over large samples of organizations. The principles governing this variability have yet to be established convincingly, and it may be that the growing practice of replication and comparison will be helpful, especially when undertaken at the international level.

But in contemporary sociology no single approach to organizations commands general confidence. Theorists lacking (or misusing) empirical material, and empiricists with no taste or gift for theory, talk past each other. A similar situation exists in the applied field of 'Organizational Behaviour'.

See also BUREAUCRACY; SOCIO-TECHNICAL SYSTEM.

See S. Clegg and D. Dunkerley, *Organisation, Class and Control* (1980).

MR

**organizational choice.** See SOCIO-TECHNICAL THEORY; TECHNOLOGY.

**oriental despotism.** Term popularized by the sinologist K. WITTFOGEL in a book of that title, to describe the political structures of hydraulic societies, that is, societies whose environment and climate necessitate the management of waterworks through a state-controlled BUREAUCRACY. These conditions prevail over about three-fifths of the earth's surface, covering most of the land outside Europe and North America. Because of the need to organize irrigation and drainage systems to ensure an adequate supply of food, oriental rulers have had opportunity to set up despotic regimes, and these regimes characterize oriental societies. This thesis has been attacked both empirically and theoretically. Empirically, writers such as W. Eberhard (*Conquerors and Rulers*) and E. Leach (in *Past and Present* 1959) have

shown that Wittfogel's account of the hydraulic and social systems of China and Ceylon, respectively, are seriously deficient. Theoretically, writers such as S. EISENSTADT (*Journal of Asian Studies* 1957) demonstrate that Wittfogel's use of concepts is cavalier, and that his continual multiplication of sub-types of hydraulic society to encompass more and more cases leads to incoherence. Further, Wittfogel's thesis that the PEASANTRY in such societies was an isolated, atomized mass and that there were no important countervailing powers to stand against the despots, are historically dubious and sociologically naive.

The continuing interest in the concept and in Wittfogel's work can be explained partly by its relationship to the ASIATIC MODE OF PRODUCTION, and partly by the view, still widespread in the West and perhaps also in the East, that it is not possible to explain the histories of occidental and oriental societies with the same theories and concepts. This is a continuing and important problem for a comparative sociology intent on establishing universal general laws (see COMPARATIVE METHOD).

LS

**ORT** [Object-Relations Technique]. A PROJECTIVE TEST developed at the Tavistock Clinic in London in the late 1950s, involving interpretation by the subject of a set of standard picture-cards portraying ambiguous situations involving varying numbers of people. The pictures are less well-defined than those in the Thematic Apperception Test (see TAT) but less abstract than the inkblots of the RORSCHACH TEST.

JL

**Ossowski, Stanislav** (1897-1963). Polish sociologist, Professor at Warsaw University 1933-9 and married to the sociologist and student of ethics, Maria Ossowska. He published important works on aesthetics, RACE and CULTURE, and METHODOLOGY, and was well-known for his socialist and humanist values. During World War II he taught underground and continued his researches on Marxism, democracy and the concept of the motherland. After 1945 he was a key figure in the reconstruction of

Polish sociology first at Lódź and then at Warsaw. When in 1952 the teaching of sociology was banned, Ossowski resisted Stalinists, as he had the Nazis, by teaching clandestinely and continuing his researches. The chief product is *Class Structure in the Social Consciousness* (1957, Eng edn. 1963). When the teaching of sociology resumed in 1956 with the Gomulka era, Ossowski held the Chair of Sociology at Warsaw University until his death.

Two features of Ossowski's work deserve comment. (1) His contribution to the distinctive character of Polish sociology. In the late 1950s the insufficiencies of Marxism-Leninism were evident enough for (empirical) sociology to be introduced in most of state socialist Europe. In Poland alone this amounted more to the recovery of a long tradition of sociological study. Thus sociologists whose views had been formed in pre-socialist Poland were able to influence the development of sociology after 1956 and secure for it a sophistication and openness to western sociology unique in Eastern Europe. Ossowski was the single most eminent figure, although Szczepański also subsequently became internationally known.

(2) The analysis of CLASS. Ossowski argued that MARX used several different conceptions of class. In his revolutionary writings, a dichotomous division appears between oppressors and oppressed — in CAPITALISM, between capital and labour. But in his theoretical analyses, two different trichotomous (three-way) distinctions are made: (a) the FUNCTIONAL scheme, inherited from bourgeois political economy, according to which wage-labourers, capitalists and landowners, whose incomes derive from wages, profit and ground rent respectively, constitute the three main classes of modern capitalist society. This scheme hinges upon the relations of people to things, makes no provision for intermediate classes and, according to Ossowski, defines each class in terms of its 'relation to the various means of production'. (b) The other trichotomous scheme provides for intermediate classes by applying simultaneously three different dichotomous criteria. The first criterion (stated a little differently from Ossowski) divides society into the propertied, who own the means of production, and the property-less, who do not. The second divides those who do not work or, to be more precise than Ossowski, those who do not engage in productive work, from those who do; and the third, connected to the second, distinguishes those who exploit by buying the labour power of others without paying for the surplus value they create, from those who have only labour power to sell. This focusses upon the relations of people to other people and upon the various relations which the different classes have to the means of production. It also provides for intermediate classes, those who own instruments of production, buy the labour power of others, and engage in productive work themselves (such as craftsmen with small workshops) and those who own the means of production and work themselves but who do not buy the labour of others (such as PEASANT proprietors who rely on unpaid family labour).

Ossowski emphasized complications within Marx, the problem of intermediate classes, and continuities between Marx's trichotomous schemes and what he called simple and synthetic gradational theories of stratification (which order classes in terms of the distribution of one or more values, such as income and education). Thus, along with Hochfeld and others, he opened up a space for the analysis of structured social inequality in a STATE SOCIALIST society, supplying some of the terms with which to conceptualize 'the non-egalitarian classlessness' proclaimed by STALIN. The study of stratification in Poland has been extended by Wesolowski and his fellow researchers, whose formulation of the theory of the decomposition of status attributes (see STATUS COMPOSITION) falls within Ossowski's conception of gradational theories of stratification. See also CLASS (particularly *Neo-Marxist theories*).

CGAB

# P

**palimony.** See DIVORCE

**paradigm.** An example or pattern, for example of a grammatical form. The term was used by Thomas Kuhn (1922- ) in the *The Structure of Scientific Revolutions* (1962) to describe 'universally recognized scientific achievements that for a time provide model problems and solutions to a community of practitioners'. Though Kuhn uses the word in a variety of senses, his basic concern is to emphasize the social and cognitive integration of communities of scientists. Far from being heroic individualists, constantly trying to falsify established theories, scientists are conservative and conformist. Scientific development is usally a matter of what Kuhn calls 'normal science', operating within the assumptions set by a paradigm. Only when an established theory generates too many anomalies is it likely that an alternative (if one is available) will replace it in a sharp break called a 'scientific revolution'. Kuhn stresses the discontinuity between one period of normal science and another; successive theories are (or at least may be) 'incommensurable'. Much discussion has centred on whether, as Kuhn believes, his account is compatible with the idea of scientific progress.

Kuhn's own work has been something of a paradigm for the history and sociology of science. His view of the social sciences, however, is that they are in a 'pre-paradigm' state in which a variety of fundamental orientations are still in competition with one another. Others have used the term paradigm to characterize the prominence of FUNCTIONALISM in Anglo-American sociology in the 1950s and early 1960s or of Marxism in Soviet and Eastern European sociology.

See also I. Lakatos and A. Musgrave (eds.), *Criticism and the Growth of Knowledge* (1970); B. Barnes, *T.S. Kuhn and the Social Sciences* (1982).

WO

**Parametric Statistics.** See MEASUREMENT.

**Pareto, Vilfredo** (1848-1923). Italian economist and sociologist. Pareto was born in Paris: his mother was French and his father an Italian political exile. Educated in Italy, he subsequently worked as an engineer and railway company director for twenty years. Increasing involvement in the Italian Free Trade controversy at the end of the 1880s brought him into contact with the economist Maffeo Pantaleoni. Receiving an inheritance, he left business to devote himself fulltime to the study of the new mathematical economics of Walras. In 1893 he succeeded Walras as Professor of Political Economy at Lausanne. From 1900 he lived as a recluse in Switzerland, though shortly before his death he was appointed a member of the Italian Senate by Mussolini.

Known equally for his work as an economist and as a sociologist, Pareto saw both disciplines as complementary parts of a unified social science constructed on similar methodological principles to the natural sciences as a system of inductively derived uniformities. His main contribution to economics was the theory of equilibrium and the idea of the maximum efficiency of an economy as a condition where it is impossible to improve any one individual's utility without damaging another's (Pareto optimality or EFFICIENCY). The distinctive theories of economics which, he believed, assumed a standard of means-end rationality among economic agents required complementing by a recognition of the pervasiveness of the non-rational in social behaviour (theory of non-logical action), by an understanding of politics and power (theory of elites), and by an elucidation of the interdependence of different social elements (concept of the social system). All this formed the province of a general sociology, such as he developed in his *Trattato di sociologia generale* (1916, translated as *The Mind and Society*).

According to Pareto a large part of human behaviour is non-rational. It is the task of the social scientist to penetrate the variety of theories (or 'derivations') which people use to rationalize their behaviour, so as to identify the more fundamental sentiments or states of mind which underlie them. An analysis of these will reveal certain recurrent tendencies (or 'residues'). The basic components of society — knowledge, interests, residues and derivations — are all manifestations of sentiments. Pareto does not always distinguish clearly between 'residues' and 'sentiments'. 'Sentiments' refer generally to mental processes other than logical reasoning and frequently to instincts or innate human tendencies. The study of sentiments is the province of psychology. 'Residues', intervening between sentiments and acts or expressions, are analytic sociological concepts which refer to diverse explanations of the constant elements occurring in social phenomena. 'Derivations' refer to diverse explanations of the constant elements which legitimize non-rational activity by portraying it as rational (there is a contradiction between man's desire to act logically and the non-logical character of most actions). Pareto divides residues into six classes — the instinct for combinations, the persistence of aggregates, the need to manifest sentiments by external acts, residues relating to sociability, the integrity of the individual, and sexual

residues. Most social behaviour is determined by a combination of residues.

Pareto distinguishes between logical and non-logical action, dividing the latter into two categories. 'Logical action' is directed towards an objectively attainable end via the best objectively available means. 'Non-logical action' refers to actions failing to meet these criteria. The first category of non-logical action is that determined by factors independent of its subjective qualities (instincts, needs, drives of the organism). The second category includes cultural normative factors other than those forming part of the actor's logico-experimental knowledge. Residues and derivations are elements of non-logical theories. There is a close connection between residues and theories transcending experience and between derivations and pseudo-scientific theories. Science must reject METAPHYSICAL and religious thought and philosophical essentialism, defining all its concepts in terms of observable realities. Sociology should employ a logico-experimental scientific method based upon observation and logical inference. Logico-experimental knowledge cannot determine the ultimate ends of action and social science cannot provide scientific solutions to social problems.

Pareto's concept of 'interest' is derived from economics and it is associated with behaviour most closely approximating logical action. Individuals and groups are prompted by reason and instinct to seek material goods and honours. Interest implies the desire to attain a political or economic goal. Pareto examines logical and non-logical action in his theory of social utility, using the concepts 'ophelimity' and utility. 'Ophelimity' refers to economic satisfactions obtained by the individual in accord with his own hierarchy of preferences and 'utility' to satisfaction in a broader social sense. Ophelimity assumes the incomparability of individual wants. Utility permits the comparison of wants with reference to the welfare of the social system and to its distributive problems. Pareto's analysis of utility calls for a new mode of social integration transcending individual economic interest.

In criticism of MARX, Pareto argued that class struggle does not arise solely from conflicts over ownership of the means of production but is also shaped by conflicts over military force and over the STATE. Pareto rejected the idea that the super-structure is largely determined by the economic base. Society is shaped by four major, mutually interdependent variables — interest, residues, derivations and social heterogeneity. 'Social heterogeneity' implies a separation (and opposition) in all societies between the masses and the ELITE. Pareto's theory of the circulation of the elites maintains that social equilibrium is upheld by elite renewal and circulation. SOCIAL CONFLICT ensues from the accumulation of superior elements in the lower classes and inferior elements in the upper classes. ARISTO-CRACIES are fundamentally unstable and lose vigour. The governing elite is then strengthened by the loss of its degenerate members and absorption of vigorous new lower class members. The advent of a new elite to power produces a new social equilibrium. Elite composition alternates cyclically between a predominance of foxes (whose rule is based on guile) and lions (whose rule is based on brute force). Just as politics is subject to a process of elite circulation, so other areas of social life experience their own cycles of disturbance and restored equilibrium. These views were popular in the USA in the 1930s, influencing Homans and PARSONS. Pareto's concept of 'equilibrium' provided links with Parsonian structural FUNCTIONALISM. His equilibrium theory was utilized by W.J. Dickson and F.J. Roeslisberger in *Management and the Worker* (1939), the study of a Western Electric industrial plant at Hawthorne (see HAWTHORNE STUDIES). Pareto, together with MOSCA, was a precursor of modern elite theory, which is linked with liberal democratic pluralism, but he emphasized the undemocratic aspects of elites. His conception of the masses as passive instruments of an all-powerful ruling elite has affinities with C. Wright MILLS. Pareto's conviction that the overthrow of capitalism would only result in the creation of a new privileged elite claiming to represent the proletariat has had great resonance in modern analyses of stratification in the Soviet Union (see STATE SOCIALISM).

Pareto's work is a complex mixture of historical erudition, brilliant insights and unverifiable assertion. For all his insistence on scientific method, his own lack of methodological rigour has prevented him from attaining the same status in the sociological canon as his contemporaries WEBER and DURKHEIM.

See ELITISM; RATIONALITY; SOCIAL SYSTEM; WELFARE ECONOMICS.

DB, JW

**Pareto distribution.** A statistical distribution, originally proposed for high incomes, that is widely found as an empirical description of the size-distributions of social entities such as cities, firms, production plants and wealth, and remarkable for its occurrence in different times and places. The distribution of a variable $x$ is defined by the number of cases of size $x$ or larger being equal to $kx^{-a}$, where $k$ is a constant and $a$ is a positive parameter measuring how quickly the distribution decays away to zero. A number of general STOCHASTIC PROCESS models of growth have been proposed to explain the occurrence of the distribution over different subject areas.

See also INCOME; NORMAL DISTRIBUTION.

JL

**Park, Robert Ezra** (1864-1944). American sociologist who created, led and held together the CHICAGO SHOOL OF SOCIOLOGY which flourished in the 1920s and early 1930s, and turned American sociology in a markedly more empirical direction. Park grew up in Red Wing, Minnesota, where his father was a businessman. He studied with DEWEY at Michigan, worked for 11 years as a newspaper reporter, studied again with William James at Harvard and with SIMMEL at University of Berlin, and worked for nine years as secretary to the Black American leader Booker T. Washington. At the age of 50, in 1914, he accepted an invitation from W.I. THOMAS to teach in the Department of Sociology at the University of Chicago, where he remained for 20 years. His influence upon the development of sociology has been great, partly through his writings, to a greater extent through his students. He supervised a great deal of empirical research, particularly in urban sociology and race relations, pioneering the method of PARTICI-

PANT OBSERVATION. He introduced the ideas of Simmel to the USA, and (with Ernest Burgess) wrote the influential textbook *Introduction to the Science of Sociology* (1921). Park was responsible for those sections of the book that dealt with questions of race, and for the prominent place given to concepts derived from the nascent science of ecology, which was growing as the significance of DARWIN came to be appreciated. According to Park, there were four great types of interaction: competition, conflict, accommodation and assimilation. Society was created by competitive co-operation which determined the distribution of the human population territorially and vocationally through the division of labour. Thus competition was the process through which the distributive and ecological organization of society was created. The moral and political order, which rose upon this basis, was the product of the other three types of interaction. In periods of crisis, when men were making new and conscious efforts to control the condition of their common life, competition might be converted into CONFLICT. Accommodation was the process by which individuals and groups made the necessary internal adjustments to social situations; whereas accommodation was a characteristic of outward behaviour, assimilation implied a thorough-going transformation of the personality, a process of interpenetration and fusion in which persons and groups acquired the memories, sentiments, and attitudes of other persons and groups, and by sharing their experience and history were incorporated with them in a common cultural life.

Park's theories were at first important to sociology in the interwar period, when the subject was trying to free itself from both social DARWINISM and a kind of philosophy of history. His journalistic experience gave him the confidence to send his students out to observe the lives of occupational groups and special localities in the teeming city that surrounded them, and his concepts were of more use in guiding their observations than other conceptual schemes currently available. Thus Park played a formative part in the foundation of a distinctive urban sociology. Much of his writing consisted of occasional essays and prefaces, some of them developing seminal notions like those of a race relations cycle, social distance, etiquette and the marginal man.

Some of Park's formulations were defective, and his view of the types of interaction is no longer followed closely. His ecological conception of competition was derived from studies of plants, insects and non-human animals, which may struggle with one another for resources but do not struggle consciously, whereas in human society most forms of struggle are influenced by an awareness of rules of conduct. While there can be no sharp distinction between competition and conflict, it is often said, as by Kingsley Davis, that competition is a patterned form of struggle, regulated by rules behind which lie a common set of values superior to the competitive interest. Those who break the rules may be suspended or eliminated from the competition. When the struggle is no longer regulated by rules expressing common values, then it is more appropriate to speak of conflict.

Accommodation used to be paired with assimilation, in that an immigrant group might either adapt outwardly to its new environment by simply conforming to the expectations of the majority (accommodation), or might change inwardly as its members came to internalize the values of the majority (assimilation). The concept of accommodation is now little-used, while that of assimilation has come under severe attack for oversimplifying the processes of ethnic change. Prior to World War I the word was used to denote the process of becoming similar, but usage changed after the war, when public opinion in the USA became agitated about the Americanization of immigrants and the desirability of restricting the influx of those groups of migrants who did not Americanize easily. It was assumed that immigrants would change to resemble the established population and that the latter would not change. This is only one possible form of assimilation, since usually both groups change as a result of contact, though the speed and direction of change vary in different areas of social life (language, religion, costume, eating habits etc) and in different local circumstances (e.g. in relation to the size and power of the groups). But American sociologists came to equate assimilation with Americanization, and to define it as a process whereby a minority was absorbed into a majority which itself was unaffected by the process. This has been criticized as showing a bias towards the majority's outlook and contrasted with the 'melting pot' model in which all groups change to produce a new culture, and with the PLURALIST model in which groups retain a distinctive identity. Outside of the field of race relations, after his retirement in 1934, Park's influence and that of Chicago declined, with the rise of other centres such as Harvard (PARSONS) and Columbia (MERTON and LAZARSFELD). However, the influence of Chicago sociology remains strong, particularly through Park's students and colleagues Everett Hughes and Herbert Blumer, and their students such as Howard BECKER.

See F.H. Matthews, *Quest for an American Sociology: R.E. Park and the Chicago School* (1977).

MPB, MB

**Parsons, Talcott** (1902-79). American sociological theorist, leader of the FUNCTION-ALIST school which dominated American sociology from the 1940s until the 1960s. The son of a clergyman and college teacher, Parsons was an undergraduate at Amherst College and a postgraduate at LSE (where his teachers included MALINOWSKI) and at Heidelberg where, though WEBER had died some years before, the Weber Circle was still active. In 1927 Parsons accepted an appointment at Harvard, where he spent the rest of his career. His graduate students included Robert MERTON, Kingsley Davis, Wilbert Moore, Marion J. Levy Jnr., Neil Smelser, Harold GARFINKEL and many other prominent sociologists. In the last two decades of his life Parsons's work was heavily criticized, but even in disfavour it has influenced theoretical discussions.

Parsons attempted to synthesize many disparate elements into one overall conceptual framework for the social sciences. He first made his mark with *The Structure of Social Action* (1937), a study chiefly of Alfred Marshall, PARETO, DURKHEIM and WEBER. He argued that though they had started from different intellectual traditions

— British UTILITARIAN economics, French POSITIVISM and German HISTORICISM — they had converged upon 'the voluntaristic theory of action'. Contrary to the psychological theory of BEHAVIOURISM, a largely American derivative of positivism, people are not totally conditioned by social experience, but orient themselves towards social situations (see VERSTEHEN) and purposefully employ the means available to them to pursue ends (see ACTION THEORY), in accordance with values.

Parsons regarded his subsequent work as a development of this theory, though his critics detect discontinuities. In the 1940s he studied FREUD to understand more deeply the psychological processes by which social values are internalized within the PERSON-ALITY. However, Parsons's version of internalization processes is devoid of the tension and conflict of the Freudian original; as D.H. Wrong later pointed out, Parsons produced 'an oversocialized conception of man'. Indeed, in *Toward a General Theory of Action* (1951), written in collaboration with Edward Shils and a group of anthropologists and psychologists, Parsons flirted with behaviourism.

*The Social System* (1951), attempts to demonstrate that CONSENSUS on shared values is essential to social order. It also outlines his PATTERN VARIABLES and, as the title implies, the conceptualization of patterns of action as SOCIAL SYSTEMS is an attempt to blend action theory and functionalism.

In *Working Papers in the Theory of Action* (1953), written with Robert Bales and Edward Shils, the 'AGIL' scheme makes its appearance. AGIL stands for Adaptation, Goal-Attainment, Integration and Latency, and was derived from Bales's work on 'phase-processes' in small groups. 'Latency' later became known instead as 'Pattern Maintenance and Tension Management'. The four are kinds of functional problem or exigency which, according to Parsons, all social systems (later all personality and cultural systems too) must meet if they are to exist and maintain themselves. The AGIL schema raises all the problems of functionalist theory, including that of TELEOLOGY, but it was pivotal to Parsons's work from the 1950s to the end; it is associated with a decline in the intellectual level of Parsons's work.

In the 1960s, to counter the criticism that his theories were unable to account for change and development, Parsons dabbled with theories of EVOLUTIONISM. He also developed a curious conception of POWER. He made the useful distinction between distributive power (i.e. of A over B, where for A or B to gain power the other must lose) and collective power (the power of A and B co-operating together to increase both their powers). He criticized correctly MILLS for over-emphasizing distributive power, but then became exclusively pre-occupied with the other type, collective power — thus betraying his functionalist bias.

In addition to his strictly theoretical work, Parsons wrote a large number of more empirical essays, many of which are amongst his finest work (see FAMILY). Among the most influential have been those in the sociology of MEDICINE. For good examples, see MEDICAL PROFESSION and SICK ROLE.

SJM

**participant observation.** The research method of studying intensively a small social collectivity over a period of time by joining it and participating in its activities. This type of research is also known as ethnography or field research. It is typically used in the study of small communities, gangs, total institutions, informal groups and other small scale settings. The research techniques employed include informal interviewing of participants and of informants (selected individuals who provide detailed interpretations of the setting being observed); participation of the researcher in the activities being studied, and observation of key events in the life of the collectivity.

Crucial phases in observational research are the initial negotiation of RESEARCH ACCESS and initial entry into the research setting, where the researcher has to establish his or her *bona fides*. Although occasionally the researcher's role has been completely concealed to facilitate entry, the researcher's purposes are usually open and a relationship of trust with those being studied is developed. Once in the field, the researcher has to develop a role or roles which enable continued participation in and observation

of the setting. Data may be recorded in various forms, but typically it involves extensive note-taking and long written accounts. Research in this style is predominantly qualitative rather than quantitative, though it need not be so. Analysis of data poses particular problems of selectivity, abstraction and generalization.

Critics of participant observation point to its possible biases and the UNRELIABILITY of data; the lack of adequate criteria of proof; its tendency to produce purely descriptive accounts; and the frequent use of the literary style of the 'omniscient narrator', who sees into causes and motives without explaining how. Its proponents argue that it provides a depth of insight and penetration into social settings which other methods cannot match. Its usefulness is generally agreed in areas which are inherently difficult to research, and where covert and deviant behaviour predominates.

See CHICAGO SCHOOL OF SOCIOLOGY; PARK.

See R. Burgess (ed.), *Field Research: A Sourcebook and Field Manual* (1982).

MB

**pastoralist.** The pastoralist type of economy is based on the care of herds of domesticated livestock, and is often combined with agriculture. It represents a cultural system which entails a characteristic use of the environment. Nomadic or semi-nomadic pastoralists can co-exist with societies with other types of economy by exploiting a particular niche in the total ecology, as Frederick Barth described the Gujars of north Pakistan. Pastoralism is often described in ecological terms as a symbiosis between the social group and the herd from which it gains virtually all its subsistence needs.

JE

**path analysis.** See CAUSAL MODELLING.

**patriarchy.** Rule of the father. In political theory patriarchy refers to particular organizations of the FAMILY in which fathers have the power of life and death over family members; a weaker version points to the father's right to exact obedience and punish disobedience. In ancient Rome the family was patriarchal in the first sense; in 17th-century England it was patriarchal in the second. Although the father's right to chastise his wife has been abolished in Britain and America, the lack of legal intervention on behalf of the wife implies, at the very least, that the family still embodies *de facto* patriarchal rights for the husband.

Feminists have appropriated the term for their own use, and to mean different things.

Psychoanalytic feminists, in particular those who follow LACAN'S structuralist interpretation of FREUD, use 'patriarchy' to refer to the rule of the father as the structuring principle of gendered entry into the social which occurs with the resolution of the Oedipus Complex (see Mitchell, *Psychoanalysis and Feminism*, 1974). Entry into culture is entry into a symbolic order and under patriarchy the phallus is the most potent cultural SYMBOL. It represents the separation of the child from the mother and the adoption of a gendered identity. Patriarchy is thus viewed as an ideological force or construct which has material or constraining effects. In this view, patriarchal IDEOLOGY is a relatively autonomous system, but articulated with the capitalist MODE OF PRODUCTION.

Other socialist feminists argue for capitalist patriarchy. In this theory the capitalist mode of production is structured by the patriarchal sexual DIVISION OF LABOUR. Capitalist class relations and the sexual division of labour are considered to be mutually self-enforcing.

Radical and revolutionary feminists equate patriarchy with male domination, a system of social relations in which men as a CLASS have power over women as a class. These power-relations are social constructs, not biological givens. This power can be economic, the right to be serviced; sexual, as in compulsory heterosexuality, MARRIAGE, motherhood and so on; cultural, as in the devaluation of women's work or achievements; and ideological, such as the representation of women as natural, biological creatures inherently different from men.

This view has been criticized for being a-historical and for wishing to 'abolish' men. In its defence one can argue that certain elements of patriarchy such as the right of males to be serviced by females and male violence towards women are both trans-cultural and transhistorical elements of patriarchy. Patriarchy thus cannot be periodized in accordance with, for instance, Marxist modes of production, or Weberian notions of MODERNIZATION and rationalization. A counter-argument to the idea of abolishing men as the solution to patriarchy is that men and women are viewed as social classes, not two biological sexes. In Marxist theory the identification of the capitalist class does not imply the socialist abolition of individual capitalists, but of capitalist, exploitative social relations. Men constitute a class not because they share common physiological features, but because they share a common position of power vis-à-vis women.

See Z. Eisenstein (ed.), *Capitalist Patriarchy and the Case for Socialist Feminism* (1979); M. Barrett, *Women's Oppression Today* (1980); S. Friedman and E. Sarah, *On the Problem of Men* (1982).

EG

I wish to add a note of dissent to the above entry. Current usage of the term 'patriachy', as defined above, seems too broad, obscuring as much as it reveals. It describes the form of male domination in terms of the household authority of the father. This is an accurate description of gender relations in virtually all historical societies before the 19th century. There social power derived from two separated arenas which both enshrined such patriarchal relations: (1) 'private' relations within the household or family in which the male head exercised very broad and largely unchanging legal or customary powers over other members (2) 'public' relations (of economic, ideological, military and political power) normally between household heads from which women were almost totally absent. Only two partial exceptions existed to this. Rules of hereditary succession could give public power to a few individual women, as queens, castellans etc, if no eligible males existed. And the separation between public and private was weaker in the economic sphere, where the smallest unit of production — but not any broader economic power relations — was often a household in which men and women worked alongside each other (see WOMEN AND THE LABOUR MARKET). With these exceptions, however, power in society was little more than a conglomerate of household power, hence the appositeness of the label 'patriarchy'. But in the 19th and 20th centuries the form of male domination changed considerably, as three principal 'universal' (see PATTERN VARIABLES) power relations diffused right across the old public-private barrier: (1) labour was a commodity, so it mattered little to the employer whether it was male, female, or indeed juvenile; (2) CITIZENSHIP was a property of an individual, at first of males with certain property qualifications, but increasingly of all adults, whether or not household heads, and eventually regardless of gender; (3) LIBERAL-ISM and SOCIALISM, both enshrining notions of fundamental human rights and powers, regardless of household position and gender, became the dominant IDEOLOGIES of the 20th century. Thus the form of male domination has changed considerably. It has been generalized and politicized right across the public-private barrier. Important patriarchal elements remain, but they now require considerable, detailed, and ever-changing political legislation (see WOMEN AND THE WELFARE STATE) and public socialization (see WOMEN AND EDUCATION). Thus patriarchy is much less appropriate to describe the current totality of male domination. Many also argue that these changes in form have also reduced the extent of male domination, but this is more difficult to measure and is bitterly contested by some FEMINISTS. It might be added that such problems and the theoretical innovations which might result from them have very great significance for sociological theory as a whole. Having ignored sex and GENDER relations for so long, sociology can expect major developments if current debates pioneered by feminists come to fruition.

MM

**patrilineal.** See LINEAGE.

**patrimonialism.** Literally 'inheritance from ancestors' but given a specific meaning by WEBER in his theory of LEGITIMATION of AUTHORITY to refer to any type of government that originated from a royal household. In such systems the ruler treats all matters of state as his or her personal affair, officials are personal servants and subject to the arbitrary power of the ruler, and the ruler may dispose of the military forces at will. Patrimonial regimes are necessarily unstable: the larger and more successful they become, the greater the potential for decentralization of functions and the emergence of relatively autonomous and countervailing powers. Weber clearly recognized this, and contrasted patrimonialism with FEUDALISM (as well as with BUREAUCRACY of a rational-legal type). Because of the numerous economic, social and political systems which appear to be compatible with some degree of patrimonialism, the term is used only at the broadest level of generalization.

See BENDIX; EISENSTADT.

LS

**pattern variables.** PARSONS argued that cultural patterns force actors to make four fundamental choices between alternative modes of orientation towards social situations: between particularism and universalism, quality and performance, affectivity and affective neutrality, specificity and diffuseness. These he refers to as the pattern variables.

*Particularism/Universalism.* Is a 'social object' judged according to criteria peculiar to that one object and its particular context, or by criteria generally applicable to a whole class of similar objects? A teacher is expected to judge the ability of pupils by general or universal standards, while a parent is likely to view his or her own children differently from children in general and judge them according to particular and special criteria.

*Performance/Quality.* Does an actor judge the 'social object' according to its performance (i.e. what it does, achieves or effects); or does he or she consider it to have a quality important in itself, independently of its achievement or benefit to the actor? This is the anthropologist Ralph Linton's distinction between *ascription* and ACHIEVE-MENT, which Parsons borrowed and renamed. It is often useful in classifying the criteria by which people are recruited to RO-LES in society: in modern economies, most roles are filled by people who have demonstrated their performance or achievement by acquiring educational qualifications. Positions such as that of king, however, are still generally filled by a person to whom some inherent quality is ascribed, like being the eldest son of the monarch.

*Affectivity/Affective Neutrality.* Does the actor set his or her own emotions aside for the benefit of an instrumental relationship directed towards ends external to the relationship itself? Doctors are required to adopt an emotionally detached, effectively neutral attitude towards their patients, while it is normal for friends, lovers and spouses to take a more involved, affective attitude towards each other (see AFFECT).

*Specificity/Diffuseness.* This concerns whether people are bonded to each other in specific and limited ways — as are employers and employees, buyers and sellers — or are related more diffusely as total personalities, as are members of a close-knit family.

In earlier presentations of the pattern variables, Parsons includes a fifth choice, between self-orientation and collectivity-orientation. Later this disappeared, or rather was incorporated into the AGIL schema (see PARSONS) as a distinction between processes internal and external to a given social system. Parsons linked the four main pattern variables to AGIL in a complicated way.

According to Parsons, the pattern variables were derived from TÖNNIES'S conceptualization of modern and pre-modern social patterns as GEMEINSCHAFT and GESELLSCHAFT. In the course of studying the MEDICAL PROFESSION in the USA, Parsons recognized that doctors were expected to behave in certain respects in ways characteristic of the Gemeinschaft model, in others in conformity with Gesellschaft patterns. This led him to break Tönnies's simple dichotomy into the four (or five) separate pattern variables. Particularism, quality, affectivity, diffuseness and collectivity-orientation are typical of *gemeinschaftlich* relationships; universalism, performance, affective neutrality, specificity and self-orientation are *gesellschaftlich*.

He claimed that these four (or five) were logically exhaustive and universal choices to be made in all social relationships — a claim which reflects the influence of the philosophy of KANT, but would not be accepted by most sociologists. Nevertheless, the pattern variables have proved widely useful. For a use by Parsons, see SICK ROLE.

SJM

**peasant.** Subsistence cultivator of agricultural land. There is little agreement over the precise definition of the term, which frequently covers a wide range of agricultural cultivators whose particular qualities may vary considerably. For example, they may be owner-occupiers or tenants, participants or non-participants in the market. Some writers (for example, Chayanov) have attempted to isolate a distinctive peasant economy; others (for example, REDFIELD) stress the notion of a peasant culture.

Shanin has suggested four factors which contribute to a broad sociological definition of the peasantry. (1) The family provides the labour for the farm. Economic action is thus closely interwoven with family relations and the motive of profit maximization in money terms seldom appears in its explicit form. (2) Cultivation of the land is the main means of livelihood. Food production thus renders the family farm relatively autonomous. (3) A specific traditional culture exists which is related to the way of life of small communities. (4) The underdog position — the domination of the peasantry by outsiders. Their political subjection interlinks with cultural subordination and economic exploitation.

The view of the peasantry as inherently backward and incapable of radical political transformation is now discarded, especially in the light of numerous peasant-based revolutions and liberation movements of the 20th-century THIRD WORLD. Detailed analysis of the peasantry has emphasized economic and cultural diversity, making generalizations difficult. Despite frequent predictions to the contrary, there are few signs of the peasantry becoming obsolete, yet its position in society remains difficult to theorize. The notion of a separate peasant MODE OF PRODUCTION is not generally accepted.

See also COLLECTIVIZATION; RENT.

See B. Galeski, *Basic Concepts in Rural Sociology* (1972); T. Shanin, 'Defining Peasants: Conceptualisations and De-Conceptualisation', *Sociological Review* 1982; T. Shanin (ed.) *Peasants and Peasant Societies* (1971).

HN

**pedagogy.** The principles and methods used in teaching something, normally used in connection with teaching school subjects. It is possible to distinguish between the expressed pedagogy that a teacher claims he/she will or does use and what he/she actually does in the classroom. Both BERNSTEIN and BOURDIEU have made much use of this term. Bernstein extended the concept by speaking of 'invisible pedagogy' to parallel the idea implicit in 'invisible' CURRICULUM, thus referring to the UNINTENDED CONSEQUENCES or hidden principles and methods of teaching. Two commonly met IDEAL TYPE pedagogies are the traditional and progressive, the former giving priority to formal academic teaching, competition, hierarchy and punishment, the latter to informal, egalitarian, non-repressive methods of teaching and to reward.

PWM

**peer group.** Strictly, peer means equal and therefore a peer group consists of equals, but in practice the term has come to refer to a group consisting of members of the same age and other relevant social characteristics, and especially of children and adolescents. Such peer groups play an important part in the socialization process, because in them those involved experience for the first time a group consisting of single-aged members. Previously they have experienced the largely hierarchical relationships of their families, consisting of mixed-aged members. All such peer groups have the characteristics typical of any other small group, a system of NORMS preserved by sanctions against DEVIANT members and sub-groups. Thus young persons can learn how to interact with similarly aged persons who are not members of their family. More particularly, they learn how to treat the opposite sex. This eases movement towards a stable family relationship.

PWM

**Peirce, C.S..** See SEMIOTICS.

**penis envy.** See PSYCHOANALYSIS.

**penology.** A great pursuit of the 18th and 19th centuries. The word was invented in the most significant period of English penal reform; appearing in 1838, it was intended to distinguish the activities and interests of a particular group of reformers and lawyers, a group which sought to establish a science of crime prevention and control. It acquired a connotation of engagement in the practical politics of courts and prisons. The penologist, having assessed the effectiveness of different judicial and custodial measures, may confirm the wisdom of a policy or purpose alternative strategies. Penological thinking has moved through a series of cycles during the last two centuries. Emphases have shifted from the simple 'warehousing' of inmates to the spiritual and moral rehabilitation of the offender and back to warehousing. The ends of imprisonment have themselves oscillated between treatment, 'incapacitation', deterrence and retribution. Current penological orthodoxy maintains that 'nothing works': all known modes of treatment, correction and intervention have failed to make a demonstrable and significant impact upon standard indicators of reconviction. Prisons themselves are in disfavour and intervention have failed to make a demonstrable and significant impact upon standard indicators of reconviction. Prisons themselves are in disfavour and there has been a pronounced drift towards 'depenalization' or DECARCERATION in a number of policy circles in the USA, Holland, Canada and elsewhere. There is more dispute about the independent efficacy of diversion programmes, intermediate treatment, community treatment and the like. Some champion the use of correctional measures outside institutions. Others assert that such measures do not 'work'.

There are criminologists who work in penology, and the analysis of punishment, deterrence and reform is still usually identified as penology, but there is no separate academic discipline called penology. The word tends to refer to an application of criminology or sociology, not to an independent occupation or branch of learning with its own institutions, departments and membership.

PR

**perfect competition.** See MARKET STRUCTURE.

**personal construct theory.** Developed by G.A. KELLY, this theory is concerned with the way individuals construct and reconstruct the categories with which they apprehend the world, categories which are considered an immediate determinant of behaviour. According to the theory, the set of categories an individual uses is personal, and changes with time and situation. It is oriented to the future, to the anticipation of events, the individual using personal constructs to construe future events as similar to those experienced in the past. Hence current personal constructs are understood by their orientation to the future, not through their history, and change is an attempt to improve the anticipation of events.

The basic assumption is summed up in the philosophy of 'constructive alternativism': '*all* of our present interpretations of the universe are subject to revision or replacement' by alternative constructions, some of which will be more useful in anticipating events. The form of the constructs is a finite number of dichotomous distinctions, with ordinal relations (see MEASUREMENT) between them, higher order constructs embracing lower-order constructs. When individuals construe each other's construction processes, a social form is produced, individuals participating in common in a social process.

The substantive content has not been much used in sociology, but has been assimilated to the general idea of cognition as an active and ongoing process which structures and defines both the world and action (see SYMBOLIC INTERACTIONISM, PHENOMENOLOGY). The associated REPERTORY GRID TECHNIQUE developed by Kelly to map out personal constructs has been seen as a way of investigating subjective meaning, and one which frees 'psychological space' so defined

from the Euclidean form imposed by measurement scales.

See DIMENSION; SCALES.

JL

**personal documents.** First-hand accounts written by participants in the form of letters, diaries, autobiographies or life histories. They give an account of social experience from the point of view of the actor, emphasizing the actor's definition of the situation. Such documents may be contemporaneous (e.g. letters, diaries) or retrospective (e.g. autobiography); they may be spontaneous (e.g. letters not written for publication) or elicited by the researcher (as in life histories, documents written for the researcher giving an account of a person's life).

Personal documents were first extensively used in THOMAS and Znaniecki in *The Polish Peasant in Europe and America 1918-20*, and were popular in the 1920s. They fell into disuse, but have recently enjoyed a renaissance. Their failings include possible lack of REPRESENTATIVENESS, low RELIABILITY and the extreme subjectivity of approach. Their strengths include the richness and vividness of their portrayal of social life, and the insights provided into the actor's frame of reference (see ACTION THEORY).

See K. Plummer, *Documents of Life* (1983).

MB

**personality.** Literally, the totality of attributes characterizing an individual person. The dominant use of the concept in sociology and social psychology is more specialized: it emphasizes those relatively stable characteristics of individuals which may underlie individual differences in behaviour and may be used to predict or explain them. This view derives most immediately from the interwar American social psychology of ALLPORT and his students, who developed a view of personality in terms of TRAITS and ATTITUDES, neuro-psychic structures linked to repeated complexes of behaviour. Some authors go further and define personality through the formula Behaviour is a function of Personality and Situation or $B = f(P + S)$.

There has been little or no agreement among theorists as to the nature of the object of study, its appropriate constituent parts, and the methodology by which it should be studied. Some see personality as a collection of general psychological processes to be explain by the laws of general psychology; others as a specific combination of psychological elements interacting in a qualitatively unique way to be explained by a 'personology' distinct from general psychology. Theorists differ over the components of personality: Id, Ego and Superego (FREUD); needs (Murray, Maslow; see NEEDS, HIERARCHY OF); traits and attitudes (Allport), cognitions and beliefs (FESTINGER) or PERSONAL CONSTRUCTS (KELLY). Methodologically, there are general disagreements between a BEHAVIOURIST and an organismic approach, and specific disagreements over the usefulness of clinical and experimental methods, and techniques such as personality QUESTIONNAIRE, FACTOR ANALYSIS and PROJECTIVE TESTS.

Writers, particularly philosophers, have always discussed the characters and qualities of individuals, but the origins of personality theory as distinct from philosophy must be seen in the work of Freud and his disciples, especially JUNG and Adler. Freud and his followers disagreed violently among themselves, but they had in common what later writers called a psychodynamic approach: the personality is an energy system, in which psychic or libidinal energy is continually structured and re-structured, channelled, stored, and discharged (see PSYCHOANALYSIS). Clinical psychoanalytic methods (see PROJECTIVE TESTS) are to be used in investigation, and the primary interest is not behaviour but to unravel this energy system and to understand its dynamic development from early childhood.

In the USA by 1920 the first university-trained psychologists were emerging. They were not vested in psychoanalysis and had not themselves been psychoanalysed, and they saw the psychodynamic approach as rendered invalid by its reliance upon abnormal cases and the admission of other than objectively observable behaviour as evidence. Allport, while accepting the need to look at normal rather than abnormal cases, rejected both the radical form of this new behaviourism and the Freudian psychodynamic view. Trait theory steered a middle

course: traits were closely linked to observable behaviour, but were not reducible to it, being seen as underlying and generating it.

Allport's conception of personality was eclectic and flexible: 'the dynamic organization within the individual of those psychophysical systems that determine his unique adjustments to his environment'. However, subsequent work in the USA picked up on the concepts of trait and attitute as immediate predictors of behaviour, and effort concentrated on techniques for their accurate definition and measurement and on investigating their correlations with social action and behaviour. Cattell (see TRAIT) introduced factor analysis to identify the inter-correlated response patterns corresponding to traits and attitudes, which he saw as principal components of the factor solution. The need for numerical scores on the response DIMENSIONS leads this approach to stress scaling methods and the need for reliable correlations, and to the use of large-scale questionnaire data rather than detailed case-studies. An individual personality corresponds to a specific profile of scores on the factor dimensions, a psychometric conception of personality associated in Britain particularly with EYSENCK.

A flow of ideas from Europe in the 1930s, spread by refugees from fascism, countered this trend in the USA. The ideas of psychoanalysis, of gestalt theory, topological psychology (see LEWIN; FIELD THEORY) and general systems theory began to influence Anglo-Saxon psychology. During World War II the large opportunity for clinical work in the processes of mobilization coupled with the impetus to understand the fascist personality (see ADORNO; AUTHORITARIAN PERSONALITY), fostered a dynamic-organismic approach, treating the personality holistically as a developing system. In the early 1950s, behaviourist experimental psychology began to gain ground as the wartime clinical services were run down. Conflict was sufficiently acute that in 1957 the American Psychological Association split into two, clinical versus experimental psychology; since then, in the USA, clinical or psychoanalytic approaches have been ousted from the mainstream of psychological theory.

Anglo-Saxon personality theory has subsequently been dominated by low-level theories and by the explicit following of a POSITIVIST model of scientific method. Theories have emphasized the social determinants and correlates of personality and have tended to stress cognition and the formation of belief-systems as central to the understanding of these aspects (e.g. Festinger, Kelly). Attempts to model these belief-systems use formal methods such as those of mathematical logic and computer simulation.

European theory has differed considerably from American, with British theory sharing elements of both. Allport suggests that European theory is more concerned with 'character', from the Greek for 'engraving', whereas American theory is concerned with the 'persona', from the Greek for 'mask', with those elements of the individual that adapt to changing social conditions. European theory has been less concerned with positivist models of science, more with the generation of ideas, and has tended to view the mind as self-active in the German tradition of Leibnitz (e.g. Hans Thomae, Karl Jaspers, Erwin Roth) rather than as a reactive tabula rasa in the English tradition of LOCKE.

In sociology, personality theory has appeared in a number of different ways. Marxism has generally had little time for personality theory, regarding it as a misleading form of psychologism, attempting to make trans-historical generalizations about individuals divorced from the context of the concrete historical processes within which they live. However, the post-Freudians Fromm and Reich attempted to incorporate Marxist elements into personality theory, emphasizing the role of social structure in shaping personality. In the past 20-30 years there has been some attempt to produce a neo-Marxist personality theory (e.g. Lucien Séve).

Freud's theory of personality directed attention to the role of the immediate family in the development of personality, and in the 1920s and 1930s sociologists and anthropologists became interested in the extent to which these theories would apply in cultures with different kinship systems. In the USA a number of studies were carried out on Indian cultures (see KROEBER) and led to a more general interest in the dominant personality type produced by, or suited to, a given culture. In the late 1930s and during World War II these studies were extended to Europe and Japan (see BENEDICT) and formed the basis for analysing national character, of direct interest in wartime.

In many areas of sociological theory, personality trait variables have been added in an ad hoc way to explain differences in behaviour or attitudes within social classes or groups; for example, difference in prejudice in political, religious or work attitudes. In the area of sexual differences, radical feminists and others have in recent years highlighted the deficiencies of the conventional conceptions of masculinity and femininity as personality traits. There has been a re-awakening of interest, much of it critical, in Freudian and psychoanalytic theory, but in a sociologized form as a theory of the operation of paternalistic culture and economic exploitation within the individual. See also PSYCHOANALYSIS.

JB

**petite bourgeoisie** (often semi-anglicized as 'petty bourgeoisie'). The CLASS of small business proprietors and self-employed artisans and tradesmen. In some countries (though not usually in the UK or USA) the term is extended to cover peasant proprietors and small farmers. MARX expected that under the pressure of capitalist competition and economic CONCENTRATION the petite bourgeoisie would collapse into the WORKING CLASS and thereby add to class polarization. This happened in most countries only to the artisans, who became employed skilled workers. Other small proprietors have held their own in absolute numbers, though driven increasingly from manufacturing industry into building and services. Their survival is due partly to their efficiency in dealing with cheap, low-technology, non-mechanizable areas of the economy, partly to their ability to raise the level of EXPLOITATION of voluntary family labour. Thus this class has a high level of familial organization, unusual within capitalism.

Where given leadership by peasant proprietors the petite bourgeoisie have been able to generate powerful political movements of diverse types, from POPULISM to FASCISM through DEMOCRATIC SOCIALISM (in Scandinavia). Where exclusively urban, however, they have shown considerable dependence upon the 'bigger' bourgeoisie, hence the faintly derogatory tone of the term 'petty bourgeois' in English. The term is sometimes used less precisely to indicate a broader 'lower-middle class' stratum including also clerks, salespersons and minor functionaries, especially to a supposed common culture, centring on a concern for propriety, cleanliness, conformity and sexual repression. But there is less evidence of this than much general writing about culture acknowledges.

See BOURGEOISIE; CLASS: *Neo-Marxist theories*; MIDDLE CLASS(ES).

See Bechhofer and Elliot (ed.), *The Petite Bourgeoisie* (1981).

MM

**phenomenology.** The study of the various forms and varieties of consciousness and the ways in which people can apprehend the world in which they live. Edmund HUSSERL, the philosopher most commonly connected with the development of phenomenology, argued that analysis of the constructs of mind was not only a science but, necessarily, the 'first science', in that all other disciplines, including logic as well as physics, depended on the prior conceptual excavations of phenomenology. Phenomenology could reveal not only the structure of our conceptual apparatus but also the ways in which we exist as human beings as opposed to mere physical entities. For example, whereas experimental psychology might have a concern with the correlation between 'food imagery' and 'hunger', phenomenology has the prior concern with the more general question of what exactly is to count as 'an image', or a case of 'remembering' and the like. The phenomenological task is thus the *a priori* description of the structures and constituents of the ways in which people think, act and live in the world. And there are many such ways.

A central feature of phenomenology is the doctrine of *intentionality*: any form of consciousness is always a consciousness *of*.

For the phenomenological philosopher contemplating the table before him, he is conscious *of* the table; there are not two separate 'things' — the 'table' and a 'conscious mind' which must be brought into alignment. There is no separation of subject and object and, therefore, as a corolary, what an object *is* will be constituted by the particular kind of intentionality through which it is experienced. The gold wedding ring of a deceased spouse pawned out of necessity is a different object for the widowed husband than it is for the pawnbroker who weighs it for a 'valuation'. The reactions of the former to the ring will be different from those of the latter. The one might place the ring along with other belongings of his dead wife and occasionally take them out, reminiscing about the days they had spent together. The pawnbroker might simply place the ring in a drawer with others awaiting redemption. The ring has different 'aspects' for each.

There are thus many ways in which objects in the world can be constituted. For Husserl, the 'scientific' and mathematical approach to the world as typified by physics is only one way in which the world can be regarded though this approach to reality had become dominant in Western civilization. In *The Crisis of European Sciences and Transcendental Phenomenology* Husserl argues that, beginning with Galileo, there has been an impetus to discover and describe the world in terms of an idealized mathematized form. However, such discovery and description was also a form of concealment. (1) It concealed from itself that the way that science produces discoveries and descriptions of the world in terms of the idealized mathematized form is due to the very logic and procedures of scientific discovery and description, rather than having anything to do with the properties of nature in itself. The 'correctness' of any scientific description of the world is sustained not by comparing that description with the world but by ensuring that the scientific procedure were indeed followed. Hence the circularity and ungrounded basis of scientific method. (2) The mathematized form of description conceals that there is a world having a prior existence to that described by science — the *Lebenswelt*, the Life-World or everyday world of mundane existence. It is in this *Lebenswelt* that we participate and from which the scientific approach is derivative.

One of Husserl's followers, Alfred SCHUTZ, argued further that the procedures and rational features of science are incompatible with the procedures and common-sense logic used by people in the everyday world. Thus science is particularly unsuited to the discovery and description of the social world and it falls to phenomenological investigation to seek to describe the various structures which operate in the social world.

The acceptance of phenomenology into the Anglo-Saxon world has been slow. The ideas are often expressed in tortuous language, and concepts such as 'being-in-itself' and the search for 'essences' are too exotic for most tastes. Second, there is the problem of accounting for the manner in which mutual understandings are obtained between individuals in the establishment of the primacy of the everyday world. Initially, Husserl proposed the notion of 'empathy' to account for this fact but later, given the difficulties with this solution (difficulties seen by WEBER) he proposed the existence of a 'transcendental ego' in which all individual egos participated. Many find this notion uncongenial as a solution to one of sociology's traditional problems.

Many of the insights of phenomenology have been expressed and made relevant in the linguistic or analytic philosophy of writers such as Austin, Ryle and WITTGENSTEIN. While these writers gave no direct guidance as to the manner in which an empirical social science could be conducted, they have been important in freeing areas of the social sciencs from the restrictions of a closed and positivistic approach to empirical enquiries.

The legacy of Husserl's phenomenology for sociology has resulted in many varied positions. SCHUTZ'S examination of WEBER'S methodological writings (in *The Phenomenology of the Social World*) indicated that certain phenomological insights could be brought to bear upon many of the central questions in the social sciences that Weber had addressed, such as VERSTEHEN and the subjective-objective dimension in the description of social action (see ACTION THEORY). How those insights have been

developed empirically are markedly different. What has come to be understood under the general rubric of 'phenomenological sociology' is certainly not a unified position, ranging from the almost EMPIRICIST aspects of certain works in CONVERSATION ANALYSIS, through 'insightful' PARTICIPANT OBSERVATION research to the studied conceptual contemplation of Socratic/Platonic intent. But this is to be expected. The structure of the social world is demonstrably heterogeneous, and it would be surprising if one approach alone were sufficient to enable that structure to be described in all its richness and detail.

See HERMENEUTICS; KNOWLEDGE, SOCIOLOGY OF; PERSONAL CONSTRUCT THEORY; SYMBOLIC INTERACTIONISM.

DBn

**phenotype.** See GENE.

**pillarization.** A translation of the Dutch *verzuiling*, this term describes the process whereby in Dutch society the dominant religious expressions (Calvinism and Roman Catholicism) became the focus for other forms of participation in social institutions. Initially this was a reaction to the efforts of a ruling liberal bourgeoisie to extend education on a secular basis. Later the two religious faiths were joined by a further ideology, socialism. Each ideology established a range of organizations to ensure satisfactory facilities for its adherents in almost every sphere of social life: schools, universities, political parties, trade unions, mass media, welfare agencies etc. Thus there are three types of schools: public, Protestant, or Roman Catholic. Within each pillar there may be further splits between conservatives and liberals; the non-religious bloc may sometimes separate into liberal-bourgeois and socialist, and may sometimes combine with liberal Protestants. Unlike Northern Ireland, where segregated confessional blocs in a constant relationship of domination and subordination have produced enduring conflict, the Dutch *verzuiling* have achieved a high degree of 'segmented integration' for the society as a whole. While each confessional bloc seeks to insulate its own adherents, leaders of different blocs collaborate with each other to secure influence in national decision-making and a share of national resources, under the prevailing cultural ethos of civility and CONSENSUS which militates against the expression of conflict.

RW

**phobia.** See MENTAL ILLNESS.

**pleasure principle.** See PSYCHOANALYSIS.

**pluralism.** There are three broad meanings of this term. (1) Descriptions of societies that are stratified on racial or cultural grounds (see PLURAL SOCIETY). (2) Descriptions of medieval or feudal societies where political authority was dispersed among the governing ranks of society, including an independent Church. This usage was employed by German historians such as Gierke to attack the 'Hegelian' absolute state and by British historians (e.g. G.D.H. Cole and Harold Laski) to criticize the absolute powers of the Government during World War I. (3) The most common use of the term refers to the STATE in those capitalist industrial societies that are not dominated by any single group or type of group (i.e. a single CLASS). The state is in most circumstances neutral between groups that accept the rules of the political game; most people have a vote; politicans compete for those votes; governments are constituted from politicians who win a pre-decided proportion of valid votes cast; governments may be replaced by general elections held every few years. The actors in this description may be thought of as individuals, parties, groups, etc, or coalitions of these. Plural theorists (e.g. R. Dahl, D. Truman), in describing the working of capitalist DEMOCRACY assert that practically all public policies are the outcome of compromise. No group that wishes to affect outcomes lacks resources (votes, money, intelligence or access) and each may therefore be effective on some issues. The interests of people inattentive to the political arena are not necessarily neglected since the wise politician takes them into account when formulating policies lest the apathetics arise and favour other politicians.

Critics of the theory abound. They assert that (1) this is not an accurate account of capitalist society, since the state is systematically biased and resources to affect outcomes are heavily concentrated among limited groups, which may be either dominant classes or elites. The reason for widespread apathy is that any other response is a waste of time. (2) It is an account not only of capitalist society but of any technologically advanced society. In such societies all policies have technical implications and technologists must therefore be consulted. (3) It totally neglects the classical Greek emphasis on politics as a moralizing experience and involvement in the polity as both the mark of the free person and the object that any decent society should actively promote: participation is not simply about groups or individuals or defending and advancing interests.

See also CLASS: *Marx on* and *Neo-Marxist Theories*; ELITISM.

RED

**plural society.** A concept introduced by the economist J.S. Furnivall (*Colonial Policy and Practice*, 1948) in defining the distinctive characteristics of the societies created in Burma and Indonesia under imperial rule. In these societies a variety of peoples — European, Chinese, Indian, and the various native groups — were physically, linguistically, religiously and culturally different, and occupied quite different places in the DIVISION OF LABOUR. Each group sought its own ends and felt no loyalty to the whole society which was maintained because it suited the convenience of the various sections and was backed by the power of the imperial country. In World War II these societies offered little resistance to the invading Japanese. Afterwards the native peoples mobilized greater political power, took over control of the state apparatus and expelled or restricted immigrant groups. Though no longer strictly plural in Furnivall's sense, some societies, like Malaysia, remain pluralistic in that the minorities are sufficiently powerful to be able to maintain societies of their own within the national framework.

Other writers have employed Furnivall's concepts to analyse the multi-racial societies of Southern African and the Caribbean in terms of social and cultural pluralism. This causes confusion because in American political philosophy PLURALISM is used in a different sense.

See C. Geertz, *Old Societies and New States* (1966).

MPB

**Polanyi, Karl** (1886-1964). Hungarian economist and historian, a life-long socialist (though attached to no party) and polemicist against market-derived (UTILITARIAN) theories of society. Polanyi spent most of his life in exile, first in Austria and then, from 1936, in the UK and USA. He first taught economic history for the Workers Education Association and the Extra-Mural Departments of London and Oxford Universities. This led to *The Great Transformation* (1944), a brilliant account of the rise of the capitalist market system in England which led him on to argue that (1) economic determinism was largely a 19th-century phenomenon, the product of a European market system, now disappearing; (2) the market system violently distorts our views on human beings and society; (3) this distortion is a major obstacle to solving the problems of our civilization. In 1946 he was appointed Visiting Professor of Economics at Columbia University, New York where he stayed until his retirement in 1953. During these years and in retirement he conducted a study of 18th-century Dahomey, published posthumously as *Dahomey and the Slave Trade* (1966) and worked with a group of associates on what became known as the 'substantivist' theory of the economy. This opposed the 'formal' model underlying modern economies, which saw economic activity as maximizing utilities and 'economizing' in a situation of material scarcity. Polanyi argued that this was only appropriate in modern market economies. A substantive model started more simply from the way in which material wants, subsistence needs, were satisfied. He identified three IDEAL TYPES: reciprocity, redistribution and exchange. RECIPROCITY is a movement of goods between related symmetrical groups, the activity being legitimated by kinship ties (as MALINOWSKI had described). Redistribution entails a centralized system, in which goods are moved towards a central agent, usually a chief or a state with authority to

reallocate them among societal members. Exchange is restricted to contractual arrangements between agents who are related only through a system of price-making markets. The last is characteristic of capitalism alone. These ideas are expounded in Polanyi, Arensberg and Pearson, *Trade and Market in the Early Empires* (1957) and in a posthumous collection of essays, edited by Pearson, *The Livelihood of Man* (1977). They have influenced anthropologists, archaeologists and ancient historians, and in those fields are currently being developed further (see STATE, ORIGINS OF). They are an alternative view of the way that economics are 'embedded' in social structures to Marxian MODES OF PRODUCTION theory.

MM

**political, the.** Distinctions between the STATE and SOCIETY or CIVIL SOCIETY, between politics and society, or between economy, polity and religion are fairly recent in European thought, and normally not present in non-European ideas. The formative period for these distinctions occurred with the rise of states in Europe claiming total authority within their boundaries, claims that were disputed by a national or extra-national CHURCH. Some relationship of a local territorial kind had to be worked out to replace the medieval relationship between regnum and sacerdotium, which was in principle universal. Depending on the relative strengths and acuity of the contending parties the outcome varied from total subordination of church to state (Russia); the uneasy division of the world into the 'moral' and the rest, with the former at the partial disposal of an official church (UK, Prussia); the same division, but with no official church (France from the mid-19th century); more or less uneasy concordats with the universal church (Italy).

From about the middle of 15th century, and more obviously in 16th century, states claimed that they were sovereign — in the final analysis all institutions and behaviours were temporally subordinate. The divisions suggested above were usually attempts to limit the full implications of sovereignty (spelled out by both HOBBES and Grotius) whether thought of as deriving from the people, from the prince or from the logic of power. If finally the state did not possess a legal monopoly of power then who or what in a world of scarcity and enemies was to guarantee internal peace and freedom from external aggression?

The effort to answer this question constitutes much of the intellectual effort and capital of European CONSERVATISM and LIBERALISM. Three solutions were offered. (1) Identify the interests (properly understood) of the population with those of the state (the political). This solution includes the national liberalism of Germany and France as well as NATIONALISM and FASCISM. (2) Demarcate the proper sphere of the political from that of the economic and the social while, often, building constitutional guarantees — normally variants of divided powers — against a strong state, an idea stemming from LOCKE. The liberal concept of *laissez faire* makes sense only if there is a recognizable economic activity to be left alone and a power that otherwise would not leave it alone. (3) Approaches derived from MARX argue the logical and historical priority of the social or the economic, and claim that eventually the state/political becomes otiose or unbearably burdensome and society re-absorbs those functions.

Even if we can get agreement in principle about what characterizes the economic or the political or the moral, it is usually much more difficult to allocate any particular behaviour to a category. In cases of disagreement, what authority has power to arbitrate? Implicitly, and often explicitly, British and American liberalism and liberal thinking foundered on the questions of a sovereign authority — albeit with balanced powers of various kinds — accepting self-imposed limits on its jurisdiction. On the whole, British conservatives did not think about the question, being content with *ad hoc* formulations about the sovereignty of the monarch and Parliament.

The political has also proved an elusive concept to define since also involved are ideas like POWER, AUTHORITY, LEGITIMACY and organization in WEBERIAN usage, and surplus, exploitation and state in its Marxian form. However, there is considerable agreement that the political exists when people cannot agree voluntarily about allocations of all kinds in societies. When agreement is not automatic — as is sometimes thought to be the case in kinship and market allocations — then some binding arbitration or settlement is required or, better, likely to appear. The neutrality or otherwise of this allocation — binding because backed, ultimately or immediately by power or force — is a vexed issue. Broadly, liberals believe that the political, when organized in the form of a state, may be captured by elements — sinister or partial interests — which distort its neutrality, or that the state apparatus itself may develop a self-interest. Broadly, conservatives may believe any of the above possibilities as contingent but not necessary and if necessary, then a price worth paying for restraining people.

Formulated in this way the question of why the political emerges, what it is that lies underneath and causes disagreement, is left open. So is the investigation and analysis of the emergence of various political forms — states, empires, 'tribes' or groups — and the question of what influences are at work in causing the behaviour of the political agency (state, empire, leopard-skin chief, moiety elder etc) and the recipient of the binding judgement (citizen, slave, subject or corporation). The only specifications, in line with Weber, are that the political ('the state' in his formulation) cannot be defined by what it does, and that by the 'legitimate use of physical force' it is able to command sufficient force to get its allocation accepted. Organizations characterized by this are political. Other organizations which may seek to influence or themselves make allocations do not have this quality and, hence, in the final analysis may be refused influence or have their allocatory functions withdrawn by the political agency.

RD

**political corruption.** To be corrupt implies a standard from which those so accused have deviated. The major conceptual problem is specifying the standard. If the standard adopted is something like that of Western legal systems controlling BUREAUCRATIC behaviour, broadly as specified by WEBER, the analyst is likely to be accused of ethnocentrism. If the standard adopted is TRADITIONAL behaviour, the analysis rapidly becomes bogged down in a morass of competing claims about what is or is not traditional behaviour. Furthermore, a behaviour that is normatively sanctioned or even mandatory in one society, such as nepotism or showing gratitude, will be regarded as corrupt in another more bureaucratized society. Since most analysts come from such societies most studies are implicitly or explicitly ETHNOCENTRIC. The usual defence of this position is that nearly all countries have similar legal definitions of political corruption. Such definitions centre upon the abuse of public office for private — not necessarily individual — gain.

An implication of this view is that a public good is not necessarily a private one. If the public good could be specified and universally agreed there could be no problem of corruption, provided a state followed that agreement. No political or economic theorists have succeeded in such a specification and no state has followed an unequivocal common good. In view of these two difficulties much academic and journalistic writing tends to be either an examination of the sources of corruption or case studies of examples of it.

Given a non-homogeneous population, the impact of the state will vary. Sections of the population will then have different incentives to avoid its rules by, for example, bribing officials concerned to implement or enforce a behaviour. From this point of view political corruption is an attempt by a group, individual or population to revert to a mode of distribution other than the bureaucratic one, i.e. to a market or kin mode.

It follows that by definition any allocation by a STATE is different to that which would be achieved via a kin or market system. Further, any LAW is a potential source of political corruption and, inferentially, the more laws, the greater the potential scope for corruption. This reasoning covers state laws as wide as Gosplan (the economic plan of the USSR) or as narrow as those prohibiting pornography, both notorious sources of political corruption. The fewer the restraints on public behaviour the fewer the opportunities for political corruption.

The more 'alien' the state the less its officials can be corrupted; a state is alien when its priorities are at variance with local custom and its officials, reference groups and

values lie elsewhere. A Martian conquest state on earth would be uncomfortable but not corrupt: a European conquest state in the THIRD WORLD would presumably be less corrupt than an independent successor state which, in attempting to change people's behaviour with officials, would by definition be in some measure sympathetic to those it was seeking to change. Equally, conquest states — and all states are, or have in some measure been such — are more or less alien; in attempting to consolidate or homogenize a heterogeneous population they are subject to counter-pressure (including political corruption) from the population (e.g. the Italian South).

Similarly, in a Marxist analysis the state protects and defines the general, common, or long-term interest of the dominant MODE OF PRODUCTION and its corollary social formation. Dominant social formations are not unitary — otherwise no compulsory definition of interest would be needed — and those that have their interest sacrificed (by higher tax, by pollution regulations, by curbs on business) have an incentive to avoid behaviour change and to bribe inspectors etc. Equally, such formations have a strong incentive to 'buy' politicans, hire lobbyists and so on to get a law changed, usually to generalize the cost over the whole society or to direct the cost elsewhere. Conjunctoral circumstances will determine the success of this but the state will have to act to control behaviour.

Although this outcome is certain its form is not. This is equally true of democratic capitalism within which a semi-autonomous, part-pluralist state — partly responsive to proletarian demands and partly attending to its own interest (see PLURALISM) — makes allocations that, looked at internationally, are not in the long-term interest of the national capitalist formation. Such allocations include price regulations, high taxes, social security measures of various kinds, limits on capital export and concomitant bureaucratic expansion. In the UK and USA, efforts have been to reduce or limit this growth at the expense of welfare programmes. This induces greater desperation amongst the poor who have an additional incentive to bribe inspectors and a stronger incentive to avoid the tax system and get into the black economy which is a source of corruption among officials. However, most corporate subsidies are untouched or only lightly touched by such retrenchment — the state is indeed only semi-autonomous. As generally defined, the analysis of political corruptions cannot deal further with this problem.

Further questions have included (a) is political corruption necessarily a bad thing? (b) if it is, what can be done about it?

Non-moralizing answers to the first question usually argue that politically disadvantaged groups may use corruption to alleviate their lot, that corruption may humanize a distant bureaucracy, and that the priorities of governments are not necessarily either admirable or in the public interest. The first two are trivial but true; the third is non-trivial but also non-falsifiable.

Answers to the second question are equally unilluminating. It is usually assumed that state planning (altering or attempting to alter behaviour on a large scale) is necessary in Third World countries, given scarce resources etc. But this assumption is only made by those who will not be subject to planning (foreign academics) or those who will do the planning (local bureaucrats). It is argued that what is needed to combat corruption are (1) better plans, (2) better bureaucrats and (3) a better-educated population. The last of these is predicated on the grounds that if one knows the law as well as the law officer knows it there is less opportunity for extortion; this proposition is clearly false. The second proposal is either true by definition, or is a plea for more resources to train bureaucrats better (i.e. to give an even larger share of national resources to the bureaucracy) or for better supervision of existing officers — but *quis custodes?* The proposal for better planning is absurd unless 'better' is related to some agreed concept of common interest, and those who are to be planned are never seriously consulted.

More important theoretical questions about political corruption concern areas such as: how is it possible to derive a neutral view of the common good (i.e. make plans or regulations that people respect); who or what benefits from the plethora of laws controlling access to pornography, drink and gambling; who or what benefits from a wide range of laws in Third World countries concerning driving cars or buses, running small businesses etc; is it sensible to include matters like corporate subsidies from the state, which are perfectly legal, but obtained from a state systematically biased toward corporations, under the heading corruption; and if not, is the study of political corruption intrinsically trivial?

RED

**political culture.** The interaction between the individual and the history, tradition, values and NORMS of a community (whether the size of a neighbourhood or state) in the political sphere. Political culture is not necessarily homogeneous. A large community may contain sub-groups which have incongruent political cultures. The dominant political culture may emanate from political or social leaders, and need not be that of the majority, while both dominant and secondary political cultures may be supportive, or potentially destructive, of stability in the political system.

Measurement is difficult, but attempts have been made, notably by Almond and Verba (*The Civic Culture*, 1963), who examined the orientation of a sample of individuals in five nations towards those nations and their political institutions. They found that a combination of respect for authority and independence from it were the most supportive towards a DEMOCRACY. They called this optimum the *civic culture.*

This study was the first major examination of political attitudes across national boundaries, but it fails to show that a stable democracy results from the presence of this civic culture, rather than *vice versa.* The use of a longitudinal sample (see SAMPLING) would have allowed the investigators to infer causal relationships rather than stop at description. They also failed to define democracy in a sufficiently rigorous way. Their statement that 'if democracy means anything, it means that in some way governmental elites must respond to the desires and demands of citizens' is more a government-sustaining prescription than a definition of democracy.

The importance of political culture lies in its all-pervasiveness, influencing individual decisions on whether to vote and who to support, the propensity to join political organizations, and attitudes towards the political institutions of nations. However, this pervasiveness also brings problems to those seeking to measure it and understand its relationship with other parts of the social system.

See CLASS CONSCIOUSNESS; CONSENSUS; CULTURE.

AMcC

**political messianism.** A term devised by J.L. Talmon (*The Origins of Totalitarian Democracy*, 1952) to denote political doctrines and movements which expected a dramatic transformation of society by revolution, analogous to the eschatological transformation of the world at the coming of the messiah. Talmon applied this term to Rousseau and others whom he accused of TOTALITARIANISM.

See MESSIANIC MOVEMENT; MILLENNIAL MOVEMENT.

MMG

**political obligation.** 'Why, or under what conditions, is one obliged to obey the state?' is perhaps the central question of political theory. Political obligation is commonly regarded as one type of moral obligation, yet unlike most other moral obligations, enforcing a person's compliance with it is considered morally permissible and often obligatory. The many different answers to the question can be classified as substantive and authoritative. Substantive reasons for obeying the STATE (i.e. the law) are that the laws themselves correspond to or amplify the requirements of moral principles. Theories of JUSTICE and UTILITARIAN theories, require correspondence as the condition of justified obedience. An authoritative reason for political obligation is that laws issue from a source vested with the moral right (AUTHORITY) to subject persons to enforceable obligations. Accounts of the basis and location of such a right are in theories of divine selection and in SOCIAL CONTRACT theories.

HIS

**political socialization.** The process or processes through which a person acquires a political repertoire broadly consonant with the POLITICAL CULTURE(s) of his or her politically relevant milieu. In structural-functional analysis the successful induction of people into a national political culture was regarded as a prerequisite of any political society and a determinant of social stability, or whatever is the independent variable. The idea of socialization into a culture as a source of stability also has a Marxist resonance ('the ruling ideas of an age' etc) and echoes GRAMSCI'S confused notions of hegemony.

The structural-functional emphasis generated a considerable body of empirical research into such areas as sex roles and voting patterns; childhood experiences with authority figures and 'consequent' adult behaviours; the relationship between authority patterns in school, home, work and adult orientations to politics; racial stereotyping; inter-generational voting patterns etc. These studies were usually technically tight and well-presented, but by the mid-1970s a number of crippling objections had been advanced against the structural-functional version. (1) The findings were either inferences about adult behaviour from pre-adult data or 'descriptions' of pre-adult circumstances from adult recall data i.e. the findings were not based on longitudinal panels (see SAMPLING). (2) The studies were predicated on the idea that CULTURE was neutral: the earlier studies did not even consider the possibility of different and competitive political cultures. The Marxist notion 'ruling ideas ... ruling classes' addressed this possibility, but failed to deliver empirical studies or to meet the objection that ideas do not belong to a class. However, the notion that working class political culture is an imposed one has led to fruitful controversy amongst Marxist historians. (3) No descriptions of what people think — or say they think — account for physical behaviour which may be role or circumstance-limited: thus white fascists, if they work in the post office, sell stamps to black liberals, and black liberals may get few chances to vote Liberal. Adult behaviour is based upon adult circumstances. (4) The QUESTIONNAIRE — a usual tool of this type of analysis — is inadequate to elicit a useful response about complex phenomena, and political behaviour, attitudes etc. are complex.

RED

**political violence.** A contradiction in terms: if 'war is a continuation of politics by other means' then politics is the solution of social problems without the use of violence. But if politics is a bargaining process, violence is one of the means available to improve one's position. Political violence needs to be distinguished from WAR between states, and from 'criminal' violence. However, there is something artificial in this distinction, exemplified by Andreas Baäder, car-thief turned international revolutionary, or by the training of revolutionaries by states who wish to undermine the government that the trainee also wishes to overthrow.

A further problem is that of morality: 'one man's terrorist is another man's freedom fighter.' Some studies of political violence condemn any violence as inimical to the freedom of the individual. Others argue that the covert violence of the state is such that an individual can only be free when being violent. The problem of LEGITIMACY is central to the discussion of political violence.

Sub-categories of political violence range through civil war, state terror, REVOLUTION, COUP D'ETAT, terrorism, assassination, kidnap, hijack (is a peaceful hijack political violence?) down to throwing a brick on a demonstration (is a sit-in political violence?). Often all tactics, including non-violent ones, by groups prepared to use violence to overthrow the state are considered political violence, just as all tactics used by the state to subdue them can be placed in the same category.

A general definition of political violence could be: the use of force in circumstances such that the behaviour of individuals is modified in such a way as to affect the processes of decision-making for the whole society. But definitions adopted for the term POLITICAL differ, and the level of activity considered as violence also differs on a continuum from killing, down to speaking harshly.

In his empirical work on patterns of political violence, Tilly distinguishes two main schools of thought on what he calls 'collective violence'. (1) The first sees it as a result of societal 'breakdown' — antisocial behaviour results from the uncertainties and strains of wholesale structural changes such as industrialisation. (2) The 'solidarity' school argues that producing political violence are the same as those that produce other types of collective action in pursuit of common interest. To examine the relevance of these schools Tilly studies Italian, German and French society 1830-1930. By analysing changes in patterns of political violence in a period of industrialization and urbanization he intends to throw light on the relevance of the 'breakdown' $v$ 'solidarity' debate. He finds in all three societies a shift from reactive to proactive violence over time: instead of reacting to events, more groups choose to initiate change. He also finds that high levels of repression produce low levels of collective violence, but that an important part of violence occurring during collective action is due to specialized repressive forces. Industrialization and urbanization do not produce violence because of breakdown; they produce new structures of power, and Tilly comes down on the 'solidarity' school's side. Violence is an ineffective strategy for a group in the short run, because it frightens away possible members. Powerful groups rarely choose violence, unless to cripple an important opponent. Powerless groups, however, will find that violence sometimes pays, since violence can provide publicity and hence support from power holders. Powerless groups also have very few possible actions available, and are often illegal. Hence they must choose between doing nothing and doing something that will provoke repression. Powerless groups can also magnify their power by discrediting a government whose repression is weak or indifferent. Tilly concludes that violent repression works. It is not true that a tyrannized population will revolt due to frustration. Violence is more effective for government than for challengers. However, all these conclusions may vary from one political system to another.

A general definition of political violence could be 'the use of force in circumstances such that the behaviour of individuals is modified in such a way as to affect the processes of decision-making for the whole society'. But definitions adopted for the term

'POLITICAL' differ, and the level of activity considered violent can differ from killing to speaking harshly.

In empirical work on patterns of political violence, Tilly distinguishes two main schools of thought on what he calls 'collective violence'. The first sees it as a result of societal 'breakdown': antisocial behaviour results from the uncertainties and strains of wholesale structural changes such as industrialization. The second, the 'solidarity' school, argues that political violence is produced by the same factors that give rise to other types of collective action in pursuit of common interest. Tilley examined Italian, French and German society between 1830 and 1930, analysing changes in patterns of political violence during a period of industrialization and urbanization. He finds in all three societies a shift from reactive to proactive violence over time: instead of reacting to events, more groups choose to initiate change. He also finds that high levels of repression produce low levels of collective violence, but that an important part of violence occurring during collective action is due to specialized repressive forces. Industrialization and urbanization do not produce violence because of breakdown; they produce new structures of power, and Tilly comes down on the side of the 'solidarity; school. Violence is an ineffective strategy for a group in the short run, because it frightens away possible members. Powerful groups rarely choose violence, unless to cripple an important opponent. Powerless groups, however, will find that violence sometimes pays, since violence can provide publicity and hence support from power holders. Powerless groups also have very few possible actions available, and are often illegal. Hence they must choose between doing nothing and doing something that will provoke repression. Powerless groups can also magnify their power by discrediting a government whose repression is weak or indifferent. Tilly concludes that violent repression works. It is not true that a tyrannized population will revolt due to frustration. Violence is more effective for government than for challengers. However, all these conclusions may vary from one political system to another.

The Kerner Commission's report on the 1967 riots in the USA concluded that violence occurred because of the accumulation of grievances, sharpened through organized protest movements to a point where small incidents were enough to set off an explosion. This is a 'breakdown' approach, and has been challenged more recently. Feagon and Hala argue that violence occurred because of a 'failure of the existing urban political system to respond adequately to their [the ghetto inhabitants'] desires and aspirations'.

Gurr produced a comparative historical study of crime and conflict in London, Stockholm, Sydney and Calcutta since 1800 to provide some insight into the decline of public order. His major conclusion was that 'public order depends more on basic socio-economic and political circumstances than on conditions controlled by the law, the police, the courts, or the prisons'.

BT

**polygraph.** See LIE DETECTION.

**Poor Law.** The English Poor Law established a system of help for the needy based on local administration and local taxes. Its origins date back to a number of different pieces of 16th-century legislation, eventually incorporated in the Elizabethan Act for the Relief of the Poor (1601). Major changes were made in 1834 with the Poor Law Amendment Act: the country was divided into Poor Law unions, each administered by a locally elected Board of Guardians but acting under a framework of centrally established principles and regulations. The most important principle was that of 'less eligibility': the able-bodied were only offered help under conditions that were 'less eligible' than those of the lowest-paid worker. The principle was put into practice through the workhouse test. The able bodied were no longer offered outdoor relief but could only gain assistance by entering a workhouse. Conditions in the workhouse were designed to discourage entry, and in some workhouses were extremely harsh, though despite the attempt to ensure common standards there were major variations between areas.

The Poor Law began to break down with the establishment of a network of social services from the beginning of the 20th century. A great deal of the credit for these developments can be assigned to social reformers like The WEBBS, who played a major role in the review of the operation of the poor laws undertaken by Royal Commission on the Poor Laws (1905-9). The Poor Laws were not finally abolished until 1948.

Some argue that some of the Poor Law principles, such as less eligiblity and the distinction between the deserving and the undeserving poor, are still influential. The poor laws, and in particular the way they were operated in the interwar years are remembered by many and colour attitudes towards the social services, in particular the acceptance of means-tested benefits (see MEANS TEST).

MPJ

**Popper, Sir Karl** (1902- ). Philosopher of science. Born in Austria, Popper emigrated first to New Zealand and then to London, and taught at the LSE from 1949 until 1969. He took British citizenship, and was later knighted. Main works: *The Logic of Scientific Discovery* (1935/1959), *The Open Society and its Enemies* (1945), *The Poverty of Historicism* (1957), *Conjectures and Refutations* (1963), *Objective Knowledge* (1972). Popper believed that his principle of falsifiability resolved the problem of INDUCTION. Following HUME, one could never prove an argument by VERIFICATION, but a single disconfirming case would falsify it. It also expressed a classically liberal suspicion of dogmatism which inspired his own (highly dogmatic) attack on what he called HISTORICISM — the belief that it is possible to make and act upon long-term predictions about social development. The social sciences should set themselves less ambitious goals, contributing to modest exercises in 'piecemeal social engineering'. He is close to logical POSITIVISM, though he diverges from it on important points. His philosophy was the principal target of the Frankfurt School's criticisms in the *Positivismusstreit*. His account of scientific development has been severely criticized in both historical and philosophical terms (see FEYERABAND; PARADIGM), but it remains influential.

WO

**population pyramid**. A graphic representation of the age-and-sex distribution of a population, current births forming the foundation and the oldest members the apex, males and females being divided by the central vertical of the pyramid. The slopes of the pyramid faces show the rates at which the numbers of males and females in the existing population fall off with age: they do not represent the mortality to be expected of any individual generation. Departures from symmetry between the distributions for males and females are readily detected when they are adjoined in the form of a pyramid, and bulges or gaps in the age distribution show up against the mostly smooth profile of its faces.

The age-and-sex distribution of a population is absolutely essential for DEMOGRAPHY, as populations with similar size but with differing distributions subject to the same intensity of MORTALITY and FERTILITY will have differing birth and death rates. Age and sex form the most fundamental categories for the organization of social relations, and changes in the relative sizes of these categories can have consequences in all areas of social structure. Disaggregation by age and sex is the first step in any sociological analysis of population. Changes in overall population size are accompanied in the short and medium term by changes in the age-and-sex composition, and it is often in this way that they have their most important sociological effects.

See DEMOGRAPHY; SEX RATIO; SOCIAL DEMOGRAPHY.

JL

**population theory.** The central aim of population theory is to provide a general explanation of the levels of population to be found in different societies at different times, and of changes in these levels. DEMOGRAPHY concerns itself largely with the arithmetical aspects of population processes, and remains almost entirely empirical, while the general area of population studies tends to be merely descriptive. The paucity of sound theory in this area has come to the attention of sociologists and others, especially in the light of the general interest in the increase in population of developing countries, seen as a population explosion (see DEMOGRAPHIC TRANSITION). Existing theories have ben examined with renewed critical interest in sociology, but the problem has displayed more complications, as social, cultural and political factors have been added to the economic and material ones previously seen as explanatory.

Modern population theory must be traced back to MALTHUS, and can mostly be seen as an attempt to improve or elaborate his theory. Malthus held that the level of population was proportional to the means of subsistence, and was retained at this level against an over-adequate tendency to breed by the positive checks of death and disease, and the preventive checks of abstinence and delayed marriage. An increase in the means of subsistence led to more and earlier marriages and an increase in births, restoring population to proportionality. Later writers have expanded the means of subsistence to include all resources, and have recast the adjustment of population to the material base in SYSTEMS THEORY terms as a HOMEOSTATIC mechanism, but have retained the central emphasis on material and economic factors as determining overall population size, with FERTILITY, MORTALITY and MIGRATION as merely alternative regulating mechanisms.

However, the difficulty of establishing what the relevant resources are, and of distinguishing movements about equilibrium from change of equilibrium, lead many to see the homeostatic view as having little explanatory power. The relevance of material factors in determining population levels may vary across societies and may itself be determined by the structure of those societies, a matter for empirical investigation. It seems likely that material limitations are less important in controlling population in modern societies than in the past.

Both MARX and the 19th-century classical economists were critical of Malthus. The destitute surplus population which Malthus saw as concrete evidence of the control of population was seen by Marx as a structural property of CAPITALISM, produced independently of population levels, the tendency to increase fixed capital limiting variable capital, and hence the demand for labour. The classical economists objected

that the 'law of diminishing returns' which ensured the pressure of population upon subsistence did not apply to manufacturing industry, and hence that population growth need not necessarily be limited by impoverishment. Later economists, including KEYNES after World War I, elaborated these ideas but produced no new general theory of population.

A parallel approach, pioneered by Quetelet, sought general mathematical laws of population growth. Verhulst (1838) proposed a general S-shaped curve of population increase, an idea pursued by Pearl and Reed in the 1920s. Mathematical theory was advanced enormously, even if in an artificially limited situation, by Alfred Lotka (1880-1949), who proved that for a one-sex population subject to constant fertility and no net migration, a stable population would be reached. The age composition, size and vital rates for this population could be calculated, and have achieved a degree of empirical support. Stable population theory forms an important continuing line of research in mathematical demography.

Neo-Malthusian theory lumps together as regulating mechanisms processes that are widely different in their degree of mediation by purposeful social action and social structure, from the mainly biological processes of death and disease, through the mixed character of fertility, to the purely social process of migration. Sociological analysis has attempted to understand the role of social factors in determining the course of these processes, treating them as having some causal efficacy over population levels, rather than merely as regulatory responses. The sociology of fertility has been most studied, partly because the demographic transition model suggests variations in fertility as more important for population size than variations in mortality, and partly because of economic models of rational child-bearing which can be related to the rich field of family sociology.

See also SOCIAL DEMOGRAPHY.

JL

**population turnaround.** The process of migration from cities to the countryside which has characterized the population of many advanced capitalist societies. This reverses the centuries-old prevailing pattern of MIGRATION in many cases (see DEMO-GRAPHIC TRANSITION).

HN

**populism.** The generic name given to diverse political movements, the main common feature of which is an appeal to the people as a whole, with an emphasis on the ordinary citizen as opposed to big business and giant trade unions. Populist rhetoric is much more widespread than are populist organizations and is adopted by some politicians within orthodox parties, especially those challenging the leadership and received ways of thinking. For populists, the people are the source of political virtue but are beset by remote, powerful and malign enemies. In addition to the belief in a conspiracy against the ordinary man in the street, populism has had the following features: support from those who are normally the backbone of centre and liberal parties; an extremist language and behaviour in politics; a reactionary programme which by seeking to reverse and deflect the dominant trends of modern times becomes, paradoxically, revolutionary; and a spectacular comet-like path across the political heavens. Though a narrow characterization of populism would confine the term to the Russian Narodnik groups of the 1880s and the American People's Party of the 1880s and 1890s, it has been applied to FASCIST and national socialist movements, Poujadism, Peronism and even McCarthyism, Plaid Cymru and the Scottish National Party.

See NATIONALISM.

JS

**positive economics.** The dominant method of economic analysis, in which theoretical predictions are tested against empirical evidence. Positive economics is concerned with what is or will be the case, in contrast to normative economies (see WELFARE ECON-OMICS) which employs ethical judgements about what ought to be the case. Examples of positive statement include: a reduction in the price of a good will lead to an increase in the

DEMAND for it; a rise in social security benefit will reduce the total number of hours worked by the labour force; an increase in the money supply will lead to a rise in the general price level. The veracity of all of these statements is capable of being tested by an appeal to the facts.

See EMPIRICISM; POSITIVISM.

RR

**positivism.** At its most general, the view that empirical science is the only valid form of human knowledge. COMTE saw knowledge as developing from a 'theological' to a 'metaphysical' and finally to a 'positive' stage. Positive science rejects supernatural forces and abstract, speculative principles; it records the objectively given relations between observable phenomena and codifies these in universal and certain LAWS. This knowledge forms the basis for the prediction and control of natural and social processes; it therefore sustains a scientific or positive politics which can organize social life on a rational basis. Positivism, Comte believed, should literally become a religion which would replace the established churches.

Comte's full political and social pro-gramme inspired substantial social move-ments in the later 19th century but was rejected by a number of writers, from J.S. MILL onwards, who broadly accepted his view of the nature of science. This con-ception, whose roots can be traced back well beyond Comte himself, was extremely influential in the philosophy of natural science and was often extended to the emergent social sciences by, for example, DURKHEIM.

*Logical positivism* or logical empiricism is a doctrine developed in the 1920s and 1930s by the VIENNA CIRCLE, which drew heavily on the philosophies of Ernst Mach (1838-1916) and Bertrand Russell (1872-1970). The Vienna Circle concentrated on the analysis of scientific statements, whose meaning consisted in (or, in later formula-tions, depended on) the possibility of their VERIFICATION. Science is made up of empirically verifiable propositions recording isolated atomic facts (see EMPIRICISM). The theory of language underlying this philo-sophy of science was largely demolished in the later work of Wittgenstein, who inaugurated the tradition of linguistic analysis in post-war Anglo-Saxon philosophy. It took time, however, for the implications for science to be worked out. Despite its manifestly inadequate account of EXPLANATION, a modified form of logical positivism, strongly influenced by POPPER, remained predominant in the philosophy of social science. More recently this consensus has been shattered by the growth of REALIST philosophies of science and by the revival of HERMENEUTIC and MARXIST approaches to the social sciences. Perhaps the most explicit confrontation was the *Positivismusstreit* (positivism dispute) between the neo-Marxist Frankfurt School (see CRITICAL THEORY) and Popper and his supporters.

See P. Halfpenny, *Positivism and Sociology* (1982).

WO

**post-industrial society.** A term coined by Daniel BELL, indicating an updating of INDUSTRIAL SOCIETY theory. In the last third of the 20th century several of the richest capitalist countries reached a position in which the proportion of the labour force employed in manufacturing industries had declined to less than a half the total labour force and the proportion in service occupations, such as workers in health, education and welfare, communications and leisure, and finance and secretarial staff was constantly rising. This led to theories that societies in which this is happening are post-industrial, no longer dominated by the industrial imperatives of capitalism but by other (usually technical and/or cognitive) imperatives, and that the traditional forms of economic, political and ideological organization could not survive in this new era. The notion is sometimes generalized to STATE SOCIALIST societies in an updating of the convergence thesis of Industrial Society theory. It is too early to assess the salience of these views, particularly in a period when most capitalist economies are in recession rather than post-industrial affluence, when manufacturing jobs are being lost due to slumps in demands rather than technological obsolescence, and when welfare services are being stretched, but not by leisure. The crisis of

basic resources being consumed at a rate faster than they can apparently be replaced may turn the world into a post-industrial society in a way not envisaged by the theorists.

The term is also used as a synonym for 'post-capitalist' society in which case it operates as a critique of the Marxist theory of the capitalist MODE OF PRODUCTION. Here the argument is that CAPITALISM has transformed itself without a proletarian revolution into a society in which the problems of affluence can be more easily resolved. SOCIAL STRATIFICATION and/or CLASS STRUCTURE in such a society is not predicated on relations to the means of production but on access to knowledge or information or other cognitive assets. Against this view some Marxists and others have argued that all these developments can be assimilated to a more traditional view of advanced capitalism and nation-states, and that in essentials the class and state structure and the propensity for crisis of the capitalist and international system have not changed.

LS

**Potlatch.** See RECIPROCITY.

**poverty.** Early studies by BOOTH and ROWNTREE attempted to assess the numbers of people who had insufficient income to maintain physical efficiency, that is, subsistence or absolute, poverty. This assumes that a poverty line can be constructed at a level which permits expenditure necessary to subsist, or to be physically able to work, but no more. In the THIRD WORLD today a similar concept is that of basic needs (see NEEDS, BASIC). The notion of subsistence poverty has been criticized. Despite the appearance of scientific objectivity, it is based on arbitrary judgements about exactly what items are necessary for physical efficiency, and similarly it fails to take account of how families actually spend money and ignores social, cultural and psychological factors.

These criticisms have led to the discussion of relative poverty. A person is considered poor if his/her income is so much lower than that of the rest of the society that he/she cannot afford the kind of goods and conditions accepted as essential in that society. This definition involves comparison with others rather than with an abstract definition of adequacy; it recognizes the importance of social, culture and psychological factors, and that there can be no once-and-for-all definition of poverty. What is considered being poor in one society at one point in time will not be poor in the same society at a different point in time or in a different society at the same point in time.

Relative poverty is necessarily based on value judgements, but unlike discussions based on subsistence poverty, this is explicitly recognized. It is fair to question whose value judgements are and should be used. Public discussion of poverty normally is based on the value judgements of external researchers and commentators rather than on the views of those with low incomes. P. Townsend's *Poverty in the United Kingdom* (1979) constitues a major empirical discussion of the extent of both absolute and relative poverty, and argues that relative poverty prevents participation in the life of the COMMUNITY and creates RELATIVE DEPRIVATION of a moral as well as material type (*see* UNDERCLASS).

See also F. Lafitte, 'Income Deprivation' in R. Holman (ed.), *Socially Deprived Families in Britain* (1970).

MPJ

**poverty trap.** The situation facing low-income families who are also in receipt of MEANS-TESTED benefits. A rise in income may mean that they lose some or all of their means-tested benefits. This may off-set some or all the benefit of the increased income. This problem is exacerbated if the rise in income means that the persons have to start paying income tax when they did not do so before.

In the UK there is a wide range of benefits offered on a means-tested basis, including FAMILY INCOME SUPPLEMENT and rent and rates rebates. Not all these benefits will be adjusted immediately to when income rises, so the effect of the poverty trap may be delayed. Tax thresholds are also raised regularly, so that complications posed by entry into income tax brackets will not always occur. Nevertheless, those whose incomes are close to the tax threshold often lose a considerable proportion of any increase achieved. This can be worsened by INFLATION, which raises money incomes. Thus a person who attempts to increase a low income by working more hours may find that the combined effect of the withdrawal of several means-tested benefits (as his or her income rises) and increased income tax payments means a marginal TAX rate of more than 100 per cent.

MPJ, RR

**power.** According to WEBER's classic definition, power is 'the probability that one actor within a social relationship will be in a position to carry out his will despite resistance regardless of the basis on which this probability rests'. Power is an aspect of all relationships of social interdependence, from the intimate interdependence of husband and wife to the interdependence of larger social units such as nation-states. Power is always relational: it is meaningless to say that a person or a group 'has power' without specifying in relation to which other people or groups they have it and what it enables them to do. To exercise power it is necessary to have some control over whatever it is that others desire, to be able to withhold what they need. This control is generally to some degree reciprocal, though by no means necessarily equally reciprocal. It is essential to think in terms of balances and imbalances of power. Thus, wherever two or more people or groups perform specialized functions for each other (see DIVISION OF LABOUR), each has a measure of potential power over the other; but the balances of power between them may be relatively equal or unequal, relatively stable or constantly fluctuating, and they change and develop through continual trials of strength. Power is a social process rather than a fixed structure or entity. The more nearly equal the balances of power within a web of social interdependence, the more the concept of power shades over into that of constraint, which people inevitably exert over each other simply by reason of their interdependence.

Weber's definition is deliberately un-specific about the resources which can be used in the exercise of power. In fact, anything which gives one person or group a degree of control over what others want or need can be seen as a power resource. Among resources discussed by sociologists are ownership of the means of production, income, STATUS-honour, sacramental and MAGICAL capacities, scarce SKILLS or knowledge, and CHARISMA. What works as a power resource depends on the type of society: for instance, ownership of the means of production is less significant in a HUNTING-GATHERING society than in a CAPITALIST society, while control over sacramental or magical rites is less significant in modern industrial societies than in many pre-industrial societies.

Weber discussed CLASSES, STATUS-GROUPS and parties as three kinds of social grouping found within patterns of SOCIAL STRATIFICATION, each of them charactertized by its position in relation to the control of certain kinds of power resource: economic resources in the case of classes, the distribution of 'status-honour' in the case of status-groups (this implies the capacity to exact deference as a power-resource), and access to the politico-legal apparatus of the state in the case of parties. Weber did not write about 'class, status, and power' — a common misunderstanding — but about three kinds of social grouping linked to three kinds of power resource.

The distribution of power resources of various sorts tends to become organized and institutionalized into relatively stable patterns of domination charactertistic of societies of particular historical types. An important element in this process of INSTITU-TIONALIZATION is the growth of LEGITIMACY. Control over resources can yield domination with which people comply for the sake of expedience, without considering it legitimate. Domination which the dominated accept as legitimate, in terms of their values, is usually called AUTHORITY. Weber distinguished three pure types of authority by the grounds on which they claimed legitimacy. Rational-legal authority rested upon 'a belief in the legality of enacted rules and the right of those elevated to authority under such rules to issue commands'. Traditional authority rested on 'an established belief in the sanctity of immemorial traditions and the legitimacy of those exercising authority under them' (see TRADITION). Finally, charismatic authority rested on 'devotion to the exceptional sanctity, heroism or exemplary character of an individual person, and of the nor-mative patterns or order revealed or ordained by him'. BUREAUCRACY is the exemplar of rational authority. PATRIARCHA-LISM, PATRIMONIALISM and FEUDALISM are among its traditional precursors. Charismatic authority has repeatedly created social movements through history; it is a revolutionary force in state and church, but inevitably becomes transformed or 'routinized' into one of the other forms of administration when the charismatic leader himself is no longer present.

The greater the degree of legitimacy accorded a pattern of authority, the less likely is it that overtly coercive means will be necessary for the exercise of power. This point has been taken up by a number of modern Marxist writers. GRAMSCI analysed the role of a whole network of cultural institutions in establishing the HEGEMONY of a ruling class, by creating the mass consent which reduces the level of coercion necessary for the maintenance of its domination. Similarly, ALTHUSSER argued that in capitalist societies 'ideological state apparatuses' function to inculcate 'respect for the socio-technical division of labour'. ADORNO spoke of the 'total reification' of the social consciouness which prevented the formation of independent critical consciousness.

Studies of the distribution of power in modern societies have been much concerned with the existence or non-existence of stable ELITES. C. Wright MILLS's *The Power Elite* (1956) attempted to demonstrate the coalescence of a single (albeit loosely co-ordinated) military-industrial-political complex at the pinnacle of power in the USA, arguing that the power elite owed its coherence in part to its members being drawn from similar social backgrounds. That argument entered Ralph Miliband's *The State in Capitalist Society* (1969), which provoked a considerable debate between Miliband and Nicos Poulantzas, a follower of Althusser, who argued in *Political Power and Social Classes* (1973) that it was largely irrelevant to study the social backgrounds from which members of powerful elites were drawn, because these could change without in any way changing the way power worked in capitalist society.

Other empirical studies have focused on

local communities. Robert Dahl's *Who Governs?* (1961) sought to demonstrate that in New Haven, Connecticut, there was no single power elite, but rather a PLURALIST pattern of politics in which different people were involved in decisions on different issues (see DECISION-MAKING), the whole system held together by democratically-elected politicians. Later authors argued that in focusing on decisions Dahl had failed to take account of the capacity of some groups to ensure that certain issues never appear on the political agenda and remain 'non-decisions'. Still less had he taken account of the hegemony of ideological assumptions which shape the workings of power. This controversy is surveyed in Steven Lukes, *Power: A Radical View* (1974).

SJM

**pragmatism.** A theory of meaning and truth largely developed by American philosophers, in which the truth of a statement is a matter of its practical usefulness in 'help (ing) us to get into satisfactory relations with other parts of our experience' (William James).

See also DEWEY; MEAD; SYMBOLIC INTERACTIONISM.

See N. Reschen, *Methodological Pragmatism* (1977).

WO

**praxis.** A Greek word meaning practical action, 'doing'; generally contrasted with contemplation, 'thinking'. The word entered modern thought principally through Hegelian Marxism, Lukács and the Frankfurt School. In this tradition the primacy of 'material' praxis is asserted EPISTEMOLOGICALLY: objective knowledge is discovered through practical action in the sphere of material production, usually by a CLASS rather than by isolated individuals. Other sociologists often share the general epistemological preference but do not restrict the discovery of knowledge to the economic sphere or to classes (e.g. P. Berger, *The Sacred Canopy*, 1967).

MM

**PRE.** See ASSOCIATION, COEFFICIENTS OF.

**prediction.** In natural science, statements about future events which are deductions from general laws confirmed by empirical verification, such as statements about the path of future movements of the planets around the sun. In social science, deductions from social LAWS which are conditional statements about future events in the social world. Few successful predictions of social events have been made, for the same reasons that social laws have not been developed, and the additional reason that if a prediction about society is made, human beings may act to prevent it occurring. In statistics (e.g. REGRESSION ANALYSIS) the term refers to the ability, given the values of one variable, to estimate or guess the values of another variable with which the first variable is associated.

MB

**prejudice.** A negative, unfavourable attitude towards a group or its individual members which stems from psychological processes within the bearer of the attitude rather than from reality-testing of the attributes of the group in question. The beliefs about the group towards which prejudice is directed are usually STEREOTYPED. Some forms of prejudice are the expression of what may be considered personality weaknesses: the prejudiced person may need to vent aggression on a scapegoat to balance other elements within his own make-up; such characteristics are associated with AUTHORITARIANISM. Similar attitudes can result from the experience of growing up in a group whose members share them, and they may be better regarded as illustrations of ETHNOCENTRISM. Hostile attitudes can also be cultivated as a result of opportunism, when ethnic distinctions are utilized in order to advance an economic policy or a political career. Attitudes and behaviour may also be role-determined, as when the holder of a particular post is required by his employer to discriminate; where people feel under pressure to behave in an expected manner they often develop attitudes that justify what they have to do. Thus prejudice may lead to discriminatory behaviour and discriminatory social patterns encourage the growth of prejudice (see ALLPORT).

MPB

**pressure groups.** The role of pressure groups in society was given academic prominence by A.F. Bentley, who argued that an understanding of government is only possible when groups and their activities have been identified. Political outcomes result from the interaction of groups: 'all phenomena of government are phenomena of groups pressing one another, forming one another and pushing out new groups.'

Pressure groups have been increasingly studied with the development of PLURALISM. It is argued that they perform a democratic role by aggregating and articulating interests, bringing pressure to bear on governments to respond to popular demands. This implies both equality of group access to government and of finance and organization, a 'balance' of interests represented, and a correlation between the importance and/or urgency of issues and the degree of influence achieved by groups concerned.

Pressure groups have been categorized as 'sectional' and 'promotional'. Sectional groups exist to continuously advance or protect a sector of society on any relevant matters; for example, business (Confederation of British Industry, National Association of Manufacturers), labour (National Union of Mineworkers, United Auto Workers) and agriculture (National Farmers' Union). Promotional groups have a membership with more socio-economic variety, existing to advocate change in one particular policy area such as morality (National Viewers' and Listeners' Council), environment (Friends of the Earth) and consumer standards (Campaign for Real Ale). These may concentrate greater attention on publicity campaigns and lobbying non-governmental organizations such as the media (NVLC) or the breweries (CAMRA).

This categorization may be inappropriate: many groups have a sectional membership and operate within a specific policy area: for example Gingerbread (one-parent families), the Automobile Association (motorists), Age Concern (the elderly).

Critics of the traditional understanding of the term argue (1) it takes insufficient account of institutional groups (e.g. government departments may compete to influence policy-making); (2) it ignores those who can exercise influence without using formal organizational structures; (3) it is of little use in comparing political influence in pluralist societies with developing or communist societies, where interests may coalesce on tribal or institutional bases.

JWM

**prestige.** See OCCUPATIONAL PRESTIGE; STATUS.

**Prices and Incomes Policy.** A policy which aims to restrain the rate of increase of prices, especially during periods of cost-push INFLATION. In the UK, between 1965 and 1971 such a policy was administered by the National Board for Prices and Incomes. The Prices and Incomes Act (1966) gave the Board statutory authority to review wage and price increases, and the Government power to enforce the Board's recommendations. Since 1972 prices and incomes policy has been operated in a variety of forms, ranging from 'freezes' and specified percentage 'norms' to the Labour Government's 'Social Contract' with the Trades Unions, whereby the Unions agreed to moderate wage demands in return for the adoption of certain social and industrial policies. At the same time the Price Commission had the power to regulate certain proposed price increases. The Conservative Government of Margaret Thatcher rejected prices and incomes policy in favour of a MONETARIST approach to the regulation of inflation. Critics of this policy, who favour a return to some form of incomes policy, claim that only an incomes policy can combine income and price stability with full employment (see UNEMPLOYMENT). Others reject this view, claiming that at best incomes policy achieves temporary wage/price stability at the cost of a subsequent 'explosion' in prices.

See MINIMUM WAGE POLICY.

RR

**price system.** See MARKET SYSTEM.

**primary process.** See PSYCHOANALYSIS.

**Prisoner's Dilemma.** See GAME THEORY.

**probability.** In statistical theory, the theoretical relative frequency of an occurrence of a certain kind of event in the long run. Probability theory is central to STATISTICS, and is the theoretical basis of random SAMPL-ING and the NORMAL DISTRIBUTION.

MB

**problematic.** Widely used as a noun by German and French writers to denote an entire framework of theoretical questions, assumptions, methodological prescriptions etc. It expresses the HOLISTIC view that individual statements must be understood in terms of the framework or universe of DIS-COURSE within which they occur.

See L. Althusser, *For Marx* (1965), *Reading Capital* (1965).

WO

**problem family.** A term widely used especially in the 1950s and 1960s, but a precise definition has never been offered. It was based on the belief that there were a number of families with multiple problems (especially CHILD CARE) which were resistent to measures of general social amelioration. The impression was given that their family life was disorganized, behaviour (especially by the parents) was compulsive, and financial crises recurred regularly. The idea has links with a strong tradition in British social thinking, but was most closely associated with the Pacifist Service Units, which dealt with bombed-out families considered unfit for rehousing during World War II, and later with the Family Service Units, which built on this experience and offered intensive service to clients in over 20 British towns. The idea influenced a number of official Committees of the 1950s, including the Ingleby and Younghusband Reports. The term fell into abeyance in official circles in the mid 1960s, but reappeared in the early 1970s with discussion of the CYCLE OF DEPRIVATION.

MPJ

**production systems.** The notion that characteristic methods of organizing the LABOUR PROCESS profoundly affect the attitudes and behaviour of workers dates well back into the 19th century; much discussion occurred over the 'factory system'. With the appearance of systematic research and theory in industrial sociology, efforts were made from the mid-1950s to classify the main forms of production system in modern industry and specify their probable consequences for industrial behaviour. Technology proved an important

point of reference; yet the notion of production system embraces a wider set of facts than this equipment. The simples IDEAL TYPES commonly in use are unit production, mass production, and process production systems.

Unit production involves 'one-off' articles, either relatively simple (a made-to-measure bookcase) or more complex (a specialized radio-transmitter) or highly elaborate (a space satellite). It tends to depend on a specific customer-order, to be craft or specialist-based, and to require a relatively lengthy and error-prone production period. Mass-production is linked to standardized articles produced in great volume. Here, a fairly dependable market exists, or can be developed through marketing campaigns. Innumerable products are of this type, from plastic buckets to automobiles. Production relies frequently on moving conveyor-belts, assembly lines and packaging equipment, giving rise to a large number of semi-skilled tasks. With more complex products, co-ordination of the flows of sub-assemblies can generate severe pressures: a minor breakdown can bring to a halt a whole department or factory. Process production is characteristically associated with liquids, gases, pulps, powders, or molten metals. It conjures up images of an integrated steel plant, a paper-mill, above all of oil refineries. Here too, markets for the product tend to be stable, at least up to the medium term. The fluid nature of the material being worked permits an elaborate, sometimes highly automated technology. Maintaining this equipment requires a large workforce of skilled operatives. Those involved in production may frequently be concerned with monitoring instruments, preparing shift reports, or making occasional adjustments to maintain the quality of the product.

Most actual plants or factories do not fit any one of these three ideal types perfectly, while some contain elements of all three. Efforts to create more complete classifications are frequent, particularly to better understand the consequences of automation. But there appear to be important differences from one country to another over how the human work associated with a given product or level of technical complexity is organized in detail.

See also ALIENATION; LABOUR PROCESS; ORGANIZATION; SOCIO-TECHNICAL SYSTEM.

MR

**productivity.** See EFFORT BARGAIN; HUMAN RELATIONS MOVEMENT.

**professions.** Originally signifying the 'liberal professions' (traditionally the Law, the Church, Medicine and the Armed Services), the number of occupational groups (see DIVISION OF LABOUR) now considered professions or laying claim to possess professional status is very broad. No complete consensual sociological definition exists, nor is any precise 'official' definition offered by the state. However, the state is in practice directly involved in the achievement by an occupational group of socially recognized and legally valid professional status. Any service requiring high expertise, and able to argue that its exercise involves ethical discretion and a measure of 'disinterestedness', tends to seek from the state a delegated right to monopolize training and authenticate qualification in its area of specialism. To reinforce its claim it may elaborate codes of practice and ethics (desirably supported by sanctions) to govern its practitioners' conduct. Once a monopoly right to certify and discipline practitioners is granted, it will generally be vigilantly enforced.

But the autonomy of some professions from the state is enigmatic. Certification may be undertaken by bodies in which state agencies have a major voice, as with school-teaching or nursing (not to mention the ancient 'liberal' profession of commissioned service in Arms). A further problematic area (from a practical as well as conceptual viewpoint) is the distinction between professional bodies and TRADE UNIONS. Craft unions amongst manual workers attempt to monopolize certificate via APPRENTICESHIP and to discipline members. Organizations such as the British or American Medical Association negotiate rewards and conditions on behalf of doctors. Such complexities are a reminder that concepts like profession are socially defined, and vary in accepted popular content according to the success of groups in pursuing their occupational strategies. That Public Relations persons have sought recognition as 'professionals' is an ironic reminder of the role of ideology in this sphere.

MR

The focus of the sociological analysis of professional occupations has shifted during this century. An early concern was the identification of the special characteristics of professional activity which set it apart from ordinary work and from entrepreneurial employment. These included:- a systematic body of knowledge inculculated through a specialized intellectual training, high ethical standards including a selfless, non financial orientation of service to the public interest and autonomy over work.

Writers like Carr-Saunders (*Professions: Their Organization and Place in Society*, 1928) and Marshall (*Class, Citizenship and Social Development*, 1964), following DURKHEIM, saw in their perception of the altruism of the professions the prospect of co-operative as opposed to competitive exchange in the division of labour. Like MARX's proletariat or MANNHEIM's intellectuals, the professions were capable of leading the way to a more progressive social order. This vision is echoed by theories of SOCIAL DIFFERENTIATION. The growth of professionalism was an integral part of the increasing complexity of the division of labour consequent on the development of scientific knowledge and technique. At a time when belief in the political impartiality of science was still largely intact, the privileges of professional offices, including monopoly rights or practice, were functional for both the individual client and for society.

The challenge to this came from sociologists who were less content to accept the professionals' own ideal representations of themselves, and more interested in exploring the empirical reality of professionals at work. Their research threw up an alternative view of the professions as self-interested occupational groups seeking to protect a monopoly terrain within the division of labour and using as instruments to maintain, if not enlarge, their sphere of influence those very organizational attributes which made up the beneficient ideal type of professionalism in earlier theories.

Everett C. Hughes (*Men and their Work*, 1952), one of the earliest and most influential spokesmen of this view, redirected attention on the benefits of occupational monopoly and immunity away from the client and towards the practitioner. The safeguards which are said to be necessary to shield vulnerable clients from inept or unscrupulous practice also serve as a defensive screen for the professional. By representing their clients as incompetent to judge their own best interests or when they have been served, and by insisting upon peer review as the only legitimate basis for work evaluation, the professions uphold the fiction that their product is of a uniform quality. By the same means individual work performance is screened from critical inspection and from possible adverse judgements on the part of the client.

This perspective conceptualizes professionalization as a device employed by occupational groups to secure effective control and autonomy over work conditions. More recently, attention has been turned towards the analysis of professional autonomy itself. Neo-Marxist writers, in the search for a means of drawing the boundary between the exploiting and exploited classes in highly differentiated occupational structures, have challenged the image of autonomy, arguing that the source of the ideological power of the higher professions is to be found in their incorporation in the ruling class. The hub of the argument rests on the extent to which the monopoly rights of the professions depend on the gift of the state. Those who oppose this view (e.g. E. Freidson, *The Profession of Medicine*, 1970) draw attention to the processual development of professional organization and power, and the capacity to generate direct public sanction. When a profession achieves the status of MORAL ENTREPRENEUR it has diversified its power base to a degree that renders it independent of any single form of sponsorship.

See especially MEDICAL PROFESSION.

See also CLASS: *Neo-Marxist theories*; IATRO-GENESIS; LAW: *Legal Profession*; MIDDLE CLASS; PSYCHIATRY.                    NH

**projective tests.** A class of psychological test, named by H.A. Murray and L.K. Frank in the 1930s, where the respondent is invited to attribute his or her own meanings onto a collection of standard but deliberately vague and ambiguous elements. The tests aim to reveal latent or even unconscious patterns of the PERSONALITY through the low level of awareness characterizing the interpretation of ambiguous, ill-defined material.

The theoretical roots of projective techniques can be traced to FREUD's theory of dreams and JUNG's studies of word association, but it was Jung's disciple RORSCHACH who was responsible for the first and most commonly used projective test, the Ink-blot or Rorschach Test. Other tests require the attribution of a narrative to the characters in a series of drawings (e.g. the THEMATIC APPERCEPTION TEST) or the completion or ordering of drawings and pictures (as in the Tomkins-Horn picture arrangement test).

Projective techniques developed in the context of clinical case studies, where detailed attention could be given to the interpretation of the flood of response typically elicited. The wide variety of social and psychological factors reflected in those response has made projective tests useful in social psychology and anthropology, despite a lack of emphasis upon objectivity and replicability in their interpretation. At the same time, the sensitivity of projective techniques to external factors and the unique features of personality diminishes their usefulness as standardized indicators of personality.

While the response to projective tests may involve projection in the Freudian sense of the attribution to others of the Id's unacceptable impulses (see DEFENCE MECHANISMS), they usually do not. Interpretation relies upon comparing test results with established case studies or constructing index scores from the relative frequencies of selected types of response. More recently, a concern with objective scoring has favoured tests that lend themselves to SCALING methods, such as picture-ordering techniques, and in many social science contexts KELLY'S REPERTORY GRID TECHNIQUE or Osgood's SEMANTIC DIFFERENTIAL have replaced projective tests in the measurement of individual meaning, at least partly because of their scaling properties.

See also AUTHORITARIAN PERSONALITY; ORT.

**property.** Something which is privately owned; ownership concerns the legally enforceable right to benefit from, control or alienate (i.e. transfer to another) property. When these rights are fully developed, it is often customary to describe it as absolute property.

Embedded in the notion of property are a complex set of legal RIGHTS. The sociologist is concerned with the derivation of these rights and their exercise within society. Property rights are not only rights authoritatively defined — which introduces crucial sociological questions of POWER and LEGITIMACY — but are a set of rules affecting the allocation of resources and hence life-chances. From a Marxist standpoint, property rights allow the expropriation of the surplus and legitimate the bourgeois social order.

Although sociologists have been reticent in dealing with the concept, sociology assesses the extent to which the proliferation of legal categories of ownership has resulted in real changes in control and benefit, or the extent to which they are a legal mystification. In particular, sociologists do not reduce the discussion of property rights to purely technical (legalistic) exercise and place this discussion in a broader social context, relating to the structure of inequality, distributional justice and the balance between individual and communal rights. This is important as the complexity of property rights is increasing in all advanced capitalist societies (*see below*).

See C. Macpherson (ed.), *Property* (1978).

HN

*History of Property.* Absolute property is comparatively and historically rare. In most primitive and historical societies, private property elements have co-existed with more communal forms in which families, LINEAGES, villages or STATES have possessed collective ownership rights. From Melanesia (see MALINOWSKI) to Mesopotamia to medieval Europe (see FEUDALISM) these complex inter-penetrations have provoked scholarly disputations about the nature of property and power therein. The concept of absolute property was pioneered by Roman Republican Law (SEE MODE OF PRODUCTION, ANCIENT). This survived tenuously through the medieval period to influence, and be enormously boosted by, the advent of CAPITALISM. The late 19th century and the 20th century developed various quasi-socialized property forms, some representing collective organizations of capital (stock exchanges, joint-stock corporations; see CONCENTRATION), others representing wider social groups (state investment and intervention, trade union 'property rights' to jobs). Thus in modern capitalism it is uncommon to find private absolute property rights attached to particular objects (apart from dwellings and personal CONSUMPTION items): property is diffused both through the capitalist CLASS (see BOURGEOISIE, MIDDLE CLASS) and through and even beyond the NATION-STATE. Thus rights to property are almost always more complex than the dominant IDEOLOGY of our time asserts.

MM

**Protestant Ethic thesis.** The name given to a set of ideas presented by WEBER in a series of essays and lectures in which he explored one distinctive feature of modern capitalist society, that is, its peculiar ethos or mentality, the spirit of CAPITALISM, and sought to locate its origins. Though forms of capitalism had existed before, modern capitalism had adopted a uniquely RATIONAL form. It was a form of enterprise employing wage labour in which the maximum profit over the long term was sought on a continuous basis through the organization of production by means of effective calculation of costs and returns and the reinvestment of profit. Avarice had been a feature of societies long before the emergence of modern capitalism; speculative and booty capitalism, financing risky enterprises or exploiting those subjugated in warfare, had been widespread. Even isolated cases of rational capitalistic enterprise existed prior to the Reformation. What Weber sought to cast light upon was the emergence on a large scale, as 'a way of life common to whole groups of men', of a form of rational capitalistic enterprise dependent upon restraint, upon willingness to defer gratification and to reinvest profits rather than enjoy them in conspicuous CONSUMPTION.

Weber argued that the spirit of modern capitalism involved a distinctive set of attitudes toward work, profit and consumption. The medieval attitude to work had viewed it as a necessary evil, to be undertaken to sustain traditionally appropriate standards of consumption. The modern capitalist viewed work as a virtue and an obligation. Industriousness was a major sign of respectability and a worthy character. The medieval attitude to interest and profit had been suspicious, viewing the pursuit of gain as of dubious morality. (The loaning of money at interest was so morally reprehensible that it could only be practised by a non-Christian.) But the ethos of modern capitalism viewed it as laudable, a calling to be followed by the most respected and expected of the humble.

A further feature of the capitalist ethos was that intense devotion to making money was an end in itself. Profit was pursued not for the enjoyment that could then be had from disbursing it in gratification or display. Profit was sought for further profit through reinvestment. The traditional attitude to profit often involved some measure of guilt, leading to its being expended on religious ceremonial to assuage the feelings of an offended God or on communal festivity to assuage the feelings of offended neighbours. In the absence of guilt, economic surplus would be expended on immediate personal pleasure or conspicuous show. The spirit of modern rational capitalism rejected such notions, seeing immorality in the failure to pursue an opportunity for profit, and therefore also in any unnecessary expenditure which could not be devoted to further investment.

What was the source of this non-TRADITIONAL syndrome of attitudes? Weber points to the similarity between the attitudes and prescriptions for conduct which form the spirit of capitalism and those found in the behaviour of the more puritan of the Protestant Reformers. Luther had developed the conception of the 'calling': God's will lay in the fulfilment of those worldly duties which derived from the circumstances in which He had placed us. No honest circumstance was intrinsically more worthy than another, hence the ideal was not renunciation of the world for the monastic life of dedication to God, but the dedication of one's life in this world entirely to Him.

The Reformation, particularly in its more Puritan forms, also promoted a massive rationalization of the religious ethic of its adherents. It eliminated essentially magical forms of salvation such as confession, penance, intervention of saints and the virgin, indulgences etc. Hence the Puritan was faced by a distant and demanding God, and was obliged to live in the temptations of the world and suffer the temptations of the flesh without recourse to any magical remedies (*see* MAGIC) or means of turning aside God's wrath should one succumb. The Puritan was thus forced by his religious doctrine to submit himself to a life of this-worldly asceticism, rigorously controlling his desires and conduct, not exposing himself to any avoidable temptation but methodically committing his life to a disciplined regime of moral conduct.

Right conduct was not seen as being a means to salvation by the Puritans. They rejected the notion of salvation by works for that of salvation by faith alone. Hence there is a puzzle as to why the Puritan should conform to this rigorous ethic. Weber believed the vital factor was the 'psychological sanctions' which derived from the need for *proving* one's faith and salvational status. This took two forms. In the case of Calvinistic forms of Protestantism, the doctrine of predestination dictated that the Elect had been chosen by God for all time. They displayed no outward signs which differentiated them from the damned, and even an inner conviction of salvation might not be conclusive. Hence arose a pressing concern for certainty as to one's standing. While works could not affect one's standing, it was reasoned that since the elect were placed on earth to glorify God through this worldly activity, diligent pursuit of one's calling provided the surest means of dispersing doubt. Since only the elect could truly glorify God by the fruit of their labour, those who seemed to augment the resources given them by God (as in the parable of the talents) could feel some confidence in their election.

John Wesley too stressed the importance of conduct as a sign of true conversion, but in the Protestant sects the rigorous and ascetic conduct of the believer was less important as a source of reassurance to oneself, and more a source of reassurance to others as to one's standing. Weber points to the role here of the concept of the 'believer's church', the idea of the community of the saved, of which the individual must show himself worthy through his conduct, and also to the importance of asceticism as a repudiation of worldliness and a means of stilling the flesh in order to hear the voice of God.

The main thrust of Weber's early discussion of the Protestant Ethic and the Spirit of Capitalism was to point to the congruence, or 'elective affinity' between the two, though the reader assumes that Weber regarded the latter as a direct product of the former. Subsequent criticism of Weber's thesis centred largely on the issue of whether Weber was claiming Protestantism to be the cause of capitalism. In later lectures and writings Weber made it clearer that his view was that capitalism was the result of a multitude of factors including the availability of natural resources, the development of technology, the cost of transportation, availability of a market, and even the climate. There remains to be explained the issue of why large groups of men should begin to live their lives in a manner marked by its diligence, frugality, rational appraisal, and methodical self-denying character. Weber believed that the Protestant ethic, to be found particularly in the development of Calvinist and sectarian practice and doctrine, was the major initial source of the mentality and style of life which gave modern capitalism its distinctive rational character.

Although forms of capitalism, even isolated cases of rational capitalist enterprise, may have existed elsewhere, and although some form of capitalism might have developed in Western Europe even in the absence of Puritan asceticism, Weber believed that the growth as a dominant way of life of rational bourgeois capitalism could largely be seen as a result of the encouragement and legitimation given to such a style of life by the Protestant Ethic.

There is now an enormous literature of exposition and controversy on the Weber thesis. Many critics assume him to be asserting something that he is not, such as that Protestantism causes capitalism, or that Calvinist doctrine encouraged capitalistic enterprise. Others misunderstood Weber's use of the term 'rational capitalism', or fail to appreciate that Weber agreed that forms of

capitalistic enterprise can be run in a traditionalistic manner, and thus without the 'spirit of capitalism'. Still others take him to task for failing to consider the ways in which Calvinist doctrine and practice were themselves susceptible to adaptation as a result of the economic interests of adherents. There is not space here to debate all these issues, which often rest on superficial readings of Weber's texts and misunderstandings of his purpose. However, it must be said that Weber's writings on this topic are fragmentary, occasionally oblique, and sometimes downright cavalier in their treatment of evidence and the reader. If Weber has not always been understood, the fault is partly his own.

See G. Marshall, *In Search of the Spirit of Capitalism* (1982). RW

**psychiatry.** The specialism of medicine concerned with the range of conditions now termed MENTAL ILLNESSES. The term began to be used in England and the USA around the middle of the 19th century, and came to embrace a diverse range of emergent and often competing specialists, then known as asylum doctors, alienists, neurologists and medical psychologists, whose names were as varied as their client groups, institutional locations and theoretical approaches. Medical interest in mental disease was long-standing and specialization in the field was not new, but in the 19th century distinctive PROFESSIONAL groups developed, gaining important legal rights and powers, and establishing professional associations and journals. In England, the Association of Medical Officers of Asylums and Hospitals for the Insane was founded in 1841, the parallel Association of American Institutions for the Insane was established in 1844. This professionalization was closely linked to the establishment of a secure institutional base for specialist practice — the asylums — and to the increasing professionalization of medicine as a whole.

As medical specialists, psychiatrists share a common medical training and clinical role that ensures important general correspondences between psychiatry and medicine. Both share a commitment to the cure of the individual patient's sickness, focussing on AETIOLOGY at the level of the individual, and a commitment to science as the means of providing the explanatory and therapeutic tools for helping the patient. However, the distinctiveness of psychiatric work — the identification and cure of mental and behavioural pathologies — and the establishment of separate institutions for the insane have ensured that psychiatry has remained largely separate from the rest of medicine, and has differed in important respects from its parent. It has been difficult to subject mental and behavioural processes to the sort of scientific analysis, modelled on the natural sciences, demanded by medicine. This has led many to turn to organic accounts of mental illness, but has also encouraged great theoretical diversity and eclecticism among others. Since asylums and mental hospitals have often served as places of last resort for the chronically infirm, the role of psychiatrists has often been custodial and administrative rather than therapeutic. This is reinforced by the powers of compulsory detention historically associated with such institutions.

During this century there have been increasing efforts to change this situation and integrate psychiatric work more fully with medicine and the health services. There has been considerable stress on the inter-relationship of physical and mental illness, and there have been active attempts to model mental health services on those for physical illness — by trying to make the custodial asylums hospitals for acute mental illness (often at the expense of chronic cases), by making voluntary admission the norm, and by diversifying the range of services available. Greater affluence and the development of the WELFARE STATE in the post-war period led to the increased use of non-specialist medical services and public outpatient services in mental health, and there has consequently been a marked expansion of medical and psychiatric work in the field. Both institutions and individuals have turned to medical experts for help with mental and behavioural problems that would formerly have received little medical attention, except perhaps amongst the upper classes. In the UK psychotherapy is almost entirely restricted to the private sector; public sector psychiatry relies heavily on physical methods of treatment, especially drugs.

Psychiatry, like medicine, has come to occupy an increasingly prominent position in contemporary society. It has not escaped criticism any more than medical activities *vis-à-vis* the insane, let alone institutional and legal procedures, did in earlier periods. FREUD complained that medical practitioners lacked the psychological skills and training to understand the psychological aspects of mental pathology and suggested that there could be non-medical psychoanalysts. This has been followed by EYSENCK'S BEHAVIOURIST argument for a divorce of the psychological parts of psychiatry from medicine proper, with psychiatry restricting its attention to mental illnesses with an organic aetiology. During the 1960s writers such as Thomas SZASZ and R.D. LAING, arguing from divergent philosophical stances, asserted the need for a distinctive science of persons in understanding mental disorders and questioned the nature of judgements that define sanity and madness. More recent Marxist critics (e.g. Navarro) have seen both psychiatry and medicine as depoliticizing sickness by focussing on bodily, mental or social processes at the level of the individuals at the expense of the structure and nature of the society that underlies them.

See also WOMEN AND MADNESS.

JB

**psychoanalysis.** Specifically, the set of ideas elaborated by FREUD. The term psychoanalysis, whose first published use came in a paper by Freud in 1897, may refer to any one or all three components of Freudian thought: (1) the general theory of individual psychological functioning, both normal and pathological; (2) the technique of therapy; (3) the method of study of the individual pysche. More generally, the term refers to the ideas of a number of different schools of psychology, including those of JUNG and ADLER, which share certain common features, four of which are important to the psychoanalytic approach: (1) an assumption of psychic or psychological determinism; (2) an emphasis on the purposive, goal-directed nature of human thought and action; (3) a belief in the importance of the unconscious features of mental life; (4) a concern with the genetic or developmental process.

*Psychic Determinism.* All mental events, whether bizarre or irrational thoughts, slips of the tongue, jokes or any other psychological event, have a cause and are a meaningful expression of the individual's psychic life. Since any mental event is meaningful in terms of the individual's psychology, not only is it psychologically determined, but it can also be interpreted. It is therefore possible not only to understand and explain the origin of mental symptoms but also, if desired, to get rid of them. Many mental events, Freud claimed, are *overdetermined*: they have more than one cause, and these multiple causes often operate simultaneously in the causation of an event. The psychoanalytic stress on the meaningfulness of all human psychic life diverges from the canons of POSITIVISM. It introduces problems of reconciling an analysis in terms of meaning with a causal analysis. It also created problems for Freud, who as a doctor trained in the methods of natural science was anxious to relate psychological events to psychical processes in the brain.

*Purpose and Goal-Direction.* The assumption of the purposive, goal-directed nature of human thought and action is given differing content by different psychoanalytic approaches. Freud conceptualized the motivations of human conduct in two different ways that were not properly integrated: in terms of biological drives or instincts that energize and direct human thought and action, and in terms of desires and wishes, a shift between the language of science, causality and objectivity, and a language of meaning, interpretation and subjectivity. The common theme of both is the importance of sexual motivations and the hypothesis of infantile sexuality, an emphasis rejected by other psychoanalysts. Freud's own theorizing of instinctual life changed considerably. His early formulation contrasted the sexual drives related to the need for the preservation of society through reproduction, with the ego drives related to biological needs for survival and hence to self-preservation. The former, whose energy he termed *libido*, operated according to the *pleasure principle*, seeking immediate gratification of its basic needs, and the eradication of tension from them. The *ego drives*

function according to the *reality principle*, seeking to deal with the environment in realistic ways and postponing immediate satisfaction in the interests of long-term advantages. The process whereby instinctual energy comes to be invested in an object — that is, a thing or person — is called *cathexis*. Forces directed at the control of libidinal cathexes are 'anti-cathexes'. In later formulations Freud broadened the concept of sexual drives to include the life-giving drives, giving the term *Eros* to this constellation, now contrasted with the death-giving, destructive forces of the personality, *Thanatos*. In both formulations these drives constitute the dynamic forces of personality and are the source of tension and conflict within the psyche; hence the common characterization of psychoanalytic theory as a 'psychodynamic' theory of personality.

*The Unconscious.* The assumption that much of mental life is unconscious is for many the hallmark of psychoanalytic ideas. By the unconscious is meant not simply what a person is not aware of at a particular moment in time — such psychic material is 'preconscious' — but what is not available to the consciousness by any process of introspection because it is actively repressed (see DEFENCE MECHANISMS). Consequently special techniques are needed to study unconscious mental life. Freud attached importance to two methods of studying the unconscious: free assocation and dream analysis. PROJECTIVE TESTS have also been used by some psychoanalysts and psychologists for a similar purpose.

The technique of *free association* originated in the therapy of one of Freud's early cases, Elizabeth R. The individual is encouraged to relax normal controls on thought, saying everything that comes to mind, regardless of its content. The analyst then selects themes to pursue and interpret. The flow of conscious materials may be subject to unconscious *resistance*, producing a blockage of ideas. Resistance serves to maintain the repression of unacceptable material in the unconscious, and so may itself be a matter for interpretation. Dreams, according to Freud, were the 'royal road' to the unconscious and in dreams the influence of the unconscious is continually present.

Since the unconscious operates according to the principles of the *primary process*, using symbols, condensing or telescoping ideas (condensation) and employing substitutions, the interpretation of dreams as a means of identifying unconscious thoughts, feelings and desires is complex and difficult. The unconscious is structured like a language, but the text of the dream relates to the language of the unconscious in no clear or simple way.

Freud's early theorizing incorporated a topography of mental life that featured three areas: the conscious, the preconscious and the unconscious. In this model the sexual drives were unconscious and the ego drives preconscious. Later he developed a different topography to characterize the structure of the personality, differentiating the *id*, the *ego* and the *superego*. The id is the reservoir of the inherited drives, both Eros and Thanatos, and is unconscious, functioning in accordance with the pleasure principle. It uses energy either in reflex action or in wish fulfillment (the creation of the image of the instinctual object) but it cannot distinguish fantasy and reality. The ego is the representative of reality and develops through interaction with the environment; it functions in accordance with the reality principle and employs rational thought (the *secondary process*). It aims to maintain the individual in the face of demands not only from reality but also from the id and the superego — demands that are often conflicting. The ego that has to divert libidinal energy to serve its own more culturally acceptable and desirable end. Freud called this *sublimation* and saw this process as the basis of civilization and cultural achievement. Both ego and superego play a part in sublimation. The superego develops through *identification* with the parents, that is, coming to empathize with their attitudes and feelings. This results in the *internalization* — the taking in — of their attitudes and standards. The superego has two components: the *conscience* and the *ego-ideal*, the former representing the internalization of what is bad, the latter of what is good.

*The Genetic Process.* Psychoanalysis assumes that the individual's present thoughts, feelings and ways of acting are the result of earlier experiences. For Freud the earlier years of childhood were crucial in determining the subsequent development of personality. He delineated stages of psychosexual development, differentiated in terms of the dominant object of sexual gratification — the focus of libido. At each stage the personality reaches a particular level of organization. Freud assumes an initial bisexual disposition — the possession of the characteristics of both sexes — and a primary narcissism — a self-love. A child's first source of gratification and pleasure is the mouth, and satisfaction comes from sucking and later chewing and biting. This oral stage lasts approximately eighteen months and is followed by the anal stage, the period when satisfaction comes in control of defecation, and toilet-training dominates. This lasts until the child is about three, when the focus of libidinal energy shifts to the genitals and the first phase of genital orientation occurs, the phallic stage. The development of boys and girls now begins to diverge, and the sexual attachment to the parent of the opposite sex becomes especially marked. For boys it is the period of the *Oedipus complex*, for girls of the *Electra complex*. Initially both male and female infants become attached to their mothers, the first love object. For the boy this attachment becomes more libidinal when he enters the phallic stage. The father becomes a more powerful rival, whom in fantasy he fears might kill or castrate him for his choice of love object, the castration complex. The boy also fears the loss of his father's love, hence he represses his desire for his mother and comes to identify more with his father, and his superego develops. The superego is the 'heir of the Oedipus Complex'. Girls do not fear castration, but come to realize that they have already been castrated and to desire a man's penis. *Penis envy* leads both to hostility towards their original love object, the mother, whom they blame for the lack of a penis, and to attachment to the father, who can provide them with a child, the equivalent of or substituted for a penis. In this process the sexual focus shifts from the clitoris to the vagina. The resolution of this rivalry with the mother for the father's love leads to identification with the mother and to the development of the superego. But for the girl, since castration cannot be feared, there is less pressure to overcome the oedipal rivalries, and superego development may be retarded. Freud claimed that the female superego did not attain the strength and independence of the male. This phallic stage, dominated by the Oedipus and Electra complexes is followed by the latency period of relative quiescence in sexual gratification that lasts from about the age of six until puberty. Finally, with puberty the child enters the genital stage, the period of full adult sexuality, which lasts until death.

*Psychopathology.* Psychoanalysis views the symptoms of mental illness as adaptive responses to underlying, often unconscious, dynamics of mental life. They can be explained by the same principles that can explain all mental life, for there is a continuity between normal and abnormal psychological functioning. Pathology occurs when the distribution of energies within the personality becomes unmanageable with the techniques the personality has established.

For Freud, the stages of psychosexual development are crucial to the emergence of a normal, healthy personality and consequently to an understanding of psychopathology. There is a tendency to cling to a particular stage of development, a tendency he describes as *fixation*, and, under adverse circumstances, to return to the point of fixation, *regression*. Pathology arises when in certain circumstances, faced with some frustration — when the individual is unable to secure satisfaction of some desire — the libido regresses and seeks satisfaction in a form suitable to an earlier phase of development, the point depending on earlier fixations. If satisfaction at this level is also impossible because of the demands of the ego or superego, then the libidinal impulses find expression in symptoms. The type of pathology that is manifest depends on the point of fixation and hence on the degree of regression that occurs. Freud himself thought that psychotic symptoms belonged to the pre-Oedipal period before the ego had properly developed. Depressive states represent a fixation at the oral level, schizophrenic or even earlier narcissistic states. Neuroses involved regressions to the anal and phallic stages of development.

*Therapy.* Psychoanalysis as a method of therapy developed in the context of private office practice in which resources were available for an extensive form of therapy. It is a lengthy process, normally requiring 50-minute sessions five days a week for three years or even longer. The therapeutic procedure consists primarily in the transmission to the patient of the analyst's explanations of the patient's mental life in the form of interpretations of the material the patient communicates to the analyst. The aim is to study unconscious processes which do not manifest themselves in direct form and require interpretation. This process of making the unconscious conscious transforms the communication of an explanation of the patient's mental life into a therapeutic process. Consequently the link between explanation and therapy is very close. However, since what is part of the patient's unconscious has been repressed, any attempt to make it conscious is likely to meet with resistance; resistance can be overcome through *transference*: the transferring of emotions and feelings, originally provoked by one person, situation or object on to another, in this case the analyst. These feelings may be both positive and negative. Positive transference aids the analyst because it provides a fund of libidinal energy on which the analyst can draw in overcoming resistances as they are encountered. But negative feelings can also be used by the analyst, for they constitute a miniature, aritifical neurosis focused on the analyst, in which the patient relieves his or her most fundamental conflicts, that can become the object of study.

While the existence of transference is an essential component of successful therapy, its counterpart, *countertransference* — the transferring of the analyst's unconscious feelings on to the patient — is problematic, since it may affect the analyst's judgement and capacity to interpret the patient's communications. Techniques were introduced by Freud to facilitate the analyst's awareness of the problems of countertransference and secure emotional detachment from the patient: training analysis itself, asymmetry in the transmission of personal information, and physical detachment, in which the analyst is out of direct view of the usually supine patient. Some psychoanalysts do not advocate this impersonal stance, arguing for the importance of give-and-take in the analytic relationship, whether it be of emotional warmth or personal information or communication.

Transference in psychoanalysis permitted, although it did not require, a shift of focus from exploring the early experiences of the patient to the immediate relationship of the patient and analyst. Psychoanalysts diverged between those wishing to explore the patient's past and those willing to concentrate almost exclusively on the current feelings and emotions — the 'here and now'. The latter focus is encouraged where time and resources dictate a shortened form of psychoanalysis. Hence much psychoanalytically-oriented psychotherapy focuses on the patient's present rather than past relationships.

*Evaluation.* The development of psychoanalysis in a clinical context of private medicine permitted the development of treatment that was more responsive to the content of patients' thoughts and feeling, allowing them to be examined in depth over a long period of time. It also ensured that both the theory and the method of psychoanalysis, like other medical treatments, would not be subject to systematic scientific evaluation. Medical treatments are largely empirical: few are based on precise knowledge either of the causes of the illness or any rigorous assessment of their value. This is equally true of psychoanalysis. The clinical context does not facilitate rigorous comparison of alternative treatments given to matched samples of patients, even were there agreement as to what constitutes improvement and cure. No studies have evaluated psychoanalytic therapy with proper randomized controlled trials and double-blind procedures. Philosophers such as POPPER and behaviourist psychologists such as EYSENCK argue that psychoanalytic theory does not conform to the canons of positive science, because concepts such as the unconscious cannot, by definition, be observed, and *post hoc* interpretations of behaviour cannot be tested (see POSITIVISM). Against this others argue that the standards of positive science should not be applied to human behaviour and assess psychoanalysis from either a REALIST or CON-VENTIONALIST philosophy of science.

Equally important have been criticisms of the substantive content of psychoanalytic ideas. Two themes have been important: the asocial and a historical character of psychoanalytic ideas, and its sexism. For many writers, psychoanalysis, especially in its orthodox Freudian version, puts too much emphasis on the biological drives underlying behaviour and too little on social relationships. The development of *ego psychology* represents an attempt to redress this balance, for the instinctual forces of the id are given less prominence. Ego psychology counterposes the reasoning, thinking individual relating to the social world with the unconsciously motivated, biologically driven individual. Its focus is still on the individual psyche rather than on interpersonal, social relationships located in a particular social and historical context. From this point of view the defect of psychoanalysis is to offer a general theory of human psychology, whereas the content and concerns of the human psyche are socially given and vary across time and place. This links with criticism of psychoanalysis's reliance on clinical data to support its theoretical and methodological claims. In terms of clinical practice the criticism has been that psychoanalysis, by virtue of its theoretical and therapeutic focus on the individual, must effect the adjustment of individuals to their social milieux rather than focusing on the defects and deficiencies of the milieux that create problems for the individual. Recent attempts have been made by writers such as LACAN to see the id not as the reservoir of biological drives but as the locus of unconscious ideas, socially created and part of the IDEOLOGY of society.

The debate about the sexism of psychoanalysis largely raises similar issues. According to Freud the development of boys and girls begins to diverge once the phallic stage is reached. In this period both GENDER identity and sexuality are determined, and particularly the development of a feminine identity. Accusations of sexism follow from the fact that Freud sees these developments as dictated by girls' physiological characteristics and as both necessary and desirable. Juliet Mitchell in *Psychoanalysis and Feminism* (1974) attempts to rescue Freud from this accusation. Building on Lacan's interpretation of Freud, she argues that Freud provides an account of how sexuality and gender are socially constructed in PATRI-ARCHAL societies. Hence there is no claim as to biological inevitability only the framework for a social psychological analysis.

See also DEFENCE MECHANISMS; FREUD; GENDER; JUNG; KLEIN; PERSONALITY; SEXUALITY.

JB

**psychopathy.** See MENTAL ILLNESS.

**psychoses.** See MENTAL ILLNESS.

**public goods.** Those goods and services which, once the decision has been made to supply them, cannot be withheld from those CONSUMERS who choose not to pay for them. Individuals who consume such goods but are unwilling to pay for them are known as free riders or free loaders. Because there is no way of excluding free riders, private firms would be unwilling to supply these goods. Consequently they are usually supplied by the Government and financed by TAXES, which are able to be levied on all potential users. Examples include national defence, street lighting and, to some extent, public broadcasting. A public good is non-rival, or non-zero sum: one individual's consumption does not reduce the amount of the good available for consumption by others. Unlike private goods, there is no OPPORTUNITY COST of consumption once a decision to supply a given amount of a public good has been made. Though there are few pure public goods in the sense that they are completely non-excludable and non-rival, many goods have some of these properties. These are referred to as quasi-public goods. For example, domestic law enforcement could be performed by private police forces offering protection to subscribers only, but such a system would present difficulties. Many services presently supplied by the State (e.g. health care and education) are not public goods as they could be, and in many cases are, provided adequately by private firms.

RR

**purges and Terror.** These terms are often confused. A purge is either the sacking of employees, usually government employees, or the removal of party membership from individuals in a one-party state either to produce a more active membership or to remove a particular faction from the party. Terror is a deliberate attempt to intimidate the population by means of violence, either on the part of the state, or by a party wishing to overthrow the state. It involves the fear of sudden death and causes individuals to withdraw from political activity. The confusion is partly due to the attempts by TROTSKY and his followers to explain their political defeat in Russia in the 1920s by analogy with the French Revolution: Stalin represents the 'Thermidorean reaction' (i.e. Napoleon) to Robespierre's Terror, as well as being Robespierre himself. Trotsky's analysis was later seized on as an intellectual weapon by Western 'cold warriors'.

Immediately post-revolutionary purges should be distinguished from purges occurring some years after victorious revoutionaries have entrenched themselves in power. In the former case people who are obviously political opponents of the revolutionaries are removed from positions of influence. In the latter, the people removed often tend to be the remnants of the original revolutionaries. In non-revolutionary societies a similar effect can be produced by a decision to expand rapidly the state sector of employment, especially if this involves the recruitment of personnel with a different ideological background to that of the existing bureaucrats (e.g. the New Deal). Just as original idealist revolutionaries tend to be purged at a later date, so too can the recruits of the period of state expansion (e.g. the Loyalty Security Program and McCarthyism).

'Purging' can lead to a condition of 'Terror'. The two phenomena are not mutually exclusive, but are worth distinguishing for the purposes of comparative analysis.

See COUP; POLITICAL VIOLENCE; REVOLUTION.

BT

# Q

**quasi-experiment.** See EXPERIMENT.

**questionnaire.** A systematic, ordered and purpose-designed list of questions by means of which information is obtained from respondents about such topics as their objective characteristics, their past and present behaviour, their attitudes, values and beliefs, their standards for action, and their reasons for acting in a particular way. Usually a questionnaire is set out in an ordered and logical sequence starting with simpler 'factual' questions, progressing to more complex, subjective or sensitive questions.

Question-wording, as S.L. Payne has shown, is an art. Particular care must be given to question construction to avoid suggesting a possible answer (leading) in the way the question is asked. Trial interviews to pilot questions are essential before using a questionnaire in a large-scale survey. Usually piloting considerably modifies the original questions. The best questions use a simple and straightforward vocabulary and style, do not assume too much knowledge on the part of the respondent, avoid emotionally tinged words, and are phrased so as to maintain the subject's interest. More complex matters, such as ATTITUDES, are often measured by means of SCALES.

In framing questions, different degrees of structure may be used. Fixed-choice questions are precoded so that the respondent is either given a pre-set choice when it is asked (e.g. Agree/Disagree/Neither agree nor disagree) or the answer is recorded in a predetermined category (e.g. the age of 24 is recorded in the age-group 20-29). Open-ended questions do not have fixed-choice answers, and are analysed and CODED after the event. Fixed-choice questions are easy to administer, quick, efficient and cost-effective in a large-scale survey; however, they involve limiting the respondent's freedom of reply, may exclude certain alternatives, and do not permit qualifications to answers. Open-ended questions avoid these disadvantages, but in turn are difficult to administer consistently, are less efficient, and do not always yield comparable data. Special types of questionnaire distinguished by A.N. Oppenheim include PROJECTIVE TECHNIQUES, SEMANTIC DIFFERENTIAL and REPERTORY GRID TECHNIQUES, and social network analysis.

See A.N. Oppenheim, *Questionnaire Design and Attitude Measurement* (1966).

MB

**QWL movement.** An international network of work designers, managers, consultants and academics whose stated aim is improvement of the quality of working life in modern organizations through INDUSTRIAL DEMOCRACY and reform of the DIVISION OF LABOUR. Critics assert that QWL is merely the 1980s guise of HUMAN RELATIONS, and is concerned principally with technical efficiency and financial profit, rather than with humanizing these ends. Governments have supported QWL aims since the early 1970s, but less keenly since the economic recession began. Trade unions have treated QWL cautiously, though there has been significant union interest for some QWL aims in countries as different as Norway and Italy. The character and outcome of the QWL Movement have important implications for the Braverman's 'degradation of work' thesis.

See also SELF-ACTUALIZATION THEORY; SKILL; WORK ETHIC.

MR

# R

race. A group or category of persons connected by common origin. The word came into the English language at the beginning of the 16th century and from then until early in the 19th century was used primarily to refer to common features present because of shared descent. It was also used more loosely to denote other likenesses (as with Charles Lamb's 'the two races of men: the men who borrow and the men who lend'); this usage, though infrequent, continues in literary contexts. A second major sense in which the word has been used can be discerned from early in the 19th century; this equates race with 'type', a category of persons of permanently distinctive character (see RACISM). This conception was destroyed by DARWIN's demonstration that there were no permanent forms in nature: each species was adapted to its environment by natural selection, so that people of one racial type who migrated to a new environment would there undergo modification. Darwin recognized 'geographical races or sub-species' as local forms and in this sense the word is still employed in biology; it designates a subdivision of a species, whose members can mate with members of other subdivisions of the same species and produce offspring but who because of their geographical isolation and cultural preferences usually mate within their own sub-species. Since the rise of population genetics in the early 1930s, biologists have used 'population' to designate the group or category under study and have described its characteristics statistically, relating the frequency of given characters to the processes of natural selection (see CLINE, GENE). 'Race' has been primarily a classificatory term, lacking the explanatory power of the concepts employed in population genetics, and so has been dropping out of use in biology. In social life, 19th-century ideas about racial characters are still employed by members of powerful groups to set at a distance members of weaker groups (see RACISM); race is sometimes used as a category in population classification (see BLACK; RACE RELATIONS); and 'racial group' is legally defined in laws directed against racial DISCRIMINATION.

See also ETHNICITY; ETHNOCENTRISM.

MPB

race relations, ethnic relations. The assumption that there is a distinctive field of academic study that can be called race relations or racial relations dates from around 1930 in the USA. This entry will consider how that assumption arose and how it is viewed half a century later. Its starting point is the question 'how do relations between people regarded as being of different race differ from relations between people of the same race?'

The thesis that inter-racial relations differ from intra-racial relations originated in the mid-19th century with the theory of racial typology according to which each individual was to be seen as a representative of a permanently distinct human type; the character and capacity of the type determined the relations between representatives of different types. Later it appeared in a

318

substantially revised form in the selectionist theory, which presented races as incipient species developing through natural selection (see RACISM). The first distinctively sociological alternative to such theories can be discerned in the writing of PARK, who advanced an ecological theory according to which groups migrate and then, in competition with others, seek to establish control over ecological niches which they can exploit. Racial characters develop as a result of territorial isolation and selection, but racial consciousness is an acquired trait stemming from competition between and within groups. According to Park, race relations are not so much the relations that exist between individuals of different race as between individuals conscious of these differences, and in this sense there were no race relations in Brazil. A different answer to the general question is found in the work of writers who contend that inter-racial relations differ from intra-racial differences only because people have been taught to classify one another racially. The main development of this view is a class theory. It holds that the idea of race was developed in the 19th century by the ruling classes of Europe and North America to justify the exploitation of people of non-European origin and hinder co-operation between white and black workers. From this standpoint there can be no distinctive field of 'race relations' and the problems constitute a subdivision of the study of SOCIAL STRATIFICATION.

Recent theory elaborates elements in the ecological and class theories by building upon the concept of the PLURAL SOCIETY, arguing that competition within a split labour market is the main source of hostility and analysing the ways in which the rational choice of actors modifies the boundaries between racial groups. These theories assume that inter-racial relations are distinctive only in so far as a person's category membership is highly visible and reinforced by popular beliefs about the significance of racial difference. The demarcation of a field of race relations study is seen as a matter of academic convenience.

A weakness in many discussions is the implication that the nature of race relations is determined solely by the more powerful group. A minority group may be set apart by the prejudices of the majority, but the experience causes the minority members to develop a consciousness of belonging together so that they may change from being a CATEGORY to being a group. Appreciation of this has led sociologists in the UK to draw a different distinction between race relations and ethnic relations. In the USA the population is officially classified by both race and ETHNICITY. The racial categories are: (a) American Indian or Alaskan native; (b) Asian or Pacific Islander; (c) Black; (d) White. The last two are subdivided by ethnicity: (i) Hispanic origin; (ii) not of Hispanic origin. The usage in sociology is similar. Italian-Americans, Irish-Americans, Polish-Americans etc, are regarded as ethnic groups; relations between them are counted as ethnic; relations between them and Black Americans are considered racial relations. This makes the distinction depend upon the nature of the groups involved and people's consciousness of them; it means also that relations between two such groups must be either racial or ethnic. In the UK, many sociologists prefer to base the distinction upon the nature of the social relations. Sikh immigrants from the Punjab can be seen as an ethnic and religious MINORITY within the larger South Asian minority that is perceived as racially distinct by members of the native British population and is the object of racial DISCRIMINATION. But the Sikhs are also a community held together by internal bonds and shared culture and to this extent they constitute an ethnic group. On this view relations between white British and Sikh immigrants can be both racial relations and ethnic relations.

See also BLACK; ETHNICITY; RACE.

MPB

**racial integration.** Integration is a mathematical term used to designate a process of making whole or entire. In sociology it is variously employed in connection with measures of consistency and conformity. Since World War II it has been used in place of assimilation to identify processes whereby members of different ethnic groups may participate equally in the public aspects of collective life while remaining distinct in the private aspects.

MPB

**racism, racialism.** The word 'racism' was introduced in the 1930s to refer to doctrines of racial superiority, particularly to the thesis that race determines culture; it continued to be used in this sense until the 1960s when it was given a wider connotation. Though some detect attitudes which they consider racist in earlier sources, the first clear racist doctrines were formulated in the 1860s by Robert Knox, Arthur de Gobineau and Josiah Nott. These are sometimes referred to as scientific racism but are more accurately described as *racial typology*. According to the typologists, variations in the constitution and behaviour of individuals were the expression of differences between underlying permanent types, each one of which was suited to a particular continent or zoological province. A NATION was therefore an expression of a racial type. The nature of a type determined the kinds of culture and relations with other groups which its representatives could create.

The assumptions of racial typology were invalidated by DARWIN. A new theory then appeared which may also be considered racist though of a different kind. This *selectionist theory* held that (1) evolution may be assisted if inter-breeding populations are kept separate so that they can develop their special capacities (as in animal breeding); (2) racial prejudice serves this function and in so doing reinforces racial categories in social life; (3) therefore racial categories are determined by evolutionary processes of inheritance and selection. Where the typologists claimed that there had originally been pure races, the selectionists see racial purity as something in the process of creation. This theory offers an explanation of inequalities within as well as between races and has recently been given new life in SOCIOBIOLOGY.

If 'racism' is used to designate a doctrine, it can be distinguished from racialism. Actions which appear to be expressions of racism can be designated racialist.

In the 1960s some Americans began to designate as racist any policies which they regarded as maintaining the subordination of a racial group, distinguishing 'institutional racism' from individual prejudices. In this perspective, members of a subordinated group can never be racist. Other authors write about 'racist societies' without specifying how a racist society is to be defined. Since these formulations are based upon the social utilization of popular beliefs about the nature of RACE rather than upon scientific knowledge, it is difficult to find a satisfactory basis for a definition of racism in this wider sense.

MPB

**Racliffe-Brown, Alfred Reginald** (1881-1955). British anthropologist who together with MALINOWSKI was largely responsible for the structure and development of modern studies in social anthropology. He studied Moral Sciences at Cambridge University until 1901. The pioneering Cambridge Expedition to the Torres Straits Islands in 1898 to study all multidisciplinary aspects of the social life of a 'primitive' people had been organized by the zoologist Haddon and included the psychologist W.R.H. Rivers. As an undergraduate, Radcliffe-Brown associated with both and was influenced by their ideas about the importance of studying societies *in situ*. His own work on the Andaman Islanders was published in 1922, 12 years after he had carried out extensive fieldwork, and was dedicated to Haddon and Rivers. This did not have the impact of Malinowski's *Argonauts of the Western Pacific* published in the same year, yet it reveals the outlines of the theoretical structure of the discipline which Radcliffe-Brown was later to teach thoughout the world. As an undergraduate, Radcliffe-Brown was influenced by W. Whewell's theories of the philosophy of science, particularly with respect to the importance of the 'inductive' method. Throughout his academic life Radcliffe-Brown asserted the need for scientific method in the discipline and regarded social anthropology as a comparative sociology in which the task was to derive generalizations about social structures and social systems from empirical data. His philosophical background also included studies of COMTE, MONTESQUIEU and SPENCER and, particularly in the formative years of writing up his Andaman Island data, he was influenced by DURKHEIM's school of sociology.

Radcliffe-Brown stimulated and organized research by other anthropologists and received many distinctions. By all accounts a brilliant teacher, his complex character possibly contributed to the rivalry with his more flamboyant contemporary Malinowski.

He held chairs of social anthropology at Cape Town (1920-8), Sydney (1925-31), Chicago (1931-7), Oxford (1937-46), and was visiting professor at Yenching (1935) and Sao Paulo (1942-4). He returned to Oxford 1946, held an appointment at Farouk I University of Alexandria (1947-9) and had a special appointment at Rhodes University South Africa (1951-4). He was also associated at various times with the Universities of London, Birmingham and Manchester. Few contemporary social anthropologists were not taught or influenced by him.

His written works are few but include *The Andaman Islanders* (1922); *The Social Organisation of Australian Tribes* (1931); (with Darryl Forde) *African Systems of Kinship and Marriage* (1950); *Method in Social Anthropology* (1958) and *Structure and Function in Primitive Society* (1961).

Radcliffe-Brown's holistic FUNCTIONAL-ISM, despite coming under attack particularly since the 1960s, still provides the framework within which social anthropology is taught. During his time in the USA his dissemination of ideas of structural functionalism was largely responsible for the development of the initial ideas of a 'Chicago School' of Social Anthropology, somewhat anomalous in the culturalist traditions of American anthropology. Particularly in the work of Lloyd Warner, but also in the researches of Sol Tax and Fred Eggan, this school approaches the study of systems and order rather than those of culture and values. Through Warner's influence, a number of studies of North American and European social groups were carried out and laid the foundation for a tradition of community studies which still continues (see COMMUNITY, CLASS *as category and scale*).

See also FUNCTIONAL THEORIES OF RELIGION; RELIGION; TOTEMISM. JE

**radical non-intervention.** A political strategy or recipe flowing from the more absolute versions of libertarianism and LABELLING theory, recommended by Schur (*Radical Non-Intervention*, 1973). Labelling theory tends to a relativism which denies the legitimacy of any moral judgement. Moreover, certain strains in the theory suggest that practical action cannot but amplify or exacerbate DEVIANCE. Labelling is thereby represented as little more than a self-fulfilling prophency, and much crime — juvenile DELINQUENCY in particular — becomes an improper subject for formal social control. Radical non-intervention is the ensuing policy, advocating therapeutic abstinence.

PR

**rank correlation or determination.** See ASSOCIATION, COEFFICIENTS OF.

**rationalism.** In a very general sense, an exaggerated belief in the RATIONALITY of human beings, or the belief that all reality can in principle be understood by the human mind, that there are no ineluctable mysteries. Hence a further sense of rationalism is the rejection of religion and superstition.

In philosophy, the term has been applied to an EPISTEMOLOGICAL doctrine which, in opposition to EMPIRICISM, stresses the importance of deductive reasoning and *a priori* theory in the creation of knowledge. Knowledge itself is seen as ideally forming a single, logically coherent system.

See M. Hollis, *Models of Man* (1977).

WO

**rationality.** (1) Applied to thoughts, actions, people and systems of organization which conform to the rules of logic or to consistent maxims of practically efficacious action. It has been claimed, in opposition to cognitive RELATIVISM, that we must assume the existence of some basic and universal criteria of rational thought if we are to be able to understand an alien culture. At a lower level, we may choose, for the sake of theoretical simplicity, to assume that people act in an economically rational manner even if we know that the IDEAL TYPE of rational economic action is never fully instantiated in reality. Rational action is easier to understand than action which is consistent, perverse or self-defeating. To assume, however, that people always act rationally may be criticized as RATIONALISM.

See M. Hollis and S. Lukes (eds.), *Rationality and Relativism* (1982); M.K. Farmer, 'Rational Action in Economic and Social Theory' in *Archives Européennes de Sociologie* 1982.

WO

(2) Within sociology, the concept of rationality was most developed by WEBER. In the first chapter of *Economy and Society* he classified social action as (1) instrumentally rational (*zweckrational*), where object and persons are used as relatively efficient instruments or means for attaining one's own rationally pursued and calculated ends; (2) value-rational (*wertrational*), where an end is pursued for its own sake, regardless of its prospect of success; (3) affectual, determined by emotion; (4) traditional, determined by ingrained habit. Actually the last two may fall close to the limits of meaningful social action in Weber's sense. Weber related these to social institutions, especially in his classification of POWER and in his comparative studies of religion (see PROTESTANT ETHIC). His broadest historical generalization concerned the rise of instrumentally rational action and the decline of TRADITIONAL action in modern Western society. This rationalization process subjected ever-greater aspects of social life to precise means-end calculations: in the economy through the rational cost-accounting and commodity calculations of CAPITALISM; in the state through BUREAUCRACY, an expression of rational-legal domination (see POWER); in religion through successively more calculative forms of Christianity, and even in music. Weber saw this as a very pervasive evolutionary trend, and refused to assign causal priority to any part of it. He also became worried about its eventual end, seeing a possibility that Western society might become imprisoned in an 'iron age' of formal rationality but substantive irrationality. This line of his thought has been extended by the Frankfurt School of CRITICAL THEORY, especially by HABERMAS.

MM

**reaction formation.** See DEFENCE MECHANISMS.

**realism.** In the philosophy of science, and in the sense used elsewhere in this work, the view that reality consists of things, structures and mechanisms which may or may not be observable, and that the purpose of science is to describe them. Realism is thus opposed to the view that scientific THEORIES are merely convenient fictions for generating testable predictions. Causal relations, in particular, are seen as grounded not in constant conjunctions of observable events (as they are for EMPIRICISM) but rather in real mechanisms in nature or society. The effects of these mechanisms may only be present as tendencies, if their operation is blocked by countervailing mechanisms; the principal purpose of experimentation is to isolate causal mechanisms from the open systems in which they occur in observable reality and which may conceal their operation.

Elements of a realist philosophy of science can be found throughout the history of philosophy, but its strongest post-war form is represented by the work of Rom Harré and, more recently, Roy Bhaskar. In *A Realist Theory of Science* (1975, 2/1978) and *The Possibility of Naturalism* (1979) Bhaskar provides an exposition and defence of realism and its application to the social sciences (see NATURALISM). Realism is currently influential in sociology through STRUCTURALISM and structural Marxism (see ALTHUSSER).

See W. Outhwaite, 'Towards a Realist Perspective' in G. Morgan (ed.), *Beyond Method* (1983).

WO

**reality principle.** See PSYCHOANALYSIS.

**reciprocity.** Anthropological and sociological interest in reciprocity derives first from the French sociologist Mauss. In *The Gift* (1925) he argued that a gift, despite its appearance of being voluntary and disinterested is, in fact, obligatory, interested and sanctioned ultimately by the use of force. Mauss drew upon examples of gift-giving collected in ethnographic accounts of the late 19th and early 20th centuries. The best-known examples are the kula ring described by MALINOWSKI and the Potlatch ceremonies studied by BOAS and his associates.

The kula ring is a system of extensive intertribal exchange between Melanesian islands which Malinowski described in *Argonauts of the Western Pacific* (1922). Within the 'ring' of islands, goods of great symbolic valuè circulate perpetually without ever being owned, although possession at any one time confers prestige. *Soulava* (necklaces) travel in a clockwise direction and are exchanged for *mwali* (armshells), which circulate anticlockwise. Exchange takes place between established kula partners, who are obliged to reciprocate by returning *soulava* for *mwali*, or *vice versa*. Each exchange entails the celebration of public rites and ceremonies. The long voyages between islands also entail political alliances and the secondary function of trade and barter of subsistence goods.

Potlatch is a system of ceremonial and competitive gift exchange among Indians of the Northwest coast of America. It has sometimes been claimed that potlatch activity accelerated in the wake of colonial contact and was a substitute for warring activities prevented by the new administration. Potlatch is the conspicuous consumption or gift-giving of a wide variety of goods at a feast to which one's rivals are invited in order to shame them with one's munificence and gain personal prestige. The shamed rival is then obliged to give a further feast in order to regain prestige.

Malinowski suggested that the kula might represent a 'fundamental type of human activity'. But others, particularly Mauss, compared it with potlatch and pointed to the fact that both institutions are examples of the use of conspicuous surplus to maintain equilibrium between groups in an atmosphere of rivalry and latent hostility. Yet for Mauss kula and potlatch were not simply political mechanisms but rather facets of systems of total prestation, which embraced the entire cultural life of their respective systems.

Reciprocal systems need not be equal, and the return made on a gift may be delayed. Mauss's work and further studies, particularly in Melanesia, amplified these ideas. Ceremonial exchange is an economic institution linking potentially hostile groups:

reciprocity does not so much make friends as prevent emmity. The inequality of some exchanges emphasizes status difference between exchange partners or promotes or decides competition between rivals. Moreover, if one partner renders more in an exchange, the delay in reciprocating an equivalent or greater amount can ensure the continuation of a relationship or alliance. Reciprocal exchange systems can thus provide a network of alliances, which ensure a degree of political stability in societies in which there is no stable system of rank or institutionalized means of succession to authority. Recent work by anthropologists working the kula ring area have caused a revaluation of Malinowski's ethnography and analysis, without as yet fundamentally altering Mauss's theoretical formulation of reciprocity.

One criticism of Malinowski suggests that he paid insufficient attention to the bartering of subsistence goods which took place at the same time as the symbolic exchanges of the kula. A school of thought which attempts to analyse traditional economic systems in their own terms (substantivist) rather than in terms of (formalist) modern market systems has associated the term 'reciprocity' with patterns of economic, rather than symbolic, activity (see POLANYI).

See also INCEST.

JE

Gouldner (*American Sociological Review*, 1960) de-limited DURKHEIM's and PARSON's arguments concerning normative CONSENSUS. The 'norm of reciprocity' was necessary to social cohesion. It consisted of the maxims '(1) people should help those who have helped them, and (2) people should not injure those who have helped them.'

MM

**Redfield, Robert** (1897-1958). American anthropologist, one of the founders of American cultural anthropology. Redfield was educated at the University of Chicago and was later Professor of Anthropology there. He married PARK's daughter and was both influenced by and closely associated with the CHICAGO SCHOOL. Major works:

*The Folk Culture of Yucatan* (1941); *Peasant Society and Culture* (1956).

Redfield is best remembered for the series of community studies he carried out in Mexico in the 1930s and 1940s. From these he developed the IDEAL TYPE of the FOLK SOCIETY and the FOLK-URBAN CONTINUUM. In the late 1940s one of his graduate students, Oscar Lewis (see CULTURE OF POVERTY), conducted a re-study of Tepozthan, one of the villages studied by Redfield which formed the basis of 'the folk society'. Lewis's findings were radically different to those of Redfield, provoking a significant debate on the relationship between theory, methodology and research findings in the social sciences.

HN

**reductionism.** The claim that a complex thing is 'nothing more than' or can be wholly understood in terms of some simpler things of which it is composed. Thus the kinetic theory of matter reduces gases, liquids and solids to aggregates of molecules; WEBER held that 'the state' could mean no more than a complex of individual actions. This doctrine of METHODOLOGICIAL INDIVIDUAL-ISM is the most important form of reductionism in the social sciences. Another is the BEHAVIOURIST reduction of intentional ACTION to a response to stimuli or the reduction of psychological processes to physiological ones. The most dramatic claim was that of some logical POSITIVISTS that the laws of every science, including sociology, should be ultimately reducible to the laws of physics (physicalism). Reductionism is conventionally opposed to EMERGENCE: the claim that complex entities have emergent properties which are not reducible to those of their component parts. For example, the STATE is not an original social form, but once it emerges it may play an autonomous role in history. This is contested by various reductionist theories.

See A. Koestler and J.R. Smythies, *Beyond Reductionism* (1969).

WO

**reference group.** A term introduced by Hyman in 1942 to denote a group, collect-ivity or person which an individual takes into account in determining his or her behaviour and attitudes. It can be the same as or different from the group of which he/she is currently a member. The basic concern is to explain a person's activities and beliefs in terms of subjectively significant relation-ships. This also adds a time dimension: a person's reference groups will be determined by his/her past, while present actions may be carried out with reference to a desire sub-sequently to join a group.

Reference groups can be of two main types. (1) A 'comparative reference group' is used by an individual in making evaluations of him/herself or others. This concept has been notably used in studies of RELATIVE DEPRIVATION. (2) A 'normative reference group' establishes and enforces standards for an individual. This has been developed by SYMBOLIC INTERACTIONISTS, notably Strauss and Shibutani, who define a reference group as 'any collectivity, real or imagined, envied or despised, whose perspective is assumed by the actor'. It is that group whose outlook is used by the actor as the frame of reference in the organization of his/her perceptual field. Seen as a perspective in this last way, the con-cept has much in common with MEAD's 'gen-eralized other'. This refers to the organized community or social group which gives to the individual unity of self — the attitude of the generalized other is the attitude of the whole community. It is a component of the 'Me' (see SELF). As individuals take the role of the generalized other, so their conduct is con-trolled and shaped. In the acquisition of self, the person moves progressively from being able only to take the role of one other (Mead's 'play phase') to several others simultaneously (Mead's 'game phase') to that of a whole community (Mead's 'general-ized other phase' or the reference group phase).

Mead's notion differs from Shibutani's in that he tended to see the generalized other as embodying the attitudes of the whole society, where Shibutani emphasizes that mass society produces multiple perspectives (often conflicting) or social worlds which can constitute multiple generalized others. The study of reference groups thus becomes the study of the construction and influence of delimited social worlds.

See T. Shibutani, 'Reference Groups as Perspectives', *American Journal of Sociology*, 1954; R.L. Schmitt, *The Reference Other Orientation* (1972); W.G. Runciman, *Relative Deprivation and Social Justice* (1966).

KP

**regression.** A statistical technique (allied to CORRELATION) for examining the degree of ASSOCIATION between two VARIABLES. The scores are represented on two axes of a graph and the data plotted as for correlation. But a regression analysis aims to fit to the data the best straight line which will enable the scores of the dependent variable to be predicted from the scores of the independent variable.

A regression coefficient measures how much higher is the mean value of the dependent variable for a given value of the independent variable than when that value is one unit lower, all other variables remaining constant. Therefore regression is always of one variable on another, with the aim of producing a regression equation which gives the best 'fit' in the circumstances.

In multiple regression analysis more than one independent variable is used to explain variation in a single dependent variable. The scores for each independent variable are weighted according to the contribution which that variable makes to the overall result, after all the other variables are taken into account.

Regression requires MEASUREMENT at the interval or ratio level. It is therefore more widely used in economics (where money is a variable) than in sociology. However, it is possible to create dichotomous 'dummy' variables with nominal level data to overcome this problem.

The term was introduced by Francis Galton (1822-1911), a man of wide interests in biology and a cousin of DARWIN, to express the way the size of the seeds of daughter sweetpeas regresses on the average toward the mean. This theory of regression was developed by Karl Pearson and published in the journal *Biometrika* that Galton helped Pearson found. The ordinary least squares (OLS) estimators employed in regression were introduced in their modern form 1821 by the German mathematician Carl Gauss, who proved that they have certain optimal properties — minimum variance amongst unbiased linear estimators. OLS estimators choose coefficient values to minimize the sum of squared deviations from the regression line or plane (in the multivariate case).

It has been argued that the regression coefficient, unlike the correlation coefficient, has causal significance in sociology as it implies that 'if the independent variable were to increase by one unit, then the dependent variable would increase on average by so many units'. However, no direct evidence as to this COUNTERFACTUAL CONDITIONAL statement is supplied by the regression, which effectively redescribes the trend of the mean in sub-populations of the existing data, and says nothing about the effects of changes or about circumstances that do not occur there. It has also been argued that as the regression coefficient is mathematically only a simple transformation of the correlation coefficient, unlike the correlation coefficient, has causal significance in sociology, as it this transformation, which depends on the relative variances of the variables, does introduce a new element which can vary while the correlation remains constant (and *vice versa*). So as long as counterfactuals are not introduced it seems permissible to treat a regression coefficient as measuring the rate of increase (or decrease) in a statistical relationship, and the correlation coefficient, or rather its square, as measuring the degree of it (*see* ASSOCIATION, COEFFICIENTS OF).

See H.J. Loether and D.J. McTavish, *Descriptive Statistics for Sociologists* (1974).

MB, JL

**regression** (in psychology). See DEFENCE MECHANISMS.

**reificiation.** Coined by Lukács to describe what MARX called the fetishism of commodities. In a commodity-producing economy, social relations between human beings assume what Marx called 'the fantastic form of a relation between things'. In *History and Class Consciousness* (1923) Lukács extended this idea to characterize the relations of cultural as well as material production under capitalism. Bourgeois thought, he argued, isolates discrete moments out of a complex and changing totality and wrongly attributes them a thing-like status. This is because the BOURGEOISIE, as a class, adopts a defensive position as capitalism develops; the proletariat is in principle able to have a non-reified under-standing of social change because it has an interest in change. The concept of reification is also central to the work of ADORNO, who argued that reification had become all-pervasive in modern capitalist societies and thinkers like himself could only oppose it indirectly.

See also SIMMEL.

WO

**relations of production.** In Marxist analysis relations of production, together with the means of production (roughly, technology) constitute any given MODE OF PRODUCTION (feudalism, capitalism etc). Under CAPITAL-ISM, the social relations of production are characterized by the purchase, in return for a wage, of the labour capacity of 'property-less' labourers by employers who legally own the means of production and the commodi-ties produced (see EFFORT BARGAIN; LABOUR PROCESS; MANAGEMENT). The concept applies not only to the hierarchical relation-ship of employer and employees within the enterprise, but also to its extensions into social and political life generally, thus defining the antagonistic classes of BOUR-GEOISIE and PROLETARIAT. The phenomena of INDUSTRIAL CONFLICT in the enterprise (especially strikes) are thus often portrayed as the classic manifestation of class conflict.

MR

**relative autonomy.** See ALTHUSSER; MODES OF PRODUCTION; STATE.

**relative deprivation.** Following research by Stouffer on *The American Soldier* (1949), MERTON refined the concept of relative deprivation and located it within REFERENCE GROUP theory (see R.K. Merton, *Social Theory and Social Structure*, revised edn. 1957, chapter 8). According to this view, individuals consider themselves deprived when they compare their personal circum-stances with those they believe to prevail in their reference group. Deprivation is relative because it is measured not against some

absolute or constant standard, but rather against a variable, the standard allegedly prevailing in a reference group at a particular time. The relative deprivation of a group increases, for example, even though its situation improves, if the improvement is less than that attributed to the reference group.

Relative deprivation is often invoked to explain why some groups challenge their place within given social, economic or political orders. It is a difficult concept to use effectively: most people know of others who fare better than themselves, though they are scarcely more deserving; we are all relatively deprived. Much therefore hinges on which comparisons are made, how long they have been made and how they are justified.

In the UK, W.G. Runciman (*Relative Deprivation and Social Justice*, 1966) used the concept in research on the relation between institutionalized inequalities and awareness or resentment of them. He found that respondents typically compared their situation with that of others quite near to them in the objective hierarchies of class and status so that their relative deprivation was much smaller than it might conceivably have been. Townsend (*Poverty in the United Kingdom*, 1979) further emphasized conditions of deprivation relative to others, rather than feelings, in an analysis which distinguished between objective, normative (collectively acknowledged) and subjective (individually acknowledged) deprivation (see CAPITALISM; POVERTY).

CGAB

The term is often used to explain the rise of social and religious movements. Since every-one experiences a sense of deprivation at some time or other, deprivation theorists such as Glock and Stark, and Aberle, have sought to distinguish various types of relative deprivation: economic, social, organismic, psychic etc. These types are often ambig-uous, difficult to apply with precision, and often appear to be invented to fit in with the salvational commodity or message being offered by the movement in question.

Moreover, the evidence for the alleged condition is often entirely circumstantial. Since the notion of relative deprivation as contrasted with absolute deprivation crucially refers to a felt or experienced disparity between aspirations or expectations and reality, it is not legitimate to take the objective circumstances of a group as the sole evidence for the actors' interpretations of the situation. We can no more conceive of someone joining a social movement who wanted nothing at all from it than we can conceive of an effect with a cause. Hence that someone who joins a social movement feels deprived of something (or he/she would not have joined), becomes a truth of logic rather than empirical fact. Just as we continue to examine every effect (or event) until we find its cause, sure in the knowledge that one must turn up, so we can continue to examine every recruit to a social movement, sure in the knowledge that he/she wants something from this movement and thus will be relatively deprived of that want. Any general statements to the effect that 'relative deprivation is the cause of social movements' or that 'a particular social movement emerged in response to relative deprivation' become tautologies, without explanatory power.

RW

**relativism.** The sceptical doctrine that there are no absolute standards of true or false (cognitive relativism) or of right or wrong (moral relativism). Since individuals and societies differ in their judgements of what is or ought to be the case, such judgements are relative to those individuals or societies. The paradox of relativism is that this claim itself takes an absolute form. MANNHEIM's sociology of KNOWLEDGE holds that beliefs must be relativized to their social base, that is, the social position of those who hold them, but that the sociologist of knowledge can escape the sceptical consequences of relativism by relating these various 'perspectives' to one another (relationism).

See K. Mannheim, *Ideology and Utopia* (1929); M. Hollis and S. Lukes (eds.), *Rationality and Relativism* (1982).

WO

**reliability.** The extent to which a method of data collection gives a consistent and reproducible result when used in similar circumstances by different researchers and/or at different times. In the measurement of ATTI-TUDES much effort is devoted to ensuring the reliability of SCALES. Techniques include test-retest reliability (two measurements on the same population with the same instrument used at different times), multiple forms (where alternate forms of the same instrument are administered to the same sample) and split-half reliability (where one half of the sample is given one half of the items, the other half is given one half, and the results are compared statistically).

The use of standardized questions in SOCIAL SURVEY research is a necessary precondition for ensuring the reliability of data collected, though it is not sufficient. In other types of research, such as PARTICIPANT OBSERVATION, problems of data reliability can occur because of the lack of checks when using unsystematic and personal methods of data collection. The reliability and the VALIDITY of data are distinct; high reliability indicates nothing about validity.

MB

**religion.** Defining religion for sociological purposes is difficult, both because of the considerable variety of beliefs and practices and because of the normative importance of religion. Sociological definitions of religion take two main forms: substantive and functional. Substantive definitions identify religion in terms of something it is, functional definitions in terms of something it does.

Substantive definitions, particularly those which draw the boundaries of religion quite narrowly, have developed from the tradition of 19th-century anthropologists such as Tylor, who saw religion as primarily involving a belief and institutions directed towards deities or other superhuman beings such as ANCESTORS or nature spirits. The virtues of this definition are that it includes what is construed as religion in common-sense terms and is straightforward to apply. Definitions of this type are sometimes criticized on the grounds that they rest on a distinction between the natural and the supernatural (or superhuman), the empirical and the supra-empirical, which the actors may not themselves make, and which may vary between observers in different social contexts or historical periods.

Sociologists, however, sometimes bring to bear on social actors categories and concepts which actors do not possess. Judgements as to whether or not something is supernatural can only be made in terms of the observer's own conception of the empirical. Hence there may be disagreements about whether or not something is supernatural (superhuman). This is only significant if the sociological explanations offered differ for religious and non-religious phenomena, for the supernatural and the empirical. Few sociologists now claim that to explain why someone holds a belief that is non-empirical requires a different type of explanation from why someone holds a belief that is empirical. Most people acquire their beliefs, whether empirical and supernatural, in the same way, on the authority of others. Similarly, sociologists today do not assert that since a certain practice cannot produce a particular effect we have to find a different explanation for its being performed than for one that does produce the effect. Both are performed because they are believed by the performers to be effective. One may wish to ask why an inefficacious practice continues to be performed, or a false belief to be held regardless of the evidence, but that is as true for secular inefficacious practices and false beliefs as it is for religious (or magical) ones (see MAGIC).

The definition of religion in terms of superhuman or supernatural beings or entities is a relatively exclusive, substantive definition. It excludes beliefs and practices oriented to supernatural forces and powers of an impersonal kind. More inclusive definitions of religion seek to contain these in some such formulation as 'beliefs, values and practices that focus on supernatural beings, worlds and forces' (John Wilson). However, inclusive definitions erode the worthwhile distinction between religion and MAGIC. It is clearer to regard religion as one element of a religious-magical, transcendental or supra-empirical domain. Religion and magic can be analytically distinguished within this domain by relatively exclusive definitions, while recognizing that many beliefs and institutions will contain elements of both.

Functional definitions of religion arose principally from DURKHEIM's rejection of the Tylorian approach. Durkheim sought a universal definition of religion, but felt that Buddhism was excluded from definitions stressing gods and spirits because it had no such beliefs. His assumption concerning Buddhism was mistaken, and whether religion is a universal property of all societies is properly a matter for empirical investigation, not for definitional stipulation. Durkheim erected an alternative definition which is partly substantive ('a unified system of beliefs and practices relative to sacred things, that is to say, things set apart and forbidden') and partly functional ('beliefs and practices which unite into one single moral community called a church, those who adhere to them'). Durkheim's substantive definition is difficult to employ. Many things which are 'set apart' and 'forbidden' are not evidently sacred (e.g. alcohol for legal minors), and even if they are 'sacred' they are scarcely religious (e.g. elite men's clubs set apart from and forbidden to women). Moreover, 'things set apart and forbidden' are not necessary components of religious belief and practice in many contemporary churches and denominations.

There are also problems with the functional element of Durkheim's definition. It is of value in drawing our attention to both the collective and the moral character of religions (as contrasted, for example, with magic), but beliefs and practice which unite their adherents into a single moral community may be secular in character. Political beliefs and practices may have this result.

Durkheim has been followed by sociologists of the FUNCTIONAL school, who see the essential character of religion as its promotion of solidarity. Religion, it is argued, achieved this end through embodying in its beliefs the common value system of the community or society, answering the major and ultimate questions faced in that society, and through its practices revitalizing commitment to those values and identity in the social group which shared them (see FUNCTIONALIST THEORIES OF RELIGION). Functionalists have defined religion in terms of beliefs and actions related to 'ultimate concerns' or symbols which formulate 'conceptions of a general order of existence'. But though religion has usually done these things, today quite diverse meaning systems such as psychoanalysis, Marxism, humanism or science may do them equally well for some people or some societies. There are many similarities between the 'moral community' of Freudian analysts and that of a church, or between the sacred heroes and rituals of Catholicism and those of the Bolsheviks. Different substantive phenomena may produce the same functional consequences, but they are not in any useful sense religions. Drawing attention to such similarities is worthwhile, but not worth broadening the term religion so far as to incorporate ideologies which are opposed to it. The virtue of the definition is that it legitimates a Durkheimian belief that religion is a functional universal in all societies, but it achieves that goal at the cost of any substantive content. For all their stress upon the definition, functionalist writings on religion are typically based upon conventional substantive conceptions of religion.

Definitions cannot be true or false, only more or less useful. Hence a definition of religion should not close off sociologically interesting problems, as do some functionalist definitions, which make religion a logical component of definitions of society itself, thereby inhibiting the analysis of SECULARIZATION. Functionalist definitions can draw attention to the continuities between religion conventionally conceived and other ideological sources of social solidarity, but they are not necessary for that purpose. For most sociological purposes a substantive definition will prove to be adequate, relatively simple to apply, and less encumbered by accompanying theoretical (and theological) entailments than functionalist definitions.

See CIVIL RELIGION; COMMON RELIGION; EVOLUTIONARY THEORIES OF RELIGION; FUNCTIONAL THEORIES OF RELIGION; INVISIBLE RELIGION; NEO-TYLORIANISM.

RW

**rent.** Payments, in money or in kind, derived from the ownership of land.

In agrarian societies (including those of the FEUDAL era) rent is the mechanism whereby a surplus is expropriated by one class from another. Under CAPITALISM, where land becomes a COMMODITY and LANDOWNERSHIP is sanctified by capitalist PROPERTY rights, ground rent has two components: *differential rent* and *absolute*

*rent*. (A third monopoly rent, has been suggested but is not widely accepted).

Most writing on rent has been from a Marxist standpoint, although much of MARX's own analysis was derived from Ricardo. In recent years two aspects of this issue have received particular attention: the complex problem of conceptualizing feudal rent within Marxist categories of analysis, and the capitalist development of the city. In each case land is capable of furnishing ground rent because it is fixed in supply, immobile, and protected by property rights from the dispersal of benefits.

*Differential rent* derives from the super-profits accrued from land of high natural productivity. It enables the function of landownership to be separated from that of agricultural commodity production. The immobility of land and the exclusivity of property rights together ensure that the benefits of high natural productivity accrue to the owner of the land rather than the cultivator, whose rights are limited by a tenancy agreement and who hands over the super-profits in the form of rent.

*Absolute rent* also derives from the local monopoly over land. In certain circumstances landlords are able to require payment for the use of land, regardless of whether super-profits are generated there. This absolute rent exists because landowners refuse to release land for production without a payment. It is thus dependent upon the private ownership of land.

See Murray in *Capital and Class* 1977/1978.

HN

**repertory grid technique.** Developed by KELLY to investigate the relationships between an individual's personal constructs, the distinctive categories that he or she uses to order the environment. It is a generalized form of his original Role-Construct Repertory Test, designed to elicit the organization of categories by which an individual, at a specific time, orders his or her close interpersonal relationships, that is, his or her role-constructs. The subject is presented with 20 to 30 cards upon each of which he or she has written the name of a person important in his or her life. By selecting the cards in sets of three and getting the subject to say in what way two of the people are similar and differ from the third, a set of binary distinctions personal to the subject is built up. Each of these verbal distinctions is then applied in turn to all the set of cards, generating a row of Yes's and No's, or I's and O's, which put all together produce a table of I's and O's. The process of eliciting distinctions continues until no new profile of I's and O's is produced, or no pattern not contained in an earlier one. 20 or 30 distinctions will suffice, Kelly says, except in some cases of schizophrenia.

According to Kelly, the relationships between the personality-constructed categories are preserved in the relationships between their corresponding rows of I's and O's. Thus the structure of personal psychological space can be represented by the space (not necessarily normal Euclidean space) that can be generated by mathematical techniques from the matrix of I's and O's. The new verbal labels attached by the subjects to the distinctions or categories involved cannot be taken as interpretatively adequate by themselves, but must at least figure in any interpretation of the psychological space produced by the test. In the generalized repertory grid technique a set of stimulus 'events' replaces the persons in the original test, a set of events specifically chosen to suit the area of study and produce a repertory grid related to the specific problem. The technique is intended to reveal the pattern of a person's constructs, not to detect or diagnose mental disorder, though Kelly devised the technique in a clinical context while providing a clinical service for high school and college students in Kansas.

JL

**replication.** See RELIABILITY.

**representativeness.** The extent to which the results derived from a particular empirical study are generalizable to a larger population. This depends on the way in which the units studied have been selected. If random SAMPLING has been used, then there is a degree of control over possible biases in selection of units. In many types of case study research, using PARTICIPANT OBSERVATION, there is considerable uncertainty about the criteria used to select cases for study and hence about their relationship to a larger population. Bias may very easily enter, and the cases studied will not necessarily be at all typical of the wider population. In historical research using original documents there is the different problem of selective survival. What still exists is unlikely to be a random sample of what existed in the past, but there is little the historian can be do about it (see HISTORICAL METHODS).

MB

**repression.** See DEFENCE MECHANISMS.

**research access.** The social researcher often has to negotiate access either to a population list which will provide a SAMPLING frame or to an institution or organization within which to carry out research. The gaining of research access is a little-discussed and poorly codified aspect of the research process, but one of great practical significance. Factors to be considered include the sponsorship of the study and institutions at which it is based, the qualifications and qualities of the researcher seeking access, the research bargain struck, the conditions under which access is granted and the way in which the researcher is introduced upon arrival in the research setting. Particular care needs to be taken in certain situations (e.g. industrial relations) to avoid over-identification with one side; and researchers should hesitate before giving bodies granting access a right of veto over eventual publication of their work as part of a research bargain.

See R.W. Habenstein (ed.), *Pathways to Data* (1970).

MB

**research design.** The plan of a piece of empirical research, specifying the manner in which data are to be collected and analysed in order to test hypotheses derived from theory, or to develop insights into the problem being investigated. It combines relevance to the problem with economy in procedure. The design stage is the most crucial phase of the research process. A particular design may involve EXPERIMENT, SOCIAL SURVEY, PARTICIPANT OBSERVATION, other methods, or a combination of more than one procedure.

See C. Sellitz *et al.*, *Research Methods in Social Relations* (1965).

MB

**research ethics.** A matter of the principle involving sensitivity to the rights of others, particularly the subjects of research. It involves the consideration of the possible effects of research upon those being studied, including the effects of such factors as manipulation, deception, stress, invasion of privacy and the exposure of sensitive feelings. Being ethical will limit the choices investigators can make in the pursuit of truth: while truth is good, respect for human dignity is better, even if in some circumstances this means that it is not possible to carry out research.

Ethical problems have arisen particularly over laboratory EXPERIMENTS and over the use of deception (e.g. covert PARTICIPANT OBSERVATION), but there are ethical aspects to all types of social research.

See J.A. Barnes, *Who Should Know What?* (1979).

MB

**response rate.** See SAMPLING.

**restriction of output.** See INCENTIVE PAYMENTS.

**revolution.** A concept derived from 17th-century mechanistic approaches to society and politics. Its simplest meaning is a 'turning-over' of society, as of a wheel: the rulers are replaced by the subjects. The Oxford English Dictionary selects the overthrow of the Commonwealth in 1660 and the restoration the monarchy in England, the replacement of James II by William and Mary in 1688, the overthrow of British sovereignty over the United States, and the fall of the fall of the monarchy in France as worthy of the title; all these events were referred to as revolutions by contemporaries. As well as these primarily political events authorities also use the term of such phenomena as the INDUSTRIAL REVOLUTION, the Cultural Revolution and other events where 'revolution' is used as a synonym for change of a far-reaching and complex character.

'The Revolution is' is a MILLENARIAN concept in frequent use. No political, social or economic change has ever provided a panacea, and so no revolution thus far has been *the* revolution.

19th-century writers concentrated on the French Revolution as the archetype. For political thinkers and activists this event draws a sharper line across history than its English and American forerunners. These grew more out of the assertion of existing rights, whereas the French Revolution and its successors were about obtaining new rights and changing social and economic as well as purely political relationships. In the early 19th century writers concentrated on describing new revolutionary utopias constructed as institutional solutions to perceived contemporary problems; after Marx the focus changes.

For MARX, the need to put revolutionary theory on a scientific basis takes priority. *The* revolution is the socialist one — a combination of a liberation of mankind from its general alienation from its true nature, with a liberation from the particular evils of capitalism — whereas *a* revolution is merely the replacement of one MODE OF PRODUCTION by another and one ruling class by another. Occasionally Marx allows his use of the term to slip, describing merely the passage of power from one group to another, without accompanying economic changes. *The* revolution occurs when the proletariat 'has nothing to lose but its chains', when the ruled are in the depths of misery and can lose nothing by revolting.

Marx fits his theory of revolution into a total theory of history, proving the inevitability of the revolution. His successors created a new type of revolution in order to escape the deterministic trap of the theory of history. This is known as the permanent revolution which, though no Trotskyite would agree, is almost synonymous with the Stalinist 'revolution from above'. Partly due to revolutionary impatience, partly due to the non-appearance of the necessary preconditions for revolution in Marx's theory (the decline in living standards of the working class to the point where it has no choice but to revolt), TROTSKY changed the theory. He argues that feudal societies may not be able to produce a bourgeoisie strong enough to initiate capitalism, and instead of waiting passively for a revolutionary opportunity revolutionaries may have to seize power and make the revolution permanent. By this he means that society must be driven through a period of capitalism without capitalists, direct to socialism. A scientific understanding of the principles of social dynamics as provided by Marxism will make it possible to escape historical determinism. There is some authority for this in Marx's writings of 1849 about the possibilities of revolution in Germany. LENIN added his analysis of IMPERIALISM to make the 1917 Russian revolution possible, but it was STALIN who really carried out the first 'permanent revolution' after 1928 — a deliberate attempt to change socio-economic relations through centralized planning and the collectivization of agriculture. Because this revolution was carried out by the state against the people, Stalin called it the 'revolution from above'. It provides interesting problems for Marxist theory as an example of the superstructure changing the base. MAO's later Cultural Revolution is a similar attempt, following on the failure of the Great Leap Forward.

Because of their apparent ability to produce successful revolutions, Marxist accounts of revolution were predominant until the Cold War brought a counter-attack from American academics. First to come under pressure was the explanation of why revolutions occur. In the 19th century De TOCQUEVILLE had suggested that revolutions occur when social conditions are improving, not when they are at their worst. J.C. Davies suggested that revolutions occur 'when a prolonged period of objective economic and social development is followed by a short period of sharp reversal'. T.R. Gurr combined notions of rising expectations and deteriorating reality into his thesis of RELATIVE DEPRIVATION. This states that revolutions occur when the provisions of goods and services by a society fails to keep up with the expectations of its members. For Lenin the problem was easier — revolutions occur when the lower classes no longer wish to continue in the old way and the ruling classes can no longer continue in the old way. Kumar takes this further: it is only when the upper classes struggle among themselves that new political forces the ruling classes cannot

control are created. (There is a chicken-and-egg danger here.)

The other major area of attention is the course, as opposed to the causes, of the revolution. All writers discussing revolutions other than *the* revolution agree that the consequences of revolutions are unpleasant, due to the logic of events. Most outlines derive from the French Revolution. Crane Brinton (*Anatomy of Revolution*, 1973) provides a modern statement: an initial period dominated by the moderate bourgeoisie, who are superseded by the radicals; there follows a reign of terror, then a Thermidorean reaction, and finally the establishment of a strong central authority and military rule. He considers revolution as akin to a fever.

Most accounts provide chronologies, not explanations. Kumar argues they begin to make sense if revolutions are understood as interruptions in the pattern of sovereign rule. The events seen by commentators as revolutions are really the final stages of a much longer revolutionary period during which the ruling authorities lose control of their subjects. Once the authorities are physically ousted, the country is in a state of war. So many factions dispute the right to rule that it is easier to overthrow governments than to deliver on promises. The revolution moves to the left, and becomes increasingly dictatorial until it has created enough opponents to halt it. The revolution is thus doomed never to fulfil itself, never to provide the freedom promised.

All these accounts have difficulty with the 1917 revolution and its successors. Stalin becomes simultaneously Robespierre and the Thermidorean reaction to himself — before he even launches the purges. The danger in imposing a pattern on revolutions is that revolutionaries are even more assiduous students of revolutions than academics: they try to avoid past mistakes once in power. The rural guerilla-type revolution associated with Mao is quite different from the urban coup of Lenin. Mao needed majority support to win his protracted struggle, whereas Lenin was well aware of the need for his minority party to strengthen its position with deliberate terror. As Tilly has shown (see POLITICAL VIOLENCE) repression is successful and whoever first successfully imposes repression wins a revolution in the cities.

The most frequently used typology is Chalmers Johnson's six-fold classification (*Autopsy on People's War*, 1974). All his categories are IDEAL TYPES. He distinguishes between revolutions on the basis of the targets of attack, on whether the event is carried out by the masses or the elite, and on the goals and ideologies of the participants. His categories are (1) the jacquerie or spontaneous mass PEASANT uprising, such as the Pugachov rebellion; (2) the millenarian rebellion, a jacquerie with a utopian dream and a living messiah, such as Savonarola; (3) the ANARCHISTIC rebellion, a reaction against progressive change, harking back to an idealized previous age, exemplified in the Vendée; (4) the Jacobin communist revolution, which involves sweeping political, economic and social change (some of Johnson's examples here are Jacobin, but not Communist, and Stone suggests reverting to Pettee's category of 'Great Revolutions', though Johnson's examples include the Russian and French Revolutions); (5) the conspiratorial COUP D'ETAT — a small ELITE that takes power and begins a programme of social change, such as the Nasserite revolution in Egypt; (6) the militarized mass insurrection, a mass revolutionary war guided by an elite, such as Vietnam or Yugoslavia.

See also POLITICAL VIOLENCE; PURGES AND TERROR.

BT

**revolutionism.** A term employed by Bryan Wilson (*Religious Sects*, 1970) in his typology of religious SECTS referring to a form of sectarianism in which God is expected to bring about a major transformation of the world. It is subsumed under the term MILLENNIALIST or MILLENARIAN MOVEMENT by other writers.

RW

**Rho.** See ASSOCIATION, COEFFICIENTS OF.

**Rickert, Heinrich** (1863-1936). German philosopher. Rickert and Wilhelm Windelband, who both taught in Heidelberg, were the leading figures in Southwest German NEO-KANTIANISM. Main works: *Die Grenzen der Naturwissenschaftlichen Begriffsbildung* ['The limits of natural-scientific conceptualization'] (1902), *Kulturwissenschaft und Naturwissenschaft* (1899), translated as *Science and History* (1962). Rickert was the main, though by no means the only influence on WEBER's philosophy of social science.

WO

**rights.** Legal and judicial discourse is expressed as a contest of 'rights' in which the establishment of a legal right is a precondition for securing a legal remedy or other form of legal intervention. The right is thus a legally recognized or established claim attached to or appropriated by a 'legal' subject (a citizen or a legal personality such as a company or charity).

*Property Rights.* One fundamental set of rights found in Western legal systems is that of rights in property. The function of much law and legal practice is related to the preservation of property rights; these function to protect the interests of those endowed with rights and to exclude those without. Thus the interests of property holders are secured against the interests of the propertyless. The nature of rights is, today, essentially individual rights in property rather than communal rights in property (see, e.g., C.B. MacPherson, *Property*, 1978).

The ideological strength of property rights may be illustrated in recent debates about welfare rights. Some argued that the claims of the poor on the resources of society might be better protected if they came to be regarded as a kind of new property right. A similar argument has been advanced in the context of employment protection on the issue of whether employees may be said to have a property right in their job. See PROPERTY.

*Human Rights.* The individual possessive character of rights has much engaged legal theorists. The dominant POSITIVIST tradition has viewed rights as necessarily created or given by legal institutions or legislatures. The alternative contention is that rights exist independently of formal legal recognition or enforcement. This underlies discussion of human rights as a set of claims or entitlements that can be mobilized in criticism of the denial of such rights by political systems. Such arguments are closely related to earlier writings on natural law. Human rights issues have in recent years become a general issue in international politics. In a number of countries a similar case has been made by those who argue that Bills of Rights similar to those in the Constitution of the USA, are needed to protect basic human rights and fundamental freedoms. Opponents of Bills of Rights, particularly at the national level, argue that to create such Bills is to disguise as legal issues that are essentially political.

AJH, MP

**rites of passage.** A term first introduced by the Dutch anthropologist Arnold van Gennep (*Les Rites de Passage*, 1908) to refer to particular RITUALS which mark the progress of an individual between relatively fixed and stable, culturally recognized states of rank, status, office, calling or profession. There are three ritual stages in the process he described: (1) separation, in which symbolic behaviour denotes detachment from the previous state; (2) the liminal or ambiguous state between old and new status; (3) aggregation or consummation as the individual assumes the rights and obligations of the new stable state.

A typical example would be the ceremonies surrounding circumcision among many peoples to mark the change from pubertal boy to adult male. Often this symbolic change takes place not at the actual age of puberty but according to the availability of a ritual expert or the initiate's social worthiness or ability to pay for the ceremony. In many African tribal societies groups of young men may be initiated together at intervals of some years. The resulting cohesion between initiates can form a political unit, an age set, adherence to which may cut across ties of KINSHIP.

It is critical to van Gennep's theory that the liminal period of instability between two stable states is imbued with particularly sacred qualities. This stress upon the related ideas of order and chaos links him to the sociological interests of DURKHEIM. More recently, other anthropologists have explored the ambiguity of initiates within this liminal period: for example, Victor Turner's

examination of ritual and symbol among the Ndembu of East Africa, and Mary Douglas's study of the sacred and the profane in her *Purity and Danger* (1966). Sociologists in the tradition of the CHICAGO SCHOOL have also used the concept widely, often preferring the term 'status passage'. B. Glaser and A. Strauss (*Status Passage*, 1971) attempt to outline a formal theory and suggest a number of properties that need to be considered in any such status change. These include whether or not the transition is regularized, scheduled, prescribed, desirable, inevitable, reversible, repeatable, collective, aware, voluntary, legitimate, clear or disguised.

See also DIVORCE; STRESS.

JE, KP

**ritual.** The performance by one or more persons of actions designed to express some range of meanings, these actions being permeated by symbolic content and highly constrained by the character of that content. When these actions are performed on subsequent occasions they will be rigid and stereotyped. Arnold van Gennep noted the importance of rituals marking important and anxiety-creating transitions in the life cycle, which he termed RITES OF PASSAGE. Rituals of this type assist an individual in making the transition from one status to another (child to adult, unmarried or married), and facilitate acceptance of the new status by other members of society. They may, as in the case of funerary rituals, help individuals to come to terms with the transition of a loved one from life to death, and their own transition to widow, orphan etc. Other rituals have been referred to as rites of intensification in which a social group experiences some revival or reintensification of sentiments or emotion, for example a stirring religious service, Encounter Group, saluting the flag or singing a national anthem.

Rituals of this latter type lend weight to DURKHEIM's view of ritual as essentially integrative in character, leading to heightening of social solidarity. Rites of passage and rituals performed prior to embarking upon some dangerous enterprise (for example prayer before battle) lend weight to MALINOWSKI's view that ritual relieves the anxiety provoked by dangerous or precarious activities. This draws upon FREUD's conception of ritual as a collective version of the obsessive behaviour of the compulsive neurotic, sublimating through ritual unacceptable emotional impulses; see JOKING RELATIONSHIP.

RW

**Rokeach, Milton** (1918- ). American psychologist, known for his research papers on dogmatism *The Open and Closed Mind* (1960). Born in Poland, Rokeach became a naturalized American and was educated at Brooklyn College and the University of California. Since 1951 he has worked at Michigan State University, where he has been Professor of Psychology since 1957.

Rokeach's initial interest was in intellectual dogmatism. He wanted to extend the study of right-wing authoritarianism embodied in ADORNO's *Authoritarian Personality* into a general study of AUTHORITARIANISM and shift the focus from the content of belief systems to their structure. The FASCISM (F) scale of Adorno's study was replaced by a dogmatism scale. This involves a pencil-and-paper test inviting acceptance or rejection of the propositions included in 66 scale items. The score is intended to measure the degree to which an individual's mind is open or closed, that is, 'the extent to which the person can receive, evaluate, and act on relevant information received from the outside on its own intrinsic merits, unencumbered by irrelevant factors in the situation arising from within the person or from the outside'.

JL

**role.** There are two broad approaches to the study of role. The first stems largely from anthropology and focuses upon the rights and duties — the normative expectations — attached to positions in a social structure or social system. In a classic statement, Ralph Linton remarked that 'status is simply a collection of rights and duties' while role 'represents the dynamic aspect of status'. Thus 'student' is a STATUS while 'studying', 'writing essays' etc are the dynamic expectations of the role. Listing such expectations becomes a standard feature of this kind of role theory. Its major sociological proponents were PARSONS (e.g. on 'the sick role') and MERTON, who developed *role set*, 'the complement of role relationships which persons have by virtue of occupying a particular social status', and *role conflict*, where incompatible expectations are held. This anthropological or structural FUNCTIONAL approach generally proceeds by mapping out the standardized expectations of a culture. It is often criticized for being overly conformist (in presuming such expectations are clear and consensual) and deterministic (in presuming people slot themselves into such expectations).

A contrasting approach emerged from the SYMBOLIC INTERACTIONIST account of MEAD. The focus switches from standard expectations in a culture to the more active processes by which people make their roles and play out their parts. This involves the process of 'role-taking' (see SELF), and uses the metaphor of the stage (see DRAMATURGY). GOFFMAN is noted for this use (in his *Presentation of Self in Everyday Life* and *Encounters*) and for developing the concept of 'role distance' to depict peoples' ability to free themselves from the standard demands of roles by playing at them tongue-in-cheek: a teacher, for example, may crack jokes or 'dress down' to reveal that he or she is more than just a teacher. This view is often considered to suggest that humans are self-conscious, even cynical, manipulators of social conduct: by selecting the appropriate role performance in a social situation, desired outcomes may be attained.

Both versions of role theory were prominent from the 1930s to the 1960s, but as the terminology became part of popular culture and the theory became associated either with cultural conformism or cynicism, it fell out of favour in sociology during the 1970s.

See J.A. Jackson (ed.), *Role* (1972).

KP

**Rorschach, Hermann** (1884-1922), **Rorschach test.** Swiss psychologist, inventor of the most widely used of psychological PROJECTIVE TESTS, the ink-blot test which bears his name. Born in Zurich, the son of a drawing-teacher, Rorschach studied medicine, graduating at Zurich with a thesis on hallucinations. After working briefly in

Russia he returned to Switzerland where he held posts in cantonal mental hospitals.

While a student under the Freudian Eugen Bleuler, Rorschach had begun investigating reactions to ink-blots, an interest he developed at school where he had the nickname 'ink-blot'. Influenced by JUNG, then at Zurich, and particularly by the method of free association (*see* PSYCHOANALYSIS), Rorschach developed empirically the use of ink-blot reactions to measure unconscious emotions. *Psychodiagnostics* (1921) contains four hundred case studies with Rorschach's analysis of each. He also used these to carry out studies of the leaders of Swiss religious sects, historically important in the development of the PROTESTANT ETHIC THESIS.

The *Rorschach Test* asks the subject to describe what he/she sees in a set of 10 symmetrical black, grey, or coloured ink-blots. The responses are used, with or without a scoring system, to investigate the subject's personality by comparison of the response with norms established over a number of clinical case-studies. Responses are classified according to their location on the ink-blot, the emphasis placed on form or colour, and the content of what is seen. Similar tests have since been devised, such as the 45-card test of W.H. Holtzmann. An extensive literature has accrued around the Rorschach test, including numerous scoring systems: see O.K. Buros, *Personality: Tests and Reviews* (1970) and *Mental Measurements Yearbooks*.

JL

**Rousseau Jean-Jacques** (1712-78). French writer and philosopher, author of *Du contrat social* [*The Social Contract*] (1762). Rousseau believed that human beings' natural independence and amorality are transformed into morally corrupting mutual dependence by socio-economic inequality, which arises through the development of the institution of private PROPERTY. Although such natural independence is, for economic reasons, not recoverable, individual moral integrity can be attained by subjecting social life to regulation by a certain form of political arrangement: namely, direct DEMOCRACY. Each person surrenders all his private claims to (negative) LIBERTY to an assembly of

which each person is a member (see SOCIAL CONTRACT). The laws made by such a body can thereby be understood as self-legislation and their enforcement on any individual constitutes no restriction of (positive) freedom — 'forces him to be free' — since they express his own wishes. Rousseau imposes the further condition on such laws that they must apply equally to all and must aim to secure the common good, and not merely subserve the aggregation of private interests. Legislation satisfying these conditions is an expression of the sovereign 'General Will' which, through its exercise of unlimited AUTHORITY, confers moral autonomy on each individual by ensuring that conduct conforms to universalized standards prescribing what is in his real interest. This was an identifiable influence upon DURKHEIM's view of the conscience collective.

HIS

**Rowntree, Benjamin Seebohm** (1871-1954). An industrialist with a major interest in unemployment and social welfare which led him to undertake a series of surveys on the extent of POVERTY in York.

As an industrialist Rowntree played an important role in the Quaker family firm, first as a director and then from 1923 to 1941 as chairman. The firm was well-known for its interest in developing industrial management techniques and industrial welfare. It was initially associated with SCIENTIFIC MANAGEMENT but later with techniques developed from industrial psychology and with profit sharing (HUMAN FACTOR).

Rowntree's poverty studies, inspired by BOOTH's in London, were undertaken from the end of the 19th century to the 1950s to assess the extent of poverty in York. Like Booth, Rowntree adopted a subsistence definition of poverty (*see* POVERTY), but made a distinction between primary and secondary poverty. Primary poverty was the position when 'total earnings are insufficient to obtain the minimum necessaries for the maintenance of merely physical efficiency'. Secondary poverty was the position when 'total earnings would be sufficient for the maintenance of merely physical efficiency were it not that some portion of them is absorbed by other expenditure, either useful or wasteful'. The first survey published in

1901 found that over 15 per cent of wage-earners were living in primary poverty. This was seen as confirmation of Booth's findings.

Rowntree, like Booth, made a significant contribution to both an understanding of poverty and the development of empirical research. In some ways Rowntree's work was an advance, for the definitions used were more precise and better-developed techniques were used for data collection.

In his later studies in 1935 and 1950 Rowntree updated subsistence standards to take account of contemporary notions of necessity. Rowntree's work was used by BEVERIDGE in developing the subsistence standards on which his report on the social services was based.

See B.S. Rowntree, *Poverty: A Study of Town Life* (1901; 2nd edn. 1922); *Poverty and Progress: A Second Social Survey of York* (1941); (with G. Lavers), *Poverty and the Welfare State* (1951).

MPJ

**Rule of Law.** See LAW, RULE OF.

**rural-urban continuum.** A typology of communities which relates their social characteristics to their special location. From the 1930s to the 1960s the rural-urban continuum represented the major organizing scheme for the codification of empirical material in rural and urban sociology and geography. Its origins lay in TÖNNIES's *gemeinschaft/gesellschaft* typology. This was concerned with a type of relationship, irrespective of geographical location, but subsequent writers attempted to relate ways of life to specific geographical locales. The rural-urban continuum was established in Sorokin and Zimmerman's *Principles of Rural-Urban Sociology* (1929) and later extended by REDFIELD in his notion of a FOLK-URBAN CONTINUUM.

Empirical research from the 1950s increasingly questioned the validity of its major premise — that settlement patterns are associated with life-styles. In the 1960s Gans and Pahl demonstrated its obsolescence, concluding that any attempt to tie the patterns of social relationships to specific geographical milieux was misconceived. Where settlement patterns and ways of life coincided this was due to a third, antecedent variable which concerned choice within the housing market.

See R.E. Pahl in *Sociologia Ruralis* 1965.

HN

# S

**Saint-Simon, Comte Henri de** (1760-1825). Early French sociologist who greatly influenced subsequent theorists, including COMTE and MARX. Saint-Simon was born in Paris of a branch of the French aristocracy that traced its ancestry back to Charlemagne. The ideas of the Enlightenment proved formative influences upon his thought. He entered the army at seventeen, and fought in the American Revolution. His life was threatened during the French Revolution and he was imprisoned from 1793-4. He subsequently built up a large fortune through land speculation, and his Paris salon attracted intellectuals and scientists. By 1804 his wealth had been dispersed, and he spent the rest of his life in near penury. His career as writer and social reformer was forged largely in the latter period. He collaborated closely with Comte between 1817 and 1823, producing *Plan of the Scientific Operation Necesssary for the Reorganization of Society* (1822). *Le Nouveau Christianisme* (1825) caused a final break with Comte.

Saint-Simon's main concepts emerged prior to his collaboration with Comte. His UTOPIAN SOCIALISM was influenced by MONTESQUIEU's and Condorcet's fusion of Enlightenment ideas with a POSITIVIST conception of society. Society as 'organic-equilibrium' is examined within an evolutionary framework (see EVOLUTIONISM). Under the law of the three stages knowledge and society progress through theological, metaphysical, and positive stages. Each stage contains the seeds of its own destruction. Saint-Simon traced the European line of development from polytheistic Rome and Ancient Greece through FEUDALISM and the more rational theology of Catholicism, to industrial society. He coined the term INDUSTRIAL SOCIETY. In the 15th century the growth of free urban cities fostered the rise of a new 'industrial class'. This term has a dual sense. It refers both to all involved in industrial production and to this group minus the proletariat. In the former sense, industrial society consists of a single CLASS in which subjugation of nature replaces the oppression of men. In all preceding stages of society class differences arise from domination by an exploitative minority. The STATE as an instrument of class oppression will be superseded by a scientifically managed welfare system and the exercise of authority will be restricted to the administration of things. SOCIAL STRATIFICATION is a meritocracy of differentials in wealth and power. Saint-Simon attributed to the decline in religion and tradition and the rising secularism of science and industry, a contemporary social crisis based on moral deregulation. He proposed a new secular religion to fill the moral void and regulate the economy (after his death this inspired a reformist movement in his name). Contemporary class conflict was merely a reflection of the problems of the inevitable transition to the new industrial order: a change which social physics (scientific sociology) should hasten.

Two major lines of sociological development may be traced back to Saint-Simon: Comtean positivism and Marxist socialism. Whether Saint-Simon's ideas were a major influence upon Marx has been disputed, since Saint-Simon is not concerned with the

338

specific nature of CAPITALIST industrial society. Comte's thought is greatly indebted to Saint-Simon, from whom he drew his law of the three stages and the idea (later developed by PARETO into the doctrine of the circulation of ELITES) that there is an antagonism between the instincts of conservation and innovation. Saint-Simon's preoccupation with the problem of order provides a direct line of continuity to PARSONS via DURKHEIM, upon whom he was a formative influence. Durkheim's conception of the crisis in industrial society as one of authority, as well as his theory of ANOMIE, is indebted to Saint-Simon. Saint-Simon's belief that progression towards more humane ethics and co-operative production is dependent upon the formulation of new ideologies by far sighted elites helped to promote an elitist conception of social change. This, with Saint-Simon's conception of a one-class industrial society and his emphasis upon the technical imperatives of social organization, provides links with modern theories of stratification such as technocratic and convergence theory, EMBOURGEOISEMENT and POST-INDUSTRIAL SOCIETY.

JW

**sampling.** Most social research inquiries, except CENSUSES and some types of OFFICIAL STATISTICS, are based on cases selected from a larger population, so the question arises of how REPRESENTATIVE the cases studied are of the population from which they are drawn. The statistical theory of sampling, itself based on PROBABILITY theory, provides a rigorous means of checking on representativeness, provided that certain conditions are met.

Probability or random sampling requires the selection of units from a population in such a way that each unit has a known and non-zero chance of selection. Selection is usually made from a list of the population, if it is available, such as the Register of Electors for a national survey; this list is known as the sampling-frame. Selection uses either a table of random numbers, or a random starting point and then units selected at fixed intervals according to the proportion of the population being sampled (the sampling

fraction). The latter procedure is known as systematic sampling.

The resulting list of units selected is known as the sample. It may be a list of individuals, but it could equally well be a list of institutions, groups, or other collectivity, depending on the subject of research. Selection according to strict principles of randomness, as defined above, is essential if correct statistical inferences are to be made from the sample to the population. Haphazard selection of units, however carried out, cannot be random in the statistical sense.

Different types of sample design are possible. (1) Multi-stage samples: in national surveys, regions or counties may be sampled at the first stage; cities, towns or their subdivisions sampled within first-stage units at the second stage; and households or individuals sampled within second-stage units at the third stage. This achieves considerable economies in interviewing. (2) Multi-phase sampling: drawing a general sample as a first step, then among those selected, identifying those with certain specifed characteristics for detailed interviewing (e.g. in a study of fertility, women of child-bearing age). This type of design may be used where no convenient sampling frame of a special group exists.

Stratification in sampling takes account of factors known to be likely to affect the results of a survey (e.g. regional, social class differences, age, sex etc). Prior to the sample being selected, the sampling frame is reordered according to the factors by which the sample is stratified. Thus in the sample selection, the proportion of the sample drawn from a given stratum is known, and can be varied if the stratum is small.

Provided that random sampling is used, then reliable ESTIMATES may be made from the sample to the population from which it is drawn, including the calculation of confidence intervals and the sampling error.

Sample size is very often determined by practical considerations such as time and money. No rules exist for determining the size of sample, though in deciding upon a target sample size, account should be taken of the precision of the results sought (what margin of sampling error is tolerable) and the type of MULTI-VARIATE ANALYSIS to be performed upon the data. Sample size, too, must take account of the response rate.

The size of the sample will not usually correspond to the number of interviews eventually completed. The number of completed interviews as a proportion of the original sample is the completion rate or response rate. Non-response in survey sampling may be due to individuals who are not-at-home (due to being at work, always out, in hospital, on holiday, dead etc) and those who refuse to participate in a survey (for whatever reason). In practice these shade into one another, and there are conditions in between (those who are too young or too old to be interviewed, don't understand the interviewer etc). The achieved sample is likely to be smaller than the original sample selected. Completion rates for mail surveys are considerably lower than those for personal interview surveys.

These procedures rest upon probability theory and the use of the central limit theorem to make inferences from a sample to a population, using the properties of the NORMAL DISTRIBUTION. Some forms of sampling do not use random selection, in which case none of the foregoing applies. Quota sampling, widely used in market research, gives interviewers quotas of particular types of people to be interviewed (e.g. by combinations of age, sex, and social class) but leaves it to the interviewer to make the selection of individuals to be approached. This can result in bias in selection, but it also means that sampling errors cannot be calculated, nor a completion rate worked out. Other types of sampling (e.g. snowball sampling) do not even possess the controls provided by the use of quotas, and are only recommended in sampling rare populations to which it is difficult to gain access.

The use of random sampling, particularly in social survey research, gives the social scientist an extremely powerful means of meeting the criterion of REPRESENTATIVE-NESS in research. Its use, particularly in large-scale surveys, is however costly and labour-intensive.

See C.A. Moser and G. Kalton, *Survey Methods in Social Investigation* (1971).

MB

**Sapir-Whorf hypothesis.** See LANGUAGE.

**Sartre, Jean-Paul** (1905-80). French philosopher, writer and critic, France's leading post-war intellectual. Co-founder, with MERLEAU-PONTY, of the Marxist journal *Les Temps Modernes.* Sartre's existentialist PHENOMENOLOGY, presented in his novel *Nausea* (1938), his main philosophical work *Being and Nothingness* (1943) and his essay *L'existentialisme est un humanisme* (1946) draws on the philosophies of HEGEL, HUSSERL and HEIDEGGER. His main contribution to Marxist thought is his massive but incomplete *Critique of Dialectical Reason* (1960), which incorporates an earlier article, *The Problem of Method* (1957). The latter is a critique of vulgar Marxism and an attempt at a more adequate conception of Marxist method. The *Critique* continues this theme as it applies to the formation of a collective revolutionary consciousness, though this has barely influenced sociological conceptions of CLASS CONSCIOUSNESS. Sartre's other major work is a biography of Flaubert, also incomplete, entitled *L'idiot de la famille* (1971).

WO

**Saussure, Ferdinand de** (1857-1913). Swiss linguist. Founder of the Geneva school of STRUCTURALIST linguistics. Main work: *Cours de linguistique générale* (1916).

WO

**scales.** The construction of scales is a method of MEASUREMENT (at ordinal or interval level) used particularly in the study of ATTI-TUDES. It rests on the assumption that there are underlying DIMENSIONS along which attitudes can be ranged. Scaling is a method by which each respondent's attitude can be assigned a numerical value to indicate his or her position on the dimension of interest.

Techniques of attitude-scale construction are concerned particularly with identifying the underlying dimension as homogeneous and linear (so that only one attribute is being measured, on a straight line) and with devising reproducible RELIABLE and VALID research instruments. In many scales, an attempt is made to have equal intervals on the scale so that interval-level measurement is possible.

Several well-known scales are called after their inventors. Thurstone scaling uses judges' ratings of a number of attitude statements to construct a multi-item scale dimension. The main characteristic of Likert scaling, also using multiple items, is its five-point scale for each item: strongly agree / agree / uncertain / disagree / strongly disagree. Gutman scales place greatest emphasis on the cumulative nature of the measure of attitude used. All share the aim of devising a linear metric of attitudes, giving quantitative precision to the subjective states of mind of individuals.

Scaling as a procedure is not confined to the measurement of attitudes, and may be used to gather other kinds of data — for example, systematic reports of behaviour.

See also SEMANTIC DIFFERENTIAL.

MB

**Scheler, Max** (1874-1928). German philosopher and sociologist. Main works: *The Nature of Sympathy* (1913), *Ressentiment* (1915), *Die Wissensformen und die Gesellschaft* (1926) and *Man's Place in Nature* (1928). A PHENOMENOLOGIST, Scheler was concerned to sustain an OBJECTIVIST ethics; this theme also influences his sociology of knowledge (see KNOWLEDGE, SOCIOLOGY OF).

WO

**schism.** The process by which a religious or other collectivity divides into two or more units which disagree sharply on some matter(s) of belief, practice or authority. The term implies that the secessionary group departs of its own volition rather than, say, as a result of mass expulsion. Schisms may develop as a result of recruitment or social changes among members producing social differentiation and consequent conflicts of interest. They may result from the pursuit of power or independence among competing leaders. Schisms are likely to occur within ideological groupings which regard themselves as uniquely legitimate (see SECT), as paths to the truth or salvation. A leader who claims to possess the complete truth can scarcely tolerate rival claimants, who will be forced into schismatic secession if they command support. Schism is more common the more available are means of legitimating claims to authority. If access to the supernatural is widely available, as in Spiritualism or Pentecostalism, dissenting leaders are able to legitimate challenges to established leadership in a manner impossible in a movement with a single CHARISMATIC leader such as the Nazi movement (see FASCISM).

RW

**schizophrenia.** See MENTAL ILLNESS.

**schooling.** EDUCATION covers a wide range of processes of which that part undertaken in formal organizations, especially for those up to the age of about 18, can strictly be referred to as schooling. In some circumstances, even as late as the early 18th century in England, the term 'school' did not necessarily indicate that a special building existed, but referred to the group within which the process of schooling occurred and which, particularly at times of persecution, might meet in a succession of different places. This early meaning of school, whereby the term was not tied to a building, is still used in relation to either a body of persons taught by or following one great thinker or those following, for instance, one set of general artistic or philosophical principles (e.g. the Frankfurt School, a group of social scientists associated with teachings emanating from that city in the interwar years).

Under formal schooling systems the age of entry and of leaving school, and therefore of compulsory schooling, are legally specified; in the UK today they are 5 and 16, but these ages and the period concerned vary between societies and even within the states of some societies (e.g. Australia). The divisions of schooling have come to be divided by age into primary (ages 5-11 in England and 5-12 in Scotland), secondary (11/12-18) and tertiary. In the UK until the EDUCATION ACT (1944) the system was divided by status into the Elementary Schools, which catered for the whole age range to 18, but were less well-equipped and of lower status, and the Secondary Schools, catering mainly for those over 11, which were better equipped and of higher status; a similar division still exists in some other European countries. Schooling in the UK for about 95 per cent of pupils is provided by the state or by the state in co-operation with other bodies, usually religious. But it may also be provided by private bodies alone, often also religious in aim, in independent schools, though these are usually, as in Britain, regulated to a degree by the state; the best-known example of the latter category is the English Public School.

See also CHILDHOOD.

PWM

**Schutz, Alfred** (1899-1959). Austrian-American philosopher and sociologist, the principal founder of sociological PHENO-MENOLOGY. Born in Vienna, Schutz served in the Austro-Hungarian army during World War I, and then studied law and social sciences at the University of Vienna. There he came under the twin enduring influences of WEBER and HUSSERL, the latter becoming a close friend.

His single major work was published in 1932 and eventually translated in 1967 as *The Phenomenology of the Social World.* Anticipating Hitler's *Anschluss* he emigrated in 1938 to Paris and in 1939 to New York, joining the New School of Social Research there. However, he pursued a full-time career in business management, leaving scholarly activities for his leisure time. This partly accounts for the piecemeal and un-organized character of his voluminous writings in America. Having retired from business he was preparing a new major work at the time of his death. Much of his writing was collected and published posthumously between 1962 and 1966 as three volumes of *Collected Papers.* In his American period Schutz was much influenced by G.H. MEAD. It was his contribution to combine European phenomenology and American SYMBOLIC INTERACTIONISM into a distinct perspective.

Schutz's work was an attempt to specify the subject matter of sociology. Both knowledge and social reality were constructed by men themselves through inter-subjective experiences. Thus sociology must reconstruct the concepts and the typifications by which common-sense knowledge is built up. According to Schutz, we cannot find any abstract laws of knowledge or

consciousness, so philosophical methods, such as Husserl's 'radical abstraction' can be abandoned. Sociology can get on with empirical study of the creation and maintenance of intersubjectivity.

All humans learn and carry around in their minds rules, conceptions, recipes and information built up through intersubjective experience. These constitute 'stock knowledge at hand', a notion derived from Husserl. Stock knowledge *is* reality as we experience it. It acquires a taken-for-granted chaacter normally shared with others. This gives a 'reciprocity of perspective' and a presumption that we share a common world. Such presumptions are what holds society together.

Extending Weber's IDEAL TYPE, Schutz argues that presumptions are activated through 'typification'. We categorize one another ideal-typically, which saves us having to start from scratch by minutely observing and assessing one another. Though this shares much with symbolic interactionism, it is rather more 'idealist' in character: the presumption (that is the belief itself) in a common world is more important in upholding social order than the actual content or substance of the shared belief. This may offer a way out of the difficulty that FUNCTIONALIST theory found itself in when it was demonstrated empirically that CON-SENSUS on substantive values and norms does not usually exist in societies. It has been taken further by ETHNOMETHODOLOGY.

Though Schutz aspired to create a method and a theory which would be general for sociology as a whole, his approach has not yet been absorbed into the main stream. His work is the inspiration for definite pheno-menological and ethnomethodological factions within sociology, and it informs many studies of direct interaction situations. But whether social order considered more broadly is maintained in the way he claimed remains largely untested. This is partly because Schutz himself wrote at a rather abstract, universal level, and partly because his legacy had been claimed by ethno-methodologists who tend to ignore the existence of major structures, institutions and power actors in society. But Schutz's approach could, perhaps, be used to examine the way in which such agencies as states, classes, churches etc continually reproduce themselves and are occasionally challenged.

See also BERGER AND LUCKMAN.

MM

**Scientific Management.** (1) A set of management techniques; (2) a movement and its associated 'philosophy' originating amongst American engineers around 1900. F.W. TAYLOR was by far their most important source of inspiration until the 1920s. Scientific management technique, as expounded by Taylor, has three principal aspects. (1) *Organization*. The structure of work should be studied, broken into simpler elements, and taught to workmen as a strict routine. Such rationalization would also be extended upwards in the organization, though for Taylor this was never a priority. The resulting detail tasks would be strictly supervised by specially trained foremen and managers, and through more elaborate formal controls. The conception of a task was split from its execution, and managerial control of workers' behaviour would become much tighter as objective information about work operations and work performance was accumulated in the corporation's 'Thinking Department'. (2) *Motivation*. Taylor recognized that workers might resist such a programme, at least initially. Once they grasped the great consequent gains in overall productivity, they would accept them provided they shared sufficiently in the gains. For Taylor, workers were rational 'economic men' concerned with careful calculation of the monetary main chance. He thus advocated a system of payment-by-results which promised workers significant gains in earnings and adamantly insisted that his methods would never work unless workers were actually granted enhanced rewards for performing rationalized work. Workers were also to be carefully selected to match individual abilities to the task performed, and to be trained and constantly retrained in rationalized operations. Every worker could become a 'first class man' at some task or other. (3) *Ideology*. The source of industrial inefficiency, and industrial conflict is lack of management competence. Once managers, by adopting 'science' instead of

'rule of thumb', showed themselves to be truly competent, workers would abandon their resistance to managerial control. A 'mental revolution' would occur, as workers and managers collaborated ('willingly' and 'heartily') to increase the size of the product instead of squabbling over their relative shares. This collaboration would be endowed with exceptionally high legitimacy, for submission to 'the rule of Science' was also submission to 'the rule of Law'.

Such prescriptions were less than immediately successful. Early Scientific Management had to contend with oppostion from trade unions horrified by their loss of control over the labour process, from managers unenthusiastic about acquiring 'competence' (and even less so over paying incentives), and even from the American Congress, which called for an enquiry into 'Efficiency Systems' in 1913. Later, industrial psychologists were to demonstrate the real dangers to health in much rationalized work (see HUMAN FACTOR TRADITION), while the HUMAN RELATIONS movement objected to the economistic, divisive implications of the preoccupation with individual incentive payments, and the stress upon technical efficiency as the exclusive goal of human collaboration in work. Yet Scientific Management gradually gained 'respectability' as its more objectionable applications were abandoned, or modified, in the light of new contributions and syntheses. In practice, worker opposition successfully mitigated some of its effects, though how far depended on local circumstances. It was hailed with enthusiasm by personalities as varied as Lenin and Mussolini (and, together with Henry Ford's mass-production flow techniques, by GRAMSCI). For half a century the essential Scientific Management 'programme' was increasingly implemented, leading to a general growth in rationalized tasks in every industrialized economy (though perhaps this is less than some pessimists argue) and a tightening of management control over events at the point of production. A growth in the legitimacy of management authority over workers as a consequence of this penetration is far harder to demonstrate, as is the claim that the truly 'scientific' manager is a 'technocrat' whose values diverge from those of dominant groups in his society, be it capitalist or state socialist.

In more recent years, Scientific Management strategy has been subject to varied, vocal, and occasionally effective criticism. There is a growing acceptance that 'excessively' rationalized work routines, by killing the producer's interest and involvement in his or her task, is counterproductive in terms of scientific management's own narrow logic. Similar claims, though they posess weaker cost-accounting foundations, have been made about the true 'efficiency' of rigid chains of command and the exclusion of subordinate personnel from the DECISION-MAKING process in corporations. Though more muted since the onset of the current economic recession in the advanced industrialized countries, such criticisms are sustained by worker resistance to highly rationalized labour processes. The origin of this resistance lies in generally rising expectations about the quality of working life. Scientific Management remains a topic of high research priority.

See also  BUREAUCRACY, EFFORT BARGAIN, EXPLOITATION, HUMAN FACTOR TRADITION, INCENTIVE PAYMENTS, LABOUR PROCESS, SKILL, TAYLOR.

See M. Rose, *Industrial Behaviour* (1975).

MR

**Scottish Enlightenment.** A group of intellectuals active at the end of 18th century, usually regarded as the cradle of the social sciences in Britain. They were generalist in outlook and their writings spread over several now distinct disciplines: philosophy, sociology, anthropology, political economy, law, psychology, ethics, linguistics. Adam SMITH in political economy, Adam FERGUSON and John Millar in sociology, and David HUME in both, were key figures who followed the scientific lead of Newton in their inquiries into human nature and the social world. They used an empirical method of inquiry which began with observation, introspection and history, and ended with explanations couched in the language of rules, principles and laws. They presumed, like Newton, that worldly phenomena had an order which could be discovered by empirical means.

Society was both a natural and a moral order. Human beings were by their nature social, and their behaviour was understood by reference to 'passions', 'senses' and 'interests' which were mediated by 'laws', 'principles' and 'rules'. The Scottish Enlightenment philosophers rejected the egoist view of human nature presented by HOBBES and Mandeville as either wrong (Hutcheson and Ferguson) or one-sided (Smith and Hume). They criticized the 'state of nature' theorists (Hobbes, LOCKE) who postulated a presocial human being, an individual apart from society. They had an instrumental concept of reason, and located the basis of moral judgement not in the rational faculty (as KANT did) but in the passions. Reason was the tool for discerning the principles operating behind observations, or for determining the most advantageous means to a specific end. Society was also a moral order because Nature and Nature's Author were presumed to be good and to have moral attributes. Human history was also thought to display an ordered, reasonable or benevolent design.

Enlightenment history, like the ethical theories of the period, was strangely ahistorical and unself-critical. The aim of the Scottish Enlightenment philosophers was to explain why the world was the way it was, and their basic assumptions were generally unproblematic. Virtue, passions and human nature were taken as given, unchanging and uncriticizable. Ultimately this basic belief, buffered by the empirical method, precluded a systematic and fundamental critique of the contemporary social order.

Most were born into the social circle of the lower nobility and professional middle rank, which included civil servants, ministers and lawyers. Many attended the universities of Glasgow or Edinburgh, and travelled on the Continent. All were preoccupied with the social nature of human beings, and were concerned with the place of virtue in commercial society. They constituted an intellectual elite who used the fundamental categories of the Enlightenment to understand the rapidly changing  social and economic  world  around  them.  Their influence  was  not  local — they  had  few Scottish  successors — but  worldwide, providing one of the main thrusts furthering the development of the social sciences in Europe and America.

BJB

**secondary process.** See PSYCHOANALYSIS.

**sect.** A form of minority ideological collectivity, typically religious but sometimes political, occasionally medical or scientific, which claims to possess a monopoly of access to the truth or salvation. Sociological concern with sects may be dated from the scattered observations of WEBER in his analysis of the PROTESTANT ETHIC. Weber distinguised the sect from the CHURCH by its achieved rather than ascribed bases of membership (see ACHIEVEMENT). The sect is exclusive in character, accepting only those who display specific criteria of suitability or worth. It imposes a test of merit upon potential members; the church is inclusive, seeking to exercise its domain over all members of a society.

TROELTSCH saw the sect as the social expression of an ascetic, radical and eschatological variant of the Christian tradition. He stressed the opposition between sect and the world. The sect sees itself as a separated community whose members seek not to be 'yoked with unbelievers'. Its appeal is primarily to the lower classes. Subsequent writers have noted that Troeltsch's view of the sect was based on a limited sample drawn almost entirely from prior to the 18th century.

A difficulty with many early definitions of the sect lay in the stress on achieved membership, taken to mean that the sect could only exist for a single generation before the need to absorb a less committed second generation set it on the path to becoming a DENOMINATION (see also DENOMINATIONALIZATION). However many sects such as the Hutterites in North America, the Jehovah's Witnesses etc have survived over several generations without any appreciable shift towards denominationalism. Hence the notion of 'established' and 'institutionalized' sect have been introduced to accommodate such groups.

However, denominationalization also posed for Bryan Wilson (*Religious Sects*, 1970) the problem that the concept of sect glossed a range of important distinctions within this category. Wilson argued that types of sect could be distinguished by their view of salvation. The CONVERSIONIST sect seeks to change the world by transforming individuals through evangelism. The REVOLUTIONIST sect is pessimistic of the potential for reforming an evil world and expects the world to be transformed by drastic supernatural intervention. INTROVERSIONIST sects reject the world and separate themselves from it in order to preserve their own purity and cultivate their own holiness. MANIPULATIONIST sects largely accept the world's values but offer superior, esoteric means for achieving them. THAUMATURGICAL sects offer personal benefits in this life through supernatural and miraculous interventions. UTOPIAN sects withdraw from the world in order to construct a new model upon which it can be rebuilt. Reformist sects believe there is some hope for ameliorating and mitigating the evils of the world through charity and service to others.

Contemporary accounts of the sect generally stress its TOTALITARIANISM; its self-conception as an elect or ELITE: its exclusionary policy regarding internal dissenters, doubters or heretics; and its hostility towards, or separation from, the STATE or society. The sect claims to possess unique and privileged access to the truth or salvation. The truth must be protected, and extensive control is legitimated over those to whom access is permitted, as is the exclusion of the unworthy. The remaining believers see themselves as of proven and tested worth subordinating their self-interests in the service of the truth. Hostility to the state also readily follows: the state demands acceptance of its own version of the truth in some particulars and may thus threaten or conflict with the sectarian's notion of what constitutes the truth or right conduct in respect of such matters as the payment of taxes, military service, education of children, medical practice etc. The sect defines through authoritative revelation what constitutes truth and error. Although frequently emerging in this form sects may sometimes develop from CULTS as a result of the successful centralization of authority by one or more leaders.

RW

**secular analysis.** See COHORT AND PERIOD ANALYSIS.

**secularization.** A contentious concept, largely because there is so little consensus as to what it is that constitutes RELIGION.

Approaches to secularization broadly follow the two approaches to the definition of religion. Those who identify religion in terms of belief and action oriented to supernatural beings (the substantive approach) regard secularization as the process in which the thought and behaviour of members of a society are less influenced by religious concerns, symbols and institutions. Such a notion does not entail the idea of a 'Golden Age of Faith' or a religious UTOPIA in which society was fully religious compared to some other stage when it will become fully secular. It simply entails the presumption that at some point religious meanings, practices or institutions were more powerful than they are at some later point. Hence, this notion does not entail that secularization is unidirectional, nor that it is inevitable, although a number of thinkers (e.g. FREUD, FRAZER) have held this view. Secularization is not a unitary or unidimensional phenomenon. It has a number of different dimensions: changes in beliefs, practices, religious institutions and in other social institutions in the degree to which, for example, they have recourse to religious legitimations. Hence there will be different indicators of the process in different settings. While in Europe statistics on membership of religious institutions, or usage of their facilities, are often referred to in support of the claim that secularization has occurred, these are not the only indicator of secularization, nor are they even necessary. There is therefore no contradiction in the claim that England has become more secular and that this is shown by declining numbers who belong to or attend the major Protestant churches, and the claim that the USA has become more secular even though the numbers of church members have increased through much of this century. Secularization can take different forms. In most European Protestant societies, and to a lesser extent in industrialized parts of Catholic Europe, church membership has declined dramatically; religious institutions have become less

prominent; their personnel have lost status and authority, and supernatural beliefs have become less widely accepted though some — such as belief in God — retain significant support. In the USA there has been increasing church membership but many of these churches have become more secular, defining their activities in terms of the provision of social facilities for integrating their members into the community and providing them with psychological support. In their beliefs the major American churches have become increasingly this-worldly, stressing the psychological comforts of religious belief, peace of mind, health and happiness, and adjustment.

While substantive approaches to religion regard secularization as having been a major feature of the development of advanced industrial societies, functional approaches to religion take a different view. They do not dispute that religious institutions and supernaturalistic beliefs have become less important in industrial societies. FUNCTIONALIST theorists regard religion as a social universal. Every society has some set of common values (CONSENSUS) answering ultimate problems (see FUNCTIONAL THEORIES OF RELIGION) or providing meaning for the world of everyday life and a world-view whereby man's biological nature is transcended (see INVISIBLE RELIGION). Religion may change its form but cannot disappear, nor even decline significantly. Religion in contemporary industrial societies is taking a new, less institutional, more individualistic, less theistic form, in which meaning is found in such themes as self-realization.

Substantive views of religion and secularization are usually informed by WEBER's conception of the role of rationalization in the West (see RATIONALITY, sense 2), of which secularization is one facet. Christianity, it is argued, was more prone to secularization in its early differentiation of the church and the world, the religious domain and the secular, liberating the profane world for rational scrutiny. Such distinctions are less readily made in Hindu or Buddhist cultures. Christianity, possessing a radically transcendent god, was also less magical in character than most world religions, and this rationalism was dramatically enhanced by the Reformation with its hostility to indulgences, penances, confession, and other beliefs and practices inhibiting the emergence of a fully rationalistic ethic and a demythologized cosmos.

The rationalizing effect of modern industrial production, particularly when combined with the disruption of traditional community, has been a powerful source of declining attachment to traditional religious beliefs and institutions. Industrial societies tend to be more secularized than agrarian societies; urban dwellers more than rural dwellers; men more than women; working women more than housewives etc. Religion can remain particularly influential in a society when it becomes a focus for NATIONAL or cultural identity, especially when faced with an external threat to that identity. Poland and Ireland display an extremely high level of continued commitment to the Catholic church because of its role as a focus for resistance to the political and cultural imperialism of Russia and England.

See D. Martin, *A General Theory of Secularization* (1978).

RW

**Seebohm Report.** In 1968 the Committee under the chairmanship of Sir Frederick Seebohm proposed a major change in the organization of social work services in England and Wales. Social work functions undertaken in a number of different local authority departments should be brought together 'to secure an effective family service'. The changes were made two years after the Report, when social services departments were established in England and Wales. A similar change had been made two years earlier in Scotland as a result of the 1968 Social Work (Scotland) Act. In Scotland, the new departments were called 'social work' rather than 'social services', and included probation work, excluded in England and Wales.

The unification of social work services has had major implications. For example, social workers now accept much broader responsibilities (previously they specialized in child care, medical social work, psychiatric social work etc) and 'generic' training is encouraged. Similarly, clients are not faced with a number of different specialist workers

from separate departments. Assistance is offered from a central source with contact from one social worker.

Some critics claim that the pressure for a unified service came from social workers, not clients, and that in part the pressure arose because of social workers' PROFESSIONAL aspirations and the desire for a better career structure. They claim that the unification of departments restricts the number of sources of help available to the client and increases the power of the social worker over the client.

The reorganization of social work services was one of a number of moves in a similar direction in British social policy: the reorganization of the health services and local government took place at about the same time.

MPJ

**segmentary societies.** See ACEPHALOUS.

**segregation.** The geographical separation of groups, more particularly of ethnic or racial groups (see ETHNICITY; RACE) whereby the weaker group is forced to reside in a restricted area or to use separate facilities (e.g. separate railway coaches, waiting rooms, lavatories and water fountains).

MPB

**selection.** Many social systems, either because purposefully structured or as an UNINTENDED CONSEQUENCE of their structure, divide members or those who pass through them into categories by socially defined characteristics. This constitutes social selection. The criteria may be biological: only males over a certain height and of good physique can be selected into Guards regiments. More usually criteria are social: only males with certain academic competence and particular religious motivations can enter seminaries, and only those who succeed in certain higher-level academic tests and are seen to possess certain traits of personality will be selected to enter the priesthood. An example of a less consciously planned process of social selection is that operating through SOCIAL MOBILITY within the class system. The part played by INTELLIGENCE in social selection is a controversial topic. Some believe this to be a biologically inherited characteristic, while others see it as entirely or largely environmentally determined. In this case the belief held will greatly influence the position taken as to how certain selection processes should be planned. This is particularly so in regard to formal EDUCATION. If environment can have much influence on the level of intelligence, students with low intelligence as now measured never need give up hope that they can achieve the high level needed for elite positions; the opposite will rule if intelligence is largely biologically determined. In the latter case improved tests will be needed to measure levels and types of intelligence so that social selection through formal education can be more efficient or so that the choice of upward mobility is at least made available to those found capable of it.

See also  WOMEN AND EDUCATION.

PWM

**selectivity.** It is frequently argued that to give social services benefits to everyone is wasteful and that instead they should be concentrated on those in greatest NEED, applied selectively. However, one of the central problems raised by selectivity is the assessment of those deemed to be in need. Such assessment, as through MEANS TESTS, can stigmatize recipients and lead to a low take-up of benefits. If selectivity is applied to areas like health care, it might lead to the development of two different services, one for those who can afford to pay and one for those who cannot, with the latter inferior to the former. Selectivity tends to be associated with a particular political philosophy: those who argue for selectivity are also arguing for a reduction in state expenditure on welfare.

Nevertheless, some who support a universal basis of social service benefits would not rule out all selectivity. TITMUSS, for example, believed that universal benefits were not sufficient to break down the barriers of economic and social discrimination and combat neglect. He favoured positive (selective) discrimination, applied to ensure that the recipient did not associate it with personal failure or individual fault. One answer was to make discrimination impersonal for example between groups and areas rather than individuals. Such views fit in with those who favour territorial discrimination, such as the educational priority areas suggested by the Plowden Report (see COMPENSATORY EDUCATION).

MPJ

**self, the.** A central, but elusive concept in social psychology, with many different meanings. Psychologists often use it to depict human potential (as in Maslow's self-actualization theory; see NEEDS, HIERARCHY OF) or beliefs held about oneself (the self concept). In sociology 'the self' is most frequently used in SYMBOLIC INTERACTIONISM to bridge the problem that people are unique, creative, experiencing, biological beings, yet simultaneously socially constrained regulated and predictable creatures. The self is seen as a process involving two phases — the 'I' and the 'Me'. The 'I' is that phase of the self which is the subject and which actively experiences, organizes and acts on the social world (comparable, in some writings, to the ego): it tends to be either more psychological (the motive force) or metaphysical (the 'soul'), and the concept is often criticized by sociologists for being too vague and general. The 'Me' is grasped more readily as that phase of the self which is the object of experience: it is the cluster of attitudes held towards oneself which tend to regulate and structure conduct. The 'Me' is composed of attitudes about oneself, perceptions of the attitudes of others to oneself (often termed significant others), and perceptions of the whole community to oneself (the generalized other). The process by which an individual imaginatively constructs the attitudes of the other — and thus anticipates the behaviour of the other — is known as ROLE taking, and human COMMUNICATION is contingent upon this ability.

William James in *The Principles of Psychology* (1890) clearly distinguished between the 'I' as subject and the 'Me' as object, but G.H. MEAD developed the idea and argued that it is the self that 'makes the distinctively human society possible'. For Mead, the self 'has the characteristic that it is an object to itself ... it is reflexive and indicates that which can be both subject and object'. BLUMER subsequently interpreted this work for sociologists. Much empirical work has now been conducted on the self either using measurements such as the TWENTY STATEMENTS TEST or PARTICIPANT OBSERVATION. Among the latter is N. Denzin's study of the acquisition of self in children (*Childhood Socialization*), and GOFFMAN's research on the self conceptions of mental patients in asylums.

See K.J. Gergen and C. Gordon, *The Self in Social Interaction* (1968).

KP

**self actualization theory.** A theory of work behaviour and organization based on a notion of a definite 'hierarchy' of human needs with 'self-actualization' at the top; sometimes known as 'neo-human relations' (see HUMAN RELATIONS). Once a 'lower' need (e.g. physical survival) has been fulfilled the subject will seek to fulfil the next need in the ladder of priority. Applied to work, the central postulate is that an unfulfilled lower level, or sometimes a 'hygiene' need (above all, for adequate pay) will generate discontent but, once met, will not produce positive motivation because the subject's needs become directed towards 'self-actualization' (a sense of achievement and personal worth). Organizational forms and personnel practice need to be transformed in order to answer such needs (for example, through job-enrichment programmes). Interesting in some of its practical applications, the theory in general (there are numerous variants) has received insufficient scientific validation. How exactly is one need identified and distinguished from others? Why should it occupy the exact precedence allocated to it in the hierarchy? Are needs differentially distributed throughout the population? How do they evolve in line with altering expectations that are culturally transmitted? Sociologists, with their belief in the plurality and changeability of value-systems, remain suspicious of any essentialist theory that plays down social (and even individual) diversity.

See NEEDS, HIERARCHY OF.

MR

**self-reliance.** The theory of self-reliant development probably originated in the People's Republic of China during the Great Leap Forward in 1957. Its popularity derives from the Arusha Declaration (1967) when President Nyerere of Tanzania used the term self-reliance in a promising salute to the aspirations of his own nation and those of the entire THIRD WORLD.

Upon independence, most Third World countries had found themselves deeply entangled in a system of international specialization and trade which, they argued, increasingly blocked their chances of independent development and industrialization (see CENTRE-PERIPHERY; DEPENDENCY). Self-reliance became at once a political force uniting the ex-colonial countries and a programme of independent development strategies.

As a political ideology, it complemented NEO-COLONIALISM, which had already begun to bring the emerging Third World countries into one camp in the international political arena. Neo-colonialism was in essence only an 'anti'-ideology, but self-reliance held out the promise of something positive, inspiring the Third World to believe it could do things for itself.

'Self-reliance' has two main planks. (1) De-linking: a gradual disengagement from the international specialization which had left so many countries dependent on the export earnings of one or two primary agricultural commodities. This is complemented by diversification of agricultural production with an emphasis on self-sufficiency in food production, and by IMPORT SUBSTITUTIVE INDUSTRIALIZATION to reduce dependency on manufacturing imports from the technologically advanced countries. (2) Rural self-help programmes, especially central in the original Tanzanian self-reliant development plan. It was planned to build viable socialist communities in the rural areas (the so-called Ujamaa villages) not by direct government intervention and tutelage but based on a democratic system of local government.

*Collective self-reliance* is a logical extension of this concept. It was soon realized that many Third World countries were individually too small, too poor and lacking in resources and potential markets to make self-reliant policies, especially de-linking, a practicable option. Only when such countries joined together in trade and economic co-operation, could self-reliance become a real alternative to dependency upon the advanced countries.

This concept first surfaced at the 1972 Conference of the Non-aligned Movement (see NEO-COLONIALISM) in Lusaka, Zambia. On the eve of a decade of debates on a New International Economic Order, the developing countries also recognized the need to enhance their collective bargaining power vis-à-vis the developed world. The concept of collective self-reliance captures both the notions of Third World economic co-operation and collective bargaining power.

AH

**semantic differential.** A type of ATTITUDE scale (see SCALES) introduced by Osgood, Suci and Tannenbaum in 1957. It attempts to measure the meaning of an object — a person, political issue, institution, concept or thing — to an individual. The individual is asked to rate the objects in question on seven-point bi-polar scales such as fair-unfair; good-bad; strong-weak; active-passive; fast-slow. FACTOR ANALYSIS suggests the scales relate to three basic DIMENSIONS of meaning — evaluation, potency and activity. The technique is designed to facilitate comparisons of the meaning of various objects to the individual — 'me as I am' for instance, compared with 'me as I would like to be'. However, it can also be used to compare the attitudes of different groups by averaging scores on the scales.

JB

**semantics.** See LANGUAGE.

**semiology, semiotics.** A projected science of the use of signs in human and animal life. The term 'semiology' originated with the French linguist SAUSSURE, and 'semiotics' with the American philosopher C.S. Peirce (1839-1914). The subject aims at a generalized logic governing all types of sign use, both linguistic and non-linguistic, and shares with STRUCTURALISM both a preoccupation with the coding and decoding of meaning, and a number of common influences.

By a sign is meant a three-termed relation formed when, for somebody, something (the signifier) stands in for something else (the signified) in some context (the ground). The signifier may point directly as an index (using Peirce's terminology) to the signified (e.g. smoke-fire); it may resemble it as an icon (e.g. a picture); or it may be a purely conventional SYMBOL (e.g. a word). While in human social life LANGUAGE with its conventional symbols occupies the most noticeable position, semiology directs our attention to other forms of signification, such as dress, manner of speech, gesture and decor, working both within and without language. From the semiological point of view, all social actions and patterns are communicative, and the way they are put together can be studied as analogous to linguistic structure.

While semiology can be traced back to VICO, in its present form in the social sciences it derives from the reinterpretation of Saussure by Roland Barthes, and of the structural linguistics of Roman Jakobson's 'Prague School' in LÉVI-STRAUSS's structural anthropology. Threads from these sources, as well as the American work of BOAS, Sapir, Whorf *et al.* on American Indian languages and world-view, are gathered together to form the basis of contemporary semiological theory. Barthes, like Lévi-Strauss, treats MYTH as a second-order system of signification underlying the level of language, and in this spirit in sociology semiology has been largely confined to the analysis of discourse, linguistic passages of greater than sentence length, such as works of literature. The study of signification in the social actions of everyday life has achieved much less attention.

JL

**senile dementia.** See MENTAL ILLNESS.

**service class.** A term applied by Renner to the functionaries of both private corporations and the civil service who serve the capitalist by assisting the development of capital. DAHRENDORF removed the Marxist element and began the practice of using the term for all public and private sector bureaucrats, people who provide neither leadership nor technical skills but who simply administer, playing their part in the ever more minutely subdivided process of authority. As such they constitute part of the new MIDDLE CLASS. Goldthorpe, in *Social Mobility and Class Structure in Modern Britain* (1980), extends the concept further to all higher professional, higher-technical, administrative and managerial occupations. These, he argues, constitute the major expanding class of the mid-20th century, just as the PROLETARIAT was in the mid-19th century.

See BOURGEOISE; MIDDLE CLASS.

CGAB, MM

**sex ratio.** In demography, the sex ratio expresses the ratio of males to females in a population or sub-population. Biologically, there is approximately a 5 per cent surplus of male births over female, but differential MORTALITY and migration of males act to alter this ratio in the population as a whole and in particular age-groups. When mortality is high, with an expectation of life of about 30 years (see LIFE EXPECTANCY) — typical of many historical and pre-industrial societies — the surplus of males is eroded to give an overall surplus of females. But when mortality falls to the levels of modern industrial societies, with an expectation of life of about 70 years, the surplus of males is carried on into the population to give an overall predominance of males. The effect of population growth, characteristic of much of the world, coupled with patterns of male and female mortality, is to increase the shortage of males, particularly in young adulthood. The proportion of males conceived is independent of the age of the mother, but varies inversely with the age of the father.

The relative abundance of men and women of different ages affects individual marriage-chances, the ages of partners, the proportions unmarried (see NUPTIALITY), the composition of households, the ratio of producers to consumers, the availability of military man-power, the inheritance of property and the structure of the labour-force. The sex ratio may be altered by losses in war of young men, such as occurred in World War I, giving rise to a cohort carrying forward a surplus of females. MIGRATION typically decreases the sex ratio in the area of origin and increases that of the area of destination. INDUSTRIALIZATION and URBANIZATION create a range of new employment opportunities for men and women, and the movements of population involved distorts the established urban and rural sex ratios.

Differing cultural evaluations of male and female children may lead to the mis-reporting of sex in some countries (e.g. China), and may also affect the sex ratio through neglect or evan infanticide of females.

See also WOMEN AND THE LABOUR MARKET.

JL

**sexuality.** Until the early 1970s sociologists rarely studied human sexuality and the field of inquiry was dominated by three main traditions. The first, symbolized by FREUD, was the clinical tradition, and examined the emotional development of the individual person by means of intensive analytic work on childhood memories and the unconscious. The second, symbolized by Masters and Johnson, was the experimental tradition, which examined the nature of sexual arousal by means of controlled laboratory experiments and which led to the growth of the sex therapy industry. And the third — symbolized by Kinsey — was the social book-keeping approach, which examined the frequency and social distribution of sexual behaviours through interviews, questionnaires and statistical computation. When sexuality was discussed in sociological writings, it was usually masked by a wider concern such as the FAMILY OF DEVIANCE, and it was not taken as a problem in itself but as a given — usually a biological or Freudian drive. Significant work in England, such as Michael Schofield's *Sexual Behaviour of Young People* (1965) was predominantly in the social book-keeping tradition; while theoretically the main frameworks adopted were either FUNCTIONALISM — as in the writings of Kingsley Davis — or else were informed by Freudianism (some of the writings of Wilhelm Reich, for example, attempted to merge Freud with Marx).

Since the 1970s however, and largely as a result of the growth in interest around deviance and GENDER divisions, there has been a substantial expansion of research in this area, primarily in the USA. Distinguishing sexuality from gender, the main theoretical approaches came from SYMBOLIC INTERACTIONISTS (notably John Gagnon and Willian Simon in *Sexual Conduct*, 1974), who reconceptualized sexuality as essentially symbolic and evoked the metaphor of 'script' (see DRAMATURGY) to analyse it; from feminist sociologists who, using either interactionism, Freudianism or social book-keeping, analysed the changing constructions around female sexuality; and from various kinds of STRUCTURALISTS and SEMIOLOGISTS who analysed sexuality as both a DISCOURSE or a form of coded desire built up through language.

Although there are many differences between these approaches, they all agree that human sexuality should be studied as a socially constructed meaning which can change dramatically across cultures and throughout history. Sexuality is thus not assumed to be a powerful biological drive constant through time and space, but a very specific product whose form and shape becomes the topic of investigation.

See M. Brake (ed.), *Human Sexual Relations : A Reader*, (1982).

KP

**shadow prices.** The implicit prices used to value COSTS and benefits when market prices do not reflect true opportunity costs and benefits. They are used widely in COST-BENEFIT ANALYSIS when market prices are distorted by monopoly (see MARKET STRUCTURE) or where they reflect disequilibrium in a market, as in the case of UNEMPLOYMENT. They are also used to value items that affect social welfare but are not marketed and therefore do not have a market price. Travel time savings, noise nuisance and pollution are examples of items which fall into this category.

RR

**shamanism.** The shaman is a religio-magical specialist in technologically simple, undifferentiated societies. Unlike the priest found in more technologically developed and differentiated social milieux, the shaman is typically a part-time practitioner otherwise engaged in the subsistence activities of society. The shaman exercises personal CHARISMA in contrast to the charisma of office displayed by the priest. His powers derive from direct personal contact with supernatural forces which are mobilized on a professional-client basis for the treatment of illness, or to safeguard or improve the crops

or hunting of the client. Although, like the priest, the shaman employs rituals, he or she cures or secures other good effects directly by mobilizing supernatural power, while the priest conducts rituals to propitiate the supernatural entities causing the disease.

The shaman may be assisted by spirit helpers, and often secures ends by going into a trance in which the soul is thought to leave the body, ascending to the spiritual realm or into the underworld. Illness is often thought to be caused by the theft or loss of the sick person's soul, which the shaman retrieves.

While the behaviour of the shaman may appear to comprise psychopathological symptoms by Western standards, such behaviour may be largely conventional in character in the society in which it occurs. Nonetheless, individuals recruited to shamanistic roles may be unduly liable to states of trance or have an unusual propensity for states of ecstasy which make them seem peculiarly suited to the role.

See MAGIC, WITCHCRAFT.

RW

**sick role, the.** It is a mark of Talcott PARSONS's penetrating originality that he brought forward an apparently natural event, the process of becoming ill and seeking medical treatment, as an appropriate object of sociological analysis. The concept of the sick role first appeared as part of a case study of modern medical practice to illustrate the interrelationships of the principle elements of the SOCIAL SYSTEM (in his book of that title, 1950). The maintenance of health is an overriding practical necessity for all societies. In a complex division of labour sickness and healing are well-developed social activities involving publicly organized insurance schemes and large-scale total institutions for housing the sick. This is so because illness represents a form of DEVIANCE from normal duties. But, unlike some other forms of deviance, being sick does not necessarily carry negative sanctions. Indeed, within the value system there may be a positive encouragement, if not obligation, to withdraw from normal social roles. By providing a motivation to deviance on the part of the sick, the social system improves the conditions for the restoration of health and, at the same time, isolates the (transient) deviant in a specialized role system. This has the effect of reducing the visibility and the attraction of the deviant role to others. The social regulation of sickness is entrusted to the physician who is invested with the authority to admit and discharge individuals in their passage through the sick role. In carrying out this role the physician's behaviour is subject to three basic norms: affective neutrality (social and emotional distance), universalism (equality of treatment), and functional specificity (narrow technical specialization) (see PATTERN VARIABLES).

The sick role has four principle elements, two rights conditional upon two obligations. (1) Depending on the severity of the sickness, the individual is exempted from normal obligations and (2) is not held personally responsible for his condition. He cannot help it, recovery is not a matter of volition, and it involves the intervention of others. But (3) at the same time the sick person should view his condition as undesirable and should not take advantage of any secondary gain from being the centre of concerned attention to prolong his indisposure. (4) As part of this, there is a related obligation to seek technical qualified help and to co-operate in prescribed therapy.

That the concept of the sick role has attracted a large volume of (mostly negative) critical attention is testimony to its importance, especially in the development of medical sociology. But in providing a paradigm for the analysis of the doctor/patient relationship, it has tended to be separated from the systematic model of social structure of which it was intended as no more than an interdependent part. Critics have been quick to point out that the empirical evidence of sickness and its treatment deviates in substantial ways from Parsons's IDEAL TYPE, which seems to be founded on the narrow organic disease model of positivist medical science. As such it embodies an image of sickness as acute, morally neutral and objectively observable, of the sufferer as the incompetent and passive professional client, and of the physician as an altruistic practitioner who puts relief of suffering above all else.

All of these assumptions carry problems.

Disorders of health are frequently chronic, if not permanent disabilities, which involve personal initiative and adjustment rather than medical cure. In such cases the incumbency of the sick role is not a temporary interlude and it may therefore involve long term deviance. Equally, many conditions, for example venereal and smoking-related disease, are not free of moral valuation. Some others may never even be recognized as legitimate disease either by their victims or by those with the authority to diagnose. So the sick role is relevant to only a limited range of sickness and even then there may be obstacles to deter the would-be incumbent, such as the high cost of available medical care.

The shortcomings of the sick role as a paradigmatic model have acted as inspiration in the development of research on the doctor/patient relationship. Most studies have focused on the degree of mutuality in interaction. The best-known, that of SZASZ and Hollander (*Archives of Internal Medicine*, 1956), distinguishes three ideal types according to context and type of medical problem: (1) activity/passivity, appropriate to treatment of medical emergencies when the patient is not even conscious; (2) guidance/co-operation, appropriate to on-going medical treatment where the sentient patient respects and follows doctors' orders; (3) mutual participation appropriate to chronic conditions where treatment depends on a high degree of involvement on the part of the patient. Underlying each of these is an assumption of an harmonious reciprocity of interests which other research has called into question. Freidson points to a fundamental tension arising from the discrepant expectations of doctor and patient. The detached approach of the doctor to what is no more than a mere case must clash with a committed involvement of the client, for whom the consultation might be a matter of life and death. That such encounters would provoke anxiety, even conflict, has been frequently verified in research and it seems that disappointment with role performance is not confined to patients. Doctors also report their own frustrated expectations of patients who are insufficiently discriminating in the problems they bring to the surgery, insufficiently deferential in consultation, and frequently non-compliant in the process of treatment. Other research presents professional practice in a more sinister light, revealing the techniques of information control employed by physicians to induce ignorance and uncertainty on the part of clients and thereby to protect the process of treatment from critical scrutiny.

The empirical record thus casts some doubt on the fit between the ideal attributes of the sick role and the real experience of illness and its treatment. In reviewing the sociological utility of the concept a distinction should be drawn between its usefulness for the analysis of the doctor/patient relationship on the one hand and for the force of medicine as an agency of social control on the other.

See also MEDICAL PROFESSION; ROLE.

NH

**significance test.** A general term in statistics referring to the use of probability theory to test hypotheses about one or more sets of data. A test has the following general form. (1) The researcher states his or her assumptions, usually in the form of a null hypothesis. (2) A significance level and critical region is selected to determine whether or not the results of the test will be accepted or rejcted. These levels (most commonly in sociological research the 5 per cent and 1 per cent levels) are selected in terms of the PROBABILITY of the distribution of data in a matrix occurring by chance. At the 5 per cent level, for example, there is a 5 per cent probability that any pattern in the data has occurred by chance, a 95 per cent probablity that it has not. (3) The test statistic is computed. (4) A decision is made on (1) in the light of (2) and (3). The researcher, in selecting the significance level, runs the risk of committing Type I or Type II errors. Type I errors consist of rejecting assumptions which are true; type II errors in accepting assumptions which are in fact false. It is impossible to minimize the risk of both types of error simultaneously.

See R.E. Henkel and D.E. Morrison (eds.), *The Significance Test Controversy* (1970).

MB

**signified, signifier.** See SEMIOLOGY.

**Simmel, Georg** (1858-1918). German sociologist, the principal figure in the 'formal' school of sociology. Simmel was born in Berlin, the son of a Jewish businessman, and studied philosophy, history, psychology, and Italian language and culture at Berlin University. His first dissertation on music and folk psychology was rejected, but in 1881 he gained his doctorate with a dissertation on KANT. His pursuit of an academic career was assisted by private means. In 1885 he became a *privatdozent* at Berlin University, and lectured on philosophy and ethics, gradually setting up courses on the new discipline of sociology. In 1900 he became a titular professor in Berlin. In 1910 he founded the German Sociological Society with WEBER. He gained a full professorship at Strasbourg University in 1914. Simmel wrote extensively on philosophy and much of his sociology was produced within one decade.

One of the early pioneers of ANALYTICAL sociology which favoured the construction of a unified comprehensive social theory, Simmel was the principal representative of German sociological FORMALISM. He made important contributions in the development of microsociology. Simmel wanted to encourage the growth of an independent scientific sociology with a concrete object of its own and, to this end, he was especially concerned with the precise definition of the boundaries between sociology and related disciplines. Simmel opposed all contemporary claims that sociology held a necessary interconnection with other sciences and should stand at their head.

Philosophy is not distinguished by its subject-matter but constitutes a specific method of analysis applicable to the objects and epistemology of other disciplines. Its method displays a world-orientation and a grasp of the totality of being. Simmel saw the historians' quest for evolutionary laws as bringing history close to sociology. His early interest in HISTORICISM and social DARWINISM influenced his work on the philosophy of history and morals, and social differentiation. In his main sociological texts, Simmel rejects the search for social laws (see LAW, SOCIAL). Participating in the revival of Kantian philosophy in Germany, Simmel followed Kant in the belief in *a priori* categories, arguing that history can never be a precise reproduction of all that has passed. Rather it is the product of selective perception and the imposition of order upon the creative flux and rich variety of human life. Simmel distinguished between sociology and the philosophy of history or social philosophy, contending that METAPHYSICS belongs exclusively to the latter. Psychology studies the psychological content of social actions on the level of individual motivation and existence.

Simmel's sociological formalism turns upon a distinction between the form and content of social life. Asking the question 'How is society possible?' Simmel bases his answer upon METHODOLOGICAL INDIVIDUALISM. Society is neither organism nor irreducible real totality, but consists of the sum total of reciprocal interactions and interdependencies between individuals. 'Forms of sociation' refer to stable, patterned aspects of social life discerned within varied situations and 'content' refers to variable aspects of social interaction such as individual interests, drives and goals. The content of social interaction is the subject-matter of the other social sciences. Simmel contrasted philosophical and formal sociology. Formal sociology must restrict itself to the analysis of pure abstract forms of social interaction, producing social laws based upon descriptive generalizations of regularities which occur in the forms of social organization. Such generalizations are harder to achieve within sociology because of its subject-matter but may be sought through comparison of similar forms regardless of their specific historical context. Simmel's formalism drew an analogy with geometric forms which neglected rather than rejected historical analysis. He attributed permanency to some forms which were actually relative to a particular historical period. Simmel is also criticized for failing to distinguish between the object and methods of sociology, and for drawing a distinction between form and content which excludes from formal sociology the cultural content of forms and of the material base of society.

Simmel's analysis of social interaction draws upon four basic principles — form, relativity, dualism, distance. 'Form' refers to the structure imposed upon the social world by the mind of the observer. 'Relativity' implies that every phenomenon achieves its meaning and existence relative to some other phenomenon. 'Dualism' refers to the determination of a social situation through the counterbalancing of its contrasting elements. 'Distance' refers to the degree of separation between one person's private space and another's. Distance of the observer from the object is significant in the production of different modes of experiencing those objects and the increasing desire for distance is a distinctive features of modern culture. Modes of experience may be scientific, aesthetic, religious, metaphysical, sociological.

Simmel published 31 books and numerous articles and essays in philosophy and sociology. *Social Differentiation* (1890) examines the historical growth of individuation. The replacement of primary groups by larger, specialized groups increases the incidence of multiple-group membership, creating impersonal and partial relationships governed by abstract rules and offering greater personal freedom. Drawing upon the SPENCERIAN EVOLUTIONISM he subsequently abandoned, Simmel offered a FUNCTIONALIST explanation of social development — that social differentiation arises from the tendency of the organism to achieve greater efficiency. In *The Philosophy of Money* (1900) Simmel examined the relationship between CAPITALISM and the RATIONALITY of science and looked at the impact of a monetary economy upon society. *Sociology* (1908) examines CITY life, the role of the stranger, dyads and tryads. Arguing that forms and objects created to satisfy human needs come to master them, Simmel is criticized by Marxists for believing ALIENATION to be inherent in all social life. He influenced LUKACS's interpretation of Marx (see REIFICATION).

Simmel's formal sociology was only taken up by a Cologne group led by Leopold von Wiese. Weber borrowed some of Simmel's concepts. Simmel's methodological individualism, and microsociology had some impact upon social ACTION THEORY, SOCIOMETRY and CONFLICT THEORY. Coser's *The Functions of Social Conflict* (1956) is indebted to Simmel. Influenced by Kant, HEGEL, Schopenhauer,

NIETZSCHE, Bergson, COMTE, SPENCER, MARX, HUSSERL and DILTHEY, Simmel never produced a systematic sociology, believing that it would be wrong prematurely to codify an emergent discipline.

JW

**skill.** A slippery concept, usually defined in 'technicist' terms by reference to a combination of learnt expertise in a repertoire of actions or activities, together with the mental ability to apply them effectively and resourcefully. The model is that of traditional craft lore. More loosely, 'skill' means little more than relative dexterity in performing some manual task. Activities recognized in practice as 'skilled' normally depend somewhat on social definitions or other conventions. Official CENSUS CLASS categories such as 'skilled', 'semi-skilled' and 'unskilled' reflect these complexities. The outstanding political influence is found in the characteristically low evaluation of women's work, however technically complex it may be. Also some occupations where relatively little expertise is now required continue to be regarded as 'skilled' because of their industrial influence, while others requiring a great range of complex abilities (e.g. traditional farm-labouring) have often been classified as 'unskilled'. New manual craft groups are often called 'technicians'. An additional complexity is the relation between natural aptitudes and skills. Undoubtedly some link exists, but the actual division of labour does not in any sense accurately reflect the distribution of innate 'talents': nearly all semi-skilled tasks could be performed by nearly all workers. The distribution of 'skills' and 'skill levels' closely follows the 'demands' of the economy but these are mediated by technological innovation and production engineering, which have usually aimed at minimizing demand for authentically skilled labour (see LABOUR PROCESS). Most historical analyses of skill stress the disappearance of ancient crafts, but an over-romantic view of pre-industrial days should be avoided: handloom weaving was wretched, monotonous drudgery.

The most forceful 'deskilling' thesis has been propounded by H. Braverman in *Labour and Monopoly Capital: The*

*Degradation of Work in the 20th Century* (1974). He argued that capitalist industrialism irresistibly breaks down skill of all employee groups, but especially that of manual workers, not just to safeguard profits but also with the aim of ensuring control of the WORKING CLASS by capitalists. Critics of this 'degradation of work' thesis object that (1) Braverman overstated the resources, knowledge and will capitalists possess to pursue such a strategy successfully; (2) new skills and specialisms do appear, and the historical evidence for long-term de-skilling is inadequate; (3) some worker groups have organized themselves to protect their skills from rationalization; (4) no alternative model of advanced socio-economic development was delineated.

MR

**slavery.** A social institution which legitimates a relationship in which one person is at the disposal of another. It cannot be sharply differentiated from other forms of servile or dependent labour enforced from the earliest historical times and in many different cultures. In medieval Europe, for example, the FEUDAL manor operated with some slaves who could be sold, but most agricultural workers were in differing degrees bound to the soil. How each person was related to the soil decided whether he or she could marry, what services he or she had to render, and whether he or she could leave the estate. One way of distinguishing slavery from such other forms of dependent labour is to restrict its application to circumstances in which the slaves were from a different ethnic group, either captured in warfare or purchased. This separates genuine slave societies, like classical Greece and Rome, the American South and the Caribbean, from slave-owning societies such as were found in the ancient Near East (including Egypt), India and China. But the distinction does not sit easily with the prevalence of debt bondage in historic societies, where those who could not pay their debts were enslaved, or with the readiness of the House of Commons to agree, in 1547, that persistent English vagabonds should be enslaved and branded with a large S. The idea of white slavery was not repellent to the Tudors, nor limited by them to savages and heathens. The law failed, and was replaced, not because vagabonds were of the same ethnic group but because there was no economic demand for slave labour.

Slavery has been economically and socially important only in a few societies, when the dominant group has been able to gain by the procurement of unfree labourers from elsewhere, when it has been able to control their utilization, and when there were insufficient workers closer to hand who could be so utilized. These conditions were exemplified in classical Greece and Rome and in the colonial Americas. Marxists often refer to these cases as slave MODES OF PRODUCTION.

*Classical Greece and Rome.* At its height, slavery comprised around one quarter or one fifth of the population of some Greek city-states and of the late Roman Republic and early Principate. Generally sold as prisoners of war, slaves worked either as domestics, urban labourers, craftsmen (and sometimes professionals), miners, or as field hands on plantations. As M. Finley has argued (*Slavery in Classical Antiquity*, 1960) there was not one single uniform slave status. Slaves could differ quite dramatically in their ability to reside, travel, sustain relationships, and own goods. Despite degrees of freedom for some slaves, in the main they were treated as investments and, particularly in mines and plantations, ruthlessly exploited and generally worked to death in the periods when they were cheap to replace. The distinction is drawn between helots (whole groups sold into slavery collectively), debt bondage (usually co-nationals working off a debt through slave labour; abolished in 6th-century BC Greece and 4th-century BC Rome before the peak periods of classical slavery) and chattel slavery (the slave as a commodity). In practice, any man, woman or child delivered into slavery was exposed to the arbitrary power of a master and custom. Law or morality offered only occasional and uncertain protection. The Romans permitted large numbers of slaves to buy their freedom (manumission). In both societies slavery decayed as the sources of supply dried up — there was no extensive reproduction of slaves.

*The Caribbean and Brazil.* From the start of slavery in the 15th century until its abolition in the 19th century as many as ten million black slaves were forcibly exported from Africa to the New World, principally to labour in the sugar, coffee, tobacco, cotton and rice plantations and in Brazilian mines, as domestic slaves, and in a host of other urban and rural occupations. The early modern history of the New World countries is largely the history of colonialism and slavery. The variations in their slave systems is explicable in terms of the difference between the colonial powers and how they reacted to indigenous conditions in their colonies. Some of the major differences include: (1) The date and scale of slave imports. Barbados, settled in the 17th century by a solid white artisanat and a largely resident planter class, developed a relatively stable social order. Jamaica (whose golden age of sugar fell in the mid-18th century at a time when slaves outnumbered the white population by ten to one and the planter class was generally absent in England) experienced many slave revolts. (2) External events in the colonial system. In Cuba a combination of the British occupation of Havana in 1763 (which opened it up for the slave trade), the economic reforms of Charles III of Spain (1759-88) and the slave revolution of 1789 in Santa Domingo (which destroyed that island's lucrative sugar and coffee production) turned the island into a massive slave-based plantation economy. (3) Cultural and religious differences between Catholic and Protestant colonial masters. The thesis of F. Tannenbaum (*Slave and Citizen*, 1947) is that by actively seeking to save their souls, protect family life, and give them a basic education, Catholic slave-owners prepared their slaves for citizenship, particularly in Brazil, whereas Protestant slaveowners in the British West Indies and the USA did not. (4) The degree to which the various slave systems permitted social space to their slaves. Jamaican slaves were expected to provide some of their own food. Many traded in the products of their garden plots. But slaves on Brazilian coffee and Cuban sugar plantations were more or less incarcerated. Such differences and the questions they raise are also relevant to slavery in classical antiquity.

*The Southern States of North America.*
Beginning with a few negro slaves cultivating
tobacco in the British settlement of Virginia
from 1619, in the next two hundred years the
slave economy came to dominate the south.
Whites and Indians could not be made to
labour so productively. Land was abundant,
labour scarce, so that any free labourer was
inclined to work independently. The advantages of large-scale production could be
enjoyed only by enterprises based upon free
labour. By 1860 about 94 per cent of slaves in
North America were field hands, unskilled
labourers or domestics, and while three-
quarters of these worked on plantations of
less than fifty slaves, the large staple-
producing plantations constituted 'the slave
power' (the title of J. Cairnes' influential
book of 1862).

The enslavement of BLACKS in the USA
was distinguished by the extent to which
slaves were regarded in law as chattels
possessed of no more right than farm
animals. Unless state law forbade him, a
master could therefore kill or castrate a slave
as well as sell him. A slave could own no
property, raise no lawful family nor testify
against a white person in either a civil or a
criminal case. In practice, state legislatures
and courts did restrict a master's power,
holding him liable for manslaughter:
'Negroes are under the protection of the
laws, and have personal rights, and cannot be
considered on a footing only with domestic
animals.' Yet legal protection was not to be
relied upon (especially if emanating from a
distant government) and was a lesser safeguard than local conditions, especially the
master's interest in preserving his investment: his return compared well with other
possible avenues of investment in the 19th
century. Because they were profitable, slaves
in the USA were relatively well looked after.
They were also allowed to reproduce. Thus
there was a substantial natural growth in the
black population.

But considerable controversy has arisen
over the treatment of slaves in North
America as opposed to middle and South
America. E. Genovese (*In Red and Black*,
1971) distinguishes three aspects of the
treatment of slaves: (1) day-to-day conditions; (2) social, religious and educational
opportunities available to slaves; and (3)

manumission (the ability to achieve freedom
at some point). He concludes that good
treatment on one of these dimensions may
not necessarily have entailed good treatment
on the others. Evidence suggests that
plantation slaves, wherever they were,
tended to be worse off than urban slaves.

Other North *v* South and Central debates
which have aroused interest include the
psychological impact of slavery on both
masters and slaves; the profitability of
slavery; the causes of abolition; the resistance of slaves to oppression; the links
between slavery and RACISM; and the moral
problem of slavery for Western culture. For
all of these debates see the contributions to
A. Weinstein and F. Gatell (eds.), *American
Negro Slavery* (3rd edn, 1978).

The tensions associated with slavery were
a major factor in the American Civil War of
1861-5. Slavery there was formally brought
to an end by the adoption of the Thirteenth
Amendment in 1866. But in areas of the
Americas where abolition occurred in conditions of excess demand for labour, it was
followed in several parts of the Caribbean by
massive importations of indentured workers
from India and China.

Western moralism has emphasized the
wickedness of a system which permits one
person to own another while forgetting that
some slaves in history were rather better off
than some legally free peasants or workers.
Nevertheless this moralistic concern, allied
with the connection between slavery and
racism, accounts for the high level of interest
in the subject in the social sciences today.

MPB, LS

**Smith, Adam** (1723-90). Moral philosopher
whose writings included the history of
science, jurisprudence, *belles lettres*, ethics
and political economy. He was born in
Kircaldy, Scotland; his father, who died
before his birth, had held the position of
Commissioner of Customs for Scotland after
a career as a high-ranking civil servant.
Smith's mother was the daughter of Robert
Douglas MP, and raised her son among the
lower nobility and the professional middle
rank, which included lawyers, ministers of
religion and civil servants. From this stratum
of society were drawn most of Smith's
associates throughout his life.

Smith attended the University of Glasgow in 1737, and studied under Francis Hutcheson. In 1740 he left Glasgow for Balliol College, Oxford, where he spent six unhappy years. He returned to Scotland when the SCOTTISH ENLIGHTENMENT was gaining momentum, and quickly associated himself with HUME, FERGUSON, Alexander Carlyle, John Millar and William Robertson among others. In 1751 he became Professor of Logic, and then Professor of Moral Philosophy (a post previously held by Hutcheson) at Glasgow. He lectured on a wide range of topics: natural theology, jurisprudence, ethics and politics. Smith retired in 1763 to become private tutor to the young Duke of Buccleuch. He spent the next two years touring France, and met the leading French intellectuals of the day (including ROUSSEAU). In 1766 he returned to London, where he studied Britain's strained relations with the American colonies, and was elected a Fellow of the Royal Society. In 1777 he became the Commissioner of Customs and Salt Duties for Scotland. He died famous and well-respected, in Kirkcaldy. Smith published in his lifetime two major works in what are now distinct disciplines.

*The Theory of Moral Sentiments* (1759) addressed the question of how one makes moral judgements. It articulated a moral and social psychology based on introspection, social observation and customary rules, mediated by the fundamental beliefs of the Scottish Enlightenment. Its theory of moral judgement comprised the principle of sympathy (the tendency for people to place themselves in another's position), and the notion of an 'impartial spectator' (an imagined figure within, who can judge right and wrong allegedly independent of personal prejudice).

*An Inquiry into the Nature and Causes of the Wealth of Nations* (1776) propounded the basic principles of the market economy. The DIVISION OF LABOUR, its effect on the extent of the market, the necessity for exchange, and an analysis of commodities were central topics of this work. It criticized the rapaciousness of the rich, and anticipated MARX in recognizing the potentially dehumanizing effects of the division of labour on labourers, as well as attacking mercantilism. The UNINTENDED CONSE-QUENCES of self-interested individuals ultimately culminated in the common good, through 'the Invisible Hand'. Smith also anticipated HEGEL and Marx in his theory of the evolution of society, where he distinguished four stages based on the prevailing mode of subsistence: hunting and fishing, pastoral, agricultural and commercial.

BJB

**social area analysis.** A method of study, widespread in urban sociology and urban geography until the 1970s, which builds up an overall description of urban society through a detailed empirical, statistical, sociographic analysis of small neighbourhoods.

HN

**social articulation/desarticulation.** An unfortunate pair of terms because of the double meaning of the verb 'articulate', which may mean either 'to express' or 'to join together'. In political sociology the word has been used in the former sense; more recently, especially in development studies, the second sense has predominated, and will be discussed here. The concept resembles that of social integration in that it refers to the joining together of parts within the SOCIAL SYSTEM. It is usually found in Marxist literature, where it refers primarily to the relationship between different MODES OF PRODUCTION within a social formation. It became popular as neo-Marxists rediscovered the co-existence of capitalist and pre-capitalist modes of production in contemporary developing societies. At an economic level the pre-capitalist subsistence sector may be articulated to the modern capitalist export sector (e.g. providing it with cheap food and a cheap, abundant labour force), but at the social level the two parts are often desarticulated. The cultural tastes and life-styles, the social institutions and the political values prevalent in the capitalist 'modern' sector are oriented to and indeed integrated with the wider world capitalist system, but do not touch the traditional life of the subsistence sector at any point. See DUALISM.

AH

**social behaviourism.** A branch of thought developed by G.H. MEAD in response to

Watson's BEHAVIOURISM, the basic unit being the social ACT. Like Watson, Mead is concerned with the observable actions of individuals, but in contrast he is also concerned with tracing these overt behaviours back to covert ones; without doing this, distinctly human conduct cannot be grasped. N. Denzin (*The Research Act*, 1976) has named Mead's view 'naturalistic behaviourism'.

KP

**social change.** So ubiquitous and varied in its form that nothing very useful can be said about it as a general concept. The notion of 'social change' as a special and distinct area of sociological study is largely a legacy of FUNCTIONALISM. In developing a theoretical approach centring on the analysis of self-maintaining social systems, functionalists contrived to make processes of change seems peripheral to the sociological task, and something of this attitude still lingers on in American sociology. British anthropoligical functionalists also tended to perceive the causes of social change as emanating from outside the societies they were studying; but change is immanent in all societies, especially in large-scale and complex ones. In effect, functionalism inherited Herbert SPENCER's concern with 'social statics' without taking up his equal concern with 'social dynamics'. But most of the 'founding fathers' of sociology in the 19th and early 20th centuries were chiefly concerned with explaining how patterns of social organization had changed and developed through history and pre-history. References to particular aspects and theories of social change will therefore be found throughout this work.

See CONFLICT THEORY; COUP; DURKHEIM; ELITISM; EVOLUTIONISM; MARX; MODE OF PRODUCTION; PROTESTANT ETHIC THESIS; REVOLUTION; SECULARIZATION; WEBER.

SJM

**social contract.** In political theory, a conceptual device employed by INDIVIDUALISTIC theorists to explain, justify or set limits on political AUTHORITY. They consider individuals as 'naturally' or morally endowed with certain rights whose exercise is regulated or restricted by the state. The logic is that such restrictions are morally permissible because consented to by rights-holders themselves. Under the terms of a minimal social contract (see LOCKE), individuals agree to pool their entitlements to enforce their NATURAL RIGHTS in a common agency — the STATE — which is thereby authorized to perform only that function. A more inclusive social contract is posited by theories that regard individuals' moral entitlements as capable only of adequate specification by political decision-processes (see HOBBES, ROUSSEAU). The state authorized by such a contract is less limited in its range of legitimate functions. Contracts are commonly treated not as actual once-for-all historical events, but rather as either recurring actual events (through constitutional arrangements for popular sovereignty) or as hypothetical events, which rational or moral persons would perform if given the opportunity to do so. These practices have surfaced in various guises within sociology (see EXCHANGE THEORY, UTILITARIANISM; for a critique, see DURKHEIM). Contract has also been regarded as the IDEAL TYPICAL relationship of modern capitalist or INDUSTRIAL SOCIETIES, contrasted (as in Maine) with STATUS typical of earlier societies, or (as in TÖNNIES) an essential part of GESELLSCHAFT as opposed to GEMEINSCHAFT. Such distinctions were broadened by PARSONS into his PATTERN VARIABLES.

HIS, MM

**social control.** A term so diffuse in meaning that it has lost specific or even practical definition. 'Social control' refers promiscuously to all constraints and patterns which generate discipline and social order, and is virtually synonomous with social ORGANIZATION. It has been held that social control inheres in the physical alignment of bodies, the character and arrangement of space, in language and vocabulary, in the most basic systems of definition and classification, in the assumptions of everyday life (SCHUTZ), in the petty etiquette of social interaction (GOFFMAN), in ritual (DURKHEIM), in gossip and JOKING, in nicknaming, in the structures of conversation (CONVERSATION ANALYSIS), in informal association and in the formal institutions of police, army, courts and prisons. Marxists maintain that the constitution of economy and thought is a powerful foundation for social control (Lukács, ADORNO). PHENOMENOLOGISTS would argue that every social artefact can stand apart from its creator and exercise restraint. 'Social control' is probably most commonly confined to the influence exerted by official agencies, and it would be sensible to assume that definition unless a contrary one is clearly demanded. The control vested in those agencies is itself complex and diffuse, embracing much dramaturgical work and a complicated symbolism as well as coercive intervention. The apparatus of controls includes police, courts, prisons and, possibly, psychiatric and social work agencies.

*Social control ideology.* Originally given salience by Lemert, the 'social control IDEOLOGY' has two connected meanings. (1) The arrangement of perspectives which arise within a particular agency or institutional setting. The police constitute a more or less bounded social world with an accompanying ideology which enables them to classify and order the populations they encounter, define their task in situationally specific ways, and devise recipes for practical action. Collectively, those definitions and recipes flow from and uphold joint motives and justifications for police work. Such ideologies are not completely resolved or dominant systems of thought: there is usually some scope for openness, play, division, and private and public dissent or innovation. (2) More generally, wider assumptions about discipline, DEVIANCE and institutional practices. Control agencies are part of a larger universe of processes which reflect broad historical movements. Thus Western prisons, asylums, religion, factories, armed forces and schools are represented as diverse expressions of a common ideology. There is a shared emphasis upon particular versions of social restraint, personal growth and education (BOURDIEU).

As yet unsystematic, control theory is undergoing vigorous development and will loom large in the making of policy. It stresses the part played by external restraint in checking the commission of CRIME. Explanation has concentrated on the constraint exercised by television cameras in public places; the design of public housing and the planning of public space; the influence of

attachment or commitment to particular groups; the effects of policing practices, and parental supervision or 'chaperonage'. The principal theme has been that criminal conduct is a product of rather specific situations; opportunity and the possibility of detection are critically important; and the explanation of crime has been rendered unnecessarily complicated by a sociology which cites the influence of political organization, social structure, patterns or motivation and other more general concerns.

See T. Hirschi, *Causes of Delinquency* (1969).

PR

**social democracy.** A term first used by various Marxist parties who believed in contesting elections and pursuing limited reforms within the existing political and economic system as a gradual means to achieving REVOLUTIONARY change. It is now applied generally to democratic socialist parties, such as the German SPD, the British LABOUR PARTY and Euro-COMMUNIST parties, all of which believe that their aims can be achieved by the ballot-box but differ greatly in their definition of socialism and in their adherence to Marxist doctrines. In Britain, the term is also used more restrictively for those within the Labour Party who downgrade the importance of the ownership of the means of production on the ground that the state can be used to control the owners of capital, and who regard the pursuit of social EQUALITY as their principal goal.

DRS

**social demography.** That area of the study of population whose concern is the interrelationship between the social structure and development of societies and the population processes occurring within them. Under this label, it is a recent development stemming from the late 1950s and the widely read work of Hauser and Duncan, and Kingsley Davis. It takes the form either of a search for causal dependencies between demographic and social variables, or of a SYSTEMS approach in which population acts as one of the aggregate variables characterizing the social system.

DURKHEIM and Halbwachs in their 'social morphology' analysed the relation between population and social phenomena, and in the

USA HUMAN ECOLOGY included research within the area of social demography. However it has only emerged as a focus of interest since World War II, stimulated most importantly by interest in the relationship between population growth and economic development, and in explaining variations in FERTILITY. In both cases, social factors have increasingly been seen as important in determining the overall outcome.

Population growth has both favourable and unfavourable economic effects: positive in that it increases the size of the economy, allowing specialization and the support of complex systems of transport, education and research; negative in that in the context of fixed resources a MALTHUSIAN law of diminishing returns operates. Technology reduces MORTALITY, but at the same time increases productivity and decreases fertility, through the availability of contraceptive technology and the modernization of family structure. As Easterlin argued in 1967, the form of the overall relationship between population and economic growth is determined by social and political arrangements and the systematic changes in these structures which accompany economic development. Social demography aims to provide the interdisciplinary approach required to understand such relationships.

Since World War II it has been increasingly apparent that the uniform decline in fertility expected from the DEMOGRAPHIC TRANSITION model is an over-simplification. Births take place at the heart of the system of family life and, forming one of the central events of the family development cycle, combine both meaningful and objective aspects in a way which demands sociological analysis. In addition, the perceived traditional resistance of certain societies or groups to the introduction of birth control has acted as a stimulus to interest among policy-makers in the sociological analysis of fertility.

The employment of women in the labour market may alter age at marriage, overall family size and the timing of births, and reciprocally, changes in the age-and-sex structure of the population alter employment opportunities. MIGRATION may also affect these variables, as it tends to occur differentially in certain age-and-sex groups and is often a response to the labour market.

MORTALITY rates are most clearly related to social structure in the case of infant mortality, the differences reflecting both the differing protective abilities of the social relationships upon which the infant is dependent and the nature of the prevailing child-rearing practices (see CHILDHOOD). Reduction in mortality rates alters the age-and-sex structure of the population, and both the increasing numbers of old people in industrial societies and the preponderance of young people in developing societies constitute significant social phenomena. Family make-up is affected, as is the ratio of producers to consumers, the demand for public services, and political behaviour.

Adult mortality rates vary with CLASS and occupation, but in an ill-understood way. The occupational and SOCIAL MOBILITY of individuals provides a trajectory through time which interacts with individuals' demographic chances to render inadequate the available simple correlations of stated class or occupation with mortality. Medical records, where they exist, are the result of social practices which incorporate many taken-for-granted assumptions in their classificatory methods. Marking occasions upon which health services are invoked, medical records will also reflect the uneven development of health services between societies and the differential distribution of health care within them.

JL

**social differentiation.** A dictionary definition is 'make or become different in process of growth or development', applying it, inter alia, to organs and FUNCTIONS. Sociologists speak of social differentiation in this sense. The organs, functions, groups and categories which are made, or become, different in the course of social development take countless forms. Some of the differences involve ranking and hierarchy and therefore SOCIAL STRATIFICATION, but differentiation need not be hierarchical, and indeed some sociologists use it only to indicate non-hierarchical differences. In this sense, the MEASUREMENT of differentiation is at a nominal level, while stratification is measured at least at an ordinal level.

Vertical differentiation characterizes ETHNIC, religious, linguistic or other distinctions playing a major part in the structuring of social relations where the ethnic, religious and linguistic communities concerned are not ranked or ordered in a hierarchy. The Netherlands in the 1950s and early 1960s provide an example: Catholics and Calvinists still maintained their extensive networks of separate schools, welfare services, political parties, trade unions, media etc at a time when differences in the class composition and income profile of each community were being steadily eroded (see PILLARIZATION).

Social differentiation is synonymous with what DURKHEIM called the DIVISION OF LABOUR in society, as distinct from the division of labour in production and other economic processes.

CGAB

**social disorganization.** Often cited as an implicit or explicit cause of DELINQUENCY, CRIME and other forms of pathology, the concept has acquired rather different meanings according to the working assumptions of particular sociologists. Generally, it refers to the disturbance of pattern, tradition and discipline which accompanies or composes SOCIAL CHANGE. That disturbance can, in turn, upset SOCIAL CONTROL.

Applied by Marxists, radicals and Durkheimians, it points to the collapse of order and moral restraint alleged to attend the rapid development of industrial capitalism. Disorganization is akin to ANOMIE; it is the result of social displacement, a new brutality, unfamiliar practices and a dislocation between economic and social life. It leads to drunkenness, crime, cruelty and the breakdown of stable family life.

Applied by FUNCTIONALISTS, disorganization refers to a chronic or temporary lack of integration between the moving parts of a social system in change (PARSONS). Society may be marked by strain, conflict and uneven development (see CONFLICT THEORY). More particularly, it may contain innovation which has not been accomodated. Such disorder is identified as DEVIANCE.

Disorganization has also been presented as similar to a fault in geological strata. The urban sociologists of the CHICAGO SCHOOL emphasized the tendency of neighbourhoods to become socially detached from their fellows. Different areas can acquire their own relatively discrete functions, populations, reputations and forms of moral and social order. If an area becomes independent in certain ways, it escapes some of the control that emanates from conventional institutions. It will no longer be minutely and effectively regulated from without by state, church and schools. That break in relations and design is disorganization, though the area and its environment are both highly structured (see PARK, WIRTH, Whyte).

More persistent has been a conception which turns to the sense of order maintained by a group. Certain situations can subvert or prevent a vision of the world as predictable, structured and secure. In response to disaster, accelerated change or an absence of social cohesion, people may systematically withdraw trust in their dealings with one another. Relations can become comparatively rudimentary, predatory and amoral. Reduced to their starkest form, they can acquire the feral properties of the Ik, a dislocated people who displayed little concern for one another. Creative strategies for dealing with such disorder may be defensive or evasive but are equally likely to be deviant. Disorganization does not signify a want of social structure. Indeed, Rainwater's description of the Pruitt-Igoe housing project and Erikson's analysis of a flooded mining area furnish extremely detailed models of social organization. Disorganization inheres in people's perspectives.

'Social disorganization' appears to be a neutral term which could be used for various purposes by different sociologists. In practice, it has been criticized and defined as an awkward idea which ought to be handled gingerly: reference to disorganization indicates a failure to discern social order or diversity. The term has had a history of acrimony.

PR

**social distance.** See GRAPH THEORY; SOCIOMETRY.

**social indicator.** OFFICIAL STATISTICS which are combined in comprehensive, aggregative form into systems to provide output measures of the effectiveness of social policies.

They are developed on the model of economic indicators such as the Retail Price Index or Gross National Product to provide up-to-date evidence of the state of society. In theory, social indicators provide a concise, comprehensive picture of changes over time in key social VARIABLES.

In practice, there are considerable difficulties in constructing satisfactory social indicators. Lacking the measurable and unifying unit of money as in economics, there is less coherence to the phenomena being measured. Many social phenomena (e.g. health, crime) are not easily compressed into a single index number representing the state of a society in a given year. The normative overtones of such statistical series, and the political uses and abuses to which they can give rise, have led to considerable wariness about their potential.

See M. Carley, *Social Measurement and Social Indicators* (1981).

MB

**social insurance.** In the UK, dates back to 1911 when it was introduced as one of a series of measures that heralded major state activity in the social services (see WELFARE STATE), although it is often claimed that the first British insurance schemes were influenced by developments in Germany in the 19th century. One of the attractions of social insurance was that it seemed to encourage individuals themselves to provide for future contingencies rather than to rely on others for help. Since 1911 the principle of social insurance has been widely used. It has something in common with private insurance: both seek to guard against possible future problems through regular payments. However, social insurance does not apply individual risk rating in the way that private insurance tries to do, and is compulsory whereas the latter is not. Further, the actuarial basis has often been abandoned in social insurance (e.g. in the UK, insurance payments now cover only a small proportion of the cost of the National Health Service). Nevertheless, the principle of social insurance can still have value: individuals may be more willing to make insurance payments than straightforward tax payments, and the belief that contributions have been made may mean that benefits are more likely to be accepted than if they had been offered on an assistance basis.

See SOCIAL SECURITY, WELFARE STATE.

MPJ

**socialism.** There is no universally accepted definition of socialism: whether as a favourable or a derogatory term, its use is politically contested. A number of distinctions can be made. (1) Between those who believe that socialism is compatible with the continuance of private capital, and those who do not. For the former, the anarchy and inequalities of the market can be overcome without extensive nationalization: by state regulation of the economy, by measures of redistributive TAXATION, by a comprehensive WELFARE STATE. These goals can be attained piecemeal and progressively by political pressure from organized labour. Socialism means the abolition of CAPITALISM's inhumanity and injustice without the abolition of capitalism itself. To others (including Marxists) this is self-contradictory. Class EXPLOITATION and CLASS CONFLICT, production for profit instead of need, the human waste of mass unemployment, are all inseparable from capitalism; socialism can only be realized beyond capitalism in a society in which productive enterprise is socially owned and managed, and where the goal of production is use, not profit. Though such a society cannot be created overnight, it requires a decisive political struggle by the WORKING CLASS against private capital and its associated bastions of power in society and state. Such a struggle, involving expropriation of the major sources of financial and industrial capital, cannot be contained within existing parliamentary forms.

(2) Between those who see the collective ownership of the means of production as the sufficient condition for socialism, and those to whom it is necessary but not sufficient. According to the former, there can be no exploitation without private property, and nothing except socialism beyond capitalism. The Soviet Union, China etc. can thus be designated socialist societies. The alternative view is that in the absence of thoroughgoing democratization of decisions about production, including the extent and use of any

surplus product, wage labour and exploitation will continue and new forms of privilege will emerge, based upon a monopoly of decision-making functions. On this view DEMOCRACY is intrinsic to socialism, not an optional extra, and socialism remains an ideal which is nowhere yet fully realized.

See COMMUNISM; SOCIAL DEMOCRACY; STATE SOCIALISM.

DB

**social mobility.** Movement from one stratum to another; in practice, usually movement from one occupational group to another. Mobility occurs within a hierarchy or graduation and is usually deemed upward or downward, though some is movement between groupings on the same level and some is ambiguous, especially where transformations of the occupational structure call in question the hitherto established social grading of occupations.

Mobility may be individual or collective. The movement of individuals (or families) is typical of advanced capitalist societies. Collective mobility refers to the movement of a stratum or socio-economic group vis-à-vis other strata or groups: for example, the movement of CASTE sub-groups in India, claiming treatment appropriate to members of the superior caste to which they really belong, and the collective elevation of skilled workers in eastern Europe and the Soviet Union.

Intergenerational mobility refers to an individual's movement in relation to the social position of his or her parents (usually son compared with father, but see below). Intragenerational mobility refers to an individual's movement in relation to a social postion occupied earlier in his or her (working) life (often present occupation compared with first). The range of movement (short, medium or long) is also important, although the possibilities here are connected with the number of levels in the stratification model employed, as is the relative possibility for movement, the degree of openness and closure within the structure as a whole or particular parts of it.

Exchange mobility refers to movement from one stratum or group to another which is compensated by a comparable movement the other way. The classic example is upward mobility balanced by a comparable amount of downward mobility. Exchange mobility is most easily identified when there is a movement within a structure whose contours are stable — that is, when the relative size of each stratum or socio-economic group remains constant. Structural mobility is generated by changes which reconstitute the overall structure: for example, contraction of the peasantry or of agricultural labourers and the expansion of the industrial working class; the change in the ratio of manual workers to managers and technical staff, and the contraction of the manufacturing sector vis-à-vis the expansion of the service industries.

A study by Glass et al. after World War II (*Social Mobility in Britain*, 1954) established the limited extent of social mobility in Britain. In the 1970s major research (on men only) by Goldthorpe et al. revealed considerable upward mobility, especially into the SERVICE CLASS, in conjunction with changes in the occupational structure, but little downward mobility, especially on the part of those of higher class origins.

Wherever there are several determinants of class position or socio-economic group membership, movement may take place with respect to one or more factors, but not to all: e.g. the poor Jewish immigrant who makes good economically but who is not fully accepted in leading social circles. Here the study of social mobility shades into the study of STATUS COMPOSITION.

R.H. Turner (*American Sociological Review* 1960) concentrated on different modes of mobility, sponsored and contest, which he related to the different school systems of Britain and America at that time. *Contest mobility* is a system in which elite status is the prize in an open contest and is taken by the aspirants' own efforts. While the 'contest' is governed by some rules of fair play, the contestants have wide latitude in the strategies they may employ. Since the 'prize' of successful upward mobility is not in the hands of an established elite to give out, the latter cannot determine who shall attain it and who shall not. Under *sponsored mobility* elite recruits are chosen by the established elite or their agents, and elite status is *given* on the basis of some criterion of supposed merit and cannot be *taken* by any amount of effort or strategy. It is like being sponsored for a private club.

Four basic difficulties confront mobility analyses. (1) Mobility is a process in time. Its examination is easiest where the relative standings of different groups remain constant through time — which they seldom do. (2) Upward and downward mobility refer to movements between strata or groups which are hierarchically related and therefore differentially evaluated. Their analysis is easiest where there is general agreement about the evaluations involved. In practice, matters are usually less clear. One dilemma concerns the relative standings of skilled manual workers and routine white-collar workers in capitalist societies. The majority or a significant proportion of each group may consider its own group superior to the other (see OCCUPATIONAL PRESTIGE). (3) Inter-generational studies acknowledge that parents may themselves have been socially mobile. But the studies must make a more or less arbitrary decision about the point in the parents' (working) lives which is to serve as the basis of comparison. (4) The analysis of individual social mobility (like much of the sociology of stratification) moves uneasily between the individual and the family or household as its unit of analysis. In the past it may often have been culturally correct to regard the husband's class or socio-economic position as determining that of the wife. This is no longer acceptable.

See CAUSAL MODELLING; GENDER STRATIFICATION; SOCIAL STRATIFICATION.

See Goldthorpe *et al.*, *Social Mobility and Class Structures in Modern Britain* (1980); Heath, *Social Mobility* (1981).

CGAB

**social security.** A term used to refer to a variety of systems of income support. In the UK it covers retirement pensions; sickness, injury and maternity benefits; invalidity benefits; unemployment benefits; supplementary benefits; child benefit; and FAMILY INCOME SUPPLEMENT. Of these, retirement pensions, child benefit and supplementary benefits are the most important, both in amount spent and numbers covered. The system was reshaped after 1945 (see BEVERIDGE, WELFARE STATE) though many provisions date back before this time and a number have been significantly altered since.

Some writers have argued for a different definition: social security is not simply an all-embracing term for systems of income support, but is a concept which differs from social insurance. Whereas social insurance is a means of providing for defined risks on the basis of benefits linked to contributions, social security assumes a broader attempt to provide for all the community against all social risks. However, as the links between contribution and benefit and the actuarial basis of many SOCIAL INSURANCE schemes has become weaker the practical impact of this distinction has lessened.

See WELFARE STATE.

MPJ

**social stratification.** The division of a society into a number of strata, hierarchically arranged groupings. These groupings have assumed numerous historical and cultural variations, of which CASTES, ESTATES and CLASSES are the most familiar. In the 1960s and 1970s attention also turned to ETHNIC and then GENDER stratification.

Stratum has a different connotation in Eastern European writings. In deference to a usage originated by Stalin, the intelligentsia (INTELLECTUALS and PROFESSIONAL and white-collar workers) is often deemed a stratum (in contrast to the workers and the private or collectivized peasantry, who constitute classes) because its members do not engage directly in productive work. Sociologists in Eastern Europe also accept that their societies are stratified, but usually reject the suggestion that they are also class societies because the latter are deemed the product of economic exploitation, which is said to have been abolished. Western sociologists rarely accept this reasoning.

See also FUNCTIONAL THEORY OF STRATIFICATION; GENDER STRATIFICATION

See Bendix and Lipset, *Class, Status and Power* (rev. 1966); Beteille, *Social Inequality* (1968).

CGAB

**social stress.** See STRESS.

**social structure.** Though one of the most frequent terms in sociology, this has no specific and universally accepted meaning. Nevertheless, it reveals one of the basic sociological insights: although societies and countless social groups within them are never long composed of the same individuals, their patterns of social interdependence show continuity over time. That is as true among students in a university, where a 'generation' of under graduates lasts only three or four years, as it is in human society as a whole. But though patterns may be continuous they are not static — patterns can change abruptly and even disappear altogether. Social structure denotes patterns which change more slowly than the particular personnel who constitute them. They are produced and reproduced by the interweaving of numerous individual people acting in accordance with their own plans and strategies, yet social structure is rarely planned and intended by them: it results from the UNINTENDED CONSEQUENCES of action.

If individuals possess 'free will', how do their separate actions intermesh to produce social structure? This is one of the oldest questions in social and political thought. Although it is conventional to distinguish several traditional answers, and in the recent history of sociology schools of 'CONSENSUS', 'EXCHANGE' and 'CONFLICT' theory have been identified, all acknowledge in one way or another the constraint imposed upon individuals' actions by their interdependence with each other in society. The process of socialization which begins at birth and continues throughout life is one means by which individual behaviour is moulded to established social patterns. It is accorded a prominent place by adherents of FUNCTIONALISM, SYMBOLIC INTERACTIONISM, so-called consensus theory, and followers of PARSONS. But relations of social interdependence are rarely equal. Usually, as other theoretical traditions have emphasized, some people have a greater capacity to shape the actions and behaviour of others than the others have to shape theirs. The socialization of infants takes place within a highly unequal relationship of interdependence, in which the parents initially have much greater power over their children. It is misleading to think of the relationship

between 'individuals' and 'social structure' as if they were separate and distinct entities in which 'individuals' all possessed 'free will' but miraculously used it to create 'social structure' with recognizable continuity. On the other hand, it is absurd to contend, as ALTHUSSER and his followers have done, that individual actions are the programmed 'agents' of social structure, and that the appearance of 'free will' is delusion. The question is one of degree. All human beings are interdependent with other human beings from birth, and their interdependence to a greater or lesser extent imposes limits on freedom of action. The extent of these limits and constraints cannot be established by philosophical speculation, but only by sociological analysis of the balances of power embodied in particular social structures in particular times and situations.

Many familiar sociological concepts are used to denote aspects of social structure. Parsons defined the components of social structure as being ROLES, NORMS and VALUES, together with 'collectivities' (i.e. groups of people sharing common values). Sociologists less tied to a consensual view of social order regard social CLASSES, ELITES, patterns of social conflict, and mechanisms for the unequal allocation of scarce resources as basic components of the social structure of societies. Formal and informal organizations and institutions also fall within the broad notion of social structure.

But it is less important to define components of social structures than to be clear what it is not. It is not to be identified solely with social harmony or social order in the sense of 'law and order'. The interdependence between enemies in social conflict and in wars, or between criminals and their victims, may very likely form relatively persistent patterns over time and thus constitute an aspect of social structure.

Nor is it the opposite of ANOMIE. The absence or the decay of rules or norms does not necessarily mean that social behaviour is unstructured and unpredictable. Predictions may be made about the incidence in such situations of, for example, suicide — as DURKHEIM argued.

Social structure is not static; stability is always relative. There are indeed long-term processes of social change, such as the

DIVISION OF LABOUR, INDUSTRIALIZATION, URBANIZATION, and population growth, which are a continuing aspect of many societies over many generations. It is not conventional to speak of them as aspects of 'social structure', but they are structured processes of change. They constrain, and indeed exert compelling forces over, the behaviour of people caught up in them.

SJM

Within STRUCTURALIST anthropology social structure has acquired a further meaning through the work of LÉVI-STRAUSS. The structure of society is not arrived at by the collection of empirical data, but through the interpretation of such data to arrive at a conceptual model which has three characteristics: (1) it is systemic, being made up of independent units; (2) it is possible to derive from these a series of transformations resulting in similar models; (3) it is possible to predict the results of modifications in one or more units. Such a model should be explanatory of the empirical data collected, rather than drawn from a classification which is derived from the data.

JE

**Social Survey.** The collection of social data by means of a purpose-designed inquiry in which a SAMPLE of the population is interviewed on a particular subject using questions standardized in a QUESTIONNAIRE. The resulting data is then usually analysed quantitatively, after coding and editing, to provide descriptive information about the VARIABLES studied and/or to search for ASSOCIATIONS or CORRELATIONS between two or more variables. The Social Survey is the most commonly used research technique in sociology, and is also widely used in governmental, commercial and independent non-profit social research.

The main phases of a social survey are: (1) definition of the problem and specification of CONCEPTS; (2) formulation of hypotheses (if any); (3) selection of the sample; (4) development and piloting (preliminary testing) of the research instrument (usually a questionnaire); (5) administering the questionnaire by an interview to the respondents selected in the sample; (6) coding of the data (where questions are not

pre-coded) and editing of the data; (7) data processing of the quantifiable results of the survey using an electronic computer; (8) analysis of the results, using appropriate statistical techniques; (9) writing up the results in a thesis, monograph or report.

A particular type of social survey is the mail or postal survey, which does not employ interviewers. Instead, sample members are sent by mail a covering letter with a questionnaire which they are asked to complete and return by mail in a pre-paid envelope. Postal surveys are much cheaper than personal interviews but suffer from several disadvantages, including the need to keep the questionnaire short, the need to avoid complex questions, lack of spontaneity, and the likelihood of a poor response rate, which is significantly lower for postal surveys than for surveys using personal interviews.

Many of the techniques of MULTI-VARIATE ANALYSIS have been developed to handle survey data. The systematic use of CROSS-TABULATION was developed by LAZARSFELD and is the most widely used method of analysis. CORRELATION, REGRESSION and FACTOR ANALYSIS are used where the data are suitable. More recent developments such as LOG-LINEAR ANALYSIS also show considerable promise. The basic form of presenting survey data has been the TABLE, and SIGNIFICANCE TESTS have been widely if controversially used in interpreting the meaning of such tables.

Critics such as Cicourel and D.L. Phillips have pointed to the limitations of Social Surveys in terms of MEASUREMENT of social phenomena and VALIDITY of data. Many well-known research monographs are based on survey data, however, and the survey remains the most powerful, efficient and cost-effective social research method available.

See D.P. Warwick and C. Lininger, *The Sample Survey: Theory and Practice* (1975).

MB

**social system.** Often used loosely as a synonym for SOCIAL STRUCTURE. The word system means a complex whole, or a set of organized and connected things or parts, so 'social system' implies stable interconnections between institutional patterns within society. Functionalist writers tended to use the term in a more specific sense: for them, a social system was a TELEOLOGICAL or goal-directed system, containing social mechanisms analogous to a thermostat, so that the system was self-regulating and self-maintaining. Few such mechanisms were ever rigorously demonstrated.

See FUNCTIONALISM, COMTE; CYBERNETICS; PARSONS; SYSTEMS THEORY.

SJM

**societal reaction.** Identified with the social pathology of Edwin Lemert: societal reaction is a public response appreciable enough to create or confirm deviant phenomena, be experienced as fateful by the deviant, and produce the possibility of secondary deviation (see DEVIANCE). 'Societal' refers to representative institutions of formal control such as the police and courts. It would also encompass any other mobilization of a socially consequential response. Its precise reference is a little unclear. But it focuses attention upon the ability of powerful audiences to define, maintain and transform aberrant behaviour. After DURKHEIM, Lemert portrayed deviation as a social process which became significant only when it entered the public arena. Societal reaction gives deviance its sociological interest and form.

See E. Lemert, *Social Pathology* (1951).

PR

**society.** Used by sociologists in two different ways. When they speak of *a* society, they usually have in mind a social unit such as a TRIBE or a NATION-STATE which has its own political, economic, familial and other institutions relatively independent of those of neighbouring societies. This usage has been strongly influenced by the old notion of sovereignty in political theory. It can be misleading: few societies in the modern world — whether stateless or STATE-societies — are truly independent of each other; the ties of social interdependence spread across political boundaries in much closer and complex ways which sociologists cannot ignore (see TRANSNATIONAL).

'Society' is also used in a more general sense to designate the object of sociological investigation; in this sense it is more or less synonymous with SOCIAL STRUCTURE.

SJM

**sociobiology.** This type of social DARWINISM has aroused some interest, particularly in the USA, since Edward Wilson's *Sociobiology: the New Synthesis* (1975) which combined two biological traditions, population genetics and evolutionary ecology, with ethology and animal behaviour. Sociobiologists study the biological basis of social behaviour not only through the observation of the behaviour of animals, particularly primate groups, but also through the examination of genetic evidence for the natural selection of particular behavioural traits. Sociobiology has aroused great controversy and has been criticized for its biological determinism, particularly by FEMINISTS. Few sociologists or anthropologists accept many of its arguments, regarding it as a form of REDUCTIONISM.

See also GENDER AND BIOLOGICAL SEX.

JE

**sociologie du travail.** Literally, sociology of work, but unlike the 'Sociology of Work' as understood in English-speaking countries, French *sociologie du travail*, which flourished 1950-1965, went beyond a concern with the structure of occupational life, to the meaning of work to the subject and thence to grapple with even bigger questions such as: How does the work done in a society help define the character of that society? What determines that society's work is done in the way it typically is done? How far can the likely evolution of work be foreseen and its possible effects evaluated? Prominent amongst its exponents were investigators such as Michel Crozier, Pierre Naville, Georges FRIEDMANN, Serge Mallet (see WORKING CLASS) and Alain Touraine. The answers provided to the key questions were varied, and sometimes showed an impatience with empirical data. All tended to view technical change as a primary cause, and to accept that it evolved according to some inner logic of its own.

See M. Rose, *Servants of Post Industrial Power* (1979).

MR

**sociology.** Defined in dictionaries as the science or study of society. The term was coined by COMTE (1830), linking the Latin *socius* (originally a people, tribe or city allied to Rome, but later a SOCIETY) to the Greek *logos* (reason or knowledge). The term spread rapidly and is now used in virtually all languages to denote any relatively rigorous, reasoned study of society — which is looser than the POSITIVIST notion of 'science' employed by Comte. The question of what is the proper subject matter of sociology has been hotly and continuously debated in the 19th and 20th centuries. Broadly, the answer is to be found in the whole contents of this Encyclopedia. More precisely, the entry for EMERGENCE delineates the two principal objects of study: social facts and social processes. Whether these define an object that is peculiar to sociology and no other discipline is also hotly debated. Such a belief is only found in modern societies. In the 20th century sociology constitutes a major source of humanity's knowledge of itself.

MM

**sociometry.** An early method of GRAPH or network theory devised by, and associated with, Jacob Moreno, an Austrian-American psychiatrist. It is based on asking respondents to rank five other people in order of their desirability and/or their undesirability as associates. Choices were graphed on paper in 'sociograms'. A useful method for dealing with hierarchies among small groups, it is parallelled in studies of larger, secondary groups by social distance scales, pioneered by E.S. Bogardus. He asked respondents whether they would approve of a person of a given nationality as a member of a club, as a neighbour, as a kinsman through marriage etc. Responses were scored hierarchically. Both types of method were later superseded by more complex computational techniques (see MULTI-DIMENSIONAL SCALING), but the core techniques are still found in many areas of sociology e.g. associational measures of SOCIAL MOBILITY.

See also SCALES.

MM

**socio-technical system.** Concept developed by the Tavistock Institute of Human Rela-tions in London to guide its approach to the study — and the modification — of behaviour in organizations. It posits interdependence between the social relations (and their psychological aspects) associated with any given productive system and the technical means selected to operate that productive system. Social relations are not viewed as narrowly determined by 'technology'; but the technical apparatus, if used productively, sets limits to the forms of social organization that can occur, or are allowed to occur. There is usually a range of options for designing a system of work roles to exploit any given set of technical means: 'organizational choice' is possible. This is reasonable, and encouraging in the face of other assertions that any given productive technology tends to determine a unique form of social organization. Under Mao, to be sure, the Chinese experimented with systems of work roles which defied every Western practice. The plants con-tinued to operate, but at some economic cost. 'Choices' are nevertheless available, permitting a 'healthier' social organization while maintaining relative efficiency. But as used by some Tavistock Institute analysts, the concept sometimes leads towards the conclusion that the 'optimization' process in organizational choice will tend to produce new socio-technical complexes in which both social and psychological satisfactions and economic efficiency can be simultaneously raised. Such ideas need better demonstration than they have so far received.

See also ORGANIZATION.

MR

**software.** A term used in computing to refer to the programmes or systems which carry the instructions on how the computer is to process the information put into it. It is to be distinguished from hardware, the physical system of electronic components, central processor, memory etc, which realizes the logical processes defined by the software. In sociology, software typically occurs in the form of standardized packages with acron-ymic names, such as SPSS (Statistical Package for the Social Sciences) including a commonly used range of statistical pro-cedures. While these tend to dictate what techniques are used, they have also made possible a wide range of statistical techniques, such as multiple regression, which are virtually unthinkable otherwise.

JL

**sorcery.** See WITCHCRAFT.

**Spencer, Herbert** (1820-1903). Victorian theorist, the most important figure in EVOLUTIONISM and social DARWINISM, influential his time but less regarded today. Born in Derby, the son of a private teacher, Spencer was mostly self-educated and tutored by relatives. Spencer's dissenting background strongly influenced his philosophy. He became a railway engineer, and first encountered evolutionary ideas through his interest in geology and paleontology. His first article, supporting the doctrine of laissez-faire, was published in the *Non-Conformist* in 1842. In 1848 he became sub-editor of *The Economist.* His first book, *Social Statics* (1850), examined political philosophy. In 1853 he inherited moderate means and became a freelance writer. Between 1865 and 1895 he popularized the concept of evolution, achieving an immense popular and academic following in England, Russia, the USA, France and Germany. From 1871 he received numerous offers (mostly refused) of academic honours.

*Progress: Its Law and Cause* (1857) outlines a theory of cosmic and social evolution that drew upon both the Darwinian and the rival Lamarckian theories. Though retaining a Lamarckian belief in inheritance of environmentally acquired characteristics, Spencer followed Darwin in seeing 'natural selection' as the major mechanism of evolutionary change (see EVOLUTIONISM). Endeavouring to create comparative evolutionary sociology and to unify all theoretical sciences, Spencer produced *Principles of Sociology* (1855), *First Principles* (1862), and *The Study of Society* (1873). Preparing for *The Principles of Sociology* (1896), Spencer commissioned historical and ethnographic research, published as the 17-volume *Descriptive Sociology* (1873-1934). This anticipated the work of Murdock and the Human Relations Area Files (see COMPARATIVE METHOD).

Spencerian cosmic evolution moves from uniformity of structure to heterogeneity, originating in the inorganic world, and culminating in social (superorganic) evolution. *Social Statics* (1850) claims that societies (like organisms) develop from a uniform state with similar parts performing similar functions, to a differentiated state with dissimilar parts performing different functions. Subsequently influenced by Bauer's biology, Spencer saw this transition as typical of different types of organism. Attributing evolutionary change to the 'inherent instability of the homogenous' Spencer's evolutionary law was founded upon seven basic principles, some drawn from contemporary physics: the indestructability of matter, persistence of force, continuity of motion, uniformity of law, transformation and equivalence of forces, the tendency of all things to move along the line of least resistance, and the principle of the rhythm of motion. Ultimately Spencer incorporated Darwinian concepts into a FUNCTIONALIST theory of organic and social change in which the equilibrium between the parts of an organism, or between it and its environment, are disturbed, precipitating development of a new state of equilibrium.

Spencer contradicts himself over the inevitability of evolution. This is asserted in *The Study of Society*, yet *First Principles* argues that society may regress from heterogeneity to homogeneity. A unilinear series of developmental stages is identifiable within evolution; but individual societies, each adapting in its own way to the environment, display diverse lines of development. Strict unilinear development is subject to interference by factors such as customs, innate RACIAL difference, the influence of the preceding stage of evolution, and the position of the society *vis-à-vis* its neighbours. All societies need not pass through the same stage nor become identical with one another.

Spencer employs two different classifications of social evolution. (1) The evolutionary transformation of MILITARY societies based upon compulsory co-ordination into INDUSTRIAL SOCIETIES based upon voluntary co-operation. Contemporary Victorian England and laissez-faire appeared to represent the highest stage of evolution. The only future change to be anticipated was that of the elimination of coercion, producing a sort of anarchy. (2) The evolution from simple to progressively more complex societies through structural DIFFERENTIA-TION. Simple societies first differentiate with the creation of a ruling class. Gradually differentiation occurs in work tasks, sex roles, with the formation of a slave labour-force, and in the spheres of regulation, sustenance, and distribution. Societies consisting of interdependent parts amalgamate under the law of integration, and under the law of differentiation produce ever more complex, differentiated institutions to perform increasingly disparate and specialized functions. Simple societies thus develop into compound, doubly and trebly compound societies, each stage based respectively upon family, clan, tribe and nation. Increasing structural differentiation takes place in terms of occupations, functions, and in the exercise of power.

An important founding father of sociology, Spencer combined UTILITARIANISM, laissez-faire, organicism, social Darwinism, functionalism and evolutionism in his philosophy. He fused social Darwinism with the Benthamite view of happiness, arguing that unhappiness is caused by maladaption. The process of natural selection benefits the race biologically, allowing the survival of the fittest (the intelligent, industrious and healthy). The idle, sick, stupid, crippled, poor and criminal should be allowed to die out. In his final years, Spencer lost widespread support for his ideas with the growth of pragmatic philosophy, the rise of the WELFARE STATE, SOCIAL DEMOCRACY, state interventionism, and England's decline as a world power. Spencer's thought is marked by contradictions between holism (society as a natural organism, and the insistence that social competition promotes the welfare of the whole) and laissez-faire INDIVIDUALISM. He was ambivalent in his use of the organic analogy, which he has been criticized for overstretching to the point of absurdity. Spencer influenced William James and other founders of American physiological psychology, and contemporary educational scientists in England and the USA. His evolutionism influenced SUMNER and the social Darwinism which persisted into the 20th century. This influence resurfaced in the 1950s with theories of structural

differentiation in cultural anthropology and NEO-EVOLUTIONISM in the sociology of development. Spencer's functionalism influenced structural-functional sociology via DURKHEIM, RADCLIFFE-BROWN, and MALINOWSKI, a line of development in which the notion of SOCIAL SYSTEM becomes more prominent than that of evolutionism.

JW

**spurious correlation.** See CAUSAL MODEL-LING.

**Stalinism.** Often used as a synonym for TOTALITARIANISM. A description of the way the USSR was run between 1928 and 1953: central control of all spheres of life, including economic and intellectual, by a single mass party in accordance with an official ideology. Some commentators would include terror as a central concept (see PURGE)

Also used to denote rigid, slavish obedience to the Soviet line in Marxist theory and inter-Communist Party relations (see COMMUNISM).

BT

**standardization.** A statistical procedure for removing fluctuations which occur in data due to some control VARIABLE, thus permitting comparisons between data free from this contaminating effect. Applied to entire TABLES, test-factor standardization removes the effect of control variables so that the relationship between independent and dependent variables may be examined free from this source of CONTAMINATION. Standardized rates are commonly used in descriptive statistics; for instance, MORTALITY rates or FERTILITY rates are standardized for age. This is to remove the effects which distribution of a population by age may have on such rates. For example, if a steel town and a seaside resort have the same annual crude death rate (number of deaths per 1000 population), it is highly unlikely that they have the same mortality experience. The average age of residents of the seaside resort is considerably higher than that in the steel town, thus concealing the fact that the true death rate in the steel town is higher, at any given age. The true comparison can be made if the respective rates are weighted according to the age-structure of the population to which they relate. This is known as standardizing for age.

MB

**state, the.** The most usual definition is that of WEBER: an organization which successfully upholds a claim to binding rule-making over a territory, by virtue of commanding a monopoly of the legitimate use of force. But a stable state will not use coercion routinely. As PARSONS observed, the state's resources are inadequate to coerce all the people all the time: if it attempts routine coercion 'power deflation' may set in, using up its resources and threatening its survival. Thus LEGITIMACY is crucial — but has two competing meanings. (1) In FUNCTIONALIST theory, including Parsons, the people morally support the state's claim to legitimacy — its authority ultimately rests in value CONSENSUS. (2) In other theories (including CONFLICT THEORY and probably Weber), the people accept the claim as routine, normal, and thoroughly institutionalized, but do not necessarily endorse it morally: resistance would be pointless, almost unthinkable, so the direct use of force is normally unnecessary.

The definition also contains a second tension between 'functional' and 'structural' elements. (1) The state may be defined functionally, in terms of what it does (i.e. make binding 'political' rules). But in many societies, household heads or local organizations like FEUDAL manors have such political functions, sharing them with the broader territorial institutions we generally call 'states'. Functionalist theories (which include most Marxists in this respect — see below) concentrate on these political functions, wherever located, and reduce the state to more diffuse aspects of society. (2) A structural definition concentrates on the claim to territorial monopoly, arguing that it involves a particular set of centralized institutions and personnel with distinctive behaviour, power and interests. Thus the state may possess autonomous power in society and, since the 18th century, has usually been contrasted with society or, more traditionally, with CIVIL SOCIETY (see THE

POLITICAL). The rest of this entry concerns the structural definition.

*Origins.* The state was not an original social form. It emerged from stateless (ACEPHELOUS) societies. Its causes are hotly debated. Four major theories have arisen: (1) SOCIAL CONTRACT: a rationalist, functionalist view in which individuals set up a centralized authority to adjudicate their disputes and safeguard their lives, liberty and emerging property rights (e.g. LOCKE). Its principal theoretical difficulty is: given such consent, how did these individuals ever lose control of the state, for its normal historical form is not DEMOCRATIC? Hence an outgrowth into (2) the redistributive chiefdom: followers of POLANYI (anticipated also by some earlier writers) argue that groups from different ecological niches agree to exchange their goods by depositing them in a central storehouse commanded by a chief who then redistributes them. These resources enable the chief to gradually elevate his power into a monarchical state and to inaugurate major inequalities in society. (See E. Service, *Origins of the State and Civilization,* 1975) (3) MILITARIST theory. Associated classically with SPENCER, GUMPLOWICZ, and Franz Oppenheimer's *The State* (1908). A stateless social (sometimes ethnic) group defeats another, and institutionalizes its EXPLOITATION with the aid of a permanent state, constituted by its military leadership. It is successively enlarged and stratified by further conquest. (4) CLASS theory. Associated with ENGELS's *Origins of The Family, Private Property and the State* (1884). The state arises to institutionalize the *de facto* emergence of private PROPERTY in originally COMMUNIST stateless societies. Similar to (3) in its emphasis upon exploitation but concerned primarily with an internal, rather than an external, theory of SOCIAL STRATIFICATION. But private and fully communal property are now thought to have been rather rare in primitive societies. So Marxists have modified the theory: the state institutionalized the emerging power of some LINEAGE and CLAN elites over others (see E. Terray, *Marxism and 'Primitive Societies',* 1972).

Note that theories (1) and (4) tend to assign historical priority to SOCIAL STRATIFICATION over the state, whereas (2) and (3)

give the state a crucial role in originating stratification. Evidence indicates that some states have originated in all these ways and, predominately, through routes combining such processes. The relative priority of state and stratification is still controversial: for a review see J. Claessen and Skalnik, *The Early State* (1978).

*State Power.* Once in place, what is the PO-WER of the state? Does it possess EMERGENT, autonomous power or is it reducible (see RE-DUCTIONISM) to other forces, perhaps to those that caused its emergence? Most debate focuses on the power of the state. However, power can have three meanings.

(1) *Infrastructural power.* State claims may be more or less enforceable — does the state possess the infrastructure to uphold a monopoly claim? For Weber, this was only established with the rise of the 'modern state' around the 18th-19th centuries. Feudal and PATRIMONIAL states shared their real powers with other lineage and local territorial power-holders (see also EISENSTADT) even though they often claimed to be ABSOLUTIST. Only modern states can tax their subjects at source, communicate messages quickly across their realms etc. These powers are common to both democratic and TOTALI-TARIAN regimes.

(2) *Autonomous Power.* To what extent is the state an autonomous actor, and to what extent is its power reducible to the rational interests and power of domestic civil society groups? Three major theories give replies. Marxist class theories and PLURALISM broadly reduce the state to, respectively, the dominant class and the people. The first is explicitly, the second usually implicitly (through the influence of social contract theory) economic reductionism. By contrast most versions of ELITISM assert the autonomy of the political rulers. Some tie this explicitly to the state's command of military force and/ or of foreign relations between states.

Within Marxist class theories attempts were made by Poulantzas (*Political Power and Social Classes*, 1972) and others to assert only a 'relative autonomy' of the state. Its meaning has varied but generally comprised the actions of the MODE OF PRODUC-TION and class structure setting limits to state actions without positively determining them:

for example, under the CAPITALIST mode, the state cannot interfere with the requirements of capitalist accumulation (so it must protect private property, give incentives to profit etc) but whether this is done through a democratic regime, MILITARY RULE etc is determined by political processes, including state power itself. For Poulantzas, relative autonomy also occurred in a period of transition between modes of production where no single class can capture the state, as witness the 'balancing act' of Louis Bonaparte in France 1848-51, when he was able to play off class against class to use state power for himself. This is similar to Weber's analysis of the Junkers' (noble landowners in Prussia) ability to play off BOURGEOISIE against PROLETAR-IAT to retain command of the German state in the early 20th century long after their own economic power had declined. Obviously, pluralist theory could also compromise its claims by advancing a theory of 'relative autonomy'. The third pluralist variant mentioned in the entry for ELITISM is implicitly this. The major criticism is that 'relative autonomy' settles none of the traditional debates between reductionism and autonomy. How relative is relative? Do states also set limits to what is possible in a mode of production? Clear-cut answers are not yet forthcoming.

Much of the debate between the three theories of autonomy has concerned the liberal democracies of Western capitalism (for a review see R. Alford, *The Power of Theory*, 1983). Faced with other types of state, pluralism generally retreats into the pluralist variant of elitism, and the argument then rages between elite and class theories. In pre-modern states it is inconclusive. With regard to STATE SOCIALISM and FASCISM, their infrastructural power and non-democratic structure have given to their state elites a significant measure of autonomous power (though its degree is also controversial). In liberal democracy, state elites are recallable either by the people (pluralism) or by the covert pressures exerted by the capitalist class (class theory). Elitism has not fared well when dealing with their internal structure. But it does better in respect of foreign policy, especially MILITARISM. It is difficult to believe that the two World Wars or, even more, the possible destruction of the world through nuclear weapons, is the outcome of the preferences either of the people or the capitalist class (as in some theories of IMPERIALISM) or merely of the machinations of the enemy. Either the people/capitalists do control the state but are irrational, or they share state power, and may on occasion be overwhelmed by, other more militaristic and traditional elites. Contemporary states wage war and diplomacy more or less as their predecessors have done throughout recorded history: only the means used and the degree of popular mobilization have changed markedly. Thus the state's monopoly of force and its capacity to deal with foreign relations seems the principle vehicle through which an autonomous power can develop. Reductionist theories theorize the state as a single abstraction, forgetting that states normally exist in multi-state systems.

Indeed this has wider implications for state theory, leading to a third, much-neglected aspect of state power.

(3) *Territorial Power.* If states are by definition territorially located, an increase in their powers in either of the above senses will also tend to demarcate social life into state-bounded social units. Though this has not been a unilinear evolutionary process (e.g. Rome had stronger state boundaries than medieval feudal Europe), modern states have considerably territorialized social life. Indeed, most sociologists use the term SOCIETY to denote (implicitly) the modern NATION-STATE. 19th-century theorists tended to assume that this would decline with the onset of powerful TRANSNATIONAL forces. But this has not happened. Territorial states are among the most powerful social actors of modern times, a fact acknowledged (and perhaps too much taken for granted) by contemporary writers in international relations and international political economy, but as yet unincorporated into mainstream sociology, even of the state.

See also CONSERVATISM; EISENSTADT; LIBER-ALISM; POLITICAL OBLIGATION.

MM

**state capitalism.** The theory that in an attempt to stave off collapse or to improve efficiency the state takes over the running of the capitalist economy. If this means any more than that the state intervenes in certain,

albeit key, sectors of the economy, then it is difficult to reconcile with the Marxist theory of the capitalist MODE OF PRODUCTION, which is predicated on the ownership and control of the means of production by the capitalist class. If the state actually does own and control the means of production and disposes of the profits of the enterprises in the system, then it is difficult to understand in what sense this can be called capitalist at all. Notwithstanding, the term 'state monopoly capitalism' is used, particularly by the Chinese, to describe the economic system of the USSR. Many of the problems of these usages are discussed, but hardly resolved, by P. Baran and P. Sweezey in *Monopoly Capitalism* (1968) and by R. Miliband, *The State in Capitalist Society* (1973).

See also STATE SOCIALISM.

LS

**stateless societies.** See ACEPHALOUS.

**state socialism.** Originally used by European socialists to acknowledge the importance that central planning would have as against local autonomy in the transition from CAPITALISM to SOCIALISM. This sense has been almost totally submerged by the enormous growth of state power in all contemporary societies, whether capitalist or any other type. The term is now applied to the economies of Eastern European and other 'socialist' societies to indicate that control is in the hands of party and/or state bureaucrats and that the distribution of rewards is based on the criterion of 'from each according to ability, to each according to work'. The term is not necessarily one of sectarian abuse, unlike the term STATE CAPITALISM. A discussion of the problems of societies in the transition from capitalism to socialism is to be found in C. Bettelheim, *The Transition to a Socialist Economy* (1975). But if the Soviet Union and similar states are not engaged in a transition to socialism, the latter part of the term has no strict application there.

LS

*Editor's Note.* As will be evident from the entries for COMMUNISM, SOCIALISM, STATE CAPITALISM, STATE SOCIALISM and TOTALITARIANISM, no ideal, generally accepted term exists as a descriptive label for the form of society found in the Soviet Union and its satellites, China, and some of their THIRD WORLD allies. This Encyclopedia nonetheless refers to them as state socialist, to be understood as a compromise term embodying a degree of contradiction between a powerful anti-democratic state and a socialized, would-be democratic system of production.

MM

**statistics.** Historically, the practical study of the state, including counting its population, recording its occupations and estimating national wealth. This usage is now rare. Today, the numerical analysis of data collected by various means from different sources in order to make it intelligible and bring out its significance. Within the term are three main areas of meaning. (1) Descriptive statistics are concerned with the collection and presentation (usually in TABLES AND CHARTS) of numerical data. (2) Statistical method is concerned with the development and application of theoretical ideas such as the mathematical theory of probability, in order to interpret and make inferences about given numerical data. The academic study of statistics increasingly emphasizes method and its underlying theory. (3) The term is also used loosely by non-statisticians, including many sociologists, to refer to any numerical datum or any form of quantitative analysis.

Descriptive statistics involves describing collections of statistical observations, whether drawn from a SAMPLE or from a total population. Various techniques are used to summarize data, including measures of LOCATION and DISPERSION, and to look for patterns of ASSOCIATION in data (such as CORRELATION and REGRESSION). Inferential statistics, the most important statistical applications in sociology, derive from probability theory and the possibility, given random sampling, of making inferences from a sample to a much larger population. If statistical techniques are used to estimate values for a population from which a sample has been drawn, on the basis of the data from the sample, they are said to be inferential. ESTIMATION, SIGNIFICANCE TESTING and hypothesis testing are inferential procedures.

Statistics is not an easy subject. As a result, there is a good deal of misunder-standing of its role (and potential role) in sociological research. Essentially, statistics is a tool used to achieve greater clarity in the analysis of data, permitting economy and precision in interpretation and explanation. Those who make use of statistics need to understand their limitations as well as their potentialities.

See H.J. Loether and D.G. McTavish, *Descriptive and Inferential Statistics for Sociologists* (1974).

MB

**status, status group.** Used in two ways in sociology. (1) Refers to social position. In ROLE THEORY a distinction is made between status, or social position, and role, or the behaviour expected of an incumbent of a social position. Typically, social positions are differentially evaluated and this suggests the second sense of status, as (2) social honour and prestige. The difference between social honour and prestige is one of emphasis rather than substance. Social honour recalls the codified rankings of a traditional status order, including the ascribed social distinctions of the Old World of post-feudal Europe. Prestige suggests the evaluations of the New World about levels of achievement in education, work and the COMMUNITY, which are often more ephemeral. 'Esteem' is sometimes used synonymously with status but is better reserved for the evaluation of personal qualities and the quality of role performances; people, not positions, are held in high esteem.

Evaluation and ranking of social positions follow definite principles, and reproduce a status system. The stable systems of traditional societies are called status orders. In such orders titles, decorations, speech and accent, education, privileges and property are testimony to the niceties of ranking, and underwrite status distinctions. In advanced CAPITALISM, status systems are less orderly, more fragmented. Claims for status are less assured of success, though they are made no less insistently. Advertising and the media continuously display before the consumer goods and services with which to confirm old, and assert new, claims for status. Status symbols are everywhere.

The term *status group* originated not so much in WEBER as in translations of Weber.

In everyday German, the word for CLASS (*Klasse*) is reserved for the bourgeoisie and workers who so rudely called in question the traditional status order of pre-industrial Germany. By contrast the NOBILITY, the PROFESSIONS, craftsmen and PEASANTS are ESTATES (*Stände*) with values and conventions which maintain continuities with the pre-industrial order. By extension, even new groups of white-collar workers and civil servants are *Mittelstande*, literally middle estates rather than middle classes. Weber evoked this usage in his use of *Stand* (translated as status group) to refer to all who occupy a common status situation, defined as 'every typical component of the life of men that is determined by specific, positive or negative, social estimation of honour' (*Economy and Society*, II). Status groups are communities; they define the normal limits of social intercourse (i.e. intercourse which is not subservient to economic or any other pressure) and tend towards ENDOGAMY, and they are the bearers of social conventions (which sometimes impede market forces).

Translations of Weber prompt a use of status group which omits the overtones of order, codification and social honour in favour of less durable crystallizations of prestige. Nevertheless it still pertains to social relations; it takes one person to make a status claim, another to concede it. Where the status striver offends the status consciousness of those among whom acceptance is sought, a status claim fails and social distance is maintained.

See CLASS: *Weber on*; SOCIAL MOBILITY.

See R. Bendix and S. Lipset, *Class, Status and Power* (revised 1966), part 3.

CGAB

status composition [congruence/consistency/crystallization]. The idea of status congruence (and its synonyms) is derived from a revision of WEBER, according to which CLASS, STATUS and POWER constitute three equally significant dimensions of SOCIAL STRATIFICATION (see CLASS: *Weber on*). To quote Lenski, 'The structure of human groups normally involves the co-existence of a number of parallel vertical hierarchies which usually are imperfectly correlated with one another.' Lenski's study

of Detroit (1954) distinguishes four hierarchies — income, occupation, education and ETHNICITY — each of which is arranged into clearly differentiated levels. Individuals or families who occupy a similar level in each hierarchy manifest status congruence or status consistency (these are semantic alternatives), high status crystallization or the composition of status attributes. Conversely, status incongruence (or status inconsistency, low crystallization or decomposition of status attributes) occurs where there is one or more significant differences in the status levels of an individual (or family). Status incongruence has attracted more comment than congruence; examples include the Negro doctor in America in the 1940s and intellectuals in Poland in the 1960s (many of whom ranked much lower in the income than the education and prestige hierarchies). Multi-ethnic and multi-religious societies have provided the most fertile source of such examples.

Many studies of stratification have aggregated rankings in different orders or hierarchies to generate an overall status. But status incongruence theory argues that the inconsistencies concealed by aggregation contribute to the explanation of social action. Lenski hypothesized that 'the more frequently acute status inconsistencies occur within a population the greater would be the proportion of that population willing to support programs of social change'.

This has proved useful to sociologists in STATE SOCIALIST societies. It provides an acceptable means of analysing stratification in societies in which class domination and exploitation are held to have been abolished. Wesolowksi in Poland argued (1967) that in a capitalist society relations to the means of production determine levels of income, prestige and education, positions in structures of power and authority, and styles of life (a proposition which denies the validity in the West of status incongruence) whereas in a socialist society the relationship to the means of production is the same for all. Differences in income, nature of work, prestige, opportunities and political attributes cannot be determined by this common relationship. Wesolowski proposes that in circumstances such as periods of rapid social change different attributes of status, such as income, prestige, education and authority, become dissociated. Where once particular groups of occupations would have had similar rankings on all dimensions, rankings now diverge. Yet there is a possibility of the recomposition of status as socialism is consolidated and education becomes the new determinant of the other attributes of status.

See Lenski, *Power and Privilege* (1966); Wesolowski in Beteille (ed.), *Social Inequality* (1969).

CGAB

**status frustration.** A troubling condition awarded prominence by American ANOMIE theory. It is claimed that Americans, and young Americans particularly, are encouraged to acquire ambitions which they are not all permitted to realize. When the gap between aspiration and achievement becomes especially taxing, the outcome can be defined as status frustration. It is a frustration that has been used to explan the genesis of deviant SUBCULTURES, and expressive subcultures above all others. It can bring about the methodical inversion of the rejecting world and the construction of an alternative symbolic universe which assigns importance to status insignia possessed or created by the deprived.

PR

**status passage.** See RITES OF PASSAGE.

**stereotype.** A belief that is oversimplified in content and unresponsive to evidence which, on rational criteria, indicates that it needs to be revised. Also used more loosely to refer to preconceived ideas about individuals, groups or objects, when these preconceptions are shared by members of particular groups or societies.

See AUTHORITARIANISM; RACISM; ROKEACH.

MPB

**stigma.** In LABELLING theory, developed by GOFFMAN in his book *Stigma* (1963). It refers to a relationship of devaluation in which one individual is 'disqualified from full social acceptance'. Research in this area focuses particularly on the problems generated by stigma for individuals and groups and on the coping mechanisms they employ. Stigma can be physical (syphilitic infections), documentary (a prison record) or contextual ('bad company'), ascribed or achieved (see ACHIEVEMENT). In some instances, the stigmatized have relatively little control over the character or display of their disfigurement. In others, appearances may be so organized that revelation is suppressed or ambiguous in its import. Its sociological significance resides in its importance for the analysis of information-management, ascribed DEVIANCE, and the conventional character of SOCIAL CONTROL. See MEANS TEST.

KP, PR

**stochastic process.** A process or, more exactly, the model of a process, in which the successive states in time are linked by probabilistic rather than deterministic laws (see PROBABILITY). Interest focuses on the distribution over the states of the process at different times, on its long-run behaviour, on the existence of stable states and on typical trajectories.

Stochastic processes have been widely used in MATHEMATICAL SOCIOLOGY, for example to model SOCIAL MOBILITY (see MARKOV PROCESS), promotion within organizations, the outbreak of riots, the growth of populations (see BIRTH-AND-DEATH PROCESS) and the diffusion of innovation. Stochastic process models in sociology have the strength that they can deal with uncertainty and variability encountered in social phenomena. But they do so by treating this as an essential randomness; and insofar as uncertainty is due to freedom of choice or the indeterminacy of action in the face of others, critics see them as at best a temporary measure and at worst as misrepresenting the nature of social reality.

JL

**Stouffer, Samuel A.** (1900-60). American sociologist. Born in Sac City, Iowa, he studied English at Harvard, worked as a journalist, and gained his PhD from the University of Chicago in 1930 for a comparison of case-study and statistical methods of studying attitudes. Stouffer's principal contribution was as a quantitive methodologist, a subject he taught at the University of Wisconsin (1931-5), the University of Chicago (1930-1; 1935-46) and Harvard University (1946-60). During World Ward II he directed social research in the US War Department. His influence lay in advancing the use of quantitative methods in sociology, in demography (the concept of intervening opportunities in MIGRATION) and above all in the four-volume result of his war work. *The American Soldier,* which made major contributions to social psychology and group dynamics, to the methodology of SOCIAL SURVEY research and introduced the concept of RELATIVE DEPRIVATION. Stouffer did not establish a school, nor have many disciples, but he fostered a strongly scientific conception of the social role of sociology.

See S.A. Stouffer, *Social Research to Test Ideas* (1963).

MB

**stratification (in sampling).** See SAMPLING.

**streaming.** Formal educational organizations tend to be set up to ensure efficiency on certain criteria relating either to the forms of knowledge to be taught or to the measured or perceived competence of the pupils concerned. In the first case there are, for example, purely academic and technical or applied scientific institutions. In the second case pupils may be divided into those who have been found to have the necessary entry knowledge or to have a level of measured intelligence believed necessary to cope successfully with the intended CURRICULUM. This second method of organization is normally referred to, particularly in secondary schools, as streaming. The usual aim given for the division of pupils into streams in schools, often designated by successive letters of the alphabet (e.g. A,B,C) is that the curriculum and the PEDA-GOGY can be matched to the nature of the pupils so that the process of learning is more efficient. However, mistakes of allocation to streams within schools or to what are in effect streamed schools within an overall educational system occur even when using the most efficient measuring tests available. The UN-INTENDED CONSEQUENCES of such streaming systems are that many of these wrongly allocated pupils are LABELLED in such a way that a pupil may come to see him/herself to be less or more intelligent than might otherwise have been the case. Many consider the effect of streaming to be socially unacceptable. There are other less severe forms of streaming. Thus 'setting' refers to a system whereby a whole age-group within a school is regrouped for each subject or for groups of subject; this method is used most often for 'difficult' subjects such as mathematics or languages. 'Broad ability banding' covers such cases as where a 12-class entry to a school is divided into three or four wide bands of measured intelligence. These methods of organization also suffer, though to a lesser degree, the disadvantage already referred to in that they operate as a form of self-fulfilling prophecy.

PWM

**stress.** The human reaction to threatening life circumstances, involving physiological, psychological and social processes in an individual. A broad, even blanket concept, but one which encapsulates the basic thesis that the observable symptoms of disease are the end product of a causal chain of reactions in which the antecedent stimulus or stressor is of a social character.

Stressors take the form of threatening changes in life circumstances; sociologists call them 'life events'. Among them, those which appear to evoke the most stressful response are bereavement (particularly becoming widowed), separation and divorce, marriage, unemployment and imprisonment.

Physiological stress typically involves endocrinal secretions which in excess may themselves produce symptoms of disease. If this happens it constitutes an example of a disease of adaptation in that it is part and parcel of a body's own attempt to protect itself. Physiological stress may occur as a reaction to a physiological stressor, such as heat or noise, but it is also part of the body's response to psychological or social stressors. Psychological stress is manifested in a cognitive response. As some writers have emphasized, particular life events only involve stress to the degree that an individual perceives and defines them as threatening. It is their symbolic relevance to a particular psyche which determines the stressful force, and a successful response requires psychological mastery through the positive redefinition of events initially perceived in a threatening light. But clearly some life events cannot be made to seem less threatening purely as an act of mental will. They require direct manipulation of the social or economic environment rather than manipulation of cognitions about that environment. These are social stressors.

The action mounted by an individual confronting a threatening life event has been called 'coping'. Coping is an intervening variable mediating between stressor and potential disease and transforming a static relationship into a dynamic one. To cope is to attempt to offset the onset symptoms. As a capacity it is strengthened by the individual's access to supportive relationships such as a network of significant others, and to material resources, each of which may act or be employed to lessen the impact of life events or aid in processes of redefinition or direct social action. Social isolation and poverty are therefore likely to act as impediments to successful coping. But variables such as these may also have an impact on the social distribution of the stressors, the life events, which are the potential triggers of the disease process. Thus the incidence of threatening changes of life circumstances as well as the severity of their impact may be expected to vary alongside such factors as occupational class and race, producing differentials of vulnerability in a society or population. By a similar process of reasoning, however, a stable experience of deprivation might be less productive of the personal upheavals which give to life events their threatening character.

There is a growing volume of empirical findings revealing the association between social stressors and the onset of diseases such as leukaemia, multiple sclerosis, anaemia, heart conditions, cancer and tuberculosis. Similar associations have also be found for psychiatric conditions. In each case there is no evidence of a specific stressor-symptom relationship. Demonstration of the AETIO-LOGICAL significance of these recorded associations presents enormously difficult problems, since most of the data are culled from the retrospective self reports of those already exhibiting symptoms. Even so, life event research and the stress model of illness constitute a promising challenge to the dominant model of explanation and treatment.

As an alternative social paradigm for the explanation of disease onset it shares certain parallels, possibly owes a debt, to PARSONS's conceptualization of illness as a disturbance of the individual's capacity and readiness for task and role performance. See MEDICAL MODEL; SICK ROLE.

See H.G. Wolff, *Stress and Disease* (1953); G. Brown and T. Harris, *Social Origins of Depression* (1978).

NH

**structural balance theory.** See COGNITIVE CONSISTENCY THEORY; GRAPH THEORY.

**structural differentiation.** See DIVISION OF LABOUR.

**structural equations.** See CAUSAL MODEL-LING.

**structuralism.** A mode of analysis first developed in linguistics between 1900 and 1930. Since the late 1960s it has gained prominence in a number of fields in the social sciences and humanities, especially in France. Modern practitioners include the anthropologist, LÉVI-STRAUSS, the cultural analyst and literary critic Roland Barthes, the Marxist philosopher ALTHUSSER, the psychoanalyst LACAN, and the philosophers Michel FOUCAULT and Jacques Derrida. Only the first of these would unreservedly accept the label 'structuralist', and the last-named is regarded as the inspirer of 'post-structuralism'. Nevertheless, these thinkers share a common 'structuralist' vocabulary and methodology, due to the influence of SAUSSURE's pioneering work in SEMIOLOGY (the science of signs). Saussure suggested that many aspects of social life besides LAN-GUAGE could be treated as signifying systems. His actual treatment of language, and the revolution he wrought in his own discipline, has come to be regarded as exemplary of the way in which other areas of the human sciences could be approached. 'Structuralists' share a conviction that social phemonema are structured in the same way that Saussure perceived language to be structured.

Thus, structuralists stress the systemic and relational nature of social phenomena. Items to be studied are not defined by innate qualities, so much as by their relations to, and differences from, other items in the same system. Following the work in the 1920s and 1930s of the Russian linguist Roman Jakobson, much use is made here of the notion of 'binary opposition': items are classified according to whether they do or do not display a relevant characteristic. Lévi-Strauss suggested that the tendency to classify in this way is a universal feature of the human mind. When an item changes its identity, this is explained neither causally, as the effect of one item on another, nor TELEO-LOGICALLY, in terms of the imputed 'goals' or 'purposes' of the system. Rather, change is explained as resulting from a 'structural transformation', by which one system of relationships is transformed into another. In analysing social phenomena as systems, structuralists rarely examine 'surface' phenomena, but assume that these are generated and explained by the workings of underlying, 'deep' or 'hidden' structures.

The influence of Saussure is also visible in the preference for a 'synchronic' as opposed to 'diachronic' approach. Saussure's revolution in linguistics is a shift from the 19th-century emphasis on historical, evolutionary studies of language, to one in which language is studied as a structure of relationships existing at a single moment in time or, more strictly, atemporally. Saussure argued that language was a system of signs. Each sign could be analysed into two components: the 'signifier' (the sound of a word), and the 'signified' (the idea to which the word refers). As different languages use different signifiers for the same signified, the relation between them is arbitrary. Over time, changes take place in both signifier and signified: words change their meanings, and meanings come to be expressed in different words. There is thus no natural, essential element to either signifier or signified. Neither can be defined in fixed terms which are unaffected by historical change. Saussure concluded that it was unenlightening to study language historically. He established a distinction between *la langue* (the underlying structure of a language as it exists at any given moment), and *parole* (the actual

speech-acts of a language in daily use), and argued that language was best studied by focusing on the former at the expense of the latter.

The historical, synchronic nature of the structuralist method raises something of a paradox for many modern practitioners. Such a mode of analysis would surely be strongly opposed to Marxism, hitherto a supremely historical and diachronic form of analysis. Most modern structuralists, however, maintain a relationship with Marxism. To be sure, Lévi-Strauss's Marxism is really only added on to his structuralism. For him, synchronic structuralism and diachronic dialectical materialism refer to different dimensions of social reality, as Saussure's synchronic *langue* and diachronic *parole* refer to different dimensions of language. Others have been less circumspect. Although Althusser denies he is a true structuralist, its influence clearly extends to many aspects of his work. In his claim to demonstrate that MARX abandons the notion of ALIENATION, for example, he attempts to dispose of the embarrassing fact that Marx continues to use the term in his later works, by claiming that it must be defined relationally, and that alienation does not mean the same thing in the context of the structure of Marx's early thought as it does in the later PROBLEMATIC.

Althusser's interpretation of Marx raises another structuralist point: its 'theoretical anti-humanism' and its argument for 'the disappearance of the subject'. Increasingly, structuralists have argued against humanist doctrines which see humanity as an active, conscious force in the historical process. According to Foucault and others, this whole conception of humanity is false. Man is not the subject of history, or of the social sciences; rather, structural forces are the causal agents, and ought to form the subject-matter of scientific enquiry.

Although structuralism has been widely disseminated outside France during the 1970s and early 1980s (indeed, it is penetrating some English-speaking areas just when it is on the wane in France), its spread has been hindered by the difficulty of much structuralist writing. In part, this is a deliberate reaction by some practitioners against what is perceived as the dominant (and dominating) French bourgeois virtue of clarity. Especially in the fields of literary and philophical criticism, structuralists have made much of the productivity of language, and of the difficulty and undesirability of assuming that language can provide us with fixed and essential meanings. This thesis may well hinder rather than advance the dissemination of structuralism, if structuralists prefer to exemplify the argument rather than explain it.

AM

**structure.** A concept widely used in sociology, but in senses either too specific or too general to permit simple agreed definition. Primarily, structure is distinguished from simple aggregation or conglomeration of elements by features loosely grouped into three linked categories. (1) A set of elements is connected by relations to form a whole, with new properties not possessed by the elements alone. (2) Substitution of new elements for old is possible without necessarily altering the nature of the structure. Substantively different phenomena may be seen as possessing a similar structure, and vice versa. (3) The ways in which the structure may be transformed serve to define it in a way equivalent to its internal relations.

The new properties associated with a structure are seen as dependent more on the nature of the relations linking it together than on the substantive nature of the parts (see SYSTEM). Substitution, as long as these relations are preserved, will have little effect on the structural properties. Some degree of HOMEOSTASIS is thus possible. From the structural point of view, a part is specified by its position within the whole. Transformations (e.g. inversions) of one or more areas of the internal relations will be systematically linked to transformations of the remaining areas. The nature of these links can give an exact image of the structure.

Human social groups possess all the above features. A set of persons, families, roles or whatever elements are chosen, is linked by social relationships, direct or indirect, of communication, obligation, power etc into a whole, which may behave in ways in which none of the elements would behave. The group may incorporate or lose members without thereby losing its identity

or form, a crucial feature of social organization. The group is subject to transformations, either concrete, historical, diachronic changes, or as hypothetical, abstract, synchronic comparisons. For example, inversion of part of a hierarchy will be connected to inversion of some or all of the rest, and the rules governing this process define the nature of the hierarchy equivalently to the internal relations of super- and sub-ordination.

At a more abstract level, LANGUAGE, and, it may be argued, all of CULTURE, possesses structure in the above senses. In a sentence, words or phonemes are connected in order into a grammatical unit which may express meaning, a meaning dependent on the arrangement of the words. Words are arbitrary symbols, and could be substituted without destroying the capacity of a sentence to transmit meaning. Sentences can be transformed in ways characteristic of their structure. Thus 'Mary loves Bill' could transform into 'Bill is loved by Mary', but the superficially similar 'Mary loves Bill's pianoplaying' cannot transform into 'Bill's pianoplaying loves Mary', defining the difference in structure.

See CHOMSKY; GRAPH THEORY; MATHEMATICAL SOCIOLOGY; SEMIOLOGY; SOCIAL STRUCTURE; STRUCTURALISM.

JL

**subculture.** Subcultural theory has been the almost exclusive property of those sociologists of DEVIANCE who have chosen to emphasize the social learning of behaviour (e.g. SUTHERLAND, Cohen, Cloward and Ohlin). A subculture was a more or less coherent assembly of beliefs and perspectives which borrowed its form and content from the wider CULTURE in which it was embedded. It was symbolically dependent, representing not opposition, independence or substantial innovation, but an exaggeration or accentuation of ideas available to all members of society. Thus everyone is exposed to hedonism, but not everyone is a bearer of a subculture given over to pleasure; everyone is aware of violent themes, but not all adopt violence as a communally-approved solution to routine problems. Subcultures are stripped of conventional contexts of meaning and are portrayed as simple structures which lack irony or counterbalance.

Subcultures mediate between social structure and the individual. Usually lodged in a framework of pathology, they constitute collective solutions to the structural problems which people encounter. Drug-taking became an attempt to accomplish style in a symbolically impoverished world. Street gangs were answers to blocked opportunities: once established, they provided the possibility of a response to recurrent dilemmas, privations and uncertainties.

The character and presence of a subculture have sometimes been merely deduced from a geographical concentration of behaviour or the assumed existence of a social problem. Thus an abundance of violent incidents in an area may be thought to demonstrate the workings of a subculture of violence, which is little more than a mechanism for the production of a subculture to explain any problem.

Its employment in deviance studies has taken two major forms. (1) The first, emerging from the ANOMIE theory of MERTON, was extensively adopted in the 1950s and 1960s in American criminology and less emphatically in British studies. The distinctive analytical assumption was that deviant (and especially DELINQUENT) subcultures emerged as solutions to socially structured 'problems' encountered by a sufficient number of interactants to generate a group response. The classic example remains A.K. Cohen's theory of 'status frustration' whereby the school system is deemed to nurture ambitions among working-class boys which the social structure cannot accommodate (*Delinquent Boys*, 1956). The 'solution' to this 'problem of adjustment' is the delinquent gang, which enables boys so circumstanced both to hit back at the system which has stigmatized them as failures, and to acquire status in terms of 'expressive' oppositional values which they can more readily meet. Others produced alternative means-ends schemes to account for variations in delinquency over time and in other societies and locations, but the major premise — that the subjects had first been socialized into the NORMS and values of the 'dominant' (or MIDDLE-CLASS) culture —

remained (as in anomie theory) relatively unproblematic. Since these theories tended towards a 'zero-sum' formulation of the genesis of social problems, the appeal waned when middle-class deviations (drug-use among hippies, the resort to tactical violence by radical groups such as the Weathermen) became too highly visible.

(2) Despite much overlap, the second view is more indebted to MARX than to Merton, and is much more a British than an American development. It is chiefly distinguished by the relations presumed to exist between changes in the dynamics of CLASS conflict and the emergence of deviant (especially youthful) subcultures. In a seminal paper (*Journal of Cultural Studies* 1972), P. Cohen linked the emergence of successive youthful subcultural styles to changes in working-class inner-city experience. Subcultures are accredited with a more creative and actively resistant function than the earlier stress on adaptation and status reassurance. Analysis of style draws on SEMIOLOGY and the concept of bricolage. Due weight is accorded to symbolic resemblances to a variety of 'parent' cultures as well as to differentiation from them. Analysis extends to middle-class as well as working-class subcultures, both of which are sited in the context of CAPITALIST social and economic contradictions. Intentionality remains a crucial problem, however, since forms of consciousness tend to be inferred from stylistic display rather than grounded in ethnography or more formal techniques.

*Inmate subculture.* Penologists have described how imprisonment inflicts distinctive pains and losses upon inmates. Prisoners in the West are deprived of freedom, initiative, diversion, diversity, information, sexual pleasure, comfort, a sense of personal worth and the like. As a limited answer, inmates may build an informal world for themselves which displaces or complements the social structure organized by officials, and provides some of the goods, services and symbolic materials otherwise withheld. Of particular importance is the construction of a hierarchy of esteem and power, the creation of new ROLES based upon a clandestine morality, and alternative perspectives to those offered by the ideologies of correction and rehabilitation. Together, those ideas and morals constitute the inmate subculture. It can receive a measure of *de facto* recognition from prison staff. Legitimation may be exchanged for inmate co-operation in a working compromise of power and authority.

This view is an appealing explanation of facets of prison organization, but empirical work has progressively reduced the scope of the first arguments of Sykes, Clemmer and others. Its description also mirrors peculiar features of long-term, American male prisons of the 1950s and 1960s. It requires substantial modification to apply to female prisons, short-term prisons, therapeutically-directed establishments, or even to all the inmates of American institutions. See PENO-LOGY.

PR

**suburbanism.** The culture of suburbs, popularly conceived as a life-style of relentless conformity to MIDDLE-CLASS norms of conspicuous consumption, a hyperactive affiliation with voluntary organizations, daily commuting to work (typically a bureaucratic occupation in the office of a large corporation), ersatz neighbourliness and privatized affluence. This stereotype entered sociological discourse through works such as W.H. Whyte's *The Organization Man* (1957). Subsequent research demonstrated that this stereotype is exaggerated and over-generalized — it is a 'myth of suburbia'. There is no evidence to support the view that there is a necessary causal connection between a shift in the location of residence to suburbia and the adoption of a particular life-style.

*Suburbanization* is the growth and re-location of residential and industrial functions from the centre to the periphery of towns and cities. This began in the late 19th century aided by new forms of mass transport. It is particularly extensive in the USA and Australia. As it has proceeded, so suburbs are subject to internal differentiation, for instance between industrial and residential suburbs.

See D. Thorns, *Suburbia* (1972).

HN

**sub-imperialism.** A term coined to characterize distinctive features of INDUSTRIALIZA-TION of fast-growing developing countries such as Brazil, Mexico, South Korea, Taiwan and Iran before the Islamic Revolution. These are: (1) rapid industrialization of the import-substitutive or export-oriented sector under the control of multinational capital; (2) close political and military association with Western imperialist countries; (3) autonomous finance capital active not only internally but internationally.

The term does not refer to IMPERIALISM (in the export of capital version). Sub-imperialist countries typically import capital but do not (as yet) export it on any significant scale. But the term indicates a definite place in the unequal hierarchy of the international division of labour. For example, Brazil manufactures Volkswagen cars under licence and exports them for final assembly to less developed countries such as Nigeria. Sub-imperialist countries thus act as a go-between or relay station for imperialist capital. Politically too they may act as 'sub-hegemonic' powers, a role expressedly assigned to Brazil and Iran by former President Nixon. Such countries are singled out for special military support and are sold the most advanced military technology on the understanding that they fulfill a policeman's role in the region.

AH

**sublimation.** See PSYCHOANALYSIS.

**substantivism.** See POLANYI; RECIPROCITY.

**Sumner, William Graham** (1840-1910). One of the founders of American sociology. Born in Paterson, New Jersey, Sumner was the son of an English immigrant whose trade in England was ruined by the industrial revolution. He studied political economy at Yale, French and Hebrew at Geneva, ancient languages and history at Göttingen, and Anglican theology at Oxford. He was ordained an Episcopal minister in 1869, but left the ministry in 1872 upon his appointment as Professor of Political and Social Science at Yale. He occupied this post until his death. Towards the end of his life, Sumner succeeded WARD as the second president of the American Sociology Society.

In the 1890s Sumner's interests increasingly shifted from economic theory to sociological research. He was a firm advocate of laissez-faire and economic INDIVIDUALISM, opposed to SOCIALISM, state intervention, and social reformism. He extended the influence of SPENCERIAN EVOLUTIONISM into the early 20th century. This heritage, increasingly discarded by social scientists, shaped early contributions to the sociology of law (see LAW). In 1880 Sumner's introduction of Spencer's *Study of Society* as a textbook at Yale marked his conversion to evolutionism and, at a time when the competing claims of religion and science were hotly debated, nearly resulted in his dismissal as a suspected atheist. In his social DARWINISM the law of evolution, producing the 'survival of the fittest', is unilinear and irreversible. CLASS struggle will lead not to socialism but to a superior form of adaption based upon 'antagonistic co-operation'.

Sumner's main work *Folkways* (1906) combines ethnography and UTILITARIANISM. Its wide-ranging description of social customs reflects his Oxford experience in its preoccupation with the construction of an inductive social science. The unfinished *Science of Society* (1927) was completed posthumously by Albert Keller. Sumner's work had some influence upon the work of Roscoe Pound and the school of sociological JURISPRUDENCE and his views on law and political economy influenced Karl Llewellyn, the proponent of American Legal Realism (see LAW), which conceived of law as a form of social utilitarianism. Sumner stimulated Llewellyn's concern with legal anthropology, and his interests in cultural evolution and the science of society shaped the work of Murdock, the American anthropologist.

Sumner introduced the distinction between 'in-groups' and 'out-groups', emphasized cultural relativism, and is usually (incorrectly) credited with coining the word ETHNOCENTRIC (see GUMPLOWICZ). Social change occurs as 'folkways' (expedient customary acts) evolve. Some are elevated into 'mores' (coercive ethical principles). Sumner's treatment of voluntarism *versus* DETERMINISM in social life lacks

clarity, since he emphasizes the constraints of folkways whilst advocating economic individualism. His CONSENSUS model of LAW as a reflection of the mores rejects the notion of law as an instrument for social change.

JW

**superego.** See PSYCHOANALYSIS.

**supervision.** See HUMAN RELATIONS MOVEMENT; SCIENTIFIC MANAGEMENT.

**supply.** The amount of a good or service that producers are willing to offer for sale in a given period of time. The supply of any good will depend upon, *inter alia*, its price and the producers' COSTS of production. A supply curve or schedule is a diagrammatic representation of the relationship between supply and the good's price, on the assumption that all other conditions remain unchanged. The simultaneous interaction of market supply and DEMAND conditions (often depicted by supply and demand curves) establishes the equilibrium market output and price for a particular good. The elasticity of supply is a measure of the responsiveness of supply to changes in price or other determining variables (see also elasticity of DEMAND). In those markets such as housing where supply changes only slowly (i.e. it is inelastic) an increase in the demand for a good will lead to price increases rather than increases in output. This may lead governments to introduce price controls.

RR

**Sutherland, Edwin** (1883-1950). After receiving his PhD from the University of Chicago in 1913, Sutherland taught at the Universities of Illinois, Minnesota and Chicago before becoming head of the Sociology Department at the University of Indiana. His work bears much of the impress of the CHICAGO SCHOOL, having been shaped by the ideas of PARK, BURGESS, THOMAS and COOLEY. He sustained a distinctively sociological approach to the explanation of CRIME during the 1930s and 1940s, when criminology was dominated by other disciplines. He trained, recruited and sponsored a number of people who were to become eminent, including Cressey, Cohen and Lindesmith. He thus preserved what was threatened. He was also a substantial scholar, producing theories of lasting virtue, especially DIFFER-ENTIAL ASSOCIATION (1939) and WHITE COLLAR CRIME (1949).

PR

**symbol.** In social anthropology and socio-logy, the term can be used loosely to indicate almost any kind of indirect representation or, more precisely, as part of a theoretical approach which is derived partly from lin-guistics and partly from PSYCHOANALYSIS. Early theories of symbolism were concerned with finding out how people interpreted their own symbols and deducing from this a symbolic order which functioned as the basis of the moral order by providing a set of public meanings and values. Thus the anthropology of RELIGION was concerned to discover the meaning of symbolic actions, words and objects within particular RITUALS and relate these to systems of thought and values within a society.

STRUCTURALIST anthropology is more concerned with the manner in which mean-ing is achieved than with providing a set of interpretations. The fundamental principles are derived from SAUSSURE's work in lin-guistics and FREUD's work on dreams. Symbols are connnected within a system analogous to LANGUAGE systems. The symbolic function is an essential part of the process of thinking, the ability to use lan-guage, and thus the way in which people relate to society. There are two principles of symbolism. Either one sign or object is used to represent another (metonym or displace-ment) or a single symbol stands for a whole complex of ideas (metaphor or condensa-tion). The former is simple substitution, and is relatively easy to interpret, but in the latter each symbol reverberates with meaning by evoking systems of related ideas. Although such theories have been influential in anthropology since the 1960s, they have not entirely displaced earlier formulations: it is often more useful to rely upon more prag-matic explanations of ritual action. In addition, some writers — most notably students of the Cambridge anthropologist Sir Edmund Leach (b. 1910), an elaborator of the work of LÉVI-STRAUSS — have suggested that the symbolic function is not necessarily

systematic. It would be more correct to study symbols in their manifestations and effects than through their meanings. See SEMIO-LOGY.

JE

**symbolic interactionism.** An influential American social psychology — often called the sociologist's social psychology — gene-rated during the hey-day of CHICAGO SCHOOL sociology (1920-35) and revitalized through the rise of LABELLING THEORY in DE-VIANCE during the 1960s. During the 1970s it came under heavy criticism, but it was also formally codified in textbooks and institu-tionalized through the Society for the Study of Symbolic Interaction and its house jour-nal, *Symbolic Interaction.*

It stands opposed to all social science traditions which theorize without having a close, first-hand intimate involvement with those phenomena about which they theorize. Strongly empirical, it advocates a wide range of research tools (especially PARTICIPANT OBSERVATION, LIFE HISTORIES and depth interviewing) to gain this. Such work is guided by three concerns. (1) Humans are distinctive in being complex symbol-manipulating animals. Though they inhabit objective material worlds as well (including their physiological bodies), the social scientist must adequately grasp the distinc-tive meanings that humans construct in their social encounters. (2) Such meanings are not universal, fixed or absolute. Rather, there is a plurality of meanings which shift through time (history), space (culture) and bio-graphy. Meaning is ambiguous, never to be taken for granted. It has to be investigated as it emerges or is negotiated between groups. The theory thus places a strong premium on studying processes rather than more static structures. Many of its key concepts — SELF, CAREER and negotiated order (see NEGOTIA-TION) — stress this. (3) It emphasizes the interactive unit — providing a bridge between the strictly biological and psycho-logical (which in focussing upon the indi-vidual tends to ignore the social) and the strictly sociological (which gravitates towards the structural and hence ignores the individual). Humans possess selves which render them persistently capable of 'taking the role of the other' and 'seeing themselves through the eyes of others'. Without this ability human communication and, with it, social order would break down. An isolated human being is a fiction. At the same time, humans are not merely determined by the definitions of others since they inevitably have their own unique biological endowment and interactive history which renders them capable of responding in different ways to the definitions of others. The theory is hence a synthesis of voluntarist and determinist thought, as well as a synthesis of the social and individual, and the symbolic and the material, and it is precisely here that its appeal has centred.

There is controversy as to the origins of symbolic interactionism. Some claim it derives primarily from the philosophical pragmatism of MEAD, particularly his theory of the self. Others claim it derives from the work of PARK under the influence of the formalism of SIMMEL. Park and Mead were contemporaries at the University of Chicago in the 1920s and it is undoubtedly here that the seed-bed for the theory lies (see CHICAGO SCHOOL OF SOCIOLOGY). The term was coined by BLUMER in 1937, and he has been considered its chief proponent, though there have been distinctive breakaway groups (e.g. the Iowa School, who favoured a more positivistic, operationable and hence testable theory (see TWENTY STATEMENTS TEST). Most recently, some have seen DRAMATURGY, PHENOMENOLOGICAL sociology and ETHNOMETHODOLOGY as breakaway variants.

The theory has been criticized and then defended on many grounds. It is most commonly accused of neglecting power, structure and history and being overly social psychological in focus. Interactionists claim that far from neglecting such areas, they have derived distinctive versions of power centring on symbolism, of structure centring on NEGOTIATION, and of history centring on perspectivism — all of which are more faithful to the empirical world than other accounts. Symbolic interactionists are incapable of making analyses that transcend situations and perspectives and which can grasp totalities and absolutes — but then the theory suggests that such goals are impossible to attain.

See BECKER; BLUMER; LABELLING.

See J.G. Manis and B.N. Meltzer *Symbolic Interaction: A Reader in Social Psychology* (3rd edn., 1978).

KP

**symbolic realism.** Robert Bellah has argued that the major social scientific theorists of RELIGION have adopted one or another form of REDUCTIONISM in their approach to the subject. They have explained religion away by arguments that: (*a*) religion is false and therefore can only be understood by examining its consequences ('consequential reductionism'); or (*b*) that religion contains an element of truth lying behind its SYMBOLS ('symbolic reductionism'). Those who argue that the dietary taboos of Leviticus were the expression of an intuitive medical awareness; or that religion is no more than the projection of the oedipal complex onto the cosmos; or that it is the representation of society to its members, practice symbolic reductionism.

Bellah advocates the alternative approach of 'symbolic realism'. This, he says contentiously, takes the view that 'religion is true'. By this he means that religious symbols are ways in which individuals and societies 'express their sense of the fundamental nature of reality, of the totality of experience'. Thus they cannot merely be reduced to projections of individual psychodynamics or social structure. They have a subjective reality, and therefore 'truth', independent of the sociological and psychological factors implicated in their explanation.

RW

**syncretism.** Reconciliation of, or attempts to reconcile, different systems of belief. First coined to refer to attempts to combine different forms of Christianity. Today more usually applied to the blending and fusion of native beliefs and religious practices with taught Christian religions and institutions in (ex-)colonial countries. Syncretic attempts to reconcile local with imposed religious forms are in evidence throughout Africa in an immense variety of 'nativist churches' and SECTS. Christian beliefs and practices are harmonized with local purification rites, taboos, and most frequently, spiritual healing practices.

See RELIGION.

AH

**syndicalism.** A movement or tendency which emerged in Western Europe in the first decade of the 20th century. It embraced the idea that the TRADE UNION, not the political party, was the appropriate vehicle for the revolutionary transformation of society. It opposed SOCIAL DEMOCRACY and revolutionary Marxism alike, on the grounds that both sapped the revolutionary energy of the working class, the former by class collaboration, the latter by economic determinism and the assumption of an inevitable capitalist collapse. Its distinctive tenets were: the need to maintain the exclusively proletarian character of the socialist movement, free from bourgeois elements and influences; an emphasis on revolutionary will and action; the idea of the general strike as a political weapon to bring about the overthrow of capitalism; a confidence in the trade unions to provide the structure and personnel to organize production in postcapitalist society. Since its heyday before World War I syndicalism has become intermingled with other socialist currents such as the movement for workers' control.

See INDUSTRIAL DEMOCRACY; LENIN; SOCIALISM.

DB

**syntactic.** See LANGUAGE.

**systems theory.** A system is a set of VARIABLES so interconnected that a change in the value of one of the variables has a determinate effect on all other variables. Sociologists see society and other smaller social systems as open systems, existing in environments and receiving energy from outside themselves. In an open system initial conditions do not completely determine the state of the system at some later point, for this is affected by inputs from the environment. If an open system has permanence, then it will maintain equilibrium in the face of environmental pressure. To identify an equilibrium one must identify its mechanisms.

A systems analysis specifies the set of principles that govern the interconnection of the system's parts. Most systems theorists are attracted by 'tough-minded' or 'hard-nosed' assumptions about people, such as economic self-interest, to connect the parts. Then the organization of the system is described and how it maintains various equilibria is specified. Next, the effects of a change in the value of one of the variables forming the system is considered. The repercussions of the change are followed through the system, and the new system resulting described. By using the principles that govern how the system parts are interconnected the stability of the system can be assessed. If unstable, the repercussions of the change must be followed through further, until either a stable system is reached or the system is destroyed.

A systems theory is as good as the set of principles that governs the interconnections of the system parts. Theories as diverse as Marxian and KEYNESIAN economics can be formulated as systems theories. The strength of formulating theories in this way is that one is forced to consider the organization of the whole system. Particularly for considering the effects of changes on a society, say a new social welfare policy or a change in the bank rate, this approach forces one to fully think through the repercussions of the change. The weakness of the approach is that any set of principles interconnecting the system's parts tends to make the relationship mechanistic.

See SOCIAL SYSTEM.

KM

**Szasz, Thomas S.** (1920- ). Psychiatrist and psychoanalyst who achieved prominence in the 1960s with his critique of the concept of MENTAL ILLNESS and of much of established psychiatric practice. Sometimes termed an anti-psychiatrist, Szasz actively rejects the label on the grounds of its unselective negative connotations and, more importantly, of its identification with the work of writers like R.D. LAING and David Cooper, to whose political philosophy he is strongly opposed.

Born in Budapest, Szasz received his University education in the USA, obtaining an AB in Physics at the University of Cincinatti in 1941 and his MD in 1944. He took up a psychiatric residency in University of Chicago clinics, and underwent psychoanalytic training at the University of Chicago Institute for Psychoanalysis (1947-50). He then joined the staff of the Institute. Since 1956 he has been Professor of Psychiatry at the State University of New York at Syracuse.

Szasz's second book, *The Myth of Mental Illness* (1961), together with a short, more polemical, article under the same title, published a year earlier in *The American Psychologist*, set out the main outlines of his argument, and brought him considerable publicity. The focal point of his attack is the appropriateness of the notion of mental illness. The term mental illness is, he argues, but a metaphor for what should, more accurately, be called 'problems in living'. Except for the obvious organic mental illness, which have identifiable physical causes and are properly viewed as brain diseases and not mental illnesses, what is termed mental illness is actually behaviour that breaks social, ethical and legal rules. Consequently to talk of illness mystifies what is in fact a moral judgement; it suggests a scientific and objective assessment of sickness based on identifiable physical pathology. Yet in the case of functional mental illnesses no such physical pathology exists. The definition of thought or action as symptomatic of mental illness is essentially a judgement about conformity to socially established rules and norms, and its evaluative nature should be made explicit. Underlying Szasz's argument is the assumption that the phenomena of mental illness belong to the realm of human thought and action; consequently, he claims, they cannot be explained or understood in natural scientific terms. The ideas and ways of thinking of the natural sciences, including the language of cause and effect, are both inadequate and inappropriate. Instead, Szasz argues, problems in living require an analysis in terms of rule-following and role and game playing, that gives proper attention to meaning, language and communication and locates them in their social context. In *The Myth of Mental Illness* he provides an analysis of hysteria along these lines.

Szasz's anti-POSITIVIST stance has its roots in his political philosophy. He is an 18th-century libertarian with an overriding belief in individual free-will and a commitment to the autonomy and liberty of the individual (see INDIVIDUALISM). One of his objections to the notion of mental illness is that by locating human action within the realm of medicine and the natural sciences it helps to undermine these beliefs and values. The label illness, when applied to human thought and action, suggests that the behaviour in question should be viewed as outside the individual's control and responsibility; it diminishes individual liberty and autonomy. The ideal for Szasz is to maximize autonomy and self-control. His objection is not to psychiatry's control of behaviour *per se*, but to the fact that the control is hidden and unacknowledged, and is exercised by others in their interests rather than in the individual's. If the individual does need help (and those with 'problems in living' may) this should not be provided by what he calls Institutional Psychiatry. This serves the interests of society, the FAMILY, or the STATE. The only acceptable psychiatry is Contractual Psychiatry (see SOCIAL CONTRACT). This follows the traditional fee-for-service model, the paradigm of PROFESSIONAL practice. The individual as a client freely enters into a relationship with a therapist, directly paid by the client who thus has control over what goes on. Social control of the individual (i.e. control exercised in the interests of others) is sometimes necessary, but its nature should be made explicit, as in the criminal system. Szasz objects strongly to the compulsory commitment of the mentally ill, calling it 'a crime against humanity'. The exercise of repressive social control is distorted and mystified in the domain of scientific medicine, where the individual's interests and scientific objectivity are supposedly paramount.

Szasz's initial critique of mental illness was the starting-point of a broad and increasingly vociferous attack on various aspects of psychiatry and medicine, developed and elaborated in a number of books. These cover topics such as the legal procedures governing commitment of the mentally ill (*Law, Liberty and Psychiatry*, 1963) comparisons of the contemporary treatment of the mentally ill with the earlier persecution of WITCHES (*The Manufactures of Madness*, 1970); and the medical treatment of drug addiction (*Ceremonial Chemistry*, 1974), as well as specific mental illnesses (*Schizophrenia*, 1974). Provocative and stimulating though much of Szasz's work is, it has not escaped either academic or political criticism. Features of his ideas, such as the mind-body dualism, his rejection of causal explanation of human thought and action, his inadequate theorizing of the social, and his claims about client control in fee-for-service professional practice, have been questioned. There has been strong criticism of his underlying political philo-

sophy by those who see it as essentially reactionary in its attack on the public provision of mental health services and its demand for private, free-market psychiatry, as well as in its suggestion that mental symptoms and sufferings can be a matter for individual self-control and responsibility. During the last decade more sociologically and historically informed analyses of psychiatry and medicine have largely replaced his ideas.

See also PSYCHIATRY; PSYCHOANALYSIS; SICK ROLE.

JB

**tables and charts.** Descriptive statistical methods of presenting data which are basic tools of social science. A table is a data matrix in which the columns and rows intersect to form cells. Cases are classified into cells according to what VARIABLES are shown in the table and how they are categorized. A typical two-dimensional table has the following structure:

|  |  | VARIABLE A | | |
| --- | --- | --- | --- | --- |
|  |  | Category 1 | Category 2 | Total |
| VARIABLE B | Category 1 | cell | cell | |
| | Category 2 | cell | cell | |
| | Category 3 | cell | cell | |
| | Total | | | |

Tables may be of one, two three or four DIMENSIONS; more than four variables cannot be easily shown in a single table. Their size can vary considerably. Repository tables (e.g. CENSUS tables) may be very large, intended to be a store of information for future use. Analytic tables, intended to show a particular relationship, tend to be small and simple in structure. Data in tables may be presented in numbers or in percentages. Zeisel suggests as a rule that tables should always be percentaged in the direction of the independent variable. The proper analysis of tabular data is difficult and time-consuming, but one major strategy for the analysis of social survey data (developed by LAZARS-FELD) depends on it (see CROSS-TABULATION).

Charts are a way of presenting statistical data visually, as a picture rather than as a set of numbers. Charts are also known as graphs or diagrams, and take various forms including histograms, bar-charts, population pyramids, line graphs, frequency polygons and scatter diagrams. Basic to any chart is a co-ordinate system, lines (usually) at right angles to each other which form two scales (or axes) onto which the values of a distribution on one or more variables may be plotted. A histogram is a one-dimensional graph; a POPULATION PYRAMID is a two-dimensional graph showing the sex and age structure of a population. Charts are often an effective way of presenting information, but are susceptible to distortion if not designed with care. Compared to tables, some loss of detail is involved in a chart.

See H. Zeisel, *Say It With Figures* (1948).

MB

**taboo.** First used in the West by Captain Cook in his description of the Polynesian institution called *tafoo* or *tapu* which involved the proscription of contact with valued persons, objects or places, non-observance of which resulted in sanctions of either a direct supernatural kind or mediated by human action. The term has been extended from its original context to apply to a complex of institutions and practices in many different cultures in which avoidance is enjoined — objects that may not be touched, comestibles that may not be eaten, places that may not be entered, words that may not be spoken, things that may not be seen or done — because of the danger or pollution which may result from contact.

Taboo has been the focus of considerable debate. A widely respected contemporary approach is that of Mary Douglas (*Purity and Danger*, 1966), who sees taboos as aspects of human intellectual attempts to grasp the confusion of the cosmos. All human societies erect systems of classification which divide phenomena into a range of mutually exclusive categories. However, not all phenomena fall unambiguously into these constructs. Such phenomena, threatening the very basis of human grasp of the world in societies where there are no alternative cognitive systems, are simply excluded from the world. Thus where human beings are seen to produce single births and animals multiple births, twins may be taboo and may even be killed at birth. Where creatures that fly have feathers while creatures that have no feathers do not fly, bats may be taboo and therefore unclean. Where women have long hair and men short hair, long-haired men may be the object of moral outrage and even forcible attempts to restore the exhaustiveness of the categories by physical assault and hair-cutting.

Such cognitive systems assume that the categories are immutable, thus nature has produced anomalies which should be eliminated. This constrasts directly with science, in which the cognitive system and its categories are merely tentative, designed to find the underlying order of the cosmos. On the scientific view there can be no anomalies in nature, only mistakes in the conceptual system.

Douglas's approach is a powerful solution to the problem of the nature of taboo, although it may not account for all cases which fall under this loose rubric.

See also MEDICAL PROFESSION.

RW

**take-off.** Coined by W.W. Rostow in his influential *Stages of Economic Growth* (1960). His model of industrial development delineates five stages: traditional society, the preconditions for take-off, the take-off, the drive to maturity, and high mass consumption. Where the other stages involve gradual cumulative changes, take-off is marked by such a rapid increase in the rate of change as to amount to a leap forward.

AH

**TAT (Thematic Apperception Test).** A PROJECTIVE TEST widely used clinically and in social science research for the assessment of PERSONALITY. The subject is presented in turn with 20 black-and-white cards depicting vague scenes of human action, and is invited to say what is happening, what led up to it, and what followed. These narrative responses are typically interpreted by attributing to the subjects elements of what is projected onto the central characters in the stories. Several scoring systems exist, but the ability of the technique to elicit coherent patterns is its main strength.

The test was developed in the later 1930s by H.A. Murray at the Harvard Psychological Clinic expressly for personality research on normal subjects. In social science research, it has been used in studies such as McClelland's of ACHIEVEMENT MOTIVATION, and in investigating the social aspects of personality it has proved perhaps more useful than the RORSCHACH ink-blot test, mainly used in clinical context.

JL

**Tau-b.** See ASSOCIATION, COEFFICIENTS OF.

**tautology.** See ANALYTIC.

**Tavistock Institute of Human Relations.** See SOCIO-TECHNICAL SYSTEM.

**tax.** A mechanism for transferring money from the private sector to the Government. The object to which a tax is applied is known as the tax base: thus direct taxes are levied upon INCOME and WEALTH, whereas indirect taxes take the form of surcharges on the prices of goods and services. The sources of tax revenue in the UK in 1979/80 were: taxes on personal income (59%), taxes on company income (7%), taxes on the transfer of wealth (2%), and taxes on goods and services (32%).

Taxation policy has three main objectives. (1) It is part of macro-economic stabilization policy to regulate cycles in economic activity and avoid excessive UNEMPLOYMENT and INFLATION (see KEYNESIAN ECONOMICS;

MONETARISM). (2) It is used to influence the allocation of goods and services. It directs expenditure away from highly taxed to less highly taxed goods. Also, tax revenues are used to finance the direct SUPPLY of various goods and services (see MERIT GOODS; PUBLIC GOODS). (3) It is used to redistribute economic resources (notably income) between different groups within society.

A tax is described as progressive if the proportion of the tax-payer's income paid in tax increases as income increases. Conversely a tax is regressive if the proportion of income paid in tax falls as income increases. If the proportion remains constant, the tax is described as proportional. Generally, direct taxes tend to be more progressive than indirect taxes. In the UK income tax system, the marginal income tax rate increases with income, whereas the major expenditure tax — Value Added Tax — remains a constant proportion of the price of a good irrespective of the quantity bought or the income of the buyer. In studying the effect of a tax, it is necessary to distinguish between those taxpayers who have legal responsibility for paying a tax and those who bear the final burden. For example, a tax may be levied on a firm but it may be able to pass on the tax in higher prices to its CONSUMERS. Tax incidence refers to the point at which the tax burden finally rests.

RR

**Taylor, Frederick William** (1856-1915). 'Taylorism', especially in continental European countries, is often used as a synonym for SCIENTIFIC MANAGEMENT. Taylor himself resisted this practice and it is more illuminating to regard him as the best-known figure in the 'efficiency movement' whose first major impact occurred in the USA shortly after 1900. Family background instilled into Taylor the principal values of the PROTESTANT ETHIC, particularly regularity of habits, individualism and obsession with time, and childhood experiences may have been largely responsible for the exaggeration of such traits to almost psychotic proportions (throughout his life Taylor suffered from severe psychosomatic illness). Yet no appeal to psychological explanation is required to understand the interest aroused by his 'system' of rationalized work and organ-

ization. His early attempts to reorganize tasks, payment methods, and industrial discipline in the 1880s at the Midvale Iron Works were strikingly successful in raising output. There were followed by a period of consultancy at the Bethlehem Steel Company, where Taylor continued this work, as well as some spectacularly successful research into mechanised steel-cutting. It was here that he conducted his experiments with a Dutch immigrant labourer, Schmidt, whom Taylor described as possessing the mentality of an ox, albeit a singularly money-oriented one. Following Taylor's revised working routine, this subject increased the quantity of pig-iron that he loaded daily on to railway trucks by around 400 per cent. For this, he received 60 per cent higher wages, but appeared content with the arrangement.

Subsequently, Taylor became an independent consultant, propagandist, and defender of Scientific Management, as trade unions and humanitarians mounted an increasingly vocal attack on his methods and those attributed to him. Taylor was obliged to fight battles on several fronts simultaneously, for the majority of 'experts' in scientific management who suddenly appeared had no ability or intention of implementing his 'system' in full. Above all, they eliminated the incentive payments for performing rationalized work on which Taylor insisted. Taylor castigated employers and managers for being duped by these 'charlatans', and the paranoid element in his character responded to the growing public controversy that focused around his name and imputed aims. Finally, Congress was obliged to mount an enquiry into 'Efficiency Systems'.

Frequently dismissed as typical of both capitalist and technocratic ideologies, the social philosophy inherent in Taylor's corpus of writings is indeed confused, and its grasp of sociological realities is weak. But his impact as a practitioner, and as a symbolic figure, was sufficient to dramatize core problems of technical rationality shared by all industrial societies.

See also BUREAUCRACY; ORGANIZATION.

MR

**technological society.** General and rather loose term to describe the application of science and technology to the solution of economic, social and political problems of advanced societies. For some, the progress of society lies precisely in the extent to which technological solutions are found to society's problems and although the so-called Technocracy Movement (which had some success between the wars in the USA) now appears very outdated, there are still many for whom science and technology remain the most important driving forces in modern civilization. In recent years, however, and particularly since the dropping of the atom bombs on Hiroshima and Nagasaki, the raising of public concern on environmental pollution, and widespread fears about the effects of civilian and military uses of nuclear power, the idea of the technological society has come to bear an increasingly péjorative image. This is well summarized by J. Ellul, *The Technological Society* (1965) and by large numbers of other works documenting the limitations of technological solutions. The technologist E. Schumacher in *Small is Beautiful* (1973) argued that the proper strategy was to adapt whatever technological facilities were available to the scale appropriate to the human needs that the technology was supposed to be satisfying. His notion of 'intermediate technology' has proved to be of value, particularly to THIRD WORLD countries, but this strategy runs counter to the expansionary requirements of the multinational corporations. The rapid depletion of natural resources in the world today has, paradoxically, encouraged proponents of the technological society to seek ever more ingenious technological solutions, and encouraged opponents of the technological society to predict its inevitable demise.                                    LS

**teleology.** Once the claim that the universe is pursuing some purpose laid down by God, the world spirit, destiny, historical necessity etc. Now used to distinguish EXPLANATIONS in terms of purposes and goals from those in terms of antecedent CAUSES. The relation between these two sorts of explanation is a matter of considerable dispute. Some writers argue that the former are merely a shorthand

for, and are REDUCIBLE to, the latter; others hold that the behaviour of at least human beings and the higher animals, if not other organisms, can be given a basic explanation in teleological terms. An important object of contention is the use of FUNCTIONAL explanations in sociology, for these often imply that societies as a whole have purposes.

See C. Taylor, *The Explanation of Behaviour* (1964).

WO

**territorial justice.** A concept developed by the geographer David Harvey in *Social Justice and the City* (1973). It is a principle for guiding the allocation of resources in such a way that the needs of the population within each given territory are met, inter-territorial multiplier effects are maximized, and extra resources are allocated to help overcome special difficulties stemming from the physical and social environment.

See COST-BENEFIT ANALYSIS.

HN

**Terror.** See PURGES AND TERROR.

**Thanatos.** See PSYCHOANALYSIS.

**thaumaturgy.** The production of miracles. Bryan Wilson has used this term to refer to one of the major forms of religious response to the world (see also CONVERSIONISM; INTROVERSIONISM; MANIPULATIONISM; REVOLUTIONISM). The advanced industrial world, in its preoccupation with causal efficacy, its reliance on empirical investigation and its faith in science, is less conducive to the emergence of thaumaturgy than technologically simpler societies, where movements of a magically oriented type are extremely common.

Such movements direct themselves primarily to the relief of specific and immediate ills and misfortunes such as childlessness, the cure of sickness, the improvement of crops or livestock, or relief from the threat of witches and socerers. Witch-finding movements have been common in Africa. For example, the Mcape or Bamucapi movement observed in Nyasaland in 1934 involved the sale of a magical powder, consumption of which gave protection from witchcraft. In simpler societies, a magical element is often a part of more organized forms of religion such as the Aladura Church in Ghana, Nigeria, Sierra Leone and Liberia, whose 'Cross-Bearers' can heal the sick and raise the dead. It forms an important part even of more revolutionist movements, such as the Hau Hau which emerged among the Maoris of New Zealand in the 1860s, in response to the constant encroachment of the white settlers. The Hau Hau believed themselves possessed of a magical shout, which would ward off bullets.

In the industrial world, thaumaturgical sects sometimes appear in the form of healing movements which appeal to desperate and unsophisticated social groups. Various types of 'psychic' or 'spiritual' healer flourish; snake-handling churches still thrive in the rural southern states of America, but the major thaumaturgical religious movement in the West is Spiritualism, which involves contact with the spirits of the dead through the agency of a medium. In the context of the Catholic Church, thaumaturgy is a major aspect of such shrines as Lourdes.

See MAGIC; WITCHCRAFT.

See B. Wilson, *Magic and the Millennium* (1973).

RW

**theodicy.** Originally a theological concept used to refer to the problem posed by the co-existence of a god that was all-knowing, all-powerful, and all-benevolent, and the fact of evil and suffering in the world. The problem was most acute in the case of apparently underserved suffering. WEBER took over this term (and others such as CHARISMA) in his analysis of world religions, and broadened it in scope to apply to (1) the problem posed by suffering, injustice and imperfection; and also (2) the solution offered by religion and ideas related to this problem. Some writers (e.g. Obeyesekere) advocate restricting the term to the first usage, while others (e.g. Peter Berger) employ it in the second sense. The need to endow suffering and evil with moral meaning and purpose is an issue addressed in various ways by religions. Christianity offers various resolutions to the

problem of theodicy: misfortune may be a means of testing faith or of returning the thoughts of a backslider to God; it may be an attack by the Devil; the visiting of iniquity to the seventh generation; or insignificant in comparison to eternal glories and rewards. Non-christian resolutions to the problem of theodicy may cite WITCHCRAFT, inauspicious astrological formations, or the act of evil spirits as the cause. The Hindu and Buddhist doctrine of Karma explains present misfortune and suffering by reference to deeds performed in a previous life (i.e. misfortune is only apparently undeserved). Resolutions to the problem of theodicy are of varying scope. Witchcraft explains a particular occurrence of misfortune but leaves unresolved the explanation for the existence of the evil of witchcraft. The power of the devil does not resolve the problem of theodicy entirely if God is held to be all-powerful (why does he permit the devil to act in this way?). Moreover these two solutions do not resolve the question of why misfortune falls upon this particular person. The doctrine of Karma is a particularly powerful resolution of the problem of theodicy since it is construed as merely a universal law of cause and effect (thus not leaving any ill-motivated agent still to be explained) and accounting for all misfortune as a consequence of prior acts by the sufferer (there is no unjust suffering, we have brought it all upon ourselves by actions in our previous lives). See CASTE.                      RW

**theory.** A body of law-like generalizations, logically linked to one another, which can be used to EXPLAIN empirical phenomena (compare MODEL). But, as has been stressed by 'linguistic' philosophers of science, most theories are not as logically neat as their idealized representations in text books. In the social sciences the term 'theory' is used very loosely, and may mean no more than a set of assumptions or concepts, or a relatively abstract inquiry distinguished from empirical research or practical recommendations. Books and courses on 'sociological theory' generally use the term in these looser senses.

See R. Merton, *Social Theory and Social Structure* (1949, enlarged edition 1968, part I).

WO

**Third. World.** This term has five referents.
(1) Geographically, it refers — somewhat
imprecisely — to the countries on the continents of Africa, Asia and Latin America. (2)
Economically, it refers, equally loosely, to all
the 'poor' countries of the world. (3) Ideologically, it captures the self-awareness of
newly emerging nations on these continents
wishing to develop an economy and society
different from the 'models' presented by the
Western capitalist countries (First World)
and the state socialist countries of Eastern
Europe (Second World). (4) Institutionally,
it refers to the association of countries on
these continents, traceable from the
Bandung Conference of African and Asian
countries (1955), which laid the foundation
for the 'Non-Aligned Movement', to the
formation of a caucus group of Third World
countries at the first UNCTAD conference
(1964) when Latin American countries
joined with Asian and African countries in
presenting advanced countries with a determined negotiating 'bloc' (Group of 77). (5)
Politically, the term refers to a Third Force in
international political relations against the
backdrop of the cold war between East and
West, communism and capitalism.

Recent economic differentiation of the
Third World between rapidly growing
economies (OPEC and so-called Newly
Industrializing Countries), and stagnating or
declining economies (FOURTH WORLD) has
eroded the institutional cohesion of the
member countries, and shed doubt on the
usefulness of the concept as a descriptive
term of existing realities in the world political
and economic order.

See the debate between Worsley, Muni and Love in
*Third World Quarterly* 1979 and 1980.

AH

**Thomas, William Isaac** (1863-1947). One
of the most important figures in the CHICAGO
SCHOOL OF SOCIOLOGY. Born in Russell
County, Virginia, the son of a farmer and
Methodist preacher, Thomas majored in
literature and classics at the University of
Tennessee during the 1880s before studying
at Göttingen and Berlin (1888-9). Starting
his academic career, he became 'strongly
impressed by Spencer's sociology', and was
one of the first students in the newly

established sociology department of Chicago
University. In 1895 he was an instructor, by
1910 a professor, but in 1918 he was forced
to leave after a public scandal. During this
period he was at his most productive and
influential, especially through his collaborative work with F. Znaniecki, *The Polish
Peasant in Europe and America, 1918-
1920.* This is now remembered less for its
developed theory (the four wishes — recognition, new experience, mastery and security
— through which men form societies; the
three personality types — Philistine,
Bohemian and creative) than for its seminal
concepts and methods: the PERSONAL DOCU-
MENT, the LIFE HISTORY, and the DEFINITION
OF THE SITUATION. In 1927, he served as
president of the American Sociogical
Society.

See M. Janowitz (ed.), *W.I. Thomas on Social
Organization and Social Personality* (1966).

KP

**time preference.** A person's preference for
benefits in the present compared with
benefits in the future. Positive time preference implies that a person will value a £ or $
accruing today more highly than a £ or $
accruing in the future even if there is no risk
associated with the future £ and $ and zero
INFLATION. It may be a fundamental psychological trait for a person to prefer instant to
deferred gratification, and/or that most
people expect their INCOMES to increase
through time, and as increments of income
are subject to diminishing marginal UTILITY,
a £ or $ in the future will yield less utility than
one today. The second reason is more widely
held by economists, and provides the rationale for DISCOUNTING. The time preference
rate expresses the rate at which future costs
and benefits are discounted. In public sector
project investment appraisal (see COST-
BENEFIT ANALYSIS) a social time preference
rate is sometimes employed which is less than
the private time preference rate. A government which acts as a custodian of the
interests of future generations should attach
more importance to the future (i.e. will
discount it less heavily) than private individuals acting separately would tend to do.

RR

**Titmuss, Richard Morris** (1907-72). One of the most influential figures in the academic study of social policy in Britain. The son of a small farmer, he left school at the age of 15 and after a job as an office boy at Standard Telephones worked in the insurance industry. Though still in insurance until 1942 he had started to write books and articles a number of years earlier.

His written work ranged widely, dealing with issues like poverty, health care and migration. Much was contained in essays, though from the 1950s he published a number of influential books, such as *Problems of Social Policy* (1950), *Essays on the Welfare State* (1958), *Income Distribution and Social Change* (1962), and *The Gift Relationship* (1970).

Appointed Professor of Social Administration at the LSE in 1950, he was responsible for developing the strength of his own department and the subject more generally. He was also influential in British politics through his association with the Labour Party, and served on a number of government committees, such as the Finer Committee on one-parent families. He was Deputy Chairman of the Supplementary Benefits Commission from 1968 to 1973.

In his writing, Titmuss developed strong support for a basic universalist system of social services, though by themselves such services were not a solution for inequality and injustice. While he accepted that selective provision could have a role to play (see SELECTIVITY) he opposed the use of MEANS-TESTED benefits.

See also GIFT RELATIONSHIP.

MPJ

**Tocqueville, Alexis de** (1805-59). French statesman, historian, political thinker and sociologist. A member of an old landed family, Tocqueville entered the magistracy as a young man. Ostensibly to study the American prison system, he visited the United States in 1831-2. He later became a member of the Chamber of Deputies, and after the Revolution of 1848 served for a time as Foreign Minister. After Louis Napoleon's *coup d'état* of 1851 he withdrew from public life. Principal works: *Democracy in America* (Part I, 1835; Part II, 1840); *Recollections* of the 1848 Revolution

and his own period in government (published posthumously in 1893); *The Ancien Régime and the French Revolution* (1856). He also published reports on prisons, slavery and colonialism.

*Democracy in America* is the classic discussion of the social foundations of DEMOCRATIC politics. Tocqueville constantly compares the over-centralized and over-powerful apparatus of the French STATE with the (then) very decentralized mode of government in the USA. He emphasizes the importance for the maintenance of LIBERTY and democracy of the myriads of voluntary associations by which Americans ran their affairs. He was not, however, entirely uncritical of America, for he recognized the dangers of 'the tyranny of the majority', and foresaw that SLAVERY in the South would precipitate a crisis for American democracy. The second part of *Democracy in America* contains a brilliant discussion of the cultural consequences of democracy — its effects on literature, the arts and sciences, and manners — which constitutes a veritable sociology of knowledge (see KNOWLEDGE, SOCIOLOGY OF).

*The Ancien Régime* is a study of the origins of the French Revolution. Toqueville depicts the growing power of the state machine under the *ancien régime*. All men, were made relatively equal in their subjection to it, but his analysis of French class structure also demonstrates the obstacles which prevented the emergence of a strong MIDDLE CLASS conscious of its common interests.

Tocqueville's writings still stand as models of the COMPARATIVE METHOD. Though he avoided over-abstraction they contain many general insights: they are one of the main sources of the theory of MASS SOCIETY, and his discussion of why REVOLUTIONS tend to occur not when social conditions are at their worst but when they are improving is recognized as an early statement of the principle of RELATIVE DEPRIVATION.

SJM

**Tönnies, Ferdinand** (1855-1936). German sociologist who coined the terms GEMEINSCHAFT and GESELLSCHAFT. Born in Schleswig-Holstein, northern Germany, the son of a prosperous farmer. Related through his mother to a family of Lutheran pastors, Tönnies became increasingly interested in the unifying potential of a new universal religion. He attended the universities of Strasburg, Jena, Bonn, Leipzig and Tubingen, receiving a doctorate in classical philology in 1887. His postgraduate studies were in Berlin and London. In 1881 he became a *privatdozent* for philosophy at Kiel University where he occupied first a chair in economics and statistics (1913-16) and then, in 1921, became Professor Emeritus in sociology. With SIMMEL and Sombart he founded the German Sociological Society, acting as President from 1910 until 1933, and also joined the American Sociological Society. He participated in the Hobbes and Spinoza Societies and the Society for Ethical Culture. He was interested in social problems and political philosophy and supported Irish and Finnish independence movements; in 1933 he lost his professorship at Kiel because of his attacks upon Nazism and anti-Semitism.

Tönnies's major work, *Gemeinschaft und Gesellschaft* (1887), was published in English as *Fundamental Concepts of Sociology* (USA, 1940) and *Community and Association* (UK, 1955). He regards social phenomena as products of human thought and will: social groups express the collective will of their members through NORMS and rules. He distinguishes two types of will differing in their relationship to means and ends. Essential or Natural Will (*Wesenwille*) is instinctive, exhibiting varying degrees of RATIONALITY, arises from innate drives, habits, or the value *per se* of the action willed, and corresponds to the affectual, traditional and value-rational orientations in WEBER's typology of social ACTION. Under Natural Will, social groups arise because individuals value their interrelationships *per se*. Tönnies's Rational or Arbitrary Will (*Kurwille*), like Weber's purposive-rational orientation, implies conscious selection of an act as means appropriate to an end. Social relationships arise instrumentally in the pursuit of common goals. Rational Will is typical of the upper and business classes, scientists, persons in authority, men and older people. Natural Will is typical of peasants, workers, women and young people. This concept was influenced by Schopenhauer and Wilhelm Wundt, and Rational Will by HOBBES and natural law philosophy.

Preoccupied with the transition from FEUDALISM to industrial capitalism, Tönnies distinguishes '*gemeinschaft*' (community) and '*gesellschaft*' (association, society). They are widely used today, usually in their German form. They are IDEAL TYPES denoting forms of social order and relationships. *Gemeinschaftien* relationships and societies arise from Natural Will and share a 'community of fate' or total life in which relationships *per se* are valued. Confident, affective, co-operative social ties based on intimate personal contact are cemented by common values which are upheld by customary law and religious sanctions. The socio-economic nexus centres upon reciprocity, barter, and exchange. Under these conditions relationships of equality may be found, as well as relationships of domination. Tönnies looked at the family, the neighbourhood, and friendship groups as examples of *gemeinschaftlich* relationships. With industrialization there is an increasing shift towards *gesellschaftlich* relationships based upon Rational Will. Such relationships are segmented, transitory, instrumental, contractual, impersonal and impoverished. Intimate personal contact is replaced by contact between strangers, traditional reciprocal forms of exchange are replaced by depersonalized ties based upon contract, contractual delimitation of conflict replaces a strong common morality, secular sanctions replace religious sanctions, and statute law becomes more important than customary law. The formal equality of all citizens co-exists with delegated authority. The city and the STATE were examples of *Gesellschaft*.

Tönnies initially intended to use the two to analyse the historical evolution of societies from primitive agrarian communism through contemporary capitalism to a socialist *Gemeinschaft* of the future, which might culminate in the formation of a world-wide political system. He never fulfilled this programme, focusing primarily upon the impact of INDUSTRIALIZATION within Western Europe, the formation of the modern state and the growth of contemporary social problems with the breakdown in traditional structures.

Tönnies's contributions include the analysis of the effects of business cycles, demographic problems, and social problems such as CRIME and suicide.

*Gemeinschaft und Gesellschaft* was not widely read until the interwar years, when it began to exert widespread influence upon sociology. Tönnies believed he had successfully incorporated the rival contractualist and organicist conceptions of society in his theory of social change, but was criticized by DURKHEIM for too UTILITARIAN a conception of INDUSTRIAL SOCIETY and a corresponding neglect of its need for moral solidarity. Tönnies's voluntarism has affinities with developments in PHENOMENOLOGY. His emphasis upon the dehumanizing effects of industrialization and urbanization is echoed in the work of Wirth (see URBANISM) and in the modern concept of an alienated MASS SOCIETY. Tönnies's influence upon anthropology was revived by REDFIELD in the 1940s. Tönnies helped to shape the ideas of the CHICAGO SCHOOL in the 1930s, and his influence is reflected in the work of MacIver and COOLEY, rural and urban sociology, and in community studies.

JW

**totalitarianism.** The term 'totalitarian' was first used by Mussolini to describe the distinctive FASCIST conception of the state as the supreme value which alone gave the individual life any significance. Subsequently it came to be used by political sociologists to characterize features common to the political systems of Hitler's Germany and Stalin's Russia. Both were seen to differ from previous dictatorships in the total claims made by the state over society, in the politicization of all aspects of social life, and in the degree of control exercised over individual behaviour through a combination of pervasive ideological manipulation and ruthless terror. They stood at the opposite pole from LIBERALISM with its idea of the limited state, its PLURALISM of parties and opinions, its INDIVIDUALISM etc.

The idea of totalitarianism correctly identifies the novel powers available to 20th-century states to control their populations. However, the degree of control actually exercised by these regimes was nothing like as total as the term implies; it obscures the very different aims and dynamic of the Nazi and STALINIST systems by its assumption that the striving for total power is a self-evident goal; it was popularized during the Cold War period, when the origin of Fascism in a distinctively capitalist crisis became obscured. As an explanatory concept totalitarianism fails, yet as an image of the frightening possibilities towards which modern states can degenerate, and in certain respects historically have done, it offers a salutary warning. In this Encyclopedia STATE SOCIALISM is preferred as a descriptive label for societies like the USSR, FASCISM for Nazi Germany and Mussolini's Italy.

See also SECT.

DB

**totemism.** A complex of ideas thought to involve a relationship between a social group, such as a clan, and some class of natural objects, usually an animal or plant, the totem. The totem was believed to be sacred for the social group, such that it might not be killed or eaten except under ritual circumstances. Members of the group were believed to regard themselves as descended from the totem, which also protected them from danger. The emblem of the totem was employed as the symbol of the group, which united in collective ritual to ensure the increase of the totemic animal or plant.

DURKHEIM used these elements as the basis of his theory of the origins and function of religion (see FUNCTIONAL THEORIES OF RELIGION). He argued that the origins of religion are to be found in totemism and believed that beginning as the badge of the clan the totemic emblem came to possess mysterious and supernatural powers when the native people were inspired by the emotional 'effervescence' of collective ritual. Totemism, and therefore religion, was a means by which social groups represented the powers of society which appeared external to, and constraining upon, the individual, and integrated the social group.

Many later commentators, such as RAD-CLIFFE-BROWN began to question the degree to which totemism could be seen as a single phenomenon. He argued that totems represented valued elements in the life of the society, such as important food sources.

Goldenweiser argued that totemic ideas were not as universal as formerly thought, nor did they always possess the syndrome of characteristics originally thought; he argued that totemism had its origin in the need for social groups to distinguish themselves from each other.

One of the more controversial approaches was FREUD's *Totem and Taboo* (1913). Freud presents a mythological account of the origins of religion and culture, which he believed to lie in the Oedipus complex. Freud explained clan exogamy, INCEST taboos, and the prohibition against eating the clan totem in terms of a myth of the primal horde in which the father monopolized the available women, rousing the envy of the sons who eventually rose up and killed and ate him. Overcome with remorse and guilt they henceforth prohibited sexual contact with their female kin, and periodically . commemorated their deed by a ceremonial sacrifice and meal of the father-substitute, the totem. Freud is suggesting that culture (and religion as part of culture) arises from the frustration and repression of instinctual desires. He is identifying the distinctive features of human as contrasted with animal life, of culture contrasted with nature.

LÉVI-STRAUSS is engaged in a similar enterprise in his approach to totemism. He argues that the assimilation of totemism to religion is a mistake and that previous accounts have tended to conflate together disparate phenomena. The relationship between natural species and human groups is part of the classificatory procedures by which primitive peoples classify and make cognitive sense of the natural and social world. Its forms derive from universal underlying structural features of the human mind.

RW

**trade union.** According to the WEBBS (1920), a 'continuous association of wage earners for the purpose of maintaining and improving the conditions of their working lives'. Standard distinctions between craft unions (grouping 'labour aristocrats' in skilled trades), industrial unions (organizing all workers in one industrial branch), and general unions (federations of workers from numerous industries and occupations), are useful in sociological anlysis (especially one that is historically or internationally comparative). In case-studies, organizational and other specificities of particular unions may also loom large.

Sociologist's main interest in trade unionism relates to its broader social impact, or the bearing of internal trade union affairs on particular sociological hypotheses. The relationship of trade unionism to the formation of CLASS CONSCIOUSNESS is a particularly important theme. To what extent does trade unionism itself express, or relate to political expressions of class-consciousness? Different ideological traditions and forms of organization of trade unionism in different societies are an important point of departure, leading to a consideration of the deeper institutional and structural bases of such phenomena. A second perennial issue is related to the practical question of 'union democracy'. It derives from MICHELS's hypothesis that the internal dynamics of organizations in the labour movement (unions and radical parties) are subject to an 'iron law of oligarchy' whose outcome is the emasculation of an original radical programme, and the relative estrangement of rank-and-file members from the leadership.

See also INDUSTRIAL CONFLICT; INDUSTRIAL DEMOCRACY; ORGANIZATION; UNANTICIPATED CONSEQUENCES.        MR

**trade union consciousness.** According to LENIN (*What Is To Be Done?* 1902), that degree of consciousness of its own position and interests which the proletariat spontaneously achieves by its struggles for economic goals. Broadly, this is economism — striving to improve wages and conditions while leaving the wages system itself unaltered. It is the task of Communists, outside intellectuals, to bring to the working class political explanations of its struggles, thus developing in it a revolutionary CLASS CONSCIOUSNESS. His view that trade unionism falls a long way short of radical class consciousness is nowadays very widely accepted (but see SYNDICALISM).

See also FALSE CONSCIOUSNESS.

MMG, MM

**traditional.** In ordinary speech, a solemn version of custom, to which clings the prescriptive force of age-old continuity. But the meaning of the term — and more especially of its derivate 'traditional' — has expanded to include every trait of social organization, cultural orientation and individual behaviour which contrasts with 'modern(ity)'.

WEBER argued that since the 16th century Europe had been shaped by a cultural value system diametrically oppositional to that of medieval Europe or indeed any other existing civilization. The modern cultural value system was geared to rational action in the world, 'involving the explicit definition of goals and the increasingly precise calculation of the most effective means to achieve them'. This instrumental (or utility) RATIONALITY of the modern world had a religious basis in the inner-worldly asceticism characteristic of the PROTESTANT ETHIC. It contrasted with the 'substantive (or value) rationality' of the traditional world, where other-worldly orientated religious principles dictated modes of conduct designed to cherish and preserve social relations, beliefs and practices.

Weber's highly original IDEAL TYPE itself started a sociological 'tradition'. The contrast of tradition *versus* modernity became a much-elaborated theme, especially influential in studies of development and MODERNIZATION. Weighed down by substantive rationality, traditional people lacked all the fastmoving, goal-setting attitudes of modern man such as openness to new experience, readiness for social change, awareness of a diversity of opinion, a present and future time-perspective, aspirations and achievement orientation, forward planning, and a belief in a calculable world (see for example A. Inkeles in M. Werner, *Modernisation: The Dynamics of Growth*, 1966).

Quite independently from the Weberian focus on the different cultural and psychological orientations which separate modern from traditional man, social EVOLUTIONISM had already habitually contrasted 'modern' from 'primitive' or 'traditional' societies. Indeed, the very simplicity of the contrast encouraged a blurring of terms: simple, primitive or traditional was all the same, namely not 'modern'. Thus, in social structural terms 'traditional' societies were said to be small in size and simple in organization, unlike modern societies, which are large and complex. They are agricultural societies based on limited social division of labour and organized around an ascribed status structure: ROLES, obligations and privileges are assigned on the basis of sex, birth and descent, rather than on ACHIEVEMENT and merit. SOCIAL MOBILITY is limited: traditional societies are 'closed' societies.

PARSONS's contributions to NEO-EVOLUTIONARY theory, the Weberian and the evolutionary traditions merge into one overall theoretical structure.

AH

**trait.** A personality trait is an enduring, general characteristic of a person underlying a specific set of types of behaviour associated together in a single pattern and repeated over time. ATTITUDE and trait are not entirely distinct, but in general an attitude has a more specific object.

Early work on personality traits was done by ALLPORT, who compiled a list of 18,000 trait names in the course of his research. He distinguished common traits, shared by individuals to different degrees and abstract in nature, from individual traits, later called personal dispositions, identified with neuropsychic structures. The distinction between common and individual traits is retained by the quintessential trait-theorist, the British-born American psychologist R.B. Cattell. A student of the statistician Spearman in London, he used Spearman's technique of FACTOR ANALYSIS to identify traits underlying scores on numerous personality attributes. A common trait he identified with a general factor underlying numerous individual's scores, and an individual trait with a set of mutually inter-correlated attributes unique to that person. (See also EYSENCK; INTROVERSION-EXTRAVERSION.)

The trait approach to personality is primarily concerned with the identification and accurate and objective measurement of characteristics correlated with behaviour, in order to explain and predict what that behaviour will be. It is much less concerned with the inner life of the individual and theories of personality dynamics and development.

See DIMENSION; PERSONALITY.

JL

**transcendentalism.** Tendency in philosophy which, following KANT, asserts the dependence of our experience on *a priori* categories. The Kantian and post-Kantian use of the 'transcendental' should be distinguished from 'transcendent', used of entities such as gods or platonic forms which are 'beyond' rather than directly present in the world. Kant's transcendentalism does not go beyond (transcend) experience; it is prior to it but serves only to make experience possible. A transcendental argument aims to elucidate what must be the case for something to exist which is known to exist.

See A. Arato, 'The Neo-Idealist Defense of Intersubjectivity', *Telos* 1974.

WO

**transference.** See PSYCHOANALYSIS.

**transformational grammar.** See CHOMSKY.

**transnational.** Relationships which occur across, and without reference to, national boundaries. To be distinguished from international: relations between national actors. Most of the basic sociological theories of social development have been transnational. The classic theorists expected processes such as CAPITALISM, INDUSTRIALIZATION, MODERNIZATION and URBANIZATION to sweep across national boundaries almost without reference to them. Alternatively, most sociologists in practice discuss these abstract processes in relation to the experience of a single NATION-STATE — which comes to be equated implicitly with the term SOCIETY. In the second half of the 20th century these traditions cannot be sustained. The strength and structuring role of nation-states seems to have increased (if unevenly) as the WORLD SYSTEM has itself developed. In the field of international political economy, considerable debate now occurs over the relative strength of national *versus* transnational forces: are multi-national corporations transnational or are they the internationalization of the stronger national economies? are the acronymic world agencies (IMF, GATT etc) global actors or committees of national representatives? are regional organizations like the Common Market transnational power blocs or loose federations of nation-states? etc. The very identification of modern society has become problematic and fundamental re-thinking is now required.

See INTERNATIONAL DIVISION OF LABOUR.

MM

**triangulation.** A term invented by D.T. Campbell to suggest that a proposition which is confirmed by two independent sources of data is more convincing than one which is only confirmed by a single source. If a proposition can survive the onslaught of several imperfect measures (each with their own errors and biases) rather than a single measure, then the uncertainty of its interpretation is reduced. Triangulation is now commonly used to refer to the use of more than one method (e.g. the SOCIAL SURVEY ad PARTICIPANT OBSERVATION) to investigate a particular problem. It is linked to E.J. Webb's advocacy of unobtrusive measures and the critique of the interview and QUESTIONNAIRE as the sole sources of sociological data. Efforts in the social sciences at multiple confirmation often yield disappointing and inconsistent results. The ideal of multi-method confirmation is a simple one, widely used in other disciplines (e.g. HISTORICAL RESEARCH), but the difficulty of its achievement points to the inherent difficulty of achieving VALIDITY in any social MEASUREMENT.

See D.T. Campbell, 'Factors relevant to the validity of experiments in social settings', *Psychological Bulletin* 1957.

MB

**tribe** [tribalism, detribalization]. The meaning of this concept shifts uneasily with changing world views. Its earliest and possibly still most colloquial usage refers to a group of people who live in 'primitive' or even 'barbaric' conditions under a chief or headman. In the late 19th century, when the belief in EVOLUTIONISM accompanied colonial conquest and administration, anthropologists defined the social organization of overseas peoples to contrast it with 'modern' societies. The KINSHIP basis of social organization struck Henri Maine (*Ancient Law*, 1861) and Lewis H. Morgan (*Ancient Society*, 1877) as a significant contrast with the territorial foundation of the modern state (see TRADITIONAL). 'Tribe' came to mean a group connected through descent from a common ancestor, organized around an ascribed status structure, contrasted with the principle of voluntary contract which appeared salient in modern societies (see SOCIAL CONTRACT). These contrasts gained the concept of tribe the pejorative overtone of 'primitiveness'.

The needs of colonial administrators to count and classify subject people for taxation and government prompted social anthropologists in the beginning of this century to undertake more detailed study of social groups, especially in Africa. They traced ethnic origins and examined patterns of culture and language, both of which came to be included in the concept of 'tribe'. Of crucial importance in view of later controversies is that it was necessary for administrative puposes to assign individuals to social units larger than the village community which embraced, indeed enclosed, most people's daily lives. Villages might be loosely connected on the basis of common recognized descent, even language and customs, but rarely shared a common social purpose in activities such as trade and warfare. They were an ethnic cultural grouping, rather than a social, political or economic organization. Colonial administrators imposed administrative unity upon these cultural and ethnic groupings, creating and naming 'tribes'.

Nevertheless, in contemporary post-colonial Africa tribes do exist, and are relevant in the study or design of national development — despite the rhetoric wisdom of most African political leaders, as well as the deeply held conviction of many African writers. Indeed, social scientists everywhere have started to shun the word 'tribe', preferring the less politically sensitive 'ethnic group'. Yet the very fact that the colonial administration gave no recognition to what were perhaps only loosely connected ethnic and cultural groupings made the tribe an objective reality which has imposed limits to national development in post-colonial Africa.

*Tribalism.* The subjective awareness of one's membership of a tribe. As in any group dynamics, the sense of belonging and security associated with the 'we' group derives strength and vitality from the contrast and the conflict with the 'they' group, as SUMNER argued. Tribalism refers to tribal rivalries in the context of the fragile national alliances of contemporary African states. Paradoxically, inter-tribal conflict and warfare has increased since independence. For all the colonial powers 'creation' of the tribes, their mutual antagonism toward the colonial rulers held the people of diverse tribes together in a common cause which has not yet been replaced by allegiance to a national community.

*De-tribalization.* With the spread of modern (Western) values, of industrialization, and of urbanization with its associated phenomena of geographical and social mobility, tribal people increasingly participate in a wider, more generalized culture and in a plural social community. As participation and mobility reduce the degree of social cohesion of the tribe and the tribal commitment of the individual, we speak of de-tribalization.

AH

**Troeltsch, Ernst** (1865-1923). German philosopher, best known for his contributions to the sociology of religion. Born in Augsburg, the eldest son of a physician, Troeltsch studied theology at Erlangen, Gottingen and Berlin. From 1891 he lectured at Gottingen and Bonn, and in 1894 was appointed Professor at Heidelberg, where he taught for 21 years. In 1915 he moved to Berlin to teach philosophy. In his intellectual life he was influenced by KANT, Fichte, HEGEL and Schleiermacher, among others. In politics he was conservative and, like WEBER, initially supported German's military aims in World War I. After the war he helped to found the German Democratic Party.

In *The Social Teachings of the Christian Churches* (1912) Troeltsch was concerned with the interaction of material and ideal factors in the development of Christianity. He argued for the treatment of religious belief as an independent variable which should be located in a web of influencing material conditions. Christianity was characterized by two opposing tendencies — accommodation and protest — institutionalized in the CHURCH and the SECT. A less wellknown work, *Protestantism and Progress* (1906) is a contribution to the PROTESTANT ETHIC THESIS.

See also HISTORICISM.                           RW

**Trotsky, Leon** (1879-1940). Russian revolutionary and Communist theorist. Born in the Ukraine, Trotsky played a leading role in the St Petersburg Soviet of 1905 and the Bolshevik revolution of 1917. He was the founder of the Red Army and War Commissar throughout the Civil War. He led the opposition to Stalin both internally and, after his exile in 1929, from abroad; he was assassinated in Mexico on Stalin's orders. An outstanding writer and theoretician, Trotsky developed MARXIST thought in a number of directions. His theory of permanent REVOLUTION (*Results and Prospects*, 1906; *Permanent Revolution*, 1930) argued that the democratic revolution against Tsarism, led by the PROLETARIAT and PEASANTRY in the absence of a strong BOURGEOISIE, would be forced beyond its bourgeois content to become a socialist revolution. The construction of SOCIALISM itself, however, could only be achieved with help from the industrialized countries of Western Europe, and thus depended on the internationalization of the revolution. Stalin's idea of socialism in one country was the antithesis of this, involving the subordination of the international proletarian revolution to the power interests of the ruling stratum in the USSR. *The Revolution Betrayed* (1936) analysed STALINISM as the inescapable product of material and cultural underdevelopment and revolutionary isolation; the ruling BUREAUCRACY became the historical substitute for the proletariat in leading industrialization. It would require a second, political, revolution to abolish the

power and privileges of this parasitic stratum.

In the period up to 1933, Trotsky was one of the first Marxists to develop a cogent analysis of Nazism and a coherent united front strategy for preventing it (*What Next?* and *The Only Road*, 1932). His exclusion from influence in the COMMUNIST movement made his warnings of no avail. Among other intellectual achievements should be mentioned his development of Marxist historiography and literary criticism (e.g. *History of the Russian Revolution*, 1931; *Literature and Revolution*, 1923). Still awaiting rehabilitation in the USSR, Trotsky's influence continues to thrive in the West, both politically and theoretically.

                                               DB

**Twenty Statements Test.** A research tool pioneered by Manford Kuhn and the more 'scientific' SYMBOLIC INTERACTIONISTS (often called the Iowa School). It operationalizes the SELF by asking subjects to list the first twenty answers to the question 'Who am I?' that enter their heads. These are then coded, most frequently with distinctions organized around self categories generally agreed upon, such as woman or husband (consensual), and those much more ambiguous like 'happy' or 'bored' (subconsensual). It is sometimes called the 'Who am I' test.

The test is criticized for not adequately appreciating how the self changes in social contexts and is hence more appropriately studied through PARTICIPANT OBSERVATION. The 1964 and 1966 issues of the journal *Sociological Quarterly* contained various discussions of the Test, and of the Iowa School, by Kuhn, Tucker, Mulford and Salisbury, and Quarantelli and Cooper.

                                               KP

**Tylor.** See NEO-TYLORIANISM.

**typology.** See IDEAL TYPE.

# U

**unanticipated consequences.** People's actions have social consequences which they themselves did not foresee. This idea is prominent in the tragic drama of classical Greece and in the history of social thought it is found in Adam SMITH's 'invisible hand', and in HEGEL's 'cunning of Reason'. In modern sociology, it is associated especially with MERTON, in whose work it is a prominent *Leitmotiv*. The idea of unanticipated consequences is closely linked with the distinction between manifest and latent functions, also introduced by Merton (see FUNCTIONALISM).

Merton's extended and explicit discussion of unanticipated consequences in *Social Theory and Social Structure* has led to too narrow an interpretation of their place within sociological theory, because he focuses mainly on the special case of 'self-fulfilling prophecies'. These occur where people's actions are based on a false perception of a social situation, but have consequences which subsequently make that definition accurate. One of Merton's examples is of white American trade unions, which earlier in the 20th century often excluded blacks from union membership on the grounds that blacks accepted lower wages than whites, acted as blacklegs, and would not submit to union discipline. But if that were true, it was largely a consequnce of blacks being excluded from union membership; later they proved as good union members as whites.

Merton also mentions in passing the case of the 'suicidal' prophecy — really a 'self-contradicting prophecy' — where an erroneous perception of social realities leads to actions which have consequences opposite to those anticipated. One example is the Prohibition experiment in the USA: many Americans initially supported the banning of alcoholic drink because they wished to reform their cities and the liquor industry was linked with crime and corruption, but under Prohibition liquor production passed into the hands of gangsters, and crime and corruption were exacerbated.

But unanticipated consequences of action are of much more general theoretical significance. People's actions are likely to have unforeseen consequences whenever their perception and understanding of their social situation is inaccurate or incomplete. That is almost always, for the workings of social processes are rarely totally transparent to those involved, but are usually opaque. A better simile for unanticipated consequences than the boomerang implied by Merton is the image of ripples spreading outwards across a pool: the consequences of people's actions travel along chains of social interdependence until they lose sight of them. The longer and more complex the chains of interdependence, and the more advanced the DIVISION OF LABOUR, the more prevalent will be unanticipated consequences. In the modern world, localized events can have consequences for the lives of people in another hemisphere. Less obviously, opacity and unanticipated consequences will tend to be greater where power balances are relatively even. The larger the number of interdependent people, and the more equal their interdependence, the less likely is the outcome of their interweaving actions to

405

resemble the plans of any single person or group of people.

The study of unanticipated consequences in inseparable from the sociology of KNOWLEDGE. The way in which people understand social situations and social events, and therefore the assumptions on which they base their actions, depend upon the standard ways of thinking and speaking about them which are gradually developed in their society. These are in turn intimately connected with developments in social structure. For example, MARX argued that a prerequisite for the emergence of full CLASS CONSCIOUSNESS was the simplification of the lines of conflict between capital and labour — with the decline of the PETITE BOUR-GEOISIE and reduction of skilled to unskilled workers. The workings of the capitalist system had to become less opaque, more transparent, to permit workers to achieve an understanding of their common situation. Before then the connection between alternative courses of action and their consequences would be unclear, and that would inhibit united action.

It is one of the prime tasks of social science to clarify the workings of society, and thus enable hitherto unanticipated consequences to be anticipated. But does that mean that people change their behaviour when the unforeseen consequences of their actions are revealed to them? Not always. To say that consequences are unanticipated and unforeseen is not necessarily to say that they would have been unintended if recognized — people may be quite happy with the outcome of their actions, or they may feel quite indifferent to them: they do not necessarily care. Or they may be unable to change their actions because SOCIAL STRUCTURE limits the freedom of action of interdependent individuals. But sometimes the exposure of unanticipated consequences leads to people acting in new ways and to important implications for policy. For example, the economic theories of J.M. Keynes helped to reveal the unrecognized consequences of economic policies based on earlier theories, and Keynes provided an important tool for new government policies (see KEYNESIAN ECONOMICS).

JM

**unconscious.** See PSYCHOANALYSIS.

**underclass.** A term sometimes used for the poor who are also denied full participation or CITIZENSHIP in their societies. It may refer to employed workers who do the least desirable jobs and are also denied the basic legal, political and social rights of the rest of the labour force. Illegal migrant labourers are the most-cited example, but the term is sometimes extended to cover all or most of those in the 'secondary sector' of a 'dual' LABOUR MARKET. Alternatively, it may refer to particular groups whose POVERTY derives from their non-employment: the long-term unemployed, single-parent families, the elderly. Membership of these is often ascriptive: black or brown skin, females, the elderly. Such long-term poverty is felt to exclude them from the full life of an overall affluent community (see Townsend, *Poverty in the United Kingdom*, 1978). Some sociologists believe that the traditional WORKING CLASS is being increasingly stratified internally into an employed, institutionalized, unionized working class, sharing in the gains of modern capitalism, and an excluded underclass.                           CGAB, MM

**underdevelopment** [undevelopment]. It is controversial whether this refers to a state or a process of backwardness thought to be typical of the countries of Africa, Asia, and Latin America. The state of underdevelopment is conventionally measured in terms of a number of economic and social criteria. The economic criteria summarize the existing and potential wealth of a nation, including per capita income, annual growth rate, share of industrial activity and employment in total output and employment, degree of diversification in external trade etc. The social criteria assess the degree to which productive achievements are translated into improved standards of living of its people, and include measures of health, life-expectancy, education and, more recently, income distribution.

Underdevelopment is one of a pair, development and underdevelopment, indicating a continuum. The assessment of points on this continuum can only be relative. If the share of industrial activity in total output is 20 per cent in country X and its level of literacy is 10 per cent this can only be considered as indicating 'underdevelopment' if there are other countries where the share of industrial activity in total output is greater and literacy rates are higher, and if these levels are taken to be the 'reference-point'. Empirical referents for 'underdevelopment' are by virtue of a comparison with 'development'.

Critics argue that this epistemological weakness of the concept reveals its ideological bias: it is designed to sell to developing countries 'Western patent solutions to basic human needs' (Illich). The reliance on Western 'patent' solutions, from cars and trucks to Coca-Cola, refrigerators, cement factories, heart-transplant machines and schoolbooks, creates markets for Western products. The need to pay for these products ties the entire production and export structure of an underdeveloped country to that of the Western 'developed' ones. This two-way DEPENDENCE in a historically evolved pattern of unequal division of labour and exchange (UNEQUAL EXCHANGE) makes underdevelopment a process of becoming underdeveloped, rather than an original state of affairs, for which 'un-development' would perhaps be more accurate. Dependency critics claim that this process has continued since the 16th century and that internal developments in the societies overseas became disrupted, stunted and distorted, while those in the Western capitalist societies were greatly stimulated.

See H. Bernstein (ed.), *Underdevelopment and Development* (1979).

AH

**unemployment.** A situation that exists when some people who wish to work are unable to find employment. Thus it is involuntary. Unemployment tends to be categorized in terms of its causes. (1) Frictional unemployment refers to those workers who are temporarily unemployed as they move from one job to another. As this process cannot be synchronized perfectly, some frictional unemployment is an inevitable feature of a MARKET economy where workers either choose to change jobs or are redeployed. (2) Cyclical unemployment arises because of the well-known trade cycles in aggregate econ-

omic activity. Much government stabilization policy of the post-World War II period has aimed to reduce the amplitude of these cycles and hence the incidence of cyclical unemployment (see KEYNESIAN ECONOMICS). (3) Structural unemployment is caused by long-term changes in the pattern of DEMAND and/or the nature of production. Its impact is often severe because industries experiencing long-run decline tend to be concentrated in areas where there are few alternative employment possibilities. Regional policy — which seeks to attract new firms into these areas — and retraining schemes designed to provide the long-term unemployed with new skills are examples of government policies designed to alleviate structural unemployment. Recent commentators have expressed concern about the possible structural unemployment implications of the widespread introduction of microprocessors.

Unemployment statistics only record those workers who register for unemployment benefits; they do not include anyone who is unable to find work but does not so register. Married women who would like to work represent the largest group within this category; their unemployment is known as disguised unemployment.

RR

**unequal exchange.** Central to discussions of trade relationships between the advanced industrialized countries and the less developed countries.

The exchange between two parties is unequal when they exchange goods or services which are not of equivalent value. This begs the question: how does one define value? Broadly speaking, there are two contrasting perspectives: marginalist economists define value in terms of an 'exchange' or 'market' theory of value; Marxists define value in terms of a labour theory of value. For the former, value is a function of the laws that govern the formation of prices in a free, competitive, market; for the latter, it is a function of the cost of labour time. The two schools have come to different assessments of, and explanations for, the inequality in trade relationship between rich and poor countries. While few marginalists believe that inequality between rich and poor countries is a necessary feature of their exchanges, some have accepted that the trading position of less developed countries has deteriorated over a relatively long time period. The 'deterioration of the terms of trade argument' is associated with Prebisch and Singer (see R. Prebisch, *Towards a New Trade Policy for Development*, 1964, and H.N. Singer in *American Economic Review*, 1950). Poor countries typically export primary products (i.e. foodstuffs and raw materials) while importing manufactured goods from the advanced countries. However, in an economically growing and industrializing world, raw materials and foodstuffs experience a relative decline in demand as compared with manufactured products, because of: (1) substitution by industrial products and replacement by synthetics; (2) the income inelasticity of the demand for foodstuffs; (3) the declining ratio of raw material inputs to industrial outputs.

These are typical 'marginalist' arguments: they focus on the laws that govern the price formation in the markets of the specific commodities traded. Though the exchange between rich and poor countries is unequal, it is not fundamentally unequal, residing as it does in the nature of the commodities traded. As soon as poor countries develop and diversify their trade with the advanced countries, inequality will disappear. Unequal exchange here is associated with an unequal INTERNATIONAL DIVISION OF LABOUR which can be corrected by a 'new' division. Demands for such a new division have formed a main plank of less developed countries' demands for a New International Economic Order.

Within this group of economists there is a further distinction between those who see this international specialization as a 'natural' historical evolution and those who attribute it to political interventions in the world market (e.g. colonialism and neo-colonialist policies) which impose upon poor countries an international division of labour which is advantageous to the advanced world.

Prebisch also introduced a Marxist type of explanation of unequal exchange. His CENTRE-PERIPHERY model attributed the worsening trade terms in part to differential evolution of wages in rich and poor countries. During each period of prosperity, wage-earners in the rich countries obtain wage increases made possible by increases in productivity; unionization prevents these incomes from falling during phases of depression. But in the primary producing countries, the constant surplus of labour prevents both unionization and the increase of wages. The change in relative prices brought about by differences in the cost of labour should lead to an increased demand for exports from less-developed countries. But this is countered by Prebisch with reference to a long-term decline for the commodities produced by poor countries.

In A. Emmanuel's *Unequal Exchange* (1972), the differential evolution of wages becomes the fundamental cause of unequal exchange. He attaches little importance to demand factors in explaining the worsening terms of trade of poor countries. Applying Marx's labour theory of value to international exchanges, he argues that (1) the prices of goods produced in any country are determined mainly by the level of wages in that country: (2) the level of wages reflect historical and social conditions which vary in place and time; (3) equalization of wage costs at the international level is unlikely to occur, because of the immobility of the factor labour (in contrast to the mobility of the factor capital). Because advanced countries are more developed, their price of labour reflects the higher standard of living already obtained. Successful class struggles and labour emancipation have seen to it that what Marx called a 'historical' or 'ethical' wage has replaced the physiological wage still evident in less developed countries. This becomes a 'normal' wage, not easily relinquished, even during recession. No matter what poor countries produce, no matter how comparable their levels of productivity, their exports will always be non-equivalent in value compared with exports of advanced countries. Inequality of exchange increases with the passage of time because of the cumulative effect of interaction between wage levels and economic development. By transferring, through non-equivalent exports, a large part of their surplus to rich countries, poor countries deprive themselves of the means of accumulation and growth. Lack of economic growth creates stagnant and narrow domestic markets which discourage domestic investment, leading to substantial unemployment which depresses wages levels further, and so on.

Emmanuel's thesis has been hotly debated in Marxist studies of IMPERIALISM. One worrying implication was that it placed the workers of the advanced countries firmly in the camp of the exploiters. Their high wages keep the poor countries poor: 'people's imperialism' has become reality. Emmanuel denies the existence or relevance of class struggles inside industrialized countries, claiming that trade union struggles there are no more than a settlement of accounts between partners. A further implication of his thesis is that unequal exchange explains the supposed exploitation by rich of poor countries independently of and even prior to 'imperialist' exploitation. Exploitation is commercial, not a result of the rich countries' investments inside the poor countries. This does not acknowledge the role of production relations in reproducing the conditions necessary for these (unequal) exchange relations. If exchange is so unequal, why do poor countries continue to exchange cocoa and bananas for trucks and television sets? Who is doing the exploiting inside these countries? Who reproduces the labour ready to work for a 'physiological' wage? Why does the reserve army of unemployed not decrease through starvation, instead of increase? Critics point out that to answer these questions we must look not merely at exchange relations but also, and more importantly, at production relations inside the poor countries. These are complex structures made up of foreign-induced capitalist relations (e.g. the existence of wage-labour and of land as a saleable commodity) which dominate and exploit pre-capitalist relations (e.g. FEUDAL relations of servitude and communal ownership of land). Some writers (e.g. S. Amin, *Class and Nation: Historically and in the Present Crisis*, 1980) see the fundamental cause of exploitation in the interaction of capitalist with pre-capitalist production systems, which has a depressing effect on wage levels. The pre-capitalist subsistence sector subsidises wages paid in the foreign-dominated capitalist export sector, for example by performing the functions of

social security and feeding the worker's family on the land while he migrates to the capitalist sector in the towns. As a result of this 'super-exploitation' the commodities which the poor countries exchange embody hidden 'transfers of value' from the pre-capitalist sector. The capitalist sector inside the poor countries thus acts as a channel to drain the surplus from the pre-capitalist sector to pass it on to the advanced countries.

This leads to political positions and alliances radically different from Emmanuel's position. The articulation of capitalist with pre-capitalist sector requires the collaboration of local COMPRADOR classes willing to deputize for imperialism. Chiefs sell the land that is not theirs to sell, and so help turn tillers of the soil into mineworkers. State marketing boards compulsorily purchase staple foods from subsistence farmers to sell cheaply to the workers in the towns. The government outlaws or undermines unionization, while local entrepreneurs participate in joint ventures with textile manufacturers from overseas. The deep gulf between rich and poor is not caused by unequal exchange between commodities (as in marginalism), nor between countries (as in Emmanuel's thesis) but by exploitation between classes inside countries. Instead of national populist alliances against imperialist countries, what is needed is a democratic alliance of workers and peasants in poor countries against the imperialist alliance of their own bourgeoisie.

AH

**urbanism.** The culture of towns and cities. Its characteristics were put forward by Louis Wirth (1897-1952), a German-American sociologist and member of the CHICAGO SCHOOL, in his influential paper 'Urbanism as a Way of Life' (*American Sociological Review*, 1938). Wirth offers an ordered and coherent framework of theory which accounts for urban ways of life by discussing the major social characteristics of the city. These are: (1) *Size of population*. This promotes a greater social differentiation, expressed geographically in the formation of different neighbourhoods according to social CLASS, ETHNICITY etc. The size of population in cities also made relationships impersonal, superficial, transitory and segmental. All urban relationships tend to be utilitarian, producing one of the central paradoxes of urbanism — the tendency to create individual loneliness in the midst of huge crowds. (2) *Density.* Wirth drew from HUMAN ECOLOGY the view that increasing physical contact due to increasing population density, would, when combined with decreasing social contact, produce increasing social conflict in cities. (3) *Heterogeneity.* The urban population is more heterogeneous due to the increasing DIVISION OF LABOUR and greater mobility. Within this 'fluid mass' the individual is more likely to seek out other similar individuals in order to partake in collective action to effect social change. These characteristics of urbanism were regarded by Wirth as becoming culturally hegemonic and would eventually characterize the culture of even those who live in rural areas.

Wirth's ideas remain a benchmark for the discussion of urbanism, but they have been revised by subsequent research. Three criticisms are: (1) Wirth is describing not the culture of urbanism but the culture of capitalist industrialization, which is made most manifest in cities. This line of attack on Wirth is common among recent Marxist urban sociologists (Castells, Lojkine). (2) Wirth's characterization of urbanism is misfounded since urban neighbourhoods form a basis for GEMEINSCHAFT, communities consisting of personal, stable, face-to-face, meaningful relationships — in Herbert Gans's term, 'urban villages'. (3) The distinguishing feature of urbanism is the strong separation of the public and the private social world of the inhabitants of cities (Richard Sennett, influenced by ELIAS).

*Urbanization.* The process whereby an increasing proportion of the population of a society becomes congregated in towns and cites. It is a process which may or may not be associated with INDUSTRIALIZATION.

*Under-Urbanization.* Used to describe the process, common in Eastern Europe, whereby INDUSTRIALIZATION proceeds without commensurate urbanization. This entails the industrial labour force being drawn from the surrounding countryside creating a new class of peasant-workers.

HN

**urban managerialism.** An approach to the study of urban social and spatial inequality, associated with the work of R.E. Pahl (*Whose City?*, 1970) and others, which relates the 'spatial logic' of the city to the conscious decisions and policies adopted by the managers or gatekeepers of the urban system, either on their own account or agents, in controlling access to important resources and facilities. It is associated with the growth of interest in CORPORATISM during the 1970s.

HN

**utilitarianism.** As a moral doctrine, the view that all moral values are mutually commensurable and can (in principle) be weighted numerically. This has been taken to imply that there is ultimately only one moral value (pleasure, happiness, preference-satisfaction etc) and the utilitarian political injunction is that its aggregate/social magnitude be maximized. Utilitarianism is historically associated with the rise of political economy. Many early utilitarians embraced LIBERALISM as they believed that the state's minimal interference with individuals' rationally self-interested activities furnished the necessary conditions for maximization (see MILL). More recent technical refinements in utilitarian reasoning have demonstrated the theoretical possibility (anticipated by HOBBES) of 'market failure', that is, circumstances in which individuals freely pursuing maximizing activities will each secure a less valuable outcome than could be attained by their being coerced to co-operate. Attainment of a socially optimal result under such circumstances can thereby serve to justify, on utilitarian grounds, greater state intervention in social affairs. Within sociology, utilitarianism influenced SPENCER and was revived in EXCHANGE THEORY and rational choice theory (e.g. studies of VOTING). However, its appeal was strongly reduced by DURKHEIM's attack on SOCIAL CONTRACT theories in general.

See UTILITY.

HIS

**utility.** The subjective satisfaction or sense of well-being that a person obtains from consuming a good or service. Early classical economists such as Jeremy Bentham (1748-

1832) thought that utility was a measurable entity, but modern economists take the view that while it is possible for a CONSUMER to rank the states of utility associated with the consumption of different combinations of goods, it is not possible to measure them absolutely; that is, utility is amenable to ordinal but not cardinal MEASUREMENT. A fundamental proposition of consumer theory is that the utility (or BENEFIT) which an individual derives from consuming a good increases at a decreasing rate as the consumption of the good increases. This is known as the theory of diminishing marginal utility (or the diminishing marginal rate of substitution if it is expressed in terms of indifference curve analysis); this is the basis of the expectation that a person will DEMAND more of a good as its price falls. It is widely held that the marginal utility of income (see INCOME) also falls as a person's income rises. This has implications for the measurement of costs and benefits in COST-BENEFIT ANALYSIS where the money values placed upon costs and benefits by individuals with different incomes are used as a basis of valuation.

See PARETO.                                    RR

**Utopia.** From the Greek for 'nowhere'. First used by Thomas More in 1516 as the name for an imaginary and perfect society, this term was used by MANNHEIM for 'all situationally transcendent ideas ... which in any way have a transforming effect upon the existing historical-social order'. Utopia differs from other types of ideology in containing the unfulfilled tendencies of the age rather than being simply an intellectualized justification of the existing social order.

Utopian communities are intentionally formed collectivities to realize the perfect social order and ideal social relationships. A secular example is Robert Owen's New Harmony founded in the early 19th century.

Other communities were founded on the basis of the social thought of Charles Fourier and of Etienne Cabet. In more recent times, utopian communes were founded in large numbers during the late 1960s and early 1970s, often on ANARCHIST principles, but with a wide range of ideological bases, even including the behaviourist psychologist B.F. Skinner's reinforcement theory of learning, as presented in his utopian novel, *Walden Two*. Most of these have survived no more than a few years. Of greater longevity have been religious utopian communities, such as the Oneida Community (see ANTINOMIANISM). Bryan Wilson (see SECTS) identifies utopianism as one type of sectarian response to the world. It differs from INTROVERSIONISM in encouraging withdrawal from an evil world in order to found a better model of society which will convert the world progressively to its evident superiority.

MARX and ENGELS criticized the early socialists as utopian on the grounds that SOCIALISM was the product of historical development, not of theorists' blueprints. The proper starting point for social theory was not the elaboration of ideal schemes for the future, but the scientific analysis of the present and the tendencies implicit in it. Yet they could not avoid giving some idea of what a socialist or communist order would be like, and this in turn has been criticized as utopian. For conservatives, any idea of radical or revolutionary social change is utopian: it must generate as many evils as it eliminates. This use of the term as a general derogatory concept confuses quite different kinds of alternative thinking. Properly, utopian theorizing is precisely about 'nowhere'; an exercise in literary imagination rather than social engineering, its aim is to heighten the critical consciousness of its readers, rather than provide a precise blueprint for implementation.

DB, RW

# V

**validity.** The extent to which a method of data collection represents or measures the phenomenon which it purports to represent or measure. This is a basic problem in social research; do the INDICATORS devised to represent particular concepts actually do so satisfactorily? Are the MEASUREMENTS made in a research study a true representation of the underlying attribute which the investigator wishes to measure? Is occupation, for example, a satisfactory proxy measure from which to classify people by social class? However high the RELIABILITY of a measure (e.g. an intelligence test), does it actually measure the underlying trait which is of interest (e.g. INTELLIGENCE)?

Two distinct types of validity have been identified by Campbell and Stanley. Internal validity is concerned with whether the methods used made a difference to the specific results. External validity is concerned with the generalizability of a study.

There are several methods of attempting to establish the validity of measuring instruments. Content validity involves making a judgement about how adequately some specific domain of content is sampled. Face validity involves judging the extent to which an instrument seems to measure what it is supposed to measure. Construct validity is concerned with the extent to which a measure gets at the underlying theoretical term, and is of greatest interest to sociologists. No single procedure can establish this, and evidence from a number of sources has to be combined.

MB

**value judgements.** It is often held that science is concerned with factual statements, not with evaluations of a state of affairs as good or bad. WEBER is perhaps the most famous defender of this view, which he called 'value-freedom'. He held that scientists should make it clear in their public utterances that value judgements were not entailed by their scientific analyses. At the same time he upheld a doctrine of value-relevance, in which the selection of objects of scientific investigation is governed by the values of the scientist and his or her culture, or by the scientist's judgement that something is interesting or problematic when seen in terms of an actual or hypothetical set of values.

The doctrine of value-freedom has been increasingly questioned in recent years. Some philosophers have doubted the possibility of drawing clear distinctions between description, appraisal and evaluation, while social scientists have argued that theories are both penetrated by, and themselves generate, evaluations of their subject matter. It has also been suggested that the doctrine of value-freedom, quite against Weber's intentions, has encouraged scientists to adopt an irresponsible attitude to the consequences of their actions.

WO

**variable.** A technical term used to refer to the representation of any distinct social characteristic or social factor (such as age, sex, income, education, occupation) in empirical research. A variable is constructed by defining a concept and developing a satisfactory INDICATOR (or indicators) for that

412

concept. The idea of a variable is very pervasive in sociology; it is basic to the analysis of CAUSALITY, of explanation, of theory, as well as to RESEARCH DESIGN, MEASUREMENT and STATISTICAL INFERENCE. A standard method of data presentation is case-by-variable analysis.

Variables may be constructed from the MEASUREMENT of objective characteristics, reports of behaviour, subjective statements of values, beliefs on attitudes, or by inference from more than one item in a research instrument. In SOCIAL SURVEY research the basic items of factual information asked for at the beginning of the questionnaire are known as 'face-sheet' variables.

MB

**Veblen, Thorstein B.** (1857-1929). American economist and sociologist, now principally remembered for his theory of 'the leisure class'. As Professor of Economics at the University of Chicago from 1892, Veblen founded a school of 'institutional economics' to study the development of the economic institutions of society rather than the atomized, hedonistic individual of neo-classical economics. He concentrated on studying the business enterprise. He believed that 'the instinct of workmanship' was essential to the technological development of society, but was now being thwarted by a dominant leisure class sheltered from direct contact with the economic environment by 'absolute ownership' (a term he coined, along with others describing characteristics of the leisure class such as 'conspicuous consumption' and 'ostentatious display'). Veblen developed a theory of CONFLICT in modern society which was a radical development of SAINT-SIMON: the basic conflict was between 'pecuniary employment' (the owners and financiers of industry) and 'industrial employment' (the engineers and workers concerned with production and efficiency rather than with profit). Veblen identified strongly with the latter. Their drive to innovate constantly threatened the value of the owners' capital, and so generated conflict between them.

Veblen's writings are lively, polemical and political, and he has been widely read, especially in the USA, though his influence within academic sociology and economics

has not been great. Major works: *The Theory of the Leisure Class* (1899); *The Theory of Business Enterprise* (1904); *The Instinct of Workmanship* (1914); *Absentee Ownership and Business Enterprise in Recent Times* (1923).

MM

**verification.** The discovery that a statement is true or valid. Logical POSITIVISTS held that science advances by the verification of HYPOTHESES, and (in one version) that statements are only meaningful if it is possible to verify them. Perhaps the most serious of the many difficulties of this principle is that statements of the form 'all swans are white' can never be conclusively verified, however much supporting evidence one collects. They can however be falsified by a single counter-instance — in this case, a black swan. POPPER therefore replaced verifiability by falsifiability as a criterion for distinguishing scientific from non-scientific statements. He argued that MARXISM and PSYCHOANALYTIC theory are pseudo-sciences, not because there is no evidence in their favour, but for the opposite reason that there is nothing which can count as conclusive evidence against them. Genuine sciences expose themselves to the risk of falsification in the light of empirical evidence, and successful sciences survive repeated attempts to falsify them. More recent work in the philosophy and history of science has shown that Popper's principle is impossibly strict.

See PARADIGM; RESEARCH PROGRAMME.

See I. Berlin, 'Verification', in G.H.R. Parkinson (ed.), *The Theory of Meaning* (1968); P. Halfpenny, *Positivism and Sociology* (1982); K. Popper, *The Logic of Scientific Discovery* (1935).

WO

**Verstehen.** The German word for 'understanding' came to be used in the 19th century to denote an imaginative penetration into religious and other historical texts. German philosophers of history opposed the POSITIVIST view that history must simply discover LAWS resembling those in natural science. The idea that we can understand texts and human actions other than by identifying causal regularities (see CAUSE) was developed especially by DILTHEY and applied in the sociology of SIMMEL, WEBER and the psychology of Karl Jaspers (1883-1969) and others. Where other writers distinguished sharply between verstehen in the human sciences and causal explanation in the natural sciences, Weber saw verstehen as a necessary part of causal explanations in social science, which are however no less 'scientific' than those of the natural sciences. Verstehen is not merely a method, but also the way data of the social or human sciences present themselves to us. Social scientists differ in their judgements about what follows from this and whether, in particular, it excludes the possibility of NATURALISM.

See NEO-KANTIANISM; PHENOMENOLOGY.

WO

**Vico, Giambattista** (1668-1744). Italian philosopher of history. Professor of Rhetoric at the University of Naples. Main work: *Scienza Nuova* (1725). Vico anticipated later themes of anti-NATURALISM, HISTORI-CISM and EVOLUTIONISM. Because the 'world of nations' had been made by human beings, it could be understood in a way in which only God could understand the natural world. With this principle Vico tried to relativize the claims made for the CARTESIAN method. His conception of history is often presented as a spiral: he retained a cyclical theory of historical change but combined it with a notion of secular development. The under-standing of past ages is, therefore, a difficult HERMENEUTIC task. The principal stages of social development anticipate those of SAINT-SIMON and COMTE, though his writings were not known to them. The first stage was theo-cratic: society was explained in religious terms and dominated by feelings, not reason. The second was aristocratic, dominated by MILITARISM. The third was monarchical or republican, humanistic and more rational. Vico was extraordinarily original and pres-cient — probably excessively so, because his theories lay largely forgotten for over 100 years until rediscovered by the German his-toricists.

WO

**victimology.** One of a number of deceptively innocent academic terms. It seems to define a solid discipline which is central to an array of institutions, departments, staff, traditions, practices and accomplishments. There is no such discipline. Instead, victimology refers to a nuance or focus adopted by some crimino-logists in their analysis of particular problems. Those problems stem from the observation that victims of crime are socially organized, that they are to be found in certain special segments of society, and that their conduct can encourage and influence the development of criminal activity. Victimo-logy was championed by those who wished to promote the criminological analysis of the presence, distribution, behaviour and effects of victims. In its most exaggerated guise, it proceeded to the argument that victims are the active cause of crime.

See CRIME; CRIMINOLOGY.

PR

**Vienna Circle.** A group of logical POSITIVISTS based at the University of Vienna in the 1920s and 1930s and founded by Moritz Schlick. The group published a manifesto in 1929, entitled 'The Scientific World-View: the Vienna Circle', written by Otto Neurath, and a journal, *Erkenntnis*. Its best-known philosopher was Rudolf Carnap (1891-1970). He and others of the group emigrated to the USA after the Nazis occupied Austria in 1936, and later became known as 'logical empiricists' (see EMPIRICISM). They held that philosophy was purely ANALYTIC and quite inappropriate for discussing religious and moral statements, which were METAPHYSI-CAL and therefore meaningless.

WO, MM

**vocabulary of motive.** A concept pioneered by Hans Gerth and C. Wright MILLS (*American Sociological Review*, 1954, and *Character and Social Structure*, 1954) to depict the observable words that people evolve in specific contexts to interpret their conduct. Such a vocabulary is always bound up with a particular historical culture and ideology (motives acceptable at one period — e.g. 'I am driven by demons' — may not be acceptable at another) and a particular social context (e.g. how a shoplifter explains a theft to a court may differ from how he/she explains it to a friend). Socially situated vocabularies must be distinguished from the more orthodox (biological and psychological) view of MOTIVATION as the inner springs of action (like instincts, needs of traits), although the relationship between such 'motives' and 'vocabularies' is an acknowledged research problem.

A great deal of the research in this tradition describes and classifies various patterns of vocabulary: Sykes and Matza (*American Sociological Review* 1957) depict five NEUTRALIZATION techniques employed by delinquents to explain away their deviance (denying responsibilities, denying the victim, denying injury, condemning the condemners, and appealing to higher loyalties), thereby showing the social functions of motivational talk. Related terms include 'accounts' (the justifications and excuses people offer when the course of interaction has been disrupted), 'quasi-theories' (the explanations people construct in social interaction to account for various kinds of problematic situation) and 'disclaimers', the 'verbal' device employed to ward off and defeat in advance doubts and negative typifications which may result from intended conduct (see J.P. Hewitt and R. Stokes, *American Sociological Review* 1975).

Such vocabularies are part of the sociology of KNOWLEDGE — by asking how 'motives' are socially produced; part of the sociology of LANGUAGE — by asking about the patterns and functions of talk; part of the sociology of DEVIANCE — by examining the 'motivations' stated by deviants to explain their conduct; and part of SYMBOLIC INTER-ACTIONISM — by showing the changing meaning of motives in interaction and the connection of such motives to the SELF.

KP

**voluntarism.** See METHODOLOGICAL INDI-VIDUALISM; PARSONS.

**voting.** The act of expressing a choice — categorical or preferential — between competing alternatives, which are usually policy proposals (e.g. in a referendum or within a legislative system) or candidates for elective office. The act of voting, and the choice it reveals, may be individual or collective (on the part of an electorate or subset); in either case it represents a critical point in a decision process. Voting is conducted by ballot or by some physical act of the voter.

Studies concentrate on what explanatory VARIABLES are ASSOCIATED with voting (as opposed to abstention) and what variables are associated with specific patterns of voting. Alternative perspectives include the psychological (analysing voting in terms of needs and predispositions), sociological (in terms of social groups and categories), ecological and geographical (in terms of spatial factors), and rational/UTILITARIAN (in terms of goal attainment). The main findings of such studies are: (1) Among mass electorates, habitual abstainers are encountered mainly among individuals or groups with a low education and political information, a low sense of political efficacy, weak identification with the overall political system and with any party in it, and limited or loose familial and organizational ties. Habitual voters show a high score on these variables. There is a CORRELATION between these relationships and social CLASS: the higher a self-assigned position on a class scale, the more likely to be a habitual voter. (2) Specific voting patterns are more variable, due to widely contrasted social structures and party systems in different polities. Left-wing voting is strongly associated with the urban working-class male trade union member who is not SOCIALLY MOBILE, lives and works in an industrial environment with a left-wing political SUBCULTURE, and holds a SECULAR view of politics (whatever his private religious beliefs). Conversely, right-wing voting is associated with the middle class, self-employed, artisan and skilled working class who are socially ambitious, live in a non-industrial environment, and whose view of political morality is inspired by religious belief.

Voting patterns within legislatures are primarily outcomes of conflicting pressures on legislators, such as the peer group, the party, the constituency, interest group demands, personal value systems, career prospects etc.

See DEMOCRACY; PARTIES; PLURALISM.

JP

**voucher schemes.** Educational schemes favoured by advocates of the MARKET SYSTEM which, it is claimed, combine the main advantages of that system with a guaranteed minimum quantity of a good or service for every household irrespective of their ability to pay. Experiments with these schemes have been carried out in education by Kent County Council in the UK and by the Alum Rock School District in California, USA. Under an education voucher scheme, the Government issues families with a standard voucher for each of their children; these vouchers can be used to 'purchase' education at a school of the families choosing. In some schemes, families may supplement the standard voucher with cash if they wish to buy more than the minimum quantity of education. The main advantages claimed for the system are that by offering CONSUMERS freedom of choice they produce an education system which is responsive to consumer DEMAND, and that through competition a high standard of education is achieved in each school. Critics claim that the system would increase inequality by producing segregation and a hierarchy of schools.

RR

**war.** See MILITARISM.

**Ward, Lester** (1841-1913). Early American EVOLUTIONIST sociologist. Born in Illinois, the son of a mechanic, and largely self-educated. He became a farm-worker, fought with the Union Army in the Civil War, and commenced government service as a clerk in the Treasury Department in 1865. He attended evening classes at the Columbian (George Washington) University, majoring in botany and law. In 1881, he joined the US Geological Survey as assisant geologist, becoming chief paleontologist in 1892, and engaged in original research in geology and paleobotany. During the 1880s he served as Professor of Botany at Columbia University. In 1903 he became president of the International Institue of Sociology and in 1906 Professor of Sociology at Brown University, and the first president of the American Sociological Society.

Ward founded psychological evolutionism in the 1880s. This was developed further by GIDDINGS, but Ward's thought, opposed to the dominant philosophy of laissez-faire, made little impact upon the development of sociology. He favoured a classificatory rather than a quantitative sociology. Supporting state interventionism and social reformism, Ward injected a humanitarian content into evolutionism, rejecting SPENCER's rigid determinism as well as social DARWINISM. Modifying Comtean POSITIVISM, he claimed that purposive human action is a product of evolution. Social science should base social reforms upon discovered social LAWS. Ward supported the trade union movement, left-wing parties, and the emancipation of women. He deplored class inequalities and believed the distinction between producers and non-producers formed the most important division in society. But egalitarianism would be achieved through compulsory public education, not state socialism.

Ward described four stages of evolution: cosmogeny, biogeny, anthropogeny and sociogeny. Following COMTE and Spencer, he distinguished between 'social statics' and 'social dynamics' with greater precision, and contrasted 'pure' and 'applied ' sociology. His principal concepts include 'genesis' (blind spontaneous evolution arising from natural selection) and 'telesis' (purposive social intervention or adaption based on artifical selection). 'Synergy' refers to universal principles of creative synthesis operating throughout nature and producing the transition between evolutionary stages.

His belief that social forces are basically psychological influenced American social psychology and the writers of the first sociology textbooks such as Small and Vincent (1894), E.A. Ross (1920), PARK and Burgess (1921). Ward's main works were *Dynamic Sociology* (1883), *Psychic Factors of Civilization* (1893) *Pure Sociology* (1903, and *Applied Sociology* (1906).

JW

**wealth.** The value of a stock of resources at a point in time. The main forms of personal wealth are physical possessions such as cars, houses and other consumer durables, and financial assets such as bank and building society deposits, shares, government bonds and life insurance and pension fund rights. Many types of wealth generate INCOME in the form of interests, profits and dividends. Wages and salaries are also enhanced by the possession of the particular form of wealth represented by HUMAN CAPITAL. Statistics on the distribution of wealth indicate the way in which the total stock of personal wealth is divided between the members of society: in 1970, the top one per cent of the wealth holders in Great Britain owned approximately 32 per cent of the total wealth, whereas the top 10 per cent held approximately 70 per cent of the total. These estimates may be compared with those for 1938, when the top 1 per cent of wealth holders owned 55 per cent and the top 10 per cent owned 85 per cent of the total stock of wealth. Personal wealth may be accumulated through lifetime acquisition (notably, saving or capital gains) and through inheritance. In the UK, inheritance is the more important source for top wealth holders. Under present UK TAX arrangements wealth is taxed when it is transferred from one person to another, via the capital transfer tax and when capital gains are made. Unlike many countries Britain does not have an annual wealth tax, although several proposals for one have been put forward in recent years.

RR

**Webb, Sydney James** (1859-1947) and **Beatrice** (1858-1943). From very different backgrounds, Sydney and Beatrice Webb wrote, researched and campaigned together. They were extremely influential both academically and politically.

The Webbs wrote on a wide range of different subjects. Some of their earliest works were centrally concerned with industrial relations: *The History of Trade Unionism* (1894) and *Industrial Democracy* (1897) are classics and have had a major impact on subsequent work. They also published a nine-volume history of English local government (1906-1929) and a two-volume study of the development of communism in Russia (1935). It is impossible to separate completely their academic writing from their political influence. As important figures within the Fabian Society they wrote large numbers of pamphlets. As a member of the Royal Commission on the POOR LAW, Beatrice Webb was instrumental in the publication of the Minority Report which set forward a programme for the break-up of the Poor Law.

Initially the Webbs looked on the LABOUR PARTY with suspicion, but they became convinced that extensive social reforms could only be put forward by a party which shared their collectivist ideals. In 1922 Sydney was elected as a Labour Member of Parliament for the Seaham Division of Durham, and in the 1924 Labour Government he became President of the Board of Trade. Though he decided not to stand for Parliament at the next election, in 1929 Webb agreed to become Secretary of State for Dominion Affairs and the Colonies in MacDonald's Government and accepted a peerage. He remained in the Government until 1931.

The Webbs' political influence cannot be measured by their direct interventions. It was much more keenly felt through their writings, their membership of committees, commissions and pressure groups, and their informal contacts.

See SOCIALISM; TRADE UNIONS; WELFARE STATE.                                    MPJ

**Weber, Max** (1864-1920). German sociologist. With MARX and DURKHEIM his influence pervades all of modern sociology. He was born in Erfurt, the son of a prominent lawyer and Liberal politician. The family moved to Berlin when he was a child. Weber attended the universities of Heidelberg, Berlin and Göttingen, studying history, law and economics. Not until near the end of his life did he accept the label 'sociologist'. His doctoral dissertation was on medieval trading companies, and his *Habilitationsschrift* (a higher doctorate) on the agrarian history of ancient Rome. His first chairs were in economics, at Freiburg and at Heidelberg. His earliest publications included essays on the stock exchange and on labour relations in the agrarian areas of eastern Germany. In 1897 he had a serious nervous breakdown following the death of his father; this marked a turning point both in his personal life and his intellectual interests. He was unable to return to his university post, and until 1918 largely lived as a private scholar. Though passionately interested in politics, usually as a non-party liberal nationalist, he was also unable to take part in public life. From these years, and perhaps arising from these frustrations, came the flood of writings which had a profound influence on sociology.

In 1902 Weber began writing on the methodology of the social sciences. He became joint editor of the journal *Archiv für Sozialwissenschaft und Sozialpolitik* in 1904 and in 1905 his most famous long essay, *The Protestant Ethic and the Spirit of Capitalism*, appeared. While continuing to publish on a staggering range of topics, Weber started work in 1910 on *Economy and Society*, a systematic presentation of his sociological research. This remained incomplete and was published only after his death. During the World War I he was briefly involved in military hospital administration, but also published his work on the religions of India, China and ancient Palestine. He helped draw up the Weimar Constitution. In 1919 he at last accepted a university chair, in sociology at Munich. From this last period of his life date his great twin lectures 'Science as a Vocation' and 'Politics as a Vocation', as well as the great *Economic History* (published posthumously from his lecture notes). Weber died unexpectedly of influenza in 1920.

The range of Weber's knowledge is unrivalled among modern sociologists. He brought to it a remarkable consistency of approach, but did not emerge with a simple set of conclusions. He has had a lasting impact across the whole subject, from methodology to each of the numerous empirical fields to which he contributed.

Weber played a prominent part in the debates about the philosophy of social science which raged in Germany around the turn of the century (see his *Methodology of the Social Sciences*). The prevailing (German) view opposed the POSITIVIST doctrine that the natural and social sciences shared the same methodological goal of discovering general LAWS, explanations of a causal nature. They argued instead that history and the social sciences aimed at the 'interpretative understanding' (VERSTEHEN) of unique sequences of events. Weber, while not representing the procedures of the

natural and social sciences as identical, partly bridged the distinction between them by arguing that through the process of interpretative understanding of patterns of social action, sociologists arrived at a causal explanation of sequences of action. Moreover, through the use of IDEAL TYPES, they could progress from the study of unique events to cautious generalizations about the common features of institutional patterns in social development. Weber also debated the question of OBJECTIVITY, 'detachment' or 'value-freedom' (*Wertfreiheit*) in social science. His views are more complex than is sometimes represented. While he advocated scientific detachment in the course of research itself, he admitted that values could and should influence the choice of problems to be investigated, and that the results of social scientific research could and should be relevant to political action. See also NEO-KANTIANISM; PHENOMENOLOGY.

It is sometimes wrongly suggested that Weber's work was 'a debate with the ghost of Karl Marx'. His incomplete remarks in *Economy and Society* on 'Class, Status and Party' have provided the basis for most modern non-Marxian approaches to SOCIAL STRATIFICATION (see CLASS, *Weber on*). More particularly, the PROTESTANT ETHIC THESIS has often been seen wrongly as an attempted refutation of the materialist theory of history, though it is an important qualification to cruder Marxist arguments current in his own time that values are merely reflections of economic forces which provide the engine of history. Weber suggested an 'elective affinity' between the two value-systems, the Protestant Ethic on the one hand and the spirit of CAPITALISM on the other; he did not say that 'protestantism caused capitalism', though this interpretation has been rendered plausible by certain idealist currents found elsewhere in his sociology — most notably his metaphor, drawn from railways, in which he said that 'ideal interests' are the switchmen of history, changing the tracks of historical development.

*The Protestant Ethic* is the key to Weber's great subsequent studies of the economic ethics of the world religions (in their English editions, *The Religion of China, The Religion of India, Ancient*

*Judaism, The Sociology of Religion* and unfinished fragments on Islam). These were designed to show that whatever their material basis, other civilizations had failed to produce the (instrumental) RATIONALITY which permeated so many aspects of Western culture and institutions and was the core of the immense dynamism of Western society. The breadth of Weber's learning can be seen in his technical discussion of how rationality had affected even Western music (see *The Rational and Social Foundations of Western Music*). These studies end somewhat ambiguously in relation to the MATERIALISM *versus* IDEALISM controversy, for they trace the evolution of the 'rationalization process' in economy and ideology alike.

*Economy and Society*, though unfinished, presents a degree of systematization of Weber's historical and comparative sociology. It begins with a conceptual exposition of the nature of rational action, and proceeds to trace its gradual embodiment through processes of social development in economic institutions and markets, religious institutions, rational law, cities, and forms of domination (see POWER). Weber's sociology of the STATE, in which he discusses many historical forms of domination — CHARISMATIC and legitimate AUTHORITY, PATRIMONIAL administration and FEUDALISM, rational-legal BUREAUCRACY and so on — has been immensely influential. Weber himself viewed the growing role of the state and the pervasive rationality of modern culture with disquiet, and spoke of 'the disenchantment of the world'. He saw the Russian Revolution as only enhancing the bureaucratization of modern society, and increasingly looked to less rationalized elements of Western society for future development — especially to capitalists' pursuit of profit and to the emergence of charismatic political leaders within liberal democracy.

Weber achieved towering status among German social scientists during his lifetime. After his death a 'Weber Circle', centring on his widow Marianne, his brother Alfred Weber, and his close colleague Ernst TROELTSCH, continued to meet in Heidelberg. PARSONS encountered Weber's work there in the 1920s, and his *Structure of Social Action* (1937), more than any other book, was responsible for making Weber known in the English-speaking world. Parsons put disproportionate emphasis on Weber's methodological and conceptual ideas. So did SCHUTZ, through whom Weber had some influence on PHENOMENOLOGY in sociology, tending to exaggerate the subjectivistic and mentalistic side of Weber's thinking. Both took up 'timeless', abstract qualities of Weber's writing which were fitted into the prevailing a-historical climate of sociology in the 1950s and 1960s. Weber's greatest achievements, however, lie in his comparative and historical studies of large-scale social institutions. Few scholars have matched his breadth of learning, but his work has inspired many more limited investigations, and this style of sociology has returned to fashion in the 1970s and 1980s. His influence is now growing, especially among comparative and historical writers like Anderson, Skocpol and Wallerstein, whose work derives ostensibly from the Marxist tradition. The richness of Weber's analyses, and his refusal to imprison them within the theoretical framework of any particular orthodoxy, will always appeal to ambitious sociologists regardless of their own theoretical preferences.

SJM

**welfare economics.** A branch of economics in which alternative economic situations are assessed in terms of their effect upon society's state of well-being or welfare. This requires a criterion in terms of which social welfare may be evaluated. The most widely accepted criterion is that of Pareto EFFICIENCY: in evaluating two situations, A and B, A represents a higher level of social welfare than B if, in situation A, at least one person is better off than in situation B without anyone being made worse off. Although all welfare criteria inevitably involve ethical judgements, the PARETO criterion seeks to minimize them by excluding comparisons between situations where some people are made better off and others are made worse off, and hence avoiding inter-personal comparisons. Unfortunately, this restriction precludes consideration of the majority of economic policy choices as most options benefit some people and impose costs on others (see

COST-BENEFIT ANALYSIS). In an attempt to overcome this restriction the Kaldor-Hicks criterion states that social welfare will increase as a result of a change if those people who benefit from the change could compensate fully those people who incur costs and still remain better off. (This criterion does not require the compensation actually to be paid.) A more general approach to the problem of interpersonal comparisons was developed by A. Bergson in his formulation of the social welfare function, a theoretical construct which enables society's preferences about the different levels of welfare associated with all possible economic situations to be ranked; it is thus the social analogue of ordinal UTILITY. As an aid to policy-making, however, the social welfare function suffers from the major defect that it does not specify how information on social preferences is to be derived. Critics have pointed to its naivity as a political model in which decision makers (i.e. politicians or civil servants) are in some sense able to specify 'society' preferences. This highlights one of the dilemmas of welfare economics not encountered in the area of POSITIVE ECONOMICS, where claims (or predictions) are tested against empirical evidence. In welfare economics, predictions about alternative states of welfare derive directly from ethical premises and are not testable. For this reason, greater attention is devoted to the reasonableness of welfare assumptions and premises.

RR

**welfare rights.** The welfare right movement is in part a response to the complexity of social service provision and legislation. It is an attempt to ensure that those who are eligible for benefits from any of the social services should understand their entitlement and be helped to obtain them. Some of the first moves to develop a system to assist those eligible to claim benefits were made in the USA. These moves were mirrored in Britain, particularly in the 1970s. The movement has campaigned for simpler procedures to assist in the claiming of benefit, for the better provision of information, and for the establishment of appeals procedures. Welfare rights offices and stalls have been widely established and some have been supported directly by local authorities.

MPJ

**welfare state.** A term first coined in the 1930s, though not widely used until the early 1940s. The origins of the British welfare state are usually traced to the BEVERIDGE Report of 1942, though Beveridge himself disliked the use of the term, preferring 'social service state'.

A series of legislative acts introduced between 1944 and 1948 form the basis for the British welfare state. They include the EDUCATION ACT (1944), the FAMILY ALLOWANCE Act (1945), the National Insurance Act, the National Insurance (Industrial Injuries) Act and the National Health Services Act (all of 1946), and the Children Act and the National Assistance Act (1948).

Apart from legislation on family allowances, the others were extensions of earlier legislation. For example, a state system of education can be traced back to the 19th century (the Elementary Education Act of 1870 gave locally elected school boards the right to provide and maintain elementary schools out of public funds); health and unemployment insurance were introduced through the National Insurance Act of 1911. The national assistance scheme represented a break with the old POOR LAW, though moves had been made to dismantle that law since the beginning of the century, and the establishment of the Unemployment Assistance Board in 1934 (which took over responsibility for the long-term able-bodied unemployed unable to claim unemployment insurance benefits) represented an important step in the direction of a system of national assistance. State concern with the welfare of children can be traced back well into the 19th century (e.g. through Factory Acts which sought, among other things, to regulate the employment of children), while child welfare services were developed throughout the early 20th century under poor law, education and health legislation.

Explanations for the development of the welfare state vary considerably. Many link moves to improve provision for the poor to the work of charities, and charitable organizations were important in the early development of many social services (see CHARITY). Others see the development of social services as linked to the changing nature of society: changes in technology and methods of production and the growth of large urban areas resulted in major social problems which could only be tackled by the provision of state-based social services. Many such explanations have links with FUNCTIONAL-ISM. Others stress working-class pressure: the role of trade unions and other working-class organizations can be seen throughout the development of social services and in some areas (e.g. health care, social insurance) working class organizations pioneered schemes themselves. The development of social services might have been a reaction on the part of those in power to the threat of social unrest: by dealing with the worst social problems the controllers of power managed to reduce some of the fervour of the attack on them. Such explanations are partly based on CONFLICT THEORY. The debate includes many strands and cross-cutting themes. In many cases the explanations contained in narratives are implicit rather than explicit, but the debate over the growth and development of the welfare state reflects the different views and assumptions of most major schools of thought in sociology, and remains unsettled.

See CAPITALISM; CITIZENSHIP; SOCIAL INSURANCE; SOCIAL SECURITY; WOMEN AND THE WELFARE STATE.

MPJ

**witchcraft.** Sorcery and witchcraft form part of the domain of MAGIC. The two terms are often used interchangeably to refer to the use of magic for the production of socially disapproved ends, but a distinction between them is widely accepted. Sorcery involves the use of magic for evil ends of a merely occasional kind by the utilization of a spell, potion or ritual, while witchcraft is a more or less permanent characteristic of the witch. Sorcery is something that somebody has done; witchcraft is attributed on the basis of what somebody *is*.

Belief in the existence of witches — except among small groups of eccentrics who occupy their leisure with rituals alleged to have magical significance — has almost entirely disappeared in industrial societies. Prosecutions for witchcraft disappeared virtually everywhere throughout Europe in the 18th century. In pre-industrial societies, the belief was so widespread that it must have

appeared independently in quite distinct and widely separated societies. Witchcraft beliefs are a common feature of small-scale pre-industrial societies where life is lived in closely knit, intimate communities in which relationships are little mediated by impersonal institutions.

Witchcraft occurs between individuals who have an existing social relationship with each other. In some tribal societies, witchcraft accusations are most typical between individuals related to each other by marriage, for example two wives in a polygamous household. In Europe and colonial America, the 'victim' and the alleged 'witch' were usually well-known to each other, and almost always members of the same community. Thus the relationship is a personal one. Anthropologists such as Max Marwick have argued that accusations of witchcraft are usually directed between individuals in strained personal relations with each other. While the exact character of the strain will vary from one society to another, typically the witch is believed to be motivated by hatred, envy, or a desire for revenge. The witch is believed to attack those whom he (or more often she) has reason to hate.

Accusations usually emerge in more or less the following way: some misfortune occurs and the victim reflects on the cause. Does someone have reason to wish him harm? With whom has he quarrelled recently? To whom has he failed to render some traditional obligation or service? Who has he made jealous? Witchcraft accusations therefore explain the occurrence of misfortune by connecting it to disturbances in interpersonal relations.

Witchcraft is one of a range of possible explanations for the causes of unfortunate events invoked by people whose world-view construes the universe as a moral realm, that is, one in which all events can be seen as having some morally endowed purpose. The universe is seen to be filled with active, intelligent agents and powers of a non-human kind — God, spirits, ghosts, or planetary configurations — which can be identified as the ultimate cause of events as well as other persons. In this context, events can provide occasions for reflecting on the moral meaning and the purposeful agency involved in their causation. If disaster of a cataclysmic or widespread kind occurs, then only an agent with an appropriately wide domain could be responsible (God, for example). If the events are related to a personal moral failure, God may again be responsible (for example, illness may be a judgement for backsliding). If the individual sees — or wishes to see — no reprehensibility in his/her own behaviour, then he/she may cast about for someone or something else to blame. In small, close-knit rural communities, resentments, feuds and jealousies may seem tangible and oppressive facticities and readily provide the basis for a belief that another would wish to cause one harm by occult means. The mobile, individualistic, transient, role-articulated character of urban industrial societies has decisively weakened the plausibility of a belief in the power of others to influence one's fortunes supernaturally. Connections with others in our community no longer possess the weight of moral significance they did in the past, and neighbourly opinion has relatively little tangible causal efficacy in a more impersonal and anonymous world.

See M. Marwick (ed.), *Witchcraft and Sorcery* (1970).

RW

**Wittfogel, Karl** (1896- ). German sinologist and comparative sociologist. Born in Hanover, Wittfogel was on the staff of the Institute for Social Research at Frankfurt 1925-33, where he received his PhD in 1928. He left Germany in 1933 and from 1934 to 1947 worked at Columbia University, New York. Since 1947 he has had a variety of distinguished teaching and research posts.

Wittfogel was trained as a sinologist and published two important works on China, *Economy and Society in China* (1931, in German) and *History of Chinese Society* (1949, with Feng Chia-Sheng). His fame rests largely on his book *Oriental Despotism* (1957) and the controversy it aroused.

See ORIENTAL DESPOTISM.

See G.L. Ulmen, *Science of Society, Toward an Understanding of the Life and Work of K.A. Wittfogel* (1978).

LS

**Wittgenstein, Ludwig** (1889-1951). Austrian philosopher. He worked under Bertrand Russell at Cambridge before World War I, but abandoned philosophy temporarily after the war, though remaining on the fringes of the VIENNA CIRCLE. He returned to Cambridge in 1929, where he worked until 1947. Main works: *Tractatus Logico-Philosophicus* (1921), *Philosophical Investigations* (1953), and a variety of other posthumous works on problems of philosophy, logic and mathematics. Wittgenstein's shift from the crudely representational theory of language in the *Tractatus* to the more sophisticated account of 'language-games' presented in the *Investigations*, along with the work of J.L. Austin, inspired the concern with language of post-war ANALYTIC philosophy.

WO

**women and crime.** Women commit far fewer crimes than men and female DEVIANCE tends to be defined as madness (see WOMEN AND MADNESS). Female criminality is closely connected with women's ROLE in society. Shoplifting is a common female crime, and is associated with women's roles as housewives and mothers, and as consumers.

Soliciting is another female crime, although prostitution *per se* is not a criminal offence. It is not a crime for men to solicit prostitutes. Thus the criminalization of soliciting by female prostitutes reflects the double standard of sexual morality, and the division this imposes on women: good women marry and bad women become prostitutes. In the USA it is illegal for men to pick up prostitutes, but arrest and conviction statistics demonstrate a *de facto* implementation of the double standard: clients very rarely get arrested. In Britain, the USA, France and other countries, prostitutes have organized pressure groups to publicize this legal sexism and abolish prostitution laws.

Women rarely commit violent crimes. If they do, they tend to be punished more severely than men, especially if those crimes are considered to be opposed to allegedly 'natural' feminine behaviour, such as husband, child or father murder. The reasons behind women's relative non-participation in criminally violent behaviour lie in socialization into predominately caring nurturant behaviour, sexual divisions in leisure (young women are less likely to join male gangs) and the confinement of women to the private sphere of the home and their exclusion from the public sphere where, according to the criminal statistics, most violent crimes occur.

However, women are the victims of violent crimes and of violent acts not considered criminal and it is in the private sphere that the majority of these assaults on women occur. Women as wives are victims of wife-battering, a crime estimated as occurring within at least 30 per cent of marriages. Around 25 per cent of recorded violent crime is wife-assault, and about 75 per cent of violent crime within the family is wife-assault. Wives are victims because of the power relations between husbands and wives within the FAMILY. It is considered so normal for a husband to beat his wife, that police treat wife-battering as a 'domestic dispute', urge the woman to initiate civil proceedings, and only charge the husband themselves if the wife is considered an 'honourable victim' — that is, if she did not deserve it! The difficulty with civil remedies lies in the fact that the wife remains with her husband under the same roof if she has nowhere else to live. Separation and divorce are also not easy options under PATRIARCHY, where women are deemed responsible for family relations, for keeping the family together, and where wives are blamed for 'provoking' their husbands.

INCEST is another instance of the police refusing to admit that crime is taking place. Father- (or other male caretaker) daughter incest is both the commonest form of incest, and a very commonly occurring crime. Kinsey estimated that 25 per cent of women in America were victims of incest. Girl children and women are not believed; in fact, FREUD sanctioned this disbelief by declaring that all women fantasize about being raped by their fathers. This scepticism about women's truthfulness is compounded by WELFARE STATE interventions in support of the family unit. It is deemed better for the girl child who is a victim of violent sexual assault to remain in the family, and for the male assaulter not to go to prison. The mother is often blamed for denying her husband sexual access and thus 'colluding' in the crime.

Women are also victims of rape. In some cases rape is not a crime: husbands cannot be charged with rape, and prostitutes find it extremely difficult to press rape charges. In marriage, wives cannot withhold their consent and prostitutes are defined as permanently sexually available, hence unrapable. Rape charges are difficult to prove. Rape is defined as penetration without the woman's consent but the patriarchal model of heterosexuality, the active male with irrepressible sex urges and the sexually passive female, makes it difficult to draw the line between lawful seduction and unlawful rape. Women have to prove they did not consent. Here, as in the case of incest, their veracity is doubted, and a woman's sexual mores, her behaviour and her relationship with the rapist (e.g. whether she 'provoked' him) are all material to the issue. Thus women frequently do not report rape; the police, if they can find the rapist, often do not prosecute; and only a few prosecutions end in convictions.

Wife-battering and rape are interconnected forms of male control of women. It is a myth that rapes occur in the public sphere and between strangers. The majority of rapists are known to the woman, and most rapes occur in the woman's or rapist's home. Most rapes are also premeditated, rather than occurring on the spur of the moment. However, the myth of rape is a powerful ideological mechanism which makes women turn to a single man for protection, especially in marriage. And it is in marriage that women are most likely to be victims of violence: rape, violent assault and murder.

See C. Smart, *Women, Crime and Criminology* (1976); S. Brownmiller, *Against Our Will: Men, Women and Rape* (1976).

EG

**women and education.** In transmitting culture and recreating social hierarchies the educational system reproduces GENDER differences and relations. Girls and boys enter education with a gendered identity which is reinforced through the operation of the overt and hidden CURRICULUM.

In the 19th century, when feminists in Britain began to open schools and colleges for women, the main debate was about whether girls should be offered a gender-specific curriculum, or simply integrated into the curriculum offered to boys. The proponents of the former argued for natural differences between men and women; those of the latter claimed that women could do as well as men on their own terrain. On the whole women's education, however class-specific, tended to concentrate on the acquisition of feminine skills and accomplishments; working-class girls spent much of their time learning to sew, and middle- and upper-class girls were given a curriculum which concentrated on their future roles as wives and mothers. 'Boys' education' was offered to a minority of girls, and female educators were warned of the defeminizing and physiologically debilitating effects of this practice.

Formal equality of access to schooling for boys and girls has existed in Britain since 1944. In spite of this, they leave education and enter adult life differently and unequally qualified. Girls do better at school than boys in primary school. By the age of 16 both sexes do equally well at 'O' (Ordinary) level and in CSE's. But more boys stay on at school to do 'A' (Advanced) levels, and this is reflected in higher education, where boys form just under two-thirds of first degree students. Of those who leave school at 16, far more boys go on to apprenticeships which lead to skilled manual work, while the small proportion of female apprenticeships tend to be concentrated in hairdressing and other typically female occupations.

Teaching is a predominantly female occupation. However, female teachers are concentrated in the primary sector and in the lower-level posts and 'female' subjects in secondary schools. Higher posts in primary and secondary education tend to be occupied by men. This disparity increases further in higher education, where the small proportion of women is concentrated in the lower levels of teaching and research. The expansion of higher education in the 1960s brought about a relative worsening in the position of women academics.

Many explanations have been offered for this. There is, first of all, the issue of subject choice. Timetabling difficulties necessitate making a choice between subjects, and sex-role stereotyping encourages girls to study traditional 'female' subjects: the arts and biology for girls, science and maths for boys. Gender-specific options, such as domestic science/needlework/cookery and woodwork/metalwork are frequently offered only to girls and boys respectively. This combines to reinforce existing stereotypes, and to reduce girls' future employment opportunities. Additionally, psychological sex-differences studies purport to demonstrate innate gendered abilities. Whatever their merit, and they have been heavily criticized (see GENDER AND BIOLOGICAL SEX) it is noteworthy that in a PATRIARCHAL society boys' achievements and abilities are rewarded with job opportunities; the same does not hold true for girls.

Feminists have argued that girls are doubly disadvantaged, by sex-role stereotyping (whereby, for instance, science is deemed inappropriate for girls and taught in ways which does not stimulate their interest) and by being forced into male educational institutions which value boys and their concerns, and present 'male studies' as education. Studies conducted by feminists have demonstrated that teachers prefer boys, spend more time with them, give them more attention, and are more concerned with their success because they feel that girls will 'only marry'. This patriarchal, hidden curriculum of devaluing girls, failing to address their concerns as equally valid, and failing to provide girls with confidence in their own abilities, mirrors the devaluation of women generally. Education operates through the principle of 'male as norm'. In co-educational schools (or male schools with girls) this ideological construct severely disadvantages girls, forcing them into even more stereotyped choices than they make in single-sex schools, and confining them to feminine behaviour. In this context academic success is defined as non-feminine. Girls are used by teachers and boy pupils as a negative REFERENCE GROUP. These findings have led feminists to argue for single-sex schools.

PEER GROUPS also reproduce gender divisions. Boys and girls differentiate between gender-appropriate behaviour and reinforce gendered classifications. For instance, male counter-school SUBCULTURES place a high value on disruptive male behaviour and regard schooling with contempt, equating it with femininity. Girls have no positive space within these subcultures: education is devalued through identification with femininity, and expressions of femininity are devalued as representations of female sexuality. The latter is also controlled by the sexual abuse and harassment to which both female teachers and pupils are subjected by boys, frequently with the passive, and sometimes active, assent of male teachers.

In response to this, feminist teachers have advocated setting up women's studies (see FEMINISM) in schools. The aim of women's studies is to analyse and explain society from a feminist point of view. It identifies the school curriculum as 'men's studies', a collection of subject areas drawn up and divided according to male concerns and interests which exclude women and their concerns, but are considered to be of universal interest and application. Women's studies will not only redress the balance in favour of girls, but will also provide a basis for anti-patriarchal education in which gender is not viewed as a limiting and debilitating condition for girls.

See E. Byrne, *Women and Education* (1978); R. Deem (ed.), *Schooling for Women's Work* (1980).

EG

**women and madness.** Women's deviance is more likely to be labelled madness than CRIME. The conflation of social femininity with biological femaleness means that, when women do not conform to traditional stereotypes and ROLES, they are defined as unnatural or mad. A further reason for this LABELLING process is that under PATRIARCHY the male is the norm and the female is deficient precisely because of her feminity. For FREUD, a woman was defined by her lack of a penis. Her neuroses were ultimately located in her inability to come to terms with this lack, and thus her unwillingness to submit to her biological destiny (see PSYCHO-ANALYSIS).

Modern psychology, PSYCHIATRY and medicine reproduce these Freudian myths of the neurotic woman. In Britain, one in six women will at some point enter a mental hospital; one quarter of the female population either receives or actually takes psychotropic drugs; and very frequently a woman who goes to her doctor with a physical complaint is disbelieved, told that it is 'all in her head', and is given anti-depressants. Some sections within the MEDICAL PROFESSION even claim that menstrual cramps and painful labours are psychogenic in origin, and can be explained by the woman's fear of motherhood and refusal of femininity.

FEMINISTS have argued that it is not women who are mad, but that patriarchy makes them insane. In the first place, the woman is blamed for what goes wrong in the family, from her husband's drinking to her child's failure at school, including violent assault on her own person. To be a woman is to be normally in the wrong.

Secondly, research has shown that MARRIAGE, one of the central institutions of patriarchy, contributes significantly to mental ill-health among women. For instance, married women form the highest category of psychotropic drug takers, suicide attempts, actual suicides and mental patients. Married men, by contrast, enjoy good mental health, surpassed only by single women. Recent studies in Britain indicate that the combination of marriage, isolated motherhood and housework is likely to produce moderate to severe forms of clinical depression.

Popular stereotypes of women as passive, childlike, irrational, lacking in ambition and so on, coupled with their legal and financial dependence on men in marriage, result in severe restrictions on women's options. Madness in women who break under the strain of patriarchal femininity serves to reinforce the traditional stereotypes of irrationality, passivity and other independence-sapping personality traits. Once defined as mad, they are subjected to drug treatment and ECT. Success in overcoming insanity is defined in terms of proper femininity — grooming, becoming a good mother and housewife. The husband, who in many cases is the person who commits his wife to a mental hospital, in conjunction with psychiatrists and therapists, thus becomes the final arbiter of his wife's mental health.

See MENTAL ILLNESS; STRESS.

See J. Bernard, *The Future of Marriage* (1976); M. Barrett and H. Roberts, 'Doctors and their patients: the social control of women in general practice' in C. and B. Smart, *Women, Sexuality and Social Control* (1978); G. Brown and T. Harris,

*The Social Origins of Depression: A Study of Psychiatric Disorder in Women* (1978).

EG

**women and politics.** Most women in the world enjoy the same electoral rights as men. But just as students of politics in general do not regard voting rights alone as indicative of the distribution of power in society, writers about women's status are now more interested in their economic and social position and the ideologies that sustain their roles in society.

In the West, equal voting rights were generally extended to women after the two world wars and over half a century of campaigning. This was usually followed by the removal of laws disqualifying women from being legislators. In Eastern Europe, the USSR and China, and the independent states of the Third World, political equality for women is often constitutionally guaranteed.

By the 1950s the dominant view in the West about the status of women was one of complacency. But there were dissenters who have since become an important political movement. Varying in political outlook, they agreed that granting electoral equality had not substantially altered the material position of women. Few women anywhere held important public office. Domestic legislation still often conferred inferior status on women. The FAMILY was still the basic unit of society. And the sexual DIVISION OF LABOUR in the home was reflected, not only by male predominance in the public sphere, but also in education and in the types of paid employment into which women increasingly went after World War II: schoolteaching, nursing, office work and catering. Some occupations were still barred to women. Even when entering the same occupations as men, women were paid, on average, about half the male rate. Legislation in Eastern Europe, and now in the USA and member states of the EEC, bans discrimination of this sort, although substantial differences persist even in STATE SOCIALIST countries.

The movement for the full emancipation of women began most noticeably in the USA, particularly among white women involved in the politics of civil rights and Vietnam. Black women were at first sceptical, giving racial equality priority, but double discrimination has drawn them into the women's movement. Experience in civil rights organizations provided women with the skills needed for political lobbying. Women in the USA and elsewhere now organize around issues that affect their earning power, status and the quality of life for themselves and men, such as abortion; employment; pensions and taxes; retirement ages and paternity leave; public expenditure on nurseries, health care and single-parent families. With many of the major national economies stagnating and growth taking place mainly in societies where religion, such as Islam, particularly subordinates women, the impact of the movement has been varied. Nevertheless, women's self-esteem and expectations in many countries have been enhanced.

The growth of the movement has been accompanied by the development of theories to explain the practices and institutions under attack. Some writers postulate innate differences, others socialization processes which sustain segmented labour markets. Some argue that female equality can only come with socialism; others prefer the concept of PATRIARCHY. Some synthesize these into a theory that women constitute a subordinate class because of their relationship to the means of reproduction rather as, in Marxism, classes arise from relationships to the means of production (see HOUSEWORK).

See also FEMINISM.                    EM

**women and the labour market.** All women work, but only under a half the female population in Britain and the USA is in employment. In pre-industrial society there was no division between home and work. Women performed HOUSEWORK, and sometimes sold the excess products of this labour (for instance, spun wool or cheese). With the growth of CAPITALISM came the factory system which removed certain forms of housework, most notably spinning and weaving, from the home into the factory. With industrialization, women lost some jobs to men in factories (e.g. spinning) and followed other jobs into factories (e.g. weaving). Jobs in other industries were also open to women (e.g. mining). Capitalist

employment restructured the sexual DIVI-
SION OF LABOUR in the labour market. Job
differentiation by sex (and age) continued, as
did the time-honoured practice of paying
women half of the male wage.

Starting with the Mines Act of 1842,
which excluded women and children below
the age of 12 from underground work, a
whole series of mid-19th-century legislative
measures restructured women's employment, barring them from certain industries
and restricting their hours of employment.
This was the result of campaigning by
Victorian philanthropists concerned with the
immorality of non-segregated factory
employment, and by male workers concerned with securing the right to a family
wage, that is, the right to earn enough to
'keep' a wife and family — the right to female
domestic servicing.

This campaign was so successful that
from the latter part of the 19th century until
World War II only 10 per cent of married
women in Britain were in employment. In the
civil service, nursing and teaching a
marriage-bar operated, forcing women to
resign from their jobs on marriage. The two
world wars constituted a direct contrast. As
men were mobilized into the army, so women
were given traditionally male engineering
jobs in munitions factories. This deployment
of female labour occurred only after agree-
ments with male union leaders that the
diluted or deskilled jobs would be upgraded
and returned to men after the war. To make
employment easier for women, the government provided housework substitutes:
nurseries, restaurants, laundries etc.

The expansion in female employment,
due largely to the entry of married women
into the labour market, occurred after World
War II. It was due to early marriage, a
reduction in the number of children and
hence a contraction in the number of years
spent in childcare, and an expansion in
female jobs, notably in the clerical and
service sector. At present, married women
are almost half of the female labour force in
the UK.

The sexual division of labour operates in
the LABOUR MARKET. Women are heavily
concentrated in a small number of predominately female occupations which either
resemble housework (e.g. cleaning, catering,

textiles and footware, primary school
teaching) or service male occupations (e.g.
clerical work or nursing). Segregation by sex
in the labour market has been increasing
steadily since the turn of the century. This is
one of the main reasons why equal opportunity legislation in Britain — the 1970 Equal
Pay Act and the 1975 Sex Discrimination
Act — has not been successful in alleviating
women's labour market inequality. Both
Acts require comparisons between men and
women doing the same or similar work, but
the sexual division of labour operates to
make such comparisons generally impossible.

Before feminists began to analyse
women's employment, women were generally viewed as deviant non-males who
worked for pin money, because they wanted
to, and were unreliable, either because they
stayed at home to look after sick children or
changed jobs because their husbands moved.
Women were, in short, blamed for not
conforming to the male norm, for not being
men.

When feminists turned to analysing
women's labour market position they initially drew attention to the fact that, for
women, employment is a second or third job,
that women's primary responsibility lay in
the home. Three ways of explaining women's
position in the labour market developed. The
first was the 'dual' labour market theory,
which postulated that industrial societies are
composed of expanding, technologically
advanced primary sectors and contracting,
technologically backward secondary sectors.
Each sector requires a particular type of
labour force, and the characteristics of the
secondary labour maket — dispensability,
social differentiation, lack of training,
economism and lack of strong trade union
organization — resemble the features of
female employment. Thus women were said
to constitute the secondary labour force. The
main problem with this theory is that whatever its merits in describing and explaining
labour market differentiation, it fails to ask
why, even if a dual labour market is 'necessary', it should be women who form the secondary labour force.

Marxist feminists moved from the
domestic labour debate to analysing women
as a reserve army of labour. Since it proved

impossible to determine the necessity of domestic labour to capitalism, they argued that capitalsim needs a reserve army of the unemployed, partly to keep down wages, and partly as a pool of potential labour to draw on in times of economic growth. Thus housework, by keeping women out of the labour market but ready to enter it if employment expands, is linked to capitalism through women as a reserve army of labour. There are three problems with this view: (1) it remains FUCTIONALIST, like the domestic labour debate, deriving the persistence of housework from its necessity to capitalism; (2) it fails to address the specificity of women — capitalism may 'need' a reserve army, but that fails to explain why women should constitute that reserve army; (3) it fails to address the sexual division of labour: because jobs and labour markets are segregated by sex, women can act as a reserve army in relation only to women's jobs, and not in relation to the entire employment needs of capitalism.

A third way of analysing women's employment patterns is to address the sexual division of labour directly and question the public-private dichotomy. Women's employment cannot be analysed in terms of SKILL or educational differentials because the attribution of skill to a particular occupation is a political, not technical, matter. For example, male tailors are considered skilled workers, female machinists semi-skilled; male toilet-cleaners are considered semi-skilled and their female counterparts unskilled. Women 'carry' their low female status into jobs. It is their feminity which classifies their job, and not the other way round. Furthermore, under PATRIARCHY women perform women's work within both the private sphere (for husbands) and in the public sphere (for men as individuals or male employers): a woman who looks after a sick child at home is a mother, and a nurse if in hospital; a female therapist who listens to her male patient and her troubled husband may use the same skills — the first is work, the second marriage, and so on. Women's work moves in and out of the home, irrespective of what women may want, for instance institutionalized *versus* COMMUNITY CARE of the old. Thus women's work cannot be analysed like men's. For men the work/home or

leisure split is real; for women, the unity of employment and housework characterizes their labour. Men express their responsibility to the family through employment. For women employment is a second or third job around which primary domestic responsibilities must be fitted. The sexual division of labour structures women's work, confining women to 'female' jobs and work for men.

See R.D. Barron and G.M. Norris, 'Sexual divisions and the dual labour market' in D. Leonard Barker and S. Allen, *Dependence and Exploitation in Work and Marriage* (1976); V. Beechey, 'Women and production' in A. Kuhn and A. Wolpe, *Feminism and Materialism* (1978); J. Pinchbeck, *Women Workers and the Industrial Revolution 1750-1850* (1981); L. Mackie and P. Pattullo, *Women at Work* (1977).

EG

**women and the welfare state.** The rudimentary WELFARE STATE was greatly expanded after World War II in line with the 1942 BEVERIDGE Report. The aim of this state intervention was to remove some aspects of welfare from the market, for example health, education and housing; to provide a financial safety-net for people not in the labour market, such as the sick, unemployed, disabled and old; and to intervene on behalf of those on low wages.

The welfare state is a capitalist state. Its aim is not to abolish CAPITALISM, but to sustain it. Thus welfare provisions must not become a disincentive to employment. Capitalism operates through PATRIARCHY in the welfare state. Men are harnessed to employment through family responsibilities. To keep men in employment the welfare state protects and reproduces the nuclear family. This is done by defining women as dependent housewives and mothers. Thus married women are excluded from a number of benefits: if they pay the married women's contribution they have no right to sickness or unemployment benefit. If they pay the ordinary contribution, they still cannot claim payments for dependence. Women with disabilities do not get allowances if they cannot be employed, but can do housework.

Another way in which women's dependence on men is maintained is through the cohabitation ruling, whereby a single woman or single mother who is thought to be having an on-going sexual relationship with a man is deemed to be financially dependent on him, and hence ineligible for benefits.

It has been argued that the expansion of the welfare state contributes to the FAMILY's 'loss of functions'. Old people, the sick, the handicapped, and others have ben removed from home into state-provided care. However, the insistence on the superiority of COMMUNITY CARE simply transforms itself into 'housewife care'. Women as wives and daughters (-in-law) care for dependent relatives for free. Thus the division between state care and HOUSEWORK is not rigid, but shifts depending on government policies and expenditure. The welfare state structures housework.

Another relationship between the welfare state and the family lies in the sexual DIVISION OF LABOUR. The expansion of the service sector increased the scope for female employment. In the 19th century voluntary charity or philanthropy occupied many middle-class women, many of whom defined their role as teaching working-class women how to be good wives, housewives and mothers. Today, most social workers are women and their clients predominately female.

The response of social workers to wife-battering or sexual abuse of girls is to keep the family together. Thus within the welfare state it is women who are delegated the responsibilities for controlling women, maintaining the family for the benefit of men as husbands, and for capital. The welfare state reproduces capitalist social relations through the medium of the patriarchal family. The unpaid, financially dependent housewife is the pivot of this system.

See E. Wilson, *Women and the Welfare State* (1977); H. Land, 'Women: supporters or supported?' in D. Leonard Barker and S. Allen, *Sexual Divisions and Society* (1976).

                                                    EG

**work ethic.** WEBERIAN accounts of the rise of industrialization and capitalist social integration stress the voluntaristic aspects of human behaviour in general and the importance of social values derived from Protestantism in particular (see PROTESTANT ETHIC THESIS). Simplified versions of Weberian doctrine were once very widely accepted by Americans, and American business and industrial power were thought to have developed successfully because American culture highlighted such values as conscientious performance of work tasks, willingness to defer gratification and save earnings, individualistic striving for 'success' (e.g. via promotion at work) and the primacy of the work domain amongst other departments of social existence. It was also widely assumed that secularized forms of such a 'Protestant' scale of economic values were indispensible to any industrializing society.

Studies by Lenski (*The Religious Factor,* 1961) provided some validation of a link between economic values and actual religious conviction. But there has been insufficient empirical test of the doctrine in most of its other guises. It may be that for much of this century disciplinary structures were effective in themselves for securing compliance and productivity and that from a managerial point of view it was often unimportant what positive work values were possessed by most manual workers, provided they accepted managerial authority and responded to money incentives. But in the 1950s it was claimed that American managerial and professional employees, who had been assumed to be highly committed to the 'Protestant Ethic', were beginning to abandon it in favour of a 'Social Ethic' stressing collaborative versus individual effort, accompanied by an enfeebling dependence upon 'The Organization'. The cultural turmoil of the Sixties and the erosion of American economic might in the Seventies have redoubled alarm amongst commentators and employers that the work ethic is being discarded, to the long-term material peril of the country. Similar apprehensions exist in West European countries, such as West Germany and Sweden, previously noted for commitment to 'hard work' (which commentators seldom try to define carefully). It is even claimed that Japanese youth are beginning to reject the somewhat different traditional work values derived from Confucianism.

For some time, then, there has existed what might be called a hypothesis of 'general disenculturation' to explain the course of events. According to this, all or most employee strata in advanced countries have been discarding the value of 'hard work' because they take their personal material security for granted, while opinion-forming élites discount (or even disparage) the notion that work can and should automatically supply a sense of personal worth irrespective of its purpose or content. With the aggravation of economic recession, this interpretation has been challenged by a 'calculative recommitment' hypothesis, according to which employees will adopt work patterns and publicly held work attitudes similar to the 'traditional' work ethic thanks to 'new realism' induced by fear of material insecurity (especially unemployment).

Both these hypotheses misjudge the real level of commitment to a work ethic in the past and oversimplify the relationship between values and action. A more plausible interpretation is that of 'differential reconstruction' of the work ethic, which suggests: (1) manual workers, even in the USA, were always far less committed than non-manual workers to a work ethic; (2) prosperous professional and associated employee groups have revised their work values disproportionately fast since the mid-1960s in the 'post-bourgeois' direction of seeking increased opportunities for 'self-actualization', if necessary via more leisure; (3) the 'materialistic' rewards of work nevertheless remain highly sought, though there is occurring a significant shift in their content; (4) non-élite categories of workers seem to be importantly influenced by these value revisions amongst the élite, but in ways whose implications for behaviour at work and for the economy (and thus for political life) have still to become clear though they are potentially extensive; (5) differential reconstruction of work values is inter-dependent with massive alterations in the composition of the labour forces and in the employment practices of advanced societies, particularly those caused by the growth of female employment and by the rise in the formal educational attainment of many younger workers.

These changes are bound up with profound alterations in family structures and gender relations. Work in the sense of paid employment has in certain respects become a more powerful value to some persons. Some sections of FEMINISTS even appear to endorse

in vociferous terms the PATRIARCHAL notion that before they can be treated as complete citizens and social adults persons must obtain paid employment. Those opposed to their programme point out that, together with other radicals, such feminists regard it as their task to itemize the satisfactions and utilities they consider employees have a right to expect in performing work, rather than to state any obligations that may arise for employees to perform that work effectively. This 'psychology of entitlement' lies behind the notion of 'organizational civil rights' which, short of demands for INDUSTRIAL DEMOCRACY, has profoundly affected large American work organizations in the last decade. These developments upset key elements of the traditional work ethic; significantly, the term 'workaholic', used to designate and belittle any person seemingly unable ever to put work out of his or her head, has gone into the dictionary. But how far work as an end in itself has been 'desanctified' in the USA and in other advanced countries is not known with any precision.

See also ALIENATION; INCENTIVE PAYMENTS; ORIENTATIONS; PROTESTANT ETHIC THESIS; SELF-ACTUALIZATION.

See M. Rose, *Wars Over Work* (1983).

MR

**work groups.** From a sociological point of view, such groups are conceptually distinct from the teams, gangs, sections etc created by managers on technical grounds. Such organizationally demarcated units (sometimes called 'secondary groups') may also possess 'primary group' characteristics: personalized roles, 'private' norms of conduct, and positive and negative sanctions to enforce individual integration and conformity. Managers sometimes attempt to prevent such characteristics appearing, for example by constantly switching operatives between different units; at other times physical or technical environment (sometimes through design) excludes the growth of primary groups. In some cases primary forms of solidarity are vital supports to formal organization, especially where the environment is dangerous in a physical sense (fishing, mining, oil prospecting) or psychologically fraught (theatrical production).

Attempts to create typologies of work groups (as by L. Sayles, *The Behaviour of Industrial Work Groups,* 1957) have been only partially successful.

See HUMAN RELATIONS; INCENTIVES; SOCIO-TECHNICAL SYSTEM.

MR

**working class.** A term originating in the early 19th century to denote: (1) Those who worked in industry, mining or agriculture but did not own their means of production, as opposed to those who owned but did not work, including absentee capitalists — at the time a politically radical sense which could include active owner-managers in the working class (in sociology SAINT-SIMON used the term in this way). (2) Those who worked with their hands — only manual workers. Gradually these two senses fused. By the late 19th century, 'working class' indicated manual workers but retained the radical sense of productive workers rather than parasites, who now included all capitalists and indeed most non-manual employees. Without a radical tinge, and used by middle-class persons, the term was more conventionally used plurally, (the 'working classes'). In popular usage and in much of sociology, it still refers to manual workers, though the manual/non-manual divide is of limited sociological significance in the 20th century (see also MIDDLE CLASS).

*Proletariat* is an alternative term to working-class; it is preferred by some Marxists and is derived from the Latin *proles,* meaning offspring (literally the class who contribute only children to the state, rather than wealth or personal military service). *Lower class,* by contrast, is not a synonym for working class; sociologists and their worker respondents agree that to be working class is honourable and respectable, to be lower class is not (see also UNDERCLASS; LUMPENPROLETARIAT). The principal sociological debate concerns the unity or diversity of the working class(es). Many studies used to follow the practice of Censuses in distinguishing skilled, semi-skilled and unskilled classes (see CENSUS CLASSES). However, a more sociological view has prevailed. While a minority of workers classified as skilled by Censuses — craftsmen who through APPREN-

TICESHIP can exercise monopoly supply over entry to the trade — may have a distinctive position (see LABOUR ARISTOCRACY), other SKILL distinctions are more artifical and variable. An alternative basis of internal differentiation, much discussed by British sociologists, is Lockwood's typology of working-class SUBCULTURES: deferential, proletarian and privatized workers with, respectively, status-hierarchy, dichotomous and pecuniary images of the class structure; see M. Bulmer (ed.), *Working Class Images of Society* (1975).

But working-class unity is also provided by TRADE UNIONS and the politics of SOCIALISM and SOCIAL DEMOCRACY. Though these have recruited variable proportions of manual workers in different countries, members do not vary systematically and uniformly by skill level. Though their socialism varies considerably, they represent a collectively organized and conscious working-class movement, the core of a working class in the sense of a 'social formation' (see CLASS). Whether this adds up potentially to a class with CLASS CONSCIOUSNESS of a revolutionary kind, or whether it is a predominantly defensive subculture within capitalism, is still debated. With the INSTITUTIONALIZA-TION of unions and socialist parties and a declining proportion of manual workers in the labour force of the most advanced economies, crucial debates have turned upon lower non-manual workers. All agree that manual workers in productive industries are working class, but disputes arise over whether the working class also extends to foremen and supervisory workers in service industries, and white-collar workers (see CLASS, *neo-Marxist theories*). In addition, Mallet, Touraine and other French writers made a distinction between the old working class (manual workers in plants with traditional productive techniques) and the new (technicians, often white-coated, who monitor automated or other advanced productive processes and enjoy staff status, but whose position with respect to property and authority relations is little different from that of blue-collar workers).

Even more difficult problems have as yet been faced largely in the sociology of development. With an INTERNATIONAL DIVISION OF LABOUR and multi-national corporations, much of the working class has been 'exported' into the THIRD WORLD. What basis, if any, is there for unity between workers there and in the advanced capitalist countries? More disconcertingly, do workers in the latter benefit so much from CITIZEN-SHIP in their NATION-STATES that they are no longer really working class, in the inter-national division of labour? A more complex and particular form of these questions is posed by RACISM within the working class of the advanced countries, a form of disunity given .modern form by large-scale Third World immigration. If we add problems of GENDER disunity, it seems that for the working class to realize Marx's hopes would require the breaching of the other principle sources of stratification in the modern world besides class: nation-state, race and gender. This seems unlikely.

CGAB, MM

**work study.** See INCENTIVE PAYMENTS; SCIENTIFIC MANAGEMENT.

**world system.** The view that neither the development nor the underdevelopment of any one NATION-STATE is autonomous, but should be examined as part of a developing world economy. In the last decade world system theories have become popular. There are two different variants, liberal and Marxist.

Liberals (e.g. D. Meadows, *Limits to Growth*, 1972) are primarily concerned with the global physical limits of post-war trends of world economic growth, industrialization, increasing resource use, urbanization and population. (1) The untrammelled pursuit of material welfare by all nations, rich and poor, will come up against critical environ-mental limits: resource depletion, pollution, soil erosion, climatic disturbances etc. (2) Growth-oriented industrial and techno-logical policies of the advanced countries prejudice the chances of industrial and technical progress for the poor countries. (3) Physical consequences of economic deci-sions taken by individual nations reach far beyond their territorial boundaries; because of global interaction of economic, physical, geological, demographic and ecological vari-ables, liberals advocate the recognition of a global community of interest and planning, and a global body politic.

For Marxists (e.g. I. Wallerstein, *The Modern World System*, 1974) the problems of the world economy are neither physical nor environmental, but political and man-made. Capitalism generates riches and poverty, development and UNDEF DEVELOP-MENT (including that which results from a rapacious use of physical resources) as joint aspects of one historical process. The global capitalist system is a hierarchy of levels of production with lines of domination and subordination connecting the capital-accumulating centres with the exploited periphery (see CENTRE-PERIPHERY). Where colonialism stratified the world into rich and poor regions, multinational corporations are today the dominant organizational form of world capitalism. Since World War II, through the internationalization of produc-tion effectuated by the multinational corp-orations, the world capitalist system has become even more integrated. The global strategy of these corporations injects a greater degree of dynamism into the system. A relative shifting of positions may occur with previously underdeveloped nations now becoming relatively developed (e.g. Brazil, Mexico, South Korea) and previously advanced nations declining in status (e.g. the UK). Marxist writers disagree as to the degree of shifting that can occur. Some argue that the system remains loaded in favour of the already advanced countries because of their historical advantage and their military/political consolidation of this advantage (the 'superimperialist' variant). Others stress conflict between competing capitalist centres (USA *versus* Europe and Japan) and conclude that some Third World countries at least may exploit this conflict to their own advantage. But all Marxists differ from liberals in that theirs is a theory of inevitable conflict, while the liberal models believe international co-operation to be possible and necessary.                                    AH

The labels 'liberal' and Marxist as used above probably cover only a minority of those writing on the global aspects of CAPITALISM. Most take a mixed CONSENSUS-CONFLICT view, and if they stress conflict they do not endorse a Marxist account of this. Many political economists analyse conflicts between nation-states, national and multi-national corporations, and other TRANS-NATIONAL, international and national interest groups rather differently, giving either a multi-factor explanation of conflicts and

likely outcomes, or putting more emphasis on NATION-STATES, and less on CLASSES, as the fundamental actors of the system (see for example the journal *International Organisation*).

See INTERNATIONAL DIVISION OF LABOUR.

MM

**Yule's Q.** See ASSOCIATION, COEFFICIENTS OF.

**zero-sum game.** See GAME THEORY.